Marriage and Family

Second Edition

Marriage and Family
A Christian Perspective

Second Edition

Barbara A. Riggs, Ph.D., LMFT
Cynthia Benn Tweedell, Ph.D.

TRIANGLE PUBLISHING®
Marion, Indiana

Marriage and Family: A Christian Perspective, 2nd Edition
Barbara A. Riggs, Ph.D., LMFT and Cynthia Benn Tweedell, Ph.D.

Direct correspondence and permission requests to one of the following:

E-mail: info@trianglepublishing.com
Web site: www.trianglepublishing.com
Mail: Triangle Publishing
1900 West 50th Street
Marion, Indiana 46953
USA

The *American Psychological Association Manual* was used in this work.

Published by Triangle Publishing
Marion, Indiana 46953

ISBN: 978-1-931283-41-0

Graphic Design: Lyn Rayn
Cover Photo: © iStockphoto.com / nataq

Printed in the United States of America

Academic and Peer Review

Authors typically invest thousands of hours in the process of providing a textbook for you—drawing upon their own expertise, collaborating with others in their discipline, researching, and writing. They have collected and organized the important topics of the subject matter in a form they believe is most beneficial for your learning. In addition to the significant investment the authors make, publishers solicit the assistance of other experts and professors in their quest to provide excellent learning resources.

Excellence is enhanced through peer reviews. These reviews are a very important part of the process of publishing any textbook as experts in the field critically examine the authors' work. Reviewers read the text carefully and usually provide the publisher with dozens of pages of critical comments. These comments range from strengths such as affirmation about content and writing style to suggestions about deficiencies—chapter organization, information regarding current research, documentation, form and style matters, as well as debate pertaining to the authors' viewpoints. The authors are provided with the review comments and are given opportunity to respond—and in many cases do additional researching, rewriting, and discussing issues and questions that are raised.

This textbook is no exception to the peer review process. Many professionals in the field of marriage and family studies, including counseling, legal affairs, and teaching/learning, have invested hundreds of hours reviewing this text. The Publisher is especially thankful to the reviewers who have given their expertise, time, and wisdom in reading and commenting on *Marriage and Family*. Their contribution adds significantly to the content and quality of what you are about to study.

For your information, some of the reviewers and a summary of their involvement in the field of marriage and family studies are listed on the following page. For those academic administrators and professors who by their choice are not listed here, we truly appreciate your significant contributions as well. You know who you are.

With gratitude,
Nathan Birky
Publisher
Triangle Publishing

Reviewers

Sharon Cady received her baccalaureate degree from Indiana Wesleyan University and a Master of Social Work degree from Indiana University. She has a private counseling practice in which she enjoys strengthening marriages and families. Sharon is a licensed clinical social worker (LCSW) and holds credentials with the Academy of Certified Social Workers (ACSW). She is also an adjunct professor for Indiana Wesleyan University, often teaching Sociology and Marriage and the Family courses. Sharon has been married to Don for 27 years. They have two adult children.

Dr. Sharon Drury earned the Ph.D. in Organizational Leadership from Regent University in Virginia, and teaches Advanced Leadership and Organization Theory courses in the doctoral program at Indiana Wesleyan University (IWU). She has been with IWU for over 15 years and served previously as the Dean for the College of Adult and Professional Studies. Sharon specializes in applying leadership theory to nonprofit organizations and higher educational institutions, and in developing women for leadership positions. She committed her life to Jesus Christ as a young adult, and has been married for over 40 years to Dr. Keith Drury, Associate Professor of Religion at IWU. They have two married sons, David and John, and four grandchildren. Sharon has hiked 1,000 miles of the Appalachian Trail, climbed Mt. Katahdin in Maine and Mt. Whitney in California, and enjoys bicycling "rails to trails" with her husband.

Charles Kaufmann is professor and Social Science Department Chair at Central Christian College, McPherson, Kansas. He currently teaches several sociology courses (including marriage and family) and many U.S. history courses. He received an Associate of Arts degree from Central Christian College, Bachelor of Arts from Briar Cliff College and a Master of Arts in Liberal Studies from Wichita State University. He is an ordained minister in the Free Methodist Church and has 24 years of pastoral ministry. Charles and his wife, Lori, have been married for 35 years and are the parents of five children and the grandparents of three grandchildren. Charles enjoys road bikes (especially his recumbent), sprint triathlons, and backpacking.

Dr. RB Kuhn taught at Allegheny Wesleyan College 5 years, followed by serving as Minister of Christian Education and Principal at Faith Mission Church/Stone City Christian Academy for 19 years. Since 2001, RB has been an administrator in Indiana Wesleyan University's College of Adult and Professional Studies. His current responsibilities as Director of the School of Liberal Arts include oversight for General Education, Electives, Criminal Justice, Religion, and Addictions Counseling. He continues involvement with Triangle's author focus groups and editing, and participates in product representation in nationwide conference settings. RB is a freelance writer, musician, worship leader, and keyboard project producer—activities which span more than 32 years. He has been married to Pamela (a published author of 40 titles of Christian education curriculum) 34 years, has a teenage daughter still at home, one married daughter, and three beautiful grandchildren.

Dr. Paul Stoltzfus is currently in private practice with specialties in neuropsychology, pediatric psychology, forensic consultations, and is an adjunct professor at George Fox University. He completed an undergraduate degree in Clinical Psychology at George Mason University (Virginia), and received Master and Doctorate degrees at George Fox University in clinical psychology. His dissertation researched treatment efficacy in adolescents in residential treatment. Dr. Stoltfus' professional involvement includes being a member of the Oregon State Bar, Board of Bar Examiners, President of George Fox Alumni Board, and Elder at Newberg Friends Church. His past employment has included: staff psychologist in community mental health, clinical director in a private mental health treatment center, and the clinical director at an adolescent residential treatment center. Paul and his wife, Janette, are the parents of four children, live on a hobby farm, enjoy gardening and raise their own pork and beef. Hobbies include reading existential psychology, practicing contemplative disciplines, tennis, archery, mountain biking, and hiking. Paul is fully in love with family, friends and the wide, wild Northwest.

Dr. Judi Schwanz is the Professor of Pastoral Care and Counseling at Nazarene Theological Seminary. She also serves as Research Consultant for the Doctor of Ministry program at NTS and is the director of the Wynkoop Center for Women in Ministry. Dr. Schwanz holds a Ph.D. and M.S. in Psychology from Portland State University, and an M.A. in Counseling from Western Evangelical Seminary. She is an ordained minister in the Church of the Nazarene. In addition to her teaching responsibilities, Judi counsels NTS students in personal and professional matters. Judi has written *Blessed Connections: Relationships that Sustain Vital Ministry,* published by the Alban Institute. She has written numerous articles and speaks at retreats and workshops. Judi and her husband, Keith, are the parents of two married children and have five grandchildren.

Dr. Terri S. Watson, Psy.D., ABPP, is an Associate Professor at Wheaton College, where she coordinates the M.A. Clinical Psychology program. Board Certified in Clinical Psychology and an Approved Supervisor with the American Association for Marriage and Family Therapy, Dr. Watson teaches graduate courses in Marital Therapy, Clinical Supervision, Humanistic / Experiential Therapy, and Play Therapy. She publishes and presents on a variety of topics including integration of psychology and Christian faith, women's issues, child and family therapy, and supervision.

Additional reviewers preferred not to be listed.

Contents

Academic and Peer Review v

Preface xi

1. Why Marriage and Family? 1
2. The Changing Face of the American Family: Early History 23
3. The Changing Face of the American Family: Modern History 54
4. Dating: Getting to Know You 83
5. Love and Mate Selection: What's Love Got To Do With It? 107
6. Marriage and Family Life: The Early Years 127
7. Marriage and Family Life: The Parenting Years 158
8. Marriage and Family Life: The Middle and Late Years 197
9. Families and Work: The Juggling Act 231
10. Time, Energy, and Money: Managing Family Resources 257
11. Cultural Variations in Marriage and Family 283
12. Conflict in Families 314
13. Divorce and Remarriage 339
14. Building Strong Families 376

Epilogue: The Future of the Family 397

Glossary 404

References 416

Index 451

About the Authors 458

Preface

I urge you to live a life worthy of the calling you have received.

—Ephesians 4:1

© iStockphoto.com / nataq

The strongest influence in your life will stem from your family. A family gives more than a name—it gives identity. Through family relationships, people come to a better understanding of themselves and learn to interact with others. Whether negative or positive, their concepts of love and their choices in life are in large part due to the influence of their families, including the way they handle conflict or develop possible prejudices.

The family is an integral part of society, both shaping and being shaped by it. Every society develops some kind of family structure, however diverse these structures may be. As social groups develop culture and social order, they must provide an organized way to nurture and care for weaker members. They also must learn to interact constructively with other social groups. In today's global society, an understanding of different family forms, such as singleness, interracial marriage, same-sex couples, and other cultural variations, is crucial to intercultural relations.

Sometimes students enter a marriage and family course hoping for a "cookbook" approach—a way to find a secret recipe for a happy family life. Of course, there is no secret recipe in *Marriage and Family: A Christian Perspective.* We (the authors) challenge much of the advice given in popular media outlets, and even in other secular marriage and family texts, making this text suitable as an introductory marriage and family textbook for college and adult age groups. "*If I had only known . . .*" We have often heard our students say this in our classes over the years. This text provides students an opportunity to examine family issues within a Christian framework, in order to gain the practical knowledge and tools they will need throughout life.

Marriage and Family takes a life-cycle approach similar to Carter and McGoldrick (2005), which is reflected in the arrangement of the chapters. The authors first discuss the science and history of the American family. Subsequent chapters consider dating, love, and spouse selection; the stages in marriage and family life; cultural variations in family patterns; and family issues such as finances, careers, conflict, divorce, and remarriage. While these topics may be found in other marriage and family textbooks, what sets this textbook apart from other texts is its Christian focus. By integrating biblical principles into every chapter, *Marriage and Family* affirms the Lordship of Jesus Christ in all family relationships.

What defines a "Christian" family? How does the American family of the 1800s differ from today's family? What are the implications of those differences? Should a family with young children operate in the same way as a family with teenagers? Should an older married couple expect to relate to one another as they did when they were newlyweds?

We believe the Bible holds the answers to these questions, offering sound guidance on how to build and sustain godly relationships. Just as we all are God's unique creations—individually designed for God's purposes— our marriages and family relationships are also unique. While your marriage may not look like your parents', we believe that certain broad Christian principles should be part of every marriage:

1. *Love:* This text discusses the different types of love and how these types relate to mate selection. The authors offer guidelines for involving God in relationship decisions by showing which kind of love is most closely aligned with the love Christ modeled.
2. *Covenant:* This is what distinguishes marriage from other relationships. In discussing mate selection, *Marriage and Family* explores Christian ideals of covenant, taking as its model the covenant relationship between God

and His people. In later chapters, the text discusses ways in which this covenant is tested and deepened. The text also examines why some couples decide to dissolve their marriages.

3. *Mutual submission:* While this concept may seem anachronistic in our modern culture, *Marriage and Family* sheds light on the biblical context for mutually fulfilling relationships. Marriages rooted in mutuality will be more vital and sustainable than marriages based on unequal power and a faulty understanding of respect and roles.
4. *Freedom:* Contemporary culture often portrays marriage and family life as something that restricts personal freedom and keeps people in bondage. By applying Christian principles, *Marriage and Family* stresses that marriage ultimately is a liberating experience, freeing spouses to be all they can be for Christ.

Marriage and Family challenges the reader to think about choices in marriage and family relationships within a biblical context. In our review of different marriage and family styles, we hope to stimulate thinking about the advantages and disadvantages of each style. Throughout this theory-based but practical text, the reader will find real-life case studies of marriage and family relationships to help in defining and understanding the differences among families. Each chapter includes a Christian viewpoint, a summary, key concepts, and questions for thought.

As a result of reading *Marriage and Family*, students should develop an understanding of marriage and family life in relationship to biblical models. Seeing marriage and family life with a Christian perspective will ultimately help students make decisions which will truly benefit their own family styles.

We would like to thank the many people who reviewed this text and made helpful suggestions. Among them are marriage and family therapists and faculty members of several Christian colleges. We especially note Charles Kaufmann, Central Christian College; Scott Monsma, Northwestern College (Iowa); Susan Warner, Cedarville University; Walter Chung, Eastern College; Richard Durfield, Azusa Pacific University; Paul Stoltzfus, George Fox University; and Dan Poff, Jim Beers, and Dennis Banter, Indiana Wesleyan University. In addition we wish to thank Cheryl Vance, Stephanie Castle, and Mallory Tucker for their assistance in researching topics. We would especially like to thank our families, for without their patience and support, this book could not have been written.

Together, we have produced a marriage and family text we hope will give glory to God as the Creator and Sustainer of families.

Healthy marriages and families are the keys to a healthy society. God places people in families to help them develop as individuals first and then to learn to interact with others. Unhealthy families offer an environment which may choke individuality and create barriers for spiritual growth. It is our hope that *Marriage and Family* will enable readers to examine their own situations in light of God's desire for their families, to identify and begin to heal from past wounds and to gain the knowledge they need to help others.

—Barbara A. Riggs, Ph.D., LMFT
Cynthia Benn Tweedell, Ph.D.

Why Marriage and Family?

1

Then the LORD God said, "It is not good that the man should be alone."

—Genesis 2:18 NRSV

© iStockphoto.com / Jadin

Why Take a Marriage and Family Class?

If you are like most students, you have been involved in and surrounded by families all your life. You've observed many different family styles, including your own intimate family relationships. So why bother with a systematic study of family at the collegiate level, when you have been "living" family all along? What can such a study add to your understanding of marriage and family?

A Better Understanding of Self

Your experience with family, likely, has been "from the inside" as a son or daughter, husband or wife. This understanding is deeply enmeshed in emotions such as love, hate, jealousy, joy, and bitterness. Some of your most intense emotions occur within the context of family. A systematic study of family will enable you to untangle your emotions from your understanding of family. An objective look at the varieties of families will better equip you to understand your own family relationships. This will allow you to bypass your preconceived ideas about marriage and family, come to a better understanding of yourself and your role within your family, and make more informed choices regarding future relationships.

This text looks at the family through the lens of the transition point of the family life cycle. The family life cycle is a series of emotional and intellectual stages families go through from childhood through retirement. The family is a system that constantly changes as it moves through time (Carter & McGoldrick, 2005). The family life cycle is also a multigenerational view of these changes. For instance, as a child leaves home, the parents renegotiate their relationship with the departing child. As parents grow older, adult children renegotiate their relationships with their aging parents to accommodate their increasing need for care. Each new stage involves transition marked by a heightened period of crisis through which families must navigate. The more you understand the challenges of each stage of the cycle, the more likely you are to successfully move from one stage to the next. Carter and McGoldrick (1989, 2005) present one of the most thorough discussions of the family life cycle. They have proposed the following stages, which provide the foundation for the chapters to follow:

- Independence—This is a period of young adulthood with a focus on emotional separation from one's family of origin.
- Coupling or marriage—This stage involves developing the ability to make a commitment to a relationship and family.
- Parenting: babies through adolescents—During this stage, parents decide whether or not to have children, develop the skills necessary to parent, and balance their roles as individuals, spouses, and parents.
- Launching adult children—As children leave home, parents develop an adult relationship with them. This also requires the acceptance of new members into the family as adult children marry.

- Retirement or senior years—Welcoming new family members or seeing others leave your family are hallmarks of this stage. The subsequent freedom from childrearing responsibilities allows retirees or seniors to enjoy the fruits of their work.

A Better Understanding of Others

Taking a systematic view of marriage and family life will enable you to better comprehend the world in which you and your family operate. People are strongly influenced by their family relationships. To really understand another person, you need to begin to understand that person in the context of family. Even single persons are influenced by the family system in which they grew up. Family gives people a worldview, values, perspectives, and attitudes about how things work. If someone's worldview differs from yours, look into that person's family background and you will begin to understand the how and why of that worldview.

A Way to Derail Misconceptions

People enter marriage and family relationships with a wealth of misconceptions and misperceptions: Isn't love all we need? If both of us are Christians, won't God protect our marriage? Don't Christian parents produce good children?

This text will dispel some common myths about mate selection, marriage, and parenting. With an objective understanding of marriage and family life, you should be better equipped to prevent or derail disillusionment in your future relationships.

A Way to Minister to Others

Christians are called to make a difference in the world. What better place to make a difference than within your own family? Most people are not called to a foreign country to perform mission work; they can find mission work right in their own communities. By understanding the varieties of ways of "doing" family, students can help those around them actualize the best marriage and family relationships possible. A word of caution here: do not anticipate becoming an expert marriage and family therapist based on one course. This book will enable you to give "friendly Christian advice" to your acquaintances, but it will take years of study and practice to master the field of family therapy. If you encounter friends who need help with marriage and family issues, be ready to refer them to expert help (for example, therapistlocator.com is a site which lists professionals in marriage and family therapy).

Basic Definitions

In recent years, even the most basic definition of "family" has been the subject of much debate. Thus, it is important to ground this study of marriage and family by defining terminology as it relates to the Christian perspective. We offer these definitions not as the "last word" on the subject, but rather as a "first word" or beginning point to aid in your study of marriage and family.

What Is Marriage?

Marriage is a multifaceted institution. We define marriage as the emotional, legal, and religious commitment in which a man and a woman share emotional and physical intimacy, roles, status, expectations, and resources. In the United States today, we can define marriage as a social, economic, and legal covenant between a man and a woman.

Marriage Is a Social Arrangement. A marriage is not a private, secret arrangement. In a marriage, a man and woman present themselves as a couple in social situations. This is the function of the wedding, which is a social event witnessed by at least two others and officiated by a representative of the state. The couple is socially recognized as "belonging together." Marriage changes the way the marriage partners are perceived and the way they act in society. Part of the social covenant in marriage is its exclusivity—it excludes other intimate relationships. Married couples who act as single people in social settings are inviting problems into their marriages.

Marriage Is an Economic Arrangement. Marriage creates a unit of economic consumption and presumes some sharing of economic resources. Couples who do not wish to share everything will need to write legal contracts (prenuptial agreements) precluding joint ownership of certain properties. A variety of strategies are available to help couples manage income and spending. We will examine some of these in chapter 10. While not all strategies are biblical, all presume at least some sharing of resources.

Marriage is a social, economic, and legal covenant between a man and a woman.

Marriage Is a Legal Contract. Because of the economic component of marriage, every state has a vested interest in creating laws to govern who, when, and under what circumstances people may marry. Every wedding includes a representative of the state who officiates and affirms the legality of the marriage. When clergy officiate at weddings, they act as representatives of both the church and the state. Thus, they declare the marriage to be blessed by God and sanctioned by the state.

Each state makes its own laws governing marriage, such as age of consent, necessary medical exams, marriage license requirements, and what constitutes common-law marriage. These laws for all 50 states can be accessed at: *http://topics.law.cornell.edu/wex/table_marriage*. Likewise, each state makes laws to govern how marriages are dissolved, including establishing procedures for dividing property and ascertaining custody of the children. A summary of the divorce laws for each state is also available at this website.

Types of Marriage

Historically, various cultures have defined marriage differently. These distinct definitions are important both for our understanding, and because they carry family policy implications. For instance, we still sometimes hear the phrase "born out of wedlock." This may be accurate as it relates to a Christian definition of marriage and family. It is inaccurate as it relates to a single mother and child as a type of nuclear family, including the policy and financial considerations of health care, pensions, and tax advantages. Furthermore, in terms of policy, same-sex couples are not recognized in most states and, therefore, receive none of these policy and financial advantages.

Monogamy. Most countries today consider monogamy to be the cultural norm. Monogamy means a person may be married to only one spouse at a time. This is true in the United States, where all 50 states mandate marital monogamy. Some people in religious sects or cults may claim to have more than one spouse, but in the United States only one of these spouses is recognized by law. Even the Mormon Church no longer allows multiple spouses.

Monogamy is deeply rooted in Judeo-Christian tradition. Culture has also increased the incidence of monogamy. Many modern cultures have passed laws making monogamy the only legal form of marriage, which reflects the spread of Christianity. The scriptural basis for this tradition clarifies that, since God created only one spouse for Adam (Genesis 2) and admonishes church leaders to be the husband of one wife (1 Timothy 3:2, 12), God intends marriage to be monogamous.

Joern Gerdts / Hulton Archive / Getty Images

1953 Mormon family after the husband was arrested on charges of polygamy.

Polygamy. Christians are unique in their practice of monogamy, since most cultures throughout history have practiced polygamy, which is marriage to multiple spouses. There are two types of polygamy: polygyny (one man married to more than one wife), and polyandry (one woman married to more than one husband). Polygyny is common in Islamic cultures. Islam is the only religion to officially authorize polygamy, as the Mormon Church officially denounced the practice in 1890 (Are Mormons Still, 2001). In Nigeria, for example, a national fertility study revealed nearly 40% of marriages are polygynous (Makinwa-Adebusoye, 2001). Such marriages are common in cultures in which women are not allowed access to their own economic resources. The shortage of eligible males leads to the rationale that women must "share" a husband in order to survive economically. Polygyny is seen to offer fertility advantages as well. If a war or famine results in the deaths of many males, a culture may justify its need to populate quickly. The practice of polygyny would make full use of all available women of childbearing age.

Polyandry is a much less common marital arrangement. In most cultures, the male is considered dominant and will not allow his wife to have other husbands. Tibetan Buddhists sometimes practice polyandry. For them, biological brothers may pool their money in order to support one wife (Knox & Schacht, 1999). Such an arrangement is rationalized for its economic advantages and as a way to slow population growth.

Serial Monogamy. In the United States, serial monogamy has become prevalent, due primarily to the increase in cohabiting couples and the rising divorce rate. Serial monogamy is a sequence of spouses or partners, one at a time, over a period of time. It has become increasingly acceptable in society—although not in the church—for both men and women to have a series of monogamous partners throughout their lifetimes, which may or may not include marriage. Breakups of these unmarried relationships can have the same consequences as divorce, especially for children.

Common-Law Marriage. In the United States, common-law marriage is recognized in some states (see http://topics.law.cornell.edu/wex/table_marriage for information on your state). Common-law marriage is a mutual agreement made by a cohabiting couple to present themselves as a married couple. The states which legally recognize these arrangements as marriages do so after the couple cohabits for a certain number of years. The number of years required for the recognition of common-law marriage varies from state to state. Partners in a common-law marriage may inherit from one another or receive alimony when they part. In some states the partners are required to go through a legal divorce if children are involved.

Common-law marriages in the United States have their roots in pioneer history, when few officials were available to make marriages "legal." (In the days of slavery, for example, when officials were unavailable, slaves would "jump the broom," signifying the union of a man and woman.)

Same-Sex Unions. Few issues generate as much heated discussion as same-sex unions. It has even polarized Christian denominations. Same-sex unions are hotly debated in state legislatures across the United States. At the time of this book's publication, the states of Massachusetts, Connecticut, Maine, California, Iowa and Vermont have legalized same-sex marriage. Several other states provide domestic partner benefits in some form: New York, Rhode Island, New Mexico, Connecticut, New Jersey, Oregon, New Hampshire, Hawaii, Maine, Washington, Vermont, California, Montana, Illinois, Alaska, and the District of Columbia. The legal discussion of same-sex unions will likely continue for several years.

For more than 200 years, marriage in this country has been understood to be a union between one man and one woman. However, few federal laws actually define marriage or mandate the conditions under which it is created and dissolved. In 1996, Congress passed the Defense of Marriage Act (DOMA), which stipulates that for the purposes of federal law, marriage is a union between one man and one woman. Further, states are not required to recognize any act "respecting a relationship between persons of the same sex treated as a marriage under the laws of any other state." DOMA has been challenged repeatedly, although to date it has successfully weathered these challenges (Winn, 2006).

Individual states have also experienced difficulty in passing their own marriage protection amendments. At stake in these court battles is the fundamental definition of marriage. Christians and other pro-family groups who wish to define marriage as the union between one man and one woman are working to institute a federal marriage protection amendment (FMA). Their primary concern is to protect state marriage laws from judicial intervention. For example, on May 12, 2005, a Nebraska federal district court judge struck down the Nebraska marriage amendment which had been passed by 70% of Nebraska voters in the November 2004 election. The amendment consisted of two parts: (1) a definition of marriage; and (2) invalidity and non-recognition of same-sex civil unions, domestic partnerships, or anything similar (Marus, 2005).

What Is Family?

Generally speaking, people think of "family" as comprising a legally married couple with biologically related children. In the context of this book, we will expand the term to include single individuals, single parents, families without children, families with grown children living outside the home, or families with children who are not biologically related or biologically related to only one of the parents. A family can be as small as two people. If biological and nonbiological extended family members are included, a family can be quite large. Figure 1.1 shows a recent estimate of family arrangements in the United States.

Types of Families

In this discussion of family, you will need to understand the terminology of family types. Since there are different ways to define them. As you look at Sidebar 1.1,

Figure 1.1

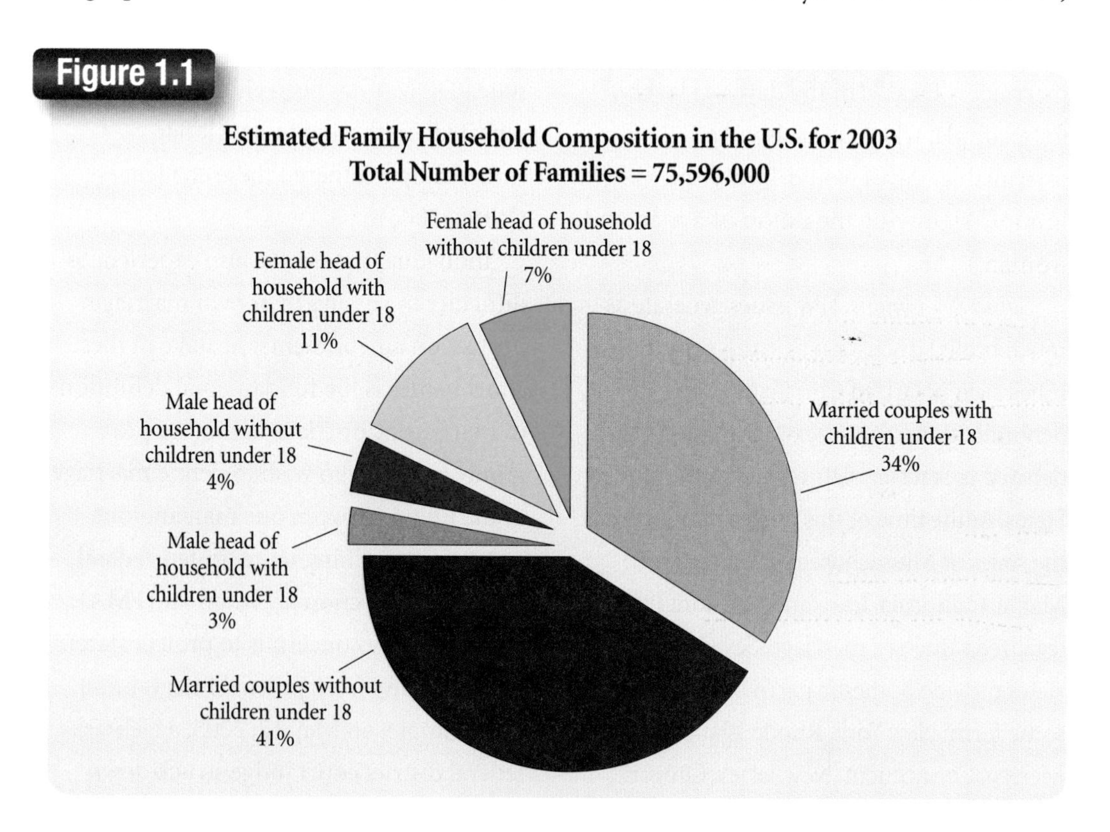

Sidebar 1.1
U.S. Census Definitions of Family

Household—One or more people living together make up a household. One of the people who owns or rents the residence is called the householder. Two types of household are defined:
Family household—At least two members related by birth, marriage or adoption, one of which is the householder. Family units that do not include the householder are called *subfamilies.*
Nonfamily household—A person living alone or householder sharing the residence with nonrelatives such as roommates or boarders.
Children—Birth children, stepchildren or adopted children of the householder. *Own children* is a subset of all children who identify the householder as parent in a household.
Family Groups—Family households plus all related and unrelated subfamilies. A person may be counted in two different family groups—a woman may be the daughter of the householder and also the mother of her own daughter living in the household.
Married—Includes both adults living and not living with their spouse but are officially married.
Unmarried—Includes all never married, divorced or widowed individuals at that time.
Cohabitation—Is indicated as an unmarried partner of the householder.

Adapted from Fields, J. 2004. America's Families and living arrangement: 2003. U.S. Census Bureau. http://www.census.gov/prod/2004pubs/p20-553.pdf (accessed June 24, 2009)

ask yourself these questions: Who decides the definition of family? Do families always live together? How do we understand "being married"? Why is a blood or an adoptive link so necessary?

Nuclear Family. A nuclear family includes parents and biological and/or adopted children living together in one household. The nuclear family is what many Americans mean when they use the term "family." The general expectation is that the nuclear family will be geographically and economically independent. According to the dominant culture of the United States, this means that when a couple marries, they are expected to live separate from their parents and support themselves. Thus, the nuclear family becomes an important unit of economic consumption. As the chapter on the history of the American family will illustrate, such expectations for nuclear families are relatively new and unique.

The nuclear family is the most common living arrangement in white middle-class culture.

Throughout most of world history and in most societies, including the United States, newly married couples lived under the economic protection of their parents. As they became economically able, they were expected to provide economic protection for their aging parents.

As we move well into the 21st century, nuclear families face increasing cultural diversity, economic restructuring, a widening of the gap between the rich and the poor, a decreasing birth rate, an aging society, and continued emphasis on equality and justice for women, minorities, and gays (Amato & Booth, 1997). As a result of this social and economic turmoil, the nuclear family, by necessity, is redefining the image of "rugged individualism" which has dominated American families since the Industrial Revolution—in favor of or more reliance on both kin and non-kin networks. In the wake of what a feminist scholar coined as "the postmodern family condition," (Stacy, 1996) multigenerational bonds are becoming as important as nuclear family ties for well-being and support over the life course (Bengtson, 2001).

Extended Family. As the term implies, the extended family includes the nuclear family and all the aunts, uncles, cousins, and grandparents. It is still true that in many American families members of the extended family only convene at special occasions, such as weddings, funerals, and holidays. In most other cultures today, and throughout history, the extended family provides an important base of emotional, economic, and social support. Many religions celebrate the value of extended family, particularly the elders, who are given a special status within the family. The functions of both the nuclear and the extended family will continue to evolve as family conditions—such as single-parent families, divorced families, remarried families, and the influx of cultures which view extended family as part of the nuclear family—continue to form the fabric of American family culture.

Extended family provides an important base of emotional, economic, and social support.

Family of Origin. Generally speaking, the family of origin is the family into which we are born and raised. In the family of origin, family members first become oriented to the world. They learn values, develop attitudes, and acquire

Whoever said "You don't marry the family" was wrong.

mind-sets. The family of origin is the strongest influence on a child's development—for better or for worse. It is important to note an increasing number of people today are raised in families in which not everyone is biologically related.

Family of Procreation. The family of procreation is the family formed when two mates have children. These children may be biological or adopted. In either case, the parents are a very important influence on the children.

Single-Parent Families. Single-parent families are formed in a variety of ways. Some occur following a divorce or after the death of a spouse. With increasing frequency today, cohabiting couples are having children and then splitting up, creating a single-parent family. In addition, some women are deciding to have children outside of marriage. In 2005, one fourth of all children were living in single-parent homes (Kreider, 2008).

Stepfamilies. When two people marry and bring a child into the marriage from a previous marriage or relationship, they become a stepfamily. In 2004, just under one tenth of the nation's children were living with one stepparent and one biological parent (Kreider, 2008).

Childless Couples. A growing number of couples are childless, either by choice or by chance. In 2004, the number of childless women age 40-44 was 19%. The higher a woman's income, the less likely she is to have children. Nearly one half of women with annual incomes of $100,000 are childless (Dye, 2005).

Fictive Kin Families. Slaves formed extensive fictive kin families to care for children separated from their parents. Today, fictive kin ties are intentional family relationships between friends. Some are formed between different genders and different sexual orientations (Muraco, 2006). Some are formed among the homeless population, who create family relationships

Fictive kin are intentional relationships formed as a family substitute.

with other homeless individuals (Pippert, 2003). This is especially true for street children who sometimes create well-structured "street families" (Molina, 2000).

Cohabiting Couples. Cohabiting couples involve two people living together in a marriage-like arrangement without the benefit of marriage. The number of cohabiting couples is on the rise, comprising an estimated 4.2% of all couples in 2003 (Fields, 2004).

When a couple's marriage does not conform to their myths, disillusionment can set in and interfere with the vitality of their relationship. We will discuss this in more detail in subsequent chapters. We mention this now as a means of prefacing the need to approach a study of marriage and family from an objective, scientific perspective. In conjunction with biblical teaching, we hope to help students develop realistic expectations about their own relationships.

The Science of Marriage and Family

By virtue of your experience in marriages and families, you already know a great deal about the subject. At least you *think* you know a great deal. Strong emotions are associated with any discussion of marriage and family topics—some good, some bad. People spend a great deal of time thinking and talking about their families and other families. They may arrive at many different conclusions based on their observations of their own families or others. This experiential knowledge is certainly valuable, but can be limited in its scope. People often derive their ideas about family from what they see on television and in films, which can be misleading. Sidebar 1.2 presents some commonly held myths about love, marriage, and sex which people are led to believe by friends, family, and the media.

How Scientific Investigation Works

The scientific method can help in finding important information about marriage and family relationships. In our treatment of marriage and family, science is not intended to replace biblical teaching. However, it can supplement the understanding gleaned from the Bible and from our own personal experiences. By using a scientific method, we can gain a more complete picture of what is happening in marriages and families today. Biblical revelation is an ongoing interpretive task that God has given us and through which He blesses us. This kind of discernment is a lifelong process of spiritual growth that allows us to form definitive conclusions on key issues like salvation. Science does not always enable us to come to once-and-for-all, firm conclusions. Scientific knowledge is

SIDEBAR 1.2
MARRIAGE MYTHS

David Popenoe lists the following as commonly-held myths about marriage. Which ones do you believe?

1. Marriage benefits men much more than women.
2. Having children typically brings a married couple closer together and increases marital happiness.
3. The keys to long-term marital success are good luck and romantic love.
4. The more educated a woman becomes, the lower are her chances of getting married.
5. Couples who live together before marriage, and are thus able to test how well-suited they are for each other, have more satisfying and longer-lasting marriages than couples who do not.
6. People can't be expected to stay in a marriage for a lifetime as they did in the past because they live so much longer today.
7. Marrying puts a woman at greater risk of domestic violence than if she remains single.
8. Married people have less satisfying sex lives, and less sex, than single people.
9. Cohabitation is just like marriage, but without "the piece of paper."
10. Because of the high divorce rate, which weeds out the unhappy marriages, people who stay married have happier marriages than people did in the past when everyone stuck it out, no matter how bad the marriage.

Source: Popenoe, D. (2002). Top ten marriage myths. *National Marriage Project at Rutgers University, New Brunswick, N.J.* accessed August 4, 2008 from http://health.discovery.com/centers/loverelationships/articles/marriage_myths.html

tentative and may change, depending on how we measure phenomena. While a variety of methods can be used in a scientific study, all scientific exploration employs certain steps (Tweedell, 2002). Combining spiritual discernment with science can inform us more completely about marriages and families.

Select a Researchable Topic. Scientists seek not only to describe how marriages and families function, but to explain why certain behaviors exist. Questions such as "who," "what," "where," "when," and "why" are all important to gain a rich understanding of social behavior. The first step in a scientific investigation is to choose a topic and frame a question that can be answered by gathering data.

Formulate Hypotheses. You may have heard the expression that a hypothesis is an "educated guess." Hypotheses are the building blocks of scientific theory. They are assumptions that scientists test and from which they draw conclusions. Scientists formulate predictions about the relationship between two or more variables in a hypothesis. Some examples of hypotheses made in the science of marriage and family might be the following:

1. Married people are healthier than single people.
2. Teenagers who marry are more likely to divorce than people who marry at an older age.
3. Firstborn children are less shy than their siblings.

In each of the above hypotheses, there is an independent variable, or a *cause,* and a dependent variable, or an *effect.* For example, in the first hypothesis, "married people" is the independent variable and "healthier" is the dependent variable. This hypothesis proposes that overall health is related to marital status. In the second hypothesis, "teenagers" is the independent variable and "divorce" is the dependent variable. Here the hypothesis suggests that being married in one's teens is a cause of divorce. The third hypothesis has "firstborn children" as the independent variable and "shy" as the dependent variable. This hypothesis suggests that birth order has something to do with shyness.

Collect Data to Test the Hypotheses. Scientists then collect data to test each hypothesis. Scientists use a variety of methods to test hypotheses. These methods will not "prove" or "disprove" the hypothesis, but merely "support" or "not support" the hypothesis. A scientist might test each of the above hypotheses using this method:

1. The scientist could use questionnaires or interviews to survey couples regarding their marital status and overall health. Sometimes the scientist will create a scale as part of the survey or may organize the data using a scale to measure the strength of responses, often assigning a numerical value of 1 to 5. Next, the scientist would use statistical analysis to compare the marital status scores in relation to overall health. If single people have more health problems, the data support the hypothesis.
2. To test the second hypothesis, the scientist could examine existing data, including public records on marriage and divorce. Using these statistics, the scientist would test the relationship between ages at marriage and divorce. Another common method would be to use a case history approach to analyze a particular family to see how family members adapt to certain challenges. Such an approach can utilize diaries, records, and other forms of existing data.

3. A scientist often collects data by systematic observation. In the case of the third hypothesis—testing the relationship between birth order and shyness—the scientist could use a two-way mirror to observe children at play. Or the scientist might set up an experiment in a lab or natural setting. Such an experiment would involve the introduction of a stimulus to an experimental group and a control group. The scientist would then compare the differences in responses between the two groups.

Analyze the Data. Scientists are interested in facts and how they fit together to explain a phenomenon. In a scientific study, each response or observed behavior is a piece of data to be analyzed. Scientists often use statistical tests to analyze these data. When using observations or conducting an experiment, scientists make careful interpretations to find regularities in the data. Such analysis gives a better understanding of the behavior being studied.

In marriages and families, it is tempting for family members to think something is highly unusual or cannot be explained. But scientists look for patterns or regularities in family behavior. In this respect, families are not as unique as they might think. This means most family members are not alone in having to face a particular "problem" in a marital or family situation.

Draw Conclusions. All scientific conclusions are tentative. For example, in the hypothetical situations above, scientists already have studied each of these hypotheses in detail. In the first situation, many studies have concluded that both married men and married women are healthier than their single counterparts. A report released in 2004 by the CDC showed married adults are less likely to be in fair or poor health, and are less likely to suffer from conditions such as headaches and serious psychological distress (Schoenborn, 2004). Can we draw from this conclusion that one of the benefits of marriage is its positive effects on health? Is this conclusion applicable to other parts of the world? To cohabiting couples?

From the second hypothesis we have learned that couples in the United States who marry in their teens tend to have a higher divorce rate than couples who marry at an older age. Is this hypothesis true or "supported" in other cultures? Was it true in earlier centuries? Regarding the third hypothesis, scientists have found contradictory data related to birth order and the personality of children. Thus, the conclusions are tentative.

We cannot know the whole truth through science. Only God knows the complete truth. Short of a right understanding of and relationship with God, we are at best speculating about facts and knowledge—truth is much more than mere information. As Proverbs affirms, "Let the wise listen and add to their learning, and let the discerning get guidance—for understanding proverbs and parables, the sayings and riddles of the wise. The fear of the LORD is the beginning of knowledge, but fools despise wisdom and discipline" (1:5–7). Our relationship to God (i.e., "fear of the Lord") is the foundation for any knowledge we seek to gain. The Bible goes so far as to declare it folly to presume to understand truth independent of its relationship (i.e., "wisdom" and "discipline") to Him.

Science enables us to understand a bit more of God's revealed truth, but we must be very careful not to draw hard-and-fast conclusions about such areas as marriage and family. Marriages and families have changed dramatically, particularly in the last 50 years. For example, as we saw earlier, a nuclear family of the 21st century may not look anything like a nuclear family of the nineteenth century. While certain biblical principles regarding marriage and family remain inviolate, we are learning that some other aspects of marriage and family once considered "carved in stone" are now seen as more pliable. Bateson, a cultural anthropologist, suggests families carry on their learning throughout the life cycle in all they do "....like a mother balancing her child on her hip as she goes about her work with the other hand and uses it to open the doors of the unknown" (1979).

A Christian Perspective

While science gathers data about what is occurring in marriages and families today, the Bible can reveal the underlying causes behind the data. For example, the condition of *personal sin* can create *social sin*, which produces marital dissatisfaction and fractured families. Science cannot "fix" sin, but God can. The Bible shows us how God's original intent for marriage and for family is based on the principles of love, covenant, relationship, and freedom.

Love

To understand love, we must first understand that all love is of God. The world talks about love in many ways, even claiming that a little bit of love is all the world needs. This is not love. Love is of God and it comes from God. He is the only source of love. Love is an attribute of God. In 1 John 4:8 we read, "... God *is* love" (emphasis added). Without the existence of God, there can be no love for others. God's love serves as the source of the love we experience and demonstrate in our marriage and family.

The real mystery is that God loves us at all. C. S. Lewis suggests that God is so full of love that it overflows, and He can't help but love us (1960). John 3:16 says, "For God loved the world so much that he gave his one and only Son, so that everyone who believes in him will not perish but have eternal life" (NLT). The Apostle Paul put it this way, "But God is so rich in mercy, and He loved us so much that even though we were dead because of our sins, He gave us life when He raised Christ from the dead. It is only by God's grace that you have been saved!" (Ephesians 2:4-5 NLT). Catching even a glimpse of God's unfathomable love for us is necessary in our understanding of love.

The love of God which we receive through the Holy Spirit is visible in us. We manifest it in how we love others. We reflect God's love for us in our marriage and family life. Scripture helps us examine what love should look like in our relationships and our marriage. Love excels in what we find hardest to do: to be patient rather than demanding, to extend tenderness even when it is not deserved, to fulfill another's needs before our own, to acknowledge our weaknesses rather than seeking compliments, to be fair and seeking truth rather than demanding our own way, and to remain faithful and hopeful even when it is easier to give up (Ephesians 5:4-7). This is the basis for love in our relationships and in marriage. We cannot create this kind of love in our own power—our love will fail. But God's love never fails.

In Colossians 3:14 we read that love is a bond which binds us together. It makes us one. Scripture refers to love as the reason "....a man leaves his father and mother and is joined to his wife, and the two are united into one" (Genesis 2:24; Ephesians 5:3 NLT). No relationship on earth takes precedence over the marital bond. The Apostle Paul ranks the marital bond as equal to the relationship Christ has with His Church (Ephesians 5: 22-23). In Scripture, no other earthly bond ordained by God carries the significance of the marriage covenant. And yet, Paul endorses singleness. In 1 Corinthians 7:7, 38, Paul comments on "His special gift of singleness," which gives people the freedom to choose marriage or singleness.

Covenant

A primary theme of both the Old Testament and New Testament is God's relationship of covenant with His people—God makes an unconditional commitment to care for and love His people, asking them to be faithful in return. In Genesis 6:18 God said, "But I will confirm my covenant with you. So enter the boat—you and your wife and your sons and their wives." God told

The marital covenant is between two people and God.

Abraham and Sarah, "I will confirm my covenant with you and your descendants after you, from generation to generation. This is the everlasting covenant: I will always be your God and the God of your descendants after you." (17:7 NLT).

Marriage is a covenant, not just a contract. It is a covenant between two people and God. It is in marriage that we are most fully made in the image of the triune God (Hahn, 2004). More than a physical act, marriage is a spiritual act in which a couple renews their marital covenant. When we renew a covenant, God releases His grace—which is life, power and His own love towards us (Hahn, 2004). God designed marriage to demonstrate His life-giving power of love.

Covenant Involves Faithfulness. Each party in the covenant vows to be faithful: "Then God said to Abraham, 'Your responsibility is to obey the terms of the covenant. You and all your descendants have this continual responsibility.'" (Genesis 17:9 NLT). God intends for couples to model their human covenants in marriage after this covenant with God (Balswick & Balswick, 1999, 2006).

Covenant Involves Intimacy. In Christian marriages, couples vow before God to love one another. Such a relationship will require grace, empowerment, and intimacy (Balswick & Balswick, 1999, 2006). Just as we repent before God, who graciously forgives sin, so too in a Christian marriage, the couple must live transparently before one another in repentance, forgiveness, and grace. A couple's love for one another in marriage fosters their ability to empower one another to grow and live as Christ intends for them to live. Intimacy in a Christian marriage goes beyond the physical level; it should follow the pattern God has set in seeking intimacy with humankind. God is interested in being more than a "best buddy." He seeks an intimacy that reaches to the depths of our souls. This is reflected in a Christian marriage when a couple is deeply connected to one another and to God.

Covenant Involves Mystery. Roman Catholicism and some other church traditions elevate marriage to the status of a sacrament. As soon as a couple freely expresses and exchanges consent, they have ratified their covenant. This sacrament is viewed as a "mystery" (Ephesians 5:31-32) in which God's involvement can never be completely comprehended by humans (Hahn, 2004). In Christian marriages, couples trust that God has a divine, holy purpose in and for their union, whether or not they understand this mysterious component.

Covenant Involves Renewal. The covenant relationship between a husband and wife carries with it roles and expectations which are then communicated to the children. This covenant is continuously renewable as a family's needs change. Thus, the marriage into which a couple weds may seem very different from the marriage in which they rear children, or the marriage in which they later care for aging parents. Yet, in the context of this text, these are all forms of a continuously renewed covenant between a man and a woman before God.

Relationship

The state sees marriage as a legal institution. Some see marriage as an economic unit. The Bible sees marriage as a spiritual *relationship* patterned after a couple's spiritual union with God. Such a relationship may defy cultural expectations that men and women act in certain ways. In Christ, a couple is free to act as God calls them to act—to be what God calls them to be. This can be a very liberating experience in a world of marriage stereotypes and expectations.

The principle of mutual submission characterizes much of the Bible's discussion of marriage. In Ephesians 5:21, Paul begins a classic passage about marriage with the theme of mutual submission: "And further, submit to one another out of reverence for Christ" (NLT). Such a relationship is possible when both marriage partners first submit

Marriage is a spiritual relationship that requires mutual submission.

themselves to the authority of Christ. Paul then describes how this concept of mutual submission works in a marriage. "For wives, this means submit to your husbands as to the Lord" (v. 22 NLT), he advises the women. To the men he says, "For husbands, this means love your wives, just as Christ loved the church. He gave up His life for her" (v. 25 NLT).

These are difficult tasks in a culture where women sometimes seek to overpower their husbands and men sometimes neglect their wives. Submission is not a way for one person to dominate another, or always get his or her way. Submission is a willful activity acknowledging the dignity of each individual. It is a willful agreement to unconditionally support the health of the relationship. When couples submit themselves to one another out of reverence for Christ, they become "fellow heir[s] of the grace of life" (1 Peter 3:7 NASB). Thus, couples can experience the fullness of God's relationship with them when they have right relationships with one another.

Freedom

As Christians, we have freedom in Christ, which leads us from sin to freedom and salvation. In Romans we read that through our acceptance of Christ, sin loses its power in our lives: "For when we died with Christ we were set free from the power of sin" (Romans 6:7 NLT). This kind of freedom differs from what the world defines as freedom—the ability to do whatever one wants to do. When we are "in Christ," we can begin to know what it means to be free—free from the distress of sin, free from worry and doubt, free from the confines of religion, free from judging and the worry of being judged, free from fear. This freedom comes through complete trust and faith in God when He brings us into union with Him. It is this union with God which allows one to be in union with a spouse in a Christian marriage.

Many in our culture view marriage and family life as limiting or restricting our personal freedom. They sometimes equate marriage with bondage. Paradoxically, the permanent nature of Christian marriage, coupled with its emphasis on unconditional love, creates freedoms unknown in other unions. In a Christian marriage, two people are totally committed to each other in all circumstances, not just in certain circumstances. Marriage is not seen as something that ends personal growth. On the contrary, in a vital Christian marriage each partner is free to continue developing individual gifts and discovering new abilities with the support and encouragement of the other. This total commitment frees Christian couples from fear of change over the years, because they are assured of working out a life together—regardless.

Summary

This chapter lays the groundwork for what is to follow. After explaining why it is important to take a marriage and family class, we define key terminology to assist in better understanding the plan of this text. Marriage is defined as a social, legal, and economic institution. Each state defines marriage differently and makes its own laws governing the conditions of marriage. One of the most volatile issues today, especially as it relates to Christians, is same-sex unions.

Marital laws in most Western countries today require marriages to be monogamous. Until recently, polygamy, especially polygyny (many wives married to one husband), was widely practiced in most cultures. The influence of Judeo-Christian principles is primarily responsible for transforming the larger culture, making monogamy the norm.

Families can be classified into different types: nuclear, extended, families of origin, and families of procreation. Different cultures emphasize different types of families. In African-American and Hispanic cultures, the extended family is usually very important. In contrast, Caucasian middle-class families are expected to be mobile and independent from their extended families.

We can learn about family in several ways. Experience can give valuable information. However, it can also propagate myths about family, which can cause people to have unrealistic expectations about marriage and family life. Science provides a more objective way to discover the facts about marriage and family life. Scientific evidence is collected utilizing standardized methods such as surveys, interviews, case histories, or systematic observation. These data are then systematically analyzed, often using statistics to test hypotheses. In this way, we gain a more complete understanding of what is currently happening in marriages and families.

While science can inform us about current behaviors in marriages and families, the Bible provides important insights about why such behaviors occur. It also gives us principles which govern marriage and family life under God's control. Such principles as "covenant" and "mutual submission" are essential in creating a spousal relationship that mirrors God's relationship with human beings.

Questions for Thought

1. What are the advantages of nuclear and extended families?
2. What scientific methods might be used to explain why someone chooses to marry a particular person?
3. How does scientific knowledge differ from biblical knowledge?

The Changing Face of the American Family

Early History

2

Diversity and change have been the only constants in the history of the American family.

—Mintz, 2001

In the beginning God created the heavens and the earth . . . Then God said, "Let us make human beings in our image, to be like ourselves." . . . So God created human beings in his own image. In the image of God he created them; male and female he created them. Then God blessed them and said, "Be fruitful and multiply. Fill the earth and govern it." . . . Then God looked over all he had made, and he saw that it was very good!

—Genesis 1:1, 26–28, 31 NLT

"Haven't you read the Scriptures?" Jesus replied. "They record that from the beginning 'God made them male and female. . . . This explains why a man leaves his father and mother and is joined to his wife, and the two are united into one.' Since they are no longer two but one, let no one split apart what God has joined together."

—Matthew 19:4–6 NLT

An old joke begins with a little boy asking his mother, "Where did I come from?" The mother pauses, takes a deep breath, and haltingly proceeds to tell the little boy about "the birds and the bees." The little boy listens patiently. When his mother appears to be through, he says, "I know all that, but Johnny came from Chicago. Where did I come from?"

Where you come from is important. In considering this issue, we can find some clues in the biblical narrative of the very first family.

Image from BigstockPhoto.com / Matthewt

In the beginning, God created the heavens and the earth.

Adam and Eve initially lived and worked in a perfect world. Imagine a world where you wouldn't dread getting out of bed in the morning, a world where you could spend time doing whatever you wanted to do. Imagine walking and talking daily with God, asking Him any questions you had on your mind. This was God's design for humanity. However, the first family fell to temptation and ushered sin into the world. A perfect relationship with God was broken.

Clearly, things *have* changed since Adam and Eve. We often hear about the "changing face" of the American family, but those faces have been changing since humanity's beginnings. Generation after generation, the history of humankind reflects a natural progression or regression, including the place and function of family. Change of any kind often triggers fear. Our generation is not the first to worry that societal change will threaten the traditional family and all the moral and cultural values it embodies. John Watson, noted child psychiatrist of the early 20th century, predicted that by 1977 the family would no longer exist (Watson, 1928).

The evidence seems to negate Watson's prediction. Despite the changes which have occurred, family remains a vital part of American culture and society, with no indication of demise. The reason is because we distinguish between the *form* of family and the *institution* of family. It is our belief that the form of family has and will continue to change, but the institution of family will remain an integral part of society.

A Nation of Immigrants: Family Life Through the Eighteenth Century

The early history of North America as it relates to family involves three primary but distinct groups of people: Native-Americans, European settlers, and Africans brought here as slaves. In this chapter, we will examine changes in the family through the cultural lens of these inextricably intertwined groups.

The Birth of a Nation: Family Life Prior to the 1600s

Native-Americans

The very first immigrants to North America were the nomadic ancestors of the Native-Americans (Brinkley, 2003). Hunters and gatherers, the first "Americans" moved south into the Americas from Siberia and Alaska to escape the cold. These early settlers arrived of their own free will. Unfortunately, as the history of North America details, that has not always been the case.

A Diverse Culture. Diversity was the hallmark of the early Native-American family. Each group shared a culture common only to its group. Family forms differed among the various groups and included nuclear family types, extended family households, clans, tribes, and other forms of kinship.

Family organization among Native-Americans generally followed one of two patterns. A matrilineal family meant the family traced its ancestry through the mother's bloodline. In a matrilineal family, the husband often joined the wife's household. In a patrilineal family, the bloodline was traced through the father; thus, the wife would join her husband's family. In some matrilineal tribes, the family consisted of female relatives and their husbands, sons-in-law, and maternal grandchildren living in a multistoried communal structure (Brinkley, 2003).

Image from BigstockPhoto.com / MWookie

The very first immigrants to North America were the nomadic ancestors of the Native-Americans.

The majority of Native-American children were loved and well-treated by their families. In contrast, early European childrearing practices tended to be much harsher than their Native-American counterparts. This led the Colonists to interpret the lavish affection and permissive treatment of Native-American children as an invitation to rebellion. However, the disciplinary practices of these people were based on their cultural norms. Rather than focus on punishment, Native-American parents used their children's mistakes to teach them lessons about life.

Image from BigstockPhoto.com / searagen

Native-American interaction with the European settlers threatened the very survival of the Native-Americans.

A Clash of Cultures. Interaction with the European settlers ultimately undermined the structure of the traditional Native-American family and threatened its very survival. The immigrants—who were to become the dominant culture—encroached upon Native-American lands and killed or displaced the residents. Eventually, by sheer numbers and with the backing of the government, they overpowered these first Americans. By the end of the 1800s, most Native-Americans resided on reservations. In the early 1900s, many of their children were sent to boarding schools to become "Americanized." This policy had disastrous effects and was largely abandoned by the mid-1900s. In chapter 11, we will look at Native-American culture as it has evolved in recent years.

SIDEBAR 2.1
WHAT COULD NOW SUSTAIN THEM

"[I] stand half amazed at this poor people's present condition. [Having] passed the vast ocean, and a sea of troubles before in their preparation . . . they had now no friends to welcome them, nor inns to entertain or refresh their weather-beaten bodies, no houses or much less towns to [restore], to seek for [comfort] . . . [All they could see was a] hideous and desolate wilderness, full of wild beasts and wild men. and what multitudes there might be of them they knew not . . . If they looked behind them, there was the mighty ocean which they had passed, and was now as a main bar and gulf to separate them from all the civil parts of the world . . . What could now sustain them but the spirit of God and his grace?"

Source: Bradford 1850.

The Young Nation: Family Life in the 17th Century

European Immigrants

In 1602, a weary band of travelers reached the rocky coast of Cape Cod aboard the *Mayflower*. William Bradford, who would later become the second governor of the Plymouth colony, recorded his observations as the group traveled across the ocean and established a settlement (see Sidebar 2.1). They began their first winter together as a group of 102. By spring, half of them were dead.

A Harsh Environment. People immigrated to the New World for many reasons: for example, to find their "fortunes," to experience a great adventure, or to escape religious or political persecution. By the early 1600s, England had become actively involved in settling or colonizing the New World. The peak period of English immigration to the young colonies was between 1630 and 1660. The rapid growth of the tobacco industry meant there was a continual need for cheap labor in the new colonies. Indentured servants (not enslaved Africans) were the main source of labor in the tobacco fields the entire century (Anderson, 1992; Gemry, 1980).

Colonial life was harsh, making it difficult for the first generations of European immigrants to sustain stable families. Because of the many fevers and diseases, a new settler had a 50% chance of dying the first year after arriving in the New World (Urdang, 2001).

Children born in the early part of the 1600s could expect one or both parents to die before the child had reached adulthood. In addition, one quarter of all children in Colonial America died before their first birthday. One-half of all marriages ended before the seventh anniversary due to a spouse's death (Mintz, 2001). This opened the door for many kinds of family arrangements. Serial marriages—a series of multiple marriages taking place after the death or divorce of a spouse—could include stepchildren from two or more unions. Because extended families were virtually nonexistent, orphans often became foster children or wards of another family. In Colonial times, it was rare for several generations of one family to live under the same roof because of the short life expectancy of the new settlers.

The earliest European immigrants were predominantly male—with many being indentured servants. Men outnumbered women 7 to 1 in those early years. Because the period of indenture was usually 3-7 years, men tended to be much older than women when they married (Urdang, 2001). This created fierce competition among males to find eligible brides.

Because men had a shorter lifespan and married at an older age, women frequently were widowed at a younger age (Urdang, 2001). This afforded women some unusual opportunities to head households and acquire property in their own names, at a time when women themselves were frequently viewed as property with few rights.

Sidebar 2.2
Early American Childrearing Practices

Early America featured some very interesting childrearing practices. Children were frequently swaddled so tightly they could be hung on a hook over the fireplace to keep them warm in the cold, drafty home of early America. Children were unswaddled and their diapers changed twice a day. Diapers were frequently dried by the fire and placed back on the infant—unwashed! Infants were bathed once a week. In an attempt to keep them warm, the water was sometimes heated so hot that occasionally the child was scalded. Crawling was viewed as barbaric, so wooden contraptions were created to suspend the pre-walking child in an upright position—often for hours on end. A very different picture of childrearing than existed later in American history.

Source: Calvert 1992.

A Perilous Time. In Colonial America, childhood was viewed as a perilous time, a time of frequent illnesses and, all too often, death in the first year of life (Calvert, 1992). Parents struggled to maintain loose affections for their children because so many died in infancy or early childhood

(Garrett, 1990). The goal of parenting was to usher children out of infancy as quickly as possible and to develop their independence. This independence was thought to be good for both children and parents. Sitting and crawling were considered demeaning and animalistic, so children's furniture was meager and made in such a way as to encourage upright posture and walking as soon as possible (Calvert, 1992) (see Sidebar 2.2). Toys were scarce, since children were pushed toward adulthood and adult activities. As adults, the focus tended to be on the present rather than reflecting back on childhood.

During this early stage of American history, children did not attend school but instead were used as a source of labor to help the family survive. Gender roles were clearly defined and enforced by the family. Boys were expected to assist their fathers in building and woodworking, as well as hunting, fishing, and growing crops. Girls were taught the skills women needed to be good wives, including grinding corn, cooking, baking, and sewing.

The Influence of Religion. The United States was the first modern nation founded by Protestants and the first to enforce strict division of church and state (Brinkley, 2003). Therefore, religion was of primary importance in Colonial culture—both as a starting point for a colony and as a method of maintaining solidarity within a colony. Religion at this time, in this part of the world, consisted almost exclusively of various Christian or Protestant denominations, many of which had been persecuted or banned in Europe.

Sidebar 2.3
Mandatory Church Attendance

In 1619, everyone in Virginia was required to attend worship services on the Sabbath. How would this requirement affect us in the 21st century?

Source: Brinkley, 2003

The Colonies were established by groups of people who shared similar religious beliefs and wanted the freedom to express them. These beliefs often became the hallmark of a colony, guiding the behavior of the inhabitants. The varied religious cultures of Early America shaped the most basic human interactions, establishing a sense of identity for both men and women, defining the spousal relationship, and instituting guidelines for rearing children. Religious beliefs also served to maintain the strict gender distinctions common in early Colonial times (see Sidebar 2.3).

Family norms tended to be regionally and religiously determined. In addition, they were related to whether a person was free, a slave, or a redemptioner (a person who agreed to a period of servitude in return for passage to the New World; a redemptioner might also serve to pay for the child's passage). Values such as hard work, discipline, and self-denial—all embraced by religious beliefs—were positive aspects of Colonial life. The Bible was often used as the basis for regulating the behavior and morality of the people. As the colonies began to form fledgling governments, religion was indispensable for maintaining order.

Free families were families of "production." A family of production was responsible for providing for its own needs. In this early time, there were no stores from which a family could purchase what it needed. All family members were involved in providing for the family. In this endeavor, it was not unusual for prepubescent children to be placed as servants in other households. In addition to being the main unit of production, families were also primarily responsible for their own education and religious teaching. The size and composition of the family determined its needs, especially its economic needs. A large family required more food and other essentials. However, a large family could also allow for a greater division of labor, especially if the children were old enough to contribute.

The Puritans and Patriarchal Authority. The early settlers of the New World brought with them their European customs of family life. While families tended to be large, their houses were small. Often, these houses consisted of only one room, and were situated close together for protection. Furniture was practical, but not comfortable—most often this included a chair for the man and sometimes a bench or stools for the others. The father was expected to teach the children to read and write, to lead prayers, and to carry on the bulk of correspondence with extended family members. He was considered the legal parent and was responsible for the actions of his wife and children. In a divorce situation, he would receive custody of the children. He was authorized to punish an insubordinate wife or unruly child and could be punished himself if he did not "keep his family in line."

Image from BigstockPhoto.com / Sue Smith

Pioneer families tended to be large and their houses small, often consisting of only one room.

Fathers also bore the responsibility for placing children in their occupations and consenting to their marriages. Love and physical attraction were not prerequisites for marriage in the 1600s. Instead, when children were old enough to marry, property, religion, and family interests were considered most important in the choice of a spouse. Fathers in the 1600s often kept their children dependent on them for years in order to aid in family production. This dependence occurred because most grown children could not fully establish their own independence until they inherited land—and fathers controlled the land (Mintz, 2007a).

Image from BigstockPhoto.com / vonora

Despite the expectation of submission, the role of women often extended beyond their expected household duties to include working side by side with men in the field.

The Role of Women. For the Puritans, patriarchal authority was considered God-mandated. Patriarchal authority is the belief men have authority over women and children and are responsible for their behavior. The spirit of this patriarchal authority is reflected in the writings of the great 17th-century poet John Milton: "God's universal law gave to man despotic power over his female in due awe" (Milton, 2001). Despite the expectation of submission, the role of women often extended beyond their expected household duties to include working side-by-side with men in the field (Kulikoff, 1986). Women who were not submissive were labeled "witches, whores, and scolds" (Brown, 1996). Certain punishments were designed especially to force women into submission.

Women tolerated this subordinate role because it was their only way to gain status as adults. Despite the requirement to be submissive to men, women were engaged in trade and domestic production, and sometimes even administered estates. Their time was limited by domestic duties and childcare; however, older daughters and servants frequently assumed the tasks of childcare, which freed the wife for other "productive" functions.

Girls were socialized against strong emotions, especially anger. Young girls were taught to share themselves, their time, and their possessions as preparation for the role they would assume as a wife in a tranquil marriage (Garrett, 1990). All children were taught the value of hard work and obedience.

The idea of patriarchal authority began to erode as early as the late 1600s among the Puritans in New England, but not until the 1700s in the middle and southern colonies. This is in part due to better health in the

Hulton Archive / Hulton Archive / Getty Images

In marked contrast to the Puritans, who forbade women to preach before men, Quakers elevated women to complete equality with men, even to preaching in meetings.

Puritan colonies, which led to a decrease in the mortality rate and an increase in the birth rate (Mintz, 2001). Other colonies were still plagued by a high mortality rate, resulting in a complicated mix of stepparents, stepchildren, wards, half-brothers, and half-sisters (Redefining Family, 2005). New England was the first society in American history in which grandparents were commonplace (Mintz, 2001).

The Role of Children

The Puritans viewed children as miniature adults; therefore, play was less acceptable in Puritan colonies than in the other colonies. To the orderly Puritan mind, playthings were unproductive and wasteful, distracting children and adults from the important tasks in life. Further, Puritans connected toys and dolls with the evil use of poppets (amulets) used in the practice of witchcraft (Calvert, 1992).

The Puritans stressed human sinfulness and what they called child depravity. Thus, they strove for complete authority over their children and used every means to "break the will" of youngsters. Their childrearing practices, therefore, tended to be harsh.

This view of childrearing was not necessarily reflected in other New World colonies. Many children grew up with very different experiences than children in New England. Other colonies were

Image from BigstockPhoto.com / ArtPixz

While the New England Puritans stressed sinfulness in their children and sometimes used harsh childrearing practices, other colonies were less occupied with sinfulness and preferred to mold and shape their children through pious moral example.

less preoccupied with human sinfulness and child depravity. Rather than break the child's will or annihilate a child's sense of self, these colonists preferred to mold or shape the wills and consciences of their children by pious, moral example.

The Quakers and Noncoerciveness. Quaker families in the Pennsylvania, Delaware, and New Jersey colonies were less patriarchal. They placed more importance on the value of women in the home and on maternal nurturance of children. They stressed affection, friendship, and hospitality. Children grew up in an environment which valued self-disciplined, non-coercive childrearing. Children were encouraged to become self-sufficient early, and parents often provided an early dowry of land for daughters and sons so they could become independent.

The Role of Quaker Women. In marked contrast to the Puritans, who forbade women to preach before men, Quakers elevated women to a complete equality with men, even to preaching in meetings. Centuries ahead of general thinking on equality of the sexes, both parents were head of the Quaker family, and the young spoke of "my father and mother's house" (Fischer, 1989).

Quaker Religious and Communal Life. The early Quakers gathered for worship in silence, without liturgy, or any appointed preacher. However, since the earliest times, Quakers have recorded (but not ordained) ministers to act as spiritual leaders. Their belief was that every person has an inner capacity to understand the Word of God and to offer an opinion.

The Quakers were strong believers in action by committees, which were appointed for everything imaginable, including attendance at weddings and funerals, as witnesses. In contrast to the Puritans, Quakers were the first to plead for religious tolerance and the first to befriend the Native-Americans and the African slaves. Later, the Quakers were instrumental in helping to abolish slavery and often provided freedom through the Underground Railroad for runaway slaves.

The Growing Nation: Life in the Eighteenth Century

A Shift in Perspective

By the late 1600s, the view of childhood began to change. It was seen as a period of preparation for life rather than a period of vulnerability. This allowed parents to take greater delight in their children's "childishness." The assumptions about a child's needs changed significantly. A new interest in child development allowed considerable freedom for children, in comparison to the earlier part of the century.

Religion continued to be a hallmark of the New World during the 1700s. Between 1700 and 1740, it is estimated 75 to 80% of the Colonial population attended churches, which were being built at a rapid pace (Religion and the Founding of the American Republic, 2006).

Religious freedom in the New World took some interesting turns during this time. While the Great Awakening (1730-1740s) was occurring—a strong evangelical thrust of Protestantism (the antithesis of evangelicalism—Deism) was arising among some upper-class Americans. Though Deists never became more than "a minority within a minority," they are just one indication of what would become a pillar of American ideology—religious tolerance (Religion and the Founding, 2006).

Family life in the colonies slowly began to improve at this time. By the mid-1700s, conditions adversely affecting the family structure of both European-born and African settlers were changing, and children were less likely to spend a portion of their childhood in a family with a stepparent and stepsiblings (Kulikoff, 1986). As life expectancy rose, the number of men and women began to equal out. Competition for available women was more civil. The downside of this change for women was that it also reduced some of the power women had managed to obtain when they had more choice in a marriage partner. As life expectancy increased, the population of the European settlers began to replace itself. White settlers were marrying earlier and having more surviving children. The overall environment became more stable, and the white settlers were enjoying a more stable course of family development. Nationally, the Colonies continued to grow because religious persecution in England and other European countries continued to drive people to the New World, where religious freedom was heralded.

Two key, but very contradictory, elements began to take root in the burgeoning American conscience: (1) a desire for independence from the Old World (England and Europe as a whole) and, (2) a growing dependence on slavery as an institution.

African-Americans

While Native-Americans were brutally uprooted from their homes and moved to reservations (where they were relegated to second-class status) they at least remained in their homeland and often remained in family or tribal groups.

Africans experienced even more shocking injustices. Torn from their homelands, separated from their families, forced into slavery, and given little more status than an animal (at best, two thirds of a human being during Colonial times), African-Americans survived and eventually overcame the terrible wrongs done to them.

Cultural Assimilation. Assimilation was virtually impossible for early African-Americans. The first African-Americans to arrive in the colonies had been captured from their home in Angola and sold in Jamestown in the early 1600s. Many of these first African-Americans were allowed to raise crops and cattle to purchase their freedom, and to marry and purchase their own farms in Jamestown. By the early 1700s, court rulings established the racial basis for slavery to apply primarily to African-Americans and occasionally to Native-Americans. These court rulings institutionalized slavery and allowed it to prosper (Hashaw, 2007). African slaves had become an essential part of the European settler's life.

Nearly all the slaves in the New World were brought from various parts of Africa. The harsh conditions in the New World were just as difficult for the new African immigrants, if not more so, than for the European colonists. Africans experienced the same high mortality rate and skewed sex ratio as the European colonists.

Africans came from various family traditions based on their national origin and religion. Because of the vast cultural differences, as well as separation from families, replication of their original family style was virtually impossible. The struggle was how to rebuild kinship in a new, unfamiliar land. How much should be African, how much should be European, and how much should be a new model based on the experiences and circumstances they encountered? The constraints of slavery will probably never be fully understood. We do know, however, that, for better or worse, African slaves were forced to adopt many of the white settlers' cultural norms, including religion.

Fictive Kin. American slaves were considered property and could not legally marry. Therefore, having a permanent family was not a guaranteed part of a slave's life. Couples frequently lived on different plantations and could see each other only with the permission of the husband's master. Children usually resided with their mothers, but mothers could not protect their children from being sold to another plantation owner (Redefining Family, 2005).

Over time, an extended kin network of blood relatives and non-blood relatives, called fictive kin, took in and cared for children who were separated from their parents. In this way, slave culture taught young people they were members of a broader community in which all slaves, whether related or not, had mutual obligations. The Christmas holiday was frequently the only holiday slaves were allowed to observe. Thus, it was an eagerly awaited time to reunite with separated family members. Even though the familial bond under slavery was fragile, enslaved men and women considered themselves married. They recognized kin by using kin names for their children rather than that of their master, which was customary. They also cared for their elderly and other relatives. Despite these difficulties, most slaves managed to create strong unions over long periods of time. The strength of the slave family is evident in the advertisements slave owners posted for runaway slaves. These advertisements revealed that one of the major reasons slaves fled their masters' plantations was to visit family members (Cayton, Gorn, & Williams, 1993).

The American Revolution (1775–1783) marked the end of British rule and the birth of the United States of America.

Cultural Interconnection. The close proximity of living conditions among masters and their slaves increased the influence of white and black families upon one another. Children of both races frequently played together until the white children reached the age of formal education, which was around 10 years of age. Young black girls frequently provided much of the childcare for white families. Sometimes the interconnection between black and white families was a matter of blood. Although laws forbade marriage between blacks and whites, interracial unions existed. Some were the result of the absolute authority masters had over powerless slaves, and some were the result of genuine affection between a black woman and her white master (Redefining Family, 2005).

The establishment of stable, nurturing slave families is the story of an unending struggle against great odds. History suggests slaves showed tenacious determination to make something good out of disastrous circumstances. As we look at various family struggles, the successful formation of the African-American family is a story of heroism in their struggle for both freedom and equality.

By the 1770s, slaves had succeeded in creating a distinctive African-American system of family and kinship. To sustain a sense of family identity, slave children were often named for a parent or other blood kin or given a traditional African name. By the latter 1700s, some religious groups (such as the Quakers) denounced slavery as against the laws of God, man, and nature, as well as being hurtful to society. Although tension increased over the issue of slavery, it was not until the United States split over the issue (North against the South during the Civil War {1861–1865}), that the Emancipation Proclamation (1863) freed the slaves in all Confederate states. The freed slaves were encouraged to join the North in defeating the South and ultimately in reuniting the country.

The American Revolution. By the mid-1700s, there was growing conflict between the Colonies and the mother country in areas of life, thought, political institutions, social customs, religious belief, and economic interests. The American Revolution (1775–1783) marked the end of British rule and the birth of the United States of America.

The Patriots were a mixed lot of the rich and poor—the common bond was their ideology of independence as a means of freeing themselves from British oppression and reasserting what they considered their rights (Nash, 2006). Patriot men were not the only ones involved in the war effort. Patriot women boycotted British goods, spied on the British, and followed the Patriot armies—washing, cooking, and tending to the soldiers—as well as maintaining the agricultural work at home to feed their families and the armies. American women willingly returned to spinning and weaving to aid the war effort—skills which had fallen into disuse (Berkin, 2005).

African-Americans, both men and women, understood Revolutionary rhetoric as promising freedom and equality. These hopes were not realized by African-Americans as the end of the war brought few changes for them, even those who fought with or assisted the Patriot armies. Many Native-Americans wished to remain neutral, seeing little value in participating in the European conflict, but most were forced to take sides. Because their towns were often attacked, one of the most fundamental effects of the war on Native-American women was the disruption of home, family, and agricultural life (Berkin, 2005).

The Age of Enlightenment: Family Life in the Nineteenth Century

The 1800s witnessed an outpouring of human knowledge in almost every field of human endeavor. Ideas which had sprung up in the mid-1700s, particularly concerning the rights of the individual, permeated what was to be called the Industrial Revolution (1750–1830). This "age of enlightenment" flooded philosophical, religious, political, and economic realms. See Sidebar 2.4 for President John Adams' comments on the age of enlightenment.

Image from BigstockPhoto.com / Jumpingsack

The age of enlightenment changed the view of family to one of a private retreat and included the father, mother, and children, rather than a household of kin groups.

Sidebar 2.4
On the Age of Enlightenment

The arts and sciences, in general, during the 3 or 4 last centuries, have had a regular course of progressive improvement. The inventions in mechanic arts, the discoveries in natural philosophy, navigation and commerce, and the advancement of civilization and humanity, have occasioned changes in the condition of the world and the human character which would have astonished the most refined nations of antiquity. A continuation of similar exertions is every day rendering Europe more and more like one community, or single family.

—John Adams (1735–1826)

Source: Kreis 2002.

During the early 1800s the commodified family was ushered in with the Industrial Age. In other words, the family itself became a commodity. With the disintegration of family farms and small family businesses, families gradually became units of consumption instead of production—consumers rather than producers. The world of work and the world of family became bifurcated as husbands and sometimes wives left their homes for substantial periods of time for work. Having "things" became more important than relationships for these commodified families, placing increasing pressure on families to bring in money to meet the family's demands for more and more things.

During the 1800s, the American family transformed from a public institution, whose function was primarily economic, into one whose role was psychological and ideological. This transformation brought about a new and more democratic family form. This new family form featured two hallmarks: (1) companionship and mutual affection between spouses and, (2) compassionate concern regarding childrearing.

A Companionate Notion of Marriage

The view of family changed to one of a private retreat instead of an integral part of the surrounding public institutions. For instance, apprentices and servants were moved out of the home into separate dwelling areas. The early part of the 1800s was marked by a rapid rise in the population, but the end of the century saw a lower birth rate. This resulted in smaller, more isolated families. This nuclear family included the father, mother, and children, rather than a household of kin groups.

A new division of domestic roles emerged as women were assigned full-time care of the children and maintenance of the home. Previously, the formality of patriarchal authority had characterized the relationship between spouses. Now, fewer spouses referred to one another as "Mister" or "Mistress" and fewer husbands used the term "Dear Child" for their wives (Mintz & Kellogg, 1988). Wives began referring to their husbands by their first name or used a pet name. With the change in attitude toward marriage, more weddings took place in churches and the ceremonies were more solemn and elaborate. Many brides began to wear a wedding band or ring, the symbol of everlasting love.

What we often call traditional Christian marriage today would closely resemble the Christian marriage of the enlightenment period. There was a growing rejection of the old notion of marriage as an economic exchange between two families (Mintz & Kellogg, 1988). Marriage increasingly symbolized an emotional bond between two people, reflecting genuine affection and equality between husbands and wives. A new, more companionate notion of marriage was emerging, as the older ideals of patriarchal authority were diminishing. The goal of this new style of marriage was personal happiness. With a growing emphasis on love in marriage, the basis for determining the success or failure of a marriage became the ability to give and receive love.

The Victorian Ideal. By the mid- 1800s, society began to change rapidly as a result of the Civil War, industrialization, and a huge immigrant influx of Irish, and later, Germans. As fathers left to fight wars and work in factories, the major cities gave rise to the more sentimental and gentle ideal of the Victorian family. This ideological change encouraged men to assume the sole responsibility of "breadwinner," a term coined in the early nineteenth century and unheard of in Colonial America. Women's roles changed to those of domesticity, a view that a woman was to devote herself to her husband, domestic duties, and childcare. Married women were not supposed to work for a wage. They were considered too pure and innocent to be out in the working world.

Ideology does not always translate into practicality. Despite the idea of a sole breadwinner, strict role divisions between the sexes, and the desire to give children a sheltered childhood, the practice of a cooperative economy continued to be the prevailing reality of the time. The wife continued to contribute economically to the family by sewing for others, selling baked goods, or performing other small tasks for income.

Innate Differences. Another prevalent idea which developed during this time was the belief there were innate differences in character between men and women. Men were thought to be more active, dominant, assertive, and materialistic. Women were thought to be more religious, modest, passive, submissive, and domestic

The wedding ceremony in the 1800s bears resemblance to wedding ceremonies today.

(Donnally, 1986). As a result, an ideal of American womanhood developed, denoted by historian Barbara Welter (1976) as a "cult of true womanhood." This cult, which was evident in much of the literature of the day, supported four basic attributes of female character: piety, purity, submissiveness, and domesticity. Piety or religion was the core of a woman's virtue and was given to her by God and nature. The essence of these ideas was that religion was a kind of tranquilizer. Young women were to pray rather than think, as they were responsible for preventing the ills of the world perpetrated by men. Thus, religion was once again used to define gender roles. It is easy to see how the double standard for men and women evolved from these ideas.

In many religious households, each morning began with prayer and Bible reading. Each day ended with the family reassembling to read the Bible or other literature out loud. On the Sabbath, the entire family attended church together. By mid-century, the idea of family vacations and family-centered holidays, such as birthdays, Christmas, and Thanksgiving emerged.

A Compassionate Approach to Childrearing

A new attitude toward children also emerged at this time. Early in the century, children were expected to contribute productively to the family. As the self-sufficient family ideal began to disappear, the role of children also began to change. By the mid-1800s, the concept of the family as a cooperative economic enterprise began to disappear. Children were still expected to help on the farm, but they were not considered a principal economic asset.

Education, Not Duties. Children came to be viewed as young innocents who needed a mother's protection from a corrupt world of sex, violence, and death. Instead of referring to an infant as "it," "the baby," or "the little stranger," as they had in the past, parents began using the child's first name. Children were now seen to need time to play. Childhood developed into an extended stage of life, and parents were not under pressure to hurry their children to adulthood. Parents accepted the fact that their children had distinctive needs and impulses (Mintz, 2004).

Communities began to place a high priority on education, and the schoolhouse became a central focus of the community. Often the teacher had little more than a sixth-grade education. Children were freed of some of their duties so they could attend school. As parents became more interested in their children's development, books on childrearing began to spring up. Child misbehavior was thought to be the result of improper supervision.

New Parenting Practices. Homes were now larger and more comfortable, with more consideration given to the children's needs. This resulted in an increase in children's toys, games, and furniture. Parenting practices changed from patriarchal authoritarianism to gentle guidance. Increased love and affection replaced the use of physical force in childrearing, which had been common in the previous century (Coontz, 1992). More mothers breastfed their own infants instead of using wet nurses. More credence was given to the effectiveness of loving, nurturing maternal discipline, rather than the paternal harshness which had previously existed. As a result, the father's role in raising the children began to decrease.

Children now stayed at home into their late teens or early twenties, which created additional burdens on the family. In theory, this was a lengthened time of training for adulthood. In reality, there were fewer opportunities than in the past for children to

As Americans began to favor city life, many men began to leave home to work in offices and factories

demonstrate their readiness for adulthood. This resulted in a separation between childhood and adulthood which had not been previously experienced. The concept of adolescence emerged from this separation during the latter part of the 1800s.

The Challenges of a New Market Economy

The new democratic family of the middle to late 1800s had two primary functions: emotional and civil. The family was now charged with the responsibility for the emotional support and happiness of its members. In addition, the family played a civil role in teaching the children the values of good citizenship, such as adherence to values, order, responsibility, and self-discipline.

This ideal-looking family form was plagued with struggles. Young women enjoyed increasing freedoms related to jobs and education prior to marriage. However, they were still subject to the expectations of their families, to put aside their own goals and to take on the goals of their husbands. Increasingly, the values of individuality and equality became the hallmarks of the new social order, but women were still expected to subordinate themselves to their husbands and children. During this period, men enjoyed the creation of male-only forms of recreation, such as saloons and red-light districts, while women still had few legal rights.

The Erosion of Parental Control. Because of ideological and economic changes in the family, parental control over children's behavior began to erode. Sons began enjoying greater freedom in their occupational choices, and daughters were marrying out of birth order — something unheard of in previous times. Parental control over sexual behavior weakened. Pregnancy, prior to marriage, and illegitimacy rose sharply. By mid-century, rapid population growth meant farms were too small to divide among the sons and still enable them to provide for a family. This inability to bestow an inheritance on children further reduced parental control over them. In addition, economic shifts produced new nonagricultural opportunities, and children began to move farther from their parents' homes.

Ironically, because of the nation's rapid material and geographic growth, the idea of family took on renewed significance as a refuge or sanctuary from the materialistic world. For Christians, the family also became the symbol of higher moral and spiritual values.

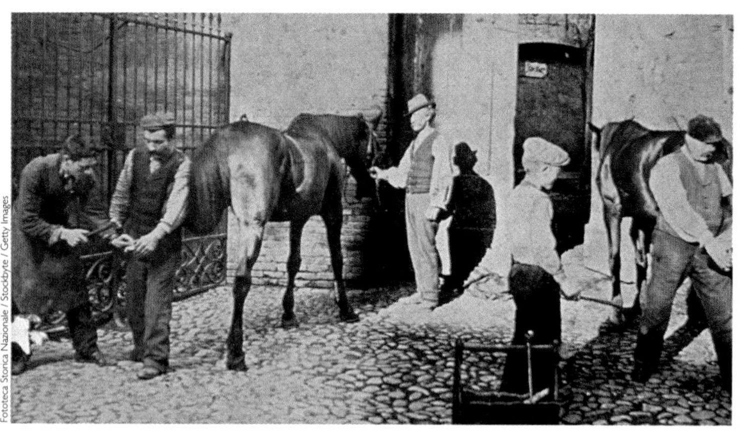
Fototeca Storica Nazionale / Stockbyte / Getty Images

Toward the latter part of the century, wages for manual labor were so low that wives and children frequently had to work just to maintain a minimum standard of living. Blacksmiths and machinists were the only laborers able to earn enough to support a family of five.

An Emphasis on Commerce. The economic transformations of the Industrial Revolution brought about further changes in men's and women's roles. As Americans began to favor city life, more men had to leave home to work in offices and factories. This brought about the emergence of two patterns of family life—the new urban working class and a return to an older pattern, the production family (Mintz, 2007b). The increase in commerce in the early part of the century caused a demand for shopkeepers and both skilled and unskilled laborers. This led to the rise of the urban working-class family with its emphasis on a cooperative family economy.

In a cooperative family economy, the family itself became a commodity, called a commodified family. Wives and children were expected to contribute about one third of the family's total income. In the poorest families, and particularly among newer immigrants, children often worked in factories or sold newspapers and trinkets on the streets. School was a luxury for these children because the child's income was needed to help support the family. Thus, even though public schools were more widely available, illiteracy rates actually rose during the early stages of the Industrial Revolution. Older children often delayed marriage so they could continue contributing to the family's income.

Toward the latter part of the century, wages for manual labor were so low wives and children frequently had to work just to maintain a minimum standard of living. Horace Greeley, editor of *The New York Tribune*, estimated a family of five required $10.37 per week to maintain a minimal existence. At that time, a textile operator earned $6.50 per week and an

The late 1800s also saw an increase in the push for suffrage (the right to vote) for women.

unskilled laborer earned only $1.00 per week. Blacksmiths and machinists were the only laborers able to earn Greeley's minimum (Mintz, 2007a).

New Worries. When husbands died or abandoned their families, women had no choice but to work outside the home. If a woman had some capital, she might open a little shop. However, if she did not have money, she often had no choice but to work in a factory. Factories came to be known as sweatshops because of the long hours and intolerable conditions. Women earned less than men doing the same job. Some women turned to prostitution, which offered more money and flourished in towns both big and small.

It was very difficult for a single mother or father to work and raise children. As a result, children of single parents were often left at orphanages or simply abandoned to the streets. This all predated Social Security, workers' compensation, unemployment insurance, retirement funds, health insurance, and other private and public programs to aid families in times of crisis.

New worries about the family emerged. The divorce rate steadily rose, and many states adopted permissive divorce statutes. Divorce had become the safety valve for a loveless, abusive marriage, at a time when marriage was based on mutual affection. In 1867, 10,000 divorces nationwide were recorded. In 1870, the rate rose to 3.1 per 100 marriages, to 4.5 per 100 in 1880, and to 5.9 per 100 in 1890 (National Center for Health Statistics, 1973).

In addition to divorce, other social ills began to plague the new nation. As the family became more privatized with less communal oversight, which included evaluating behavior based on religious principles, child and spousal abuse became more prevalent. The new market economy and the many changes taking place in the family now meant the family could become a place of violence rather than a place of retreat.

The late 1800s also saw an increase in the push for suffrage (the right to vote) for women. Early in the century, a few courageous women began what was to be a 72 year struggle for equal voting rights.

During the Civil War and immediately after, little was heard of the movement. However, in 1890, the National American Woman Suffrage Association (NAWSA) was formed from a merger between two rival factions—the National Woman Suffrage Association (NWSA) led by Elizabeth Cady Stanton and Susan B. Anthony, and the American Woman Suffrage Association (AWSA), led by Lucy Stone, Henry Blackwell, and Julia Ward Howe. In chapter 3 you will read more about the long battle to end the disenfranchisement of one half of the citizens of the United States, which changed the political and social meaning of being female in the United States.

Economic Downturn. Early in the nineteenth century, one of the indicators used to determine the health of the family—the birth rate—began to drop. By the end of the century, mothers were having an average of three children instead of the seven or eight which was common at the beginning of the century (Mintz, 2001). One reason for the decrease, children were no longer considered economic necessities. In addition, childrearing changed from one of restraint to one of nurture. The time required to care for each child increased, so parents reasoned they should reduce the number of children born into the family.

The Comstock Act (1873) was both a reaction to "the degradation of the day" and an attempt to curb the decline in the birth rate. It restricted distribution of contraceptive information and devices, as well as pornographic literature. Some states criminalized abortion. In a failed effort to curb the rising divorce rate, many states extended the waiting period for divorce and, overall, made it more difficult to obtain.

Rapid economic expansion is always accompanied by recession. The new, young Republic was no exception. Following several slumps in the economy, the first depression to hit was the crisis of 1837. Contributing to this panic were wide economic shifts and the rapid increase of immigrants from Europe, Asia, and Mexico.

Desertion and nonsupport of family were a growing problems. Eleven states made desertion and nonsupport of family felonies, and three states instituted the whipping post for wife beaters.

The Homestead Act opened up the Midwest and Plains with survival dependent on each family member.

Go West, Go Forth! With the downturn in the economy came Horace Greeley's familiar saying, "Go West, young man, go forth into the country" (McElroy, 2001), encouraging the countless numbers of unemployed—both skilled and unskilled—to think about the potential which lay to the West.

© Getty Images

Life for the early pioneers was hard. Uprooted from their previous ways of life, friends, and families, they lived in crude dwellings that served as shelter from the fierce winds that blew across the plains.

After the Civil War (1861–1865), and as a result of the Homestead Act (1862), settlers could receive 160 acres of land, provided they resided on it for 5 years. The Plains and Midwest became the new frontier, where people of little means could become landowners. This propelled family ideology back to the idea of the family as the unit of production, with Plains-family survival dependent on each family member.

Role Expectations. Life for the early pioneers was hard. They were uprooted from their previous ways of life, friends, and families. They lived in crude dwellings that served as shelter from the fierce winds that blew across the plains—homes which were impossible to keep clean in the blowing dust. Plains women suffered loneliness, food shortages, and perilous childbearing. Many communities were settled by the Mennonites, who came to the United States from Russia and Germany. By the mid-1800s, the average pioneer family consisted of a nuclear family of five—a husband, wife, and three children (McNall, 1983).

The role expectations in Plains families were clearly defined. Men did the heaviest labor—working the land, construction, and fence-building on a homestead, mining in the camps, and various big-muscle jobs in the new towns—and took off in search of other wage work when necessary. Early in the settlement of the Plains, a production ideology identified women as an economic asset. Women were responsible for the multitude of domestic duties: caring for barnyard animals, gardening, and earning cash by washing, cooking, and sewing for others. Children were a vital resource for pioneer families, filling in wherever they were needed: hunting, weeding, gathering wild plants, herding, delivering laundry, caring for younger siblings, cooking, canning, and much more (West, 1994). Women, more than men, were responsible for maintaining a good Christian home and upholding the values of society. Women also had a primary responsibility of service to others (McNall, 1983).

The image of the frontier is often viewed as one of individualism, self-reliance, and rugged adult males. But the transformation of the nineteenth-century West could be more accurately pictured as a familial conquest—an occupation by tens of thousands of interdependent households.

By the late 1800s, the Great Plains were bustling with well established cities, towns, and communities. Small-town America was basically Protestant, with the settlers' religious values mirroring their pragmatism and positive attitude toward success. The Puritan influence was evident in the individualism which marked these frontier families. However, this individualism coexisted with a cooperative spirit among individuals and families. Morality in small-town America meant being a God-fearing Christian.

African-American Families in the 1800s

During the years of slavery, most slave children lived with their mothers but knew their fathers. While many marriages lasted 20 years or more, family breakup was common—often the result of the sale of the husband or wife. Even when marriages were not broken by sale, slave husbands and wives often resided on separate farms or plantations and were owned by different individuals.

Slavery and servitude were virtually abolished between the 1770s and the 1830s in the Northern states. African-Americans in the North could legally establish families. In Northern black churches couples were married, children were baptized, and new surnames chosen by former slaves were recorded. Benevolent societies looked out for their members' welfare and sheltered slaves who escaped from slave-holding areas.

During the decades before the Civil War, most slaves lived in nuclear households, consisting of two parents and their children. In the mid-1800s, approximately three fourths of all slaves lived in two-parent families and one fourth lived in single-parent families. Another 10% lived outside of a family unit, either alone or with others of the same sex (Cayton, Gorn, & Williams, 1993).

After the Emancipation Proclamation in 1863, newly freed African-Americans struggled to reestablish family lives of their own. Many families which had been separated managed to re-form into stable units. However, it was still more likely for black children than white children to live in female-headed households. (You will see in chapter 11 this trend has continued into the 21st century.) Education was important to African-American families. After slavery was abolished, frequently both parents worked so their children could attain an education.

Constitutional Amendments. Three important amendments affecting African-Americans were added to the Constitution. The 13th Amendment (1865) ended slavery in the United States. The 14th Amendment (1868) allowed blacks to have the same rights as whites. The 15th Amendment (1870) allowed black males to vote. While restrictions still prevented many black males from voting, you will see in the next chapter these amendments were very important for the civil rights movement in the 1950s and 1960s.

Christianity and Blacks. In the early decades of the 1800s, there was little attempt to evangelize slaves. The reasons were varied, but most were based on fear—fear the slaves might take the Exodus literally, or fear of what some considered the "strange rituals and dogmas" which characterized many of the slaves' worship patterns. Some slave owners, unfortunately, did not consider slaves as having souls to be saved. Another dilemma surfaced regarding baptism. If a slave was baptized, how could a Christian slave owner justify holding a Christian slave?

The first real interest in the evangelization of African-Americans came from the Quakers, who taught friendship of all humanity. By the late 1700s and early 1800s, traveling missionaries developed among the Baptists and Methodists, and later the Presbyterians, preached to blacks and whites alike, winning over most African-Americans by attacking all evils, including slavery. Because most African-Americans already believed in a Supreme Being, drew a distinction between good and evil, and saw creation as the handiwork of a Supreme Being, conversion to Christianity was not particularly difficult. As the slaves began to accept Christian beliefs, similarities and differences arose between blacks and whites in the practice of religion. One of the most noticeable differences still evident today is the expressiveness of black religion (Matthews, 1995).

The early 1800s witnessed the birth of the independent-black-church movement, which grew out of Methodism and Baptism. One reason the conversion of blacks was so successful was the emphasis on plain doctrine and having good discipline. The black church grew rapidly. An example is the African Methodist Episcopal Church whose membership was nearly 10,000 only 8 years after it was organized (Woodson, 1921).

Asian-American Families in the 1800s

The earliest Asian immigrants were wealthy Chinese businessmen and their families who found a welcome reception among the wealthy in the young America. This changed when a series of droughts,

While the Chinese immigrants were vitally involved in the mining process during the California gold rush, they are perhaps best known for their contribution to the completion of the transcontinental railroad.

wars, and famines in China caused large numbers of Chinese to immigrate to California in the mid 1800s. These laborers, called "coolies," were hard workers and did many of the "dirty jobs" no one else would do. The Chinese immigrants were vitally involved in the mining process during the California gold rush, but are perhaps best known for their contribution to the completion of the transcontinental railroad, which physically, economically, and culturally united the young country (Daniels, 2002; The History of Chinese, 2000). Despite their contributions, the Chinese experienced severe exploitation and discrimination which continued into the mid-1900s. The hostility was so great that many fled to the coasts where they found safety and support from small groups of Chinese society. The Chinese Exclusion Act of 1882 prevented further immigration of Chinese to America; however, some still managed to find ways to enter. This was the first time a specific group of people was singled out as undesirable and presented a dramatic departure from American policy of unrestricted immigration (Wei, 1993).

The earliest Chinese communities looked much like "bachelor communities" in that men outnumbered women 20 to 1. Many of the new Chinese immigrants were married, but their wives were still living in China. This prevented assimilation into American society, since family formation is the major way acculturation occurs (Daniels, 2002). Because of the apparent rejection of American society and the lack of assimilation, pockets of Chinese culture called "Chinatowns" developed across the nation and still exist today as thriving cultural centers in many major cities (Daniels, 2002).

The economic, social, and political constraints present in the 1800s influenced the prevailing split-household Chinese family. Until the early 1900s, Chinese-American families tended to create two separate households, with the male (or males if father and son) in the United States and the wife, children, and other relatives in China. Husbands and wives led completely separate lives, with fathers having the primary economic responsibility and mothers forming the primary attachment with the children. The split-household family continued until about 1920 (Glenn, 2007).

The first group of Japanese immigrants came in the late 1800s as political refugees. Initially, immigrants were primarily male but by the early 20th century, immigrants were almost exclusively female, often marrying and establishing families with Japanese men they had never met. The Japanese immigrants worked as agricultural laborers and by the early 20th century were farming much of California's agricultural land. Although there was no exclusion act as there was for the Chinese, the Japanese, like other ethnic groups, experienced discrimination (Daniels, 2002).

Shortly after the American annexation of the Philippines in 1898, groups of Filipino students came to the United States and some of them stayed, establishing Filipino-American communities at the end of the century. Like other Asians, they too experienced discrimination.

Hispanic-American Families in the 1800s

In the early 1800s, much of the South and Southwest was part of Mexico. In 1846, war broke out between Mexico and America. The victorious Americans claimed not only Texas, but Mexican territory in California, Nevada, Utah, Mexico, Wyoming, and Arizona. Mexicans were given the chance to remain in the United States as citizens or return to Mexico and most chose to remain. These Mexicans cannot be considered immigrants because they were already living on what became American soil and, therefore, were the first Mexican-American population (Brinkley, 2003).

Mexican Americans, like the Chinese, suffered discrimination from stereotypes, such as dirty and unfair, but the booming U.S. economy lured many more across the border, creating an explosion of Mexican-American immigrants by the end of the 1800s. Most Mexican Americans were Catholic, which clashed with the predominantly Protestant American settlers, creating yet another point for discrimination (Daniels, 2002).

Mexican-American families, like Anglo-American families, demonstrated diversity in their living arrangements. Mexican-American families generally consisted of extended family, as well as a variety of others, both related and non-related, living together with a married couple. While the proportion of extended-family households has decreased since the 1800s, la familia (term which describes the close bonds of affection between kin, extended kin, and adopted kin) is still a very important part of Hispanic families today (Del Castillo, 2007).

The mid 1800s brought other immigrants to young America. The largest group of immigrants was Irish. The potato famine in Ireland resulted in an influx of Irish immigrants during the mid to late 1800s. Most of these Irish immigrants settled in the Eastern seaports. While some came as families, the Irish population was overrepresented by males. This changed over time as young, single female immigrants began to outnumber the young, single male immigrants. The massive immigration of the 1840s transformed the Catholic Church in America, swelling its numbers and increasing anti-Irish and anti-Catholic sentiment (Daniels, 2002).

A series of crop failures and a failed revolution brought an exodus of German immigrants to America. Many of these German immigrants settled in Pennsylvania, the Midwest, and the Mississippi Valley (Brinkley, 2003). While like the Irish immigrants in many ways, the German immigrants brought a foreign language and represented three different religious groups—Protestants (mostly Lutheran), Catholics, and Jews. Germans were more likely than the Irish to migrate in family groups and establish close-knit groups of German families, many of which continued speaking German. This presented a source of contention for English-speaking Americans (Daniels, 2002).

Nativism, a policy of favoring the interests of native inhabitants over those of immigrants, may seem strange in a nation of immigrants; however, the 1800s reflect numerous examples of attempts to exclude or limit newcomers. Nativists complained the newcomers drank too much, the Catholicism some of them practiced was opposed to American Democratic principles, and their willingness to work for the lowest of wages threatened the livelihood of American workers. Immigrants were blamed for their own poverty, lack of education, crime, and political corruption (Brinkley, 2003).

Nativism in the 1800s came in three phases. The first phase was anti-Catholic, aimed at Irish Catholics and to some extent, German Catholics. The second phase was anti-Asian, triggered by Chinese immigration and ending with the Chinese Exclusion Act of 1882. Finally, the third phase, anti-all immigration, began in the mid-1880s when a general restriction of immigration gained popularity. Sadly, there has never been a time in America when nativist attitudes did not exist. They existed in the Colonial period, throughout American history, and they are enjoying a revival today (Daniels, 2002).

A Christian Perspective

The Christian faith in its various forms was foundational to early American history. It was the reason most immigrants came to the New World. It framed the societal and family infrastructure of the Colonies. It fueled the Great Awakening and its evangelistic outreach across the nation and was responsible for a growing perception of the United States as a "redeemer nation . . . building on the idea of Americans as a 'chosen' people, divinely ordained by history to be a light for all humankind" (Johnson & Johnson, 2004).

Values such as hard work, discipline, and devotion to family grew out of the Christian perspective. These same values were reflected in the pioneer spirit as the country grew. Christian ethical parameters served as safeguards during the unbridled expansion of the Industrial Revolution. The Bible was often used as the basis for regulating the behavior and morality of the people. The legal framework of this young nation was based on Judeo-Christian principles, and most families reflected biblical patterns in their understanding of roles and responsibilities.

Summary

In this chapter we have seen how family has remained a vital part of American culture and society, with no indication of demise. The *form* of family underwent changes during the eighteenth and nineteenth centuries, but the *institution* of family remained an integral part of American society.

Early in the history of this country, the family was considered a unit of production responsible for its own survival. Marriage was often seen as an economic arrangement. Childhood was short and children were a commodity involved in contributing to the needs of the family. Large families were the norm, allowing for a greater division of labor.

During the Enlightenment of the 1800s, the American family was viewed less as a public institution, whose function was primarily economic, and came to be seen as one whose primary role was psychological and ideological. This ushered in a new and more democratic family form with two features: a companionate relationship between spouses, and a compassionate concern for children.

The Homestead Act propelled settlers into the West, where the pendulum of family ideology began to swing back to a unit of production, with its more restrictive role expectations. By the end of the nineteenth century, the American family was poised between small-town, God-fearing morality which honored the family, and big-city influences which was credited with the potential to breakdown the family.

Questions for Thought

1. In 1619, everyone in Virginia was required to attend services on the Sabbath. How would this requirement affect us today?

2. "From both nineteenth-century fiction and science emerges the belief in childhood as a special realm, a place to which adults can never return but which they can always remember." (Brown, 2003). This statement is said to express the overwhelming myth pervading the history of childhood in early America. Do you agree? Why or why not?

3. Which of the family types profiled in this chapter most closely fits your idea of the ideal family? Explain.

Resources

Activities:

1. Compare and contrast a classic TV/movie series (Little House on the Prairie, Christy, Bonanza, etc.) with this chapter.

2. Find your ancestors' immigration records at: http://www.ellisisland.org (accessed June 23, 2009)

3. Website: PBS quiz on daily life for different social groups: http://pbskids.org/stanton anthony/day_in_life.html (accessed June 23, 2009)

Books:

The American Girl Series: Historical fiction books for young girls about life at different times and in different cultures throughout American history. (American Girl Publishing, Inc.)

American Literature, Volume 1 by William E. Cain. This collection of American Literature includes the narrative of the life of Frederick Douglas, *The Scarlet Letter* by Nathaniel Hawthorne, some Puritan sermons by Jonathon Edwards, Anne Bradstreet's letter to her "Dear and Loving Husband," and many more poems and stories. Reading pieces from the different time frames enables a person to picture what individuals and families experienced during those times. (Longman, 2004)

Little Women by Louisa May Alcott. This novel, set during the time of the Civil War, details the lives of four sisters and the many adventures they experience as they grow from children into young women. (Tyndale House Publishing, 2004)

Movies:

Little Women. DVD. A movie based on the book by Louisa May Alcott

Online Video: African-American Lives, Part II

A series that traces the history and genealogy of famous African-Americans, including Maya Angelou and Don Cheadle. http://www.pbs.org/wnet/aalives/videos/ index.html (accessed June 23, 2009)

3 The Changing Face of the American Family

Modern History

He who brings trouble on his family will inherit only wind,
and the fool will be servant to the wise.
—Proverbs 11:29

This is not your grandfather's family.
—Swindoll, 2006

Many people reflect nostalgically on the period from the late 1800s through the mid-1900s. Television programs such as *Leave It to Beaver* and *Ozzie and Harriet* depict an idyllic family scene: a pleasant mom and dad, well-adjusted children, a happy dog, a nice house with a white picket fence, and a dependable car in the driveway. The most serious family problem could always be solved in the course of one program, including commercials. Some might suggest these were "ideal times" or "the good old days." Has the American family disintegrated since then? Is the 21st century American family, as so often depicted by the media, in deep trouble?

The American Family from 1900 to 1950

> There's an epidemic of sexually-transmitted diseases among men. Many streets in urban neighborhoods are littered with cocaine vials. Youths call heroin "happy dust." Even in small towns, people have easy access to addictive drugs, and drug abuse by middle-class wives is skyrocketing. Police see 16-year-old killers, 12-year-old prostitutes, and gang members as young as 11 (Coontz, 1999, p. 79).

Does this sound like the state of America at the end of the 20th century? Actually, according to family historian Stephanie Coontz, this describes the end of the 1800s. She explains that times were actually worse at the beginning of the 1900s than they are today. Most laborers worked 10 hours a day, 6 days a week, leaving little time for family life. Children, too, often worked full-time in mines, mills, and sweatshops. Women did not have the right to vote. Their wages were so low that some women turned to prostitution. Race riots were more frequent and more deadly at the beginning of the 20th century than in more recent times. A white child had a 1 in 3 chance of losing a sibling before the age of 15, and a black child had a 50–50 chance of losing a sibling (Coontz, 1999). Only 6% of children graduated from high school at the beginning of the 20th century, compared to 69% in 2000 (Green & Winters, 2002). Child abuse and neglect were widespread, and men who left their families rarely paid child support. Sidebar 3.1 examines other startling facts about this time in the history of the American family.

As noted in the previous chapter, the breakdown of the family was such a crisis in the early part of the century that John Watson, one of the most famous child psychiatrists of the 20th century, predicted marriage would be dead by 1977 (Watson, 1928). As late as 1977, Amatai Etzioni

At the turn of the century, wages were low and most laborers worked 10 hour days, 6 days a week, leaving little time for family life.

(1977), sociologist and member of the Research Advisory Board of the National Marriage Project, stated that by the mid-1990s not one American family will be left."

SIDEBAR 3.1
WHO WOULD HAVE GUESSED?

- The 1920s was the first time that the majority of American families consisted of a breadwinner husband, a homemaker wife, and children attending school.
- The most rapid increase in unwed pregnancies took place between 1940 and 1958.
- Teen childbearing was higher in the 1950s than today.
- The defining characteristics of the 1950s family—a rising birth rate, stable divorce rate, and a declining age of marriage—were a glitch in history—out of sync in comparison to long-term historical trends.
- Throughout the history of America, most families have needed more than one breadwinner to support the family.

Source: Coontz, 1999: pp. 79, 90, 92, 94.

Governmental Intervention

It is no wonder these fears about the future of the family were met with an increase in governmental involvement. Groups representing the medical, legal, and social aspects of family life emerged to address the problems plaguing the American family. They included pediatricians, judges in the juvenile court system, psychologists, and social workers. Each of these groups offered "expert" advice on childrearing, parenting, and social policy, in an attempt to strengthen the family.

The Progressive Reform Movement of the early 1900s sought to curb the decline of the family. This movement inspired laws enforcing compulsory school attendance, child labor restrictions, the Pure Milk Act, the first seniority systems in the workplace, as well as pensions for widows (allowing children to remain with their mothers). These broad attempts to restore the family also included the prohibition of alcohol and the elimination of male-only forms of recreation, such as red-light districts.

However, racism and prejudice also played into social policy. For example, when single white girls became pregnant, they often were secretly sent to private homes and their babies given up for adoption. Single black girls in the same circumstances were often said to be immoral, and their pregnancies were touted as an example of the "inferiority" of African-Americans. Sometimes these girls were even forcibly sterilized (Mintz & Kellogg, 1988).

The Suffrage Movement

As you will recall from chapter 2, agitation for equal suffrage (the right to vote) began in the early 1800s and the

National American Woman Suffrage Association was formed in 1890. After a courageous and persistent political campaign, the 19th Amendment was passed in 1920. This amendment gave women the right to vote and had enormous political and social significance, even though American history has given it little attention. The suffragists' deliberate rejection of violence may be one of the reasons the movement has not received the attention lavished on other more bloody periods of American history (Cooney, 2005).

Full political citizenship for women is tantamount to full human dignity. Although women would continue to be regarded as subordinate for years to come, winning the right to vote was possibly the biggest step toward equality. The right to vote embodied the recognition that women had the ability to reason, the power of judgment, and the capability for social responsibility and effective action (Flexner & Fitzparick, 1996). You do not need to be female, a feminist, or even politically minded to see the importance of the suffrage movement. The importance lies in the larger story, which is about democracy and how a powerless class of Americans won concessions and guarantees from those in power, without the use of violence (Cooney, 2005).

The importance of the suffrage movement lies in the larger story about democracy and how a powerless class of Americans won concessions and guarantees from those in power without the use of violence.

The Role of Religion

During the early 1900s and further into the century, a new missionary movement gained strength. This movement began after the Civil War when missionaries evangelized newly freed slaves (Matthews, 1995). It grew throughout the 1900s to include a strong interest in international missions (Bays, 2005). Ironically, while international mission outreach expanded, religion's power over the general American community saw a decline during the same time period. This parallels the development of the American family into a more private institution, with the practice of religion becoming a family issue.

The Impact of World War I

After World War I (1914–1918), the cooperative family economy of the previous century gave way to the family-wage economy. For the first time in history, male breadwinners were able to support their families on their incomes alone. The compassionate family became the ideal family. In an attempt to strengthen and stabilize the family, writings on marriage promoted this concept of the ideal family in the literature of the time. In many ways, this compassionate family model was similar to the companionate model of the previous century. Husbands and wives were encouraged to be both friends and lovers, and parents were instructed to be "pals" to their children. Privacy became the hallmark of the 20th-century family (Coontz, 1992).

Image from BigstockPhoto.com / ArtPixz

The Depression hit farmers particularly hard, not because they lacked products to sell, but because buyers were unable to offer enough to allow the farmers to break even.

The Great Depression. In 1929 the stock market crashed, ushering in the beginning of the Great Depression. The Depression hit farmers particularly hard, not because they lacked products to sell, but because buyers were unable to pay enough for the farmers to break even. Some farmers dumped or burned their grain or slaughtered their livestock in a desperate attempt to uphold prices (U.S. Department of Agriculture, 2009). Sidebar 3.2 illustrates how some farmers suffered and some farmers prospered. Between 1927 and 1934, one of every 10 farmers lost their farms. In the early 1930s, nearly one half of the farms sold were subject to foreclosure (U.S. Census Bureau, 1949). Over 2 million people, including children, roamed the streets looking for jobs and food (McNall, 1983).

The Family in Distress. The Great Depression is often thought of as an economic cataclysm, but the effects on the family were also significant. During this period, unemployment, low wages, and needy relatives tested the limits of the ideal (compassionate) family. As the Depression progressed, more and more men lost their jobs and were forced into the streets to look for any work they could find. Some were forced to steal food or money to feed their families (Elder, 1999). Divorce rates during the Depression fell because divorces were too costly, but the rate of desertions increased dramatically. By 1940, 1.5 million married couples were living apart (Mintz, 2001).

Many families lost their homes. Often, families were forced to share living arrangements with relatives to help make ends meet. Many families coped by returning to the structure of a cooperative family economy. Children frequently worked part-time jobs to help support their families, and wives often took in sewing, laundry, or lodgers to supplement family income. Many young people had to delay marriage or postpone having children. Because of these economic hardships, the perceived ideal of domestic life was impossible for most families to achieve. In an attempt to address the problems of the ailing economy, the government instituted the New Deal (1933–1945). This was a series of programs intended to bolster the male breadwinner role through the creation of relief programs, jobs, and the stimulation of economic recovery for the country (Brinkley, 2003).

Statue at the FDR Memorial remembering the breadlines during the Great Depression.

Sidebar 3.2

I remember my grandfather talking about the Depression. He was one of the lucky ones. He told of the day one of his neighbors was taking his hogs to be slaughtered because he couldn't afford to feed them any longer. My grandfather offered to take them for a small sum rather than have them slaughtered. As the country emerged from the Depression, my grandfather was able to sell some of the hogs, purchase more land, and become one of the largest farmers in that part of Missouri at that time.

—Anonymous

The Impact of World War II

A Dramatic Change for Women. During WWII (1941–1945), large numbers of married women began to work outside the home for the first time, many of them taking on previously male-dominated jobs (Caplow, Hicks, & Wattenberg, 2000). The poster image of "Rosie the Riveter" in work clothes, performing skilled, industrial labor, was more than a novelty. It embodied the heroic spirit of the time, women stepping into positions vacated by men who were engaged in a lengthy, horrific war.

Housing shortages, a lack of schools and childcare facilities, and the prolonged absence of loved ones placed tremendous strains on families. These wartime stresses contributed to an increased divorce rate. Thousands of children became latchkey kids, and the rates of juvenile delinquency, unwed pregnancy, and truancy escalated. To draw more women into the workplace, factories began to set up daycare centers. Women moved into increasingly responsible positions and provided support services for all branches of the military. They were paid the same as the men who had previously held these positions and received the same promotions. The impact was dramatic: married women were out of the house and earning their own money. The symbolic, domestic image of women in the late 1800s and early 1900s had now changed.

Absolute Stock Photo

Rosie the Riveter embodied the heroic spirit of the time, women stepping into positions vacated by men who were engaged in a lengthy, horrific war.

Changes in Marriage and Divorce Rates. In 1946, the year following World War II, marriages abounded. As illustrated in Figure 3.1, the marriage rate had dropped substantially from 1942 to 1944, due primarily to the war. The marriage rate then rose dramatically from 12.2 per 1,000 people in 1945 to 16.4 in 1946 (National Center for Health Statistics, 1973). Thousands of men returned home from war, and a spirit of optimism swept the nation. The first of the "baby boom" generation was born and families looked forward to a time of peace and prosperity.

The divorce rate, which had been slowly climbing from 1940 to 1944, rose from 3.5 to 4.3 per 1,000 people between 1945 and 1946 (National Center for Health Statistics, 1973). The increase in divorces was primarily due to the large number of marriages which took place just before the men shipped off to war, and the subsequent 3 or 4 year separation before their return. Most divorces in this period occurred between young, childless couples or older married couples with grown children. Figure 3.1 compares the number of marriages and number of divorces per 1000 population during the 10-year span from 1940 to 1950, while Figure 3.2 illustrates the trend in the number of divorces per 1000 population across nearly a 110-year span. Interestingly, the peaks and dips in the divorce rate reflect the times of prosperity and distress in America, indicating the susceptibility of the American family to the economic, political, and psychological climate of the country. Evidence of this susceptibility can be seen in

Married women were out of the house and earning their own money, changing the domestic image of women from earlier in the century.

the peak of the divorce rate in 1920 during the rebellious times of the roaring 20s and a dip in the divorce rate in the 1930s when couples couldn't afford to divorce during the Depression.

The American Family from 1950 to 1990

Families in the 1950s

To many, especially those of the baby boom generation, the family of the 1950s characterizes the traditional family. Similar to the traditional family of the Victorian 1800s, the post-war family symbolized a haven from a heartless world and a way to satisfactorily meet the intimacy needs of family members. The nostalgia connected to the late 1940s into the 1950s stood in stark contrast to the experiences of those who had endured the Depression and the war.

Figure 3.1

U.S. Marriage and Divorce Rate 1940–1950, per 1000 Population

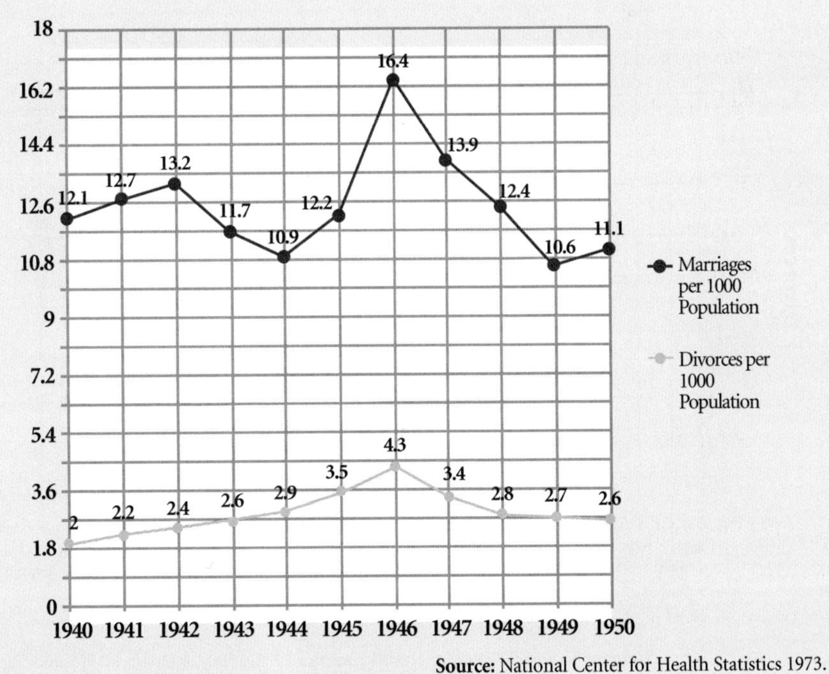

As Figure 3.3 depicts, the average age of marriage dropped in the period between 1940 and 1950, before beginning a gradual rise in the 1950s. In the 1950s, the divorce rate stabilized, the number of married women in the workforce dropped, and birthrates doubled—all indicators frequently used to determine the health of the family. More and more young women graduated from high school and went on to college instead of working to help support their families or subsidize a brother's education.

This image of the traditional family was bolstered by television shows such as *Leave it to Beaver* and *Ozzie and Harriet*. As we suggested at the beginning of this chapter, in the course of a half-hour program, fathers returned home ready to help settle any minor problems, mothers were always cheerful and loving, and children were socially and academically successful. This depiction of family life in the 1950s, while misleading, does accurately point out that, in general, families for the first time owned a house, a car, and what would become an important cultural icon—a television set. Overall, parents were anxious to provide their children with advantages which had not existed during the Depression and war. The 1950s and 1960s enjoyed unequaled prosperity in the United States. Numerous

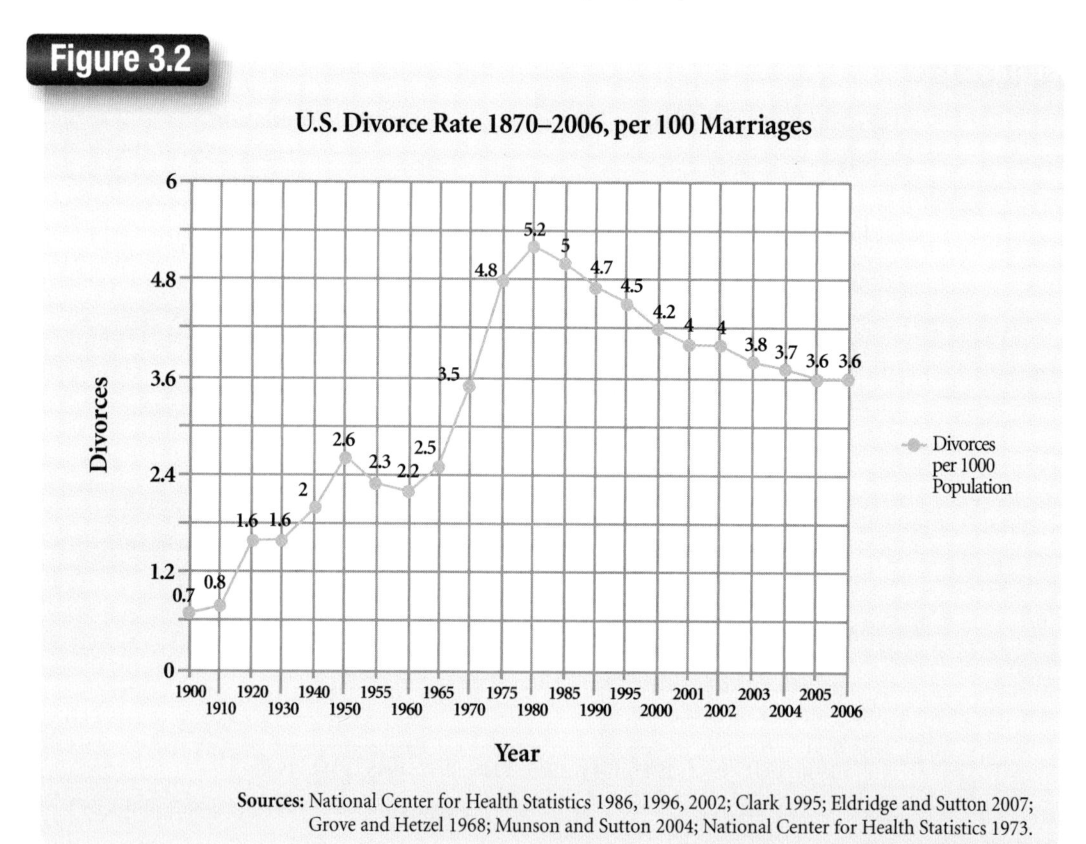

Sources: National Center for Health Statistics 1986, 1996, 2002; Clark 1995; Eldridge and Sutton 2007; Grove and Hetzel 1968; Munson and Sutton 2004; National Center for Health Statistics 1973.

Figure 3.3

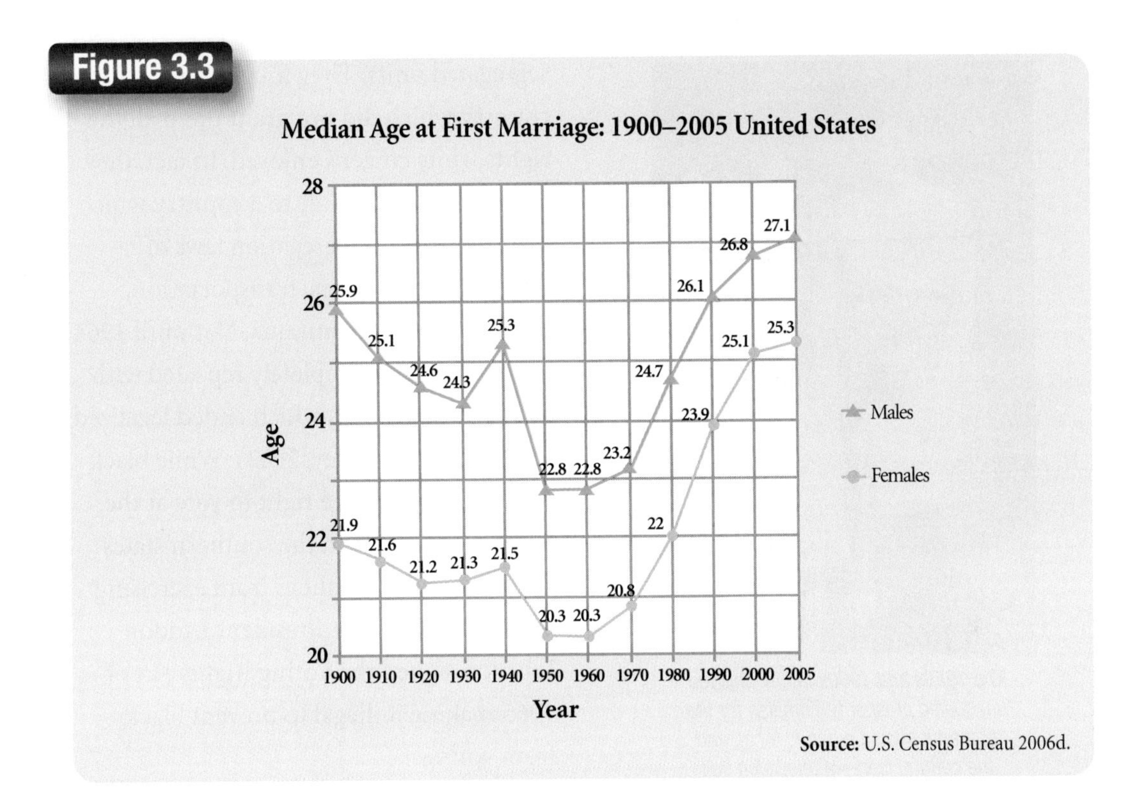

Source: U.S. Census Bureau 2006d.

factory jobs were available, the number of white-collar jobs increased, wages were high, mortgages and tuition money were available because of federal support, and goods were relatively cheap (Coontz, 1992).

However, this emphasis on prosperity in the 1950s would sow the seeds of a radical family change in the 1960s. The idealized middle-class family began to show cracks by the late 1950s.

Not all families followed these trajectories. Between 1920 and 1950, African-American families were themselves divided by education, class and gender lines; however, these differences did not fracture the black community. This is partially due to external factors of white racism, violence, and hostility, which forged the African-American community together (Taylor & Naison, 2000). In the nation's cities, housing

George Marks / Retrofile RF / Getty Images

The image of the traditional family were bolstered by television shows such as Leave it to Beaver and Ozzie and Harriet.

The 1950s and 1960s family enjoyed unequaled prosperity. Families for the first time owned a home, a car, and the cultural icon—a television set.

shortages and black population growth created segregated neighborhoods. The HOLC (Home Owners Loan Corporation) perpetuated this by refusing loans to blacks in white neighborhoods and making it generally difficult for blacks to get home loans, claiming they were poor risks (Massey, 1993). At a time when white families were able to buy a home and begin to accrue wealth, black families were often denied the same opportunities. Home ownership and the transfer of wealth from one generation to the next continued to be one of the markers of social class difference.

African-Americans also took part in both WW I and WW II, serving in segregated units. They fought for a country which did not grant them all the rights white citizens enjoyed. In fact, they returned from the war to a country which institutionalized segregation laws of schools, public places, transportation, restrooms, and restaurants. Not until 1964 were these laws completely repealed with the Civil Rights Act, which ended legalized segregation (Brinkley, 2003). While black males were given the right to vote at the end of the Civil War, the southern states found ways to stop them from exercising most of their rights. President Lyndon Johnson signed the Voting Rights Act of 1965 making it illegal to prevent blacks from voting.

Lambert/Archive Photos / Hulton Archive / Getty Images

At a time when white families were able to buy a home and begin to accrue wealth, African- American families were often not presented with the same opportunities.

Families in the 1960s

Cultural Myths. In response to the demands on men to create and support expensive suburban homes and lifestyles, a mythical world of adventure and freedom arose in popular culture. Movies about spies and western gunslingers stood in sharp contrast to the restrictive corporate lifestyles of many men. Youthful marriage and early childbearing created a culture of women in their thirties with diminishing childrearing responsibilities, but with unrealistic expectations to be all things to all people—an attractive wife to her husband, a self-sacrificing mother for her children, a prudent shopper, an imaginative cook, an industrious housekeeper with a shiny kitchen floor, as well as an active member of the community. The resulting anxieties and dissatisfaction in both men and women led to an increase in the divorce rate in the 1960s. Maintaining the middle-class lifestyle and keeping up with the Joneses often required the wife to work at least part-time outside the home. By 1960, one third of married women were working full- or part-time (Women's History in America, n.d.).

Divorce was once again on the rise. In an earlier era, a common sentiment was to stay married "for the children," no matter how uncomfortable or abusive the relationship might be. By the 1960s, the presence of children no longer hindered divorce. Parents came to believe it was better for children to live in a happier, less stressful environment than to pretend to maintain a marriage on their behalf. Child custody became a battlefield adversely affecting both children and parents alike.

Youth Culture and the Generation Gap. The ideal suburban life could be a place capable of providing comfort and emotional fulfillment for family members, but it could also be a place where young people had too much time and too little to do. Married women became self-sacrificing and isolated, while men were harried with the challenge of providing the consumer products of the "good life." Children were pressured to succeed and conform to middle-class ideals and, as a result, became rebellious and created alternative cultures. The period of childhood had

Image from BigstockPhoto.com / leaf

1960s teens listened to new forms of music, created new dance forms, developed their own slang expressions and often embraced much freer attitudes than those of their parents.

Sidebar 3.3
Fear of Rock 'n Roll

On May 4, 1966, John Lennon proclaimed, "We [the Beatles] are more popular than Jesus." My father (like many other Christian fathers) took offense at this statement and forced me to take all of my Beatles albums out back and burn them—every one of them!

—Anonymous

increased in length, but it offered even fewer ways of demonstrating maturity than in the previous century.

The combination of a lengthy childhood and delayed responsibility led to the development of a youth culture. High school students embraced new fashions which deviated substantially from their parents' styles. These teens listened to new forms of music, created new forms of dance, developed their own slang expressions, and often embraced freer attitudes toward sexuality, smoking, and drug use than their parents. What came to be known as a generation gap captured the essence of these dramatic differences between parents and teens (Caplow, Hicks, & Wattenberg, 2000). Sidebar 3.3 illustrates some of the conflicts parents faced with the new generation of children and the parent-child conflicts which ensued.

Concern over teenage delinquency, high pregnancy rates, and the perceived immorality of rock music led to laying blame on inadequate parenting, rather than on the difficulties inherent in the changing dynamics of family life in the 1950s and 1960s.

Cultural Upheavals. The emergence of the civil rights movement, the anti-nuclear movement, and the beat culture marked the 1960s as an age of rebelliousness, a

Sidebar 3.4
The Civil Rights Movement

The Civil Rights Movement was at a peak from 1955–1965. The 14th, 15th, and 16th amendments to the Constitution laid the foundation for Congress to pass the Civil Rights Act of 1964 and the Voting Rights Act of 1965, following nearly a decade of nonviolent protests and marches. These Acts guaranteed basic civil rights for all Americans, regardless of race. The television reporting of civil rights workers, sit-ins, marches and protests, and the bloody, violent, and sometimes inhuman response from police and National Guard, brought to America's conscience the severity and inhumane treatment of African-Americans (Cozzens, 1998).

Some of the more notable protests include the Montgomery bus boycott in 1955; the student-led sit-ins of the 1960s; the Freedom Ride of 1961; Birmingham in 1963; the march on Washington in 1963; Freedom Summer of 1964; and the Selma, Alabama, protest in 1964.

Additional information about the Civil Rights Movement and these protests can be found at these websites:

http://www.watson.org/~lisa/blackhistory/civilrights-55-65/index.html (accessed June 24, 2009)
http://memory.loc.gov/ammem/aaohtml/exhibit/aopart9.html (accessed June 24, 2009)
http://www.infoplease.com/spot/civilrightstimeline1.html (accessed June 24, 2009)

SIDEBAR 3.5
THE BEAT CULTURE

The Bomb, the Cold War, "mutual, assured destruction," the Korean War, Communism, McCarthyism, loyalty oaths, the Hollywood blacklist, the Rosenbergs, the "military industrial complex," Sputnik, suburbia, television, James Dean, Charlie "Bird" Parker, bebop jazz, rock 'n roll, civil rights, Emmett Till, Rosa Parks, Little Rock, Martin Luther King, Jr., Malcolm X, Lenny Bruce, Bob Dylan, Timothy Leary, and Vietnam. These people and phenomena associated with the post-World War II era, termed the Beat Generation, helped to shape an aesthetic shared by the diverse group of writers and visual artists who became known as the beat [culture].

Source: Ginsberg, 1996.

time for young people to be heard. (see Sidebars 3.4 and 3.5) "We're the young generation, and we've got something to say," sang the free-spirited Monkees in their TV theme song (Boyce & Hart, 1966). Other musicians, such as Joan Baez and Bob Dylan, probed deeper themes of rebellion and anti-war sentiment. Young people in the sixties did speak out against the "establishment." Sometimes they used radical methods to achieve their goals. Civil rights demonstrations and protests against the war in Vietnam often turned violent. However, this era of rebelliousness also ushered in a focus on "rights": groups which championed black power, students' rights, women's rights, homosexuals' rights, Native-Americans' rights, and an emphasis on environmental protection.

Men and women began experimenting with new gender roles which blurred the boundaries between masculine and feminine behavior. There were attempts to equalize the roles of men and women and to eliminate traditional marriage vows in an effort to create more personal or sexual freedom within marriage. By the 1970s, homosexuals were publicly proclaiming their right to same-sex unions based on traditional marriage models or new models involving more autonomy. Thirty-five years later, these same debates continue without resolution. Communal alternatives to marriage, open marriages, and same-sex unions all challenged the traditional marriage ideal of the 1950s by rejecting the materialism of the suburban lifestyle and experimenting with non-nuclear family forms.

Image from BigstockPhoto.com / purmar

By the 1970s homosexuals were publicly proclaiming their right to same-sex unions based on traditional marriage models.

Families in the 1970s and 1980s

The 1970s saw an erosion of the optimistic economy of the 1950s. When the husband's income did not keep up

Many women work to supplement the family income, which requires the assistance of each family member.

with inflation or a perceived standard of living, the wife often joined the workforce to pursue a career or supplement the family income. Some businesses and larger institutions removed barriers to advancement for women, but inequality still existed. Many women entered previously male-oriented professions such as medicine, law, management, and higher education. These changes sometimes shifted the balance of power within families. Men often felt inadequate because they could not support their families on their incomes alone. Those who decided to work two jobs to make ends meet found their increased absence from the home further exacerbated problems with their wives and children. Many women felt overwhelmed as they tried to be "supermoms," caring for the house, the children, and working part- or full-time. The divorce rate began to escalate in the 1970s. Cohabitation (couples living together but not married) became more common. This was especially evident among the highly visible movie stars of the time who rejected traditional marriage and childrearing arrangements. The birth rate for cohabiting couples and the out-of-wedlock birth rate soared, especially in low-income families. Conservative political movements sought to restore family values as a way to prevent the erosion of the traditional family.

The 1980s brought the reaping of what earlier decades had sown. The belief that maternal employment outside the home was harmful to children decreased as a "pro-feminist attitude" emerged (Caplow, Hicks, & Wattenberg, 2000). Women continued to enter the workforce in unprecedented numbers, creating a childcare dilemma. Latchkey children became increasingly common, as well as older children caring for younger siblings until a parent arrived home from work. Childrearing, the family's foremost

Image from BigstockPhoto.com / tobkatrina

Childrearing is increasingly assigned to parent substitutes at daycare centers or preschools.

function, was increasingly assigned to parent substitutes at daycare centers or schools—or to television, the modern age's electronic babysitter. By age 16, the average child was estimated to have watched up to 1,500 hours of TV—more time than was spent in the classroom (Boyse, 2008). Americans were being born and raised without the family support enjoyed by their forefathers.

During the 1970s and 1980s, the nuclear family felt even more economic pressure as factories closed or moved overseas, and companies began exiting older, less economically viable cities. The effects devastated entire communities. Young Americans could no longer count on stable, well-paid employment, which led to the new idea of multiple career changes throughout the adult life cycle. Education became more essential, but at the same time unaffordable for a large segment of the population. Young people often found it necessary to work while in high school or college, reducing their time for study and contributing to an overall decline in educational achievement.

African-American Families in Modern America

In the early 1900s, many blacks moved to the North from the South. The industry needs in the north created jobs during both world wars, as work in the south became less certain. This movement north created segregated areas in inner cities, generally those areas in which whites didn't want to live. Despite legislation guaranteeing equal rights, black families have been discriminated against in nearly every aspect of life. African-Americans have been the targets of race riots, the Ku Klux Klan, and other discriminatory practices which have jeopardized the formation of stable two-parent families (McAdoo, 2007).

Modern African-American families have some unique characteristics. Households are more frequently formed with the birth of a child rather than marriage. Throughout history, African-American women have outnumbered African-American men. This continues today, possibly accounting for the decrease in marriages among African-American females. The importance of extended family and kin in maintaining

Modern African-American families are frequently formed with the birth of a child rather than marriage.

cohesion in African-American families is often overshadowed by the negative depiction of African-American family life. Studies have shown African-American families have about 70 various structural formations, compared to about 40 in white families. This illustrates the variability of family structure and the flexibility of family roles in African-American families (Barbarin, 1993).

In single-parent families, the relationship between the mother and father usually dictates the amount of contact fathers have with their children. Even when there is little contact with a child's biological father, African-American children usually have contact with uncles, male cousins, and other men in their community. Grandparents, especially grandmothers, are important in the lives of African-American children and often perform some of the child-rearing functions (Barbarin, 1993). Some of the difficulties continuing to plague African-American families are high unemployment and underemployment, a high number of single-parent families, gangs, drugs, low educational attainment, and poverty (McAdoo, 2007).

Hispanic Families in Modern America

Hispanic-Americans have played definitive roles in forging U.S. history and culture. They are the largest minority in the United States, numbering 42.7 million in 2005. Hispanics constituted 14% of the nation's total population with a 3.3% increase from 2004 to 2005 (U.S. Census Bureau, 2006e), making people of Hispanic origin the nation's fastest-growing ethnic or race minority.

Family is a highly valued part of Hispanic life. There is a sense of dependence on the family unit, which extends into

Hispanic-American families tend to be tight knit extended families who embrace traditional values such as hard work, honesty, loyalty and dedication.

adulthood. Traditional family values such as hard work, honesty, loyalty, and dedication are part of Hispanic culture. Hispanics tend to view religious and political life as intertwined and often worship in ethnic congregations in both Roman Catholic and Protestant traditions.

One challenge facing the Hispanic community and the U.S. is the high birthrate among unmarried Hispanic women—the highest in the country—with over 3 times that of whites and Asians, and nearly one and a half times that of black women (Federal Interagency Forum, 2007). One reason for this may be the tight-knit extended family, which facilitates unwed childrearing; a single mother's relatives often step in to make up for the absence of the baby's father.

Asian Families in Modern America

Asian families come from a variety of different countries but have become an important part of American culture. The Asian population rose by 3% (421,000) between 2004 and 2005, compared to the black population, which increased by 1.3%, and the Hispanic population, which increased 3.3% (U.S. Census Bureau, 2006e).

Asian families tend to have hierarchical structures which value family obligation. They tend to place others' needs above their own, and maintain continuing interdependence in their relationships. Asian-American families tend to be fairly resilient in comparison to other immigrant families.

Asian-American families tend to have hierarchical structures that value family obligation.

Asian families have the highest proportion of married family units, a lower divorce rate, and a smaller number of female single-parent households than the national average (Reeves & Bennett, 2004). Asians have nearly twice the national average for holding a bachelor's degree and have 117% of the median income for white households (Reeves & Bennett, 2004), which make them a significant part of the U.S. economy. Especially among Japanese-American and Chinese-American women, their parents' marriages had been based on responsibility and obligation instead of love, which has greatly influenced their decision to remain single (Reeves & Bennett, 2004).

The American Family Today

The last half of the 20th century has seen many of the same marriage-weakening trends people have either cheered or jeered over the previous 300 years. However, these trends have decreased sharply in recent years. To illustrate, we will look at the following indicators commonly used to evaluate the health of marriage and family life in contemporary American culture: age of first marriage, birth rate, divorce rate, cohabitation, the elderly, and the economy.

Age of First Marriage

Men and women are marrying later in life than they did 30 years ago, and the proportion of adults living alone has tripled since 1950. As Figure 3.3 demonstrates, in 1970 the median age at first marriage for men was 23.2 and 20.8 for women (Fields & Casper, 2001). In 2000, the median age at first marriage for men increased to 26.8 and 25.1 for women (Fields & Casper, 2001). In 2005, the average age at first marriage was 27 for men and 25.5 for women, indicating this trend is continuing (U.S. Census Bureau, 2006d).

Figure 3.4

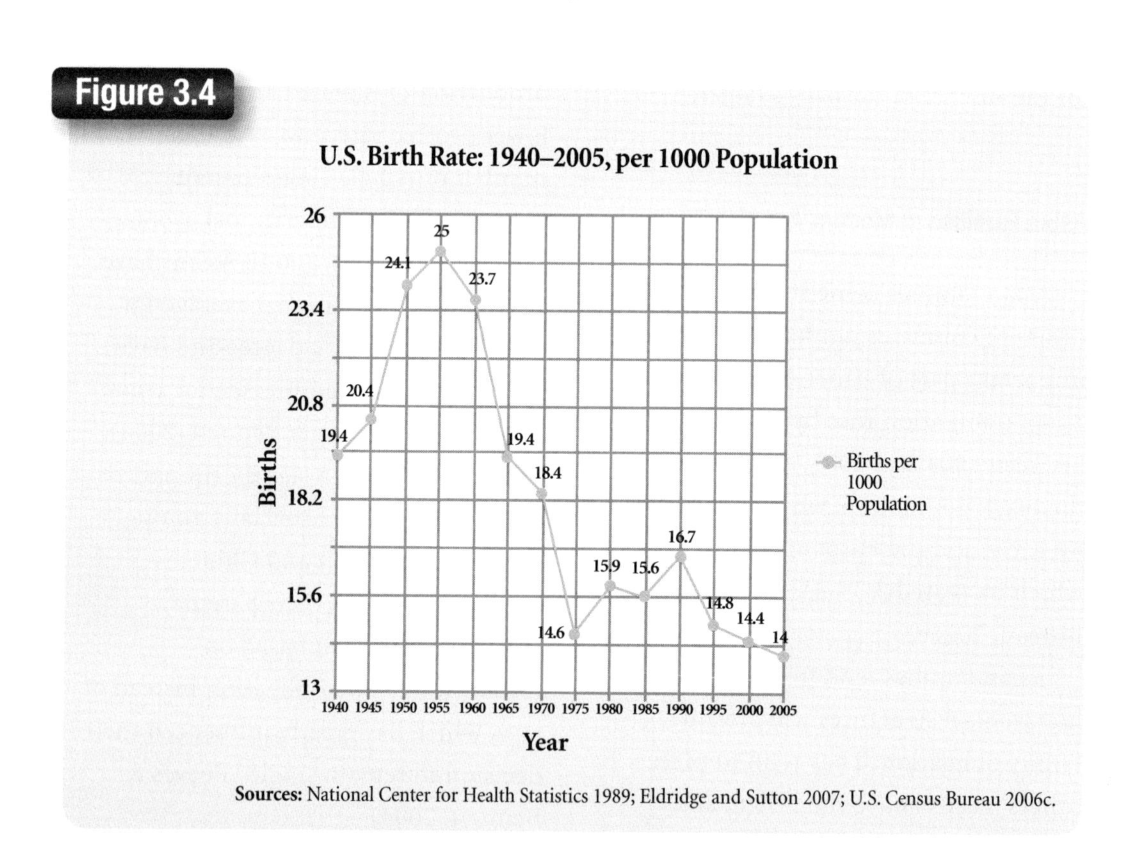

Sources: National Center for Health Statistics 1989; Eldridge and Sutton 2007; U.S. Census Bureau 2006c.

Figure 3.5

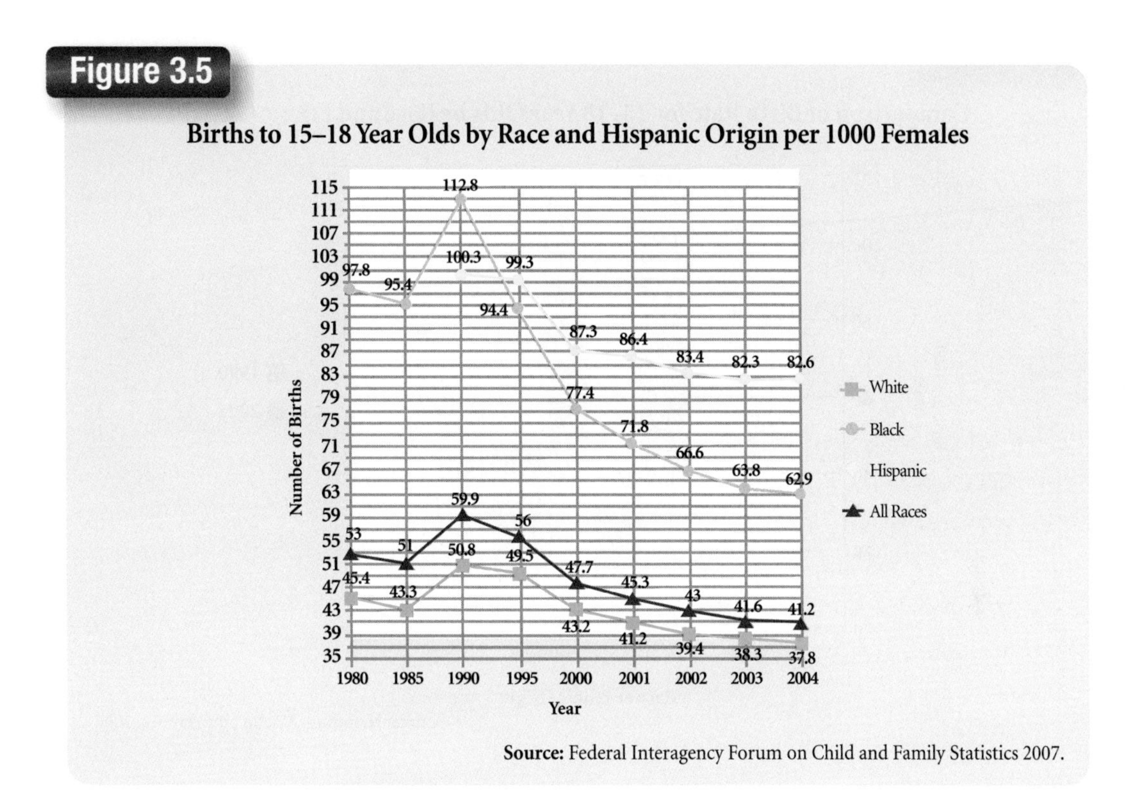

Source: Federal Interagency Forum on Child and Family Statistics 2007.

Birth Rate

Figure 3.4 shows the overall decline in birth rate, while Figure 3.5 illustrates the number of births to adolescents. Figure 3.6 compares the birth rate among all females between 1990 and 2005 by race and ethnic group. In 2003, slightly under a third of all births in the United States were to unmarried women, rising from 5.3% in 1960 to 32.2% in 2003 (Ventura & Bachrach, 2000; Hamilton, Martin, & Sutton, 2004). In 2003, 68.5% of births to African-American mothers were to single mothers, and 45% of births to Hispanic women occurred outside of marriage, compared with 23.5% for white women (Hamilton, Martin, & Sutton, 2004). The implications of single-parent families will be discussed in a later chapter.

The picture for teen births has improved (see Figure 3.5). According to Child Trends Data Bank, teen birth rates have been declining for the past decade; the preliminary 2004 birth rate for teens ages 15 to 19 is the lowest rate ever reported in the United States, at 41 births per 1,000 (Facts at a Glance, 2007). After an increase in the teen birth rate in the late 1980s, the birth rate for adolescent females has declined steadily since 1991. However, rates among Hispanic teens

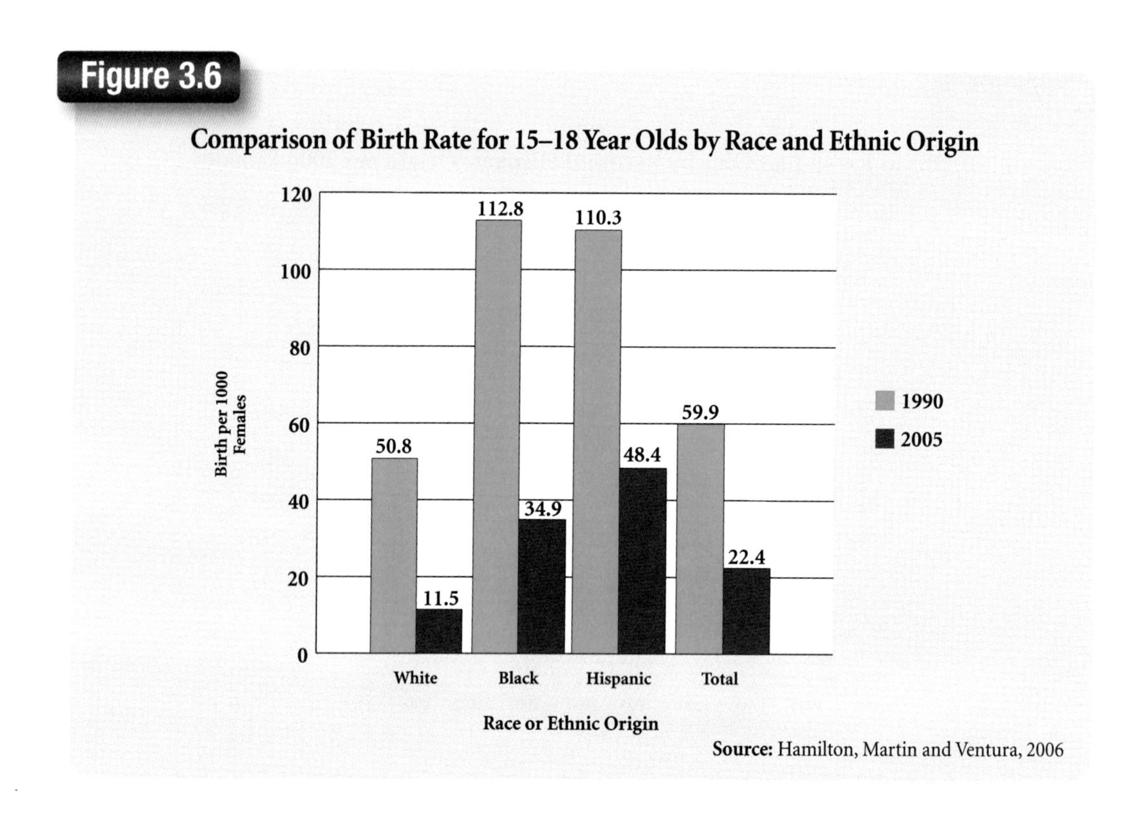

began declining later in the 1990s than rates among black or white teens, and Hispanic teens currently have the highest teen birth rate (see Figure 3.6) (Hamilton, Martin, & Sutton, 2004).

Divorce Rate

The divorce rate rose sharply in the 1970s and 1980s, but actually declined slightly in the latter part of the century. It then remained steady until the end of the century, when it began to drop slightly (see Figure 3.2). It is no longer true that half of all marriages will likely end in divorce; if present trends continue, about 4 of 10 marriages which occurred in 2000 will end in divorce. While this sounds encouraging, it is important to remember the United States still has one of the highest divorce rates in the world (World divorce statistics, 1996–2005).

In 2003, seven times more children were affected by divorce than at the beginning of the 20th century (Fields, 2003). Children who commute between separated parents have become commonplace. One in two children will live in a single-parent family at some point, and 1 in 3 children are born to unmarried parents (Children's Defense Fund, 2004). Some critics claim this collapse of the traditional family is a greater cause of poverty than any shortcomings in the

After an increase in the birth rate for teens in the 1980s, the birthrate for adolescents has steadily declined to about 4 in every 100 births.

economic or political system. Despite these statistics, 90% of all Americans marry, and most people remarry after a divorce (Mintz, 2001).

Cohabitation

Another significant change which occurred in the last half of the 20th century is the increase in the number of cohabiting couples. In 1970, households of unmarried couples made up only 1% of U.S. households, while in 2000 the rate increased to nearly 5.2% (Simmons & O'Neil, 2001). Couples who are less educated, have low religious orientation, and less economic resources are more likely to cohabit (Seltzer, 2000; Amato, Booth, Johnson, & Rogers, 2007). The probability a cohabiting union will result in marriage within 5 years is less than 50% (Lichter, Qian, & Mellott, 2006).

Premarital cohabitation has consistently been associated with an increased risk of divorce and less marital success (Kamp Dush, Cohan, & Amato, 2003; Phillips & Sweeney, 2005; Stanley, Rhoades, & Markman, 2006). An exception to the preceding is when cohabitation is limited to the future spouse (Teachman, 2003). Teachman's findings suggest women who had premarital sex and cohabitated with the man they eventually married had the same chance of divorce as those who abstained from premarital sex and cohabitation. However, according to the same research, multiple sexual partners increased the risk of divorce regardless of cohabitation.

The Elderly

From the young to the old, dynamics of the family have changed. Medical advances have increased the life expectancy of Americans; therefore, they can expect to spend a longer time in the "golden years." In 2003, people 65 and older made up nearly 12% of the American population. Projections are that by 2030 the elderly will represent 20% of the population and after 2030, the oldest old-age group, those 85 and older, will grow rapidly (He, Sengupta, Velkoff, & DeBarros,

2005). At the end of the 20th century, most elderly people did not rely on their loved ones for financial support. Instead, national averages suggest Social Security provided the largest share of income (about 40%) with personal income, pensions, and assets making up the other 60% (He et al., 2005). It is important to keep in mind this varies by race, education, and previous socioeconomic level, with some people relying more heavily on Social Security for income in their old age than others. The majority of elderly at the end of the century died in hospitals and nursing facilities, not in their own homes (Hungerford, Rassette, Iams, & Koenig, 2002).

Medical advances have increased the life expectancy of Americans allowing them to be more active and enjoy their "golden years."

The Economy

In the first half of the 20th century, the United States weathered two world wars and the Great Depression. In the second half, this country overcame challenges ranging from a 40 year Cold War with the Soviet Union to extended periods of sharp inflation, high unemployment, and enormous governmental budget deficits. The nation finally enjoyed a period of economic calm in the 1990s: prices were more stable, unemployment dropped to its lowest level in almost 30 years, the government announced a budget surplus, and the stock market experienced an unprecedented boom.

However, as it relates to family, the economy at the end of the 20th century and the beginning of the 21st century offers less security and poses more competition for workers than it did previously. Americans face modest pay increases which frequently fail to keep up with the cost of living. Educational requirements and job training have increased, many times forcing young people to delay marriage in order to prepare for careers. While not as great as in other countries, the income disparity between classes continues to increase as we move into the early 21st century. Workers at the dawn of the 21st century find themselves facing two dismal prospects: career plateauing and the potential for midlife layoffs.

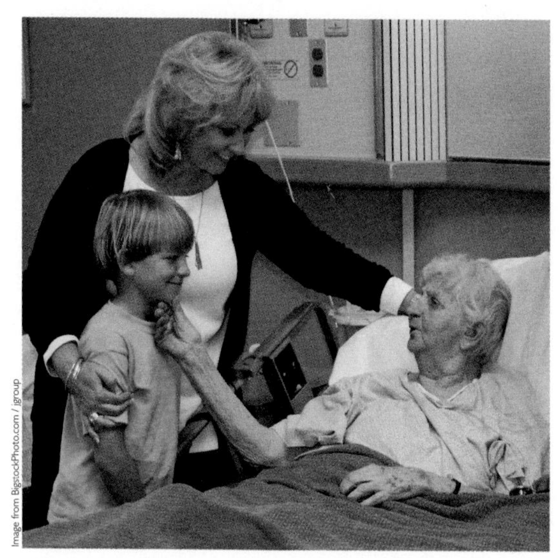

Many adults find themselves in the sandwich generation caring for their aging parents while still raising their own family.

Challenges Ahead

The American family at the beginning of the 21st century faces some profound challenges. Balancing work and family has become increasingly difficult for families with two working parents. The availability of childcare is nearing a crisis point as record numbers of mothers enter the workforce. The graying of America as the population ages has created the sandwich generation, a term which applies to adults who are responsible for raising their own children and who, at the same time, assume some or all of the caretaking of an elder family member. Conversely, the number of grandparents who are caring for grandchildren has also risen. While this may help to alleviate the childcare problem for working parents, it is also creating stress-related problems for the older generation.

As we have seen, many changes have taken place over the last 100 years which has presented families with the many challenges we have discussed. It is easy to view these changes as negative, fearing the demise of family as we know it. This is often because we compare the complex and diverse families of today with the seemingly more standard-issue ones of the 1950s, a unique decade when every long-term trend of the 20th century was temporarily reversed. Stephanie Coontz, family historian, sums up the resilience of families in these words:

> If we look back over the last millennium, we can see that families have always been diverse and in flux. In each Period, families have solved one set of problems only to face a new array of challenges. What works for a family in one economic and cultural setting doesn't work for a family in another. What's helpful at one stage of a family's life may be destructive at the next stage. If there is one lesson to be drawn from the last millennium of family history, it's that families are always having to play catch-up with a changing world (1999, p. 90).

A Christian Perspective

The nuclear family, once prized as the foundation of society, suffered heavy blows in the decades following World War II. Since the 1960s, families have grown smaller. More people than ever live alone—single young adults, divorced singles, or people who have lost a spouse. In 1960, 70% of American families were married couples with two or more children—the father was the breadwinner and the mother was the homemaker (Mintz, 2001). Currently, the married male breadwinner-female homemaker family makes up only about 22% of American households (Aronwald, 2005). More common are two-earner families (in which husbands and wives both work), single-parent female heads of households, stepfamilies, and empty-nest families. This domestic revolution has been caused by a declining birth rate, rapid entry of married women into the workforce, rising divorce rates, and an aging population.

While these indicators may appear to be bad news for American society as a whole, it may well be good news for the Church. Some feel American society has turned its back on the gospel, in part because life has been too easy—people haven't needed anyone or anything. As the last century drew to a close, this sense of self-reliance seemed to buckle. Membership in religious organizations rose from 41% in 1900 to 70% in 2000 (Caplow, Hicks, & Wattenberg, 2000). As encouraging as this may seem, the percentage of individuals attending church on a weekly basis has remained steady for this period.

This opens an avenue for churches and individual Christians to use societal trends to maximize their influence for Jesus Christ. How can churches reach those who don't fit the mold of the "traditional" family? Today, political parties pledge support for the American family, but controversy lies just beneath the surface. It periodically bubbles up (sometimes becoming a

© Jupiter Images

"If there is one lesson to be drawn from the last millennium of family history, it's that families are always having to play catch-up with a changing world."
Coontz, 1999, p. 90

steady boil) over issues such as abortion, same-sex marriage, and stem-cell research. These disagreements reflect divergent moral judgments on issues at the heart of families.

With the graying of America, today's youth and young adults will determine the future of religion in the 21st century. It is often suggested that young people are 'spiritual but not religious.' In contrast to this, researcher Christian Smith (2005) has found teenagers are not particularly influenced by post-modern, pluralistic culture. Most American teenagers are religious and, the vast majority, Christian. However, their faith is what Smith calls 'Moralistic Therapeutic Deism.' He explains this as oriented toward being good and nice in moral ways, primarily concerned with one's own happiness and comfort, and a view of God as distant except when there is a problem one needs God to solve. This type of faith is not unique to young people but reflects the less-than-passionate faith of their parents.

The influences of post-modernism are stronger in young adults, especially those who attend college. Young people are marrying older, having fewer children, are more educated, move more often, and live in more diverse neighborhoods. According to Wuthnow (2007), this creates a large group of young adults who are neither contributing to nor receiving support from local congregations. The net result is their influence on American religion is by their absence, not by their presence. Wuthnow suggests the strongest effect on church attendance is marital status. Since young people are delaying marriage and child bearing, this suppresses church attendance until they are in their early 40s. The 20s age group rates the highest in discussing religion with friends, indicating lack of church attendance is not a sign they are oblivious to spiritual concerns. On the contrary, while piecing together bits and pieces from different theological resources is characteristic of young people, Wuthnow reports core beliefs have been remarkably unchanged in the last 30 years.

It will be interesting to see if the early 21st century brings renewed interest in the Church and an increase in family-related reforms comparable to the Progressive Era of the late 19th and early 20th centuries.

Summary

Sandwiched between two lengthy world wars, the Great Depression seems to symbolize the first half of the 20th century. These were years of struggle, deprivation, and family upheaval. Women entered the workforce in great numbers, filling the positions vacated by their husbands and helping with the war effort. When the men returned, the country experienced a time of optimism and economic expansion. The nuclear family of the 1950s came to symbolize what many refer to today as the "traditional" family. Like the traditional family of the Victorian 1800s, the post-war family symbolized security from the often unstable world outside the borders of the United States.

A strong youth culture fostered by the 1950s led to sweeping political and philosophical changes which would affect the second half of the 20th century. The nuclear family came under increasing pressure as more and more women entered the workforce. The makeup of families began to change from the traditional breadwinner-father/homemaker-mother model to other more common forms.

Several indicators are used to measure the health of the family. These include the marriage rate, divorce rate, birth rate, and age of first marriage. These indicators have been used to suggest the American family is in a state of decay. However, according to family historian Steven Mintz (2001), the family is not a dying institution and in many respects is stronger than in the past. Marriage and other trends stabilized in the 1990s, after undergoing sweeping changes in previous decades.

While the headlines focus on the death of marriage, rampant divorces, and a rising infertility rate, recent data from the National Center for Health Statistics (NCHS) and the Census Bureau tells another story. According to these statistics, the fertility rate actually rose slightly between 1999 and 2000; the marriage rate stabilized after 10 consecutive years of decline; and the divorce rate continued its 20 year downward trajectory. The overall impression suggests relative stability (Fields, 2003).

Not all families survived as well as others. African-Americans struggled both socially and financially, with fewer opportunities than their white counterparts. Even after gaining the right to vote, many were prevented from exercising that right.

In looking over the history of the family, it becomes evident that, while there are problems, the increasing and decreasing trends establish a pattern—not a pattern of demise, but one of change. The *form* of the American family has changed over the last 4 centuries, but the *institution* of family remains an intact and vital component of American society today.

Questions for Thought

1. "There has never been a time when the overwhelming majority of American children were well cared for and their experiences idyllic. Nor has childhood ever been an age of innocence, at least not for most children" (Mintz, 2004). Do you agree with this statement? Why or why not?

2. What do you consider to be the greatest challenges facing the American family in the 21st century?

3. How do you think the Church can meet these challenges?

4. How would you distinguish between the form of family and the institution of family?

Resources

Activities:

Compare and Contrast the families in the popular family sitcoms:

1. Leave it to Beaver (1957-1963)
2. The Wonder Years (a story about growing up in the 1960s)
3. The Brady Bunch (1969-1974)
4. Growing Pains (mid-1980s-early 1990s)
5. The Cosby Show (1984-1992)
6. Full House (1990s)
7. Reba (2001-2007)

Movies:

The Color Purple, (PG-13). Drama that shows the problems faced by African-American women during the early 1900s including poverty, racism and sex discrimination.

A League of Their Own, (PG). DVD. A movie about the changing role of women, specifically those in the All-American Girls Baseball League- created while most able men were away during World War II.

Kramer vs. Kramer, (PG). DVD. Movie about a single dad. Online Video: Slide show of historic family pictures of a California family: http://www.youtube.com/watch?v=7cSEs Y5pNR8 (accessed June 23, 2009)

Online video:

Women in the Workforce—WWII: http://www.youtube.com/watch?v=9GarCzR_6Ng (accessed June 23, 2009)

Dating

Getting to Know You

4

A wife of noble character who can find? She is worth far more than rubies.
—Proverbs 31:10

© iStockphoto.com / egening

We tend to take dating for granted. How else are men and women supposed to get acquainted or find a spouse? However, "dating" as we know it today did not exist for most of history. It didn't emerge in America until the middle of the 20th century. Americans often see dating as a way to promote individual choice in spouse selection. But for people who seek to live a life modeled after Jesus, dating has created many dilemmas.

This chapter briefly reviews the history and cultural variations of dating, as well as the American perspective on dating. We also will explore the various stages of dating as they relate to the differences between men and women. One of the consequences of the American emphasis on dating is a dramatic increase in premarital sex. Thus, we will examine the implications of contemporary sexuality in light of God's plan for sex. Finally, we will discuss the options of remaining single and not dating—which have become increasingly popular choices among Christians.

The History of Dating

In most cultures throughout history, marriages were arranged by parents. The general thinking was teens and preteens could not make reasonable marriage decisions for themselves. Thus, the parents, who had much more knowledge and wisdom about marriage than their children, made marriage choices for them. These marriages often occurred when the marriage partners were very young. Sometimes, the marriages were not consummated until much later.

Supervised Dating: Keeping Company

As various cultures raised the age at which people could marry, young men and women began to take more and more of a role in choosing their mates. In eighteenth- and nineteenth-century America, young people, with the permission of their parents, were allowed to get to know one another before they officially became engaged. This came to be known as "calling" or "keeping company." It involved adult supervision and very strict customs regarding what activities were permitted. Calling was very much controlled by the woman, who would invite the gentleman to call. Permitted activities might include sitting and talking in the family parlor, attending church functions together, and going to the occasional community dance, along with parents and siblings (Bailey, 2004). Marriage occurred only with the permission of the parents. It became customary for the suitor to ask the woman's father for permission to marry his daughter.

Dating Independently

After World War I, dating customs began to change. As America became more industrialized, parents often worked away from home leaving young people with increased freedom without supervision. As young people became responsible for structuring their free time, dating became an activity in its own right, creating a new social institution (Olson & DeFrain, 2006). Some scholars attribute much of this change to the automobile, which made "going out" possible (Bailey, 2004; Whyte,

George Marks / Retrofile / Getty Images

Dating in the early to mid 1900's involved adult supervision.

2007). Regardless of the reasons, without the parameters of parental supervision, dating became a more private and independent way for young people to get to know one another and find spouses.

As young people became more independent, attended coeducational colleges, and developed more leisure activities, dating began to take on a life of its own. More and more people began dating for fun, rather than for spouse selection. According to Bailey (2004), a woman's reputation depended on building and maintaining her popularity. Women had to be seen with popular men in the "right" places. Dating was more about competition within the peer culture of youth. Dating and mating were two quite different things. Dancing became a competitive social function in which the male partner was responsible for the female until someone cut in. The popularity of the movie theater in the mid-1900s also dramatically changed dating activities. As the culture has moved from public movie theaters to VCRs and DVD players, dating has continued to become more private and independent of outside supervision.

Despite an increase in interracial dating, only 5% of all married couples are in an interracial marriage.

Cultural Variations in Dating

Americans often are surprised to learn that, historically, the majority of cultures have *not* included a system of dating whereby individuals are free to have relationships with different people before marriage (Madathil & Benshoff, 2008). Most nonindustrialized cultures today still practice parent-arranged marriages and have no formalized system of dating. Many young people in these cultures prefer this practice and would feel stressed if they had to choose their own spouses. In fact, nations practicing arranged marriages have lower divorce rates. In 2008, a study of arranged marriages found couples from India living in arranged marriages in the United States reported higher levels of marital satisfaction than U.S. couples who had chosen their spouse without family involvement (Madathil & Benshoff, 2008). Asian-Americans living in the United States are more likely to have family involvement in spouse selection and consequently, a much lower divorce rate (8% for men and 10% for women)

Sidebar 4.1
Race and Courtship. Are They Related?

To understand the enduring legacy of color line in our marriage choices, we must look at the political history. From 1661 to 1967, courtship and marriage were regulated by numerous state laws called antimiscegenation laws, designed to prevent racial mixing. The laws until 1967 were relatively unchanged, however the racial categories which these laws were based on changed considerably. For instance, in 1785, Virginia considered anyone less than one quarter "Negro" as white. But in the early 20th century, any drop of "Negro" blood precluded entrance into the white race. Thus a couple complying with the antimiscegenation laws in one time period could be in violation of them in another. The immediate post-war period brought new ways of thinking about race as cultural understanding of race entered mainstream America. While several states dropped or changed their antimiscegenation laws, it took the federal Supreme Court to rule in favor of Andrea Perez in Perez vs. Sharp in 1967. Perez was a Mexican-American woman considered white applying for a marriage license to African-American, Sylvester Davis after receiving permission from her Parish to marry. Some important considerations based on this case to ask yourself include: Why is the rate of interracial marriage still so low despite the absence of legal prohibitions? What does the endurance of antimiscegenation laws into the late 1960's say about the social definitions of race and how they shape the possibilities and limits of our courtship choices? Who should define who we can and cannot date or marry?

Adapted from Lubin, A. "What's love got to do with it?" The politics of race and marriage in the California Supreme Court's 1948 *Perez* and Sharp Decision. *OAH Magazine of History,* 18(4), 31-34.

than whites (23% for men and 25% for women) (U.S. Census Bureau, 2005b).

However, as nations become more economically self-sufficient, they tend to move toward freedom of choice in marriage. This seems to be related to women's increased educational attainment and economic independence. In less industrialized nations, women often are not able to support themselves and must depend on men (their fathers and later their husbands) for survival. Women in these cultures allow their parents to choose their spouses and then marry at an early age. Industrialization brings more employment and educational opportunities for women. This leads to a delay in marriage and more time for dating before marriage (Olson & DeFrain, 1999).

Many industrializing nations are now practicing a blend of the old traditions of arranged marriages and the more Westernized notion of dating. For example, young people in India are beginning to choose their own spouses through dating, but under the strict supervision of their parents. In China, couples are still formally introduced by friends and relatives, but are beginning to date and choose their own spouses. In Japan, while young people have limited contact with the opposite sex, they are beginning to date and fall in love on their own (Olson & DeFrain, 1999).

Race also has an impact on dating. With 30% of whites and 34% of blacks admitting to personal racial prejudice

(Cohen & Agiesta, 2008), race is a factor in whom one dates. Though interracial dating is becoming more popular, skin color still matters. Over half of all African-Americans, Hispanic-Americans and Asian-Americans report dating interracially, while only 35% of whites have dated interracially (Yancey, 2002). Despite increases in interracial dating, interracial marriage accounted for only about 5% of all married couples in 2000 (Fields & Casper, 2001). Hispanics and Native-Americans are most likely to marry whites, followed closely by Asian-Americans. African-Americans are least likely to marry whites, but that too is changing (Qian & Lichtor, 2007). Chapter 11 will discuss interracial marriage in more depth. Sidebar 4.1 looks at the historical impact of race and politics on dating.

© Getty Images

Dating serves four functions: recreation, socialization, confirmation of social self and mate selection.

The Functions of Dating in Today's World

The terminology of dating is changing. Whether it is "hanging out," "pairing off," "seeing someone," "hooking up," or "dating," single people get together for many different reasons. When we talk about dating in the contemporary arena, most consider dating to be an end in itself, rather than a form of spouse selection. Sociologists have identified four functions of dating: recreation, socialization, confirmation of social self, and status acquisition.

Recreation

Most people today think of dating as a fun activity. Although an individual can enjoy different dating activities (attending a movie, going out to eat) alone or with a friend of the same gender, many say it is more enjoyable to do these activities on a date. So dating has become a recreational activity, something apart from developing a long-lasting relationship. Kimmell, a senior at University of Arizona states, "The start of a relationship is thrilling, enjoyable and fun. The excitement of a new partner can make your stomach churn until you finally get comfortable with each other, and that's when all the cute text messages and frequent phone calls force many girls to put a label on the relationship" (2009, 1).

Socialization

A second function of dating is that it presents an opportunity to be socialized into the norms, roles, and values of relationships with the opposite sex. In this way, it is preparation for married life. While many parts of a relationship change with marriage, dating introduces young people to adult gender roles. Dating provides adolescents with training for adulthood (Glenn & Marquardt, 2001).

Confirmation of Social Self

A third function of dating is the opportunity to gain self-insight (Whyte, 2007). Through interactions with other people—those of the same sex and those of the opposite sex—we receive feedback about ourselves. In 1922, Charles Cooley labeled this term the looking-glass self, which is still used in the social sciences today. On a date, a man and woman see themselves through one another's eyes and can adjust their behavior accordingly. If they see approval, they will continue what they are doing. If they see confusion, they might adjust their behavior to win approval. When dating, she is trying to be the kind of woman she thinks *he* will like. He is trying to be the kind of man he thinks *she* will like. Thus, dating can become a game where the players attempt to outwit one another, trying to manage the impressions they give in order to gain approval.

Mate Selection

The fourth function of dating involves mate selection. Dating has become the socially acceptable way of finding a suitable spouse. Dating allows partners to get better acquainted and assess compatibility. Ideally, dating improves the chances a person will meet a suitable marital partner (Rouse, 2002).

Dating in America

When a young man "called" on or "kept company" with a young lady in the eighteenth and nineteenth centuries, he did so under rather strict supervision. What came to be known as "dating" in mid-20th century America was characterized by diminishing supervision and increased independence on the part of the couple (Bailey, 2004). The earlier versions of dating had as their primary goal the selection of a suitable spouse. That is not the primary goal today.

The Meaning of Dating Today

"We're dating" can mean many things in American culture today. It can mean a couple goes out together occasionally, or it can imply a committed relationship of some duration. It can be the prelude to a formal engagement or just a way to pass some time. Dating often means something

© Getty Images

Hooking up—casual sexual interaction—rarely occurs in the absence of alcohol.

different to both parties in the relationship. Usually, as time passes in a dating relationship, the nature of the relationship changes. However, it doesn't always change in the same way at the same time for both parties. Current trends show a decline in traditional forms of dating and a rise in casual sexual interaction, often referred to as "hooking up", which has become an alternative to traditional exclusive relationships for some young people (Daniel & Fogarty, 2007). "Hooking up" is vaguely defined and can include varying degrees of sexual behavior from kissing to sexual intercourse. Factors which make a young person more likely to "hook up" include both psychological and social predictors (Longmore, Manning, Giordano, & Rudolph, 2004; Paul, McManus, & Hayes, 2000). Psychological predictors are low self esteem and personality traits which include high risk taking and permissiveness, with the primary social predictor being alcohol use or intoxication. Rarely do hookups take place without the presence of alcohol use by both partners (Longmore et al., 2004). This begs the question, if hooking up is so great, why do you have to get drunk to do it?

A study of over 1000 college students found hooking up common on college campuses (Glenn & Marquardt, 2001). According to this study, dating has a variety of meanings from hanging out or just being together to a high degree of commitment. College men rarely ask women out on dates or acknowledge their relationship has progressed to the point they have become a couple. Regarding relationships and marriages, this study found college women found their relationships either too committed or not committed enough. College women have marriage as a life goal and would like to meet a spouse while in college.

Consequences of Hooking Up

Hooking up, despite the increasing popularity, is not without consequences. One's psychological well-being can be affected. The dashed hopes and lowered expectations can diminish a young person's sense of well-being (Manning, Giodano, & Longman, 2006). These short-lived, nonexclusive, no-commitment relationships can prevent young people from practicing the relationship skills and competencies they will need in future long-term relationships and marriage (Manning et al., 2006). Hook ups are associated with sexual risk taking, such as sexually transmitted diseases and unplanned pregnancy (Manning et al., 2006).

Kastner (2004), psychologist and adolescent researcher, suggests young people perceive less cost in hooking up because it eliminates the chance of heartbreak when it's over. However, the consequence to future relationships can be great. Kastner sees hooking up as "a negative mudslide" which leads to incompetence in intimate relationships.

> "If you're having casual sex at 16, you don't have the confidence to move on to dating at 18 because you don't know how," she says. "At 20, you feel even more awkward so you avoid dating even more. At 22, you're like the client I saw last Friday. She knows how to hang in bars, flirt, and go home with a hook up. She doesn't know how to spend time with a person, one on one. That scares her. She feels like a loser, she feels disconnected and empty, and has low self-esteem." (Kastner, 2004)

Perhaps the most serious consequence is spiritual. As Christians, we are called to kingdom living despite the culture around us. Sometimes as Christians, we lie to ourselves, especially about sexual sin. Young people may see hooking up as an alternative to sex. They push the boundaries of sexual behavior just short of intercourse, ignoring the psychological, emotional and spiritual side effects. Sexuality in general and sexual intercourse specifically are gifts from God for marriage. Hooking up does not embrace sexuality as the gift God intended for it to be.

Electronic Dating

Internet dating has gained increasing popularity. Of American internet users who are single and interested in dating, 74% report they have used the internet in some fashion to further their romantic interests. About 30 million Americans, or 15% of American adults, say they know someone who has been in a long-term relationship with or married someone they met on the internet (Madden & Lenhart, 2006). This can occur through an online chat room, or, more elaborately, through a service which scientifically matches people on certain characteristics. Two major questions surround internet dating. Is electronic dating effective? Can it be dangerous?

Of 10,000 internet users looking for a romantic relationship, 66% believe internet dating is potentially a dangerous activity, with females representing a higher percentage than men. Problems identified with online dating include others having

Peter Scholey / Photographer's Choice RF / Getty Images

Many people are using the internet to enhance their search for a compatible mate.

access to a person's personal information and the ability of users to lie about their identity or marital status. However, any dating relationship has risks, and with online dating on the rise, many who actually use the services are becoming more confident about its safety (Madden & Lenhart, 2006).

Meeting someone new is frequently accompanied by a great deal of excitement. However, there are some important safeguards when using online dating services. The electronic dating relationship involves stages similar to that of "in-person" dating. A couple might e-mail for a few months to get to know one another. This then may evolve into phone calls and eventually a meeting in a public place. Asking questions, especially about religion and spirituality, can prevent investing emotionally in a relationship doomed to fail. One internet dater said: "I'm learning that while online services can be a tool in the dating game, we still must trust God for all things and listen to the Holy Spirit's leading" (Everything You Need, 2005, para. 12). Another online dater gives this advice: "Make sure you don't have major unresolved problems in your life. That new significant other isn't going to fix them for you. . .If you try online dating for a couple of months and it doesn't work out, either accept that now isn't the time to be looking, or go look somewhere else. You have to accept what God has planned for you. Pray and let him lead you to the right place to find a date and/or spouse" (Everything you need, 2005, para. 15, 18).

Regardless of the concerns for safety, many find lasting relationships through online services. Estimates are that more than 120,000 marriages a year occur as a result of online dating (Online Dating Magazine, 2007). Going slowly and patience are the two most important tips according to an internet dater who married as a result of the experience. This success story goes on, "Our relationship has been an example of trusting in what God has in store for you and knowing that it may not be what you expect" (Everything you need, 2005, para. 19).

Premarital Sex

God created human beings as sexual creatures. Unlike many other species who copulate indiscriminately—much like taking in food—human sexuality is highly connected to emotional drives. God created humans in such a way that reproduction ideally requires a certain degree of intimacy. This is much more than simple biology—human sexuality is coupled with many sociocultural and psychological factors.

Authentic Sexuality. The Balswicks (1999, 2008) explain the need for authentic sexuality in order to be everything God created humans to be. Sex is highly distorted in Western culture, promoted by images which isolate the physiology of sex from the sociocultural context of sex. For example, men and women today have many opportunities to gaze at scantily clad women and men—through advertisements, television, movies, and particularly the internet. It is possible to achieve sexual gratification without ever developing an emotional attachment to the people in the images. Families, communities, and churches also may give contradictory messages about the meaning of human sexuality. For example, your family and church may give the message that premarital sex is a sin, while your community actually may encourage premarital sexual activity. Your church might assert certain types of sexual activity are sinful and other types sacred, causing you to be confused. Often, churches and families do not say much about sexuality—if it is discussed at all. These contradictory messages may cause individuals to be confused about their own sexuality. Ultimately, this confusion leads to an inauthentic, distorted sense of sexuality which is empty and far from what God intended it to be.

In order to attain authentic sexuality, it is important to balance the natural sex drive with sociocultural family teaching about sex and God's plan for sex. To facilitate this balance, the Balswicks (1999, 2008) suggested six basic biblical principles regarding sex:

1. Human sexuality is established in the differentiation of male and female and the unity between them.
2. Sexuality is a good gift meant to draw us to deeper levels of knowing (ourselves, others, and God).
3. Humans are born with an innate capacity for sexual pleasure; this capacity can best develop within an emotionally caring, trustworthy family environment.
4. Sexuality and spirituality are intricately connected.
5. After the Fall, sexuality was distorted and in need of redemption.
6. Christ offers restoration and renews our potential for authentic sexuality.

Is it possible to achieve this authentic sexuality within a dating relationship? By biblical standards, no. When you see yourself and your dating partner as children of God—destined for eternity—you cannot justify premarital sex, especially when you also consider the physical and emotional toll it takes.

The Physical Toll of Premarital Sex

Premarital pregnancy and sexually-transmitted diseases such as HPV and AIDS are among the most obvious negative results of premarital sex. Many people argue that the use of condoms and other contraceptive devices can reduce the physical impact of premarital sex. Thus, our contemporary culture often promotes the idea that premarital sex is not wrong if couples use contraception. However, just from a strictly physical standpoint the odds of so-called "safe-sex" practices are generally comparable to those of playing Russian roulette. While reducing the number of bullets in the gun's chamber can better one's odds of escaping unharmed, no one can reasonably argue the game should at all be characterized as "safe" (let alone moral), even if only one bullet remains in the chamber. The ethical standard being promoted in "safe-sex" arguments is it is not bad if you can just "get away with it unharmed." Unfortunately, many safe-sex proponents will not even entertain the proposition of abstaining from the game—of putting the gun down in favor of committing to monogamy.

Relativism. Giving credibility to this kind of acceptance of premarital sex is the worldview of relativism, which holds that ethical truths depend on—are relative to—those holding them. After years of analyzing undergraduate essays about sexual morality, we have concluded the most common ethical view in American culture is relativism. Through the lens of relativism, then, premarital sex is seen to be acceptable under the right conditions: the couple is in love, planning to marry, and using contraception.

E. Dygas / Taxi / Getty Images

Premarital sex can bring a lifetime of disappointment.

46% of teenagers report having had sex at least once.

Teen Sexual Activity. Such widespread cultural acceptance of premarital sex has produced a teen culture which promotes sexual promiscuity. According to the Guttmacher Institute (2006), 46% of teenagers in the United States, ages 15 to 19, have had sex at least once, most with someone within three years of their own age (Guttmacher Institute, 2006). Figure 4.1 gives the frequency of teen sexual behavior by age. While sex in the early teens is relatively low, sexual activity increases with age. The average age that teenagers first experience sex is 17 years old (Guttmacher Institute, 2006).

While those numbers and figures may appear bleak, they actually represent a downward trend of teen sexual activity which plateaued in 2007 (Stein, 2007). In 1993, 56% of high school boys and 50% of high school girls reported at least one sexual

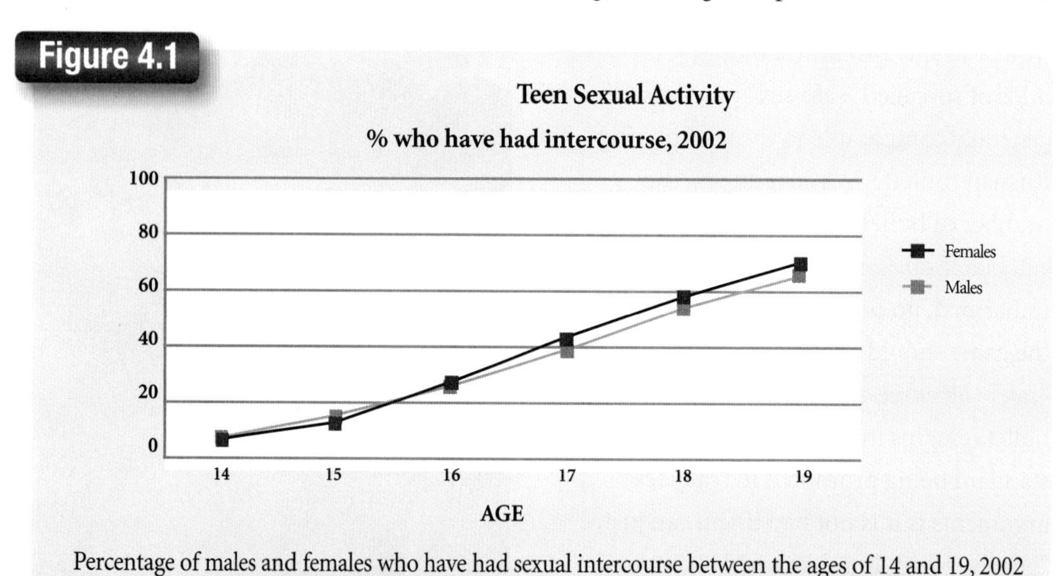

Percentage of males and females who have had sexual intercourse between the ages of 14 and 19, 2002

Source: Alan Guttmacher Institute 2006

experience in their past. By the time teens are college age, 85% of boys and 77% of girls have participated in sexual intercourse. That rate has steadily dropped to 48% of boys and 45% of girls in 2003 (Kaiser Family Foundation, 2005). A Columbia University study found teenagers who pledged to remain sexually abstinent until marriage were 34% less likely to have sex than those who did not take virginity vows. For those teenagers who did not keep their pledges, virginity vows delayed sexual intercourse by 18 months compared to non-pledgers (Bearman & Brückner, 2001).

Even though rates have been falling, teens today experience great pressure to be sexually active. Still, many teens feel very uncomfortable about having sex before they are ready to marry. The Alan Guttmacher Institute (2006) found about 10% of sexually active women, ages 18 to 24, who had sex before age 20 reported their first sexual intercourse was unwanted. The younger a girl's age at her first sexual experience, the higher the probability it was a forced act (Guttmacher Institute, 2006). Alcohol, drugs, or fatigue often lower teenagers' resistance to participate in behavior they later regret. As stories about the disappointments of teen sex begin to circulate, attitudes are changing, and more teens are starting to believe premarital sex is wrong or are at least postponing their first sexual experience.

The rate of teen pregnancy dropped 20% from 1990 to 2005 (see Figure 4.1) (U.S. Census Bureau, 2008b). Researchers attribute 20% of this decline to decreased sexual behavior among teens. The other 80% of the decline is due to the more effective use of contraceptives among teens (Alan Guttmacher Institute, 2006). The rates of premarital sex are dropping, but in a culture filled with sexual messages, premarital sex is still very common.

How do we compare with other nations? Figure 4.2 indicates the rates of teen sex in the United States are comparable to other Western nations. However, Figure 4.3 indicates that, in the United States, teen sex is much more likely to result in pregnancy and abortion. Although contraceptive use among teens has increased dramatically over the past 20 years, it is still not as high as in other industrialized nations. This helps explain why the rate of abortion is so high in the United States, despite the objections of many churches and faith-based organizations.

Attitudes toward premarital sex. Americans as a whole have become more accepting of premarital sex. In 2008, 61% of the sampled adults believed premarital sex was permissible compared to 53% in 2001 (Saad, 2008). Among teenagers, 36% had a positive attitude toward premarital sex while 37% had a negative attitude and 27% expressed no opinion. This is despite the fact that nearly 52% of adolescents in the study indicated they had engaged in premarital sex (Martin, Specter, Martin, & Martin, 2003).

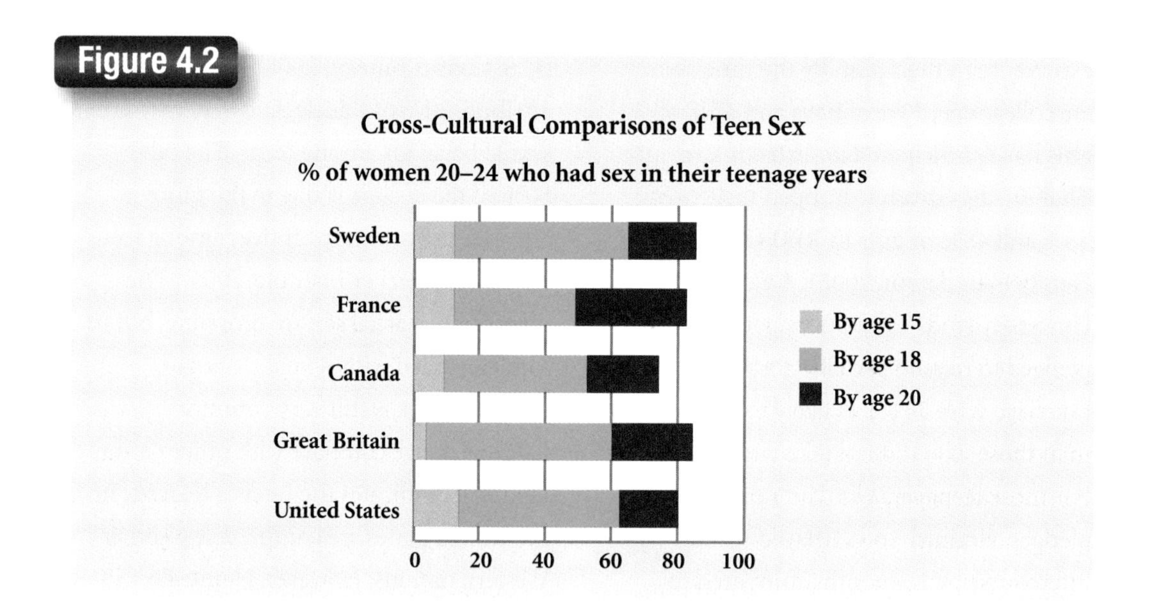

The Emotional Toll of Premarital Sex

While the physical toll of premarital sex is more overt (unplanned pregnancy and sexually transmitted diseases), the emotional toll is perhaps more dangerous (several more bullets in the Russian roulette gun's chamber). Premarital sex can subtly start a person down a road which may have a very tragic ending. Before proceeding down that road, it is important to consider some of the negative consequences of premarital sexual activity.

A Sexual Double Standard. The sexual double standard is still very much alive today. This cultural "rule" says casual sex is OK for men, but not for women (Bogle, 2007). Americans do not stone women who participate in sex outside of marriage (as was done in biblical times). However, the American culture still excuses men for having several partners, while whispering bad things about a woman who "sleeps around." While the media tends to promote sexual freedom and equality, unofficially the word in small-town America is "boys will be boys, but girls will be virgins." This sexual double standard can take an emotional toll on women who are encouraged to have sex before marriage, but then find themselves disrespected for doing so.

Incompatible Values. People can have entirely different motives for participating in premarital sex. For example, incompatible values occur when one partner is hedonistic, while the other partner is relativistic. The hedonistic partner believes premarital sex is just for pleasure and recreation; the relativistic partner believes that premarital sex is only OK when the couple is in love. He tells her he loves her in order to get sex. She thinks they are on their way toward marriage. He thinks this is just a "fling." She ends up emotionally scarred.

Confusion of Values. People often experience confusion of values after participating in behaviors they previously considered immoral. Those who engage in premarital sex often rationalize their behaviors by saying it really wasn't wrong. A good example is the tendency among some Christians to argue that the Bible never really talks about premarital sex. This line of reasoning says fornication really just refers to adultery within a marriage. (See Acts 15:20; 1 Corinthians 6:13, 18; Ephesians 5:3; 1 Thessalonians 4:3; the KJV uses the word *fornication,* while the NIV translates it as *sexual immorality*. See also the related root word

Guilt and shame often occur when people realize they have sinned.

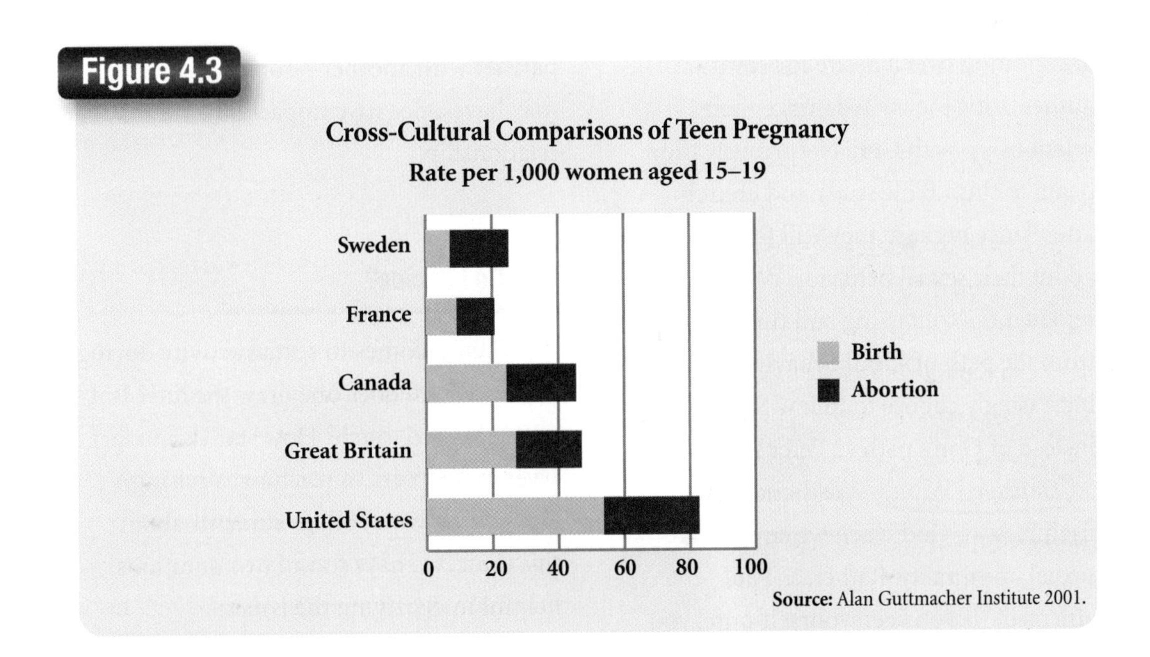

Source: Alan Guttmacher Institute 2001.

whoremongers in Hebrews 13:4 KJV, which also is translated *sexual immorality* in the NIV.) Another example is the supposition that oral sex is not really sex because it is not vaginal. Such rationalizations can confuse people into denying the reality that sex is much more than mere copulation—it is a physical expression of intimacy, designed for monogamous, committed love.

Guilt. Guilt and shame often occur when people realize they have sinned. God will forgive every sin, if the sinner confesses and accepts Christ's forgiveness. However, some Christians carry unconfessed sin, which interferes with their Christian walk. After the romance is gone, premarital sex can leave people feeling very ashamed, embarrassed, and full of guilt.

Damaged Spiritual Relationship. When believers place a desire for physical gratification over a desire for spiritual authenticity, they will damage their relationship with God. Notoriously they begin to shun Bible study and church attendance because they will feel guilty about their sexual behavior. Without repentance (confessing and turning away from the path of sinful behavior), they will increasingly choose to follow their passions instead of God's path (2 Peter 2:18–19).

Damaged Witness. We damage our usefulness to God when we engage in sexual immorality. Rather, as Paul affirmed, "If you keep yourself pure, you will be a special utensil for honorable use. Your life will be clean, and you will be ready for the Master to use you for every good work" (2 Timothy 2:21 NLT). A believer's witness (Christian example to others) becomes damaged when non-Christians become aware Christians are participating in sexual behavior the Bible forbids. The most effective Christian witness is a life of Christian purity.

Negative Repercussions. Engaging in premarital sex can have negative repercussions. Most premarital sex takes place in temporary relationships. The ensuing guilt can jeopardize the health of future relationships. A sexual relationship is designed to be unique with each couple, so what was special about one relationship cannot be recreated in another relationship. Those who have had previous sexual relationships may find themselves subconsciously comparing one sexual partner with another—something which may have a negative impact on a future relationship.

How Do I Decide?

When it comes to sexual activity during dating, where does one draw the line? Is it OK to kiss, to touch? How "far" is too far? Over many years of teaching, advising, and talking with college students about this topic, we have found two questions helpful in clarifying the issues:

1. *Can I talk about sex with my partner?* We are amazed at the number of couples who are having sex without first having really discussed the implications and repercussions. Before you even *think* about initiating a physical relationship, you need to discuss your feelings, expectations, values, the complications (contraception), and possible consequences (pregnancy, sexually transmitted disease). If you can't talk about it, *don't do it*!
2. *Can I have sex in good conscience, knowing God is watching?* If you can't do it at the feet of Jesus, then *don't do it*!

While it was written some time ago, Dr. Lewis Smedes (1976), former President of Fuller Theological Seminary, has some sound advice when making decisions on premarital sexuality, which is still relevant today. He refers to them as a Christian moral stance on sexual intercourse.

1. The Morality of Caution. Anyone trying to make a decision looks at the costs. Am I likely to get hurt? And how great are the risks? Some of the risks are obvious—pregnancy, incurable diseases, but more difficult to assess is the potential harm to an eventual relationship.
2. The Morality of Concern. While the morality of caution is concerned with one's own well being, the morality of concern asks, "Am I likely to hurt someone else?" For instance, consider the child which could result from intercourse. A concerned partner will also consider how intercourse might affect their partner as a whole person.
3. The Morality of Personal Relationships. While the previous two moralities look at personal consequences, the morality of personal relationships looks at the relationship. Two questions become the focus: will intercourse affect the relationship and will intercourse strengthen and deepen the relationship? Sexual intercourse can only strengthen a relationship if two people already have a genuinely personal relationship. When two people use each other in intercourse, they end up hurting each other and corrupting the sexual act.
4. The Morality of Law. This is the law of the New Testament. Paul made no distinctions between casual sex, sex when engaged to be married, or even sex between two mature widowed individuals. Paul makes it very clear in 1 Corinthians 7 he is referring to sexual intercourse for unmarried people. While these

verses may also refer to other kinds of sexuality, the fact he is referring to intercourse outside of marriage is unmistakable. Paul thought sexual intercourse for unmarried people was wrong because "it violates the inner reality of the act; . . . because unmarried people thereby engage in a life-uniting act without a life-uniting intent" (p. 110). Biblical teaching can still be used as a guide for sexuality. Can you trust God for His guidance in this area of your life?

How would sexual intercourse affect me, my family, my relationship and my walk with God?

Common Myths About Dating and Sex

Navigating the complex waters of dating can make for a difficult voyage. Along with peer pressure and cultural relativism, many myths also lie just below the surface, threatening to capsize our relationships, especially our relationship with God.

Myth 1: Dating Is Good Preparation for Marriage

If one's married life consists of going out to dinner and seeing a movie every night, then myth 1 is true. However, married life is much more mundane and complicated than dating ever could be. Most married couples will spend many hours discussing children and finances—topics which probably never came up when they were dating. Marriage often involves a great deal of time apart, even when both partners are in the same house. Dating is a fun-filled, temporary relationship. If dating is done well, partners have gotten to know each other's good and bad qualities in dating. Counterfeit courtship, or to be dating a person you are not going to marry, can lead to much disillusionment and broken expectations. Even when dating is done well, marriage changes things. Marriage is a long-term commitment to the hard work of building and raising a family. While dating introduces some of the roles in relationships as mentioned earlier in this chapter, it is not total preparation. The next chapter discusses the kind of relationship one must develop in order to prepare for marriage.

Myth 2: It's OK to Date a Non-Christian, If It's Not "Serious"

The Bible advises us: "Do not be yoked together with unbelievers. For what do righteousness and wickedness have in common? Or what fellowship can light have with darkness?" (2 Corinthians 6:14). A first principle: We mustn't expect to convert a partner through a dating relationship. It is more probable a non-Christian partner will pull the Christian away from his or her walk. Second, one can't always predict how serious a relationship will become. All too often Christians have awakened one morning to find themselves "in love" with their non-Christian boyfriend or girlfriend. Suddenly, they must choose between the non-Christian partner and their commitment to God.

Myth 3: When Two Christians Date Each Another, They Will Not Be Tempted to Have Sex

Everyone, Christian or not, has a sex drive. It is part of God's plan for human beings to desire one another. Dating only Christians does not make you immune from struggles with sexual temptations. In fact, some time ago researchers identified a phenomenon they call the nice-girl dilemma (Scanzoni & Scanzoni, 1981). This describes a religious woman who cannot accept her own sexual drives and then finds herself in a sexual encounter. Since she never considers she might be involved in premarital sexual activity, she does not take steps to prepare for such an encounter—even when her relationship is getting more and more sexually intimate. She sees the sexual encounter as just an isolated mistake—a sin which will never happen again. She does not seek contraception, because that would be admitting she is planning to participate in immoral activity. The couple does not

Sexual temptation is just as strong for Christians as non-Christians.

discuss the possibility they are experiencing sexual temptation. They do not take proactive measures to avoid being in a tempting situation again, nor do they discuss the consequences of their behavior. By not facing the temptation, the temptation overcomes them.

Myth 4: You Have to Date to Find a Spouse

Actually, many people today report they are marrying their best friends without going through the formalities and complexities of traditional dating activities. Instead of dating, they focus on honestly communicating with one another and sharing good times and bad times together as a more meaningful way to discover compatibility as a married couple. The following testimony illuminates how one Christian found a spouse without dating.

> When I was in college, after having had my heart broken a couple of times, I gave up on dating and focused on being a woman of God. I was involved in a great Christian fellowship group. As I became close friends with several of them, there was one particular guy who was always around when I needed to talk. We spent a lot of time taking walks and talking about our past, present, and future. After about a year, we found ourselves talking about our future *together*. Much to our surprise, we had fallen in love and were coming to realize that God intended for us to be together for life. We had never been on a formal date—in fact, he was not the type of guy I would have dated! We laughed about this, and after we were engaged, we finally went on a real date: dinner and a movie. Oh, and on the morning of our wedding day, he called me on the phone and asked me to marry him—we had just gone ahead and planned a wedding without his ever officially asking! That was 29 years ago and we are still best friends.

Intentional Singleness

In 1 Corinthians 7:38 (NLT), the Apostle Paul said this: "So the person who marries his fiancée does well, and the person who doesn't marry does even better." Are we to interpret this as advice *not* to marry? Some commentators feel Paul's thinking may have been colored by Nero's persecution of believers, which made life so uncertain. Others attribute his stance to the first century belief they were living in the end times. More likely, Paul was extolling the single life for those dedicated to Christian service.

Jesus was not married. A number of his disciples, including Paul, were not married. Many Christians advocate people who dedicate themselves to Christ's work should avoid the distractions of dating, marriage, and subsequent family obligations. Some argue it is easier to live a Christian life when you are focused only on Christ, not on members of the opposite sex.

In contemporary America, it is difficult to live life as a single person. Our culture emphasizes coupling, either in dating or marriage. People who choose to be single or who choose not to date, are often viewed with confusion or pity or judged to be of a different sexual orientation.

The reality is that, while almost all people expect to marry, people actually are spending an increasing number of years unmarried. According to the 2005 Census Bureau report, 8% of men and 33.1% of women between the ages of 25 and 29 had never been married; and, according to the same report, 26% of Americans lived alone. In 1950, only 9% of households were headed by a single person, compared to 48% in 2004 (U.S. Census Bureau, 2005b). While marriage continues to be important, and most people eventually will marry, people are delaying marriage and spending more time as singles. During this single period, they are very busy pursuing educations, careers, hobbies, travel, and other personal interests. "Single" has now become an accepted status for young people, as people are encouraged to develop their own identities before making a lifelong commitment to another person.

Remaining single can liberate one for a life of adventure.

Data indicates many Christians do not date very often. A 2004 *Christianity Today* poll of single people indicated 54% had not been on a date in the past 2 years (Courtney, 2004). Comments by Christians who are not dating indicated they preferred not to have the pressure of premature sexual intimacy and marriage. Many Christians are choosing not to date because they want to develop friendships with people of the opposite sex without the pressure of a lifelong commitment.

Many Christians fear singlehood as a lost opportunity for sexual intimacy. But Christians who are committed to celibacy find sexuality is much more than having sex. McMinn, a sociology professor at Wheaton College, (2004) says "unmarried people uniquely reflect God's inclusive, expansive, open love of others." Learning to live with the cultural challenges of singleness, including the natural longing for sexual intimacy, can bring one into a deeper dependency on God.

A dating hiatus can give one time to reflect on yourself, your relationships and your walk with God.

A Christian Perspective

American culture seems to promote the idea of a "dating game." In this mind-set, dating participants are not so much concerned about the intrinsic value of one another, but are more interested in what they can get from the relationship. Those involved in a dating relationship face incredible pressures to conform to the images they see in films and television programs. More emphasis is given to wedding plans than to preparation for the complex, hard work of marriage. Music lyrics, books, and the Internet endorse premarital sex. Too often, however, the "freedom" of premarital sex has a heavy price—sexually transmitted diseases, unplanned pregnancies, and emotional pain.

The Church can confront these issues by offering teens and single adults Christian alternatives to the dating game. Group activities insulate young people from the dangers of isolation and can cultivate more honest, meaningful relationships. The Christian abstinence movement has had a profound sociocultural impact, so much so, that it is being imitated and promoted by secular groups around the country. While helping to educate and enlighten young people about biblical principles and marriage, the Church must also teach and support the truth that the choice to remain single is a viable biblical option.

Summary

Dating is a relatively new phenomenon in human history. Historically, cultures involved parents and other elders in arranging marriages suitable for their children. Many preindustrial nations still adhere to this practice. Some industrialized nations also include varying levels of parental involvement in marriage arrangements. As nations industrialize, women are given more opportunities for education and career development. This leads to a rise in dating and a postponement of marriage. In the United States, "courting" was strictly chaperoned and intended solely for the purpose of spouse selection until the 20th century. Following World War I, the American value of freedom of choice resulted in dating not only for spouse selection, but also for recreational purposes.

Today, dating has many functions besides recreation and spouse selection. Through the process of dating, individuals find out about themselves and one another. They become socialized into adult gender roles. Dating also can become a vehicle of status attainment for young people. Dating practices continue to change as people meet via the Internet and hooking up—intimacy without strings attached—becomes more prevalent.

With increased dating and delay of marriage comes an increase in premarital sexual activity. The prevalent cultural norm in America today is relativism; thus, premarital sexual activity is generally accepted in secular culture under certain circumstances. In contrast to relativism, Christians hold to the biblical principle of authentic sexuality. Recognizing that sexuality has become distorted because of the Fall, Christians seek Jesus Christ to restore and renew their potential for authentic sexuality. God's plan for sex is that it operates within the covenant relationship of marriage, intended to draw a couple to deeper levels of knowing themselves, one another, and God.

Many Christians today are opting to go against cultural norms and take a hiatus from dating. The single life, far from being the stereotype of someone unable to find a spouse, represents a conscious decision to cultivate a deeper relationship with God and to focus on developing self-identity.

Questions for Thought

1. Dating can mean different things to different people. Discuss some of the dilemmas this presents to couples in relationships.
2. Is dating good preparation for marriage? Why or why not?
3. What does "authentic sexuality" mean for you personally? Are there ways you should be changing your behavior to be more consistent with biblical norms?
4. How can remaining single enhance or hinder someone's Christian walk?

Resources

Activities:

Visit www.eharmony.com (accessed June 23, 2009), an online dating site with success stories and information.

Books:

Passion and Purity: Learning to Bring Your Love Life Under Christ's Control by Elizabeth Elliot. A fairly conservative look at purity in dating and marriage. (Revell, 2002)

When God Writes Your Love Story by Eric and Leslie Ludy. A popular Christian book on dating and purity. (Multnomah Books, 2004)

Saving Your Marriage Before It Starts: Seven Questions to Ask Before and After You Marry by Les and Leslie Parrott. (Zondervan, 2006)

Movies:

Hitch, (PG-13). DVD. Movie about a male match-maker and his humorous and encouraging experiences,

Website/Magazine:

www.christianitytoday.com/singles (Accessed June 23, 2009)

Love and Mate Selection

What's Love Got To Do With It?

5

"What a grand thing, to be loved! What a grander thing still, to love!"
—Victor Hugo, French dramatist, novelist, and poet (1802–1885)

Love never gives up. Love cares more for others than for self. Love doesn't want what it doesn't have. Love doesn't strut, Doesn't have a swelled head, Doesn't force itself on others, Isn't always "me first," Doesn't fly off the handle, Doesn't keep score of the sins of others, Doesn't revel when others grovel, Takes pleasure in the flowering of truth, Puts up with anything, Trusts God always, Always looks for the best, Never looks back, But keeps going to the end.
—1 Corinthians 13:4–7 MSG

What Is Love?

A popular song from the early 1990s asks an interesting question: "What's love got to do with it?" This chapter will examine the meaning of love and its connection to relationships. To determine the link between love and relationships, we first must get a handle on what love is.

When you think of all the songs ever written, consider how many of them have something to do with love. Love seems to be the songwriter's predominant theme! In love songs we find some aspect of love we can relate to on an emotional level. But therein

Image from BigstockPhoto.com / Sanchezamoralex

So much of what people assume about love has to do with an emotional feeling.

lies the problem: So much of what people assume about love has to do with an emotional feeling.

Love is something for which all people long. It illuminates joyous comings and overshadows sad goings. It is the biggest drama of people's private lives, and it fuels the tabloids which report on the "love lives" of the rich and famous. So what is love, really? It is something different for every person.

The Bible speaks of love for God and for all humanity as our greatest goal (see, for example, Matthew 22:36-40). But how do

Image from BigstockPhoto.com / Paha_L

Storge love is the natural familial affection for people.

we attain this kind of love? Psychiatrist Erich Fromm recognized the complexity of love when he wrote *The Art of Loving*. He suggested that love, for most people, is about being loved rather than loving others. Love is something we must learn and practice, just as you learn and practice a musical instrument. He goes on to differentiate between selfless love and self-centered love. Selfless love is embodied in the statement, "I love you just because you are my child." Self-centered love says, "I love you when you do what I ask of you." Most of us grew up poised somewhere between these two realities. But does that adequately describe love?

What about the love between a husband and a wife? Sigmund Freud, according to some psychoanalytic writers, suggested love (libido or sex drive) is the cornerstone of our humanity—something which protects us enough to allow us to change and to grow (Gerasimos, 1991; Hutcheon, 1995). The Object Relations Theory, which is rooted in Freudian psychoanalytic principles, encourages spouses to grow in autonomy and interdependence, which allows them to develop a more authentic love (Scharff & Scharff, 2005).

Theologian, author, and church father Saint Augustine (354–430 ad) described love this way: "What does love look like? It has the hands to help others. It has the feet to hasten to the poor and needy. It has eyes to see misery and want. It has the ears to hear the sighs and sorrows of men. That is what love looks like."

The Dimensions of Love

Ancient Greek culture used four words to describe different kinds of love: *agape*, *philia*, *eros*, and *storge*. C. S. Lewis (1960) expounded on these four dimensions of love:

- **Agape**—unconditional, selfless love as personified in *commitment*;
- **Philia**—love which characterizes friendship, personified in *intimacy*;
- **Eros**—love which exemplifies romance and physical desire, personified as *passion*;
- **Storge**—love which displays a natural, familial *affection* for things and people.

While many social scientists have added to or renamed these dimensions of love, the concepts remain essentially the same as in ancient times. It is generally accepted that a combination of these four dimensions are necessary for lasting relationships. In Sidebar 5.1, the Balswicks use three of these dimensions of love to develop four relationship types.

Romantic Love

Mate selection in Western society is predominately dictated by romantic love. Recall that early in the history of America, spouse selection was based primarily on economic factors—the ability to support a family, acquisition of inherited land, and dowry, among other things. As economic factors improved, the notion of romantic love began to grow. During the early 20th

SIDEBAR 5.1
RELATIONSHIP TYPES

Complete love has an equal proportion of *eros* or passion, *philia* or intimacy, and *agape* or commitment. In Western culture, *eros* or passionate love tends to be predominant early in a relationship, with *philia* or intimacy entering in next, and *agape* or commitment following. In Christian relationships, it is important for an atmosphere of commitment to precede passion and intimacy, allowing both to grow to equal proportions prior to marriage.

Self-giving love is high in *agape* or commitment. This is seen more commonly in other cultures and in arranged marriages. Cultural constraints tend to fuse these relationships together. While intimacy and passion may develop in the relationship, they are not as necessary to keep a relationship together.

Friendship love is higher in *philia* or intimacy. Rarely does friendship alone lead to marriage; however, it is an essential component of a good relationship. Many husbands and wives describe their partners as their best friends, indicating the importance of emotional companionship. A marriage based strongly on friendship may face challenges to the development of passion, leading to dissatisfaction in the marriage.

Infatuation love is high in *eros* or passion. Many times people describe an immediate passion and sexual interest in another person. This can lead to a hasty marriage, which usually doesn't last, because the other necessary elements for maintenance of a relationship fail to grow and develop. Fortunately, most relationships that are predominately based on passion burn themselves out before a marriage takes place.

Source: Paraphrased from Balswick and Balswick 1999, 59–72.

century, people began to question the meaning of romantic love. They wanted to know how to tell if they were experiencing *true* romantic love.

Eric Fromm (1956) attempted to explain his concept of love, suggesting that people tend to see love in the context of being loved, and that loving is a skill we need to learn. He suggested love is an art to be practiced, and that people working on their ability to love will demonstrate giving, caring, responsibility, and respect—many of the agape characteristics. While few people today marry someone they do not love, love is not the only deciding factor.

Compatibility

The idea of compatibility has become a cornerstone for many in determining relationship strength. Most of us think of compatibility as the capacity to live in harmony with someone—someone we enjoy being with, who will listen and support us, and with whom we share many things in common. However, these traits are not sufficient to keep a relationship together. We have counseled numerous couples who have been married 15 or even 20 years. They describe their early relationships as full of *commonalities*, but are now talking about divorce. Love must be defined as more than a series of compatibility traits. How many times have you heard a young couple say they are moving in together to see if they are "compatible"? This is looking at love through the wrong lens.

Compatibility does not hinge on an inventory of personal traits. It is not based on commonalities. It is not something you have—it is something you make. It is a disposition, an attitude, and a willingness to work. Most of all, it is a *process* a couple experiences in their growth together. For this reason, and to minimize confusion, we prefer to call this process commitment, not compatibility.

Image from BigstockPhoto.com / vgstudio

Compatibility has become a cornerstone for decision making about relationships, but lasting relationships must be built on more than compatibility.

Making Love Last

It is not unusual for clients to come into our offices and say, "I love him [or her], but I am not *in love* with him [or her]." What does this really mean? It means the relationship has lost its

Image from BigstockPhoto.com / Mistorian

Commitment is a better indicator of a lasting relationship than the profession of love.

passion. Many couples believe they cannot regain this passion. However, with a little relationship work, we believe it is possible for couples to attain the level of enthusiasm their relationships once held.

Try to recall a time when you were very angry at someone you loved—your mother, father, brother, sister, boyfriend or girlfriend or maybe your child. At that moment of anger, you didn't *feel* love for that person, but did you actually stop loving that person? Probably not. Merely the *feeling* of love was gone, not the *essence* of your love.

Because we have found this principle to apply overwhelmingly in our counsel of couples, we no longer ask couples if they love one another. We ask them instead to explore their level of commitment to their relationship. A couple's level of commitment to their relationship seems to be a much better indicator of whether the relationship will endure than the love they profess for each other.

Laurie Hall described the difference between involvement and commitment in a relationship as the difference between bacon and eggs—the chicken is involved, but the pig is committed (Hall, 2000). This difference is poignantly described by Dr. Iannis to his daughter Pelagia in the film *Captain Corelli's Mandolin*:

> Love is a temporary madness. It erupts like an earthquake and then subsides. And when it subsides you have to make a decision. You have to work out whether your roots have become so entwined together that it is inconceivable that you should ever part. Because this is what love is. Love is not breathlessness, it is not excitement, it is not the promulgation of promises of eternal passion. That is just being "in love," which any of us can convince ourselves we are.
>
> Love itself is what is left over when being in love has burned away, and this is both an art and a fortunate accident. Your mother and I had it, we had roots that grew towards each other underground, and when all the pretty blossoms had fallen from our branches we found that we were one tree and not two (Madden, 2001).

Theories of Mate Selection

Our selection of a marriage partner is only partially conscious. Subconscious or unconscious factors also come into play. We are told beauty is in the eyes of the beholder. Why do we consider certain people beautiful, but not others? Why are we drawn to certain individuals and not to others? The answers to these questions are complex.

Theories of Developmental Process

Primary Elements. Theories of developmental process help to explain how we filter out ineligible or incompatible people. Propinquity, or physical proximity, is the first rule guiding whom we choose to date and later marry. Assortative partnering, which has its roots in evolutionary theory, relates to choosing a partner based on physical characteristics. Assortative partnering is related to homogamy, which is the concept of choosing someone with some elements of similarity to your own. When homogamy is related to demographic characteristics or resources, we use the term endogamy to suggest the choice of a spouse within one's status group.

Types of Stratification. Several factors influence our choice of a mate. The first element of stratification or grouping is race and ethnicity. We tend to marry within our own racial and ethnic group, which are examples of homogamy (Gardyn, 2002). According to the 2000 Census, the number of interracial couples in America increased from 1% in 1970 to over 5% in 2000, which is still a small percentage (Lee & Edmonston, 2005). There were nearly 4 million interracial marriages in 2006, almost double the number of interracial marriages in 2000 (U.S Census Bureau, 2007b). Most interracial couples consist of a white person and a nonwhite person, the most common being a white/Asian-American couple. The second most common pairing is white/Native-American, and the third most common is a white/African-American couple. African-American men are more than twice as likely to intermarry as are African-American women, and Asian-American women are more likely than Asian-American men to intermarry (Lee & Edmonston, 2005).

Image from BigstockPhoto.com / FeverpitchPro

Proximity, physical characteristics, resources and status are all involved in mate selection.

Social Class and Education. Social class and educational endogamy also affect our choice of a marriage partner. We tend to choose within our own class or close to it. This is partly explained by proximity. Our parents' social class determines where we live and what school we attend. Even in our work environment, we tend to be drawn to people with similar interests and educational status.

Religion. Religious homogamy, marrying within one's own religion, is more important in some groups than in others. The culture of many denominations tends to encourage marriage to someone with similar religious beliefs. The Apostle Paul advised Christians not to be "unequally yoked together with unbelievers" (2 Corinthians 6:14 KJV). Another translation calls this being "mismatched with unbelievers" (NRSV). Paul's comment to the Corinthian church suggests believers and nonbelievers have nothing in common. A marriage with such disparity will only lead to problems. God is to be the center of a Christian marriage and if half of the marital union doesn't believe this, there will undoubtedly be tension. What about the believer in a relationship with a nonbeliever who is confident they can influence that person for Christ? You probably have known a Christian involved in a relationship with a non-Christian. More often than not, the Christian is pulled down, rather than the non-

Marrying someone of the same faith persuasion can strengthen a marriage.

Christian being pulled up. It is almost as if gravity exerts its influence in the spiritual realm too.

Paul gives instruction in 2 Corinthians 6:14-15 not to be joined with those who are without faith:

> "Do not be yoked together with unbelievers. For what do righteousness and wickedness have in common? Or what fellowship can light have with darkness? What harmony is there between Christ and Belial? What does a believer have in common with an unbeliever?"

The righteousness of a Christian which Paul refers to is a gift from God which is compromised when a believer marries a nonbeliever. Righteousness is incompatible with unrighteousness; light is incompatible with darkness, and marriage between a believer and nonbeliever creates a spiritual incompatibility.

Age. Age is another important factor in spouse selection, especially in first marriages. Since many young people meet in college and marry soon afterward, the age difference at first marriage is around 2 years, with males being older (Darroch, Landry, & Oslak, 1999). When men remarry, or marry later in life, they tend to marry women considerably younger than themselves. In general, men are less likely than women to marry someone older or less attractive than themselves (Smith, 1991).

Evolutionary Theory

Darwin's theory of evolution is not accepted by many Christians. However, some social psychologists use the evolutionary theory of mate selection to explain how men and women select mates *through unconscious attraction to qualities of fitness for bearing children and continuing the species.*

Physical Appearance. When asked about beauty, men and women tend to value different traits. Pop psychology claims men are visually stimulated, while women are romantically inclined. However, such gender stereotyping is not always the case.

Physical appearance plays a role in mate selection for both sexes.

Again, individual men and women have different values and crieria for pleasing physical appearances and attractions.

Buss and colleagues (2001) identified several characteristics which both sexes consider very important in a potential marriage partner, with physical attraction being one of the most important. In a study of 728,000 Match.com members, physical attractiveness was rated as the most important characteristic, after intelligence and sense of humor (Gardyn, 2002).

Physical appearance also plays a role in what both sexes find attractive. In her article describing sex differences in mate preference, Denisiuk (2004) suggested women tend to identify attractive men as having a healthful appearance: symmetrical features, clear skin, and white sclera (the white part of the eye), which is suggestive of good genes. Masculine features such as a strong jaw, narrow hips, and muscular build, which suggest high testosterone and fertility, are also attractive to women.

Sidebar 5.2
Is It All in Your Nose?

A Swiss zoologist who tested women's responses to men's sweaty T-shirts has found that women are attracted to the scent of men who are most unlike them in an array of immune system genes called MHC (major histocompatibility complex), and that this may influence mate choice. The same type of study conducted with mice found that pregnant mice prefer the familiar odor of MHC-similar males. It is hypothesized that nesting with relatives may provide support and protection for the mother and her young. Interestingly, women who are on the Pill, which raises estrogen levels and simulates pregnancy, also preferred the odor of MHC-similar males. This brings up the possibility that odor perception in pregnancy plays a different function—that of choosing cooperative partners and would-be relatives.

So, what are the benefits of choosing MHC-dissimilar mates? It seems that MHC-dissimilar mates have a higher fertility rate, produce hardier offspring with more effective immune systems, and have a reduced risk of genetic diseases. In other words, from an evolutionary standpoint, the more dissimilar the parents are genetically, the healthier the offspring, the lower the observance of genetic disorders, and the greater the likelihood for survival. Darwin's survival of the fittest!

While this does not provide definitive answers on mate selection, it does bring up an interesting question: is mate selection in our society altered by the number of young women who are on the Pill?

Source: Wedekind and Furi 1987, 1471–1479.

Denisiuk went on to suggest men have their own criteria for judging the attractiveness of women. What men tend to find attractive in a woman are full lips, full breasts, and full hips, as well as smaller waists—all indicative of a woman's estrogen level and her ability to bear children. Sidebar 5.2 presents an interesting theory of mate selection as it relates to the sense of smell.

Parental Involvement. Some proponents of the evolutionary theory of mate selection suggest the differences in what men and women find attractive in a mate are based on their potential parental involvement. These theorists believe that since women tend to be the primary caretakers of their children, they tend to be more selective about the men they choose, in order to improve the survival of their offspring.

This evolutionary theory purports that men are generally less involved in childrearing, so they can afford to be less choosy about a mate (Eagly & Wood, 1999).

Psychodynamic Theory

According to the psychodynamic theory of mate selection, our parents have a great deal to do with our choice of a mate. Psychodynamic theory has grown out of the work of Sigmund Freud, Carl Jung (pronounced Yung), and others. It suggests

The parent image theory of mate selection suggests we choose a someone similar to our opposite sex parent.

our deepest relational needs are based on our internalized family drama. As adults, we search for the types of experience which comes closest to the patterns of interaction we experienced in our early childhood. This is an attempt to get what we feel we needed or missed as we were growing up (Scharff & Scharff, 2005).

Parent Image Theory. Various types of psychodynamic theories offer explanations for our choices. How many times have you heard someone say, "I married my father" or "She is just like my mother"? Based on Freud's work, the parent image theory of mate selection suggests we marry someone resembling our opposite sex parent (e.g., a son would marry someone who reminded him of his mother; a daughter would marry someone like her father).

Ideal Mate Theory. The ideal mate theory of mate selection grew out of Freud's theories and is the hallmark of Object Relations Theory. It suggests we form a fantasy image of our ideal mate in our minds through our childhood interactions, and then search for someone who will come close to fulfilling this fantasy image.

Exchange Theory

The exchange theory of mate selection is based on the premise: the exchange of social and material resources is a fundamental form of human interaction. All relationships have give and take, but the balance of the exchange is not always equal. Exchange theory explains how we feel about a relationship with another person based on the balance between what we are putting into the relationship and what we are getting out of it, the kind of relationship we believe we deserve, and our chances of having a better relationship with someone else.

When applied to mate selection, exchange theory suggests we select mates who are more or less our equals. This selection process is based on several things, such as similar backgrounds, financial status, physical appearance, social status, and personality traits, to name a few. Exchange theory suggests relationships continue because the partners are getting as much or more from the relationship as it is costing them. Sometimes, however, one partner chooses to maximize his or her own interests, and exploits the other partner. Clearly, this is not conducive to a loving relationship.

Equity Theory

The equity theory of mate selection is similar to exchange theory in that people should *benefit from* a relationship in proportion to what they *give to* a relationship. Fairness is the hallmark here, although how to judge what is equitable or fair for the individuals involved can be difficult.

We tend to choose a mate who is similar to us in interests, background, social status and personality.

Stage Theories

Stage theories of mate selection describe how we move through distinct stages as we develop. Instead of experiencing gradual changes, stage theories suggest we make sudden shifts to different plateaus of perception and behavior. These shifts often correlate with the epiphanies or "ahas" of personal experience.

SVR Theory. Murstein's (1987; Parsons, 1998) Stimulus-Value-Role (SVR) theory of mate selection suggests we choose our friends and partners through a three-stage model. We then filter out people at each stage who do not fit our preferences.

1. In the initial stimulus stage, we evaluate people based on physical appearance. We are usually attracted to people of similar age, appearance, and ethnicity.
2. In the intermediate value stage, we evaluate the other person's values, such as attitudes toward religion, sex, career, and family. If their values are similar enough to our own values, we can choose to continue the relationship.
3. In the role stage, we share our activities to build a working relationship. It is preferable for our likes and desires to be complementary (you do this, while I do that) and for our attitudes toward roles to be similar.

Relationship Theory. Levinger's (1976, 1999) relationship stage theory of mate selection suggests our relationships move through a series of stages as we mature. His model is based on an ABCDE acrostic:

- Acceptance/attraction. When we meet someone, our initial attraction frequently is based on beauty and similarity.
- Build-up. As we reveal more and more of ourselves, we become increasingly interdependent. We may become annoyed at one another, but the pleasant parts of the relationship keep it going.
- Continuation/consolidation. This is the stage at which commitments such as marriage are made. The couple may enter into a long-term, stable relationship.
- Deterioration. Many relationships decay due to poor effort, lack of rewards, and unavailability of alternatives.
- Ending. The relationship ends when the partners agree to separate or when one leaves.

Family Life Cycle. Unlike traditional sociological theory which looks at the family life cycle as commencing with marriage, Carter and McGoldrick (1999, 2005) begin the family life cycle with young adults. This is a cornerstone stage with the

Sharing activities is one way to build a working relationship.

primary task of coming to terms with the powerful force of the family of origin. The family of origin has a tremendous effect on who, when, and whether or not the young adult will marry, as well as impacting transition through future stages of the family life cycle. Successful completion of this stage involves separating from parents yet remaining connected, without cutting off or reactively trying to substitute the parental relationship with another. As was mentioned in chapter 3, an increasing problem in our technological society is the prolonged dependency young adults experience in preparation for the work world. This creates difficulties for both parents and young people as they attempt to renegotiate the hierarchical relationships (Carter & McGoldrick, 1999, 2005).

Same-Sex Relationships. Stage models can contribute to our knowledge of gay and lesbian family culture; however, it is important to keep in mind there are enormous differences in the social, historical and community contexts in which these families are formed. Carter and McGoldrick's family life cycle stages have been applied to the study of gay and lesbian relationships, but not without problems. The family life cycle developed by Carter and McGoldrick is child-centered and occurs in a context which receives validation and community support. The gay and lesbian life cycle is typically not child-centered and receives little validation or support in the larger context (Slater & Mencher, 1991). Other differences reside in the process of "coming out," the stages of couple development, and the stages a family goes through when they discover their child is gay or lesbian (Laird, 2005).

While all of these theories of mate selection help to explain some aspects of why we are drawn to certain people, we are still left with questions. What accounts for the intensity of love? Why do many couples have complementary traits? The deeper we look at the phenomenon of romantic attraction, the less these theories of mate selection seem to explain. As we usually find in dealing with the weighty issues of life, the more we know, the more we realize we do *not* know.

The continuation/consolidation stage is where commitments such as marriage are made.

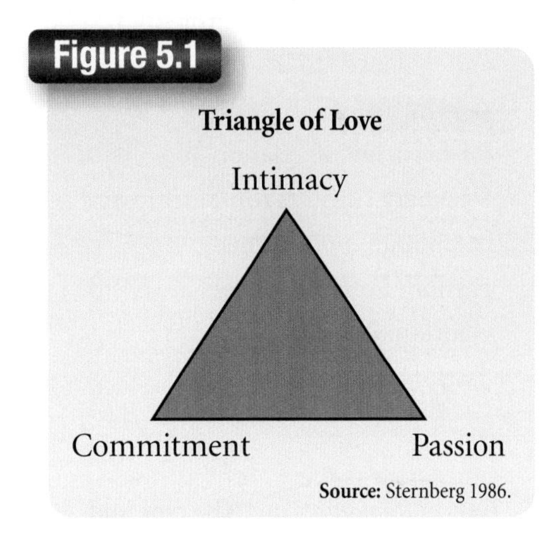

The Role of Romantic Love

If we conducted a survey to learn why people married their spouses, we would find as the predominant answer, "Because we were in love." We have already discussed that no matter how we try to define love, a definition remains elusive. There is no general consensus of what constitutes love.

Triangular Theory of Love. Robert Sternberg's triangular theory of love (1986; 2000) may further our understanding of the role of passionate love. This triangle of love, as shown in Figure 5.1, is characterized by three different elements: intimacy, passion, and commitment (1986). Although we have examined these elements earlier, to summarize,

- Intimacy is the feeling of closeness between two people;
- Passion is the drive which produces physical attraction and romance, and that leads to intercourse; and
- Commitment is the decision to further a loving relationship.
- Sternberg suggests romantic love is a combination of intimacy and passion. Romantic lovers are bonded emotionally and physically through passionate arousal.

Types of Romantic Love. The type and strength of the love is determined by the relative proportions of intimacy, passion, and commitment, as well as their interactions. Companionate love is high in intimacy and commitment. It typifies marriages in which the passion is gone but a deep affection and commitment remain. Fatuous love is high in passion and commitment, but is low in intimacy. It is exemplified by a whirlwind courtship and marriage, in which commitment is fueled by passion without the stabilizing influence of intimacy. Consummate love is the only stage which includes all three in relatively equal proportions. It is the most complete form of love and represents the love relationship couples strive for, but apparently few actually realize. Sternberg warned that maintaining a consummate love may be even more difficult than achieving it, and he stressed the importance of turning the components of love into action. "Without action, even the greatest of loves can die" (Sternberg, 1987, p. 331).

While Sternberg's triangle theory provides some description of the different kinds of love, even according to Sternberg, it still doesn't explain the phenomena of love. Sternberg and colleagues (2001) have further conceptualized a theory of "love as a story," in which one's personal attributes, as well as the environment, interact to create an internal narrative or story, which an individual then seeks to fulfill in a relationship. These stories are highly influenced by one's family of origin and the cultural messages one receives about love (Sternberg, 1998). In his research, Sternberg (2001) has found that couples with similar stories tend to be more satisfied, while couples with divergent stories tend to be less satisfied.

Image from BigstockPhoto.com / visual28

A consummate marriage consists of intimacy, commitment and passion.

Crazy in Love. Anthropologist and researcher Helen Fisher (2004) has used neurophysiologic research to study what happens to our brains when we are in love. She has found certain parts of our brains exhibit increased blood flow and "light up" on a brain scan during the early passionate stage of a relationship. She concluded that romantic passion is actually hardwired into our brains. It is not an emotion at all, but is instead a drive as powerful as our hunger drive. Fisher suggests that passion triggers the same areas of the brain which are involved in substance abuse. Likening love to a drug, she has found the same basic brain chemicals triggered in drug abuse are also triggered in love. Love affects our energy levels, our mood swings, our thinking, our behaviors, and tolerance of our partners.

This seems to substantiate why people in love sometimes do crazy things. Fisher suggests couples in the first few months of ecstasy feel madly in love and truly believe their love will last forever. During this time, they sometimes do things they otherwise would not do. Celebrities are a visible example of this phenomenon. For instance, Britney Spears married Jason Alexander on a whim. Their marriage lasted 55 hours before it was annulled. Johnny Depp tattooed "Winona Forever" on his arm in honor of Winona Ryder, later changing it to "Wino Forever" after their break up.

Maybe you have done something similar when you were in love, and later could not explain why. Brain chemistry can help explain these intense feelings of love, as well as our behaviors while we are in love, and the incredible pain we experience when love fails.

Brain chemistry can help explain the intense feelings of love, as well as the incredible pain when a relationship breaks up.

It is important to note here that while this kind of passion may feel good at the onset, it is impossible to sustain over a prolonged period of time. A review of Sternberg's consummate love tells us that while passion is important, it is only one of three necessary elements of long-term love. Time is required for all three to develop. Ted Huston (2003), in studying the relationship between the length of the dating experience and marital success, has found the closer the length of courtship comes to the average of two and a half years, the more successful the union will be. Passion may blossom first and feel very good, but it takes time for intimacy and commitment to bloom fully.

A Christian Perspective

Choosing a marriage partner is one of the most important decisions a person will ever make. This decision will have far-reaching effects on the couple, as well as many other people—parents, children, and friends. We often struggle with selecting the right partner. As Christians, we want God to be involved in our choice of a spouse.

Making the Right Choice

As most of us have discovered, passion has an uncanny ability to affect our rational thought and at times our ability to hear God clearly. So, how do we discern God's will for our relationships?

The Balswicks (1999; 2006) have suggested three guidelines for determining God's direction concerning marriage:

1. The couple should seek God's will through prayer, Bible study, and meditation.
2. The couple should seek wisdom from those who love and care about them—parents, family members, and friends. These trusted people can lend a different perspective, which can be invaluable.
3. The couple should seek wisdom from their church or a related body of believers. This will add different but very helpful input.

Neil Clark Warren, founder of eHarmony.com, offers 10 principles for choosing the right marriage partner. (see Sidebar 5.3) Although these principles have been around since the early 1990s, they are still very pertinent today.

Premarital Counseling

Marriage and family therapists attest to the value of premarital counseling in marital success. Many couples only manage a few of hours of premarital counseling with their pastors. However, to properly prepare to reap the full benefits of your relationship, couples should commit to a much longer period of time (6 to 12 weeks) with a counselor before marriage.

Premarital counseling should include an inventory such as Prepare/Enrich or FOCCUS (Facilitating Open Couple Communication, Understanding and Study) to measure strengths and deficits on a number of scales, such as roles, friends, budget issues, sex, children,

Seeking wisdom from the people who love you, as well as your church body can help you make the right choice regarding marriage.

in-laws, and family-of-origin similarities. The more similar a couple's scores are in these areas, the stronger the relationship, and the more likely the marriage will be successful. Marriage and family therapists can help couples decide if they are ready for marriage and, based on their scores, how difficult it will be for a couple to make their marriage successful. It is much better to find this out prior to the wedding than to wake up one morning and wonder just what you have done. Premarital counseling also encourages couples to talk about things

SIDEBAR 5.3
HOW TO CHOOSE THE RIGHT MARRIAGE PARTNER

1. Eliminate the seven primary causes of faulty mate selection.
2. Find a person to love who is very much like you.
3. Get yourself emotionally healthy before you get yourself married.
4. Develop a clear mental image of your "perfect person."
5. Find love that you can feel in your bones, and express it with great wisdom.
6. Let passionate love mature before you decide.
7. Master the art of intimacy.
8. Learn how to clear conflict from the road to love.
9. Refuse to proceed until you can genuinely pledge your lifelong commitment.
10. Celebrate your marriage with the full support of your family and friends.

Source: Warren 1998.

As Warren points out, couples can minimize failure in mate selection by avoiding such factors as marrying too quickly, marrying too young, not knowing your partner well, and having unrealistic expectations of marriage. Ask yourself what kind of personality, likes, appearance, goals, and dreams you want in a spouse, and then look for someone with similar values.

Don't bring "baggage" into the marriage. Make sure you are emotionally healthy before you say "I do." Make sure the love you feel comes from deep inside, then wait until marriage to express the depth of your passion.

Give passionate love time to mature before you marry, so that companionate love will have time to grow. Cultivate intimacy. It involves self-knowledge, the desire to know others, and the ability to share one another's emotional experiences. Learn how to deal with conflict. Understand that you each have your own thoughts and feelings, you need to be listened to and understood, you need to be willing to compromise, and you agree to resolve disagreements as they occur.

Be sure when you marry that you are truly ready to make a covenant to be with this person for the rest of your life. Seek input from your parents and friends regarding what they think about your marriage. They know you best and care about you and your happiness, so they can offer wisdom about who will make you happy.

they have not thought to discuss, or that are difficult for them to discuss. (see www.lifeinnovations.com {accessed June 23, 2009} or http://foccusinc.com {accessed June 23, 2009} for more information on premarital inventories.)

Several recent articles have indicated that counseling can be damaging to a marriage, since only about 17% of counselors are marriage and family therapists who have been trained to work with couples. Those seeking premarital or marital counseling should carefully investigate the qualifications of the counselors before committing to therapy. A list of certified marriage and family therapists can be found at the American Association for Marriage and Family Therapy website at http://aamft.org.

Summary

This chapter has explored the varieties of love, the difficulties of defining love, and the theories of mate selection. The ancient Greeks used four words (*eros*, *philia*, *storge*, and *agape*) to describe different aspects of love. Although terms are different, we continue to define love types in essentially the same way today.

Because of the elusiveness of a definition of love, its place in mate selection is subject to different theories of mate selection. Psychodynamic theory suggests an unconscious component to mate selection, one which is largely determined by our parents and our childhood experiences. Exchange theories view relationship formations from a more utilitarian framework, having to do with the balance between what we are putting into a relationship versus what we are getting out of it. Stage theories look at relationship formation from a developmental perspective, noting progression though particular stages of a developing relationship.

While these theories seem to hold some explanation for mate selection, the role of romantic love—what we think of as the main reason for choosing a mate—is given little attention. It is important to see the interconnection between intimacy, passion, and commitment. New research on brain chemistry confirms what we have long thought to be true: People are changed by the experience of falling in love. Thus, it is easier to understand how easy it is to make hasty, rash decisions about the choice of a mate.

Christians stress the importance of relying on God and their loved ones to confirm their decisions about prospective marriage partners. No one is in a position to make such an important decision in isolation. Premarital inventories can provide an unbiased look at the strengths and weaknesses in a relationship and provide for better decisions about the relationship. Prayer, an extended period of premarital counseling, and the wise advice of others can be invaluable in helping couples make one of the most significant decisions they will ever make.

Questions for Thought

1. What do you think are the most important characteristics in a spouse? Are some of these characteristics absolutely essential or are they just important?

2. Which of the theories presented in this chapter fit best with your thoughts on why we choose the mate we choose? Why?

3. Think about your family of origin. What impact does it have on your choice of a spouse? Do you see this influence as good or bad?

Resources

Books:

Getting Ready for Marriage Workbook by Jerry D. Hardin & Dianne C. Sloan (Thomas Nelson Publishers, 1992)

Sacred Marriage by Gary L. Thomas (Zondervan, 2000)

Movies:

License to Wed, (PG-13). DVD. A movie about one couple's outrageous adventures through pre-marital counseling.

Father of the Bride, (PG). DVD. A hilarious story about a father's saga through his daughter's engagement and wedding. Look for similarities between the father and fiancé.

The Mystery of Love DVD. PBS: In popular culture, one type of love—passionate sexual romance—is prized above all. But there are many kinds of love that give shape and meaning to life. This film explores real love stories of marriage, parents and children, romance, brotherly love, altruism, divine love, love of community, even the love of war. Actor, playwright and author Anna Deavere Smith hosts the special.

Marriage and Family Life

6

The Early Years

The man who finds a wife finds a treasure, and he receives favor from the Lord . . . .Let your wife be a fountain of blessing for you. Rejoice in the wife of your youth.

—Proverbs 18:22;5:18

Happily Ever After?

At the conclusion of the wedding ceremony, the great adventure begins! Unfortunately, too many couples are unprepared for the journey. They have put so much time and energy into planning the wedding and honeymoon, they have not thought about what happens *after* the wedding. Often there is an assumption that "if we can just find the right spouse, we will live happily ever after."

A good marriage is not so much a matter of *finding* the right mate as it is *being* the right mate. Married life takes *staying power,* something which is established in the critical first weeks and months after the honeymoon. This chapter will focus on the first few years of marriage, reviewing the changes occurring to each marriage partner's self-image, the couple's relationship to one another, and their relationships to others. Even couples who live together before marriage find their relationships change after marriage. In that context, we will explore the difference marriage makes legally, emotionally, and socially.

We also will examine biblical principles for building strong marriages. The Bible presents the framework for a successful marriage, but the couple must work out its own patterns and roles within that framework. Each marriage is unique. Thus, what worked for your parents or grandparents may not work for you and your spouse. In this chapter, we will also reveal and debunk some common myths about marriage.

Finally, we will give an overview of choices in family planning. Will the couple have children or remain childless? Will the couple use contraception? If so, what is available? If the couple chooses to have children, how many children should they have? These very important decisions must be made early in the relationship. Ideally, they should be negotiated even before marriage.

Henrik Sorensen / Stone+ / Getty Images

Couples who cohabit and then marry experience lower quality relationships and a much higher divorce rate.

What Difference Does Marriage Make?

A biblical perspective of marriage stands in stark contrast to societal acceptance of cohabitation. In chapter 4's discussion of dating, we saw that God's Word is filled with numerous references regarding sex outside the boundaries of marriage (Acts 15:20; 1 Corinthians 6:13, 18; Ephesians 5:3; 1 Thessalonians 4:3; Hebrews 13:4, for example). Couples who are sexually intimate without being married are living in opposition to God's will. In this kind of sinful relationship, they cannot experience the authentic sexuality God intended for them. Premarital sex, then, is a "disconnect" from God's intention for sexuality. It can cause confusion and lead to some real difficulties before and during marriage.

Likewise, many couples who choose to cohabit before marriage do so because they want to know what marriage will be like. However, cohabiting couples who later marry report cohabitation is different than marriage (Cohan & Kleinbaum, 2002).

Marriage tends to change the nature of the relationship. What was once casual becomes legally binding. Many engaged couples declare "marriage won't change us," but find that it does. Communication patterns and roles which were established during courtship are renegotiated after marriage. Many couples assume that once married, God will then bless their marriage and everything else will work out fine. Unfortunately, this may not be the case, since marriages following cohabitation are more than twice as likely to end in divorce in the first 5 years. Of those couples who cohabit before marriage, 49% will divorce in the first 5 years compared to 20% who did not cohabit. By 10 years, 50% of the marriages following a period of cohabitation prior to marriage will have divorced, compared to 33% of marriages which did not involve cohabitation (Bramlett & Mosher, 2002). It seems marriage changes everything dramatically.

Changes in Self-Concept

In the past, a wedding was an event which brought two families together, forming an alliance. More recently, the wedding has become an event the parents paid for, displaying their approval and support for their child's marriage (Cherlin, 2004). A common idea from both of these is the legal and social approval for having children. According to Cherlin (2004),

Lauren Burke / Riser / Getty Images

Men more commonly than women can fall into the trap of using work as their identity and avoiding the emotional connection with their family.

weddings are moving away from being a show of family support and approval for having children, to being an individualized couple event—a milestone in demonstrating the development of their self-identities. Weddings seem to be more about symbolizing the couple's personal achievements and stage of self-development rather than the final event culminating in heterosexual marriage (Bulcroft, Bulcroft, Bradley, & Simpson, 2000; Freeman, 2002).

Married people take on new patterns of thinking about themselves. Marriage presents a time of renewed identity exploration. Who am I? Who are "we"? How do we balance our individuality with our oneness? Resolution of these questions can have positive or negative consequences or a combination of both.

A common, but more negative, way some men resolve this is by assuming an

© iStockphoto.com / 4X6

God's intention for marital mutuality is reached through a reciprocating relationship in which spouses encounter their own uniqueness in relationship to God and each other.

occupational role and working at a task considered appropriate for adult males (Zemon-Gass & Nichols, 2007). They are doing the right things but in the absence of an emotional connection with the family. This phenomenon led to what was coined in the 1970s by Balswick and Peck (1971) and still used today as "[the] tragedy of the inexpressive American male". For females, the struggle can be more difficult. It is not uncommon for women to define their new identity through their husband and later their children. This incomplete resolution can be seen later in the depression middle-aged women sometimes suffer when their children leave home and they may not feel as connected to their husbands (Zemon-Gass & Nichols, 2007). According to Zemon-Gass and Nichols, both husbands and wives can experience the sense that one's individuality is being smothered by their partner, and that the marital relationship is unfair.

In a more positive identity resolution, both spouses simultaneously learn individuation and interdependence—to be separate but together—early in their marriage. Santore (2008), a sociologist at University of Albany, suggests attachments between romantic partners take place in a 'culture of intimacy'. This culture of intimacy raises the bar for marriage in which relationships support both personal growth and the fulfillment of one's spouse.

Achieving this kind of intimacy in a marriage is likely more difficult apart from a belief in a biblical marriage, which supports both hierarchical and mutual submission between a couple and God. The Balswicks (2006) describe this as a reciprocating process:

> The supreme meaning of being created in the image of God is that spouses reflect a relationship of unity without absorption. To be human in a context of marriage is to be a particular spouse in relation—distinct and unique and yet inextricably intertwined and interdependent. God's intention for marital mutuality is reached through a reciprocating relationship in which spouses encounter their own uniqueness in relationship to God and each other. Marriage serves as a sanctifying process as spouses strive for unity in the midst of their own unique differences.

You sometimes see references to "his marriage" and "her marriage." These are outdated conceptions which describe marriage for a man as involving more income, less housework, laundry, and cooking, while marriage for a woman involves increases in all of these. The fact is, both spouses benefit from marriage. These descriptions do not describe the culture of intimacy or reciprocating relationship discussed above. The new patterns of thinking necessary to support marital intimacy involve an emphasis on knowing each other, validating each other, helping each other, and sharing oneself, as new roles and rules are negotiated in the relationship.

Changes to the Relationship

Dating is fun and falling in love is exciting. While these elements should remain in a marriage, they probably will not dominate the relationship. Marriage changes the relationship. Marriage requires much more work together on mundane things like budgets, insurance payments, home maintenance, and investments. Romance often wears thin when the car breaks down, the laundry piles up, and budding careers require hours of overtime. Spouses are less tolerant of each other than when they were dating. One of the major difficulties during this early time is dealing with the expectations one had of marriage. Each partner in a marriage brings a set of beliefs and characteristics which are likely to affect their future together. Couples who have similar expectations of marriage and each other are better able to achieve their common goals, while dissimilar expectations can cause disillusionment in the marriage (Waller & McLanahan, 2005). Disenchantment is inevitable in the early years of marriage. The focus shifts from romance to commitment, perseverance and staying power.

Many people today advocate living together before marriage as good preparation for marriage. Data indicates that couples who cohabit before marriage have more marital discord, lower marital quality and are more likely to divorce than non-cohabiting couples (Amato, Booth, Johnson, & Rogers, 2007; Bramlett & Mosher, 2002; Kamp Dush, Cohan, & Amato, 2003; Stanley, Whitton, & Markman, 2004). Why? One reason is people having unconventional attitudes

© iStockphoto.com / pixalot

Disillusionment is inevitable in early marriage as the focus shifts from romance to commitment, perseverance and staying power.

towards marriage or who are poor marriage candidates may be more likely to cohabit and divorce (Amato et al., 2007). Current research suggests the cumulative experience of cohabitation (more partners for longer periods of time), can cause a reduction in esteem for marriage and childrearing (McGinnis, 2003). In addition, men who cohabit prior to marriage, report lower dedication to their spouse (Stanley, Whitton, & Markman, 2004). Cohabiting couples find marriage changes the relationship. They are often unprepared for such dramatic changes, changes which require adjustments to their communication and behavioral patterns.

Cohabiting couples generally do not make a lifelong commitment to one another. Marriage drastically changes that because lifelong commitment is what marriage is all about. A cohabiting relationship is often seen as temporary and convenient (Stanley et al., 2004). An important aspect of cohabiting couples is their duality of intention. Some partners see cohabitation as a first step toward marriage, a way to test compatibility (Amato et al., 2007). Other partners see cohabitation as a relationship with many of the perks of marriage (e.g., sharing expenses, housework, companionship, sexual intercourse) without the long-term commitment of marriage (Sassler, 2004). Therefore, one partner may have a deeper commitment to the relationship than the other. This difference in commitment is often at the root of later dissention in the relationship. In cohabitation, each person in the relationship retains a "single" mind-set. Single people think in terms of "me." A successful marriage requires a "we" mentality. This is consistent with God's intention for marriage as a covenant patterned after His relationship with His beloved children. God is completely faithful to His children and does not waiver in His commitment to their happiness.

Changes to Other Relationships

When two people marry, their relationships with friends and family change. Married couples spend more time together and less time with friends. Gerstel and Sarkisian (2006) suggest marriage is 'greedy' for three reasons. The first is material. Since married couples tend to have more money, they need less help from family and friends and as a result, give less in return. Because couples spend more time with each other, their investments in other relationships decrease. This is especially true for dual-earner couples who are already strapped for time because of their jobs. Second, because of the intense emotional connection common in early marriage, there is a decrease in their collective life with family, friends and community. A newly married couple is often so wrapped up in each other, they have little interest in others. Third, American culture encourages the expectation of self-sufficiency in marriage.

© Getty Images

Friends become 'our' friends rather than his friends and her friends.

Couples are expected to make it on their own, both practically and emotionally. While family and friends are likely willing to help, new couples are unlikely to ask. The greed of marriage causes couples to turn inward, pushing aside other relationships. Sidebar 6.1 is an example of how one couple managed to maintain their emotional connection even when apart for a period of time.

Some couples work hard to avoid this phenomenon by reserving one night a week for separate activities with their friends. Sometimes this involves a "guys' night out" and a "girls' night out." But often they find they have less in common with their single friends. Many healthy couples find themselves in new friendships with other married couples. "His friends/her friends" thinking begins to fade and is replaced by "our friends."

Sidebar 6.1
Tales from a Commuter Marriage

Both our careers were important—and we both had difficulty finding meaningful work. When I got an exciting offer 150 miles away from the city in which he owned a business, we had to make a choice. We had been married for 4 years and had no children. We had a stable marriage, so the choice was easy. I would "try out" the new opportunity, and we would see one another on weekends and on vacations. I got an apartment and moved in a little furniture. Weekends together were very romantic. In our long daily phone conversations, we seemed to talk more than we ever did while we lived together. We missed each other, but loved our work, so, overall, we were happy. After a year I was sure this job was right for me, so we sold the house and purchased a home in the new city. Now he was the one to live in smaller quarters, but he didn't seem to mind. I was glad to move all my things into our new house and began to feel more at home. He would join me on weekends. I would go to his place for vacations. This continued for 4 years until we committed to starting a family. We agreed to move back together—but how? Whose career would be sacrificed? Since he owned his own business, he had more freedom to be an "absentee owner." Together with our new baby, we would travel to his business every weekend. But his business began to require more and more of his presence, so a few months after the baby was born, he began to spend 3 days a week away from home. Then, more and more—until we were once again a commuting couple. It had become an option for us, and it was too easy to give in to the temptation to put career before family. Now after 8 years of a commuter marriage, we are happily together again. I love my career . . . he often likes his job. But we both love one another and have a very strong marriage. Those years apart taught us to truly cherish the time we have together.

—Anonymous

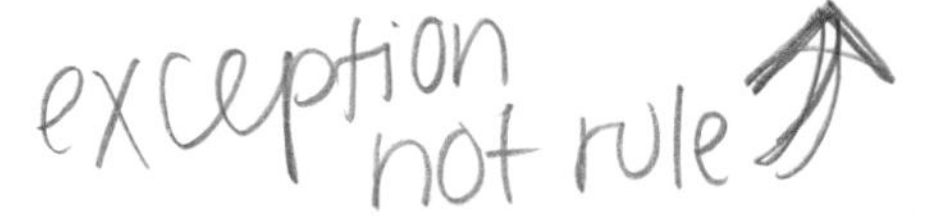

Family relationships take on a new dynamic, as each marriage partner's family circle increases to include the spouse's family. "You don't marry the family" may be a familiar adage, but it is essentially incorrect. While a dating couple often operates very independently of family (at least in America), this changes once they marry. Couples who isolate themselves from their extended families may encounter undue stress and problems in their marriage relationship. Even if she doesn't like his family, she should not try to tear him away from them. Even if he can't relate to her family, he should not keep her from maintaining her ties to them. Spouses need to accept the distinct habits, traditions, and customs of the family into which they have married. These family traditions may seem very strange to the new family member, but they must be respected—if not embraced.

Marriage also changes the nature of the relationship to a spouse's own family. A married person takes on the identity of an adult who has personal responsibility apart from the parents. This is referred to as differentiation. Parents and adult children will take on a slightly different relationship, as they balance the ongoing tensions between separation and connectedness (Sabatelli & Bartle-Haring, 2003). While parents often become important consultants for the newly married couple, problems can arise when parents become too involved in the couple's relationship. Successful marriages include an emotional separation from the parents and families of childhood (Sabatelli & Bartle-Haring, 2003). Parents can provide support by empowering the newly married couple to become financially and emotionally independent. The couple must become differentiated from their families of origin. "This explains why a man leaves his father and mother and is joined to his wife, and the two are united into one" (Genesis 2:24).

Some important negotiations need to take place regarding in-law relationships. Since the couple must divide time between two families, less time will be available for family get-togethers. Where does the new couple spend their first Thanksgiving? Their first Christmas? Their birthdays? Sometimes, negotiating these issues with extended family can go a long way toward promoting good family relations. Developing effective patterns of communication with extended family in the early years of marriage can set the stage for stable relationships in the future.

Couples have to divide their time between two extended families for family get-togethers and holidays.

Legal Implications

Cohabiting couples and married couples face major legal differences. Marriage is a legal arrangement, with specific laws regarding the joining together of property and debt. Unless there is a prenuptial agreement specifying the distribution of property and debt, each partner in the marriage may become legally responsible for all assets, income, and debt brought into the marriage.

Cohabiting couples may not have such legal footing, so they are more likely to keep their finances separate and not share fiscal decisions. Cohabiting couples sometimes retain personal ownership of property and debt, making it is easier for them to split up. Laws regulate the division of property and debt when a married couple splits. Some states have no laws for cohabiting couples who decide to separate.

It may not be legally advantageous to live together without marriage. In certain states, cohabiting couples are not eligible for jointly held health insurance, tax advantages, and other benefits. Thus, their living expenses may be higher. Unless there is a living will or other legal document specifying responsibility, cohabiting partners may not be considered "next of kin" in medical and other important decisions.

Another major difference between marriage and cohabitation involves children. Any children born to a woman who is married are the financial and legal responsibility of both the wife and the husband in the marriage, unless the husband is proven not to be the biological father. In a cohabiting relationship, any children born are the responsibility of the woman alone, unless the man is found to be the biological father.

Marriage Myths

As a husband and wife establish a new identity as a married couple, they are likely to have unrealistic expectations. Marital illusions, which feed on cultural trends, turn into marital "disillusions" when reality falls short of expectations. In the chapter on dating, we looked at some typical dating myths. Myths surround marriage as well. These myths may lead to disenchantment, especially in the early years of marriage (adapted from Popenoe, 2002).

Myth 1: Marriage benefits men much more than women

This myth was based on studies of psychological well-being and was then applied to marriage (Waite, 2001). The truth is both men and women benefit about equally from marriage. Married people live happier, healthier, wealthier, and longer lives than non-married individuals (Waite & Gallagher, 2001).

Both men and women benefit about equally from marriage.

According to Waite and Gallagher, possible reasons for the increased health benefits are married people are more health conscious and the increased financial benefits of marriage encourage better health practices.

Myth 2: The keys to long-term marital success are good luck and romantic love

Luck and romantic love are not related to long-term marital success. Marital satisfaction is a key factor in marital success. Good problem-solving skills and good communication skills have been consistently found as factors in marital satisfaction (Sharlin, Kaslow, & Hammerschmidt, 2000). Commitment and companionship are both related to long-term marital success. Additional keys to marital success include sharing dreams, handling conflict as it arises, nurturing the love connection, and repairing damage to the relationship (Gottman & DeClaire, 2001).

Myth 3: People can't be expected to stay in a marriage for a lifetime as they did in the past because we live so much longer

The truth is, the length of the typical divorce-free marriage hasn't changed significantly in the past 50 years. While people are living a little longer, they are also marrying later. Most divorces occur in the first 7 years of marriage, far short of a lifetime of marriage (Popenoe, 2002).

Myth 4: Married people have less satisfying sex lives, and less sex, than single people

The truth is, most married couples have much better sex and more of it than their single counterparts. A national survey found 43% of married men had sex twice a week compared with only 26% of single, non-cohabiting men. For women, 39% of those married reported having sex twice a week compared to 20% of non-cohabiting single women (Waite & Gallager, 2001). This doesn't change with age. For instance, many men and women remain sexually active well into their 70s and 80s, according to the University of Chicago's National Social Life, Health and Aging Project (Lindau et al., 2007).

Myth 5: Cohabitation is just like marriage, but without the "piece of paper."

Cohabitation does not seem to offer the same health benefits as marriage. Waite and Galliger (2001) suggest this is because cohabitation does not have the same level of commitment as marriage. Therefore, women do not take as strong a stand on the health behaviors of their partner as a wife does. In addition, cohabitation is less likely to produce the financial benefits afforded by marriage. This can also negatively impact health benefits.

Myth 6: Couples who really love each other will not have conflict

On the contrary, the deeper the relationship, the greater the likelihood of conflict. When you disagree with a casual acquaintance, you can just walk away and "agree to disagree." But when married couples disagree, those disagreements have a tendency to fester and annoy until they erupt into full-scale conflict. The more emotion you allow to cloud your judgment, the more you will struggle to get your way. The more couples

Couples who say they do not have conflict may have communication problems.

communicate, the greater the possibilities of conflict. Couples who say they do not have conflict may have communication problems. The Balswicks explain "marriage without conflict often signifies that one partner has given up personhood; there is agreement, but only at that partner's expense" (1999).

Models of Marriage

In the early years of marriage, a couple establishes patterns which impact the rest of their lives. Many couples begin by imitating the marriages of their parents. This can be potentially dangerous, because the two sets of parents probably reflect two different marital patterns. Couples need to differentiate themselves from their parents and develop their own unique marriage (Balswick & Balswick, 2006).

This section will review some of the common patterns of marriage relationships, as suggested by Hetherington and Kelly (2002): traditional, cohesive-individuated, pursuer-distancer, disengaged and operatic. These marriage styles or models are closely tied to the way couples express emotions, solve problems, communicate, and assume family tasks. It is important to remember that, in any marriage, you may see different aspects of more than one model, but couples tend to fit into one particular model more than the others. The first three types carry a high risk of divorce, while the last two endure because the needs of both spouses are being met.

Hetherington and Kelly (2002), along with many other marital researchers, view marriage as investing in an emotional bank account. Couples who make more withdrawals than deposits are at an increased risk of divorce. Gottman (1995, 1999, 2001), well-renowned relationship researcher, studies how people interact with each other and has discovered that happy couples make a bid for emotional connection 100 times in 10 minutes. These bids are the fundamental units of emotional connection. Bids can be a question, a gesture, a look, a touch or any single expression which says, "I want to feel connected to you." Happy couples experience 20 positive responses to these bids for every one negative response. In conflicted couples, this is reduced to 5 to 1 positive to negative and in soon-to-divorce couples it is only 0.8 to 1 (Gottman, 1995, 1999).

Pursuer-Distancer Marriage

The pursuer-distancer marriage is the most common and also the most divorce prone because it combines two conflicting types of responses. According to Hetherington and Kelly (2002), the woman is the pursuer 80% of the time. Longing for communication and intimacy, she is eager to confront and discuss problems and feelings. When she approaches her husband, he, preferring to avoid confrontation, does everything he can to avoid the interaction. In this type of relationship, if the pursuer is persistent in making bids for connection, the distancer becomes increasingly anxious until they withdraw from the interaction either physically, emotionally, or both. Especially for men, this may be used as a safety valve when feeling overwhelmed and flooded with the physiological changes (increased blood pressure and heart rate) common in marital disagreements.

Using Gottman's research, you can see how negative this type of pattern in a marriage is. She makes a bid and he responds negatively to it so as to avoid the interaction. Eventually the emotional bank account will overdraft. According to Gottman (1999, 2001), at this point, either the distancer gets angry at the nagging, or more likely, the pursuer becomes contemptuous and withdraws. Despite the fact the distancer wants the nagging to stop, they are totally unprepared for the cold contempt they encounter in their spouse.

Gottman has found pursuer-distancer strategies are persistent and will be used in a second marriage if a similar marital mismatch occurs. It is interesting to note that, if both partners are pursuers, their marriage may be intense at times but it will be stable. Likewise, if both spouses are distancers, they may never resolve anything, but they too can form a stable relationship.

Disengaged Marriage

The disengaged marriage has a high failure rate second only to pursuer-distancer marriages. In this type of marriage, it is not so much about the spouses' differences but about their similarities. This type of marriage, according to Hetherington and Kelly (2002), is a union between two people who are each self-sufficient or either fear, or do not need, intimacy for their sense of well-being. This can result when two people either can't make appropriate bids or respond appropriately to bids from their partner (Gottman & DeClaire, 2001). These may be marriages of convenience in which the couple desires children or the stability and assistance which marriage provides without the intimacy or companionship. Disengaged marriages can also result when sexual or romantic attraction is the basis for the marriage but then fades. These couples have little in common, such as backgrounds, shared interests, or life goals, which are the building blocks of successful marriages (Hetherington & Kelly, 2002).

Disengaged couples often don't really need each other so their marriage may last for several years. According to Hetherington and Kelly (2002), when the couple is in their 30s or 40s, they begin to wonder if this is all there is to marriage. As they drift apart, there is usually little emotion at the prospects of divorce. If they can find someone who shares their interests, and learn ways to emotionally connect, they may be successful in a second marriage. Often they have personality problems which prevent them from connecting with another person and they become what Hetherington and Kelly refer to as a "competent loner."

Operatic Marriage

Operatic marriages are full of intense emotion. These couples fight viciously, which leads to passionate lovemaking. These marriages tend to be between a sensation-seeking operatic man and an emotionally volatile woman. These are couples who find calm, placid relationships boring. Hetherington and Kelly (2002) found these couples to be the most sexually satisfied of all the marital types. They note, however, couples can lose the ability to distinguish the arousal caused by sex and the arousal caused by anger when their fighting is so furious and frequent.

© Getty Images

Operatic marriages are full of intense emotion.

The fighting can be so intense for these couples that they can say terribly hurtful things in the heat of an argument that cannot be taken back later. Emotional and physical abuse can also be a problem in these marriages. The divorce rate for these couples is the third highest of the five types. Often these couples break up and reconcile over and over again, finding new, less intense relationships boring (Hetherington & Kelly, 2002).

Cohesive/Individuated Marriage

Cohesive/individuated marriages are considered by most people to be a good marriage. Hetherington and Kelly (2002) suggest this is the type of marriage which reflects the values of the baby boomers—gender equality and intimacy (Amato, Booth, Johnson, & Rogers, 2007). These marriages are very good at accommodating gender differences. Chores and responsibilities are shared while maintaining autonomy within the relationship. These couples find that times spent together are the best times, and their relationship serves as a refuge from the world.

Cohesive marriages are stable and have the second lowest divorce rate. When these marriages do break down, it is frequently because one partner broke the balance of "us" and became more "me" focused. Hetherington and Kelly (2002) note that when these couples divorce, the women tend to do very well because of the emphasis in the marriage of autonomy, achievement, and self-expression.

Traditional Marriage

In chapter 3, we examined early and mid-20th century marriage types which resemble current traditional marriages. These marriages may look like something out of the past, but it does not mean they don't work. In fact, they have the lowest divorce rate of all five marriage types. In using the term traditional marriage, Hetherington and Kelly (2002) refer to a marriage in which the roles are traditional and very clearly defined. In a traditional marriage context, the wife usually assumes an expressive role, tending to the emotional needs of the family, while the husband assumes an instrumental role, providing the primary financial support for the family. Both partners must agree on these traditional values for this type of marriage to work.

The biggest problem in these marriages is change, especially if either spouse begins to behave untraditionally. According to Hetherington and Kelly (2002), in successful traditional marriages, when change occurs over a period of time, it usually changes in the direction of the husband's values rather than the wife's values. When the changes occur more in the wife, it often results in an unhappy, dissatisfied husband. If these couples divorce, it is often the first time the woman has experienced her own autonomy to discover her own strengths and talents apart from her husband (Hetherington & Kelly, 2002).

In the Biblical model of marriage, interchangeable, flexible roles lead to intimacy and interdependence.

Biblical Model of Marriage

Newly married couples have many choices available in deciding what model of marriage they will select. Will a couple choose the traditional marriage, in which the husband and wife operate with well-defined traditional values? Or will they choose a cohesive marriage, in which intimacy and equality are the hallmark and both partners contribute in all areas to the marriage? Or should they choose some combination or accommodation between the traditional and cohesive marriage?

Balswick and Balswick (2006) are critical of these choices, saying both marriage models fall short of God's design. They suggest instead a biblical model of marriage which stresses covenant, grace, empowerment, and intimacy.

According to the Balswicks (2006), traditional marriage stresses a commitment to marriage as an institution, but does not always stress commitment to a particular spouse. Therefore, traditional marriage, as interpreted by the Balswicks, is full of duties and expectations rather than mutual love and affection. In contrast, a biblical model of marriage is a covenant between partners who are mutually submissive. Earlier, we defined mutual submission as a relationship characterized by mutual giving and receiving.

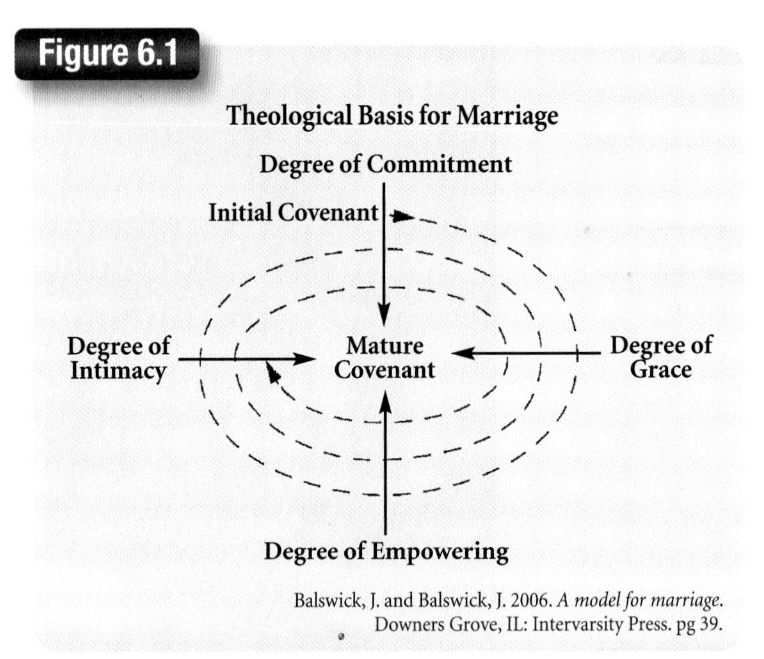

Balswick, J. and Balswick, J. 2006. *A model for marriage.* Downers Grove, IL: Intervarsity Press. pg 39.

Balswicks' depiction of the theological basis for Christian marriage, which includes covenant, grace, empowerment and intimacy. In the figure you can see how these fit together to develop a mature covenant.

There is much ongoing discussion in churches regarding a Christian perspective on marriage. One organization, Christians for Biblical Equality (www.cbeinternational.org {accessed June 23, 2009}), has many scholarly resources on gender roles in marriage and careers. While some theologians maintain traditional gender roles protect the family, others find much biblical support for mutuality in marriage.

If they are mutually submissive, the husband and wife are committed to the institution of marriage and to each other as individuals. The biblical model of marriage is exemplified by grace. This means two individuals recognize their fallibility. They fall short of God's ideal of perfect love and realize they must repent and ask for forgiveness—from God and from one another.

Partners in a biblical marriage do not make demands on one another, nor do they become possessive out of fear of rejection. Instead, they empower one another to become what God created them to be. This results in true intimacy—with one another and with God. In a biblical model of marriage, marriage partners have a positive mind-set. They are vitally connected to God, Who created them to be together and Who continually regenerates and renews their relationship. Figure 6.1 is the

Family Planning

One of the most important choices a couple faces is whether or not to have children. In nearly all cultures, childbearing is a vital function of marriage. However, in recent industrialized cultures, childbearing has become a choice, and some couples are choosing not to bear children or to delay childbearing for many years. This means they often face criticism and mixed messages from the very culture that idolizes the family. Newly married couples face enormous pressure from family, friends, and even their churches, encouraging them to have children. Western culture reveres parenting by emphasizing such occasions as Mother's Day and Father's Day, which is reflected in the greeting card industry, restaurants, department stores, and even churches. This can be a very painful experience for couples who have been unable to conceive or have chosen not to.

In a recent survey of Americans youth between the ages of 12 to 24 year olds, almost 90% expected to have children some day (Youth Happiness Study, 2007). For most newly married couples, the question is not *if* they should have children, but *when* and *how many.*

Couples today are marrying and having children later in life.

Delayed Childbearing

In the next chapter, we will consider the tremendous changes that take place when children enter the marriage scene. Couples need to take the advent of children into consideration in family planning. Couples today delay childbearing for a number of reasons. Some wait to ensure that their relationship and finances are strong enough to survive the challenges of parenting. Many couples marry later in life, which naturally results in delayed childbearing. Couples often want to get a good start on their careers before introducing children into the picture. They become involved in their careers; many become addicted to the additional income and balk at making sacrifices for the sake of having children. Thus, couples too often find themselves in their late 30s or early 40s and in a frenzy to have children before their "biological clocks" run down. Ironically, while young couples may seek technological aid to avoid pregnancy, older couples may seek technological aid in order to get pregnant. Fertility begins to decline around age 30 and declines more rapidly after 35. A woman may be unable to conceive by the time she is in her late 40s. Currently 20% of women now have their first child after age 35, so age is an increasingly common cause of fertility problems (Nouriani, 2006). Birth defects also increase as the mother ages.

Birth Control

Only in the last 50 years has birth control become legal and widely accessible in the United States. Figure 6.2 lists the most commonly used birth control methods today and their effectiveness. Each method brings with it risks and side effects.

Some see artificial birth control as a violation of God's command to "be fruitful, and multiply" (Genesis 1:28); however, others are quick to point that God's call for humanity to fill the earth is one command we've long-since obeyed. Some Christians are now expressing an interest in the rediscovery of sex for procreation without artificially controlling the outcomes of marital affection.

Not all birth control methods are artificial, as seen in Figure 6.2. Fertility awareness, or natural family planning, is a

Figure 6.2

Birth Control Methods and Their Effectiveness

Category	Method	% Effective	Advantages	Disadvantages
Hormonal	Combination Pills	98%	Convenient Effective	Must be taken on daily schedule, regardless of frequency of intercourse. Possible side effects: dizziness, nausea, changes in menstruation, mood, and weight. Other side effects rare.
	Injections (Depo-Provera)	97%	One injection every 3 months.	Possible side effects: irregular bleeding, weight gain, breast tenderness, headaches.
	Transdermal Patch	98%	New patch is applied once a week for 3 weeks. Patch is not worn during the fourth week, and woman has a menstrual period.	Similar to oral contraceptives.

Figure 6.2

Birth Control Methods and Their Effectiveness ***continued***

Category	Method	% Effective	Advantages	Disadvantages
	Progestin-only Pills (mini-pills)	98%	Convenient Effective	Must be taken on daily schedule, regardless of frequency of intercourse. Less protection against ectopic pregnancy.
	Vaginal Ring	98%	Inserted by the woman, it remains in the vagina for 3 weeks, then is removed for 1 week.	If ring is expelled and remains out for more than 3 hours, another birth control method must be used until ring has been used continuously for 7 days. Possible side effects: vaginal discharge, vaginitis, irritation. Similar to oral contraceptives—combined pill.
	Post-coital Contraception (commonly known as the morning-after pill)	80%	May be taken after unprotected intercourse to prevent pregnancy.	Prescription only. Must be taken within 72 hours of unprotected intercourse. Possible side effects include: nausea, vomiting, abdominal pain, fatigue, headache
IUD (Intrauterine device)	Levonorgestrel (LNg 20) IUD	99%	After insertion into the uterus by physician, IUD can remain in place from 1 to 10 years, depending on type.	Possible side effects: cramps, bleeding, pelvic inflammatory disease, infertility, perforation of uterus.

Figure 6.2

Birth Control Methods and Their Effectiveness *continued*

Category	Method	% Effective	Advantages	Disadvantages
Barrier Methods	Condom, male	85%	Nonprescription. Applied immediately before intercourse. Inexpensive. Offers some protection against sexually transmitted diseases (STDs).	Entails male responsibility; loss of female control. Interrupts sex. May break.
	Withdrawal	73%	Requires no purchases.	Interrupts sex.
	Condom, female	79%	Nonprescription. Applied immediately before intercourse. Offers some protection against STDs.	Expensive. Interrupts sex.
	Diaphragm with Spermicide	84%	Inserted into vagina before intercourse and left in place at least 6 hours after; can be left in place for 24 hours, with additional spermicide for repeated intercourse.	Possible side effects: irritation and allergic reactions, urinary tract infection. Risk of toxic shock syndrome, a rare but serious infection, when kept in place longer than recommended.
	Spermicide alone	71%	Nonprescription. Inserted between 5 and 90 minutes before intercourse and usually left in place at least 6 to 8 hours after.	Possible side effects: irritation and allergic reactions, urinary tract infections.

Figure 6.2

Birth Control Methods and Their Effectiveness ***continued***

Category	Method	% Effective	Advantages	Disadvantages
	Cervical Cap with Spermicide	84%	Prescription. Can remain in place for 48 hours for repeated intercourse.	May be difficult to insert. Possible side effects: irritation and allergic reactions; abnormal Pap test.
Fertility Awareness	Periodic Abstinence and Fertility Awareness Methods	75–80%	Nonprescription. Consistent with Roman Catholic guidelines. Non-artificial.	Requires frequent monitoring of body functions; e.g., body temperature.
Surgery	Vasectomy for Men	99%	One-time surgical procedure.	Possible side effects: pain, bleeding, infection, other minor postsurgical complications. Very difficult to reverse.
	Female Sterilization	99%	One-time surgical procedure.	Possible side effects: pain, bleeding, infection, other postsurgical complications, ectopic (tubal) pregnancy.
No BirthControl	No Birth Control	15%	Natural	Ineffective

Sources: Trussell and Kowal, 2004. The essentials of contraception: Efficacy, safety and personal consideration. In R. A. Hatcher et al., *Contraception Technology*, 18th ed. New York: Ardent Media, p 221-252. http://my.webmd.com/hw/health_guide_atoz/tw9416.asp?navbar=hw237867 (accessed June 24, 2009);

U.S. Food and Drug Administration. 2003. *Birth control guide.* Available online: http://www.fda.gov/ForConsumers/ByAudience/ForWomen/ucm118465.htm (accessed June 24, 2009).

method by which a woman determines her fertility window, only about 100-120 hours per month, and avoids sexual intimacy during that time to avoid pregnancy (Fertility Awareness Methods, 2008). Different methods are used to determine the window of fertility, making it nearly as effective as artificial birth control methods. These methods can also be used by couples desiring pregnancy to identify the best time for conceiving.

Another way to prevent pregnancy is emergency contraception (EC) called the morning-after pill. It is intended for occasional use and must be taken within the first 72 hours after unprotected intercourse (Mayo Clinic Staff, 2008). There is much controversy surrounding the use of the morning-after pill, sometimes called Plan B. Because there is question whether it works to prevent conception or to prevent implantation of the fertilized egg, some people consider this an abortion agent. Because it works in a similar way to birth control pills, the FDA considers it birth control, but many conservative groups disagree and are alarmed at the rapid increase in sales since it became available in 1999 by prescription and in 2006 without a prescription (Stein, 2007).

Since 1976 it has been legal for women to end their pregnancy during the first and second trimester. An abortion is a procedure used to end a pregnancy. However taboo abortion may be, abortion has become widespread in America. In 2005, there were 19.4 abortions per 1000 women aged 15 to 44 (Guttmacher Institute 2008a), which equals out to slightly more than 1 in 5 pregnancies ending in abortion. While this may seem high, the abortion rate has been steadily falling in the U.S. since 1981 (Guttmacher Institute). Christians cannot hide from these statistics, as 43% of people obtaining abortions identify themselves as Protestant and another 27% as Catholic. Most women who seek abortions have never yet married and over half already have one or more children (Guttmacher Institute).

An abortion is a procedure involving drugs or surgery to remove the embryo and placenta from the uterus. Sidebar 6.2 presents an interesting thought on when a baby is really a baby. In a medical abortion, an oral drug is taken in the first 8 weeks to abort the baby. In 2005, abortion by medication accounted for 13% of all abortions. This type of abortion was just approved in 2000 by the Food and Drug Administration, and already over half of abortion providers provide the medication option (Guttmacher Institute, 2009). A 2007 study of nearly 12,000 women concluded that this type of abortion does not increase the risk of future miscarriages, ectopic pregnancy or preterm delivery (Pruthi, 2007).

In a surgical abortion, the baby is removed from the uterus with a vacuum pump or syringe during an outpatient

Sidebar 6.2
When Is It Really A Baby?

A couple of years ago, a Canadian goose decided to nest outside our office door. At that time, though plentiful in the area, Canadian Geese were on the endangered list and so were protected by law. As soon as she laid an egg, she became vicious with anyone coming or going out of the office. She would leave the nest and fly into people on the sidewalk entrance with such force that in addition to scaring them to death, would leave large bruises anyplace she was able to strike with her powerful bill. Because this was an office and people needed to come and go, the Department of Natural Resources was called. The response of the DNR? The egg is protected under the law and anyone tampering with or disturbing that egg could be prosecuted. You can move a goose before she lays an egg, but once the egg is laid, it is protected from removal.

I have questioned since that time how we as humans can view a newly laid goose egg as a goose, with all the same rights and protection, yet we as humans grapple with when a baby is really a baby. Is it at conception? when the heart begins to beat around 5 weeks? or when the baby could survive outside the mother's uterus? Sometimes I just don't understand human logic.—A confused private practice therapist

procedure. Though it is uncommon, it is possible to cause scarring in the uterus or weaken the cervix (the entrance to the uterus) resulting in subsequent pregnancy problems (Pruthi, 2007). More controversial than abortion is late-term or partial-birth abortions which are performed after the age of viability (the age at which a baby could survive outside the womb). Late-term abortions have been banned in 36 states and 13 states ban abortions after a certain number of weeks, usually 24 (Guttmacher Institute, 2009).

We can read about God's relationship with the unborn throughout the Old and New Testament. For instance: "…I, the Lord, made you, and I will not forget you" (Isaiah 44:24). "I knew you before I formed you in your mother's womb. Before you were born I set you apart and appointed you as my prophet to the nations" (Jeremiah 1:5). "You made all the delicate, inner parts of my body and knit me together in my mother's womb" (Psalm 139:13). "But even before I was born, God chose me and called me by his marvelous grace…"(Galatians 1:15).

Knowing the Scriptures, as Christians, we can still struggle with how to respond to the abortion issue. We may have our answers down pat until it becomes a personal issue, such as when a close friend or loved one experiences an unwanted pregnancy that would devastate her current life, or is told she is carrying a severely deformed child. Then maybe we aren't quite so sure of our answers.

Based on a sermon by Hamilton, a young Presbyterian pastor, there are three things we must keep in mind as we form our Christian response to abortion (2003).

One, the Gospel favors women and children. Jesus treated women as thinking people, worthy of respect, despite the fact that it was contrary to the culture of the time. "There is no longer Jew or Gentile, slave or free, male and female. For you are all one in Christ Jesus" (Galatians 3:28). Jesus also taught "… when you did it to one of the least of these my brothers and sisters, you were doing it to me!" Certainly Jesus includes women in the "least of these" and children are literally the "least of these," without power, influence or wealth. When considering powerlessness, children have to be at the top of the list. "The irony of the abortion debate, as it stands in our church and society, is that it frames these two groups, women and children, as enemies of one another" (Hamilton, 2003, p. 605).

Two, why is it assumed that the woman is solely responsible for herself and her baby? Or the man and the woman are solely responsible? Reasons often given for abortion include fear about not being able to handle the emotional, financial and physical demands of a child, fear that having a child would destroy important relationships, and fear that it would destroy one's current life. Women who have had an abortion are likely to say, "I had no choice." If a person has no choice, are they really exercising their free will?

Three, the Christian response to abortion must reframe the issue to look at responsibility rather than rights. In the pro-choice movement, the right of the mother to choose is pitted against the right of the baby to live. The Christian response centers on the responsibility of the whole Christian community to care for the "least of these." As Christians, we know that no adult belongs to him or herself and that no child belongs to the parent. Every person is a child of God. "Because of that, every young one is our child, the church's child to care for. This is not an option. It is a responsibility" (Hamilton, 2003, pg 606).

"You made all the delicate, inner parts of my body and knit me together in my mother's womb." Even when we know the scriptures, decisions can be very difficult.

"We cannot simply throw the issue of abortion in the faces of women and say, 'You decide and you bear the consequences of your decision.' As the Church, our response to the abortion issue must be to shoulder the responsibility to care for women and children. We cannot do otherwise and still be the Church. If we close our doors in the faces of women and children, then we close our doors in the face of Christ" (Hamilton, 2003, p. 607).

Infertility

Medical science increasingly provides options for couples wishing to conceive. Infertility is defined as the inability to conceive after 1 year of trying (after 6 months for women over 30). About 12% of women ages 15-44, or about 1 out of 10, had difficulty getting pregnant or carrying a baby to term in 2002 (Nouriani, 2006). Female problems account for one third of infertility cases, while male problems account for another third and mixed—both male and female—problems account for another third. Certain factors increase the risk of infertility in both men and women. Figure 6.3 lists these for both sexes. As you look at the list, the good news is that many of them are preventable.

Many new treatment approaches to fertility have given infertile couples new hope for having a child. Assisted reproductive technology (ART) is a term used to describe several methods used to assist infertile couples. ART sometimes involves the use of donor eggs, donor sperm or previously frozen embryos. Donor eggs and sperm are sometimes used when a woman has a

Figure 6.3

Causes of Infertility

What increases a man's risk of infertility?	*What increases a woman's risk of infertility?*
The number and quality of a man's sperm can be affected by his overall health and lifestyle. Some things that may reduce sperm number and/or quality include: • Alcohol • Drugs • Environmental toxins, including pesticides and lead • Smoking • Health problems • Medicines • Radiation treatment and chemotherapy for cancer • Age	Many things can affect a woman's ability to have a baby. These include: • Health problems that cause hormonal changes • Sexually transmitted diseases (STDs) • Age • Stress • Poor diet • Athletic training • Being overweight or underweight • Smoking • Alcohol

Source: Nouriani, M. 2006. Infertility *Office on Women's Health in the Department of Health and Human Services.* http://www.womenshealth.gov/faq/infertility.pdf (accessed June 24, 2009).

Sidebar 6.3
Ethical Dilemmas in Reproductive Technology

It is fundamental to decide when human life begins in order to form consistent opinions on ethical issues such as abortion, cloning, IVF, prenatal diagnosis (PND) and preimplantation genetic diagnosis (PGD). In all of these, it is the status of the human embryo that is really at stake. If life begins at conception, then the embryo deserves all the rights of personhood. Can the embryo have these rights without usurping the mother's or father's rights?

Disease was not part of God's original plan. Disease is a consequence of the fall of man when sin entered into the world. Preimplantation genetic diagnosis (PGD) involves testing the genetic material of embryos to look for specific genetic mutations or chromosomal rearrangements. It is generally used by patients who know they are at risk of transmitting a genetic disease or chromosomal abnormality to their offspring. By testing a fertilized egg prior to implantation, modern science can now eliminate the risk of an embryo having certain genetic disease using PGD and IVF. The concern now, however, is that the technique might be used to select characteristics that range from less serious disease to purely matters of preference, such as gender (The Ethics, 2008).

Both IVF and ovulation induction using drugs result in higher numbers of multiple births (more than two babies). They have both allowed many couples to become parents of their own biological children that otherwise may have been impossible. This presents several dilemmas not the least of which is, 'are we playing God?'. Should medical technology be used to assist couples to become pregnant? Should there be an age limit? IVF is considerably more expensive than ovulation induction so there is a high push for success. With the economic factors and the push for success, should the number of embryos implanted in the uterus be restricted? By whom? If it is determined that there is a multiple birth pregnancy, should the pregnancy be aborted and start over? Should it be allowed to continue despite the high risk of complications for the babies? Should some of the babies be selectively aborted to allow the others a better chance of survival? (Multifetal Pregnancy, 2007)

Current IVF procedures often result in creation of more embryos than can be safely transplanted into a woman's uterus. There is much current debate about what to do with these embryos. For instance, can or should they be destroyed? Who owns the rights to the embryos in the case of death or divorce? What rights do all parties have if the embryos are donated to a nonrelative or unknown recipient? This also brings up the idea of embryonic stem cell research. The implantation of embryonic stem cells promises the possibility of cures for diseases and even injuries in the future. Is it moral or ethical to use these fertilized embryos that would otherwise be destroyed for this kind of research? What if this research leads to medical advances that could revolutionize the treatment of diseases, injuries, and aging? How would you regulate the research so that embryos were not being bought and sold? (Using Preimplantation, 2006)

The use of prenatal diagnosis (PND) may be less controversial but nevertheless holds ethical questions. If a genetic problem is found during an amniocentesis (a test of the amniotic fluid obtained by inserting a needle into the uterus), should an abortion be allowed, encouraged or denied? For parents, the diagnosis of genetic problems often occurs in the second trimester so a decision to abort would involve a late-term abortion. Should late-term abortions be legal in these situations? Who should decide if an abortion can or should be performed? (Diagnosing Birth Defects, 2005)

Ethical issues that arise surrounding reproductive technology is challenging for everyone. These are only a few of the dilemmas. Do you think these issues are resolvable? Who do you think should have the final say? Should the rules apply to everyone?

genetic disease that can be passed on to the baby. These techniques include (U.S Department of Health, 2006):

In vitro fertilization (IVF) – fertilization outside the body using mature eggs and sperm for fertilization. The embryos are then implanted into in the women's uterus.

Zygote intrafallopian transfer (ZIFT) or Tubal Embryo Transfer is similar to IVF but the young embryo is transferred to the fallopian tube instead of the uterus.

Gamete intrafallopian transfer (GIFT) involves transferring both eggs and sperm into the fallopian tube so fertilization takes place in the woman's body (rarely used).

Intracytoplasmic sperm injection (ICSI) is used when there are serious problems with the sperm, or for older couples in which IVF has failed. In ICSI a single sperm is injected into a mature egg, then the embryo is transferred to the uterus or fallopian tube.

Embryo adoption is another option for infertile couples. Since many eggs and sperm are harvested, and many embryos created, there is the question of what to do with the unused embryos. Currently there are half a million embryos frozen in storage in the United States, with 12% of those not currently being used by the parents (Nightlight Christian Adoptions, 2008). Sometimes couples elect to "adopt" one of these embryos for implantation into the woman's uterus. In this case, the resulting child would not be biologically related to either parent.

Christians sometimes grapple with the issue of reproductive technology. Some Christians argue that such fertility methods interfere with God's intention for our bodies. (You can read more about some of the ethical dilemmas surrounding reproductive technology in Sidebar 6.3.) Some questions to ask yourself are: is infertility the will of God or a consequence of human and environmental factors? Is fertilizing an egg outside the woman's body playing God?

Reproductive technology has given infertile couples new hope for having a child.

Adoption

Adoption has become an increasingly common practice in the United States. Approximately 1.6 million children are living with adoptive parents. These children comprise 2.5% of all children under the age of 18. Of all adopted children, 16% are black, 7% are Asian and 2% are Native-American (Child Welfare Information Gateway, 2004; U.S. Census Bureau, 2004). The U.S. adopts more children internationally than any other country, accounting for 13% of adopted children (Tarman, 2003; U.S. Census Bureau, 2004). Experts attribute part of this escalation to a number of reasons, including the fact that fewer American children are available for adoption due to abortion, the increase in single-parenting, and the preference for adoption by relatives (Tarman, 2003).

Birth parents have a number of different reasons for placing a child up for adoption, but it is usually because they want a better life for their child than they feel they can provide. Children who are eligible for adoption come from many different settings such as foster care, orphanages, birth relatives, or from the hospital after birth.

There are different ways that adoptions take place. Some are arranged through adoption agencies while some are handled independently using an attorney or private center. An increasing number of adoptions are taking place internationally with parents adopting children from other countries. There are also different kinds of adoption ranging from closed or confidential adoptions in which neither birth nor adoptive parents know the other's identities, to open adoption where there is some level of contact between the two families.

When left to medical science alone, the choices involved in family planning are very complicated and confusing. In addition to seeking medical advice, a couple is wise to seek answers through prayer, Bible study, and sound Christian advice. The husband and wife then need to commit totally to their mutual decision. If one partner feels in any way uncomfortable about a family planning choice, both partners need to renew their discussion, counsel, and prayer.

A Christian Perspective

Everyone longs to give themselves wholly and deeply to someone else and to be loved unconditionally in return. This is the ideal God has outlined for marriage. Marriage is to resemble His relationship with us.

As young people date and experience the exhilaration of falling in love, they can easily be swayed by their feelings to enter a relationship they would otherwise avoid. Dating and falling in love is great fun, but it also leads to one of the most serious issues of life—who will you choose as your life partner. This is why courtship is so important. It is time spent with each other, getting to know each other, worshiping together, sharing interests and dreams. The Apostle Paul wrote, "Can two walk together except they be agreed?" This illustrates the importance of choosing a Christian mate. Being in love is not enough. When you enter into the marital covenant with your spouse and with God, you must both start from the same place. The two must be one in Christ.

There are wonderful possibilities in Christian marriage that do not exist in secular marriage. In Christian marriage, there is physical harmony, mental harmony, and spiritual harmony. It has been said that it take three to be in a marriage—a husband, a wife and God. Reflect on what God's desires are for you, your relationships, and your family.

Summary

A couple must make many critical decisions in the early years of marriage, decisions that will have a long-lasting impact on their life together. Some of these decisions ought to be discussed before marriage, but likely will be revisited and renegotiated at various times throughout the marriage. This chapter has attempted to review a few of the most important decisions or choices a couple will make.

In deciding to marry rather than cohabit, the couple takes on a new identity that affects the way they think and act as individuals and as a single entity. Marriage changes how the marriage partners perceive others, one another, and even themselves. Because they have committed their lives to one another, they plan their future together and take action to ensure that their relationship remains healthy.

In the early years of marriage, a couple will confront some common cultural myths about marriage. If they cling to these myths, they will become disillusioned and dissatisfied with their marriage. They must grow to understand and accept more about themselves and the reality of their life together.

Couples often fall into various types or styles of marriage, based on commitment, adaptability, authority, and communication. Pursuer-distancer marriages involve one spouse being aloof and the other spouse pushing for more intimacy. This type of marriage has the highest divorce rate. A disengaged marriage is one in which the spouse places a low priority on intimacy and a strong belief in independence. These couples have the second highest divorce rate, as they just drift apart. An operatic marriage is very volatile, with heated arguments followed by passionate love-making. These marriages are prone to abuse, and have the third highest divorce rate. Cohesive-individuated marriages exemplify gender equality and intimacy, allowing personal freedom in the relationship. Renewal, affection, support, and companionship are important in these marriages, which have a low divorce rate. Traditional marriages tend to have defined roles in which husbands generally earn the income and wives raise the children and keep house. These marriages have a low divorce rate as long as both spouses agree on the roles. In contrast, a biblical model of marriage represents a covenant in which partners are mutually submissive to one another and to God.

One of the most important choices a couple makes in the early years of marriage is whether or not to have children. If so, when? How many? Numerous options for birth control include both natural and artificial means. Assisted reproductive technology is available for those couples desiring a child, who have been unable to conceive. Couples who choose ART have many difficult decisions beyond the medical decisions, which include financial, moral, ethical, and religious decisions. The theme of this chapter has been *choice*. The choices a couple makes in the early years of marriage will set the tone, structure, and patterns for their later years together. The couple needs to reevaluate and renegotiate these choices at regular intervals throughout the marriage. Before committing to any avenue of action, the marriage partners must present their questions to God, seeking answers through prayer, Bible study, Christian advisors, and deeply honest communication with one another.

Questions for Thought

1. Compare and contrast cohabitation and marriage. What would you consider to be the primary advantage(s) of marriage over cohabitation?

2. What other marriage myths would you add to the six we have mentioned in this chapter?

3. How would you describe a biblical model or style of marriage?

4. What principles or guidelines would you include in describing a Christian perspective on family planning?

Resources

Books:

The First Five Years of Marriage: Launching a Lifelong, Successful Relationship (Complete Guides) by Phillip J. Swihart and Wilford Wooten (Focus, 2006)

Intended for Pleasure: Sex Technique and Sexual Fulfillment in Christian Marriage, Third Edition by Ed Wheat and Gaye Wheat (Revell, 1997)

Rocking the Roles: Building a Win-Win Marriage by Robert Lewis and William Hendricks (NavPress, 1999)

Sacred Sex: A Spiritual Celebration of Oneness in Marriage by Tim Alan Gardner (WaterBrook Press, 2002)

Open Embrace: A Protestant Couple Rethinks Contraception by Sam Torode, Bethany Torode (Wm. B. Eerdmans Publishing Company, 2002)

Movies:

1. *Video on embryo adoption*—YouTube—Snowflake Babies: http://www.youtube.com/ watch?v=Lr2NOypbYg8 (accessed June 23, 2009)
2. *Video Activity*—Choose a Disney movie (Little Mermaid, Cinderella, Beauty and the Beast, etc.) What marriage myths does this perpetuate?

7 Marriage and Family Life

The Parenting Years

Children are a gift from the Lord; they are a reward from him.
Children born to a young man are like sharp arrows in a warrior's hands.
—Psalm 127:3–4 NLT

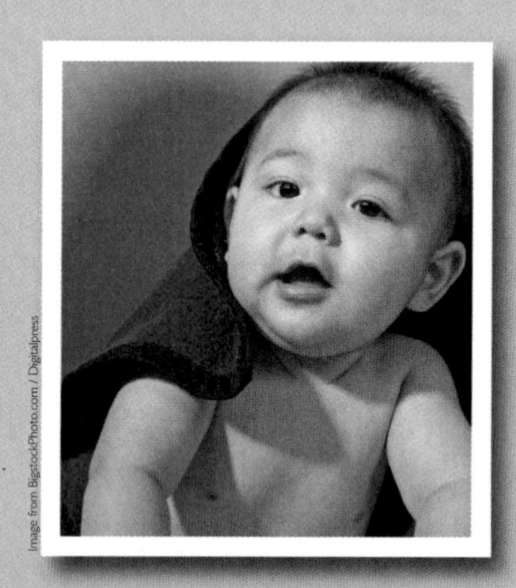

Image from BigstockPhoto.com / Digitalpress

Babies are lovable and cute. They are born with an innate ability to love their parents and will appreciate all their parents do for them. Right? Wrong! Babies come into this world helpless and completely dependent on their parents for everything. They have no capacity to love. They learn to love or not to love through the actions of their parents. No one is born with the ability to love; loving is something which must be learned. Parenting may well be the only job with no "job evaluation" for at least 18 years. That is a long time for a parent to operate without a supervisor or an instruction manual. Think of the mistakes which can be made over the course of 18 years.

Look around the next time you are in the supermarket and you will see plenty of parents making plenty of mistakes. You also will see lots of out-of-control kids. Riding the wave of popular "reality" TV shows, programs such as *Nanny 911* and *Brat Camp* focus on dealing with out-of-control children. Could it be society is on the verge of being out of control in its childrearing practices? In this chapter, we will look at some of the primary challenges facing parents today. We will see that we can change our perceptions of parenting, not by watching reality TV, but by studying some fundamentals of parenting and learning how to apply them to real-life situations.

Lessons in Kite-Flying: Parenting Goals

Parenting is like kite-flying. When you begin, you keep the kite close, work with it, and carefully control each move. But the goal of kite-flying is not to keep it close, but to watch it soar, to watch it do what kites do.

Parenting is like kite-flying. As you and the kite grow in your skill, you let the kite out farther and farther. But dangers come along—trees, wires, other kites—and then you reel in the string to bring the kite closer. You regain control and, as things stabilize, you let the string out again.

Parenting is like kite-flying. During a successful kite-flying experience with my son, we went into supper and tied the end of the kite to the clothesline. It was really up there, and we went inside to eat. When we came out again, that kite was doing exactly what it was supposed to be doing—it was soaring, and we were proud. It didn't seem to need us at all.

Parenting is like kite-flying. (Moitozo, 2005)

The kite metaphor underscores the true goal of parenting: to help children mature into healthy, independent, productive, self-disciplined, competent members of society. To this, Christian parents would add the goal of helping their children become faithful, practicing Christians.

Obedience

Many parents see the goal of parenting as getting their children to obey them. Is obedience the primary goal of parenting? In Colossians 3:20 (NRSV), the Apostle Paul told children to "obey your parents in everything, for this is your acceptable duty in the Lord." The Greek word he used for "obey" means to listen attentively, to hearken, to hear and understand. It is not the same word he used elsewhere—a military term—to mean subjection or to be subdued. The first word implies a willingness to listen and internalize what the parent is trying to convey. The second word brings to mind an unquestioning military response to a command. The true goal of parenting goes beyond simply demanding a behavior. The true goal of parenting is an internalization of what is right and wrong, good and bad, moral and immoral.

Protection

When children are young, one of the parents' primary goals is to protect them from harm. In this regard, parents sometimes must require unquestioning compliance when a child faces an imminent threat. A loving parent does not allow a small child to "choose" whether or not to run in front of a speeding car. As children grow, the parents bandage their hurts, play with them, read to them, and keep them safe. All the while, conscientious parents continue to set limits and to explain the consequences of their children's actions: "If you jump from there, you will hurt yourself"; "When you hit your sister, it hurts her." Both physically and socially, parents teach children how the world works.

Image from BigstockPhoto.com / rosesmith 333

A primary goal of parenting young children is protection.

As children grow older, the parents' goal is to transfer responsibility for protection back to the child. This means teaching children the values and skills necessary to make wise decisions of their own.

In discussing the parental goal of protection, it could be said that children have a "right" to expect their parents to protect them. Arguments about children's rights generally revolve around the extent to which children are entitled to certain rights. That is to say, which adult rights are they entitled to, and at what age do they qualify for these rights? Despite these fine points of contention, international groups such as the United Nations assert unequivocally that children have rights by virtue of their birth. For example, they have the right:

- to a loving, caring environment
- to be told they are loved
- to be listened to
- to have their thoughts, ideas, and feelings respected
- to be played with
- to have help with their learning
- Most of all, to feel cherished.

Trust

Children learn to trust their parents because mom and dad are responsible for feeding them, caring for them, and loving them. Children learn to rely on their parents for physical, emotional, and spiritual support. They look to mom and dad to make decisions regarding what is good for them. Over time, and with consistency, children learn to trust their parents' wisdom. Parents continue to earn their children's trust by nurturing them and making wise choices for them until they are ready to make their own decisions. The degree to which children learn to trust their parents lays a foundation for how they will deal with trust and respect issues in the future.

Since John Bowlby (1969) published his overarching theory of child development and attachment, researchers and clinicians have observed how nurturing children is essential to a child's physical, emotional, and spiritual growth. By attachment, Bowlby meant the intense physical and psychological connection of an infant to its primary attachment figure (parent or primary caregiver).

According to Bowlby, the attachment system essentially "asks" the following fundamental question: Is the attachment figure nearby, accessible, and attentive? If the child perceives the answer to this question to be yes, he or she feels loved, secure, and confident, and, behaviorally, is likely to explore his or her environment, play with others, and be sociable. If, however, the child perceives the answer to this question to be no, the child experiences anxiety and, behaviorally, is likely to exhibit attachment behaviors, ranging from simple visual searching on the low extreme to active following and vocal signaling on the other (Fraley, 2004).

Nurturing is a key part of child rearing which fosters attachment and trust.

Nurturing is one of the key ingredients assuring the secure attachment of children. Nurturing goes far beyond just providing food, clothing, and shelter for a child. Diana Baumrind describes nurturing or nurturance as parental responsiveness, which she defines as the "extent to which parents intentionally foster individuality, self-regulation, and self-assertion by being attuned, supportive, and acquiescent to the child's special needs and demands" (1991, 62).

Responsibility

While parents are to set limits, the goal is not so much obedience as it is teaching children responsibility, empathy, and mature understanding. Sometimes, by allowing natural consequences to take their course, parents will teach children an important lesson, such as: "If you don't wait half an hour after eating that big meal, you may get sick on the roller coaster ride."

Image from BigstockPhoto.com / Mcninch

Helping children mature involves allowing them to perform according to their abilities, even when they make mistakes.

At other times, parents may need to impose artificial consequences, after first explaining the reason: "When you hit Mindy just now, you hurt her. You do not like to be hit, right? So, you should not hit others. Now, go over there where it is quiet and take some time to think about what you did. Then, decide what you need to do next."

As children mature, they naturally want to make their own decisions. If parents prohibit children from making decisions they are capable of making, the parents undermine their children's confidence in their own abilities. Sometimes, parents do this because they actually do not want their children to grow up. This circumvents the goal of helping children mature. One of the parents' primary goals is to help their children achieve responsibility for themselves.

If children have been taught well, if they trust their parents and respect their parents' wisdom, they will come to mom and dad when necessary—not out of fear or obedience, but because they are mature, responsible, and respectful. In healthy families, even adolescents will reach out to parents for help when they are in over their heads. The adolescent who goes to a party, discovers his friends using drugs or alcohol, and calls mom or dad to come pick him up is demonstrating the kind of relationship all parents should want to have with their children.

Parenthood: The Developmental Journey

Just as E. Erickson proposed various stages of child and adult development, other research examines the stages people go through in becoming a parent. Unell and Wyckoff (2000) use a developmental perspective to examine the experience of raising children. They outline eight distinct seasons or stages of an adult parent's life based on the developmental stages of their children. These stages provide a good springboard to begin our investigation of the parenting journey.

Stage 1: Celebrity - Self-absorption of impending parenthood

The celebrity stage begins before the baby is born. Parents-to-be experience a change in extended family status related to pregnancy, creating a sense of being special, but at the same time feeling ambivalent about life and worried about personal wellbeing. In this stage, parents-to-be alternate back and forth between hopes and fears, excitement and anxiety.

Stage 2: Sponge - Surrendering former identity to the essentials of caring for a baby

The sponge stage begins with the birth of the baby and ends when the child is around 2 years of age. This is the stage in which another birth takes place—the new parent is born. Attachment to the child and identifying one's self as a parent are the primary tasks in this stage. Parents in this stage feel tremendous responsibility for the child and experience a sense of frequent depletion from constantly forgoing personal needs in order to meet the baby's essential needs.

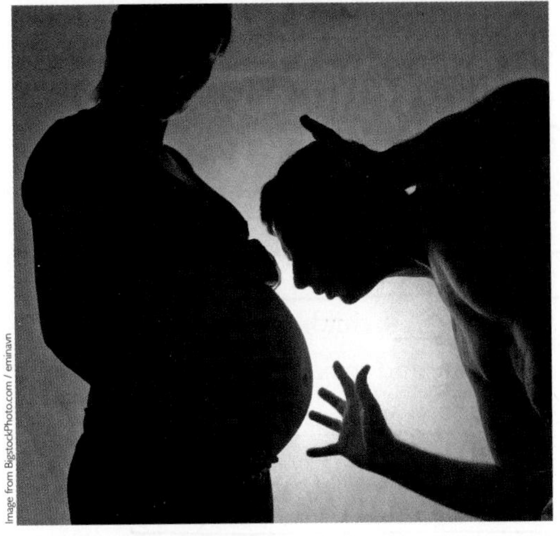

Image from BigstockPhoto.com / eminavn

In the celebrity stage, parents-to-be alternate back and forth between hopes and fears, excitement and anxiety.

Stage 3: Family Manager - Organizing and juggling life with toddlers and preschoolers

When children are between 2 and 5 years of age, parents face their fears of ineffectiveness—this is the family manager stage. The primary task of parenting is to determine the meaning of what Winnicott (1989) termed a *good-enough parent*—reconciling the desire to be a perfect parent with being a "good-enough" parent. In this stage, children are mobile, have learned language skills, and are exerting their independence. As a result, children require more of their parents' time and attention than when they were younger, resulting in an emotional, physical, intellectual and spiritual state of responsibility for the children's welfare. Parenting decisions revolve around when to say no, and following through on new rules.

Stage 4: Travel Agent - Stepping back, and stepping up, to the activities as children go through school

The travel agent stage, when children are in elementary through middle school, involves development of a new way of interacting. As children develop more autonomy and social skills, parents are required to set realistic goals, motivate their children, effectively communicate with them, and establish authority. Parents must revise their definitions of parenting as their child enters a new developmental stage.

Image from BigstockPhoto.com / Paha_L

In the travel stage, parents need to set realistic goals, motivate their children, effectively communicate with them, and establish authority.

Stage 5: Volcano Dweller - Exercising damage control in one's own life with teenagers

During the teen years, the volcano dweller stage, parents exist in a precarious state in which adolescent mood swings, demands, and hormone surges can explode without warning. It is not unlike the family manager stage (the unpredictable toddler years), but the stakes are higher. Teens wrestle with identification, responsibility, and maturity. Clashes with parents over authority are common. Parents must support their teen(s) while maintaining their own authority and responsibility for their teenager.

Stage 6: Family Remodeler - Reevaluating life as a parent of new adults

The family remodeler stage, the departure stage, occurs when the adolescent leaves home and parents are left to reflect on their past performance and their future relationship with their adult child. Much like the sponge stage, parents experience changes in their own identity as they begin to parent an adult, imagining where their children will go and who they will be with. Parents struggle with restructuring a downsized group of individuals into a family, as spouses get reacquainted with each other and begin to redefine themselves without children.

Stage 7: Plateau Parent - Reliving childhood through grandchildren

Plateau parents have raised their own children to adulthood and are often having to care for their own parents. They gain a new perspective on the first six seasons of parenting as they observe their children enter adulthood, and a first glimpse of the last stage as they watch their aging parents live through it. Through grandparenthood, parents are one step removed from the responsibility of parenting as their adult children enter their first season of parenthood.

Stage 8: Rebounder - Accepting and embracing the parent/child role reversal.

Rebounders are in the last stage of parenting as they encounter health problems, struggle to remain independent, and adjust to the need to be cared for rather than taking care of others. Unell and Wyckoff (2000) suggest three categories of rebounders: proud independents who struggle to maintain their family position; humble submissives who take a passive role in the family, expecting, but not demanding, to be included as a vital member; and aged sages who struggle to maintain their independence but are willing to ask for help and are grateful for assistance.

In the plateau stage, grandparents are one step removed from the responsibility of parents but can have a tremendous impact on their grandchildren.

This chapter will examine the first six stages of parenting. The last two stages will be covered in chapter 9.

Parenting and Boundary Transitions

Many transformations occur within the family system during the transition to parenthood. The arrival of children necessitates the need to renegotiate family identity, family boundaries, spousal boundaries, and personal identities. In looking at boundary transformations, new parents find that parenthood brings about a renegotiation of previous relationships. Carter and McGoldrick suggest this stage, families with young children, requires adults to move up a generation as they become caretakers of the younger generation (2005).

Family and Friends

The birth of a child frequently distances couples from their friends who have no children. This occurs because the new parents have less available time and are not as flexible or spontaneous as they were previously. Friends who already have children, despite their limited available time, can be a source of support and encouragement for the new parents. When couples first marry, they have to differentiate themselves as a couple in order to forge their own identity, often to the exclusion of their families. Once they have a child, roles are often renegotiated to include greater involvement with each spouse's family of origin.

Image from BigstockPhoto.com / buso 23

The birth of a child changes relationships with both friends and family often limiting time for friends and increasing involvement with family.

The Marriage

The addition of a new family member places a strain on the marriage. Available time for one another shrinks, family priorities change, and leisure time becomes *family* time. It is not uncommon to hear a new father express some jealousy, complaining that his wife cannot think about anyone but "the baby." The new role of mother can be daunting—a never-ending cycle of feeding, diapering, monitoring, and caretaking. Even with help and support from dad, a new mother can still feel an overwhelming sense of responsibility. The fatigue new mothers experience can last as long as 2 years after a baby is born. This fatigue may lessen a wife's responsiveness to the physical and emotional needs of her husband.

Research has shown that the level of satisfaction in a marriage resembles a U-shaped curve, decreasing with the birth of a child (Rollins & Feldman, 1970; Olson et al., 1983). Children are only partly responsible for this decline in satisfaction (Cowan et al., 1985). In chapter 5 of this text, we noted the level of passion falls off early in a marriage, contributing to a *feeling* of less satisfaction. We will examine the marital satisfaction curve again in chapter 8.

Work and Family

The boundary between work and family also is altered by the addition of children. Most families experience some financial strain with the birth of a child, whether the wife works or not. Men, who generally take on the socially prescribed role of provider, seem to be more affected by this than women. In the modern two-pay-check family, the life cycle challenges in this stage involve satisfactory child care and chores.

There are two clear research findings related to parental employment and the effects on health and cognitive outcomes of children: poverty is harmful to children and working parents are not (Yeung, Linver, & Brooks-Gunn, 2002; Aughinbaugh & Gittleman, 2003; Melmed, 2008). Work status is not as important a determinant for child development as a loving, supportive home environment. When new mothers need to work for financial reasons, or even if they choose to return to work, they may experience tremendous role strain. This role strain is believed to be bi-directional. The internal conflict, which produces guilt, can arise from the home domain or the work domain or both (Elgar & Chester, 2007). In other words, when mom is at work, she senses a pull to be home, feeling guilty and neglectful as a mother. When she is at home, she senses a pull to work, feeling guilty and neglectful as an employee. While maternal fatigue plays a role in satisfaction with work and family life, this kind of conflict is also detrimental to a satisfactory family life. The interface between work and family will be discussed in greater detail in chapter 9.

After the birth of a child, couples renegotiate roles and responsibilities which can create role strain.

Roles

Identity transformations which occur in the transition to parenthood are far-reaching and potentially very stressful. At the birth of the baby, parents must make a number of important decisions regarding how they will they carry out their role responsibilities, how they will raise the infant, what goals they have for the child, and how will they carry out these goals.

After the birth, role strain may exist between the husband and wife as they make these new decisions. Role strain occurs when the husband or the wife has a clear idea of what their roles and responsibilities are, but does not have the time or the energy to fulfill them in a satisfactory manner. Resolution requires a renegotiation of roles, as well as the establishment of new roles. Who is going to be the primary parent? Who will be the nurturer or playmate? Who will be the disciplinarian? Will these be shared roles and to what extent will they be shared? These are just a few of the new roles which need to be negotiated between the couple. These all involve a reworking of one's adult identity. As parents invest in these new roles, their other interests and role responsibilities will be affected. Things which were important before they became parents are just not as important anymore; new responsibilities have taken their place.

In addition to taking on new roles, parents will need to revise many previous roles. If mom stays home, will she become the primary homemaker? If she works, how will homemaking responsibilities be shared? If the couple was active in their church or community, what role(s) will they renegotiate after the baby is born? The traditional family has often encouraged dysfunctional patterns in role establishment, creating over-involvement of the mother and under-involvement of the father—often to the detriment of the child (Carter & McGoldrick, 2005).

New parents must balance their needs for separateness and connectedness, as well as meet the needs of the child.

Potential Areas of Conflict

In addition to adjusting to boundary transformations in the areas of family and friends, marriage, work and family, and roles, the transition to parenthood can be riddled with potential conflict, both internal and external.

Extended Family Involvement. The transition to parenthood means a parallel transition to grandparenthood. Intergenerational themes come into play here. Couples must come to an agreement on extended family involvement. If one spouse has had little or no involvement with grandparents or extended family, it will be difficult for that spouse to see the need for extended family time. This can become a source of conflict for the couple. The more differentiated each spouse is from the family of origin, the easier this transition will be. In the previous chapter of this text, we defined differentiation as the process through which a married person separates from the family of his or her childhood and establishes a new family. A differentiated person is someone whose emotional process is no longer dependent on others, especially parents, even in the actual presence of parents. Differentiated persons are able to live and function without undue anxiety or overdependence on others. Differentiation is a lifelong process, one we never completely finish.

The Marital Relationship. Conflict can arise regarding how the couple will maintain their marital relationship. If they pour all their energy into parenting and family, their relationship will suffer. If they neglect their child in favor of their relationship, their child will suffer. Remember the two mischievous children in *Mary Poppins*? Father worked all day at the bank. Mother was involved in lady's organizations. This left the children to be raised by the nanny. Although this is an extreme example of imbalance between the needs of the child and the needs of the parents, it serves to remind couples to maintain their marital relationship after the birth of children.

Marriage and family therapists frequently counsel couples who have poured their lives into their children for years. Then, when the last child leaves home, the parents wake up one morning and discover they are married to strangers. They were so busy being parents they forgot how to be spouses. Therapists who work with new parents often give the couple an assignment. The couple is told to establish a "date night" once a week, and a weekend away at least every 3 months. These are practical ways a couple can foster their marital relationship as they face the demands of parenthood.

Balancing the individual needs of partners for separateness and connectedness also can create conflict in the new family. If partners perceive their needs for individuality and separateness are not being met, they may notice a growing level of resentment. The more differentiated each spouse is, the easier it will be to balance these needs. As the new parents continue to foster family differentiation, they will develop a balanced level of cohesion and adaptability in their family system (Place, Hulssmeier, Brownrigg, & Soulsby, 2005).

Despite the discomfort and stress new parents experience as they make the transition to parenthood, the birth of a child ideally brings an additional sense of purpose to their marriage. Children bring meaning, fulfillment, joy, and value to life. Parents feel needed and essential to their children's well-being. These important bonds are formed early and can last a lifetime.

Parenting Styles

Control is often thought to be a parenting goal. “If I can control my child’s behavior, then we can live together peacefully in the same household.” Earlier in this chapter, we pointed out that the goal of parenting is not to control children, but to help children mature enough to make good decisions for themselves. When we control children, we get them to do what we want them to do, following our set of rules. When we nurture children, we give them the love and support they need, with appropriate levels of responsibility, in order to help them make their own decisions.

Baumrind describes control as parental demandingness, which she defines as “the claims parents make on children to become integrated into the family whole, by their maturity demands, supervision, disciplinary efforts and willingness to confront the child who disobeys” (1991).

Developmental psychologists have been interested in the correlation between parent behavior and child outcomes since the 1920s. One way to examine these effects is by studying the parenting styles of the parents. Parenting style refers to the broad pattern of parenting rather than the specific parenting practices used. Most research today is centered on Diana Baumrind’s 30 plus years of longitudinal research on parenting styles (1966, 1967,1971, 1991, 1996). Using the construct of parenting style, she seeks to capture parents’ normal variations in trying to socialize and control their children. Parenting style involves two primary elements: parental nurturing and parental control or demandingness.

A typology of four parenting styles is shown in Figure 7.1. Based on the levels of nurturing (responsiveness) and control (demandingness), the four parenting styles illustrated are indulgent, authoritarian, authoritative, and uninvolved (Maccoby & Martin, 1983).

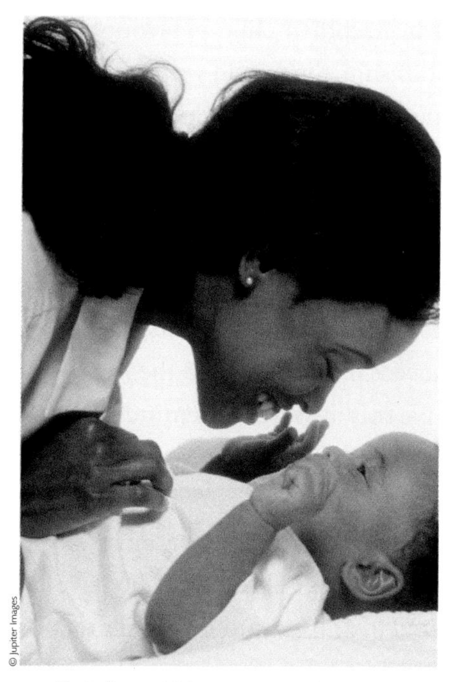

Nurturing a child means giving the love and support children need, with appropriate levels of responsibility, in order to help them learn to make their own decisions.

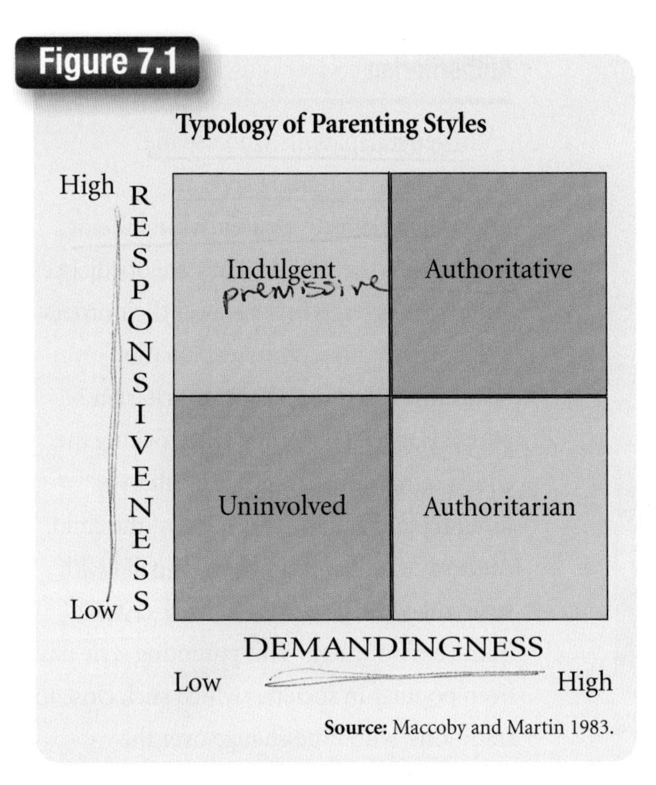

Source: Maccoby and Martin 1983.

Indulgent

Parents who employ the indulgent parenting style, sometimes referred to as permissive or nondirective, are "more responsive than they are demanding. They are nontraditional and lenient, do not require mature behavior, allow considerable self-regulation, and avoid confrontation" (Baumrind, 1991, 62). Still used by parents today, this was a popular style in the 1950s following World War II. Perhaps the harsh conditions of the war years, set against the backdrop of Nazi coercion, set the stage for this more relaxed style of parenting.

Indulgent parents give little punishment, have few guidelines for behavior, provide little structure, and avoid taking charge. Parents often fear that setting limits may stifle a child's natural curiosity and inclinations. Indulgent parents generally fall into two categories: *democratic* parents, who are more conscientious, engaged, and committed to the child; and *nondirective* parents, who provide less direction, are less available, and may exhibit disengagement with their children.

Children who grow up in indulgent homes tend to have high self-esteem, good social skills, and low levels of depression. However, they may behave irresponsibly, have little ability to handle frustration, be emotionally immature, perform at a lower level in school, and frequently exhibit behavior problems (Larzelere, 1998).

Authoritative

Parents who use the authoritative parenting style generally are demanding, but not intrusive. "They monitor and impart clear standards for their children's conduct" (Baumrind, 1991, 62). They discipline their children, not by penalizing or punishing them, but in a caring, loving, supportive way. Discipline is seen as a means to help the child learn to be self-regulating and socially responsible.

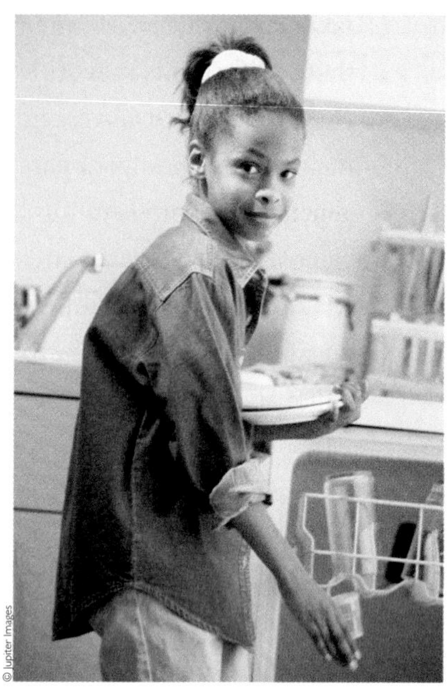

Authoritative parents are demanding but not intrusive and use discipline in a caring, loving way rather then a harsh, penalizing way.

Authoritative parents tend to realize there is no one "right" way to raise a child, especially in our ever-changing society.

Children raised in an authoritative home become good problem-solvers and have a good understanding of cooperation. They generally show more initiative and social responsibility than children raised with other parenting styles. Research shows that adolescents whose parents are authoritative rate themselves—and are rated by objective measures—as more socially competent and as having less problematic behavior than non-authoritative parents (Baumrind, 1991; Lamborn, Mounts, Steinberg, & Dornbusch, 1991; Steinberg, Darling, & Fletcher, 1995).

Authoritarian

"puritan"

In general, parents who use the authoritarian parenting style are demanding, directive parents, but are not responsive to the child. "They are obedience- and status-oriented, and expect their orders to be carried out without explanation" (Baumrind 1991, 62). An authoritarian parent is more concerned with making the child listen to the parent's ideas than in listening to the needs and ideas of the child. Authoritarian parents provide a child with strict rules and a structured, well-ordered home environment. This parenting style has been popular in societies which stick close to traditions, with little change over the generations. Children reared in authoritarian homes often have difficulty making their own decisions when they reach adulthood, since they frequently don't learn decision-making skills as children and adolescents.

Authoritarian parents are demanding, directive parents who are more concerned with getting the child to listen to them than to hear the ideas of the child.

Sidebar 7.1
To Spank or Not to Spank?

Spanking is certainly a topic that divides child researchers. On one hand, we have Murray Strauss, foremost researcher in the world on family violence. He suggests that 100% of children have been spanked and blames spanking for problems such as depression, juvenile delinquency, spousal abuse, and lowered mental ability (Strauss, 2001; Strauss & Stewart, 1999).

On the other hand there is Robert Larzelere, who has over 2 decades of research on parental disciplinary practices, and Diane Baumrind, suggesting that many studies on the use of spanking do not differentiate between spanking practiced by a nonabusive, loving parent (two swats to the bottom with an open hand) and the impact of severe physical punishment and abuse. Both researchers take a more middle-of-the-road approach, saying it is better not to spank in favor of other discipline techniques, such as time-outs or withholding a toy. However, an occasional swat on the bottom, when delivered in the context of good childrearing, has not been shown to do any harm (Baumrind, 1991, 2001; Larzelere & Kuhn, 2000). Even James Dobson, noted conservative evangelical Christian family psychologist, suggests using others means of discipline when possible. However in the case of child defiance, he advocates spanking—with clearly defined guidelines—of children between the ages of 18 months and 6 years, and seldom, if ever, after the age of 10 years (Dobson, 1996).

Finally, in the debate over whether or not to spank, Christians who trust the Bible as God's inspired Word must also weigh the rare, but direct, advice Scriptures give on parenting. It's hard to rationalize away the Proverbs warning that "He who spares the rod hates his son, but he who loves him is careful to discipline him" (13:24), as well as "The rod of correction imparts wisdom, but a child left to himself disgraces his mother" (29:15). But there is, likewise, Paul's caution in his letter to the Ephesians to "not exasperate your children; instead, bring them up in the training and instruction of the Lord" (6:4) and similarly, in his letter to the Colossians he warns parents to "not embitter your children, or they will become discouraged" (3:21). So how that "rod" of discipline (which clearly is meant to inflict some pain) is applied, and to what age, is certainly subject to interpretation; but ultimately the Bible not only allows, but encourages, contexts for "careful" spanking.

The authoritarian style of parenting can be further classified into two subdivisions: *non-authoritarian-directive* parents, who exhibit all of the typical authoritarian characteristics, but who are not intrusive or autocratic in their use of power; and *authoritarian-directive* parents, who are highly intrusive in their use of power and who often translate this to corporal punishment or spanking. Sidebar 7.1 briefly examines the dilemma of spanking. Harsh and inconsistent punishment is common in these high-control, low-responsive homes. Verbal put-downs and few explanations for punishment often occur in authoritarian homes (Hartup & Laurson, 2000).

Children raised in authoritarian homes tend to perform relatively well in school and do not exhibit behavior problems. However, they are likely to fear their parents and avoid their company (Barber, 2000). They generally have poorer social skills and lower self-esteem, and have a higher risk of depression and dysfunctional relationships in adulthood (Hartup & Laurson, 2000). Children from authoritarian homes also have a less internalized self-directed sense of right and wrong, relying more on external authority (Neuharth, 1989).

Uninvolved

As the word suggests, parents who use the uninvolved parenting style are not involved in their children's development. They place few demands on the child, so they rate low in control, but are also non-responsive. In extreme cases, this parenting style can be characterized by behaviors of rejection, hostility, and neglect. Earlier in this chapter, we mentioned the father and mother in *Mary Poppins*. Their involvement consisted of hiring a nanny to care for their children and little else. While not abusive, they demonstrate one kind of neglect seen in an uninvolved parenting style.

Children from uninvolved households have the poorest outcomes, as compared to other parenting styles. They do poorly in school and exhibit the poorest social behaviors, making them the least competent of all the groups. They also are the least self-reliant, curious, and self-controlled of any group (Baumrind, 1971). Adolescents from uninvolved households have the highest levels of psychological and behavioral dysfunction (Lamborn et al., 1991).

We can surmise from scientific studies that parental responsiveness or nurturing is a predictor of social competence and psychosocial functioning, while parental control or demandingness correlates with academic performance and child deviance. In examining the literature regarding the four parenting styles, it becomes apparent that authoritative parenting is associated with higher social competence, higher academic performance, and fewer problem behaviors in both boys and girls at all developmental stages. But what determines the type of parent someone will be? Surprisingly, as we will see next, it is not just about the parents.

The Determinants of Parenting Style

In determining what components influence certain parenting styles, we will focus on four areas: the parents' contribution, the child's contribution, parenting styles and gender, and ethnic variations in parenting styles.

The Parents' Contribution to Parenting Style

The origins of parental beliefs and actions regarding childrearing are extremely complex. One of the biggest determinants of parenting style is the ethnic and cultural heritage of the parents, the grandparents, the community, the church, and even the media. Parents tend to parent either the way they were parented, or exactly opposite to the way they were parented. An "in-between" style, while not impossible to adopt, is difficult to maintain because there is no role model for it. This explains why in an acutely heightened emotional moment, parents often revert to the way their parents treated them.

However, other factors also are important in further explaining the way someone parents. Mark Bornstein (1998), head of child and family research at the National Institute of Child Health and Human Development, has identified four parental factors and one child factor which impact how we parent.

Biological Component. First, a biological component of our parenting style seems to point to a hardwired method of relating to a baby. Have you ever watched how an adult interacts with a young baby? Often, the adult speaks to the baby in a high-pitched voice to get the baby's attention. Schore found a biological connection between the activation of the baby's brain in response to the parent, and the resulting activation of the parent's brain (1997, 2000).

Personality Component. The second parent factor involves personality traits, such as intelligence, attitudes, childcare knowledge and skills, and the parents' motivation to become involved with the child. The healthier a parent is emotionally, the more likely the parent will empathize with the baby and develop positive parenting skills, such as responsiveness and predictability. Conversely, negative personality characteristics, such as self-centeredness and depression, make it difficult to nurture effectively (Bornstein, 1998). The more positive the parents' interactions are with the baby, the more the parents will tend to engage and nurture the child (Simmons & Dye, 2003). The characteristics of the baby also play a role in parental behavior.

© Getty Images

The origins of childrearing beliefs are extremely complex but one of the biggest determinants of parenting style is how you were raised in your family of origin.

Socioeconomic Component. The parents' socioeconomic status (SES) affects the home circumstances, attitudes, and actions of parents toward their children. If there is research control for SES, parents may parent in the same way; however, parents in a higher SES have the ability to provide their children with more daily stimulation opportunities, more appropriate play materials, and more language development (Bornstein, 1998). Bornstein sites the "Zero-to-Three" survey which confirms that younger mothers, economically disadvantaged mothers, and single mothers feel particularly unprepared for the overwhelming role of new mom (*What Grown-Ups Understand About,* 2000).

Other Diverse Components. According to Bornstein (1998), the fourth parental component is comprised of divergent parenting beliefs and practices, such as family configuration, level of social support, socioeconomic class, cultural worldview, and the birth order of the child. For example, the current divorce rate means 1 in 4 children are likely to spend a part of their childhood in a single-parent home, placing strain on an already stressed parental situation (Grail, 2003). Over 6% of children under the age of 18 are being raised by grandparents who thought their parenting days were long over. About half of these children are preschoolers (Simmons & Dye, 2003). We cannot assume the neighborhoods and communities in which we live can keep our children out of harm's way. It is no longer safe to allow children to play next door or even in the front yard without close supervision.

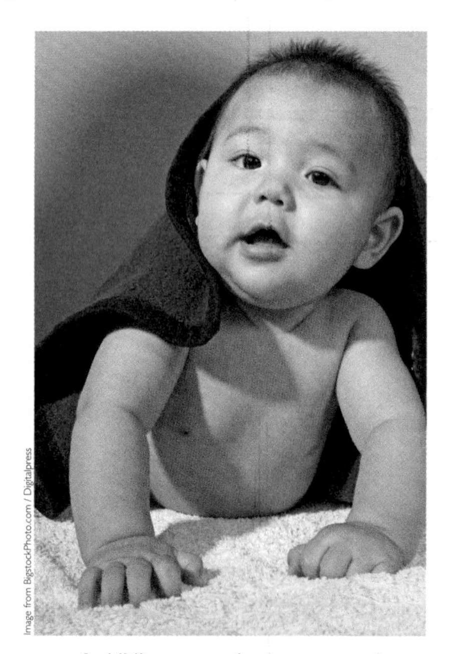

A child's age, gender, temperament, responsiveness, and appearance affect the bonding, and thus, the parenting style of the parents.

Childbirth and parenting classes are available to help build parenting skills, but many do not take advantage of these resources. The church continues to be a place of support for the family, often filling the gap left by social agencies. However, most families live a fast-paced life, finding it more of a burden to connect than to remain anonymous.

The Child's Contribution to Parenting Style

The parents' contribution to parenting style is only part of the picture. Children also influence parenting practices. The child's individual characteristics play a key role. The more obvious components are the child's age, gender, and physical appearance. Less obvious, but just as significant, are qualities such as temperament, personality, and responsiveness (Bornstein, 1998). Child characteristics can affect bonding—the intense physical and emotional connection between parent and child—and determine parenting practices for years to come.

Most parents-to-be tend to have a mental picture of what a baby will look like. The mental image, however, may not match reality. If the child is physically handicapped, premature, irritable, or colicky, parents can become frustrated and question their parental competence. Some babies have a shriller cry than others or are less consolable, which certainly challenges the patience of any parent. For example, premature babies tend to arch their backs rather than curl into their caretakers when picked up. This behavior can cause parents to find themselves thinking the baby "does not like me."

Gender and Parenting Styles

The parent's gender will determine many aspects of parenting style. Traditionally, mothers encourage intimacy, nurturing, and bonding, whereas fathers tend to encourage self-reliance. This can be seen in how parents react, play, and talk to their children. For instance, one physical manifestation is how fathers are more likely to toss a young child high in the air, wrestle, or tickle the child; while mothers are more likely to cuddle and nurture the child, both of which are important for brain development (Pellis & Pellis, 2007).

Differences between parents on childrearing practices can be a huge source of contention. It is important for both parents to be willing to compromise on what they feel is right, realizing every child is different and there is no single "right" way to raise a child. The Bible affirms this principle in the original language and meaning of Proverbs 22:6: "Train a child in the way he should go, and when he is old he will not turn from it." The implication is that parents are actually called to study and discern a particular child's way in his or her relationship to God (what Proverbs defines as "fear of the Lord") and the world. With the founding biblical premise that every human is designed to be in a right relationship with God, the question becomes not so much "What is the right way for every child?" but rather "What is the way this particular child should be going in his or her walk with God?"

Of great importance, parents should never disagree on parenting practices in front of the child. These kinds of disagreements need to take place in private, so as not to undermine the authority of either parent. One of the most effective parenting tools is a "united front," especially as children get older.

Ethnic Variations

Earlier we explained that ethnic and cultural heritage is one of the biggest determinants of parenting style. In general, authoritative parenting is a predictor of good psychosocial outcomes and fewer problem behaviors in all American ethnic groups studied: African, Asian, European, and

Hispanic. However, authoritative parenting is associated with academic performance only in European Americans and, to a lesser extent, Hispanic-Americans. Studies also have indicated that Baumrind's standard conceptualization of parenting styles is not as meaningful in some cultures. For example, the most similar style to East-Asian-American childrearing is the authoritarian style, which does not capture the idea of "training" which is more endorsed by East Asians (Chao, 1995; Ang & Goh, 2006).

Parents from different cultures differ in their expectations of when children should attain certain competencies. They also differ in the significance placed on competencies. The very heart of the concept of culture is the expectation that different people will hold different beliefs, values, motives, and behaviors. All of these factors create similarities and differences in parenting as well. More about cultural differences is presented in chapter 11.

Parenting style is also greatly affected by ethnic and cultural heritage.

Family Variations

Single-Parent Homes. With the high divorce rate and the high numbers of pregnancy outside of marriage, it is important to look at the effects on children raised in single-parent homes. While many single parents do an exceptional job of raising their children, on a whole, children from single-parent families do not fare as well as their counterparts from intact families. Research shows children from single-parent homes are more likely than those from two-parent homes to be suspended from school, become delinquent, suffer from abuse, take drugs, have repeated chronic physical health conditions, and mental health problems. (Weitoft, Hjern, Haglund, & Rosén, 2003; Amato, 2005; Bramlett & Blumberg, 2007). Single-parent families will be discussed further in chapter 12.

Gay or lesbian parents. In both social science and family therapy fields, the idea of "gays," "lesbians," and "family" have, until recently, been mutually exclusive concepts. Estimates of the number of children growing up in gay and lesbian families vary widely—from 1 million to 6 million children. The question which begs an answer is: what effect does growing up in a gay or lesbian family have on the children? While there is not unanimous agreement, according to a growing body of scientific research, children who grow

© Fotosearch

Most of the scientific research suggests children who grow up in a gay or lesbian family fare as well emotionally, cognitively, and socially, with no differences in sexual functioning, as children from heterosexual families.

up in a gay or lesbian family fare as well emotionally, cognitively, and socially, with no differences in sexual functioning, as children from heterosexual families do (Perrin, 2002, Little, 2005). There are no developmental differences or general differences in children when raised by homosexual parents compared to heterosexual parents (Paige, 2005; Alfano, 2005). However, researchers point out that thus far, there have been no comparison studies of long-term achievement in education, occupation, income or other domains of the life of children (Stacey & Biblarz, 2001). Despite these findings, most researchers agree, based on all the research, children do best when raised by two married, biological parents (Parke, 2003).

Parenting the Adolescent

Adolescence, as a part of American society, is a social construction of the 20th century. In pre-industrial times, the labor of the entire family was necessary for survival. Thus, childhood was short and adolescence as we know it was unheard of. The Industrial Revolution allowed some children to escape this cycle, especially middle-class children, who enjoyed a brief period of adolescence prior to early marriage. Savage (2007) suggests that the birth of adolescence mirrored much of what was taking place in society at the time and continues to reflect the world we live in today—living for the present, pleasure-seeking, consumerism, and the seeking of social inclusion determined by sheer volume of purchasing power.

As the American lifespan lengthened and life in general became less survival oriented, adolescence evolved into what Eric Erickson (1963, 1968) refers to as a time of crisis during which young people develop a sense of personal identity, while avoiding role confusion. In other words, adolescence is a time of coming to know who we are and how we fit into society. This involves taking all we have learned about life and molding it into a unified self-image. According to Erickson, this means integrating conflicting elements through role experimentation rather than role fixation (clinging to a role prematurely which may not fit). Erickson also contends that in Western industrialized societies late adolescence offers a time for a "psychosocial moratorium," a time of experimentation with various roles and identities before adolescents integrate them into their chosen identity. This may help parents understand some of the angst, odd behavior, and conflict they experience with their adolescents. Sidebar 7.2 expresses the frustration some parents experience while parenting an adolescence.

Marcia (1966), building on Erickson's work on adolescent identity, suggests adolescence isn't a time of *identity resolution* or *identity confusion* as Erikson claimed. Instead, this stage involves the *exploration* of and *commitment* to an identity in a variety of life domains, including politics, occupation, religion, intimate relationships, friendships, and gender roles.

> **SIDEBAR 7.2**
>
> "Oh, to be only half as wonderful as my child thought I was when he was small, and half as stupid as my teenager now thinks I am."
>
> —attributed to Erma Bombeck

Parenting can be a frustrating and seemingly unrewarding job—especially when it comes to adolescents. Few parents are ready for the contention which exists between most adolescents and their parents. Many parents are barely past adolescence themselves, and may still be feeling some tension as they work to establish their own identities. Research suggests an authoritative or indulgent parenting style is related to relatively higher levels of self-confidence and lower levels of psychological distress. Parental involvement and acceptance may be the primary contributors to the development of an adolescent's positive self-concept, psychological well-being, and resiliency (Aquilino & Supple, 2001; Sheehan & Noller, 2002; Ritter, 2005; Lee, Daniels, & Kissinger, 2006). Lower levels of problem behavior were found in authoritative and authoritarian homes, suggesting strictness and supervision may help deter the development of behavior problems. Compared to teens raised in neglectful families, teens raised in indulgent families had higher levels of competence and work orientation, and significantly fewer

Image from BigstockPhoto.com / Stuart E

Adolescence involves exploration and commitment to an identity.

psychological difficulties. However, adolescents from both indulgent and neglectful homes scored lower in school performance and displayed more behavior problems than adolescents from authoritative and authoritarian homes. This suggests indulgent and neglectful homes may be equally problematic.

Image from BigstockPhoto.com / Hallgerd

The higher the stress level and the more prolonged, the greater the likelihood of permanent brain changes.

Children Under Stress

Extended biological and psychosocial stress in childhood is associated with long-term vulnerability to a variety of mental and emotional problems (Egle et al., 2001). Michael Gurian examines this relationship in his book *The Soul of the Child*, drawing from neurobiological research and the Genome Project. He confirms what family scientists have believed all along (Gurian, 2002). Gurian describes the physical changes which take place in the brain as a result of nurturing and attachment. These changes can be seen on PET scans, which shows that all human sensations—every thought and action—are first experienced in the brain as electrical energy. The brain then translates these as feelings, actions, or words. Certain parts of the brain "light up" or remain "dark" based on electrical stimulation.

John Bowlby (1969) theorized attachment is instinctive and there is a biological control center in the brain which regulates attachment behavior. PET scans now allow neurobiologists to watch the brain of a child "light up" when their mom comes into the room (Schore, 2000). "The brain vibrates, light emissions increase, the body vibrates, signals, and reaches out for Mom" (Gurian, 2002, p. 51). Over time, when mom and dad are attuned to the baby's cues, the brain circuits grow more readily and richly (i.e., stronger and denser). If the parents are harsh or unloving toward the child, the child's circuits do not grow as readily or richly as a child with loving, attentive parents. The less rich these circuits, the less likely a child will have the full human emotional spectrum later in life (Schore, 1997, 2000). Amazingly, in a chronically stressed child, PET scans show dark spots or gaps in the brain. In a normal child, these same areas "light up."

In situations of prolonged abuse or neglect, these changes may be permanent. Interestingly, though still speculative, these children's brain scans have similar patterns to scans found in adults with borderline or narcissistic personality disorders. In spite of these similarities, we must advise against inferring causation until more research is achieved.

The cortisol (stress hormone) level in children who are under significant emotional stress also measures higher than in normal children. The longer the level remains high, the greater the likelihood of permanent brain changes (Gurian, 2002).

Child Abuse and Neglect

On almost any day, the local news documents the horrors of child abuse and child neglect, which continues to be a major problem in this country. The child victimization rate in 2006 was 12.1 per 1,000 children, down from 12.3 per 1,000 children in 2002. This translates to just under 1 million children abused or neglected in 2006. In 2006, boys accounted for 48.2% and girls accounted for 51.5%. Figure 7.2 reveals young children are more likely to experience abuse and neglect than older children. In 2006, the rate of abuse or neglect for children 3 and under was 38.6 per 1000 children of the same age group, with the highest percentage of victimization occurring in the birth to 1 year range (24.4 per 1000) (Child Welfare Information Gateway, 2007). Nearly 83% of these children were abused by their parents, with non-parental perpetrators (foster parent, daycare staff, unmarried partner of a parent, legal guardian, or residential facility staff) accounting for another 10%. (Child Welfare Information Gateway, 2007). This means over 90% of child abuse and neglect is inflicted by someone the child knows!

While the causes of abuse are not well understood, the incidence of abuse is higher in poor and extremely poor families. Certain parental characteristics also have been found in parents who abused their children. Cognitive factors such as a negative attitude, unrealistic expectations, and inaccurate knowledge of normal child behavior were seen as playing a role in abuse, especially neglect. The attitudes toward the child before birth—such as an unwanted pregnancy—are associated with subsequent maltreatment of the child. Personality attributes such as anger and anxiety—especially when compounded by other stressors, such as marital conflict, poverty, unemployment, or a difficult child—were also associated with abuse of a child.

In comparison to non-abusive parents, abusive parents displayed greater psychological reactivity, irritation, and annoyance in response to both positive and negative behaviors in their children. For example, abusive parents seemed to have unrealistic expectations and perceive their children as more aggressive, intentionally disobedient, annoying, and less intelligent, even when the observer did not see these differences (Herzog, Gara, & Rosenberg, 2006).

Parenting Effectively: Ten Principles

Having overviewed parenting goals, parenting stages, boundary transitions, and parenting styles, we offer the following 10 principles for effective parenting.

Principle 1: Be Consistent

Consistency. Consistency. Consistency. We cannot stress this enough. The biggest culprit in child misbehavior is inconsistency on the parent's part. When a parent tells a child to do something, the parent must make sure the child complies. The parent must not yell, complain, or ignore the noncompliance. If the request is not important enough to see that the child conforms, the parent should not assign the task.

Principle 2: Hold Fast to Consequences

Second only to consistency, children must face consequences for misbehavior. However, they need to know the consequences before

Figure 7.2

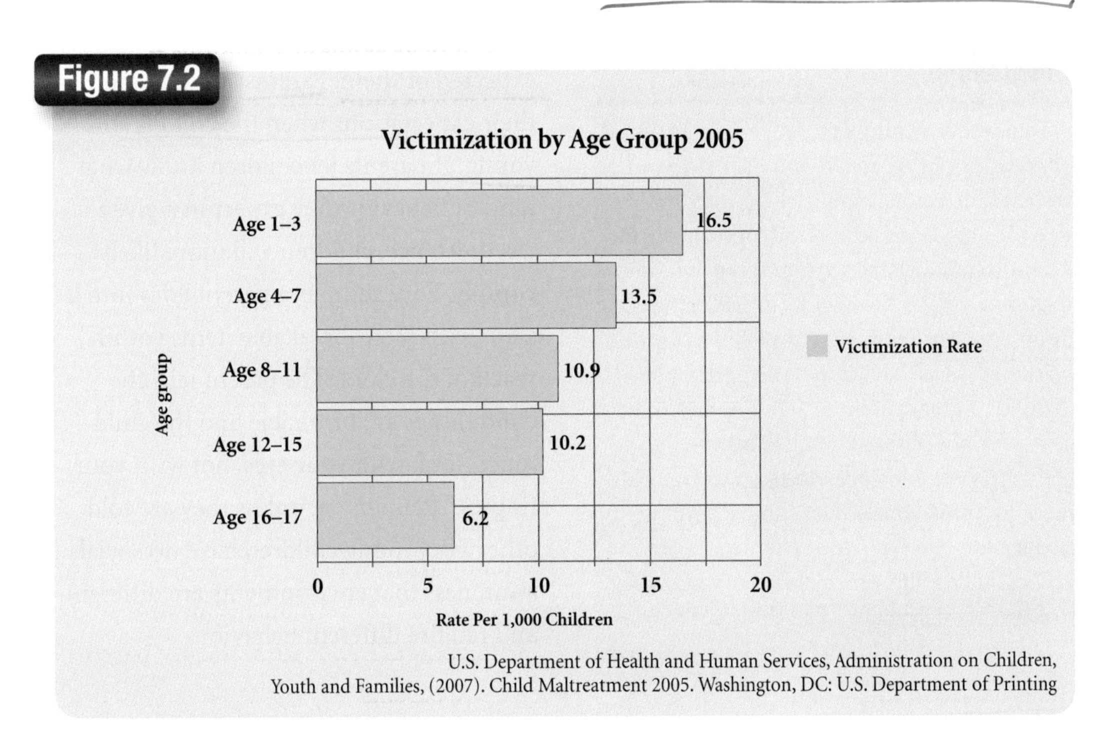

U.S. Department of Health and Human Services, Administration on Children, Youth and Families, (2007). Child Maltreatment 2005. Washington, DC: U.S. Department of Printing

they decide to misbehave. Adults know the consequences of running a red light or taking something without paying for it. They then make the decision to act or not. Children need the same information to guide their behavior. Parents must then hold fast to the consequence (even when they want to give in), so their children can learn that every action has a consequence.

Principle 3: Allow Choices

Children need choices. Parents can do this in a variety of ways. The number of choices should be consistent with the child's age. Toddlers can choose between milk and juice. Preschoolers might choose between wearing a red shirt or a blue shirt. The goal is to help children learn to make decisions—a skill many adults still have not learned. Choices can also be used to help children decide on a behavior. For instance,

> *Mom:* "If you choose to crawl under the table, you will not get dessert."
>
> *Child:* "But I want dessert."
>
> *Mom:* "It's your choice. If you choose to crawl under the table, there will be no dessert."

Of course, an important part of the parent's role in helping a child learn to choose correctly is to be consistent with the consequences.

> **SIDEBAR 7.3**
> **It's Your Choice!**
>
> I have enjoyed watching our daughter talk about choices with our 2-year-old grandson. When he misbehaves, he can tell you fairly quickly that he made a bad choice and accepts the consequence for his actions. She always talks to him about the choice he made and what other choices he had. If he gets really upset, she patiently waits until he has calmed down enough to tell her why he is being disciplined. It's hard for a grandparent to stand by and watch him cry over not getting a gumball because he did something he was told not to do, but he has quickly learned to think about his choices and their consequences. He is frequently overheard at preschool telling the other children when they misbehave that they made a bad choice.
>
> —Author

Principle 4: Define Expectations

Children need to know what is expected of them. Parents should define their expectations when the child is still young. If parents let children know what kind of behavior they expect in a given circumstance, children will more likely comply. For example, a parent goes into a shop with many breakable items within reach of the child. The parent tells the child things are breakable and the child must "look with your eyes, not with your fingers." Remember, unless they are told otherwise, young children have no social awareness that environments are different and require different behavior.

Principle 5: Tailor the Discipline to Fit the Offense

Natural consequences are always the best. (See Sidebar 7.4) Consequences which are too harsh will create fear in the child; this means when the child "minds," he or she does so based on fear of the parent, rather than an intrinsic understanding of why the behavior is wrong or right. Consequences which do not have a negative effect on the child are a waste of time for both parent and child. These kinds of meaningless consequences will not bring about the desired behaviors.

Principle 6: Do Not Threaten

Parents should never threaten to do something they cannot or will not do. Most children (except the very young) are very skilled at knowing when the parent is bluffing. Children perceive this as permission to continue doing the unwanted behavior a little longer.

Principle 7: Remain Calm

Yes, parents *can* remain calm, even when dealing with an unruly child. It takes determination on the part of the parent, which includes a willingness to take a "parent time-out" when necessary. If parents continually use a loud, demanding, or frustrated tone of voice, children will get used to it, eventually tuning it out. Just as children are skilled at knowing when a parent is bluffing, they also are very adept at triggering a parent's "flash point." A calm, even tone of voice will set a good example and effectively communicate the message. Save the stern voice for serious situations.

> **Sidebar 7.4**
>
> Shouting to make a child obey is like using the horn to steer the car . . . and you get about the same results.

Principle 8: Remember They Are Children

Parents must not expect a young child who is hungry or tired to remember the rules or to obey them. It is important to have realistic expectations of children, given their developmental age. Young children often become little whirlwinds when they are hungry or tired. Their bodies go into a kind of primitive mode and they *cannot* comply with parental wishes. Parents need to feed them, give them a nap, and see to their needs, then then the child will be able to follow directions. Adolescents, on the other hand, should be able to monitor their own behavior and, within reason, be responsible for themselves with some parental oversight.

Principle 9: Establish Curfews for Older Children

Parents need to involve older children in determining when the children should be home. Some families have a set time for every night. Other families base the curfew on various activities. We recommend the second alternative. For example, let's say the house curfew is 11 p.m. Your teen says she is going to the mall. However, the mall closes at 10. What will your teen be doing between 10 and the curfew at 11? As teens get older and begin to stay out later, parents can set an alarm clock to ring at curfew time. If the teen arrives home before curfew, he can turn off the alarm so it does not wake the parents. This allows parents to go to bed at their regular time, knowing the alarm will awaken them if the teen does not arrive home by curfew.

Principle 10: Know Your Children's Friends and Their Friends' Parents

Sadly, we live in a time when we cannot assume our children are safe at all of their friends' homes. For example, one of the authors of this text lives in a quiet, upper-middle-class, suburban neighborhood. When she checked the sex offender's registry, she found nearly 1,000 registered sex offenders within a 3 mile radius of her home! Parents need to make an effort to know the parents of the children their own kids are hanging out with, as well as the children themselves. Children may complain that this is an invasion of their privacy, but it could be considered parental neglect *not* to know this information.

Especially important is monitoring adolescents' Internet use—who the child is communicating with online. If parents don't know how to check what sites their child is frequenting, they need to learn! Even sites primarily geared to young people are hunting grounds for predators.

A Christian Perspective

What is godly, Christian parenting? After examining various sociological theories, can we find a difference between these theories of parenting and Christian parenting? The answer is yes and no. The biblical foundations for parenting support the sociological principles of good parenting.

Despite the humor (not to mention casual theology) in Sidebar 7.5, parents can find some reassurance in this fiction. If they have persistently and lovingly tried to raise their children wisely, but the children have chosen a different way, the parents should not be hard on themselves.

The reality is, even our omniscient, omnipotent, infinitely good and loving God was so committed to His children having the choice to obey or not obey that He allowed them to choose even the way of separation from Him. Even though it meant that with their choice would come death and destruction, God would not make them obey. So, how realistic is it, and more to the point, how right is it, for human parents to think they can ultimately control their children's destinies? Even the best parent, God, had children who rebelled—and at the time, those children were even innocent of sin. So, if God had trouble raising children, what makes parents think it will be as easy as a formula?

Sidebar 7.5
God as Parent

After creating the heavens and earth and all the living things, God created Adam and Eve. And the first thing God said was "Don't."

"Don't what?" Adam asked.

"Don't eat the forbidden fruit," God replied.

"Forbidden fruit? We have forbidden fruit? Hey, Eve, we have forbidden fruit!"

"No way!" Eve exclaimed.

"Yes, way!" Adam asserted.

"Do *not* eat the fruit!" God repeated.

"Why not?"

"Because I am your Father and I said so!" God replied, wondering why he had not stopped creating when he finished the elephants.

A few minutes later, God saw his children having an apple break and was he ever ticked!

"Didn't I tell you *not* to eat the fruit?" God asked in bewilderment.

"Uh-huh," Adam replied.

"Then why didn't you obey me?" demanded the Father.

"I don't know," Eve said, shrugging.

"She started it!" Adam whined.

"Did not!"

"Did too!"

"DID NOT!"

Having had it with the two of them, God's punishment was that Adam and Eve should have children of their own. Thus, the pattern was set and it has never changed!

Source: Unknown

Parenting and the Attributes of God

By looking at the attributes of God as parent, we can better understand our Christian responsibility as parents. The goal of Christian parents is to help their children mature physically, emotionally, and spiritually. God gives children to us for a short time—they are only on loan, so to speak. They do not "belong" to the parents; they are His. However, it is the responsibility of the parents to raise them in a manner pleasing to God. This involves using godly principles in childrearing practices.

© Jupiter Images

When parents love their children, children learn to love others.

Often, what has been written on Christian parenting takes Scripture out of context to support everything from abusively beating children to letting children do whatever they choose. This examination of six attributes of God provides a blueprint for what actions are appropriate for children. For easy reference, Sidebar 7.6 offers the scriptural references for the six attributes we will discuss.

God Is Life. The life given to human beings, in the scriptural sense, is different from the life given to animals. Animals are not created in God's image—human beings are. That is the vital principle which sets us apart from everything else in Creation (Genesis 1:1, 26–28). Life is a gift from God, which He gives at our birth and extends again when we accept Jesus Christ as our Savior. Children are a gift to parents from God. As parents, we are to love and care for them in the way God loves and cares for them, not in wrath, but in sound teaching (Psalm 127:3–4; Ephesians 6:4; Colossians 2:8).

God Is Loving. Love describes the very nature of God and is the greatest of all Christian virtues (John 3:16; 15:9–13). It is not just that God loves, but He *is* love personified. Love is not merely one of His attributes, but it exemplifies His very nature (1 John 4:7). Humans must learn how to love (1 John 4:7b–11). It is not an instinctive behavior. When parents love their children, children learn to love others (Isaiah 49:15; 66:13; Matthew 23:37). God's greatest desire is for His creation to love him (Matthew 22:37), yet He gives each one free will—how cheap our love for Him would be if humans were hardwired to love Him!

Yet, at the same time, discipline and instruction are vital parts of parenting. It is proof we *do* love our children (Proverbs 13:24). Children who grow up without loving discipline often feel unworthy and unwanted. At the same time, discipline must be grounded in and motivated by love, or children will grow up resentful, discouraged, and rebellious (Colossians 3:21).

God Is Faithful. Our world is broken. It is full of broken promises, failed marriages, deceit, and dishonesty. But that was not God's original design. God is faithful and true to His Word (Deuteronomy 7:9; Psalm 36:5; Lamentations 3:22–23). God's children never have to question His faithfulness to them. Human children need their parents to be faithful as well. They need to know they can trust their parents. Parents accomplish this by being consistent and true to their word. That means setting appropriate limits and consistently applying appropriate consequences. Children will learn "we say what we mean and we mean what we say." Scripture often uses the metaphor of "rock" when referring to God. Children can come to know their parents as a rock in their lives, a rock which is solid and models the faithfulness of God.

God Is Patient. God's patience is really a display of His mercy. His patience is demonstrated again and again in the Bible—with the first family in Eden, with the Israelites, toward the Gentiles, and in His judgments (Nahum 1:3a; Nehemiah 9:17; Psalm 103:8; 145:8). Christians often say, "Do not pray for patience," because the situations in which we learn patience are often painful. Yet James affirmed just the opposite—God's Word insists we should welcome such painful circumstances and even "consider it pure joy, my brothers, whenever you face trials of many kinds, because you know that the testing of your faith develops perseverance" (James 1:2–3), and perseverance, he went on to explain in verse 4, "develops maturity."

Mature patience is an important parental attribute. Children can be challenging, but James suggested those challenges should be counted as joys! Those little "joys" may know exactly when a parent is on the last nerve, and they know how to step on it! Can we see those exasperating moments as opportunities for us to mature—and to be joyful (albeit, not necessarily happy) about it?

Likewise, it's always important to remember they are children, not miniature adults—parents' expectations must be age-appropriate. (Again, that is part of the "maturity" scenario.) Learning to be patient may be as simple as lowering expectations of oneself. When parents are too busy, too overcommitted, they can forget their children are a gift—entrusted to them for a short time—time that can never be reclaimed.

> Cleaning and scrubbing can wait till
> tomorrow . . .
> for babies grow up as I've learned to
> my sorrow . . .
> So quiet down, cobwebs—dust, go
> to sleep . . .
> I'm rocking my baby, and babies
> don't keep!
>
> (Hamilton, 1958)

God Is Forgiving. One of the greatest biblical truths is forgiveness of sin (Isaiah 43:25). Forgiveness is such a powerful concept because of the enormity of sin, the cost of forgiveness—Christ's atoning death—and our complete unworthiness of this forgiveness (Colossians 2:13–14; Psalm 85:2). Parents are called to model forgiveness to their children, the kind of forgiveness, for example, which does not bring up past mistakes (Psalm 32:1; 1 John 1:9).

God wants parents to have a close, intimate relationship with their children just as He wants to with each human being.

It is important that parents understand their children to be no less deserving of God's grace than anyone else in the world, and with that understanding comes the mandate of our forgiving them as well. The caution Jesus gave in parable form of the unmerciful servant applies, likewise, to parents and their relationship with their children:

> Then the master called the servant in. "You wicked servant," he said, "I canceled all that debt of yours because you begged me to. Shouldn't you have had mercy on your fellow servant just as I had on you?" In anger his master turned him over to the jailers to be tortured, until he should pay back all he owed. This is how my heavenly Father will treat each of you unless you forgive your brother from your heart.
> (Matthew 18:32–35)

Tragically, many an unforgiving parent has likewise experienced the tortures of their own personal jailers (often self-inflicted). Bitterly they refuse to extend a fraction of the mercy God has extended to them, and the hard question

Jesus asks them in this parable is, "*How can God treat you any differently unless you forgive your child from your heart?*"

Some wounded parents might protest as Peter did, "Lord, how many times shall I forgive my [child] when he sins against me? Up to seven times?" (v. 21). Jesus' answer to parents is no less compromising: "I tell you, not seven times, but seventy-seven times" (v. 22). The Christian parent's life must be characterized by unconditional and unending forgiveness . . . nothing less is acceptable in God's sight because He gave no less to us who have betrayed Him far worse.

God Is Personal. God is a personal God. Since He first created the human race, God has desired an authentic relationship with His people (Genesis 3:8; Exodus 33:11; John 15:14–15; James 2:23). And not just to people in general. God desires a personal relationship with each one of us. It is the very reason for our existence—it is how and why we were designed, and defines what it means to be created in

Sidebar 7.6
The Attributes of God

God Is Life

In the beginning God created the heavens and the earth. . . . Then God said, "Let us make human beings in our image, to be like ourselves. They will reign over the fish in the sea, the birds in the sky, the livestock, all the wild animals on the earth, and the small animals that scurry along the ground." So God created human beings in his own image. In the image of God he created them; male and female he created them. Then God blessed them and said, "Be fruitful and multiply. Fill the earth and govern it. Reign over the fish in the sea, birds in the sky, and all the animals that scurry along the ground" (Genesis 1:1, 26–28).

Children are a gift from the Lord; they are a reward from him. Children born to a young man are like arrows in a warrior's hands (Psalm 127:3–4).

Fathers, do not provoke your children to anger by the way you treat them. Rather, bring them up with the discipline and instruction that comes from the Lord (Ephesians 6:4).

Don't let anyone capture you with empty philosophies and high-sounding nonsense that come from human thinking and from the spiritual powers of this world, rather than from Christ (Colossians 2:8).

God Is Love

Anyone who loves is a child of God and knows God. But anyone who does not love does not know God, for God is love. God showed how much he loved us by sending his one and only Son into the world so that we might have eternal life through him. This is real love—not that we loved God, but that he loved us and sent his Son as a sacrifice to take away our sins. Dear friends, since God loved us that much, we surely ought to love each other (1 John 4:7b–11).

For God loved the world so much that he gave his one and only Son, so that everyone who believes in him will not perish but have eternal life (John 3:16).

I have loved you even as the Father has loved me. Remain in my love. When you obey my commandments, you remain in my love, just as I obey my Father's commandments and remain in his love. I have told you these things so that you will be filled with my joy. Yes, your joy will overflow! This is my commandment: Love each other in the same way I have loved you. There is no greater love than to lay down one's life for one's friends (John 15:9–13).

continued

SIDEBAR 7.6
The Attributes of God

Can a mother forget her nursing child? Can she feel no love for a child she has borne? But even if that were possible, I would not forget you! . . . I will comfort you there . . . as a mother comforts her child (Isaiah 49:15; 66:13).

How often I have wanted to gather your children together as a hen protects her chicks beneath her wings, but you wouldn't let me (Matthew 23:37).

Jesus replied, "You must love the LORD your God with all your heart, all your soul, and all your mind" (Matthew 22:37).

Those who spare the rod of discipline hate their children. Those who love their children care enough to discipline them (Proverbs 13:24).

Fathers, do not aggravate your children or they will become discouraged (Colossians 3:21).

God Is Faithful

Understand, therefore, that the LORD your God is indeed God. He is the faithful God who keeps his covenant for a thousand generations and lavishes his unfailing love on those who love him and obey his commands (Deuteronomy 7:9).

Your unfailing love, O LORD, is as vast as the heavens; your faithfulness reaches beyond the clouds (Psalm 36:5).

The faithful love of the LORD never ends! His mercies never cease. Great is his faithfulness; his mercies begin afresh each morning (Lamentations 3:22–23).

God Is Patient

The LORD is slow to get angry, but his power is great . . . (Nahum 1:3a).

They refused to obey and did not remember the miracles you had done for them. Instead, they became stubborn and appointed a leader to take them back to their slavery in Egypt! But you are a God of forgiveness, gracious and merciful, slow to become angry, and rich in unfailing love. You did not abandon them (Nehemiah 9:17).

continued

His image, what it means to be a person.

Just as we must nurture our human relationships, we also must nurture our relationship with God. As we have seen in our study of uninvolved parents, a distant relationship with our children is harmful to them. It is contrary to their nature as created persons. Likewise, a distant relationship with God is harmful to us. God wants parents to have a close, intimate relationship with their children just as He wants to with each human being. As authentic love is God's primary motive with relation to us, it should be the godly parent's primary motive.

Achieving Balance

As Scripture reveals, God's love is balanced by His anger; His mercy (forgiveness) is balanced by His justice. God has given parents authority over, and responsibility for, their children. Parenting is all about balance—a balance between expectations and consequences, a balance between discipline and mercy (forgiveness)—in essence, a balance between nurture and control. When parents make a parental decision, they should ask this question: "Does this choice reflect my deepest love and commitment to my child?" If parental decisions can be made with this perspective, the path as a spiritual parent will be much less complicated.

Does this sound familiar? If we look at God's attributes in their totality as a guide for Christian parenting, we will see a parent who is patient, loving, and nurturing, who sets appropriate limits and consistently enforces them. We will see a parent who is forgiving and who uses known and well-defined consequences in a gentle, loving, but firm way. We will see a parent who encourages the internalization of knowledge, values, and morals, not one who demands obedience. We will see a parent who is available to the child, who is involved in a warm, close relationship based on trust. We will see a parent whose parenting style most closely resembles the authoritative parenting style.

Isn't it amazing the style most recommended by social scientists most resembles God's model for parenting? Isn't it amazing what has taken years of research to determine (the parenting style with the best child outcomes) was there in black and white the whole time!

This is the relationship God desires to have with His children. Shouldn't it also be the relationship parents want to have with their children?

SIDEBAR 7.6
The Attributes of God

The LORD is compassionate and merciful, slow to get angry and filled with unfailing love (Psalm 103:8).

The LORD is compassionate and merciful, slow to get angry and filled with unfailing love (Psalm 145:8).

God Is Forgiving

I—yes, I alone—will blot out your sins for my own sake and will never think of them again (Isaiah 43:25).

But if we confess our sins to him, he is faithful and just to forgive us and to cleanse us from all wickedness (1 John 1:9).

You were dead because of your sins and because your sinful nature was not yet cut away. Then God made you alive with Christ, for he forgave all our sins. He canceled the record of the charges against us and took it by nailing it to the cross (Colossians 2:13–14).

Oh, what joy for those whose rebellion is forgiven, whose sin is put out of sight! (Psalm 32:1).

You forgave the guilt of your people—yes, you covered all their sins (Psalm 85:2).

God Is Personal

When the cool evening breezes were blowing, the man and his wife heard the LORD God walking about in the garden. So they hid from the LORD God among the trees (Genesis 3:8).

Inside the Tent of Meeting, the LORD would speak to Moses face to face, as one speaks to a friend. Afterward Moses would return to the camp, but the young man who assisted him, Joshua son of Nun, would remain behind in the Tent of Meeting (Exodus 33:11).

And so it happened just as the Scriptures say: "Abraham believed God, and God counted him as righteous because of his faith." He was even called the friend of God (James 2:23).

You are my friends if you do what I command. I no longer call you slaves, because a master doesn't confide in his slaves. Now you are my friends, since I have told you everything the Father told me (John 15:14–15).

Source: All Scripture references are from *The Holy Bible, New Living Translation*. Wheaton, IL: Tyndale, 2004.

Summary

In this overview of parenting, we first examined parenting goals such as obedience, protection, trust, and responsibility. The primary goal of parenting is to help children internalize knowledge, morals, and values—not unquestioning compliance to parental demands. Parents want their children to grow and mature into healthy, productive individuals. Children need to be able to trust their parents and to rely on their wisdom, so that, as the children mature, they will come to their parents for guidance.

Parenting is a process which involves developmental stages. In the celebrity stage, parents experience changes in extended family status and a sense of being special. The sponge stage, which begins with the birth of the child, involves bonding with the child and developing a parental identity. During the family manager stage, which begins when the child is around 2 years of age, parents often feel the most ineffective, as the child begins to challenge their parental authority. The travel agent stage, from elementary to middle school, involves setting age-appropriate goals and motivating the child, as well as continuing to establish authority. The volcano dweller stage, which occurs during the teen years, involves supporting the teen while maintaining some authority and responsibility over the teen. The family remodeler stage is the departure stage, which begins when the child leaves home and ultimately involves establishing a relationship with the adult child. The plateau parenting stage involves being one step removed from parenting and reliving life through grandchildren. The final stage, the rebounder stage involves accepting and embracing the parent-child reversal as one's health declines.

The transition to parenthood also involves several boundary changes. When a baby is added to the family, changes occur in relationships with other family members and friends. Changes also occur in the marriage, including renegotiating the roles each partner has played and deciding how to maintain intimacy in the marriage. Work and family tensions are common with the introduction of a child, often leading to increased individual and marital stress.

The balance between nurturance and control forms the basis for the four primary parenting roles. Indulgent parents are high on nurture and low on control. Children from indulgent homes often exhibit high self-esteem, but are frequently immature and irresponsible. Authoritative parents are high on nurture and high on control. Children from authoritative homes fare the best, exhibiting initiative, social competence, cooperative behaviors, and good problem-solving skills. Authoritarian parents are high on control and low on nurture. Children from these homes perform well in school and do not typically exhibit behavior problems; however, they score lower in social skills and self-esteem, are more likely to be depressed, and ultimately develop dysfunctional relationships. Uninvolved parents are low in both nurture and control. Children in this type of family perform the poorest in school, are the least socially competent, and often grow up feeling unloved and unwanted.

The way we have been parented has much to do with the parenting style we will adopt. Personality, socioeconomic status, cultural heritage, and cognitive abilities also play a role in our parenting style. The characteristics of the child can affect how the parents relate to the child. The importance of this becomes apparent when examining the incidence of child abuse, which affects as high as 16.5 out of every 1000 children.

The 10 principles of effective parenting are to:

- be consistent
- hold fast to consequences
- allow choices
- define expectations
- fit the discipline to the offense
- parent without using threats
- remain calm
- be flexible with small children
- establish curfews for older children
- know your children's friends and their parents.

The Christian perspective looks to the attributes of God as a model for good parenting. God is life-giving, personal, loving, faithful, forgiving, and patient. These six attributes are most consistent with the authoritative parenting style, which was shown to result in the best child outcomes of the four parenting styles.

Questions for Thought

1. What is the difference between parenting style and parenting practices?

2. Do you think you will use the same parenting style which was used on you? Why or why not?

3. Discuss control as it relates to parenting.

4. Can you think of any other attributes of God which might apply to parenting? Explain.

Resources

Books:

Becoming Attached by Robert Karen (Oxford University Press, USA, 1998)

Parenting from the Inside Out by Daniel Siegel and Mary Hartzell (Tarcher, 2003)

Love You Forever by Robert N. Munsch (Author), Sheila McGraw (Illustrator). Heart-warming story about mother-child relationship. (Firefly Books Ltd., 1995)

Movies:

Mary Poppins, (G). DVD. Rated

Video activity:

Tape or buy a DVD set of Super Nanny from ABC to see the stress of parenting. Also find useful tools for kids at http://www.supernanny.com (accessed June 23, 2009)

Website:

For kids, teens, and parents: http://kidshealth.org (accessed June 23, 2009)

Marriage and Family Life

8

The Middle and Late Years

The glory of the young is their strength; the gray hair of experience is the splendor of the old.

—Proverbs 20:29 NLT

Image from BigstockPhoto.com / Steve Pepple

Television would have us believe that life for 20 and 30 year olds is carefree, full of friends, and replete with good times—the best stage of life. Recently, we asked a group of graduate students this question: "What do you think a person in midlife (middle-aged person) looks and acts like?" Their most common answer was this: "A midlife person is someone who is old—older than us." Ironically, the majority of these graduate students were in their thirties; yet, they did not see themselves on the threshold of middle age.

Society is fearful of growing older—especially Western societies. Consider advertisements for anti-aging products. The advertising industry adds to societal fear of aging by portraying aging in negative tones. If you are lucky, the ads say, midlife and beyond might involve a sports car, but chances are, you'll really be too "old" to enjoy it. Few ads even include older people as actors. Through the advertiser's lens, aging translates to a time when life stands still and people wait to die.

When seen in this light, midlife can become an almost desperate attempt to undo the aging process. What a distorted view of aging! This chapter examines two adult stages in marriage and family life: the middle years (midlife) and the later years. We hope our developmental lens will be more realistic and reassuring than the unrealistic lens of the advertiser.

Setting the Stage

Erickson's Eight Stages of Life

With the publication of *Childhood and Society* (1950), Erik Erickson offered the most influential theories of psychosocial development to date. He viewed human development as a lifelong process encompassing the entire life cycle, from birth to death. Dividing this life cycle into eight stages, the "stages of man," Erickson suggested each stage involved some psychosocial crisis or challenge which must be resolved before a person can move to the next stage.

Illustrated in Figure 8.1, Erickson's eight stages point out:

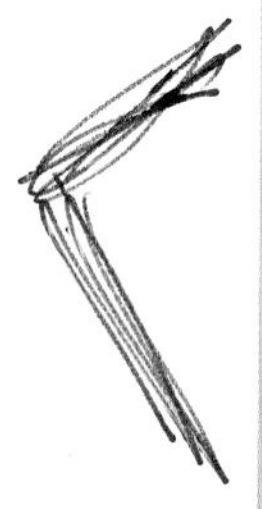

- the time period of the developmental stage,
- the psychosocial crisis of the stage,
- the predominant social setting during the stage, and
- the favorable outcomes of the stage.

The first five stages involve infancy through adolescence. For our purposes in this chapter, we will focus on stages six through eight.

The sixth stage begins in young adulthood and lasts until about age 40. The psychosocial crisis involves intimacy versus isolation. Love and intimacy are the hallmarks of this stage, the building blocks necessary for developing loving, intimate relationships. The inability to achieve these goals means the person will suffer from isolation and loneliness.

The seventh stage corresponds to midlife or the middle adult years (approximately ages 40 to 65). The psychosocial crisis is generativity versus stagnation. During this stage, the individual develops an interest in others beyond the immediate family. This interest includes concern for future generations and society as a whole. The inability to achieve generativity results in self-absorption or narcissism.

The eighth stage corresponds to old age (older than 65 years). The psychosocial crisis is integrity versus despair. People in this stage of life tend to slow down their productivity as they explore life as a retired person. During this stage of life, people contemplate their accomplishments and are able to develop integrity if they feel they have led a successful life. If they view their life as unproductive, feel guilt about their past, or feel they did not accomplish their life goals, they are likely to become dissatisfied with life and develop despair. This often leads to a sense of hopelessness and depression.

Levinson's Four Eras

Working from Erickson's theories, Daniel Levinson later identified four life stages, known as Levinson's eras, which

Figure 8.1

Erickson's Eight Stages of Psychosocial Development

Developmental Stage	Psychosocial Crisis	Predominant Social Setting	Favorable Outcome
Infancy	Trust vs. Mistrust	Family	Development of trust in self, parents, and the world
Early Childhood	Autonomy vs. Shame	Family	Development of autonomy without a loss of self-esteem
Ages 4–5	Initiative vs. Guilt	Family	Learns direction and purpose in activities
Age 6 to onset of puberty	Industry vs. Inferiority	Neighborhood, school	Acquisition of sense of mastery and competence
Adolescence	Identity vs. Role Confusion	Peer groups	Development of an ego identity—a coherent sense of self
Young Adulthood to age 40	Intimacy vs. Isolation	Partners in friendship and intimacy	Ability to work toward specific career; involvement in an extended intimate relationship
Ages 40–65	Generativity vs. Stagnation	New family and work environment	Development of concern for those outside immediate family: future generations and society
Old Age Ages 65 and over	Integrity vs. Despair	Retirement and impending death	Sense of satisfaction in looking back on life

Source: Zanden 1977, 112–113.

overlap and are broader and more inclusive than developmental stages or periods (Levinson et al., 1978; Levinson, 1997):

- First era: childhood and adolescence, ages 0–22
- Second era: early adulthood, ages 17–45
- Third era: middle adulthood, ages 40–65
- Fourth era: late adulthood, ages 60+

Levinson suggests that changing from one era to another is a lengthy, complicated process requiring a basic change in the fabric of life. In *The Seasons of a Man's Life,* Levinson says, "Adults hope that life begins at 40—but the great anxiety is that it ends there" (Levinson et al., 1978). Each era includes transitions, some of which extend through all three stages or eras. These transitions and how they change, based on the relevant stage or era, are the focus of this chapter's examination.

Criticism of Erickson and Levinson

Criticism of Erickson's and Levinson's developmental theories falls into two broad groups. The first group of criticisms revolves around its intrinsic weakness: it doesn't explain how a developmental crisis is resolved; some of the stages, particularly those in adulthood, have not been empirically demonstrated; what constitutes transition from one stage to the next is not clearly explained; and there is no explanation of how societal influences affect development (P. Miller, 1989, 2001).

A second group of criticisms focuses on the nature of the model. Feminist critics point out the theories are from a European male perspective, with emphasis on the individual and on achievement of autonomy. Both Erickson's and Levinson's theories view the male as the model for normal development.

Those who criticize these theories suggest that for women, connectedness is central to development, that it is virtually ignored in male-dominated theories, and that autonomy may be more characteristic of men's development than women's personality development (Gilligan, 1982, 1991, 2008; Hyde, 1991; Jordan et al., 1991; J. Miller, 1986; Sneed et al., 2006). The self-in-relation model or theory (Jordan et al., 1991) is a feminist model of psychological development which asserts the primary motivation for women throughout life is to establish a basic sense of connection to others.

The self-in-relation theory stresses the connection to others as essential for female identity and fundamental to their self-concept. It involves an important shift in the emphasis from separation to connection as the basis for self-experience and self-development. It also recognizes the powerful impact of the cultural context of our patriarchal society on women's lives—appreciating women's relational qualities and activities as providing potential strengths for growth and development. (Pietromonaco & Barrett, 2000; Warne & McAndrew, 2008)

Image from BigstockPhoto.com / vgstudio

As the human lifespan has lengthened over the last century, the middle years now entail a much longer period of time.

The Middle Years

Family: Changes in the Middle Years

The longest phase in the family life cycle is most often connected with the middle years. In many respects, this phase also is the most problematic, as it involves many changes. As noted in chapters 2 and 3, in the past, parents invested most of their active adult lives to raising their children. As the human lifespan has lengthened over the last century, the middle years now entail a much longer period of time. Most parents enter the empty-nest phase well before retirement. This means empty-nest parents face a long period of continued career productivity. Without children in the mix, couples also develop new activities for themselves during the middle years.

According to McGoldrick and Carter, the most significant characteristic of this period is the number of exits and entrances of family members (McGoldrick & Carter, 2003). The "launching" of children many times includes several reentries and retreats before children are finally on their own. This period also involves the introduction of grown children's spouses and the transition to grandparenting. During the middle years, our own grandparents become ill and die, and our parents become elderly, requiring increasing care. This creates additional stress, primarily for women, who tend to become the primary caretakers.

Couples in their middle years often have fewer financial struggles than in previous life stages. This can lead to new opportunities which were not available when their responsibilities focused on children. According to McGoldrick and Carter, couples experience this as a second opportunity to expand and explore new avenues and new roles. Less commonly, the middle years can lead to disturbance, a sense of emptiness and loss, depression, and general disintegration (McGoldrick & Carter, 2003). We will discuss this further in the section on midlife crisis.

Marriage: Changes in the Middle Years

It is evident to most of us that a marriage of 50 or 60 years does not remain the same through the entire length of the marriage. For that matter, a marriage which lasts 8 to 10 years does not remain the same. Change is part of the reality of marriage. The ability to adapt to life's varying circumstances largely determines the durability of any relationship, especially marriage.

The Nichols (1993) identify four stages in the marital life cycle:

Stage 1: The beginning—mating and marriage
Stage 2: The early years—expanding the base
Stage 3: The middle years—affirmation and preparation
Stage 4: Later years—consolidation and celebration

© Fotosearch

Changes in a marriage are common, such as the change to empty nest as the last child leaves for college.

In his developmental theory on the stages of life, Erickson identified psychosocial crises as the elements necessary to help move people from one stage to the next. In the Nichols' theory, the changes necessary to move from stage to stage are called core tasks. These core tasks target five areas: commitment, caring, communication, conflict/compromise, and contract (Nichols & Pace-Nichols, 1993). Using the Nichols' stages as a framework, we will briefly summarize the first two early stages of marriage before analyzing the middle years of marriage in more detail. We will then look at the Nichols' final stage in the section titled "The Later Years."

Stage 1: The Beginning—Mating and Marriage. According to the Nichols, this first stage involves separating from parents and developing an identity as a couple. The couple's core tasks are initiating the development of commitment between the partners, determining if there is a sufficient amount of caring to proceed to marriage, developing the patterns of couple communication and a shared sense of conversation, learning how to compromise and resolve conflicts which arise, and clarifying one another's expectations (contract) and learning how to interact as a couple (Nichols & Pace-Nichols, 1993). See chapter 4 on dating for more detailed information on this stage.

Stage 2: The Early Years—Expanding the Base. The Nichols suggest a "settling-into" the marriage, which includes learning how to relate to both sets of parents from an adult perspective, and identifying yourselves as a couple in the extended family network. The tasks in this second stage include deepening loyalty to one another while dealing with external attractions, redefining the nature of caring, deepening communication with one another, rebalancing power between spouses as roles change with the addition of children. and reworking the co-executive relationship of the couple. The Nichols add a parental task to this stage as well: adjusting to the addition of a child with all the realities of establishing a nuclear family and fulfilling the parental role (Nichols & Pace-Nichols, 1993). See chapter 7 on parenting for more detailed information on this stage.

© Jupiter Images

The addition of a child to the family involves establishing the nuclear family and fulfilling the parental role.

Focus on Stage 3: Affirmation and Preparation

According to the Nichols, marriage partners examine the integrity of their relationship during what he calls stage three of the marital cycle. By this time even a "good" marriage has experienced many trials and tribulations. If a couple has successfully integrated the core tasks from previous stages, their relationship will progress in a healthy manner toward the next stage. If partners fail in their core-task performance, then conflict and marital disharmony will occur. This can lead to marital dissolution.

Core Task: Commitment

The task of *commitment* during the middle years centers on maintaining a solid couple boundary and a strong couple bond (Nichols & Pace-Nichols, 1993). It is easy for a family to be caught up in the frantic pace of home life, work, children, friends, church, and community. Meeting all these needs can erode the couple's boundaries and weaken their relationship. Over time, the relationship can become increasingly fragile.

According to marriage and family therapists, many couples in their middle years seek therapy. Their complaints are common. They "are no longer in love," or "have grown in different directions," or "are just bored with the relationship." What therapists have found is the couples almost always have poured their time and attention into children, school, work, church, and other "good" activities, without continuing to nourish their marital relationship. Just as a plant will die without nourishment, so too will a marriage.

Maintaining a caring relationship is essential for a healthy marriage.

Core Task: Caring

Maintaining a *caring* relationship, despite differing interests and the general demands of life, is another core task of this third stage (Nichols & Pace-Nichols, 1993). A couple's faith in God and dedication to their marriage vows can ease this transition by fostering a determination to work on the marriage rather than abandon it. That is the key, therapists point out: Couples must work to maintain a close, caring relationship throughout the childrearing years in order to prevent complaints from becoming grounds for divorce. The Conways (2001), marriage counselors, writers and teachers for over 35 years, suggest that when people aren't working and growing, marriage grows stale. In our own practices, we, along with other therapists, have witnessed many couples in their middle years working to revitalize their marriages—and succeeding. A large number of couples even report their marriages are stronger than they have ever been. Anything of value is worth maintaining in top condition. How much more, then, than the covenant of marriage?

Core Task: Communication

Essential to a lasting marriage is communication, which involves sharing oneself with another person, as well as desiring and being willing to work to understand that other person. (Conway & Conway, 2001) Because married life in the Nichols' third stage can be so hectic, the couple's normal communication practices often suffer, especially if good communication patterns were not established earlier in the relationship. Intellectual and emotional sharing between spouses is an important core task of the middle years. Life exerts a centrifugal force on couples and families, seeking to pull them in different directions. Good communication can prevent a family's ultimate disintegration. Across the board, marriage and family therapists report they rarely, if ever, see couples seek marital counseling who already have good communication skills. Is this coincidence or an indication of a key element to marital success?

Communication, sharing oneself and desiring to understand the other person, are essential to a healthy marriage.

Core Task: Conflict/Compromise

Couples in the middle years must continue to reconcile both their personal and marital needs as they attend to the core task of communication and *conflict resolution*. At this third stage of the Nichols' marital life cycle, men and women seem to go in different directions psychologically. This is prompted by children moving out of the house and the resulting shift in energy and family dynamics. According to Carter and McGoldrick (2005), it is not uncommon for men at this stage to feel a lack of intimacy in their marriage; thus, they may turn to their wives or children to meet their needs for closeness. At the same time, women often experience a new freedom associated with not having children in the home; they may welcome opportunities to pursue their own individual interests. This creates an imbalance of needs which can lead to marital tension or even to divorce. Over the years, most couples have worked out their patterns of conflict resolution. However, with some couples, even Christian couples, one partner may feel the balance has been unequal over the history of the marriage. This spouse may either insist things change or physically or emotionally leave the marriage. Therapists have found that even in marriages of 20 to 30 years, the other spouse often claims to have no knowledge of this problem until the marriage is about to end.

Core Task: Contract

The contract task in the middle years is for the couple to rework their expectations and reexamine the bargains they have made with each other over the years. While reworking expectations can be very positive and healthy in a marriage, it can also prove disastrous if this examination does not cause the couple to make positive changes in their relationship (Nichols & Pace-Nichols, 1993).

Other Midlife Issues

Marital Satisfaction

Since the 1970s, research has indicated the level of satisfaction in a marriage resembles a shallow U-shaped curve, as portrayed in Figure 8.2. In this graph, it appears marital satisfaction decreases with the birth of a child and increases when the children are launched (Rollins & Feldman, 1970; Olson & DeFrain, 2006; Olson et al., 1983). Children are only partly responsible for this decline in marital satisfaction, however (Cowan et al., 1985). In chapter 5, we saw that the level of passion falls off early in a marriage, contributing to a *feeling* of less satisfaction. Other life-cycle factors of general life satisfaction have been shown to have an effect on marital satisfaction (Dush, Taylor, & Kroeger, 2008) These include work-family strain, competition for advancement at work, and the financial burdens which frequently occur around the time children are being born into the family (purchase of a home, a car, furniture, for

Figure 8.2

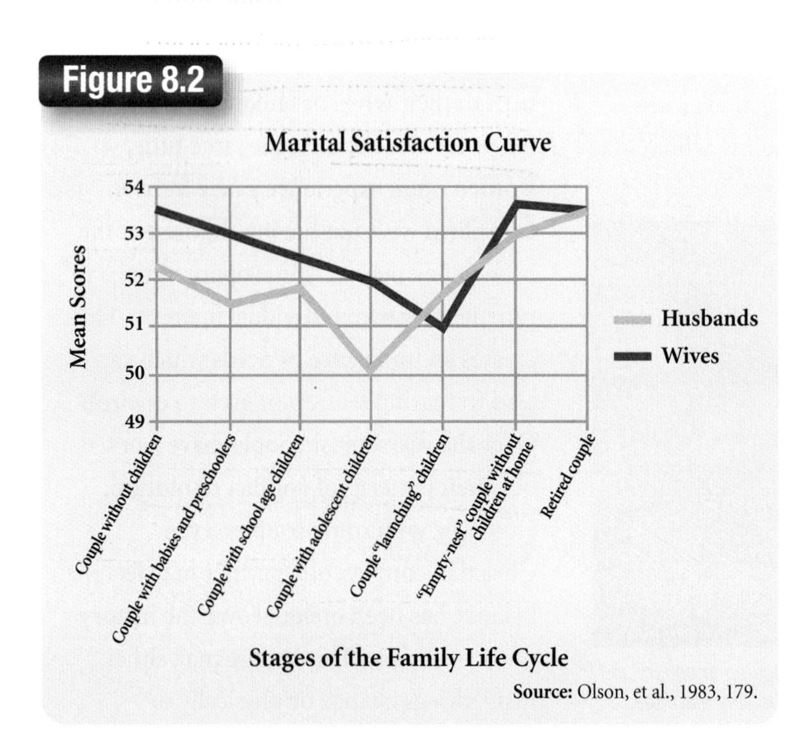

Source: Olson, et al., 1983, 179.

During the middle years, when the level of satisfaction is lower, the extent of the couple's commitment to the relationship is of paramount importance.

example) (Olson et al., 1983). Midlife identity issues also have been correlated with lower levels of marital satisfaction.

In looking at Figure 8.2, it is important to keep in mind that while midlife can represent the period of lowest marital satisfaction, it does not represent dissatisfaction with the marital relationship overall. During the middle years, when the level of satisfaction is lower, the extent of the couple's commitment to the relationship is of paramount importance. The question can become one of whether or not to continue the marriage. If couples can come to the realization that eventually the stresses of raising children and balancing work/activity routines will diminish, they would try harder to stay the course. Dissolving the marriage at this point does little to reduce life's stresses!

While the drop in satisfaction looks steep on the graph, it is important to understand it actually is a modest, gradual change. If the entire family life span were to be displayed, the U-shaped curve would appear much shallower, resembling more of a dip in the road than a pothole (R. Miller, 2001).

Midlife: Crisis or Transition?

We cannot look at marriage in the middle years without looking contextually at the life transitions which take place simultaneously. While there is nothing magical about turning 40, it does signal a time of introspection and reevaluation of life during the 40 something years. The leading edge of baby boomers, who were born after World War II and into the early 1950s, seemed to live the American dream —growing up in new homes, in new suburban neighborhoods, going off to college in record numbers, landing high-paying jobs, and buying homes at relatively low prices and low interest rates.

Is That All There Is? Ironically, while they seemed to enjoy the best of what America had to offer, they still ended up at middle age, asking, "Is this all there is?" A cartoon in *The New Yorker* illustrated this time period. In the cartoon, a couple sits at the breakfast table. The egg timer pings, the toaster pops, and the coffeepot perks. The husband turns to his wife and says, "Is this it, Alice? Is this the great American dream?" (Martin, 1973).

Without a doubt, future generations will ask the same question. In essence, the question is one of purpose—a crisis of purpose not unlike that experienced in adolescence. Adolescents struggle to develop an identity apart from their parents. In midlife, the struggle involves an intense period of introspection with respect to hopes, dreams, and goals—many of which people in midlife may have held since adolescence. In addition to introspection, the desire to leave a legacy also surfaces. People in midlife may ask themselves these questions: Who did I want to be? Who am I now? Who do I want to be in the future? How can I leave my mark on this world?

These questions cannot be addressed apart from the physical aging which becomes increasingly apparent in midlife. As signs of aging occur in the body, reflection often takes precedence in a person's life.

Midlife Crisis. Most people struggle as they make the transition to midlife. However, some people react more dramatically than others. Sidebar 8.1 lists the range of symptoms which can mark the midlife transition. Not too long ago, it seemed men had more difficulty at this age dealing with midlife crisis. This period of introspection and reevaluation of life generally occurs between the late thirties and the early fifties. It was not uncommon for men at midlife to divorce their wives of 20 plus years, begin dating right away, and sometimes marry again, often a much younger woman. Psychologically, this represents a rejection of and safeguard against aging, as in, "If I am able to attract a younger woman, then I am not as old as my years say I am."

Currently, therapists are seeing nearly an equal number of men and women leaving their marriages during the middle

Sidebar 8.1
Midlife Transition

Midlife transition is a normal part of maturing. Midlife occurs around the age of 40, give or take 10 years. The symptoms or signs of midlife can be positive or negative and can range from mild to severe. They include:

- Questioning the meaning of life
- General discontent with your life or lifestyle, when it has previously provided happiness
- Confusion about who you are and where your life is headed
- Questioning decisions you made in the past
- Greatly increased or decreased ambition and drive
- Boredom or discontent with people or activities you previously enjoyed
- Daydreaming, irritability, or unexpected anger that differs from earlier in life
- Feeling adventurous; having the desire to do something completely different
- Giving in to alcohol, food, or drug compulsions
- Greatly increased or decreased sexual desire. If sexual desire increases, this may include sexual affairs, especially with someone much younger

Sources: Goodman, Schlossberg, and Anderson 2006; Gould 1993; Lachman 2004; Levinson et al., 1978; Levinson, 1997; Sheehy 1995, 2006.

years. An increasing number of women complain their lives have been devoted to their husbands and families. Thus, now that their children are nearly grown, they want out of their marriages, so they can do what they want to do.

This may explain what is behind a startling milestone: In 2005, married couples became a minority of all American households for the first time in American history. Also for the first time, the majority of American women (51%) said they were living without a spouse, up from 35% in 1950 and 49% in 2000 (Roberts, 2007). Several factors are driving the statistical shift. At one end of the age spectrum, women are marrying later or living with unmarried partners more often and for longer periods. At the other end, women are living longer as widows, and, after a divorce, are more likely than men to delay remarriage, sometimes delighting in their newfound freedom (Roberts, 2007).

Menopause

During the middle years, both men and women undergo gradual hormonal and emotional changes associated with the aging process. For women, this period—menopause—signals the end of their reproductive years. Menopause generally is preceded by perimenopause, which begins in some women as early as the mid-thirties. Perimenopausal or menopausal symptoms include irregular menstrual periods, hot flashes, and night sweats, most of which last until about one year after the last period. Menopause "officially" begins with a woman's last menstrual period. The post-menopausal period can last the remainder of a woman's life. In addition to physical symptoms, menopause involves emotional symptoms, such as mood swings, depression, irritability, and decreased concentration and memory.

Image from BigstockPhoto.com / alwekelo

During the middle years, both men and women undergo gradual hormonal and emotional changes associated with the aging process. Exercise helps reduce problems associated with the aging process.

We often categorize menopause as a "women only" phase in the life cycle. Recent studies have reported men also experience many of the symptoms associated with female menopause. Male menopause, as it is called, involves the hormonal, physiological, and chemical changes which occur in all men, generally between the ages of 40 and 55. Like female menopause, male menopause is a physical condition with psychological, interpersonal, social, and spiritual dimensions. Whether this condition truly can be called menopause is to be determined by ongoing studies. However, we know for certain that hormonal and chemical changes do take place in both men and women during the middle years as a natural part of the aging process (Mayo Clinic Staff, 2007).

Parent-Child Relationships in the Middle Years

Parent-child relationships change across the adult lifespan as both children and adults age. What in one stage may be rocky and full of conflict can become peaceful and supportive in another stage. For our purposes here, we will refer to two phases: the *early-middle-years family*, which is characterized by the presence of adolescents in the home; and the *later-middle-years family*, also known as the empty-nest family.

The parents' sense of well-being during the childrearing years is often associated with the success of their children. To summarize briefly, the early parenting years are marked by a parent-child power gradient, in which the power rests clearly with the parents. The parents' goal is to help their children become independent. As children near school age, they become less dependent on their parents to meet all of their needs. However, the parent-child power gradient still favors the adult.

As children enter school, the parent-child relationship begins to change: peer influences increase and parental influences decrease. Parents, at this time, often feel they have little or no influence on their children. While it may seem this way to the parents, children are still listening and want to please their parents.

Early-Middle-Years Family Dynamics. During the middle years of family development, the parent-child power gradient begins to shift. Families with adolescents must negotiate new boundaries as adolescents move beyond the confines of family life. This is more difficult in present-day families due to the lack of rituals marking this period of development, and the lack of community supports which could provide structure for adolescents (Carter & McGoldrick, 2005).

Image from BigstockPhoto.com / MaszaS

Middle years parents not only deal with their adolescent's struggle for identity, but often are involved in their own midlife identity crises.

Heightened power struggles frequently define the parent-child relationship as children become adolescents and ultimately leave home (see Figure 8.1).

Adolescence is the time when children experiment with their own identities. Their identity undergoes differentiation through the rebalancing of self (identity), as well as self (identity) in relation to others—primarily parents. Simultaneously, parents not only deal with their adolescent's struggle for identity but often are involved in their own midlife identity crises. Children pull toward independence, while at the same time fearing total responsibility for themselves. In the confusion, parents sometimes pull in the reigns too tightly or let go too quickly, allowing more freedom than the child is ready to handle (Kroger, 2004).

In chapter 7 we learned adolescence is a creation of the 20th century. As the age of first marriage has continued to climb, the period of adolescence has lengthened. These 21st century children have adult bodies, drives, desires, beliefs, and abilities long before they achieve true adult status. This upward shift in age at first marriage is important to the understanding of middle-years families, since children's marital status affects so many other areas, such as childbearing, housing needs, jobs, economic independence, and relationships with parents (Wuthnow, 2007). Is it any wonder the early-middle-years family is so often under stress?

Later-Middle-Years Family Dynamics. During the later middle years of family development, children are recognized as adults by their family, whether by virtue of age, marriage, or having children of their own. It is essential for the parent-child relationship to change at this point. This period marks an equalization of power between parents and children. It also is a period of differentiation, in which adult children separate from their families of origin and reattach as an adult member of the extended family. However, parents do not want to be completely isolated from their adult children. The degree of life satisfaction for parents generally improves when children maintain frequent contact after moving out (Newman & Grauerholz, 2002).

As their children enter early adulthood, parents can either step back, supporting and commending their children's independent decisions, or they can continue to operate a parent-child power struggle, wondering why their adult child continues to crave parental affirmation. In *The Blessing*, an adult child runs beside the stretcher of a parent who has just had a heart attack—desperate for affirmation from the dying parent—desperate to hear these words: "I am proud of you" (Smalley & Trent, 2004). As Smalley suggests, this blessing is as important to us today as the birthright was to the eldest son in the Old Testament (see Genesis 25).

Paradigm Shift. As people near their middle years and their parents enter their twilight years, the balance of power once again may shift. Today, adult children are increasingly responsible for the care of their aging parents. Researchers agree daughters are more likely to assume the care of parents than are sons, with an estimated one half to two thirds of adult women assuming this role in their lifetime (Cicirelli, 2001, 2003).

This is a particularly stressful period: older adults grapple with their failing abilities and adult children wrestle with assuming the parental role for their parents. Marriage and family therapists often have the opportunity to work with middle-aged adults struggling with these transitions. Weighty questions can arise: When can Mom no longer stay in the house alone? When do we take the keys away from Dad? Should we move Mom in with us? Is a nursing home the right decision for Dad?

Middle years adults are often dealing with their aging parents at the same time experiencing the challenges of parenting adolescents.

These questions do not have easy answers. Compounding the stress, adult children who are dealing with aging parents may still be experiencing the challenges of adolescent or young adult children at home. Understandably, this generation of adults is often referred to as the sandwich generation—the period in which one assumes responsibility for aging parents, while at the same time continuing to bear the responsibility for childrearing.

Grandparents As Parents. Grandparents raising grandchildren is a growing trend in America. According to the U.S. Census Bureau, 3.2% of American children in 1970 resided in a household maintained by grandparents (Casper & Bryson, 1998). In 2006, 8% of all children lived in a household with a grandparent; the majority of these were grandparent-headed homes (Bergman, 2007). Some factors which account for the rise in grandparent-maintained households include parental alcohol and drug abuse, child abuse/neglect, parental incarceration, teen pregnancy, HIV/AIDS, poverty, abandonment, and divorce.

While children can benefit tremendously from a relationship with their grandparents, being raised by grandparents can be disadvantageous for children. If grandparents are past their prime earning status, grandparent-headed homes do not fare as well financially as parent-headed homes, with about 19% of grandparent headed homes living in

Children can benefit tremendously from a relationship with their grandparents, however, being raised by grandparents can be disadvantageous for children.

poverty (GrandFacts, 2007). However, grandparent-headed homes in which grandparents are still working are often more financially stable than parent-headed homes, because working grandparents generally earn more than the younger parents.

Family structure and dynamics can suffer when children do not live with their two biological parents. Grandmother-headed households, in which no parents are present, are more likely to be poor and receive public assistance (GrandFacts, 2007). Grandchildren in households with both grandparents present, but no parents, are more likely to have no health insurance (Kirby & Kaneda, 2002). Grandparents and grandchildren both would benefit from policies and programs intended to help families face these kinds of issues. As the number of grandparent-headed families increases, we will likely see more concessions to assist children and adults in these families.

Ethnic differences in grandparenting. Grandparenting styles vary among different ethnic groups. In white American families, there is a desire for a close, satisfying, stable relationship between grandparents, parents, and grandchildren, but at the same time, independence from their kin. Grandparents desire affection and respect from their grandchildren but do not want to be obligated to them. White American families are less likely than any other ethnic group to co-reside with a grandparent (Cherlin & Furstenberg, 1997; Simmons & Dye, 2003).

While care-giving grandparents come from all social classes, there is a higher rate of single African-American grandparents from urban, low-income households than in any other racial or ethnic class (Kelch,

Grandmothers in African-American families tend to be influential and respected by their children and grandchildren.

grandparents are #1 daycare

2008) Over half of the African-American grandparents who reside with a grandchild are responsible for their care (Simmons & Dye, 2003). This type of involved grandparenting has been a time-tested family technique with roots in the black cultural traditions and the economic and social realities of black culture. Grandmothers in African-American families tend to be influential and respected by their children and grandchildren as they teach values, encourage education, and impart religious faith (Kelch, 2008).

As in African-American families, over half of the Native-American grandparents who live with their grandchildren are responsible for them (Simmons & Dye, 2003). In these families, the role of grandparent has been shaped by a practical division of labor allowing younger women to participate in the work force. Transmission of Native-American identity is an important function of Native-American grandparents, especially those reporting tribal membership and living in a non-metropolitan area of an "Indian" state. (Mutchler, Baker, & Lee-Seung, 2007).

In Hispanic families, grandparent households are fairly common. One in 20 Mexican-American grandparents are raising grandchildren. In contrast to their non-caregiver counterparts, Mexican-American grandparents tend to be significantly younger, married, without a high-school diploma and not in the labor force (Simmons & Dye, 2003). Despite problems such as overcrowding and poverty, Latina grandmothers had higher life satisfaction than both African-American or White grandmothers (Goodman & Silverstein, 2006).

Well-Being in the Middle Years

How people rate their well-being in their middle years can affect both the immediate and the extended family. As already noted, midlife can be a tumultuous period, both individually and for the family as a whole.

Educational Status and Well-Being. People tend to define themselves and their personal achievements through educational achievement. One study found that, especially in women, lower educational levels are associated with increased psychological distress (Markus, Ryff, Curhan, & Palmersheim, 2004). Mroczek

The more satisfied couples are with their lives, the more likely they are to be satisfied with their marriages.

(2004) found people with higher educational levels tended to value self-accomplishment and have higher levels of work and marital relationship stress. For high-school-educated individuals, the emphasis was not so much on personal accomplishments, as it was on family and marital relationships, financial security, and jobs; in other words, they placed less emphasis on self-accomplishment and more on the needs and requirements of those who structured their everyday lives (Markus et al., 2004). According to Lachman and Firth (2004), people with higher educational levels feel more control than those with less education. A higher sense of control is related to higher life satisfaction and lower levels of depression. The more satisfied couples are with their lives, the more likely they are to be satisfied with their marriages. As one ages, the perceived sense of control decreases. In older adulthood, this culminates in the inability to care for all of one's own needs. Therefore, older adults experience less internal control and more external control—which can be a source of depression in the elderly.

Social Class and Well-Being. As we age, our self-esteem is at least partially related to our social class—social class has a mitigating effect on our self-esteem (Ryff, Magee, Kling, & Kling, 1999). In other words, the higher our social class, the higher our self-esteem, and the higher our sense of well-being. Not only is social class linked to well-being, it is also a factor in the health of middle adults and the aging process. It has long been established that the higher the social class, the better the overall health and longevity of individuals (Brunner, 1997; Cherkas et al., 2006; Sapolsky, 2004; Stewart-Brown, 1998). Lower social status has also been shown to speed the aging process (Sample, 2006). The stresses of being poor and the perceived sense of lack of control over one's environment are thought to be contributing factors.

Middle adults are more influenced by the contextual stressors in their lives than younger or older adults (Mroczek, 2004). One explanation for this is careers, relationships, and families dominate the lives of middle adults more than these factors dominate the lives of younger or older adults. For example, many middle adults are concerned with providing financially for their family, making plans for their own retirements, dealing with shaky relationships which can begin to fall apart, handling the demands involved in parenting adolescents, worrying about losing a partner in later life, juggling time between work and family, and balancing the work demands placed on more senior workers. While higher social class doesn't mitigate all of these, it does reduce the impact of financial strains, which allows for a greater sense of well-being.

In light of these contextual stressors, it is interesting to note that a positive

Image from BigstockPhoto.com / DNF-style

Commitment in the later years involves balancing the satisfaction achieved in life with the inevitable losses to come.

affect—outward display of emotion—continues to increase during the middle years, which may be because middle adults tend to be heavily engaged in work and relationships. This level of engagement may actually contribute to lower levels of distress and higher levels of positive well-being and fulfillment than in either the younger or the older person.

Another possibility is related to generativity. In midlife, many people blossom into more mature, integrated beings with a desire to leave a generative gift to the world (Mroczek, 2004). The middle years present a time to evaluate our spiritual lives, leading to a spiritual maturity which is uncommon in earlier stages of adulthood. Once their children are raised and they have acquired some financial security for their older years, it is not uncommon for individuals or couples in their later middle years to make decisions and life changes involving some type of part- or full-time ministry.

The Later Years

American society as a whole is afraid of aging. Advertisers, TV shows, and the media often play to this fear by portraying a stereotypical image of older people. Very few of these portrayals provide positive images of a healthy later life adjustment and can actually be detrimental to older adults psychological and cognitive functioning (Ory et al., 2003). Take a moment to think about what images "old age" generates for you. Chances are your overall assessment is rather pessimistic. Many myths about old age contribute to this pessimistic view. Listed below are some myths about aging captured in time-worn sayings:

- To be old is to be sick.
- You can't teach an old dog new tricks.
- Why change my behavior now if I have done it all my life?
- Old people do not pull their weight.

Focus on Stage 4: Consolidation and Celebration

Earlier, we examined the Nichols' four-stage marital life cycle and the core tasks which must take place in moving from one stage to the next. We briefly summarized stages one and two, then took a deeper look at stage three in our examination of midlife. By looking developmentally at the Nichols' final stage of the marital life cycle (stage four), we can better understand the family transitions which occur during the later years.

Image from BigstockPhoto.com / Image Point Photo

Communication in the later years involves the ability to talk about and share the meanings the marriage has held for each partner, as well as plans for the future.

Core Task: Commitment. According to the Nichols, this final stage of the marital life cycle is about balancing the satisfaction achieved in life with the inevitable losses to come. Typically at this stage of life, people move into retirement, which results in the loss of career identity, readjustment of the time spent together as a couple, and realignment of relationships with extended family. The commitment task in this stage, according to the Nichols, involves supporting each other in the search for meaning and satisfaction in life, as well as remaining a productive member of society. Olson and DeFrain (2000) suggest an older person's mental attitude is to some degree dependent on their accomplishments in the past and prospects for the future. For those who have worked throughout all or most of their adult lives, this can be a challenging and sometimes depressing period of making peace with the past and finding meaning and purpose in the present.

Core Task: Caring. Maintaining a satisfactory degree of couple closeness and support in the remaining years is an important core task in the later years. This involves demonstrating caring and appreciation for past sharing, as well as continued affection and concern for one another in the present. Affection and concern are important ways to provide the support necessary in the search for meaning and satisfaction in life (Nichols & Pace-Nichols, 1993).

Core Task: Communication. Deepening the avenues of communication is especially important in the later years. According to the Nichols, the core task of communication in this stage involves the ability to talk about and share the meanings the marriage has held for each partner. Couples should be able to communicate clearly with one another about their plans for the future. This includes their commitment to outside activities, boundaries regarding extended family, and long-range plans such as estate management, end-of-life issues, and how to plan for life following the death of a spouse.

Core Tasks: Conflict-Compromise and Contract. Communication is essential in facilitating the conflict and compromise task of the later years. Older couples compromise more, appear to have less conflict in their communication, and display more affectionate behavior during conflict than middle or younger couples (Henry, Berg, Smith, & Florsheim, 2007). Couples in this stage of the marital cycle often deal with fears of losing their independence and productivity. They may need to find new ways to redirect their interests and abilities. For example, many people in their later years foster an outward focus by becoming active in community or church volunteer efforts.

The contract task in the later years involves supporting one another's attempts to find meaning, as well as jointly celebrating one another's cumulative achievements. One of the difficulties older adults encounter, according to Ingersol-Dayton and Krause (2005), is when they do not accept the past and they become self-critical and incapable of accepting their limitations and imperfections. Both partners in this stage should continue to strive for fulfillment and satisfaction in life. They can be instrumental in supporting one another in this effort. In addition, couples can reach out in joint grief work to others who have lost a spouse (Nichols & Pace-Nichols, 1993).

Well-Being in the Later Years

According to the Census Bureau, about one in every eight Americans is elderly (over 65). This number will continue to grow as the baby boomers leave the midlife stage and enter their later years (Hetzel & Smith, 2001). By 2030, the number of people 65 and older will double from the number of older people in 2000, and will represent 20% of the population (U.S. Department of Health and Human Services, 2004).

So what is old? A survey of over 3000 adults of all ages found that among

Older Americans are living longer and enjoying greater prosperity than any previous generation.

Americans, nearly half of people 65 and older do not consider themselves "old" and only 15% of people over 75 consider themselves as "very old". The survey also showed that middle age is whatever you want to make it. Half of the age 65-69 respondents and one third of those in their 70's still considered themselves middle aged (Parkin, 2000).

The Best Years or the Worst Years? Among the aging myths that still abound in our society, one asserts that old age is the worst time of life. The truth is, older Americans are living longer and enjoying greater prosperity than any previous generation. In fact, a recent study found nearly 50% of 65- to 69-year-olds felt these were the best years of their lives. For people in their seventies, the percentage dropped to 44% and for people in their eighties, the percentage dropped to 33%. Among older African-Americans and older Hispanics, 60% and 57% respectively said the older years were the best years of their lives. (Parkin, 2000). One reason for these high numbers may be the increased health and financial means of people over 65, which makes it possible for older couples to do many of the things they have always wanted to do, but could not because of family and work responsibilities. While elders still face the possibility of poverty, in 2006, the poverty rate for people 65 and older declined to 9.4%, down from 35% 50 years ago (DeNavas-Walt, Proctor, & Smith, 2007).

What constitutes a meaningful, vital life for an older adult? In the survey, American Perceptions of Aging in the 21st Century (National Council on Aging, 2002), 85% of the respondents agreed family and friends were the most important contributors to a vital life, closely followed by health. Also important was a rich spiritual life, community involvement, and new learning experiences.

Normal aging is a gradual process that can lead to physical decline in several areas of functioning. With aging come certain changes in mental functioning, as well. For example, short-term memory typically declines. However, very few of these changes match commonly held negative stereotypes about aging. As people age, good mental health is dependent on stable intellectual functioning, the ability to cope with change, and the ability to engage in life and family (Goldman, Rye, & Sirovatka, 1999; Vaillant & Mukamal, 2001; Wilson et al., 2002).

Emotional Well-Being in the Later Years. Our emotional well-being is an important indicator of marital adjustment and family cohesiveness. Emotional well-being tends to improve as we age. Psychological distress and depression decrease across the adult lifespan and are the lowest in older adults. Positive affect (outward display of emotion) increases from young adulthood through older adulthood, with the highest levels found in older adults (Kessler et al., 2004).

Image from BigstockPhoto.com / Steve Pepple

Both husbands and wives benefit physically and emotionally from marriage.

Interestingly, despite losses common in the elderly—retirement, decreased or loss of sexual functioning, and loss of a spouse—psychological distress and depression continue to decrease in older adults. This may be due to a proportional decrease in stress in other areas of life. For example, if they have prepared well, older couples no longer experience the stresses of balancing work, family responsibilities, and finances. This works to the advantage of older adults, especially women, who exhibit less distress and more positive emotions than in either of the two younger female adult stages (Kessler et al., 2004).

In a study by the National Council on the Aging (NCOA), older adults reported that having family and friends was the biggest key to a meaningful and vital life, followed by taking care of one's health, one's spiritual life, and community involvement (American Perceptions on Aging, 2002). The spiritual life of the elderly, as pointed out by the NCOA, is in part where the elderly gain a sense of meaning in life. Religious participation has been found to reduce the likelihood of some illnesses (Anderson & Anderson, 2003), positively impact mood (Koenig, George, & Peterson, 1998) and actually improve longevity of life (McMullough et al., 2000). The importance of spirituality is reflected in the church attendance of the elderly, 51% higher than any other age group (Barna, 2005).

Marital and Life Satisfaction in the Later Years

As indicated in Figure 8.2, the Marital Satisfaction Curve, marriage satisfaction, which is relatively low during the early phase of the middle years, sharply increases after age 50. While both men and women benefit from a satisfying marriage, a dissatisfying marriage tends to be more detrimental for women (Gallo et al., 2003; Troxel, Matthews, Gallo, & Kuller, 2005). For women, the quality of the marital relationship is the greatest predictor for marital satisfaction, much stronger than for men (Goodman, 1999; Schmidt, Kliegel, & Shapiro, 2007).

Women report higher quality relationships with their children than men do (Antonucci & Schultz, 2003). However, men report higher quality marriages, sexuality, and financial situations than women. Overall satisfaction with children, marriage, work, financial situation, and life in general all increase with age. Satisfaction with one's financial situation and sexuality peaks at midlife. Thereafter, sexuality substantially decreases with age.

The strongest predictors of overall quality of life are the quality of a person's marriage and close relationships, the person's financial situation, their health, and living situation (Fleeson, 2004; Beedon, Southworth, & Gist, 2006). Compared to a decade ago, there has been improvement in the lives of people 50 and over; however, the improvements in the past few years have been more modest, primarily because of changes in the economy (Beedon, Southworth, & Gist, 2006).

The physiological changes taking place in the aging process affect sexuality in older adults, but do not necessarily interfere with sexual activity.

As examined in chapter 7, marital satisfaction increases to its highest level since the addition of children into the family about the age of retirement; however, marital arguments can still take their toll (Dush, Taylor, & Kroeger, 2008). Research indicates the more negative spouses are with each other during disagreements, the less the satisfaction they feel with their marriage and the more likely they are to have physical symptoms, chronic health problems, physical disability, and poorer perceived health (Bookwala, 2005). There is evidence to suggest that, in the elderly, the more negative the disagreements, the more they weaken their immune systems (Kiecolt-Glaser et al., 1997; Kiecolt-Glaser, Glaser, Cacioppo & Malarkey, 1998; Burns, 2001; Segerstrom & Miller, 2004) Since older people already have less vigorous immune responses than younger people, marital disagreements may put the elderly at greater risk of infections and illness.

The physiological changes taking place in the aging process affect sexuality in older adults. However, these changes do not necessarily interfere with sexual activity (Goldman, Rye, & Sirovatka, 1999; Zeiss & Kasl-Godley, 2001). In fact, a study reported in the *New England Journal of Medicine* found 73% of people between the ages of 57 and 64 were sexually active. This number dropped to 53% for those age 65 to 74 and to 26% for individuals age 75 to 85. (Lindau et al., 2007).

Family Relationships in the Later Years

In the later years, couples realign their relationships with extended family members, including their children's spouses and their grandchildren. This is the time when multigenerational families may include three and sometimes four generations.

One of the myths pervading the area of family relationships is that American families do not care for their older family members. The facts do not support this myth. In 1999, only 1% of adults 65 to 74 years of age resided in nursing homes. For people from 75 to 84 years of age, the number increased to 4%. For those over 85 years of age, it rose to 18% (Federal Interagency Forum on Aging-Related Statistics, 2004). The truth is American families are committed to their older members and provide a variety of assistance, from hands-on care to monetary support. Currently, approximately 1 out of every 4 households (23% or 22.4 million households) provides care for persons 50 years of age or older. This is estimated to soon reach 39 million households (Selected Caregiver Statistics, 2001).

The majority of the primary caretakers are middle-aged women who often work part-time or full-time, in addition to providing care for a family member. However, an increasing number of men are also functioning in this role. Problems occur when an elderly person has no spouse or children able to provide care, making the only option nursing home care. Another concern is the growing number of the "old-old"—those who are 85 years of age and older—whose children may themselves be old and, therefore, unable to provide the same level of care as younger relatives.

Image from BigstockPhoto.com / lisafx

Approximately 1 out of every 4 households provides care for someone 50 or older.

In addition to caring for the elderly, a large and growing number of older family members are caring for chronically mentally ill and mentally retarded younger adults (Goldman, Rye, & Sirovatka, 1999). Too little is known about how to help afflicted younger individuals and their care-giving parents. Families are eager to help themselves, and it is important for society to find ways to enable families to do so.

Grandparents are increasingly involved in the lives of their grandchildren. Since people are living longer, this leaves more years for grandparent-grandchild interaction. This relationship can bring richness and stability to children's lives. Currently, grandparents are the number one providers of childcare (followed next by fathers and then by daycare centers) for preschool children whose mothers work (Smith, 2002).

Grief and Loss in the Later Years

The elderly experience several losses as they age—the loss of many physiological functions, some loss of physical health, the loss of physical ability, sometimes the loss of their independence or their home, and the loss of family and friends to death. All too often, death and bereavement are very much a part of life for the elderly. Although people of all ages may experience the death of someone close, for the elderly, these losses occur much more frequently. Sidebar 8.2 illustrates in a humorous way loss in the later years.

> **SIDEBAR 8.2**
> **When Being at the Wrong Place Isn't "Wrong"**
>
> I remember laughing, but at the same time being puzzled by a story my aging parents told. They lived in a small rural town in the Midwest. When a mutual friend died, they headed to the funeral home. They didn't check to see which funeral home was handling the arrangements, so they found themselves at the wrong funeral home. They stayed anyway, laughing about it later. They remarked that it didn't really make much difference, because they knew *that* person too. I didn't know whether to be horrified or to look at death as just another part of life, and laugh with them.
>
> —Anonymous

Building and maintaining close relationships, such as a marriage, is related to mortality. So significant is the loss of a spouse, the chances of dying in the first 30 days after the death of a spouse increases as high as 53% for men and 61% for women. Time does help people heal and after 1 year, the risk decreases to 21% for husbands and 17% for wives after the death of their spouse (Christakis, 2006). Sidebar 8.3 tells the story of one widow's lonely struggle. Coping with the death of a spouse can be a very difficult and confusing time. In addition to grief, loss, and loneliness, the surviving spouse faces many practical considerations: arrangements to be made, financial matters to handle, sometimes children to care for, just to name a few.

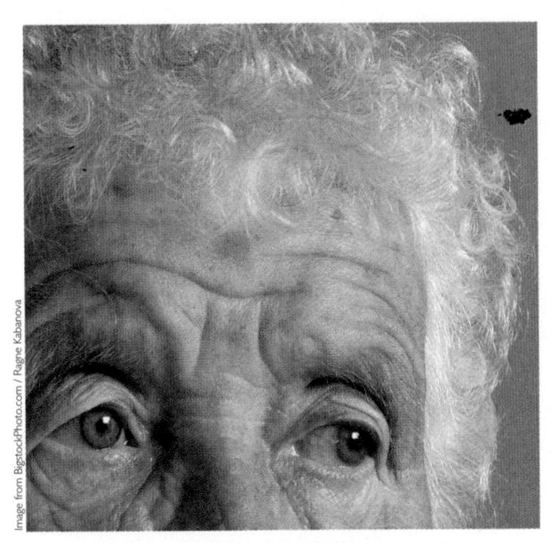

The elderly experience several losses as they age—physiological functions, physical health, physical ability, sometimes their independence, and loss of family and friends to death.

On average, women live 5.2 years longer than men, making it more likely for a wife to live beyond her husband (Minino, Heron, Murphy, & Kochanek, 2007). While women seem to fare better than men emotionally after the death of a spouse, they are more likely to suffer financially. Poverty rates for elderly women in 2006 were 11.5% compared to 6.6% of older men (U.S. Department of Health and Human Services, 2007). Social isolation and loneliness are prevalent among spouses who have lost their partners. Since a woman is more likely to live alone after the death of her husband, she should be encouraged to maintain contact with family, friends, and social networks, such as church and community organizations.

SIDEBAR 8.3
A Widow's Story

Dorothy was a vivacious woman of 69, married to Robert, who was 70. They had a good life together and shared many of the same interests. Since Robert's retirement 5 years earlier, they had traveled several times each year to different places around the world. They had participated in mission trips together on several occasions and were active in their local church. They played golf a couple of times a week and frequently got together with friends.

As Robert's health began to fail, Dorothy devoted her time to seeing to Robert's every need. They were unable to get out like they used to, and even began missing church. Within 6 months, Robert died, leaving Dorothy alone. At first, she was numb. She refused to wash his pillowcase because it still had Robert's scent on it. She cried, she screamed, she ached—and nothing seemed to relieve her grief. Soon, she could no longer smell Robert when she cried on his pillow.

The church tried to comfort her. Her children, who lived out of town, tried to get her to come stay with them. Her friends called to check on her, but she had no desire or energy to get out or see anyone, and she could not bear the thought of leaving the home she and Robert had made. Soon, the calls came less frequently. Even her children called only a couple of times a week. There were days that she did not speak to another adult. Her life felt like an empty shell.

A year after Robert died, she started to get out a little bit. But her travel companion was not there; her golf partner was not there—all the things she and Robert had shared required two people. She began occasionally going out to lunch with a friend. She started going to church again, where she sat with the other women who had lost their husbands. But life was forever changed.

One year and 3 days after Roberts's death, Dorothy died. The doctors said she died of a heart attack, but those closest to her knew that Dorothy had died of a broken heart.

—Anonymous

A Christian Perspective

Midlife and Raising Children

For many Christians, midlife can be a time to question how they are living, a time to evaluate their Christian "walk." Far too many Christians measure both their family success and their spiritual success by the actions of their grown or nearly grown children. Paternal determinism often still prevails in Christian homes. This is a belief that if you parent your children properly, they will turn out well. If a child fails, acts improperly, or even gets into serious trouble, many Christian parents question God. It is not uncommon to hear parents try to justify their own actions in the case of an unruly young adult. "He [or she] was raised in the church," they might say. "Why would God let this happen?" It is difficult for them to understand that raising their children in a Christian home will not necessarily protect these children from making poor or even devastating decisions as young adults.

In chapter 7, we referred to the analogy of kite-flying as it relates to knowing how much string (freedom) to give children. The goal of Christian parenting is to raise children to become the young men and women God wants them to be. To this end, parents are responsible for instilling character and being good role models. What the children do with these building blocks ultimately is between them and God. Parents eventually must release the kite string. Christian parents who have done their best to raise their children according to Christian principles can find reassurance in verses such as Proverbs 22:6 (NLT): "Direct your children onto the right path, and when they are older, they will not leave it."

Midlife and the Marital Relationship

One of the greatest dangers to stability in the Christian marriage is the growth of a hedonistic attitude in society. Hedonism is the belief that pleasure and happiness are the primary goals of life. Once ascribed to men, hedonism now seems to be equally appealing to women. To the contrary, there is support for the benefits of the giving of ourselves and helping others, which include health, happiness, and a longer life (Post, Neimack, & Moss, 2007).

The sad commentary is that Christians are not immune to hedonism, despite its contradiction of Scripture. Whether prompted by midlife crisis or a desperate attempt to recapture the excitement of an earlier time in their single lives, many Christian couples are calling it quits. It is alarming to note that Christian marriages end as frequently as non-Christian marriages. According to Barna statistics, among married, born-again Christians, 35% have experienced a divorce. That figure is identical to the outcome among married adults who are not born-again Christians (Barna, 2006). As Christian couples enter their middle and later years, it would be wise for them to "get back to basics" in their marital relationships. Christian counselors or pastors trained to counsel couples can help them rediscover the joy of their covenant partnership and reconnect to their full potential as marriage partners.

A Christian Perspective on Aging

God loves us throughout all the stages of our lives. He has a special love for those who are growing older. Many Scriptures refer to growing old as the culmination of a good life, in which we continue to enjoy life and family, remain productive, and continue our walk with God. Compare the following scriptures (all from the NLT) against some of today's myths, stereotypes, and fears associated with aging. Do they match?

- "Abraham lived for 175 years, and he died at a ripe old age, having lived a long and satisfying life. He breathed his last and joined his ancestors in death" (Genesis 25:7–8).
- "Today I am 85 years old. I am as strong now as I was when Moses sent me on that journey, and I can still travel and fight as well as I could then" (Joshua 14:10b–11, Caleb speaking).
- "So David son of Jesse reigned over all Israel. He reigned over Israel for 40 years, 7 of them in Hebron and 33 in Jerusalem. He died at a ripe old age, having enjoyed long life, wealth, and honor. Then his son Solomon ruled in his place" (1 Chronicles 29:26–28).
- "Grandchildren are the crowning glory of the aged; parents are the pride of their children" (Proverbs 17:6).
- "Listen to me, descendents of Jacob, all you who remain in Israel. I have cared for you since you were born. Yes, I carried you before you were born. I will be your God throughout your lifetime—until your hair is white with age. I made you, and I will care for you. I will carry you along and save you" (Isaiah 46:3–4).

- "But the godly will flourish like palm trees and grow strong like the cedars of Lebanon. For they are transplanted to the Lord's own house. They flourish in the courts of our God. Even in old age they will still produce fruit; they will remain vital and green. They will declare, 'The Lord is just! He is my rock! There is no evil in him!'" (Psalm 92:12–15).

God's view of aging certainly differs from many contemporary ideas! As we age, we should strive for quality of life. Many older people find retirement to be a time to fulfill goals they have put off—such as getting more involved in volunteer activities, mission projects, and other mind- and spirit-building endeavors.

For those dealing with the loss of a spouse, the church community becomes paramount in helping to alleviate some of the loneliness. Members of the church need to reach out to widows and widowers. Scripture acknowledges the difficulties that widows face and urges believers to care for them (1 Timothy 5:16; James 1:27).

Christians need to reach out to the older people around them. More than one widow or widower has been heard to say, "I have to go to church because it is the only place where I can get a hug." This can translate to mean "the only place that I can touch and be touched by other people." What a sad commentary on an all-too-common reality.

While the thought of death is probably far from your minds during this academic time in your life, death is a reality all people face. Christians can take comfort in the fact their lifetimes are but a second to God, and they have eternity waiting in the wings. It may seem frightening to think about death now, but as Christians age, they find increasing comfort in living peaceful lives and calmly awaiting the next with their Heavenly Father.

Ian Shaw / Stone / Getty Images

The Christian community can do a lot to ease the loneliness of the elderly by reaching out to widows and widowers.

Summary

This chapter has explored the transitions people experience from the middle to the later years of their lives. It began with a life-cycle perspective on the aging process. This included a review of Erickson's eight stages of development and Levinson's four stages or eras of development. The Nichols' model viewed marriage from a developmental standpoint. This model offers four stages: the beginning years, the early years, the middle years, and the later years.

The middle years represent a much longer period than in earlier times because of the increasing longevity of Americans. Family transitions during this time include several potential exits and returns of older children; juggling of schedules related to work, home life, church and other activities; physical changes due to the aging process; and dealing with aging parents. The middle years can be a particularly stressful and difficult period for families.

Midlife crisis represents a time of introspection and reevaluation of life, accomplishments, and goals. While this can be a stressful period of time, it also can bring about a new sense of purpose. Menopause and its associated hormonal and chemical changes seem to serve as a physical springboard, launching both women and men into a new phase of life. Parent-child relationships change considerably during this period. Children move out, marry, integrate another person into the family, and ultimately add grandchildren to the family. During this same time period, the parents often care for their aging parents. This puts a strain on families in the middle years, especially women, who are the primary caretakers.

Myths about the elderly and the aging process lend a pessimistic view of the last stage of life. From a developmental perspective, the later years represent a time when couples readjust to having increased time together and finding new interests in life. Fine-tuning communication techniques will vastly improve a couple's ability to support one another and work together to exercise their talents. While aging is a gradual process, people in their later years can expect to notice a decline in several areas of functioning. Older people can maintain a high level of emotional well-being despite these physical changes. As evidence of this, older adults experience the lowest levels of depression in comparison to adults in other phases of the life cycle. As people age, their sense of satisfaction with the quality of their marriage increases, their relationships with their children improve, and their overall view of life is enhanced. The two biggest predictors of quality of life in both sexes are their financial situation and how they view the state of their marriage.

The last stage of life is often characterized by loss. Two primary problems the elderly face are loneliness and social isolation. This is especially true of women, who, on average, outlive their husband by slightly over 5 years (Minino et al., 2007). By maintaining close ties with family, friends, church, and other social networks, the elderly can fight loneliness and continue to function as contributing members of society.

Questions for Thought

1. Sociologists and gerontologists have noted one of the fastest growing segments of society today is the age group of the "old-old," those who are 85 years of age or older. What challenges does this age group face, as compared to people between the ages of 65 and 85?

2. Do you agree that the film industry, television, and advertising companies portray aging in a negative light? Explain your answer. Have you noticed any changes recently?

3. In 2005, married couples became a minority of all American households for the first time. Do you think this trend will continue? Why or why not?

4. What do you think is the most important step a couple can take to ensure a lasting marriage?

Resources

Books:

A Grief Observed by C.S. Lewis. A memoir of C.S. Lewis dealing with the grief over his wife's death.

The 36-Hour Day by Nancy Mace and Peter Rabins (1999). A book for families caring for a person with Alzheimer's or dementia

Movies:

Failure to Launch, (PG-13). DVD. The story of a grown man who lives with his parents and what it takes for him to "launch" into manhood.

Grumpy Old Men, (PG-13). DVD. Think about Erikson's Integrity vs. Despair stage while watching this movie.

Secondhand Lions, (PG-13). DVD. The story of a young boy growing up with two old and fascinating uncles.

While You Were Sleeping, (PG). DVD. A romantic comedy that includes many scenes of a normal, yet quirky and fun, American family.

The Bucket List, (PG-13). DVD. Comedy/ drama about two terminally-ill men fulfilling their list of to-dos before they die.

Dad, (PG). Three-generational drama about reconnecting between parents and children.

Online Video:

Understanding menopause: http://www.youtube.com/watch?v=s0nAC7ag3XM (accessed June 23, 2009)

Websites:

1. *AARP* website for people 50+: http://www.aarp.org (accessed June 23, 2009)
2. *Mayo Clinic* on menopause: http://www.mayoclinic.com/health/menopause/DS00119 (accessed June 23, 2009)

Families and Work

9

The Juggling Act

I can do everything through him who gives me strength.
—Philippians 4:13

© iStockphoto.com / njgphoto

Dual-income marriages are more the norm today than the exception. The employment of wives and mothers rose dramatically from 1960 to 1990 and has since leveled off (Cotter, England, & Hermsen, 2007). Currently 65% of mothers who have children under 5 years old are in the workforce. For mothers who have children over 5 years old, the rate has hovered between 79 and 80% for the last 6 years (Women in the Labor Force, 2007). Approximately 60% of families with children younger than 18 are dual-income families—both parents in the workforce (U.S. Department of Labor, 2008a). This compares with less than one third of mothers in 1975. Working motherhood is a relatively new phenomenon for middle-class families; however, black middle-class mothers have preceded their white counterparts in the job market (Landry, 2000).

Middle-income families have undergone many changes in marriage patterns to accommodate this shift to dual-income households. Many middle-class families struggle as they attempt to create balance. Dual-income marriage is perhaps the greatest challenge facing contemporary families, producing much stress and conflict. Who is minding the children? What is the impact on the children? Each family is unique and must negotiate its own system of tending to children and housework, while the parents juggle two full-time jobs.

In this chapter, we will review the history of women who work outside the home, as well as how these women have changed the patterns of marriage and family relationships. We will look at the dual-income family today, including its positive and negative impact on children. Finally, we will offer strategies to help dual-income parents better organize their lives and manage their family relationships.

Working Mothers: A Historical Perspective

The last 60 years have seen dramatic changes in the patterns of marriage and family relationships. These changes have taken many interesting twists and turns. As they relate to mothers in the workforce, we can refer to revolution, counterrevolution, and renegotiation. Patterns of adaptation are different for first-generation, second-generation, and third-generation working mothers. Contemporary American culture is filled with families from all three of these generations operating at different levels simultaneously.

Post-World War II

During World Wars I and II, it was necessary for many women to work outside the home to fill in for the men who were at war. Women moved into jobs which had previously been the domain of men. During World War I, women in the lower classes moved from garment work to factory production (Brown, 2002). While lower-class women, including many blacks and immigrants, had always worked, especially in service jobs, World War II saw

Lambert / Hulton Archive / Getty Images

During WWII women worked in defense factories to help the war effort. When the war was over, they were expected to return home and be housewives.

women of all social classes taking jobs outside the home, seeing it as their duty to their country to help with the war effort. After the war, they were expected to return to home and family (Epstein, 2002; Yellin, 2004). And most of them did—producing a baby boom from 1946 into the 1960s. The term baby boomer refers generally to everyone born between 1946 and 1964.

Many of the women who worked during WWII found they had to take more traditional jobs after the war.

While it was common for a woman to work before she married, the middle class set the standard of domesticity for women after they were married. It was expected she would make family her priority, and any financial support would come from taking work into the home (Epstein, 2002). The number of single women in the workforce peaked during WWII and then declined sharply after the war as large numbers of single women pursued higher education

Sidebar 9.1
The Past and the Present

The following is a quotation from Casper and Bianchi's book, *Continuity & Change in the American Family,* which illustrates some of the changes that have taken place in the lives of women who work outside the home.

> Consider the life of a young woman reaching adulthood in the 1950s or early 1960s. Such a woman was likely to marry straight out of high school or to take a clerical or retail sales job until she married. She would have moved out of her parents' home only after she married, to form a new household with her husband. This young woman was likely to marry by age 20 and begin a family soon after. If she was working when she became pregnant, she would probably have quit her job and stayed home to care for her children while her husband had a steady job that paid enough to support the entire family.
>
> Fast forward to the last few years of the 20th century. A young woman reaching adulthood in the late 1990s is not likely to marry before her 25th birthday. She will probably attend college and is likely to live by herself, with a boyfriend, or with roommates before marrying. She may move in and out of her parents' house several times before she gets married. Like her counterpart reaching adulthood in the 1950s, she is likely to marry and have at least one child, but the sequence of those events may well be reversed. She probably will not drop out of the labor force after she has children, although she may curtail the number of hours she is employed to balance work and family. She is also much more likely to divorce and possibly even to remarry compared with a young woman in the 1950s or 1960s.

Source: Casper, L. and Bianchi, S. 2002. *Continuity & change in the American family.* Thousand Oaks, CA: Sage., pg 3.

(Caplow, Hicks, & Wattenberg, 2000). One legacy of WWII was the new-found independence and self-worth which married women discovered through working. Nearly half the women drawn into the workforce by the war had left by 1950; however, a significant number remained (Acemoglu, Autor, & Lyle, 2002). About 17% of those remaining were working mothers (Cohany & Sok, 2007). Many white, middle-class women with some college education were filling jobs, partly because there were not enough men to fill them, partly because they needed more income and partly because they were tired of domesticity and wanted jobs (Epstein, 2002). Women worked in primarily traditional jobs such as clerical, sales, teaching and nursing, but some women found more diversified employment in traditionally male occupations such as science, medicine and agriculture (Caplow, Hicks, & Wattenberg, 2000). The trend of women in the workforce has continued to increase since that time.

Revolution: First-Generation Women Who Work Outside the Home

The 1960s ushered in dramatic changes in families, marriages and work. Social attitudes toward women and their role in society changed after the war ended. From the mid-1960s on, married, middle-class women with children found greater acceptance in choosing to work outside the home. The dynamics of marriage subtly changed as a result, so that women were not wholly dependent on their husbands to support them (Engerman & Owyang, 2006). The common structure of marriage in this period changed from the traditional *patriarchal* marriage to a more egalitarian, companionate form of marriage (Amato, Booth, Johnson, & Rogers, 2007). This enabled women to have greater bargaining power in family decisions which is associated with higher marital quality for wives (Amato et al., 2007) (see chapter 6).

Women were still primarily responsible for the majority of housework and care of the children. Most husbands helped with household chores, but usually those chores which qualified as "man's work" (household repairs, yard work, trash). Advanced technology, such as washing machines, vacuums, and dishwashers, is responsible for the reduction in housework time and freed women to pursue outside employment (Greenwood, Seshadri, & Yorukoglu, 2005).

The Women's Revolution. The Equal Pay Act of 1963 bolstered the value of women's employment by making it illegal for employers to pay different rates for women and men who performed equal work (Brinkley, 2003). In *The Feminine Mystique* (1963), author Betty Friedan identified the enduring "problem that has no name" as the contemporary woman's need for personal fulfillment. The solution to this need was thought to be meaningful, well-paid work outside the home. Fueled by increased access to reliable birth control (e.g., the Pill), the women's revolution was on (Engermann & Owyang, 2006; Golden & Katz, 2002). Women were encouraged to let career life co-opt family life.

The women's movement challenged the culture and structures of gender equality, as well as confronted the men who expected women to abide by the rules (Epstein, 2002). As a result, the women's revolution shattered many marriages in the late 1960s and early 1970s, as women seemingly changed the rules of their marriages, spending less time on home and family and more time on outside interests. Women who fought to save their marriages found it challenging to hold on to their careers without jeopardizing family life. These women were caught in the contradiction between an economy which needed them, and a culture which continued to define femininity in terms of passivity and subservience (Epstein, 2002). Thus, most first-generation women who worked outside the home sought to "do it all." They rose early to cook breakfast and get their husbands and children off to work and school. They spent a good portion of their evenings cooking, cleaning up after dinner, helping children with homework, and tending to numerous household chores. Hochschild (1989) chronicled the long workdays of mothers and the resulting strain on relationships. She documented how women essentially worked a second job after they returned home, which she referred to as "the second shift." About one third to one half of mothers are still doing a "second shift" today, according to the research (Amato, Booth Johnson, & Rogers, 2007; Bianchi, Robinson, & Milkie, 2006).

Other Factors. Married women with children continued to move into the paid labor market in the early 1970s. Many of these women entered for self-fulfillment or to keep pace with a rising standard of living, which necessitated a rise in median

First-generation working mothers often try to do it all.

family income. However, other dynamics were coming into play. With a decrease in industrial and factory jobs, more men became unemployed, which prompted more women to enter the paid labor force. Women began to demand higher wages to replace the decrease in their husbands' wages and to keep up with the expected standard of living.

Many first-generation women who work outside the home today still succumb to the superwoman syndrome, which is the strategy of juggling home, work, and family by trying to "do it all." They are often exhausted and unsatisfied with both career and family (Moen & Roehling, 2004).

Counterrevolution: Second-Generation Women Who Work Outside the Home and the ERA

Many daughters whose mothers worked full time while they were growing up live counter to their mothers' "juggling act." They may wait to have children until they can focus more time and energy on them. They may choose to stay home with their children, deferring their careers to their post-parenting years. Others choose to lighten up on certain aspects of housework or childrearing. They may not keep a spotless house and may rely on outside services and fast-food restaurants to support their domestic duties.

In the late 1970s and early 1980s, the women's revolution was dramatically curtailed as the realities of family life without a full-time homemaker sank in. Susan Faludi reports in her book *Backlash: The undeclared war against American women* (1991) that the feminist movement was under fire for many of society's ills: rising divorce rates, juvenile delinquency, infertility, emotional illness in women, and so forth. Whether or not the employment of mothers outside the home actually caused these problems was not the issue. Many felt the need to return to the "good old days."

Women who worked outside the home often found themselves at odds with women who chose not to work outside the home. The women's movement of the 1960s often became a "woman versus woman" struggle in the 1970s. At the heart of this battle was a philosophical difference over a proposed amendment to the Constitution—the Equal Rights Amendment (ERA). The ERA was first

The Equal Rights Amendment was at the heart of the struggle to provide both men and women equal rights and bring an end to sex discrimination.

introduced into Congress in 1923. Congress finally passed and submitted it to the states for ratification on March 22, 1972. An original deadline of 7 years was extended by Congress to June 30, 1982. When this deadline expired, only 35 states (of the necessary three fourths, or 38) had ratified it. Since that time, it has been reintroduced into every session of Congress but has still not passed (Francis, 2006).

Proponents of the ERA assert this amendment is needed to give both women and men equal rights guaranteed by the U.S. Constitution. They propose the ERA is necessary to provide a remedy for sex discrimination, to give equal legal status to women, and to expand workplace opportunities for women. Supporters often point to opponents of the ERA as operating from a base of fear: fear of a military draft which would include women, and fears such as unisex bathrooms, health clubs, and sports teams.

However, opponents of the ERA—particularly conservatives—focus on other issues. They point out that women already have the full protection of the Constitution under the 14th Amendment. Further, ERA opponents are not opposed to the issue of equality itself, but are concerned about the wording of the amendment as it relates to issues of reproductive rights, abortion, homosexual rights, same-sex issues, and power shifts from the states to the federal government.

Though the ERA failed to pass, other major changes in marriage and family life had already taken place in this generation: widespread use of birth control; more single-parent, female-headed households; less-segregated gender roles. Sara Evans (1989) writes that the real battle was over the *meaning* of these changes. What were the new expectations for men and women in families and at work?

Renegotiation: Third-Generation Women Who Work Outside the Home

It is unclear how third-generation women who work outside the home will respond to the revolution and counterrevolution of the two previous generations. A strong conservative movement currently calls for a reconsideration of family values. Women are not leaving paid employment in significant numbers; it would appear the working mother is here to stay. However, families are struggling to come to a quiet resolution of the family/work dilemma without abandoning one for the other. New patterns of adaptation have emerged: family restaurants enable working parents to have quality time with children over a healthy dinner; cell phones enable families to stay connected; computers enable many to work at home either all or part of the time; and home-based businesses are on the increase.

Many third-generation marriages follow an *egalitarian* pattern, characterized by role interchangeability with respect to career, housework, and family responsibilities. Husbands and wives share the responsibility for childcare, household chores, and income production. Family responsibilities are negotiated and renegotiated. For some women, adoption of more egalitarian attitudes leads to less marital satisfaction. This is presumably because nontraditional wives negotiate work and family responsibilities that previous generations of women took for granted, creating space for conflicts and disagreements in the relationship (Amato, Booth, Johnson, & Rogers, 2007).

Despite a leveling off of the number of mothers in the workforce, over half the mothers with children under 6 years old work outside the home.

Working Mothers: The Situation Today

Currently, the dual-income family has become the norm, with over 70% of working-age women employed full time, including over half of mothers with children less than 6 years of age (Carter & McGoldrick, 2005). These women represent all three of the generations previously discussed. Some women struggle to do it all—manage responsibilities at home and at work—as "superwomen." Some women who work outside the home have lightened their burdens by hiring others to help with family responsibilities. Still others do not experience this stereotypical "struggle" because their husbands contribute equitably to the mutual tasks of balancing work and family (Deutch, Kokot, & Binder, 2007). Sidebar 9.2 is an example of how one family manages some of the household responsibilities.

There are many reasons for the large number of women in the workforce according to Cotter, England and Hermsen (2007). These include smaller families, the rise in single mothers who must work, and the fall of men's real wages (wages adjusted for inflation), making it necessary for women to work. Possibly more important reasons are the increases in women's education, better job opportunities, and more opportunity for

Sidebar 9.2

Okay, I admit it. You will find my family eating at fast-food restaurants more times per week than we eat at our dining room table. My kitchen is always the neatest room in the house—because we seldom use it. My mother, the "do it all" superwoman, would be ashamed if she were alive to see how seldom I use all the pots, pans, appliances, and china she gave me for our wedding—or maybe she would applaud because I am thinner and healthier since I don't have a lot of extra food around the house. Now are you shocked because fast food is so *unhealthy?* Perhaps so, but you can often find some healthy alternatives on the menu. And I'm tired of pushing vegetables on my children, when all they will really eat are chicken nuggets (perhaps I'm reaching here, but aren't French fries a vegetable?). I'm also tired of cooking something that only I will eat. I'm surrendering my obligation to force them to eat veggies to the peace of allowing them to choose off a menu, guaranteeing they will eat it without an argument!

I have found that my family eats better, argues less, watches television less, and talks to one another more when we are at a restaurant—even if it is fast food. And it's not much more expensive if you look for the bargains. We've actually had seniors come over and comment how wonderful it is to see a family laughing and having fun together over a meal. What a relaxing way to cap off a grueling work/school day. This is so much better than arguing over what I should cook, what we should watch on television, and whose turn it is to do dishes!

Signed,
Queen of the fast foods

—Anonymous

women to enter more exciting and satisfying careers. Since 2000, there has been a leveling off of women's employment rates, which represents a real, but very small, downturn of employment rates. Social scientists are not sure why this leveling off has occurred or what the future trends will be, but it is unlikely that, as the most affluent nation, there will be a significant decrease in the number of working women.

According to the Bureau of Labor, when families have children their outside work hours tend to change (U.S. Department of Labor, 2008b). For instance, fathers of children under 18, average 42.6 hours per week of outside work while mothers average 36 hours per week. In families where the mother does not work outside the home, fathers worked an average of 17 minutes longer per day than fathers whose wives also work full time.

Sharing the Workload

While husbands today are much more involved in household chores, the workload is still not equal in most families. The amount of time women spend on housework has dramatically declined by almost 4 hours per week since the mid-1960s, while the amount of housework performed by husbands has increased slightly and then leveled off

(Bianchi, Milkie, Sayer, & Robinson, 2000). A study of over 13,000 families found that wives spend almost twice as much time on household chores as their husbands (Lee, 2005; Axinn & Thornton, 2000). Figure 9.1 calculates the average time Americans spend on various household activities each week. These figures are very general and are affected by the number of children, family income, gender role ideologies, and the career of each partner. Further analysis by Parkman (2004) indicates the time a woman spends on these activities significantly decreases as her income increases. However, the husband's participation in these activities increases only slightly as his wife's income increases. In other words, women who earn close to what their husbands earn, or more, are more likely to rely on outside services for cooking, cleaning, and childcare. A husband's participation in household chores, while it has increased in recent years, does not equal the time his wife spends on these activities. As a result, women often have less free time than their male counterparts (Mattingly & Bianchi, 2003).

As the number of children increases, the household workload increases. The gap between men and women also increases. For example, Amato, Booth, Johnson and Rogers (2007) found men did about one fourth to one third of the housework whether there were children in the home or not. Fathers also did about the same amount of childcare. Interestingly, some mothers felt their husbands were not doing their share of the housework but were satisfied with the amount of childcare fathers were doing.

Figure 9.1

Hours Spent Per Week on Household Chores

Hours in Different Tasks				
Task	**Husband**	**Wife**	**Children**	**Others**
Preparing Meals	2.8	10.1	1.2	2.4
Washing Dishes	2.2	6.7	2.4	2.1
Cleaning House	2.2	6.7	2.4	2.1
Outdoor Tasks	5.3	2.4	1.5	1.5
Shopping	1.7	3.3	0.3	1.0
Washing, Ironing	0.8	4.6	0.8	1.5
Paying Bills	1.6	2.0	0.1	0.8
Auto Maintenance	1.9	0.3	0.2	0.9
Driving	1.4	1.7	0.3	0.8
Total	19.9	40	9.1	13.6

Source: Parkman 2004.

In egalitarian couples, husbands and wives share household responsibilities.

This may be explained in a couple of ways. Mothers may feel they are more adept at childcare than their husbands, or they may see childcare as the more enjoyable of the two activities. Amato et al. (2007) found, overall, the percentage of household work husbands were doing and the number of hours their wives worked outside the home were the best predictors of their wives' perception of unfairness in work distribution.

The level of family income tends to determine the reliance on outside services. Even though men are contributing more time to household work, women still put in the bulk of hours on household chores (Parkman, 2004). In families which hold more traditional views of gender roles, wives spend many more hours on household chores (Parkman, 2004). In families with more egalitarian gender roles, husbands do more housework—about one fourth of the housework in traditional families and about one third of the housework in egalitarian families (Amato, Booth, Johnson, & Rogers, 2007). Men or women who have jobs requiring many hours away from home will spend much less time on household chores. Studies also indicate that men spend more time in paid employment than women, which naturally accounts for less available time for household chores (Amato et al., 2007; Bianchi, Robinson, & Milkie, 2006; Married Parents, 2008; Parkman, 2004).

Occasionally husbands contribute more to household chores than their wives. For example, an unemployed husband or a single father with custody of the children may spend much more time on household chores. These situations are generally considered temporary. The "househusband" who quits his job to support his wife's career and take care of the family is a rarity—not a cultural norm. In fact, while the U.S. Census estimates 5.5 million parents stay home with their children, only about 100,000 are fathers (The Futurist, 2005).

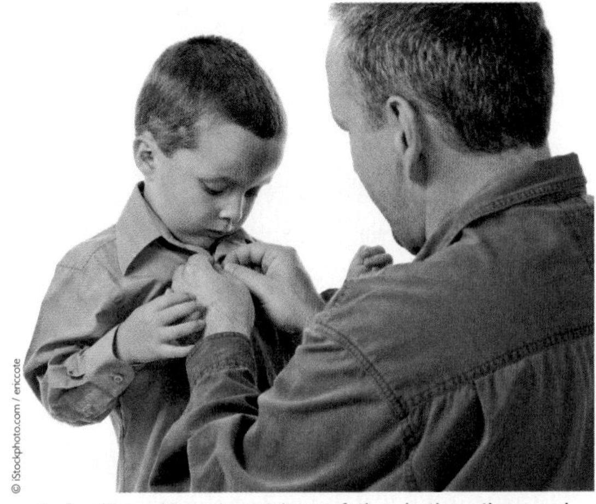

In families with a stay-at-home father, both mothers and fathers have a strong influence on their child's development.

When comparing stay-at-home-father households to stay-at-home-mother households, mothers still formed strong bonds with their children even when they worked more than 40 hours per week, according to The Futurist (2005). This same study found in families where the mother works outside the home and the father is a stay-at-home father, mothers were much more engaged in their children's day-to-day life than working fathers with stay-at-home wives. In stay-at-home-father households, child care is more likely to be distributed evenly, with fathers performing many of the roles historically associated with female homemakers. These families were found to have both a strong father influence, as well as a strong mother influence, with both parents playing an important role in the child's development. This is in contrast to stay-at-home-mother families in which the working father tends to have much less influence in child development (Baylies, 2004; The Futurist, 2005).

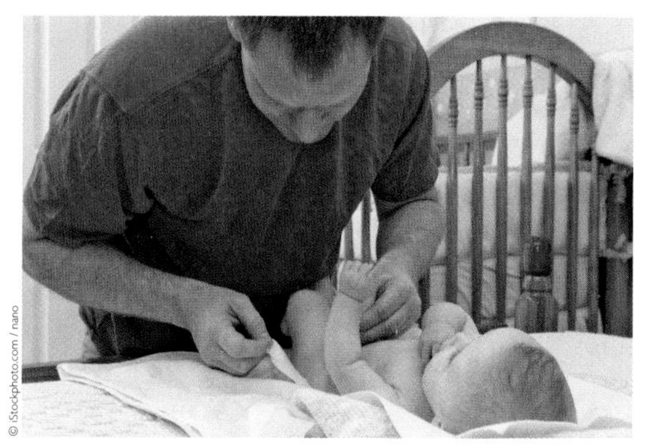

Men and women have learned to communicate and negotiate their contributions to household and family management.

The Repercussions of Imbalance

How does the "division of labor" regarding household chores affect marriage? We might assume women overall would be very unhappy about any perceived imbalance. However, divorce statistics do not indicate this. In fact, the divorce rate in the United States reached a peak in the early 1980s and has stabilized or slightly declined since then (Eldridge & Sutton, 2007). Lack of help with household chores is rarely a primary reason for divorce.

Generally, the trend follows a dual track. Many first-generation women who work outside the home often do not insist their husbands put in equal time on domestic duties. They grew up in a culture in which cooking, cleaning, and childcare were considered to be "women's work." Thus, they generally accept responsibility for these duties. Their husbands may or may not contribute to household chores, although many have been influenced by cultural expectations to at least "lend a hand."

On the other hand, the husbands of second- and third-generation women who work outside the home are much more involved in family responsibilities today than their fathers were, particularly in parenting tasks (Amato, Booth, Johnson, & Rogers, 2007; Bianchi, Robinson, &

Milkie, 2006; Parkman, 2004). Men and women of these newer generations have learned to communicate and negotiate their contributions in the areas of household and family management.

The Glass Ceiling

The 2004 elections resulted in a dramatic turn of events, ushering in America's first woman Speaker of the House. The 2008 elections saw the first woman making a close run for the democratic nomination for President of the United States and another female the republican Vice Presidential running mate. While women now have gained access to most occupations and are entering the workforce in record numbers, they still find it difficult to access top executive positions. In 2007, the number of female CEOs running major corporations grew from 9 to a record 12, however, that still represents only 2.4% of Fortune 500 companies (Jones, 2008). Social analysts refer to this phenomenon as the glass ceiling, which is a metaphor for the organizational, attitudinal, and societal barriers preventing women from advancing up the career ladder (Crutcher, 2006). Women who experience the glass ceiling are promoted to just below the top level, but can't seem to break through the invisible barrier which limits their success.

In the past, men often were seen as responsible for this subtle form of discrimination. Many men found it difficult to view a woman in a leadership role (some still do). There was an assumption that because men and women did not think alike, strategize or network in the same ways, or talk the same language, a woman could never communicate effectively with men in a leadership role. Brizendine (2008), a neuropsychiatrist, refutes these beliefs suggesting male and female brains are more alike than different, and the glass ceiling has nothing to do with raw intellect.

Interestingly, women themselves often have curtailed their own career opportunities. For first-generation women who work outside the home, cultural socialization encouraged them to place great importance on their roles as mothers and grandmothers; thus, many chose not to expend the time or effort necessary to make it to the top of the corporate ladder. They

For women, top management positions are often lonely and isolating.

often were satisfied with meaningful careers which allowed them plenty of time for family.

Thus, second- and third-generation women who are more career-oriented find few role models to help them with their ascent. Men tend to mentor each other, but women often have to go it alone. Women sometimes find a lack of social support at the top. Men get together for golf outings and happy hour after work. Often, women are not invited or may feel the need to spend that time at home. Thus, women often are lonely at the top because they may not have much in common with the men surrounding them. It is not uncommon for a woman who reaches the top to suddenly "bail out," realigning herself with her family and female friends. Concern for this "brain drain" in science prompted a study of why women scientists, engineers and technologists leave full time employment in alarmingly high numbers (Helwett, Luce, & Servon, 2008). The findings indicate there are several reasons why women leave these professions: hostility, isolation, job expectations, long work weeks, and the need for out-of-town travel. Since women in dual-income families still bear the brunt of the household management, they often leave their job rather than remain under the pressure required in the job. Brizendine (2008) suggests the lack of women rising to the top is more a matter of timing. She suggests the "go-for-it" moment occurs in one's 40s, which coincides with one of the busiest times for women with children, thus taking them out of the running for the top jobs.

A woman who takes time off from work to have children will often experience a dramatic long-term consequence. *The Price of Motherhood: Why the Most Important Job in the World is Still the Least Valued* (Crittenden, 2001) examines the long-term financial impacts (career earnings, retirement income) for women. The author notes that a woman who leaves the workforce to have two children takes a 15% cut in lifetime earnings. In a culture with a divorce rate of 40–50%—with women most often receiving custody of the children—women may find themselves in a financially tenuous position.

The Impact of Dual-Career Families on Children

Dual-career families are on the increase today. Over 55% of women with infant children work outside the home (U.S. Census Bureau, 2005c). This is still a relatively new phenomenon, and Western culture is struggling to adapt to this new family form. How are children's lives different when both parents work outside the home? Research is divided on the advantages and disadvantages for children.

The Daycare Dilemma

Who is minding the children? The daycare program is a by-product of WW II, when the Langham Act of 1941 provided money for construction and operation of child care centers for children of defense workers. While the Langham Act expired at the end of WW II, a precedent had been set regarding care of children (Zylan, 2000). With the increase in working mothers in the years which followed, daycare centers sprang up across America. Parents thought their children would be well-served by such "learning centers," as they were often called. This is a clear example of how family life is sometimes shaped by the political system and the people in power. In 1962, Congress approved daycare funding for poor mothers, and expected them to enter the workforce and leave their children with others, which bolstered the growth of daycare centers—another example of people in power shaping family life (How Welfare, 2001). Many of those original daycare centers have since closed, and the institutional option for daycare is used much less frequently today. Instead, most children of working mothers are cared for by another family member. According to a 2008 census, 66% of children under age 5 receive care from a relative. About one third of these children are cared for by a grandparent, one fourth by their father, and about one tenth by another relative. Just over 30% of children in the same age group are taken care of at an organized care facility (U. S. Census Bureau, 2008a). There has been a lot of negative publicity about infant mistreatment in some daycare centers, prompting public concern and an increase in state regulations of such centers (Knox & Schacht, 2004). The new governmental restrictions, coupled with the difficulty in finding qualified people to work at these centers, placed financial hardships on the daycare industry, prompting many to close. A growing number of children of working mothers are receiving care from an in-home daycare or family-care home, which is a private family home providing care for about 12 children. These homes are also licensed, providing parents with a safe alternative to a daycare center.

Daycare can be a place where children learn socialization skills, as well as academic skills.

Quality care for children remains a challenge, particularly if there are no extended family members available to watch them. The family with a working mother and children younger than 15, paid an average of $107 each week for childcare expenses in 2005 (U. S. Census Bureau, 2008a). Since babies and toddlers are too young to report on their treatment (or mistreatment), it becomes very risky to leave children in the care of others. The perception of a lack of reliable childcare is a dilemma which pushes many mothers out of the workforce. A parent cannot do their job effectively if they are worried about their children.

Disadvantages of the Dual-Income Family

Over the last two decades, there has been an increasing divide between those families who work too many hours and those who do not work (Hochschild, 2007). According to Hochschild (2007), both extremes hurt families. While those who do not work contribute to the growing poverty level, those who work too much experience a "speed-up" in their work lives, such that balancing work and family no longer carries any meaning.

Dual-income families have been at the heart of much heated debate over the last 3 decades. Much research on this issue emerged during the 1980s, an era of conflict between working mothers and nonworking mothers. The debate continues today, with polarized positions citing either advantages or disadvantages of dual-income families. Many people have assumed that mothers working outside the home would be harmful to children. These assumptions biased much of the early research and have become part of the popular notion about dual-income families. The press has served to foster the idea of harm by depicting these families as time-crazed, with children starved for parental attention (Galinsky, 1999). For instance, the May, 2001 issue of National Review shows angry, crying children with a caption, "Thanks Mom!" The Case against Working Mothers (Lowry, 2001). Popular talk show host, Laura Schlessinger, equates maternal employment with child abuse and neglect, calling it a societal trend which "is a disaster to the lives and emotional well-being of the child" (Schlessinger, 2000 p. 7).

Despite the negative assumptions about the effects of mothers working outside the home, research has not confirmed the damage to children. Galinsky (1999) looked at the impact of work on the family through the eyes of the children. She found over 60% of the children felt they spent about the right amount of time with their parents, in contrast to 53% of parents who felt they didn't spend enough time with their children. About two thirds of the children felt their parents worked about the right amount of time. With regard to how successful these children thought their parents were at balancing work and family, nearly 75% felt their mothers were successful and 70% felt their fathers were successful in managing work and family life. The parents in contrast were much less positive than their children with only 34% stating they felt successful and 60% feeling somewhat successful in balancing work and family.

While this is a somewhat different picture of the children in dual-income families, these families are not without other challenges. In a recent study (Haddock & Rattenborg, 2003), couples were overwhelmingly positive about the benefits, but also realistic about some of the difficulties, which can be grouped into three main themes: 1) external, from non-family oriented employment; 2) internal, from conflicted feelings about working outside the home and; 3) sacrifices in their work for the well-being of the family. Successful couples make every effort to set boundaries on work and many identified a lack of support from their place of employment as a challenge to dual-employment. While parents expressed periodic feelings of guilt regarding their dual-worker status, they did not struggle with the overwhelming feelings of guilt previous researchers had reported. The last challenge couples reported was the need to make sacrifices to balance all the work and family activities. These sacrifices sometime involved one's career and sometimes couple and individual time.

In other research, Bianchi, Robinson, and Milkie (2006) found that married mothers felt they lacked time for themselves rather than time with their children, while fathers expressed more time shortages with their children. Not surprising, of all the working parents, single mothers expressed the most strain trying to balance work and family.

A related issue is the difficulty in managing time. Stress levels can rise when parents must try to juggle their schedules to accommodate the schedules of active children. Sickness or an emergency means one parent must leave work. Stress can spill over into the marital relationship. Often, a third party (grandparent or other extended family member) must fill in these gaps.

Advantages of the Dual-Income Family

Dual-income families face a number of challenges but there are also advantages. The obvious advantage is the increase in disposable family income. Haddock and Rattenborg (2003) and others (Haddock, Zimmerman, & Lyness, 2003) found that couples reported greater flexibility for both men and women when both spouses worked outside the home. The extra income provided security in the event one partner could not work. In addition, couples felt freer to take risks with their careers. In other words, a spouse was freer to take a lower-paying job with increased job satisfaction, or they could choose to start their own business.

© iStockphoto.com / DegasMM

Children in dual-career families benefit from the increased social interaction at daycare.

Role modeling egalitarian roles is another positive result in dual-career families (Haddock & Rattenborg, 2003). When both parents work, there tends to be more commitment to equality and avoidance of gender stereotypes. Children learn a more balanced approach to power within families by observing the respect and support parents demonstrate towards each other's schedule, work goals, and parenting obligations.

Having a career in addition to childrearing can be beneficial to the development of one's identity. This is especially true for middle-class wives who do not have to work to supplement the family's income. For this group of women, working outside the home increases their confidence and self-esteem (Amato, Booth, Johnson, & Rogers, 2007; Hochschild, 1997; Haddock & Rattenborg, 2003). Work provides a social outlet, as well as providing adult interaction in an intellectual environment for women who work outside the home (Haddock & Rattenborg, 2003). However, not all women benefit in the same way. Women who must help supplement income tend to experience less job satisfaction and feel their job interferes with their family life (Amato et al., 2007).

In Haddock and Rattenborg's study (2003), many parents said working gave them a better appreciation of home. It provided a separate realm of interest away from the family which led to better parenting and overall increased happiness. Many of these working parents suggested they had more patience and were better able to give their children their full attention. Parents also mentioned that, by not having their child dependent on them all day long, it was easier to accommodate themselves to their child's changing developmental needs.

Children in families who are successful in managing the work-family interface benefit in a number of ways. Haddock and Rattenborg (2003) found children benefited from the increased opportunities for social interaction with other children during daycare and were able to interact on a more intellectual level with adults. Children also displayed an increased sense of responsibility and independence, viewing family as a team in which they contribute. Increased finances place parents in a better position to be able to afford high quality childcare, which benefits their children intellectually, as well as the ability to provide a multitude of sports and other after-school activities, which benefit children's development.

The story on working parents is not black or white. There are advantages and disadvantages when there is a full-time parent in the home, as well as when both parents are in the work place. What is important is how a family works out the work-family dilemma so that every member of the family derives benefit.

© iStockphoto.com / sparkia

Children can benefit from the multitude of sports and after-school opportunities dual-career families can often provide.

Single-Parent Families and Work

The number of single parents continues to rise to the extent we are seeing a change from a two-parent family structure to a single-parent family structure (Dunifon & Kowaleski-Jones, 2002). This shift is very prevalent in African-American families, accounting for over half of all African-American families (McCreary & Dancy, 2004). In African-American families, the kinship support common in African-American culture tends to mediate some of the disadvantages for these families, which may make them better off than their white counterparts (Durr & Hill, 2006).

As is easily imaginable, single working parents often have a more difficult time balancing work and family. Statistics suggest single mothers, in comparison to their married counterparts, tend to have less education, bear children at younger ages, and have fewer financial resources (Martin, 2000). These situations all complicate the work opportunities single parents experience. Children in single-parent families not only have fewer financial resources, but also have access to only one parent. Studies have shown single working mothers report less contentment with the time they have to devote to their children, and feel they have made more sacrifices in their family and personal lives for work than employed married mothers (Bianchi, Robinson, & Milkie, 2006). Bianchi also found that in contrast to married mothers, whose time spent doing housework has decreased by nearly half since the 1950s, the amount of house work performed by single mothers has remained essentially unchanged, nearly equal to that of married mothers. This equates to about

17 hours per week for both married and single mothers (Bianchi et al., 2006). In the same study, single mothers were found to be only slightly more stressed trying to balance work and family than either employed mothers or fathers. This could be a result of the kin network support or the increased household chores performed by older children in single-parent homes. (Romich, 2007).

Mario Tama / Getty Images News / Getty Images

African-American families are more than twice as likely to experience unemployment.

Unemployment

So far in this chapter we have been looking at families trying to balance work and family life. What about the family experiencing unemployment?

Unemployment increases the risk of poverty, contributes to income inequality, and creates a series of debilitating social effects on the unemployed person and their family (Saunders, 2002). With the current unemployment rate at 9.5%, 3.2% greater than the 10 year high of 6.3% in 2003, many American families are faced with involuntary job loss (U.S. Bureau of Labor Statistics, 2009). The effects of unemployment on all families are devastating but not all families are affected equally. Black families are more than twice as likely to face unemployment than white families (Bucks, Kennickell, & Moore, 2006), and more likely to fall from professional or managerial positions than are white employees (Kalil & DeLeire, 2002).

Unemployment negatively affects families' economic security (Kalil & DeLeire, 2002). This is reflected in how families spend money on necessities such as food, clothing, and shelter. Families may move to less expensive housing and be forced to rely on public assistance. Research has shown unemployment has negative physical and emotional health consequences (Burgard, Brand, & House, 2007; Saunders, 2002; Stack & Wasserman, 2007), and increases the likelihood of divorce (Kalil & DeLeire, 2002; Lewin, 2005).

Children are also affected by unemployment. When parents are unemployed, children's wellbeing is diminished, which can lower their academic achievement. The stress of unemployment can inhibit parents' warmth and increase inconsistent, disengaged parenting behaviors toward their children resulting in poorer child adjustment (Kalil & DeLeire, 2002).

In our current fragile economy, it appears an increasing number of families will be affected by unemployment. In the next chapter we will discuss the importance of families having some savings to help offset the financial impact of temporary joblessness.

Strategies for Balancing Work and Family

While most mothers today work outside the home, their income is no longer considered "extra" money to spend on luxuries. Many families now depend on the income of both parents just to pay for basic necessities. A growing number of families are headed by single parents who must work to support their families. What was a debate, in the 1970s and 1980s, over the impact of women working outside the home has subsided into a discussion of how to best manage the situation. Haddock, Zimba, Zimmerman and Current (2001) investigated couples with children who were successfully managing work and family. They found the following 10 strategies for managing the work-family dilemma.

Value Family

Maintaining a commitment to family should be the highest priority. This needs to be more than lip service—it must include action, as families plan their daily life activities. Families need to proactively schedule time together, create rituals, and make memories with the entire family.

The second priority is an emphasis on family happiness over professional responsibilities and advancement. To honor family happiness, parents may have to limit work hours, sacrifice career advancement, or make career changes to keep the family as the number one priority.

Strive for Partnership

Equality and partnership between the couple can be critical to the success of a dual-income family. While equality between spouses can vary, successful couples in this study had a high degree of equality. Three main components of marital equality were found to be important: the division of household labor, equal input into decisions and making decisions together, and functioning as interpersonal partners who respect, appreciate, and support each other.

Derive Meaning from Work

This can be an important part of the success in dual-income families. Spouses need to sense enjoyment and purpose from their professional pursuits. This creates energy and enthusiasm, which limits work related fatigue and burnout.

Maintain Work Boundaries

When couples maintain the family as priority, it will guide their decisions about how much effort to expend, and what work position would best support this priority. It is important for couples to maintain control over their work, rather than allowing their work to maintain control over them. There should be a conscious concerted effort to set clear boundaries on work and professional commitments.

Focus and Produce at Work

While work-related boundaries are important, it is also important to be productive while at work. Being productive at work can also make it easier to negotiate support from employers regarding limiting work hours. It is important to learn that when you are at work, you are at work, and when you are at home, you are at home.

Prioritize Family Fun

Despite busy schedules, it is important to schedule family fun time. This allows families to stay connected, relax, and enjoy each other, which reduces the stress of managing multiple responsibilities. Having a sense of humor and the ability to laugh at life promotes a family atmosphere of fun.

Take Pride in Dual Earning

It is important to believe dual earning is positive for all members of the family. Rejecting societal messages regarding working parents is an important part of this. Couples in the study did not feel guilty about not spending every minute engaging their children in quality time because they felt they had a good balance of time with their children, time in household chores, and time together as a couple.

Live Simply

Simplifying life can be beneficial in balancing work and family. This can be accomplished in several ways. One, it is important to restrict those activities which limit family time, such as television and extracurricular activities. Second, it is important to control spending so life is not full of unnecessary expenses. Third, it is important to have high, but realistic, expectations to simplify life and manage the responsibilities of a dual-career family.

Make Decisions Proactively

It is important to maintain control of life and decision making, rather than allowing the pace of life to dictate what happens. Having a clear sense of priorities can be a guide for decisions regarding marriage, children, family, and career. It is important for both spouses to be involved in decision making and maintain open communication between each other. It is also important to keep the big picture in sight. This provides a sense of direction for life and facilitates decision making.

Value Time

Awareness of the value of time, and viewing it as a window of opportunity, can assist in creating balance and happiness in the family. Viewing time as a sacred commodity allows couples to protect and choose wisely how to use time. While remaining conscious of time, it is important to live in the moment, making the most of every day.

A Christian Perspective

Over the course of the past century, much of the balancing act between work and family has centered on power struggles. Most often, research indicates the primary struggle as occurring between husbands and wives. As wives contribute more income to their families, their bargaining power increases. Men today contribute more help with childcare and domestic duties than previous generations of men. Still, many women experience frustration that they continue to perform the lion's share of these duties. Household duties can sometimes detract from more important concerns, such as quality time with family, family devotions, church activities, and special events. Parents need to focus on activities which will endure, rather than on those which are all products of vanity. Showing off a beautiful house is not nearly as important as working to be the family God calls us to be.

Much of modern family history has occurred in the shadow of women demanding "equal power." The Balswicks

(1999) note equal power often becomes no power for anyone. Such an "every person for him- or herself" environment becomes ultimately unfulfilling for all family members.

Marriage is not about the husband having more power, or the wife having equal power. A Christian marriage acknowledges God has the power. The husband and wife are servants—to God and to one another. Egalitarian marriage is not about *his* power or *her* power, but about *God's* power. According to the Balswicks (1999), there is a balance of power in a healthy home. It is an empowering model of spouses building each other up, valuing, and respecting each other, rather than dominance.

To achieve a Christian marriage, the couple has to get *beyond* power. They must seek *equity* rather than *equality.* Equity is about justice—what is fair and good. Equal power actually may not be equitable. God did not create men and women exactly the same. Only the wife can get pregnant, give birth, and nurse a baby. If she chooses to stay home to care for the baby, she gives up her ability to add income to the family. She might not be viewed as *equal* to her husband as this decision relates to income. And yet, this arrangement may be considered very *equitable*, because it affirms the way God created her. She should not feel as if she has less power in the relationship because she works all day for less (or no) pay.

Ephesians 5:21 says, "Submit to one another out of reverence for Christ." As husband and wife submit themselves to one another out of reverence for Christ, they allow God to have total power in their relationship. They put an end to the game of who does more work, who earns more, and who has more power. By getting beyond the cultural game of power, they realize true fulfillment in serving one another.

Summary

One of the most dramatic changes to family structure in the last century has been the entrance of mothers into the workforce. This continues to be one of the greatest challenges facing the contemporary family.

After World War II, it became more commonplace for married women to work outside the home as teachers, nurses, secretaries, waitresses, and stewardesses (flight attendants). Once they began to have children, however, they were expected to quit their jobs and devote their time to homemaking and childcare. The mid-1960s introduced the first generation of women who chose to work outside the home, as well as raise a family. Wives often became "superwomen," trying to excel at home and in the workplace. The women's revolution, close on the heels of the Equal Pay Act, bolstered the value of women's employment. In the 1980s a growing backlash movement caused conflict between women who worked outside the home and those who did not. The second generation of women who worked outside the home challenged the superwoman notion and began to accommodate career with family—or chose to become stay-at-home moms.

Today first- and second-generation women who work outside the home (along with some third-generation women who work outside the home) coexist in a culture which sees many different ways to accommodate work and family. More husbands are involved in sharing household chores and childcare, but women still do the bulk of the housework.

Dual-income families impact children—in both positive and negative ways. Much depends on how parents deal with the extra income and extra demands. Successful strategies shun overindulging children with luxuries the parent didn't have as a child. Many families are able to delegate responsibility for chores, so that everyone contributes to the smooth functioning of the family. Other families focus on what is really important, to help streamline household duties.

A Christian perspective moves beyond power struggles to see God as the ultimate power in the family. As family members practice mutual submission—to God and to one another—they become more of what God created them to be.

Questions for Thought

1. Why would economics (working for pay) have a great impact on a marriage?

2. Discuss strategies to juggle career and family. What other strategies would you suggest, in addition to those discussed in this chapter?

3. Use the Bible to discuss a Christian strategy to juggle career and family.

4. Discuss the advantages and disadvantages of dual-income families.

Resources

Books:

Her Story: A Timeline of the Women Who Changed America by Charlotte S. Waisman and Jill S. Tietjen. (Collins, 2008)

Movies:

Baby Boom, (PG). DVD .Comedy about a female executive who unexpectedly becomes a mom and tries to integrate the roles.

Waging a Living, (NR). Docudrama which looks at America's working poor.

Websites:

1. *News stories from ABC—Can working mothers have it all?* http://www.abcnews.go.com/2020/LifeStages/story?id=2641588&page=1 (accessed June 23, 2009)
2. *Working Moms: Help!* http://abcnews.go.com/Video/playerIndex?id=2649809 (accessed June 23, 2009)
3. *What to look for in a daycare* by American Academy of family physicians: http://familydoctor.org/online/famdocen/home/children/parents/infants/030.html

Time, Energy, and Money

10

Managing Family Resources

For the love of money is the root of all kinds of evil. And some people, craving money, have wandered from the true faith and pierced themselves with many sorrows.
—1 Timothy 6:10 NLT

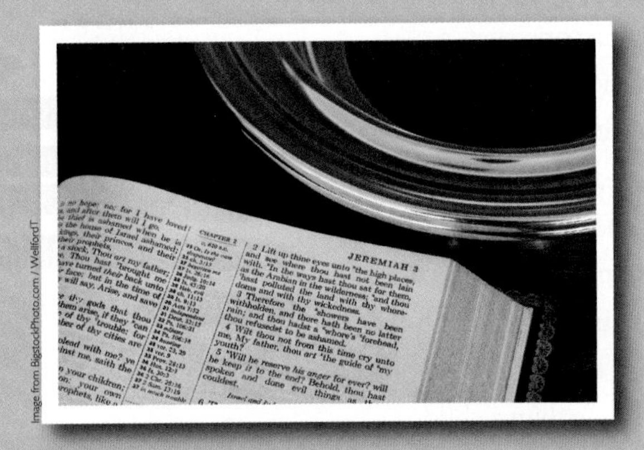
Image from BigstockPhoto.com / WellfordT

Compared to most of the world's societies, citizens of the United States enjoy unbelievable wealth and resources. Americans often live in such a way that tells others we think our resources are limitless. However, resources are finite things for which we are accountable. How a nation uses and maintains its resources is largely determined by its priorities. In the same way, families determine how to use their resources based on their family values and priorities.

When we think of family resources, we usually think of money. Money is only part of the picture. Family resources also include issues related to time and energy. In this chapter, we will examine how families manage time as it relates to the work-family interface, how they manage their energy levels to thwart the stress of busy lifestyles, and how they manage their financial situations. We also will give helpful suggestions for achieving financial peace, as well as offer a Christian perspective on living the life of a good steward.

Families and Time

Time as a Social Construct

What time is it? A simple question, isn't it? We're not usually shy about asking even a stranger this question. But what does time have to do with managing family resources? It might help to look at time as it relates to navigating the complex waters of culture.

Time is essentially a social construct. That means it has different meanings in different circumstances. That is not to say time is an arbitrary social construct. A country cannot just decide to create its own interpretation of what time it is at a given moment. Certain international standards prevent that kind of chaos. However, what significance time has can vary immensely. A man white-knuckling through traffic to get his pregnant wife to the hospital has a different awareness of time than a child quietly playing in a sandbox.

Every culture and society constructs its own meaning of time, passing its temporal awareness from one generation to the next. For instance, American, Japanese, and many European cultures tend to view time as quantitative and linear. These cultures measure time in units which reflect forward movement. Thus, time becomes a commodity ("time is money") which can be bought ("buying" time), spent ("spending" time), or wasted ("wasting" time). Time is logical, sequential, and oriented to the present. This approach to time is called monochronic, meaning time (*chronos*) has a singular (*mono*) meaning. This linear approach is structured and concrete, most often arranged in a way which is sequential ("math class first, then study hall"). In a monochronic society, people are said to be "clock-bound," and businesses stress efficiency and time management.

Other cultures view time differently. In some Asian cultures, as well as Native-American and Latin-American cultures, time has a different "feel," a sense of unlimited continuity. Time does not march forward in measured units, but rather focuses around events. This approach to time is called polychronic, which means time holds multiple (*poly*) meanings. In this respect, it is cyclical or circular ("what goes around, comes

Our attitude toward time can have profound impact on marriage.

around"; the "circle of life"). Polychronic cultures tend to view time as nonlinear; thus, people in these cultures tend to savor the experience of the event before moving on to another event. Because time is more fluid, matching specific activities with specific time periods is not a priority. The event is the priority. For example, weddings scheduled for one or two o'clock rarely start before five or six, when all the guests have arrived.

Sidebar 10.1 illustrates how differences in time perception can result in a clash between cultures.

People use time as a way to communicate with one another. How often have you heard that someone is always "fashionably late"? Others like to arrive early and "beat others to the punch." You might be a "night owl," while someone else is an "early bird." These are ways people use time as a statement of identity. Making someone wait nervously for an interview might be an exercise of time as a statement of power. Arriving early for a date could be interpreted as a statement of attraction.

Our attitudes about time are both innate and learned, and they affect how we behave. Differing attitudes toward time can have a profound impact on marriages and families. Much of the friction between spouses can be traced to different attitudes toward time: as well, time issues can foster friction between parents and their children. Hochschild (2007) suggests there are twin processes which exist—the pull toward work and the pull towards the family. It is in an emotional culture that this time squeeze in families must be resolved or conflict ensues, both between spouses and between parents and children. This conflict with time has real consequences. It affects career attainment, children,

Sidebar 10.1
A Cultural Clash

Recently, a noted North American theologian and Bible college professor was asked to give the commencement address at a Bible college in the Philippines. While he was in the country, he agreed to preach at a local Filipino church on Sunday at 9 a.m. On Sunday morning, he was ready an hour early and anxious to leave. His host told him that he did not need to arrive until 9 because the doors would still be locked. By 8:30, he was pacing the floor, so his host agreed to take him to the church. He arrived at 8:50, finding the doors still locked. At 9 someone arrived and unlocked the doors. At 9:15 the regular pastor arrived and greeted the visiting professor. At the same time, the worship team arrived and began to practice. By 9:30, they were ready to start the service.

The frustrated professor left the Philippines, wondering how the Filipino churches could put up with such inefficiency. He was unable to grasp that arriving on time for anything in the Philippines was considered rude—your host might not be ready and would be embarrassed by your punctual arrival. Fifteen minutes to a couple of hours late, depending on the event, was considered normal. You were not considered to be late unless you arrived *after* an event had started.

Since the Filipino culture is a contextual, relational culture, the custom is to wait until everyone is present before starting an event. Thus, people are rarely late.

Source: Author's personal experience

Image from BigstockPhoto.com / Mcininch

Families operate in a highly structured world of scheduled activities making family time difficult to find.

family life for both men and women, marital satisfaction and even health. (Friedman & Greenhaus, 2000; Gerson, 2007; Hochschild, 2007; Rotondo, Carlson, & Kincaid, 2003).

America's Time Crunch

Families also create their own sense of time. Quality family time in America often seems to be a sentimentalized quest. This quest too frequently clashes with actual experience, creating conflict and a sense of failure in trying to meet a deeply felt obligation. The failure to fulfill the sentimentalized idea of family time leads to disillusionment and guilt in families (Daly, 2001). This "idealized" family has ample, flexible, quiet time for a variety of family activities. The typical family time in America, however, is limited by the clock.

The reality is families operate in a highly structured world of work schedules, school schedules, after-school activities, community obligations, and church functions. Is it any wonder families feel overwhelmed and out of touch with time?

According to Families and Work Institute's 2002 National Study of the Changing Workforce (NSCW) (Galinsky, Bond, & Hill, 2002):

- 67% of employed parents said they didn't have enough time with their children, about the same proportion as 10 years ago.
- 63% of married employees said they didn't have enough time with their husbands or wives, up from 50% in 1992.
- 55% of all employees said they didn't have enough time for themselves.

What has changed? Today's families are busy. Their overloaded lifestyles mean they face unparalleled pressures. Time itself has not changed over the course of history—a day still contains 24 hours, and only 24 hours. What has changed is how families use time. More often than not, both parents are employed outside the home, working long hours and sometimes weekends. Because most parents love their children, they often push their own individual needs to the back burner in order to devote more time to their

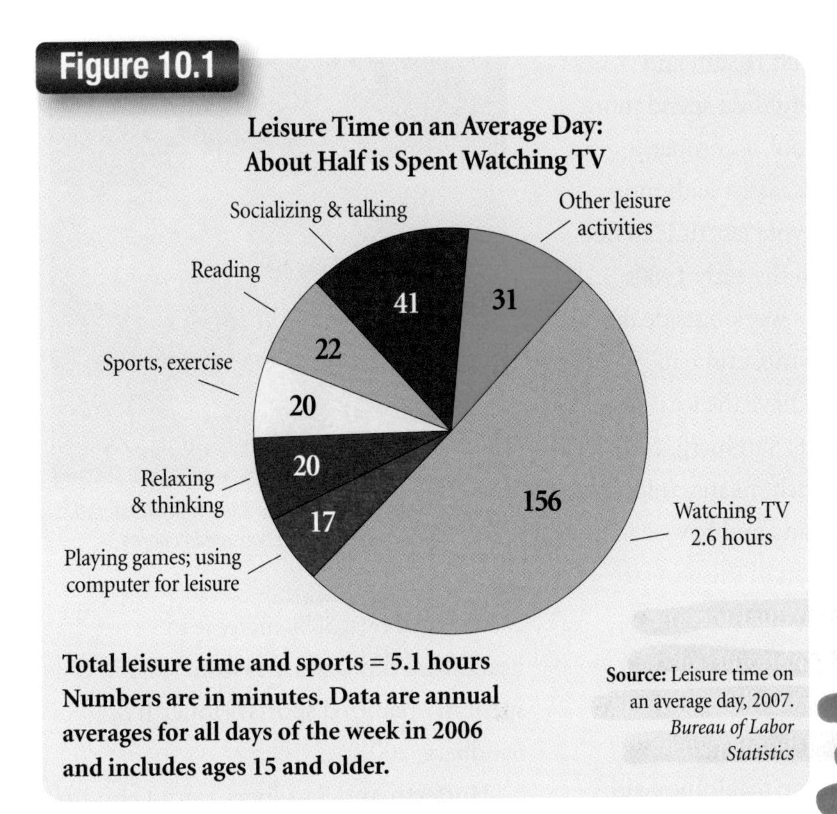

Total leisure time and sports = 5.1 hours
Numbers are in minutes. Data are annual averages for all days of the week in 2006 and includes ages 15 and older.

Source: Leisure time on an average day, 2007. *Bureau of Labor Statistics*

parenting responsibilities (Daly, 2001). Doherty (2001) suggests this competition for parental time takes precedence over their marital relationship. He stresses the need for couples to communicate their feelings about work, children, and the household, exerting the effort necessary to do something they mutually enjoy. While most parents already realize this, putting principles into practice can be very challenging.

The amount of time considered to be "family time" has remained the same over the course of several years. In 2002, parents with children under the age of 18 averaged 44 hours per week of paid work, with fathers averaging 48.3 hours, and mothers averaging 39.6 hours (Galinsky, Bond, & Hill, 2002). If parents are working more hours than in the past, how can they still have the same amount of family time? The answer is found in what parents and children are sacrificing in other areas, as well as in how they are defining "family time." Much of family time today is filled with structured child activities and household chores. Figure 10.1 illustrates how leisure time is spent by a typical individual.

In the previous chapter, we noted that, in 2004, a wife with no children averaged 28.2 hours per week in household chores, while a husband with no children averaged 18.5 hours per week. With two children in the home, the woman averaged 51.2 hours per week to the man's 23.8 hours (Parkman, 2004).

Figure 10.2 demonstrates the change in children's weekly time expenditures between 1981 and 1997 and between1997 and 2002.

Children's activities add greatly to the whirlwind pace that family's experience. According to research supported by the

National Institute of Child Health and Human Development, children spend more time in daycare and school, accompany parents on more errands, assist with more household tasks, and devote less time to free play than children did in the early 1980s. Children whose mothers work outside the home tend to spend the most time in daycare and school, and have the least free time for play (Hofferth & Sandberg, 2001).

The family time crunch means children spend 10% less time eating and have 8% less free time for play than in the past (see Figure 10.2). Children in dual-income families and single-parent homes also experience less sleep than children who live in a home with a stay-at-home parent. Children who spend more mealtimes with family and who get enough sleep, exhibit fewer behavior problems than children who don't. The time demands on children are exacerbated by a 50% increase in homework time, and a 44% increase in time spent in organized sports (Hofferth & Sandberg, 2001).

Image from BigstockPhoto.com / mandygodbehear

Much family time today is filled with structured child activities and household chores.

Hofferth and Sandberg found children in 1997 spent an average of 1.3 hours per week reading, up 19 minutes from 1981. Children who read more achieve higher

Figure 10.2

Children's Weekly Time Expenditures

	1981	1997	Change	2002	Change
School	21hr 22min	29hr 22min	8hr	31hr 12min	1hr 50min
Play	15hr 54min	12hr 58min	2hr 56min	8hr 12min	4hr 46min
TV	15hr 12min	13hr 9min	2hr 3min	14hr 30min	1hr 21min
Reading	57min	1hr 16min	19min	1hour 30min	14min
Meals	9hr 8min	8hr 18min	50min	7hr 6min	1hr 12min
Sports	2hr 20min	5hr 17min	2hr 57min	3hr 6min	2hr 11min
Homework	1hr 25min	2hr 7min	42min	4hr 6min	1hr 59min
Chores	2hr 27min	5hr 39min	3hr 12min	6hr	2hr 48min

Source: Hofferth and Sandberg 2001; Bianchi, Robinson and Milkie 2006.

scores in school than children who do not read, or who read very little. Children of educated parents tend to spend more time reading and less time watching television than children of less-educated parents. In contrast, children who spent 13 hours a week or more watching television scored lower in math and verbal achievement tests than other children (Hofferth & Sandberg, 2001).

Families and Energy

As newlyweds, a husband and wife generally are free to come and go without regard for anyone else but themselves. If they decide to run out at 10 p.m. for pizza, they grab their jackets and head for their favorite pizza place.

Once they begin to have children, the scenario changes—often dramatically. Children require structure, schedules, and supervision. No more spontaneous 10 p.m. pizza runs (unless the pizza is delivered), because the kids have to be in bed by 8:30.

The Work-Family Interface

As children get older, the schedules become more complicated. In chapter 9, we looked at how families struggle to balance work and home responsibilities. After work, a father may find himself racing to pick up Tommy, who is already late for soccer practice, then calling his wife to see if she will have enough time after Mindy's dentist appointment to pick up Dylan, who was supposed to get a ride with a friend after the speech team meeting, but is now stranded because the friend got sick and left early.

Once the after-school activities are over and everyone is home—and that is not to say everyone arrives at the same time—parents continue in high gear with meal preparation and cleanup, homework supervision, bath time, bedtime rituals, and other household activities. It takes energy to raise a family. Family energy is closely related to family time. When families are stressed by the many demands on their time, the quality of their time together suffers.

Conflict. Because family boundaries are more permeable than work boundaries, the demands of work often intrude more on family time than the other way around (Eagle, Miles, & Icenogle, 1997; Gerson & Jacobs, 2007; Rotondo, Carlson, & Kincaid,

Image from BigstockPhoto.com / amysuem

As children get older, schedules become more complicated which depletes family energy.

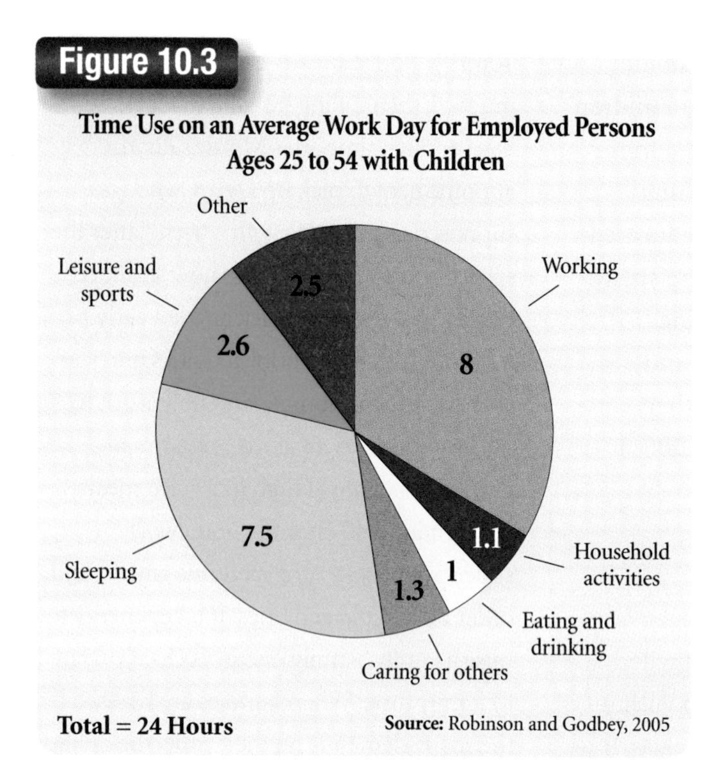

2003; Friedman & Greenhaus, 2000). For both women and men, satisfying work can benefit their relationship with their children and enhance their children's developmental outcomes (Daly, 2004). Further illustrating the work-family connection, for both men and women, positive marital satisfaction is related to higher job satisfaction, just as marital discord is related to declines in job satisfaction (Rogers & May, 2003). Figure 10.3 demonstrates time use on an average workday.

More often than not, however, conflict characterizes the work-family relationship. Our perception of the conflict between our work and our family affects the work-family interface. Thus, how we think about our work-family conflict determines the amount of conflict we experience. This includes how we achieve role balance in the work-family relationship, and how work and family enhance our role experiences. The extent of the social support the family receives, along with the family's own coping resources, can result in either work-family role strain or work-family role ease (Voydanoff, 2002).

Role Theory. To understand the work-family interface, we must look at both work stress and family stress. Role theory explains the experience of ambiguity and/or conflict within a role can lead to undesirable effects on an individual. Performing multiple roles can lead to personal conflict because the person has difficulty performing each role successfully. This conflict is due to lack of energy, incompatible behaviors among roles, and conflicting demands on time (Kahn et al., 1964).

Conservation of Energy Theory. The conservation of energy theory also helps to explain the work-family interface. This theory suggests families seek to acquire and maintain resources. Resources include the quality and length of the marriage; personal characteristics, such as self-esteem, which

© Fotosearch

Social support from other family members can buffer work-family stress.

acts as a buffer against stress; and energy resources, such as time, money, and knowledge to acquire additional resources. According to this theory, then, stress is the response to a loss of resources, the threat of a loss of resources, or a lack of expected gain in resources (Hobfoll, 1989). It is interesting to note recent research suggests that altruism, or selfless giving of yourself, not just to your family but to others as well, has been associated with living longer, happier lives, and an increased sense of well-being, (Post, 2007; Post, Neimark, & Moss, 2007). An increased sense of well-being decreases our stress level, thus increasing our energy resources.

The Effects of Stress

Stress is a commonly reported cause of headaches and sleep difficulties. It can make us vulnerable to illnesses such as colds, flu, ulcers, allergies, high blood pressure, and even heart attacks. Stress drains our energy. Long-term stress invariably leads to severe fatigue. In extreme cases, it results in depression, which has a profound effect on the entire family (Lundberg, 2005; Nakajima, 1994; Page, 1999).

Fatigue is a normal and important response to physical exertion, emotional stress, boredom, lack of sleep, and physical illness. Sleep, good nutrition, and a low-stress environment usually relieve fatigue. However, families are anything but low-stress environments. In fact, while families are supposed to be a safe haven from the world, they often are one of the major causes of stress. Key sources of family stress include conflicts between spouses, parenting

Image from BigstockPhoto.com / Velkroe

Men are participating more in child care and are therefore dealing with the additional stress of too many demands and too little time.

SIDEBAR 10.2
Risking It All

(This is a true story based on a client's experience.)

The couple came in for marriage counseling. The wife had just discovered that her husband had taken $60,000 of their retirement savings and invested it in some very high-risk investments without her knowledge. He had lost it all.

She obviously was furious. Her salary was their primary income. Thus, in actuality, it was the money she had worked so hard for. She tried for a while to make the marriage work. The fact that he had concealed this from her, and then lied to her when she questioned him, made it difficult.

The final straw came the day she learned he had cashed in their mutual funds. She was livid. After he had depleted their savings, he had the nerve to cash in their mutual funds! When he was questioned, he admitted to playing the stock market again. He had become obsessed with it over the years. When the whole story unraveled, he admitted to taking smaller amounts of money even earlier in their marriage. The amounts had increased over the years. Since she trusted him, she had let him manage the money—never having a reason to question him. Or so she thought.

This story has a sad ending. Her faith and trust in him was destroyed, and she ended the marriage. She is now single and raising their two teenage children, with only about 15 years left to save for retirement. He continues to play the stock market, thinking he will strike it rich someday, and then maybe she will come back to him. His greed and get-rich-quick mentality cost him his marriage and his family. And it cost his family the benefit of a husband and a father.

Source: Author

responsibilities, financial worries, over-scheduled calendars, and behavior problems in children. In addition, major transitions tend to increase family stress. These include job or school changes, loss of a job, family moves, the addition of new family members (birth or adoption), parent-child problems, or deaths of loved ones.

Stress in Men. Evidence suggests men's participation in family activities is increasing (Daly & Hawkins, 2005; Pleck, 1999). Historically, nurturing and childcare has been the domain of women; therefore, mothers and women caretakers experience much social and cultural support. As more men participate in these activities, they often find themselves in a largely private struggle to accommodate increasing family responsibilities with their typical male roles. Social and cultural support for them has been slow to keep pace. This is reminiscent of what working women experienced when first trying to break through the "glass ceiling." Their support network was minimal. Fathers now have to deal with the stress resulting from too many demands, too little time, and too many "to do" lists which once were thought to be a woman's domain (Daly & Hawkins, 2005).

Work Stress. The prevalence of stress in today's working environment has a direct impact on families. One-fourth of employees view their jobs as the number-one stressor in their lives (Employee burnout, 1991/1999). Problems at work are more strongly associated with health complaints than are any other life stressors—even more than financial problems or family problems (U.S. Department of Health and Human Services, n.d.; Rotondo, Carlson, & Kincaid, 2003). Work stress is related to a variety of occupational variables:

- Excessive workload demands: long hours, too many responsibilities, hectic pace, mundane tasks, or a lack of control
- Working conditions: infrequent rest breaks, inadequate light or ventilation, or dangerous conditions
- Management styles: conflicting expectations, poor communication, or lack of support from peers and supervisors
- Career concerns: job insecurity, lack of advancement potential, or rapid change for which employees are unprepared
- Hostile environment: mistreatment or workplace discrimination

Any of these variables can lead to a serious loss of personal energy and motivation for work and leisure (Feagin, Early, & McKinney, 2001). Work stress and financial stress take a heavy toll on families. Sidebar 10.2 demonstrates an example of how financial stress can lead to the breakup of a family.

Families and Money

A key area of conflict in families is related to money. Ninety-five percent of couples argue about money-related topics. Fifty-five percent of people report they always or sometimes worry about money (Statistics, 2008). Often the biggest problem is not a lack of money, but how a family spends it. Sidebar 10.2 looks at the tragic story of one couples divorce because of how money was used.

The current state of the family economy is bleak. If we were to point to one primary cause of this situation, it would be the debt load most Americans carry. See Sidebar 10.3. Sadly, Americans have been conditioned to believe debt is a normal part of life. Sidebar 10.4 illustrates the mistake a newlywed couple made in how they spent their money.

Image from BigstockPhoto.com / jas0420

Arguments about money occur with 95% of couples on a regular basis and 55% report they always or sometimes worry about money.

SIDEBAR 10.3

Debt has become big business since the late 1960s when credit cards were introduced. Consider these statistics:

- 70% of Americans are living from paycheck to paycheck.
- The median income in 2001 for all families was $39,900.
- The average American spends $1.22 for every dollar earned.
- The personal saving rate in America is 3.6%, down from 8.7% in 2000.
- 62% of all American households don't save or don't save regularly.
- Household net worth is less than $15,000 (excluding equity of the house).
- Typical non-mortgage household debt is $38,000 or more.
- Only 44% of Americans are preparing fro retirement; 62% will retire with an income less than $10,000 per year.

Source: Statistics. 2008

How American Families Spend Their Money

As bleak as this picture looks, it doesn't have to be this way. Prevention is the key. Managing family resources well, particularly financial resources, means the family must live within its means. They must learn to differentiate between "needs" and "wants," and find the courage to say no to extraneous expenses. The ability to budget money can prevent a family from becoming a statistic.

Living Expenses 1. Figure 10.4 details a sample list of expenses for a Midwestern city family of three: father, mother, and one child.

SIDEBAR 10.4
A Very Costly Lesson

Tim and I got married 3 years ago. We both had good jobs, but we also had two car payments and were trying to pay off our student loans. Tim was working on paying off some credit cards, too.

Like all newlyweds, we wanted our apartment to look nice. Tim fell in love with this great leather couch at the furniture store, but we knew we couldn't afford it. Later that day, I saw an ad for a Rent-to-Own store near us. When we went to see what they had, we saw a leather couch just like the one Tim wanted. I found the dining room table of my dreams. The store made it sound so easy—it would cost just $45 a week. We could do that. No problem! They delivered our furniture the next day.

Everything seemed great. Then I got sick and couldn't work for 2 weeks. Tim took over the household chores while I recovered. He forgot to make the Rent-to-Own payment one week, but we made it up the next week. We continued to pay promptly and were excited about going in with our final payment. The furniture would finally be ours. On the day we walked in with our last payment, the clerk told us someone would be by the next day to take our furniture back to the store. We were aghast! We had just paid it off! What did they mean by saying it wasn't ours?

The salesperson had been so nice when we first rented the furniture, but now everyone we talked to was just plain nasty. The clerk pulled out our contract. In the fine print, it said that missing a payment would void the rent-to-own contract and would render it as a rental contract only. We tried to argue, but it was no use. We had signed the contract.

We have learned to read *everything* in a contract before signing it. If we had just waited until we could afford them, we could have bought the leather couch and dining room table at the furniture store—and this terrible waste of our money would have never happened. As it turned out, we learned a very costly lesson. I hope you can learn from our mistakes.

—Anonymous

Figure 10.4

Living Expenses for a Midwestern City Family of Three: Two Parents and One Child

Monthly housing	$655
Monthly food	$448
Monthly child care	$618
Monthly transportation	$358
Monthly health care	$276
Other monthly necessities	$298
Monthly taxes	$369
Monthly total	$3,022
Annual total	$36,264

Source: Basic family budget calculator 2005.

Figure 10.5

Living Expenses for Single Parent Making Minimum Wage, Raising Two Children

Monthly housing	$805
Monthly food	$427
Monthly child care	$620
Monthly transportation	$416
Monthly health care	$68
Other monthly necessities	$162
Monthly total	$2,498
Annual total	$29,976

Source: Children's Defense Fund 2005.

The family income in Figure 10.4 is $36,264, requiring $697.38 per week ($17/hour). Overall, 29.7% of Americans have incomes below basic family budget levels required to meet their basic expenses (Allegretto, 2005).

Living Expenses 2. Now let's look at Figure 10.5, which lists the living expenses of a single parent who makes minimum wage and is raising two children.

Figure 10.5 illustrates a family needing roughly $30,000 per year just to meet its necessary expenses. This family's total income, based on the federal minimum wage, is $10,716. That is $19,000 below their expenses and $5,374 below the 2005 federal poverty level of $16,090 for a family of three (Department of Health and Human Services, 2005).

Poverty is a growing problem in the United States. The 2004 poverty rate climbed for the fourth consecutive year to 12.7% or 37 million people (Children's Defense Fund, 2007) and dropped slightly in 2006 to 12.3% (U.S. Census Bureau, 2007a). That means approximately 1 out of every 6 Americans lives below the poverty line and is unable to cover even basic expenses.

Image from BigstockPhoto.com / belinda_bw

One out of every 6 Americans lives below the poverty line and is unable to cover their basic expenses.

Figure 10.6

Children's Weekly Time Expenditures

Income	Total	Housing	Food	Trans-portation	Clothes	Health	Childcare/School	Misc.
Up to $41,700								
Age 3–5	$7,210	$2,650	$1,090	$800	$340	$500	$1,150	$680
Age 12–14	$8,070	$2,580	$1,770	$1,130	$710	$640	$290	$950
$41,700–$70,200								
Age 3–5	$10,120	$3,600	$1,350	$1,200	$400	$660	$1,860	$1,050
Age 12–14	$10,640	$3,520	$2,050	$1,540	$830	$820	$570	$1,310
Over $70,200								
Age 3–5	$14,960	$5,730	$1,760	$1,690	$530	$760	$2,750	$1,740
Age 12–14	$15,270	$5,660	$2,580	$2,030	$1,040	$940	$1,010	$2,010

Source: Hofferth and Sandberg 2001; Bianchi, Robinson and Milkie 2006.

The Cost of Raising Children

While most often children are a welcome addition to the family, they also require great expenditures of time, energy—and money. The cost of raising children is high, as illustrated in Figure 10.6. Housing represents the largest proportion of childrearing expenses (33–37%).The second biggest expense is food (15–20%).

Variations occur according to household income level and the age of the children. Younger children tend to be less expensive than older children. According to the USDA, the current cost per year of raising a child varies from $9,840 to $10,900 for a middle-income, two-parent family with two children (Lino, 2005). If we refer back to Figures 10.4 and 10.5, we will see childcare is the second biggest expense (housing is the biggest expense) for low- and middle-income families. Particularly in the case of those living at or below poverty level, this leaves little for other necessary expenses.

Families and Sound Finances

How do families achieve financial balance? How can husbands and wives tell if their financial decisions are sound? How can families avoid the quagmire of too much debt? We offer the following suggestions to help you to manage your financial resources wisely.

Get an Education

The best first step you'll ever make in achieving your financial goals is to get an education. Stay in school. If at all possible, strive to attain an academic degree. In 2005, college graduates with teaching and liberal arts degrees earned an average of $44,350 a year. People with advanced degrees earned an average of $74,602 compared to those with a bachelor's degree who averaged $51,286. People with a high school diploma averaged $18,734. (U.S. Census Bureau, 2005a).

Image from BigstockPhoto.com / yakup

One of the best ways to achieve your financial goals is by getting a college education.

Make and Stick to a Budget

Many people don't take the time to budget their financial resources. Others feel a budget is too "confining" or "controlling." The exact opposite is true. Budgets put families in control of their money. If a large company were foolish enough to operate without a budget—without controls on spending and without accountability measures—it would not stay in business very long. Operating without a budget is just as foolish for families; yet less than 30% of families follow a written monthly budget to manage household finances (Statistics, 2008). While the number of bankruptcies decreased 61% in the 12 month period ending March 31, 2007, it is not really representative of the financial problems of American families (Bankruptcy, 2007). The number of family bankruptcies increased 12.8% in the previous 12 month period ending March 31, 2006, prior to the Bankruptcy Abuse Prevention and Consumer Protection Act of 2005 (Bankruptcy, 2006). One of the simplest and best ways to avoid bankruptcy is to follow a budget.

A personal budget is a financial plan setting limits on the amount of money a family can spend on a category of expenses in a given month. A good budget accounts for expected income, outstanding debt to be retired, and retirement savings. It also includes an emergency fund.

Many people have no clear idea of how they spend a good portion of their money. They don't keep track of their spontaneous ATM withdrawals, and then are shocked to find their checking accounts drained. They don't understand why they had a wallet full of money on payday, but an empty wallet by Monday morning. When people don't track their spending, they often waste their money on frivolous purchases (wants) without even realizing it. Then they find themselves unable to meet their fixed monthly expenses (needs). A budget helps to curtail extraneous purchases by providing accountability for money spent. For example, if you realize you have only $50 available for food expenses that week, you might decide to forgo that $4 specialty cup of coffee.

Control Unplanned Spending

Impulse buying is a major budget crusher. Unfortunately, we live in a culture of "instant gratification." We see something we want and we want it *now*. We justify this, of course. Sometimes a price "just can't be beat." However, we take a beating later when we can't pay our bills. Make it a policy to avoid buying anything on impulse. Go home, sleep on it, and see if it is still important to you the following day. Rarely is the "must-have" item as attractive the next morning. If it is, then work it into your budget.

Before you make an unplanned purchase, ask yourself these questions:

- Is the purchase useful in some way?
- Is it simply a "feel good" purchase?
- Is the item serving as some sort of reward?

If the item is something you want, rather than something you need, wait to buy it until you have given the purchase more thought. If the product is useful and necessary, and if it doesn't interfere with meeting your monthly obligations, then you can justify your purchase.

Avoid Comparing Yourself to Others

People often fall into the trap of comparing themselves to others. They compare their homes, cars, salaries, job positions, clothing, and even their children. When you compare yourself to others, you generally arrive at 1 of these 3 conclusions:

1. I am better than that person.
2. That person is better than I am.
3. I wish I could be like that person, or, I wish I could have what that person has.

Scripture is full of warnings against the pitfalls of comparison. The Apostle Paul told the Galatians, "Do your own work well, and then you will have something to be proud of. But don't compare yourself with others" (Galatians 6:4 CEV). He was a bit more adamant with the Corinthians: "Their trouble is that they are only comparing themselves with each other and measuring themselves against their own little ideas. What stupidity!" (2 Corinthians 10:12b TLB).

When we fall into the trap of comparing ourselves to others or "keeping up with the Joneses," we find ourselves buying things we do not really need. Not only does this damage our budgets, but we find we don't really feel any better about ourselves. How many times have we heard it said that "the best things in life aren't things"?

Image from BigstockPhoto.com / andres

Using credit cards sparingly and paying off the balance every month can prevent you from falling into the credit card trap of owing too much to pay it off.

Use Your Credit Cards Sparingly

Credit cards are readily available. Pre-approved letters for credit arrive regularly in the mail. While they are a wonderful convenience, they also can sabotage financial stability. Credit cards may encourage impulse buying and spending money the user does not have. Instead, you can reserve your credit cards for emergencies or for purchases which require them, such as a car rental. Unfortunately, many people use their credit cards when they *know* they don't have enough money to spend on something. They tell themselves they'll pay off the credit card balance "next month" or in "just a couple of months." If you do use your credit card, make it a rule to pay the complete balance each month.

In the United States, 78% of households are considered eligible for credit. This explains the frequency of credit card commercials and the many pre-approved letters which show up in your mailbox. Of 282 million Americans living in the United States in 2002, 185 million had at least one credit card; the average number of cards per person is 6.5, the average per household is 14.3 (Statistics, 2008). According to Dave Ramsey, people who use credit cards instead of cash will spend 12–18% more (Ramsey, 2007). This may explain why so many people who use credit cards for everyday purchases declare bankruptcy.

On those occasions when you want to use your credit card, consider using your debit card instead. That way, you will know your checking balance and can spend accordingly. But exercise caution. Debit card overdraft fees can play havoc with your budget.

Never Carry a Credit Card Balance

In 2005, the total consumer credit amount totaled $2.2 trillion. The average household consumer debt is $9,000. If we exclude those households paying their bills in full each month, household consumer debt actually is closer to $13,000. Three out of five Americans carry credit card debt from month to month. The average household spent $1,700 per year on finance charges and late fees last year. Nearly half the people who carry a credit card balance pay only the interest on their balance each month (How much debt can we, 2005). Here's a sobering example of how credit card debt can undermine a family's financial viability:

> A family needs a new sofa, but can't afford to buy one. When they find one they really like, the husband pulls out a credit card. Like magic, they have a new sofa.
>
> They pay $2,000 for the sofa, using a credit card with an APR of 19.8% interest. If they pay only the minimum monthly payments, they will pay off their sofa in 31 years and 2 months. Worse yet, they will end up paying more than $10,000 for their $2,000 sofa. The interest alone robs them of $8,202. Can a sofa actually be worth paying 5 times its original value?

Save, Save, Save

Looking back at the story of the $2,000 sofa, consider this. If the family had put the same monthly payments into a simple 10% mutual fund over the same period of 31 years, their fund would have yielded $45,540. But because they had to have that sofa *right away*, they paid dearly for it.

One of the most important aspects of a budget is a savings account. Most financial planners recommend a family put the equivalent of 3 to 6 months of the regular salary into savings. Then, if the refrigerator breaks down, or the car quits, the family has an emergency reserve. Families without an emergency reserve often fall prey to "payday loan" businesses. Like credit cards, these enterprises promise convenience and immediacy. Let's examine what they have to offer:

> Let's say you need to borrow $100. A payday loan business lets you write a personal check for $115. The check casher or payday lender agrees to hold the check until your next payday or up to 14 days and gives you $100. At the designated time, depending on the particular plan, the lender deposits the check. You now must have the $115 in your checking account or you rollover the check by paying a

fee to extend the loan for another 2 weeks. In this example, the cost of the initial loan was a $15 finance charge, which is a whopping 391% APR. If you rollover the loan three times, the finance charge climbs to $60 to borrow $100. Since partial payments are not accepted, people often end up at another payday loan office to pay off the first loan, only exacerbating the problem until they are thousands of dollars in debt.

A savings account can protect a family from the above problems. If a family saves only $10 a month, they can build up a sizeable savings account in a short time. Thus, they would have $100 available for an emergency, and not have to pay a $60 finance charge. Unfortunately, all too often, when money is tight, the savings account is the first thing a family deletes from its budget.

It is also important to begin saving for retirement, especially when you are young. In 2006, social security, which averages $1,079 per month, was the largest source of income for those currently 65 and older accounting for nearly 40% of their income. For many of those over 65, it was their only source of income (McDonald, 2007). An example of the importance of saving early for retirement is what can happen to $100.00. Suppose you put $100.00 a month into an account earning 8% interest for 5 years, starting at age 25. Your friend Tom does exactly the same thing, except he is 35 when he starts to save. If you both stop investing after 5 years and hold your investment to age 60, you will have $74,430.15 at age 60, while your friend Tom will have $34,475.56. Your investment would be almost double Tom's just because you started earlier. That is the power of compounding interest.

Living the Life of a Good Steward: A Christian Perspective

Christians often give lip service to God as the One who owns their earthly possessions, especially their money. Their lives don't always reflect that lip service, however. The Apostle Paul warns the "love of money is the root of all kinds of evil" (1 Timothy 6:10) and the love of money brings out the ugliness in us. Maybe that is why the NIV has 114 references to money, among them these two:

- "People who want to get rich fall into temptation and a trap and into many foolish and harmful desires that plunge men into ruin and destruction" (1 Timothy 6:9).
- "But mark this: There will be terrible times in the last days. People will be lovers of themselves, lovers of money, boastful, proud, abusive, disobedient to their parents, ungrateful, unholy, without love, unforgiving, slanderous, without self-control, brutal, not lovers of the good, treacherous, rash, conceited, lovers of pleasure rather than lovers of God—having a form of godliness but denying its power. Have nothing to do with them" (2 Timothy 3:1–5).

The Christian who is searching for direction on how to handle finances will find excellent guidelines in Scripture. Money itself is not evil. In the gospel of Luke, chapter 16, Jesus explains wealth can be a blessing or a curse, depending on how we use it. Will we use it to exercise power over others? Will we use it for self-indulgence? Will we use it to serve others? Our perception of money can enhance or distort our values, make us selfish or selfless, encourage us to take advantage of others or help others, cause us to thank God or—sadly—to hide from God: "And some people, craving money, have wandered from the true faith and pierced themselves with many sorrows" (1 Timothy 6:10b NLT).

Manage Your Resources Wisely

In this chapter we have looked at family resources as they relate to time, energy, and money. How we exercise responsibility for our possessions is a test of character, values, and stewardship. Jesus said if we are trustworthy with little, we will be trustworthy with much (see Luke 19:16–19). The converse is also true—if we are dishonest in the little things, we will be dishonest in bigger things (see vv. 20–24).

Consider Your Body a Valuable Possession. In reviewing the effects of

Tithing is a way of recognizing God as the ultimate Provider of all we have.

stress, we learned our bodies are vulnerable to attack and stress can easily drain our energy. God places great value on the human body. The Apostle Paul calls the human body a most valuable possession because it is the dwelling place of the Holy Spirit (see 1 Corinthians 3:16; 6:19). Therefore, believers must be good stewards, giving their bodies as much attention as they do their valuable possessions. In the gospel of Mark, we find even Jesus needed to rest (see Mark 6:31–32). This underscores the importance of finding time in the busy family schedule for "free play," rather than cramming "one more thing" into an already overbooked schedule. Sometimes, we need to be a little more polychronic in our approach to time—letting time unravel quietly and loosely.

Make Tithing a Part of Your Budget. "The earth is the LORD's, and everything in it, the world, and all who live in it; for he founded it upon the seas and established it upon the waters" (Psalm 24:1–2).

To tithe means to give a portion of your income to God. Biblically, the tithe most often meant a tenth part of a person's earnings and possessions. Many Christians follow that same pattern and give 10% of their income to the church, mission group or other ministry organization. Others give a smaller or higher percentage. Some people tithe on their gross income; others on the net. Tithing is a form of worship which recognizes God as the ultimate Provider of all we "own." Our responsibility is to manage well what He has given us.

Tithing, which can be traced to the earliest times in biblical history, was meaningful because it involved giving up something of value. This often meant a sacrifice of physical belongings. We encourage Christians to find a place for tithing in their weekly budgets, and to encourage their children to offer a part of their allowances for the same reason.

Establish Your Priorities

Stewardship is how we use what God has given us. A budget is one way a family manages its income and expenses. Following a budget means we learn to prioritize our needs over our wants. That actually is a good way to exercise stewardship in all areas of life. When we prioritize, we sort through everything which assails us and we establish order. As you've often heard the self-help gurus say, prioritizing means we learn to operate *proactively* rather than *reactively*. In other words, we don't just wait for a crisis and then try to figure things out (reactive). Instead, we plan how to approach the various avenues of our life in order to prevent a crisis situation from occurring (proactive).

The way people spend their time, energy, and money reflects their priorities. Remember, though, it is not just about conservation of our time, energy, and money but also about sharing these unselfishly with others. If someone were to watch your every move over the next 72 hours, what do you think he or she would say about your priorities in life? Would that person be able to determine your values and your goals? Would that person say you are a good steward of what God has given you? Would that person say you are living a life which demonstrates your trust and faith in God?

To live life as a good steward means you need to establish your priorities. Answer these questions:

1. What is the most important area of your life right now? Where do you want to spend the greatest amount of your emotional energy—energy that it takes to plan, prepare, and follow through on your plans? This may be school, work, your church, your family, or your relationships. Are you happy about how you spend your emotional energy? If you need to make adjustments, what do you need to do? How do you want to spend your emotional energy?
2. Where do you spend most of your physical energy? This may be at work, at school, or participating in leisure activities. How satisfied are you with how you spend your physical energy? Do you need to make changes? How much emotional and physical energy have you allotted to personal activities you enjoy?
3. Think about what you did last weekend (or on a typical weekend). If you could make changes, what would they be? Was it a good balance for you? What free-time activities do you value, such as seeing friends, reading, cooking, or sports, to name a few? Do you allow enough time for these activities?

If you feel you are not living according to your priorities, answer a few more questions:

1. What gets in your way or stops you from living according to your priorities?
2. Do you believe you are not entitled to this kind of life, or do you feel selfish if you do try to realize your goals?
3. Are you unsure of what you want to do? Are there too many demands on your time? What are you willing to give up in order to gain more time for your priorities?
4. If your life doesn't represent your values, goals, and priorities, what do you need to do to bring your life in line with them?

Establishing priorities will help you manage your resources wisely. Your priorities will change over the course of your life. For example, a mother may step out of her career for a few years, until her children are in school. For those childrearing years, her priorities will center on her children. Later, she will balance her priorities between career and home life. What is important is to plan ahead and anticipate the changes, rather than let them become overwhelming.

Live Your Priorities

Living your priorities—putting them into practice—is much more difficult than talking about them. In *First Things First*, author Stephen Covey explains we need to have the discipline and willpower to exercise integrity, even in unexpected situations (1995). Sometimes, despite our best intentions, life will not always cooperate with our plans.

We offer the following suggestions to help you live your priorities:

1. Write down your priorities and your goals. Post them where they will remind you of your commitment. This helps to cement your ideas in your mind and imagination. By becoming more familiar with them, you make it easier to implement them.
2. Before you react to a situation, stop and consider your priorities. What actions are consistent with your priorities? What actions will be most pleasing to God?
3. Before committing to something which deviates from your plan, ask yourself if it is the most beneficial use of your time *right now.*
4. Have the courage and integrity to do what is right, regardless of the pressure and urgency you feel to do otherwise.

Christians who live their priorities in a way which honors God, experience peace and satisfaction. They understand their first priority is to work on their relationship with God. By placing Him first, they find their other priorities fall into place. In John 14:1, 23, 27, Christ lets the disciples know what their priorities should be and imparts comfort and the promise of peace: "Do not let your hearts be troubled. Trust in God; trust also in me… Jesus replied, "If anyone loves me, he will obey my teaching. My Father will love him, and we will come to him and make our home with him…Peace I leave with you; my peace I give you. I do not give to you as the world gives. Do not let your hearts be troubled and do not be afraid".

While Christians are not promised a problem-free life, they understand God has their ultimate well-being in mind. Living by his priorities means we will be good stewards of the resources he has given us.

Summary

In this chapter, we have examined ways families manage their resources of time, energy, and money.

Time is a social construct which has different meanings in different cultures. In North America, time is monochronic, structured, and sequential. This understanding of time makes it difficult for families to have flexible time together. Parents today are working more hours. Family time is often filled with household chores and structured children's activities. Many parents react to the stress of trying to do it all by sacrificing their personal time and time together as a couple. Children also struggle with a time crunch. They spend less time in unstructured play and at family meals, but spend more time doing homework and participating in structured activities.

Time is closely linked to energy. American families tend to be stressed, overwhelmed, and tired. Role theory and conservation theory can both be used to examine the work-family interface. Work is one of the leading causes of stress; however, the way we perceive the conflict between work and family can mitigate the strain. For both men and women, satisfying work can have positive benefits for the family.

Of all the family's resources, money can be the most problematic. It also causes the most family conflict—not so much the lack of money, as how it is spent. Families today often operate under a heavy debt load. Family members are called to be good stewards of all their resources, including money.

Children add to the financial and energy burden of families. The cost per year depends on the age of the child and the income of the parents. Currently, it ranges from $7,000 to over $15,000 a year and is rising.

Sound financial decisions keep a family on solid ground. One of the best ways a family can remain financially secure is to create and stick to a budget. To remain on track, families should avoid impulse buying, use credit cards only when they can pay off the entire balance each month, avoid comparing themselves to others, establish a savings account, and tithe regularly.

Christians recognize they are stewards of what God has given them. To be a good steward, they understand they must establish priorities and live by those priorities. If their priorities are in line with God's priorities, then they will live them in a way which honors God and brings them peace and satisfaction.

Questions for Thought

1. In what ways are family boundaries more permeable than work boundaries? How can families curtail the intrusion of work on family time?
2. Explain how role ambiguity or role conflict can cause stress.
3. Families are supposed to be a safe haven from the world. Instead, they often are one of the major causes of stress. Explain.
4. What other suggestions would you make to achieve financial balance in your life?

Resources

Books:

The Seven Habits of Highly Effective People by Stephen R. Covey. The Classic book on how to manage time, energy, and priorities. (Free Press, 2004)

The Automatic Millionaire by David Bach. A book full of sound financial advice, especially in regards to planning for the future. (Broadway, 2005)

Movies:

Financial Peace University DVD Study Kit. This can be purchased at DaveRamsey.com, where there are also many other resources on financial stability, paying off debt, and saving for the future.

Website:

Budgeting tools and more: http://www.crown.org (accessed June 23, 2009)

Cultural Variations in Marriage and Family

11

There is neither Jew nor Greek, slave nor free, male nor female, for you are all one in Christ Jesus.

—Galatians 3:28

Paul Chesley / Stone / Getty Images

God created us in His image (Genesis 1:26–27), but He did not create us the same. As God's image bearers, human beings intrinsically resemble one another. Thus, human beings cannot be mistaken for cattle. However, each human being is distinctly unique and different from any other human being—even twins are not exactly the same. People differ in appearance; we have different skin color, eye color, and hair color. We are male or female. We are born into unique families with rich cultural traditions.

The Apostle Paul tells us these differences do not matter to God (Galatians 3:28). However, humankind's history tells another story. It would appear these differences matter a great deal to us. As the result of racial and cultural variations, people perceive marriage and family patterns differently. Struggles arise when one culture asserts it is the dominant culture and identifies others as "minority" cultures.

In this chapter, we will look at how culture affects our perception of marriage and family. We will consider various ethnic and racial groups in the United States, particularly African-American, Hispanic-American, Asian-American, and Native-American cultures. We will examine the challenges created by cross-cultural marriages, as well as the impact of income level, social class, and disability on the family structure. Among the most volatile relationship issues in recent American history is the same-sex debate, which we will include as an adjunct to our study of cultural diversity. Finally, we will offer a Christian perspective on cultural variations, explaining how God wants us to live in a multicultural society.

The Terminology of Ethnic and Cultural Variations

Chapters 2 and 3 of this text include introductory material on cultural variations as they relate to the early history of this country. Throughout this chapter, you will find frequent references to the terms *race* and *ethnicity*. What is the difference between these terms?

The Difference Between Race and Ethnicity

Race is an ascribed status—it is an intrinsic part of a person's genetic makeup. It is not an internal issue but rather a political issue which serves to privilege one group of people over another (McGoldrick, 2003). A racial group is a group of people who share a common biological heritage, resulting in distinct physical attributes. Racial variations include observable human differences, such as eye color, skin pigmentation, and hair texture. Earlier in the 20th century, schoolchildren often were taught there were only four primary racial groups: black, red, yellow, and white. Even in the 1950s, many official American documents listed only three or four categories under the subheading of race. (The same was true of the category of religion; often, people filling out an official form could choose from only three categories: Catholic, Jew, and Protestant). This is quite a contrast to today's multi-category documents.

Over the course of time, particularly in America, racial mixing has resulted in very few who can claim they are "completely white" or "completely black." Most people are a mix of genetic material from a variety of races, sometimes making it difficult to distinguish among racial groups. Thus, ethnicity often becomes a more important factor than race. Ethnicity refers to a group's common ancestry which has evolved shared values and customs transmitted over generations, primarily through the family (McGoldrick, 2003). An ethnic group is a group of people with a distinct cultural heritage. This may manifest in a distinct manner of communication, religion, dress, food habits, and other mannerisms.

While we may choose to ignore all or certain aspects of our ethnic heritage, we cannot change our racial makeup. Sometimes race and ethnicity overlap—certain races develop distinct cultural patterns which relate more to ethnicity than race. A more common occurrence today is to find many ethnic groups within a single racial group. For example, in the United States, white southerners differ culturally from whites on the West Coast and southern Alabama blacks differ culturally from Chicago blacks.

Defining Cultural Diversity

Each ethnic group expresses a distinct culture, which is defined as the values, beliefs, and norms characterizing a group in a particular place and time. Included in the culture are its patterns of marriage and family life. Societies respond to cultural diversity in different ways. In some societies, a dominant culture will discourage families of other cultures from practicing their unique cultural patterns of language, dress, childrearing, and marriage rituals. A dominant culture which does this exhibits ethnocentrism, the belief that one's own culture is superior to others. An ethnocentric perspective often fails to appreciate other cultures and sees diverse family patterns as somehow "wrong." Sometimes a dominant culture will go beyond encouraging change and may force a minority culture to assimilate into the larger culture. Cultural assimilation means "to make similar," to blend into a larger culture and lose the unique norms and values which distinguish a minority culture from a dominant culture.

Many families maintain some of their ethnic traditions.

We have only to look at Native-Americans to find a history of cultural assimilation. Most Native-Americans do not speak the language of their ancestors or practice tribal customs. Only about one third of Native-American families still live on reservations (Ogunwole, 2006). Of those, most have adopted the patterns of the larger culture.

America's early history seems to point to a melting pot ideology. A melting pot nation is one in which various cultures blend together more or less harmoniously into a unified society. The cultural expectation in a melting pot nation is that the majority of immigrants will learn the language and adopt the customs of the culture to which they have moved. For example, most descendants of European immigrants do not speak the language or practice the customs of their Europeans ancestors. They have, voluntarily or by necessity, assimilated into American culture.

An alternative perspective is cultural pluralism, in which different ethnic groups coexist in the same society, with each group celebrating its unique cultural norms, while adhering to the laws of the larger society. For example, Americans of Middle Eastern descent often establish and frequent their own restaurants and stores, which sell the foods and clothing they prefer. In a pluralistic society, these different groups not only interact with one another with a certain degree of tolerance, but minority cultures are often encouraged to uphold their customs.

Many ethnic families in America practice unique customs of diet, dress, and holiday observance, which serve to solidify their ties to family and culture. These families may speak their native tongues in their homes, while speaking English in public. In contrast to the melting pot metaphor, it could be said a salad bowl image personifies cultural pluralism. A salad is a single entity comprised of individual ingredients which retain their individuality in the bowl. In a salad bowl nation, the various cultures retain their identities as they mix with one another to form a larger society.

Immigrant families face particular challenges. Ambert (2001) suggests the most successful immigrant families become bicultural. They adopt the language and norms of both cultures and can easily move back and forth between them. The children learn to respect their English-speaking teachers and do well in school. This is in contrast to immigrant families who may move into a poor neighborhood where crime, teen pregnancy, and high school dropout rates are high. Children in such families (second-generation immigrants) may experience downward social mobility—they may do less well than their parents because of the environment in which they are living.

America's Minority Groups

Whether it is called a melting pot or a salad bowl, the United States is an exciting blend of cultures. From Chinatown to the French Quarter, from simple Amish churches to technologically advanced mega churches, America's history is steeped in diversity. From colonial times on, different ethnic groups have left their mark on America's ideology, including as it relates to marriage and family.

As we examine the strengths of the American family, as well as the challenges, we will focus on the four most prevalent minority groups in America: African-Americans, Hispanic-Americans, Asian-Americans, and Native-Americans.

African-American Families

African-American families constitute a distinct cultural group; however, there is tremendous diversity within and between African-American families. The great diversity in values, characteristics, and lifestyles can be attributed to geographical origins (the country of ancestry), educational achievement, socioeconomic status, religious background, and the level of acculturation (Boyd-Franklin, 2003).

© Getty Images

African-Americans often have strong extended kin networks.

There are many challenges of racism and prejudice facing African-American families. Some of the stereotypes associated with African-Americans continue to haunt them: low income, high crime, low intelligence, promiscuous behavior. These false stereotypes are so deeply ingrained and so damaging they can become self-fulfilling prophecies—if the family does not overrule this tendency (Olson & DeFrain, 2006). In truth, African-American families are very strong. Extended family members especially become involved in children's lives and push them to achieve.

Strengths. Cultural resiliency theorists focus on the positive aspects of black family organization and have identified the following strengths of African-American families (Boyd-Franklin, 2003; Collins, 2000; Medora, 2005; Musick, Wilson, & Bynum, 2000; Sarkisian & Gerstel, 2004):

- Strong kinship bonds
- Extensive exchange of support between kin and non-kin
- Communal patterns of childcare
- Strong mother-child relationships
- Flexibility in family roles
- Strong religious orientation

African-American families tend to have strong religious roots, which sustained them during their years of slavery (see chapter 2). This has also enabled them to overcome other challenges because they are able to turn to their churches for social and spiritual support (Diller, 2004).

There are a number of barriers preventing African-Americans from forming strong, happy, enduring marriages, including: limited educational and employment opportunities, the limited number of available black men, children from previous relationships, and a tendency to mistrust each other (Chapman, 2007; Edin & Reed, 2005; Tucker 2000). Despite these barriers, African-Americans do form strong, long lasting marriages. Some of the sources of strength which help families overcome these barriers include:

- good emotional and physical health
- trust
- positive marital role models
- determination, especially of men, to be the father they did not have
- social support
- some financial and employment opportunities
- religious participation

(Chapman, 2007; Coles, 2006; Marks, 2005; Marks et al., 2005; Marks et al., 2006; Marks et al., 2008).

Challenges. A primary challenge to African-American families today is the lack of male role models. A large number of African-American families are female-headed households. According to the Census, 60% of children born to African-American women were born out of wedlock (U.S. Census, 2007d). The high frequency of female-headed households is a relatively new phenomenon, since throughout history African-American families were headed by two parents (Wilson, Kohn, & Lee, 2000). In chapter 2, we noted that, even under slave conditions, African-Americans continued to value their family connections. An extended kin network (fictive kin) took in and cared for children who were separated from their parents. Despite the terrible conditions of slavery, African-Americans fought with determination to maintain stable, nurturing families. When a man and woman were forbidden to marry, they married anyway and referred to one another as husband and wife, whether the law of the land recognized their union or not (Cayton, Gorn and Williams, 1993).

The number of female-headed households continues to increase in African-American families.

The rise in female-headed households in the latter years of the 20th century coincides with a rise in unemployment for African-

American males during the 1990s. There is an increase in the number of poor women, including black women, who are bearing children, often by choice, but choosing not to marry. This is not because marriage has lost its meaning in low-income communities, but because they want to be confident the marriage will last (Edin & Kefalas, 2005). These families attempt to overcome the challenges of childrearing by involving extended family members in childcare (Boyd-Franklin, 2003; Collins, 2000; Medora, 2005; Musick, Wilson, & Bynum, 2000; Sarkisian & Gerstel, 2004).

Recent scholarship has focused on the need for more involvement in parenthood for African-American fathers. While it is affirmed that marriage is the best arrangement for African-American parents, single fathers should be very involved in their children's lives (Clayton, Mincy, & Blankenhorn, 2003).

African-Americans have not given up on marriage. They still want to marry. However, they have separated the decision to marry from the decision to parent. One does not necessarily follow the other (Edin & Kefalas, 2005). Middle-class African-American families are building their own communities, which emphasize dual-income marriage and small family size. In their struggles to balance work and family, these families are similar to middle-class white families (Toliver, 1998).

Hispanic-American Families

Hispanic-Americans encompass several Spanish-speaking cultures, including Mexican Americans, Cuban Americans, Puerto Ricans, and others. The term *Latino* or *Latina* also refers to Hispanic-Americans. This is the fastest-growing ethnic group in America. The U.S. Census (2007e) estimates the Hispanic-American population will continue to grow and spread throughout the United States. The Hispanic growth rate was 24.3%, more than 3 times the growth rate of the total population. Projections suggest that by 2010, Hispanics will represent 15.5% of the population and nearly 24.5% by 2050 (U.S. Census, 2007e). Hispanic women also have the highest fertility rate of American women, so these families generally include many children (Downs, 2003). They also value their very strong extended family ties.

Hispanic-American families tend to assimilate readily into the larger culture. Intermarriage is common. These factors may cause a loss of cultural distinctiveness and some of the unique strengths of their highly cohesive families. As a result, intergenerational conflict is common as younger generations challenge the cultural norms of the older generations (Olson & DeFrain, 2006). For example, a Hispanic teen may resent his parents' accent, rules, and in general, being "different" from other peers.

Strengths. Hispanic families have a strong identification and attachment to the nuclear and extended family which includes intense feelings of loyalty, reciprocity, and solidarity among members called familism. Several researchers have identified the following as strengths of Hispanic-American families (Carter & McGoldrick, 2005; Medora, 2005; Ramirrez et al., 2004; Rodriguez et al., 2007):

- High priority given to family (familism)
- High commitment to marriage
- Family cohesion
- Increasing role flexibility
- Supportive kin network system
- Strong commitment to religion

Challenges. One of the major challenges facing Hispanic families is poverty (Llagas, 2003). In 2006, 27% of Hispanic children lived in poverty compared to 10% white, non-Hispanic children (Federal Interagency Forum on Child and Family Statistics, 2008). There are many struggles which accompany poverty that influence overall wellbeing, including: limited job opportunities, unequal or limited access to family resources because of the language barrier, unequal access to healthcare, and cultural insensitivity from society at large (Suleiman, 2003).

Hispanics and blacks both experience labor market discrimination and housing discrimination; however, these two groups differ in some important ways. Hispanics are more likely to intermarry with whites, which is a key sign of cultural assimilation (Bean & Stevens, 2003). Hispanics are also more likely than blacks to experience residential integration, an indication of upward mobility (Emerson, Yancey, & Chai, 2001). This may be at least in part because Hispanics tend to have lighter skin color than blacks, making them seem more similar to whites than to blacks.

Other challenges Hispanic-American families face may be related to the loss of extended family connections among new immigrants. This loss of traditional family support among new immigrants may be a factor in the high rates of teenage childbearing and out-of-wedlock births. Hispanic-American teenagers also have the highest rates of attempted suicide and

Hispanic families demonstrate a high degree of familism.

the lowest high school graduation rates of all American teens (Eaton et al., 2007). These teens may also face language barriers other American teens do not encounter.

Certain Hispanic-American groups have strict male/female roles which are related to the strengths and challenges of their families. The stereotypical dominant "macho" role for males may be related to domestic violence. For females, cultural role expectations may result in low academic achievement, since women are discouraged from careers requiring high achievement. As Hispanic families assimilate, males tend to move toward more egalitarian roles, including housework, childcare, and marital faithfulness and away from the traditional, machismo ideology (Hirsh, 2003).

Most Hispanic-American families are very religious and maintain a close relationship with their churches (mostly Catholic). They often turn to their churches in times of need, gaining social support from clergy and other church organizations.

Asian-American Families

Asian-American families place a very high value on education and achievement, so much so they often sacrifice family ties in order to achieve educational or career goals. Yet they retain a strong family orientation, particularly within the nuclear family.

Asian-Americans also have a strong identification to the nuclear and extended family. Women traditionally move into their husband's family at the time of marriage and their last name disappears from the family tree. Researchers have identified the following as strengths of Asian-American families (Carter & McGoldrick, 2005; Olson & DeFrain, 2006; Zhou & Gatewood, 2000).

Strengths.

- Strong family orientation
- Great respect for elders
- High value on education
- Well-disciplined children
- Extended family support
- Hard working

Challenges. Asian-Americans tend to be hard workers, sometimes to excess. Their high achievement motivation may place excessive pressure on young people. At the same time, Asian-American families often distrust outsiders, so they may be less likely to seek help from professionals. Family members often isolate themselves from kin as they seek to better themselves through education and job opportunities. Intermarriage is becoming increasing common for Asian-Americans.

Recent Asian immigrants from poorer, rural nations (Vietnam, Cambodia, and

Laos) are having greater difficulty adjusting to American culture than earlier immigrants from Japan, China, and Korea (Olson & DeFrain, 2006). The turmoil of civil wars and political instability has led to an erosion of traditional family values and practices among these newer Asian immigrants. Evidence of the decrease in strong family ties may be seen in the increase in domestic violence, divorce, and elder abuse in recent years.

Paul Chesley / Stone / Getty Images

Navajo mother teaching daughter weaving. Navajo Indian Reservation.

Native-American Families

Native-Americans were the first Americans. Their history is steeped in legend and tells the epic story of a proud people who were brutalized and imprisoned on their own land. The many diverse tribes encompass a wide range of cultural heritages. About one third of Native-American families live on reservations today (Webster & Bishaw, 2007). The rest have been assimilated into the larger culture, so it is difficult to make generalizations about Native-American family patterns.

For most, family remains a highly valued component of Native-American life (Sage, 2001). Those who choose to live on the reservation place great importance on the community as a larger extended family, which often operates in place of a missing parent. The tribe works together to socialize its youth into the values, language, and traditions of the tribe's heritage. Marriages are often a tribal affair, requiring the consent of the whole community (Carson et al., 1990). Elders are revered and respected for their role in transferring the tribal culture to the young. This is evidenced by a growing interest in pantraditionalism, which refers to those who had been assimilated, but who have chosen to re-embrace their previously lost native culture, values, and practices (Garrett & Pichette, 2000). This increased awareness of native culture also serves to increase family bonds.

While Native-American families continue to experience many social and family problems, a number of strengths have been identified (Joe, 2001; Olson & DeFrain, 2006; Ronnau & Shannon, n.d.; Sage, 2001).

Strengths:

- Extended family system
- Strong identification their culture
- High family cohesion
- Respect for elders
- Adaptability
- Extensive informational resource system

Challenges. Native-Americans face many challenges to family stability. In the last 40 years, female-headed households have increased, exceeding the rate of the general population (Coles, 2006). Median family income is among the lowest of all cultural groups. According to the U.S. Census Bureau, almost a third of Native-Americans live below the poverty line (Webster & Bishaw, 2007).

Lack of education and employment opportunities, financial difficulties, racial prejudice, and isolation all contribute to family instability. Some prominent examples of family challenges are depression, alcoholism, and alcohol-related health problems, such as diabetes. Suicide has become the second leading cause of death for Native-American males between the ages of 10 and 24 (Joe, 2001).

Intercultural and Interracial Marriage

Intercultural marriage is not a new phenomenon in America. America's rich cultural heritage is due primarily to this blending through intermarriage. In America's early history, white European immigrants married other white European immigrants at a high rate. Most white Americans can trace their ancestry to several European nations.

As a nation, we have a long history of intercultural marriage; however, until 1967, our society explicitly forbade racial intermarriage and discouraged intercultural relationships (McGoldrick, 2003). The number of interracial marriages has been on the rise since then. In 1970, 0.7% of all marriages were interracial marriages. This rose to 1.3% in 1980 and to 2.2% in 1992 (U.S. Census, 1994). The 2000 census included a mixed-race category and recorded 4.9% of all marriages were interracial marriages (Fields & Casper, 2001).

Whites are the least likely to marry interracially. Approximately 2% of whites have a non-white spouse, while 6% of blacks have a non-black spouse, and over 13% of Asians have a non-Asian spouse.

Interracial marriages between blacks and whites are more likely to be age discrepant.

Black-white marriages are more than twice as likely to consist of a black male married to a white female (U.S. Census, 2008b). The reasons for this are not clear. This arrangement may indicate black men feel more freedom in their marriage choices, or that they have a lower opinion of black women as marriage partners than they do of white women. It may indicate black women have a low opinion of black men, or feel more freedom to choose to remain single. Black women often resent successful black men who choose to marry white women. Others claim this situation is a crisis in the black community, contributing to the increase in the numbers of single mothers (Crowder & Tolnay, 2000; Judice Powell, 2005).

A couple who intermarries—particularly a black-white couple—is more likely to have been married before and to be age discrepant (varying widely in age; e.g., older man with younger woman) (Knox & Schacht, 1999). Intercultural couples often choose to live in an urban community which is diverse and puts distance between them and their parents.

The Challenges of Intercultural Marriage

Intercultural marriages can be problematic for ethnic groups seeking to retain their culture and traditions. Intercultural marriage partners often are at odds with both sets of families. They find it challenging to respect the ethnic traditions of both families and pass them on to their children, especially if they cannot compromise. Couples may choose to break ties with their cultural traditions rather than try to resolve family conflicts. Couples may also isolate themselves from their families, either by choice or because one or both families reject the couple for having married outside the group (Karis, 2003).

Living without extended kin relationships can be very stressful on a marriage. This places more emphasis on the marriage partners to fulfill needs which are sometimes met by extended kin. With the advent of children, couples living without the support of extended kin may find life particularly challenging. Such stresses may cause the couple to become even more isolated or may result in intensified conflict. Such stress will also be felt by children living without extended kin. Often an intercultural marriage which begins relatively stress-free can become conflict-ridden when certain events remind one or both spouses of family heritage. For example, the death of a parent often brings one back into contact with one's cultural roots. The process of mourning such a death can become very complex and stressful on an intercultural marriage (Crohn, 1998).

The Effects of Intercultural Marriage on Children

Children in intercultural families sometimes suffer from identity confusion. They may carry a heavy load of stereotypes. Racial slurs may hit them from all directions (Knox & Schacht, 1999). Sometimes children from intercultural marriages experience the stress of being raised without the benefit of extended kin, because their parents' families have rejected them (Childs, 2005). But often these children learn to be strong and self-assured. Much depends on the attitude of the parents, extended family, and community regarding the marriage.

© iStockphoto.com / bonniej

Biracial children may suffer from identity confusion and racial slurs.

In 2006, the Census counted nearly 2 million multiracial children, 4.2% of children under 18—these children no longer need to feel different and alone (U.S. Census, 2006a). The difficult truth is that many of these children are still fighting the "one drop rule" which historically meant any trace of African ancestry precluded one from being white (Newman & Grauerholz, 2002). Sometimes these children face the awkward question, "What race are you?" Many well-adjusted multiracial children simply answer, "I am multiracial."

Variations in Social Class

In addition to racial and ethnic origin, different cultural groups arise due to income differences. America does not have a rigid class system, such as the caste system in India. Social class membership is not defined objectively, but subjectively (Thompson & Hickey, 2005). In other words, Americans do not have to meet a certain income level to qualify for classification as "middle class." A person's social class is closely aligned with self-identity—social class is most often whatever that person believes it to be. However, certain broad ideologies are associated with different social classes. Sidebar 11.1 looks at some of the problems defining middle class. People in lower classes view the world and family relationships differently from those in the middle or upper classes. Different researchers use different income levels to divide the classes. For ease in understanding, we will use Thompson and Hickey's (2005) divisions, which include upper class, middle class, working class, and the lower class (see Figure 11.1).

The Upper Class

While many people dream of marrying someone rich, someone who will rescue them from a life of financial struggle, this is more the stuff of fairytales than reality in the United States. Upper-class people move in tight, exclusive social circles. They have a very strong sense of family history and traditions, which serves to reinforce their wealth. Upper-class families often discourage dating and marriage outside their social circles (Morton, 2004).

Sidebar 11.1
What is Middle Class?

Defining middle class is fairly subjective. A 2005 New York Times survey asked respondents to indicate what social class they considered themselves. Here are the results.

- 1% considered themselves to be upper class
- 67% considered themselves middle and upper-middle class
- 35% felt they were working class
- 7% identified themselves as lower class

As you look at these numbers, bear in mind that the official poverty rate in 2005 was 12.6%.

Source: New York Times, 2005. *Class Matters.* New York: Times Books.

There is a tendency in the social science field to minimize race as a factor and focus more on class variables. As you examine the following statistics, can we really ignore race as a factor in poverty or do race and class go hand and hand in understanding poverty?

	Poverty Rate by Race:	Homelessness by Race:	Homelessness by Gender	
African-American	25%	42%	51%	Single men
White	11%	39%	30%	Families
Hispanic-American	22%	13%	17%	Single women
Native-American	4%	4%	2%	Unaccompanied Children
Asian	11%	2%		

Source: How many people experience homelessness? 2009. *National Coalition for the Homeless.* U.S. Census Bureau, 2008b. Statistical Abstracts of the United States. Washington, DC: U.S. Government Printing Office.

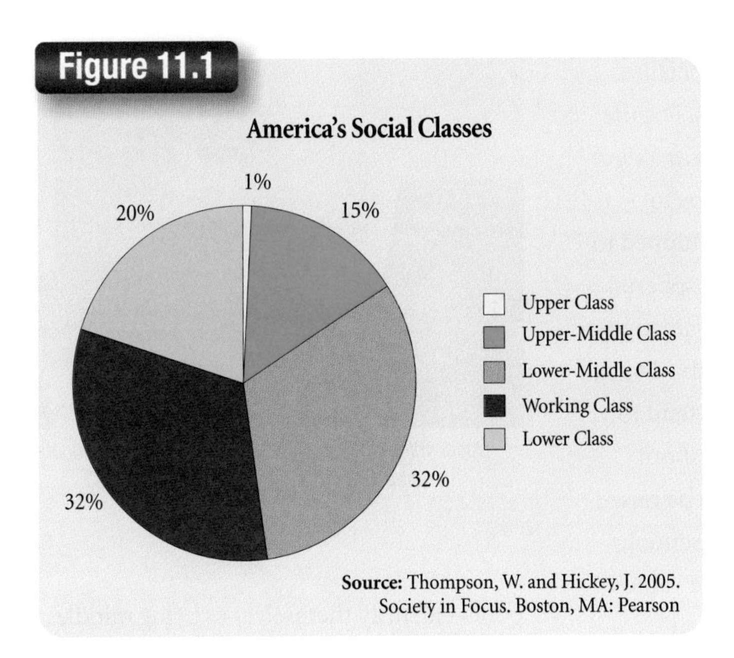

The upper or elite class accounts for around 1% of the population and is the smallest percentage of the population of the United States. The income level for upper class is in excess of $500,000 (Thompson & Hickey, 2005). People in this class usually do not engage in productive work for a living but instead manage people who work, rely on their inheritances, or live on their investments (Morton, 2004). They are almost exclusively Anglo-American and Protestant with their "old money" and power going back generations. Even the richest non-Protestants or people of color have less prestige and influence than the Anglo-Protestants whose class roots go deep (Kliman & Madsen, 2005).

Spending patterns of the upper class include buying expensive items with their vast discretionary money, and also involving themselves in various philanthropic activities. As a whole, this group is older than the general population, well-educated and married. Those in the upper-upper class maintain low visibility, live luxurious life styles, and keep their wealth within their social class. Those in the lower-upper class tend to seek out more visibility, gravitating to high prestige occupations (Morton, 2004).

Quality education, often Ivy League education, is of high importance to the upper class. Children raised in this environment will likely attend exclusive

The upper class has disposable money to pay for luxuries.

private schools, where they can socialize with other people like themselves. For the upper class, education is not seen as a door to financial success, but as a means to become a better person—ably equipped to participate in political and social spheres. Childrearing patterns emphasize creativity and individual expression (Votruba-Drzal, 2006). Many upper-class women tend to have relatively traditional beliefs about childrearing. While children may be raised by a nanny or sent to a boarding school, mothers oversee and reinforce the values associated with their social position (Newman & Grauerholz, 2002).

As a whole, upper-class groups frown upon marriage with other "lower" social groups (Morton, 2004; Newman & Grauerholtz, 2002). Women, particularly, are said to "marry down" if they marry someone from a lower class. Even the "nouveau riche" (the newly rich, especially if they come from a lower class) may not be accepted in upper-class circles because they lack the cultural values and norms of the "old rich." These differences in attitudes toward money, education, philanthropy, and childrearing may cause the dream of "marrying rich" to turn out to be a nightmare.

The Middle Class

Most people in America—from prosperous business owners to the working

Upper-middle-class professionals are highly educated, salaried, professionals, and managers.

poor—identify themselves as being middle class, making the term non-descriptive. It usually identifies the "middle income group—neither rich nor poor—which encompasses about 50% of U.S. household income. The income in this class varies from near the national median income of around $40,000 to about $500,000 (Thompson & Hickey, 2005; Williams, Sawyer, & Wahlstrom, 2005). Middle-class families are further divided into sub-groups—upper-middle class and lower-middle class.

The upper-middle class, or professional middle class, consists of highly educated, salaried professionals and managers and encompasses the upper 15% of households in the middle class. The income in the upper-middle-class household ranges from in excess of $100,000 to about $500,000 (Thompson & Hickey, 2005).

Upper-middle-class professionals usually hold college degrees and many have graduate degrees. They usually enjoy a great deal of autonomy in their occupation. Families in this class share a number of characteristics with upper-class families (Newman & Grauerholz, 2002). For instance, wives in upper-middle-class families often play a similar role to upper-class wives in keeping the home running smoothly, supporting their husbands, and moving to accommodate the husband's job. Also like their upper-class counterparts, they have the financial means to hire someone to help with the domestic chores. While many upper-middle-class wives work at least part-time, employment is often not a necessity, unlike families at the lower end of middle class.

Upper-middle-class families place a high value on the conjugal family—husband, wife, children and parents. These families tend to be small (parents and a few children), living as nuclear groups away from extended kin. They devote much of their time to their children, trying to give them skills and attitudes which will lead to good jobs and financial success (Cherlin, 2002). Upper-middle-class families place a high value on equality in marriage. While their marriages may not be more egalitarian in reality, there is greater expectation of equality than in other classes (Newman & Grauerholz, 2002). Other values stressed in upper-middle-class families are independence, non-conformity, and innovation. One of the main indicators of upper-middle class is college education in preparation for typical middle-class occupations (Thompson & Hickey, 2005).

Upper class parents stress skills and attitudes that will help their children obtain financial success.

Parents in the lower middle-class emphasize rules and conformity to social norms.

Understanding middle-class values and lifestyle is important because middle class is often equated with what is "mainstream" in American society (Pattilo-McCoy, 1999). Middle-class norms often define for this culture what is desirable and what one should strive for (Newman, 1999). For example, one of the values held by the middle class is autonomy—between adult siblings and adult children and their parents (Newman, 1999). This, therefore, becomes the norm for which individuals strive, even in the working class and the poor. Problems can arise for lower-class families, who tend to be dependent on immediate family for support, if they begin to model the autonomy they see in middle-class families on television (Newman & Grauerholz, 2002).

Lower-middle-class families often share more commonalities with the working class than with the upper-middle class. These families constitute roughly one third of middle-class households and consist of semi-professionals, skilled craftsmen, and lower level management (Cashell, 2007; Thompson & Hickey, 2005; Williams, Sawyer, & Wahlstrom, 2005). The household income in this group ranges from $35,000 to $75,000.

Most lower-middle-class families require two incomes to provide for their family as is common in the working class. People in this class usually have at least a high school education and many have some college (Fields, 2004). Most workers in this class are closely supervised and do not have the same kind of independence as those in the upper-middle class. They are also less likely to be encouraged to share their thoughts and ideas at work than professionals in the upper-middle class.

Childrearing patterns among the lower-middle class emphasize strict obedience to rules and conformity to social norms. Parents' perceptions of bad behavior and how to discipline children is strongly related to social class (Pinderhughes et al., 2000). Less likely to attend college, lower-middle-class family members are less tolerant of diverse values and behaviors (Pinderhughes et al., 2000).

The Working Class

Working-class families account for approximately 32% of total U.S. household income (Thompson & Hickey, 2005). Typically, working-class families have a strong work ethic with little expectation of work satisfaction (Carter & McGoldrick, 2005). They place an emphasis on obedience, respect for people in authority, and have little tolerance for deviance, unlike the individualistic acceptance of nonconformity of the middle class (Zweig, 2004). The major distinction between the working class and the middle class is their dependence on hourly wages, which range from $16,000 to $30,000, and account for approximately one third of America's income

© iStockphoto.com / heimphoto

The working class has a strong work ethic and little anticipation of work satisfaction.

(Thompson & Hickey, 2005). This is a vulnerable segment of the population because of the impact economic downturns, layoffs and plant closings have on these families.

Working-class people tend to get married earlier than the middle- and upper-class individuals, making them even more vulnerable to economic pressures (Newman & Grauerholz, 2002). Most mothers must work to supplement the family income. This creates a dichotomy in which parents want to be with their children but know they must work to provide a "good home." Unfortunately, children only see the absence of parents which can frequently make it a "bad home" in spite of the parents efforts to the contrary (Newman & Grauerholz, 2002). Working-class parents sacrifice so their children will *not* have the life they have, in contrast to middle-class parents who sacrifice so their children *can* have a life like theirs (Newman & Grauerholz, 2005).

The Lower Class: Families in Poverty

The lower class includes the working poor, as well as those in abject poverty. The working poor are families who have regular employment but whose wages are so low they live in relative poverty. Families in poverty lack the basic needs—food, clothing, shelter—necessary for a minimum standard of well-being and life. Families in this class account for approximately 20% of total U.S. family income and earn less than $16,000 (Thompson & Hickey, 2005). According to the 2007 Census, the poverty rate in 2006 was 12.3%, down from 12.6% in 2005. About 17.4% of the children in America fall into this group (America's children, 2008; DeNavas, Proctor, & Smith, 2007;

© Jupiter Images

1% of the American population experience homelessness each year.

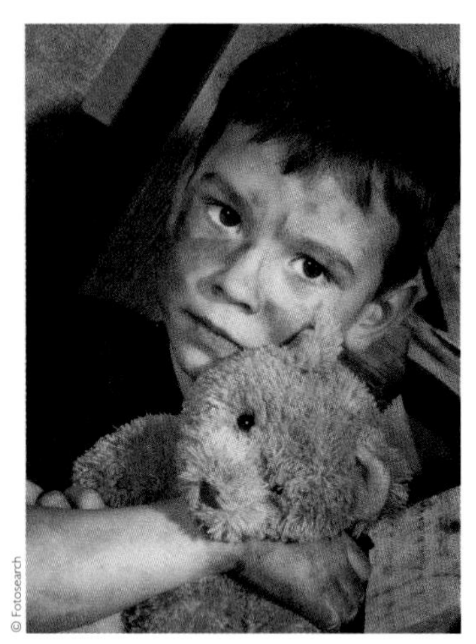

Over 17% of America's children live in poverty.

U.S. Census, 2007c).

Lower-class families often live in deteriorated housing in unsafe neighborhoods. They may be unable to afford adequate clothing for winter and may require government-issued food stamps to provide food for their family (Cherlin, 2002). Poverty exacerbates problems faced by all families. The fear of not enough money, the effects of poor housing, crime-ridden neighborhoods, poor education, and inadequate health care commonly affect lower-class families, as well as the welfare of children in these families (The Real Issue, 2005). Children growing up in poverty are likely to be ill-prepared for school, have low academic achievement, higher rate of teen pregnancy, drug and alcohol problems, poor mental and physical health, delinquent behavior, and unemployment in adolescence and young adulthood (University of Alberta, 2006; Polakow, 2006; Seaman et al., 2006; Stratham, 2007).

Lower-class men often have little or no education and few occupational skills which prevents them from finding work paying more than minimum wage. They generally have few, if any, benefits such as health care or paid time off. Lower-class women often work in low-paying service jobs or are dependent on welfare to provide for their family. A small minority of lower-class families is homeless (Cherlin, 2002). An estimated 3.5 million people, 1.35 million of them children, are likely to experience homelessness in a given year (Homelessness in the United States, 2004) This means 1% of the U.S.

Figure 11.2

Adults in Families Living Below the Poverty Level by Household Type and Sex, 2005

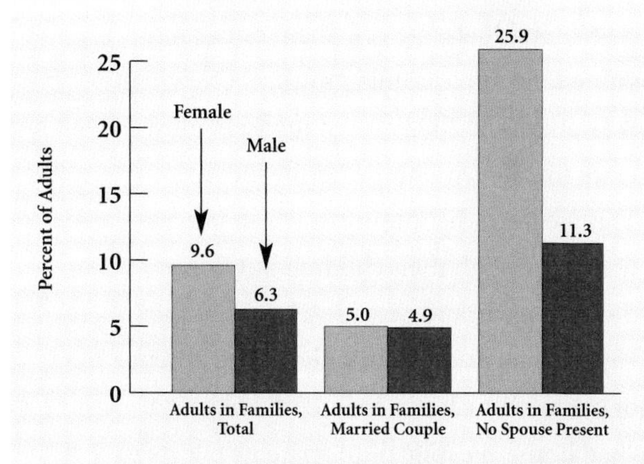

**Families are a group of at least two people related by birth, marriage, or adoption and residing together.*
***Poverty level defined by the U.S. Census Bureau was $19,971 for a family of four in 2005.*

Source: Women's Health USA, 2007 U.S. Department of Health and Human Services, Health Resources and Services Administration, Maternal and Child Health Bureau. Rockville, Maryland: U.S. Department of Health and Human Services.

population will experience homelessness each year (The Urban Institute, 2000; Webster & Bishaw, 2007).

The most common type of family in poverty is the female-headed family which led to the terms feminization of poverty and juvenilization of poverty back in the 1970s. Even when a woman works full-time, she often does not earn enough to support her family without outside assistance (see Figure 11.2). While the gender poverty gap remains large, it has been decreasing and is now about 40%. Almost 1 in every 8 women is poor, compared with 1 in 11 men (DeNavas, Proctor, & Smith, 2007).

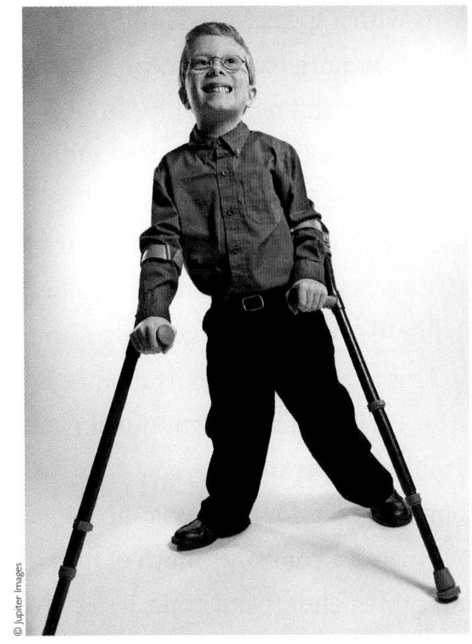

Parents of special-needs children can feel overwhelmed and trapped without respite care.

The Disability Challenge

Families with disabled members face special challenges. Often a family member's disability requires unusual physical, social, or emotional accommodations involving the entire family's support. While these challenges can bring families closer together, they can also drive them apart. The divorce rate is higher in marriages which are unexpectedly faced with a disabled family member. Domestic violence is higher among families with special-needs children (Knox & Schacht, 1999).

Many additional frustrations come with caring for family members who are considered "different" by outsiders. Stares and unwelcome whispers accompany disabled persons who participate in normal public family activities, such as eating at a restaurant, playing at a park, or even attending church. The family, by association, may experience discrimination—called "disability by association" (Burke, 2008). As a result, families with disabled members can become socially isolated, which often produces stress within the family.

For their own emotional well-being and the well-being of other family members, those who care for a special-needs person occasionally need time away from their responsibilities. If no one steps forward to offer respite care, the caregiver can feel overwhelmed and trapped.

Parents with a special-needs child especially require respite time to nurture their own marital relationship. Other siblings need to spend time alone with the parents without the distraction of the special-needs child. Churches and social service agencies can minister to families with disabled children by offering respite care. This allows other family members to care for their own socio-emotional needs.

Finding proper care and accommodations for the special-needs family member consumes much of the family's time. They spend hours in research and make many visits to professionals, all of which is a drain on the family's financial resources. Sometimes other family members are very resentful of the sacrifices parents make for the disabled member. The nondisabled family members—particularly siblings—can feel neglected and socially isolated. Parents of a child with a congenital defect, such as a mental handicap, often feel guilty and have a difficult time forgiving themselves (Roessler, Chung, & Rubin, 2006).

Despite the challenges, studies indicate disabled people do much better when family members are involved in their care and rehabilitation (Roessler, Chung, & Rubin, 2006). Caring for a special-needs family member does not have to produce isolation and resentment. When each family member is encouraged to accept some responsibility for the care of the disabled member, the family bond is strengthened. Of great importance is networking. When families with disabled members are allowed to interact with other families in similar circumstances, they develop important social relationships—for the disabled members, as well as for other family members. Burdens shared are burdens lifted. Spirituality and religion have also been noted as a crucial source of support which provides meaning, hope, and peace for families with handicapped members (Zhang & Rusch, 2005). Unfortunately, the faith community has not proven to be that helpful for these families (Gaventa, 2008).

Same-Sex Families

As an adjunct to our consideration of cultural variations, we will look briefly at a controversial family form which has

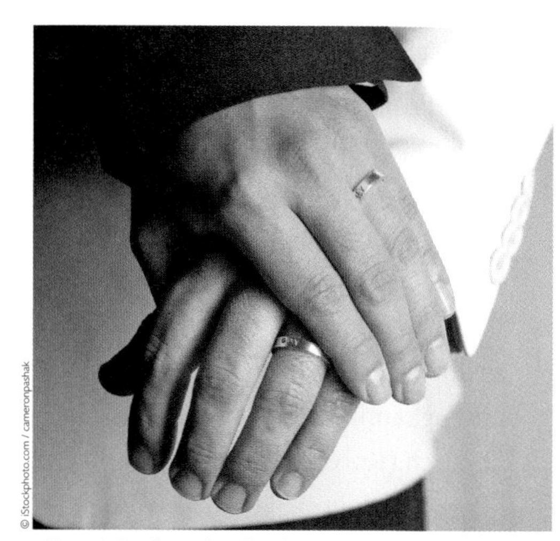

Two states have legalized same-sex marriage and 11 states have some provision to provide benefits for same-sex couples and their children.

gained much attention in recent years: same-sex couples raising children. We will attempt to present the information in a non-biased way, devoid of an agenda and reserve the Christian viewpoint on same-sex couples for the last section of this chapter. Currently, not enough data exists to confirm the percentage of families who currently live this lifestyle. According to the Census Bureau, there are about 780,000 same-sex couples, representing 0.7% of the total number of households (2006b). However, the National Center for Health Statistics reports 4.1% of American men and women identify themselves as lesbian, gay, or bisexual (Mosher, Chandra, & Jones, 2005).

In the introduction to this text, we examined some of the issues surrounding the same-sex marriage debate. The extent of rights or privileges these couples experience varies from state to state. At the current writing, two states, Massachusetts and California authorize same-sex marriages, extending all the rights of heterosexual spouses to same-sex couples. Seven states, Maine, New Hampshire, Vermont, Massachusetts, Connecticut, Rhode Island, and Iowa and the District of Columbia recognize same-sex marriages. Civil unions or domestic partnerships grant nearly all the privileges afforded by marriage and many states offer domestic partnerships, granting some of the rights of marriage. Without the legal provisions of civil unions or domestic partnerships, partners and children do not qualify as dependents for health care benefits, retirement benefits, social security, pension, or death benefits. This can cause additional strain, both financial and emotional, on these families.

The Children of Same-Sex Couples

Many same-sex couples are parents. Certain high-profile celebrities have publicized their same-sex family forms, including the addition of children by adoption or in vitro fertilization. Sometimes, the children are in the custody of one of the partners from a previous heterosexual marriage.

One of the debates surrounding same-sex couples is how it affects children. On one side, same-sex advocates suggest children will be fine and there are many studies to support their position (Bos, van Balen, & van Den Boom, 2004, 2007; Bos & van Balen, 2008; Goldberg, 2007; Golombek et al., 2003; MacCallum & Golombok, 2004; Meezan & Rauch, 2005; Tasker, 2005). On the other side of the debate, there is more skepticism. Since no longitudinal studies of same-sex households have followed children into adulthood, can we say children will be fine? Research exploring diversity of parental relationships is just beginning (Perrin, 2002). There are some studies which have shown a negative impact on children, including: 1) social exclusion and gossip which can lead to hyperactivity in boys and lower self esteem in girls (Bos & van Balen, 2008); 2) the experience of homophobic attitudes from family, friends, peers, and other parents (Fairtlough, 2008); 3) an increased risk of substance-abuse, anxiety, and depression (Weber, 2008); 4) some increase in the likelihood of being homosexual (Cameron & Cameron, 2002; Cameron, 2006); 5) a general increase in reported problems or concerns (Cameron & Cameron, 2002).

Both sides of the argument are most likely right. Children seem to be doing as well as children normally do. What we do not know, because of the methodological difficulties in the research, is if these children are representative of the general population of children raised by gay and lesbian couples. Fortunately, the research situation is improving and soon there may be more definitive answers as to the effects of same-sex parents on children.

Advocates of same-sex relationships suggest that children are doing fine.

Children seem to be doing well, but are they representative of the general population of children living in same-sex families?

The Families of Same-Sex Couples

Same-sex families face a number of challenges, not the least of which is how society views them. The stigma often marginalizes individuals in same-sex families, restricting family members from their full expression of social citizenship, humanity and personhood (Weber, 2008). Unlike the four minority groups reviewed in this chapter, same-sex couples have a choice in their arrangements. African-Americans, Hispanic-Americans, Asian-Americans, and Native-Americans have an ascribed status—their race is an intrinsic part of their makeup. They may choose to deemphasize their cultural heritage and certain aspects of their ethnicity, but they cannot choose to raise their children as "white." The decision to live in a heterosexual or homosexual relationship is a choice. Despite the growing number of same-sex families and the sometimes loud debates surrounding their lifestyle, the cultural expectation in our society is that a heterosexual couple is the norm. A homosexual couple and their family face the same stigma some interracial couples face—usually, even worse.

Same-Sex Couples

Despite the generally inhospitable social climate gay men and lesbians encounter, it is evident that being part of a couple is important to them. We will now look at some of the relevant topics for same-sex couples.

In the last chapter we looked at how couples in satisfied relationships must find some kind of balance in household labor. The same is true for same-sex couples. Research has found same-sex couples are more likely than heterosexual couples to negotiate this balance, taking into consideration different interests, skills, and work schedules (Kurdek, 2005; Patterson, 2000).

Conflict is inevitable in all couple relationships, including same-sex relationships. There are some differences, however. Gottman et al. (2003) found that same-sex couples began conflict and maintained it more positively than their heterosexual counterparts. One possible reason for this is they have fewer differences in power and status between them than do opposite sex spouses. It is interesting to note same-sex couples identify the same areas of conflict as heterosexual couples—finances, affection, sex, criticalness of each other, driving style and household tasks (Kurdek, 2004a).

Same-sex couples, in contrast to heterosexual couples, are less likely to identify family members as sources of support (Kurdek, 2004b; LaSala, 2002). This lack of family support is often viewed as a stressor. This is one of the largest differences between same-sex couples and heterosexual couples. Despite the lack of family support, same-sex couples enjoy a high degree of support from friends, which may help compensate for the lack of family support (Kurdek, 2004b).

Several studies have examined the stability of same-sex relationships. The findings indicate the dissolution rate for same-sex couples is higher than for heterosexual couples (Kurdek, 2004b; Andersson et al., 2004). Dissolution of a same-sex relationship is likely to have the same impact on children as that of a cohabiting couple with children. This is a paramount difference between the two couple types. Same-sex spouses do not have the institutionalized barriers—social, legal, and religious—that married heterosexuals have against leaving their relationship. This is one of the arguments used by advocates of same-sex marriage to legalize same-sex marriage.

Same-sex couples and families are affected by certain risk factors to a greater extent than heterosexual couples and families. Studies have shown gay, lesbian and bisexual individuals are at a greater risk of suicide attempts and completed suicides (Cochran et al., 2007; D'Augelli et al., 2005; Silenzio et al., 2007). They also report a history of more childhood psychological and physical abuse by parents or caretakers, more sexual abuse, more partner psychological and physical abuse, and more sexual assault experiences in adulthood than their heterosexual counterparts (Austin et al., 2008; Balsam, Rothblum, & Beauchaine, 2005). As a group, they have been found to experience more depression, anxiety, panic attacks, and psychological distress than heterosexual individuals (Balsam, Beauchaine, Mickey, & Rothblum, 2005; Cochran, Mays, & Sullivan, 2003). Many of these problems are explained by researchers as the result of the stigmatization and discrimination same-sex couples experience on a regular basis. Despite the higher risk of these problems, it is important to keep in mind that many same-sex couples report happy, satisfying, productive lives.

A Christian Perspective

A Christian Response to Ethnocentrism

Christians fall prey to ethnocentrism when they judge other families as "wrong" or look down on them because they speak a different language, eat different foods, dress differently, or have different beliefs. Christians may *believe* in equality, but still subconsciously *practice* ethnocentrism by alienating themselves from minority cultures or avoiding contact with other ethnic groups. Consequently, communities and churches still reflect distinct clusters of white, African-American, Hispanic-American, Native-American, and Asian-American groups.

Christians are called to witness to those who do not believe in Jesus Christ. However, Christians should not compel families to give up traditions which are unrelated to scriptural principles. Faith in Christ should transcend culture. Cultural traditions have a vital place in maintaining the stability of family life, and Jesus Christ can be affirmed in homes of many different cultures. At the same time, Christians need to exercise discernment when confronted with cultural aspects which challenge Christian principles. The early Christians lived among Jews and Gentiles and struggled with this very same thing. The Apostle Paul offered some good advice about living as a Christian in a multicultural society:

> Let us therefore no longer pass judgment on one another, but resolve instead never to put a stumbling block or hindrance in the way of another . . . Let us then pursue what makes for peace and

> for mutual up building. Do not, for the sake of food, destroy the work of God. Everything is indeed clean, but it is wrong for you to make others fall by what you eat; it is good not to eat meat or drink wine or do anything that makes your brother or sister stumble (Romans 14:13, 19–21 NRSV).

A Christian Response to Social Class

Discrimination based on social class is a subtle threat to Christian unity. Christians often subconsciously show favoritism to the rich while alienating the poor. Even children learn they are expected to belong to certain groups and operate within certain circles of people. It is human nature to form "cliques," to want to be with people "like us." But Christians are called to rise above human nature, to seek Christ's nature. Churches frequently organize along racial, ethnic, and class lines, giving children an impression the "others" are practicing the wrong religion. What did Jesus have to say about social class?

Christians especially should be sensitive to the social systems which negatively affect families in poverty. For example, as New Orleans faced the impending disaster of Hurricane Katrina in 2005, middle-class families with cars and money for gas were able to evacuate on their own, leaving poor families to rely on ill-equipped governmental agencies for survival. Christians and other faith-based groups responded quickly to fill the gaps left by social agencies. Churches opened their doors to refugees, feeding and housing them, transporting them to shelters, and assisting with their basic needs. Christians and other faith-based organizations have continued to supply relief to those whose lives were shattered by Hurricanes Katrina and Rita. Their efforts to rebuild devastated communities have made a concrete difference to thousands of devastated lives. Wherever possible, Christians need to be willing to uphold social justice by advocating public policy changes to help families in poverty.

> "But those who exalt themselves will be humbled, and those who humble themselves will be exalted" (Matthew 23:12 NLT).

A Christian Response to Disability

A key principle of the Christian faith is to uphold the dignity of human beings. Jesus often chided Pharisees for neglecting the poor and sick, and for showing favoritism to elites (see Matthew 23). He said, "Whoever wants to be first must be last of all and servant of all"

(Mark 9:35 NRSV). Paul admonished believers to imitate Christ's humility and to "regard others as better than yourselves" (Philippians 2:3b NRSV).

Those who have been labeled "disabled" by our social world face many challenges. While they may not be the most beautiful to behold or exhibit the most charming behavior, God often uses those who are weak in the eyes of the world to do great things for Christ. Disabled people, far from being a burden, often are a great blessing to their families. When Christians selflessly serve those incapable of expressing their gratitude, they honor the example of Jesus Christ.

A Christian Response to Homosexuality

While there is debate among thoughtful Christians, conservative Christians believe the Bible does not condone homosexuality or same-sex unions. The covenant of marriage is God's design for a man and a woman—not two of the same sex (Genesis 1:27–28; 2:20–24; Proverbs 31:10–31; 1 Corinthians 7:2–5). The majority of Christian scholars agree that a biblical marriage is a marriage between one man and one woman (White & Niell, 2002).

The Bible asks Christians to align themselves with God's design for relationships. While condemning the sin, Christians must not condemn the sinner. Christians must always reach out to others with a loving attitude. When Jesus ministered to the Samaritan woman by the well, He did not approach her with condemnation. He spoke the truth about her situation, engaged her in discussion, and told her who He was. Her decision to accept that truth and change her life ultimately led many others to Christ (John 4:5–42). Christians often avoid people who claim to be homosexual. Isolation can lead to elitism, which does little to promote the love of Jesus Christ. By coming alongside people from all walks of life and by modeling an authentic Christian lifestyle, Christians can have a transforming effect on those who most need God's love and grace.

↳ aim for holiness!

Summary

The issue of cultural diversity should strike home to Christians, who once were considered a minority group. In this chapter, we have focused on four American minority groups and discussed their strengths and challenges. We also have examined how racial, ethnic, and social distinctions affect family relationships. Diverse racial and ethnic groups may involve different values, customs, and behaviors, but these are not necessarily inferior to any other culture. God directs Christians away from ethnocentrism, the belief one culture is somehow superior to others. Instead, God calls Christians to appreciate cultural pluralism—the celebration of diverse cultures.

Racial or ethnic minorities in America tend to have strong families with close extended family relationships. A disturbing pattern of female-headed households continues to challenge many minority families. Minority families generally have close ties to churches, which often form the basis for their communities.

Intercultural marriage has become more common in America. The lowest rate of intermarriage occurs in the African-American population. Intermarriage still carries a stigma, which may cause some families to break their ties to extended family. Often these families form new ties in communities where intermarriage is more common.

Different cultural groups arise from different income levels. This chapter has looked at the distinguishing features between the upper class, the middle class, the working class and the lower class. Understanding middle-class values and lifestyle is important because the middle class is often equated with what is "mainstream" American society. As such it tends to define what is desirable and what one should strive for.

The number of families living in poverty has increased. The female-headed family is the most likely to experience poverty which has led to the terms "feminization of poverty" and "juvenilization of poverty".

Families with a handicapped member experience many challenges. These include discrimination, finding time away, proper care and accommodations, and the social isolation that often plagues these families.

Homosexuality is not an ascribed status. It is included in this chapter because it is a variation that increasingly challenges the conventional notion of family. Christians are encouraged to uphold the biblical definition of marriage as between one man and one woman. They also are encouraged to reach out to homosexuals with love and not with condemnation.

Questions for Thought

1. Do you consider America a melting pot or a salad bowl? Explain your answer.
2. What is God's intention for cultural diversity?
3. How can Christians provide services to families in poverty?
4. How is networking important to special-needs families?
5. Discuss a Christian response to homosexuality.

Resources

Books:

Promises I Can Keep: Why Poor Women Put Motherhood Before Marriage by Kathryn Edin and Maria Kefalas. (University of California Press, 2007)

Movies:

American Family: Journey of Dreams. The first drama series to air on broadcast TV featuring a Latino family. To find out more about listings in your area, visit www.pbs.org (accessed June 23, 2009).

Remember the Titans, (PG). DVD. Looks at family structures in different cultures, including evaluating stereotypes.

Waging a Living, (NR). Docudrama which looks at America's working poor

The Color Purple, (PG-13). Drama that shows the problems faced by African-American women during the early 1900s including poverty, racism, and sex discrimination.

Online video:

Class and family structure in the U.S—Professor from Minnesota http://www.youtube.com/ watch?v=F0Oqeov0Gcw (accessed June 23, 2009)

Website:

Wedding traditions for various cultures: http://www.weddingyellowpages.net/articles/ wedding_traditions_customs.php (accessed June 23, 2009)

12 Conflict in Families

I . . . beg you to lead a life worthy of your calling, for you have been called by God. Always be humble and gentle. Be patient with each other, making allowance for each other's faults because of your love. Make every effort to keep yourselves united in the Spirit, binding yourselves together with peace.

—Ephesians 4:1–3 NLT

© iStockphoto.com / junial

Although God has designed us as individuals, we cannot live apart from other people. We are called to relate to one another in such a way we fulfill our potential and help others to fulfill their potential as God's image bearers. Because people need one another, we gather in groups, such as families and communities. We speak often of the family as the foundational building block of society. The best cement for holding these blocks together is love—love for one another and love for God, who loves us in return.

However, our relationships with other human beings are very fragile, imbued with great potential for disagreement and conflict. The fact we are not all alike contributes intrinsically to the inevitability of diverse opinions, choices, and styles; the fact we are fallen human beings contributes to the inevitability of disagreement and estrangement.

The more we come to know another person—the closer we get to one another—the greater will be our potential for disagreement. The more intimate our relationships become, the more intense our conflicts will be. The more deeply we love someone, the more we can hurt and be hurt.

Although it is inevitable, conflict does not have to destroy relationships. We can resolve and manage conflict by controlling our reaction to conflict. The act of resolving conflicts actually can help couples build up their relationships and draw them closer together.

In this chapter, we will review basic types of familial conflict (conflict as it relates to families). We will then focus on constructive conflict management, offering important recommendations for effective conflict resolution. We will also examine how destructive conflict negatively impacts families, offering strategies for survival and change.

When conflict results in argument and violence it is destructive conflict.

Understanding Conflict

Couples cannot avoid conflict, but each spouse can decide how to respond. Will the couple allow conflict to destroy their relationship or will they use conflict to build a stronger relationship?

Some couples claim they never have any conflicts. This should raise a warning flag. If spouses never disagree, do they truly know one another? Are they truly communicating? Are they avoiding conflict by changing the subject? Does one simply give in to the other without discussion? Avoiding conflict or denying its existence is a sign of an unhealthy relationship.

When conflict results in argument and violence, it is destructive conflict. Destructive conflict involves disagreements which are negatively resolved. People who use conflict destructively use the tactics of avoidance, coercion, or violence (Cox & Gunn, 1999).

Constructive conflict means the parties involved disagree according to the rules of fair fighting. This results in deeper communication and resolution. Often, too, couples who work out their conflict constructively strengthen their relationships (Cox & Gunn, 1999).

Sources of Conflict

As a family increases in complexity (e.g., number and ages of children; stepfamily; complicated work and activity schedules), it becomes more susceptible to conflict.

Disagreements can become intense because family members live together in close quarters and often have to coordinate their activities and schedules. Small annoyances can fester and grow until they become full-scale blowups.

Knox and Schacht (1999) identify six sources of conflict in marriage:

1. *Behavior*: Some annoying behavioral habits seem to become intolerable when people live together. An increasingly problematic behavior which is the basis for major marital conflict is addiction. Drinking, smoking, drugs, and pornography are all areas which create couple conflict (Koczyriski, 2004).
2. *Cognitions and perceptions*: Differences in opinions may mean members do not always get their way.
3. *Value differences:* Values are the basis for behavior. When family members disagree on values, one member may participate in behavior another finds wrong or offensive. In addition to differences in values, conflict can result from personality differences. Imposing one's lifestyle on another and not valuing compromise have been shown to contribute to marital conflict (Koczyriski, 2004).
4. *Inconsistent rules:* Children or parents may express frustration when there seems to be different rules for different family members, or when parents disagree about rules for the children.
5. *Leadership ambiguity*: There may be struggles for power among family members, or a lack of guidance when situations need to be clarified. Power struggles within the family can be a key element in domestic violence (Yllo, 2007).
6. *Job stress:* People are often quite controlled when they are in a public situation all day, but sometimes unload stress on family members when they arrive home. Along with job stress, especially for dual career families, is the division of labor at home. Uneven distribution of duties is another major source of conflict for couples (Koczyriski, 2004).

In parallel conflict style, couples may avoid each other or give each other the "silent treatment".

When there are children in the home, conflicts can be quite intense. Couples frequently disagree over childrearing practices. The demands of small children can be stressful. Teens can create much tension and disagreement within families. Families who do not have good conflict management skills are often surprised to find themselves in the throes of destructive conflict.

Couples in Conflict

Gottman (2001) has found that a full 69% of all marital conflicts never go away. For instance, if the couple was arguing over spending too much money 10 years ago, they are likely still arguing over it today. The reason for this is couples attach different meaning to the same situations. These meanings are often deeply rooted in each person and often have their roots in the family of origin. Thus, arguments about money could really be about feelings of insecurity and fear about the future. The couple, embroiled in the argument over spending, has no idea the argument is about anything more than "what one of them spent last week."

Couples tend to develop rather predictable habits of conflict behavior. Three styles of conflict which can be destructive in a relationship have been identified (Adler, Rosenfeld, Proctor, & Proctor, 2004; Knox & Schacht, 1999):

1. Complementary style of conflict—Couples who use a complementary style of conflict behave opposite to one another. For example, he will yell and then she will listen.
2. Symmetrical style of conflict—Couples who use a symmetrical style of conflict react equally to one another. For example, he shouts insults and she shouts insults back at him. These spouses often don't really hear one another, but just try to outdo the other.
3. Parallel style of conflict—Couples who use a parallel style of conflict retreat from one another or avoid one another. For example, some couples will give each other the "silent treatment."

Types of Conflict

Personality-Based Conflict. We often blame others for a conflict, assuming if they would just change something about *themselves*, the conflict would disappear. This is personality-based conflict (Buss, 2006). For example, a husband may be agitated with his wife because she somehow always seems to cause them to arrive late to church. He insists she needs to be more punctual in order for their relationship to work.

The problem with personality-based conflict is personalities are very difficult to change. She may admit she needs to be more organized and will "work on it." Inevitably, she slips up and causes him to become even more agitated.

"I thought you said you were going to try to help us be on time!" he shouts. "No, an apology just won't cut it this time! You just don't care how this embarrasses me, do you?"

Personalities don't change overnight. Deeply ingrained patterns of behavior are very difficult to erase.

Situational Conflict. Instead of insisting a person change immediately, perhaps it would be better to encourage the person to change something about a particular situation or circumstance which tends to exacerbate a personality flaw. For example, perhaps in the situation above, the wife is trying to get the children dressed and ready to go. Instead of berating her for always making them late, the husband could pitch in to help, or could make sure everyone gets up a few minutes earlier. By sharing the burden, they allow themselves time to get to where they need to be.

Peter Cade / Iconica / Getty Images

"I thought you said you made a reservation!"

Unexpected situations can exacerbate personality flaws or it can be a time to pull together and work together to solve the problem.

Situational conflict is usually much easier to handle than personality-based conflict. For example, a wife spends over an hour commuting to and from her job every day. She is angry she has to "waste" 2 hours a day and 10 hours a week in travel time, not to mention the cost of fuel. When she arrives home after work, she is usually short-tempered with everyone. If she changes her situation and finds a job closer to home, even if it means a lower salary, it helps to defuse her anger.

While family members work to change personality flaws, they need to acknowledge that certain situations make personality flaws particularly noticeable. In the examples above, the husband was unreasonably angry because he felt his wife was making them late to church. The wife was unreasonably angry over having to commute a long distance to work. Whenever possible, people should assess the situations which inflame personality flaws. In both cases, the personality flaw was unreasonable anger. If they were not able to change their situations, they would

© iStockphoto.com / keeweeboy

When a spouse withdraws from conflict without cooperation, resentment can build which can sometimes erupt violently.

have had to look for other ways to control their anger.

Situational conflicts often occur because of differing expectations. Each member of the marital dyad comes to the marriage with their own unique version of how marital tasks should be allocated. Couples are then faced with negotiating a congruence of roles which can lead to conflict. See Sidebar 12.1 for an example of how expectations and incongruence can create conflict.

> **SIDEBAR 12.1**
> **A Humorous Example of the Incongruence of Expectations**
>
> There is an old story about a young couple who had recently returned from their honeymoon. The new wife prepared a special dinner complete with candlelight and music, they sat down to a wonderfully romantic meal. After dinner, the new husband pushed his chair back, took her hand and said, "Let's go for a walk". She instantly became angry and upset, fighting back tears. She was instantly ready to defend, but she had no idea what she needed to defend.
>
> When they were later able to discuss what had happened, he found out that in her family, the parents never fought in front of the children. They always went for a walk to argue. She found out that in his family, after a wonderful meal, the parents went out for a walk, leaving the dishes on the table until they returned or for the children to clean.
>
> After that, he learned to preface a request to go for a walk with a smile and a word of assurance that everything was fine, and she learned that disagreements, managed in healthy ways, were actually part of normal family life.

Conflict Management Styles

It is important in marriage to avoid conflict whenever possible. Downs and Downs (2003) give some suggestions to help couples avoid rather than deal with conflict. These include:

Show up for the marriage: It is important to develop dedication to the marriage which requires time spent together. It is important for couples to spend time interacting with each other with a focus on each other.

Talk about something else: It is not just about talking, but about learning what is important to one's spouse. This requires conversation about things other than the job, the children, or next week's schedule, such as art, God, politics, etc.

Heap on encouragement and praise: A

fundamental tenet is that conflict increases as praise decreases. According to Downs and Downs (2003) there are gender differences in play here. In the absence of praise, women perceive disapproval. The opposite is true for men. The absence of criticism means everything is alright. Sidebar 12.2 is an example of incongruent expectations.

Balswick and Balswick (2006) describe five styles of conflict management spouses use. While we often use a combination of styles, when tension rises, we tend to fall back on the style modeled most in our family of origin. That style may or may not have worked well in our family of origin, but in a marriage it frequently creates even more conflict. As you examine the five styles, keep in mind none of the styles are intrinsically bad. Some produce more consistently positive outcomes, but each of the styles may be appropriate in certain circumstances.

1. *Withdrawal:* A family member simply withdraws without cooperation or assertion. This is not healthy in most family situations because resentment tends to build. The family member who is practicing avoidance may allow emotions to build and may suddenly erupt irrationally. The biggest problem for the withdrawer is to come back and work on resolving the issue.
2. *Yield:* A family member yields (or gives in) to another family member. This is unhealthy when the yielder gives in without expressing their own desires, they build up resentment toward others.
3. *Win:* A family member is always trying to create conflict in order to win. These family members will spend much time arguing over seemingly insignificant issues, just because they enjoy winning and can't stand to lose. These spouses tend to be very persuasive, harsh, and demeaning to their spouse.
4. *Compromise:* Family members negotiate, each giving up a little in order to keep the peace. This may be appropriate in some situations, but at other times, compromise can undercut what is the "right thing" to do. Cooperation in finding a mutually satisfactory resolution is the goal.
5. *Resolve:* This spouse will stay with a conflict until there is a good resolution for each party. Maximum satisfaction is the goal of the resolver since they see compromise as defeat.

The Balswicks (1999; 2006) explain that at different times in His ministry, Jesus used each of these patterns of conflict management. In a biblical model of family, members exercise each of the five patterns to make decisions about when it is most appropriate to compromise, resolve, win, yield, or withdraw. Different situations call for different responses.

For example, the decision to marry should never be a *compromise*: "I'll marry you if you do _____ for me." But housework readily lends itself to compromise: "I'll do dishes tonight if you will vacuum tomorrow."

A family member might need to compete to *win* over others: "It is wrong for you to have an abortion. Here are the reasons why . . ."

It may be necessary for one family member to *yield to* another: "I will trust that you know how we should invest this money."

Sidebar 12.2
An Example of the Incongruence of Expectations

"We live by encouragement and die without it—slowly, sadly and angrily."

Source: Biography for Celeste Holm

It might be appropriate to *withdraw* to avoid conflict altogether: "I know we don't agree on politics, so we will just not discuss it."

It is certainly wise to "pick one's battles," acknowledging some things are just not worth fighting over, while other things should never be compromised.

Spouses who consistently need to win can be very harsh, persuasive and demeaning.

In the 1970s, Thomas and Kilman (1974) identified five styles of conflict resolution based on varying degrees of cooperativeness and assertiveness. These styles continue to be widely used today in describing conflict resolution and include:

Competitive: Individuals, who tend to use the competitive style, know what they want and take a firm stand on it. They usually operate in a position of power which may create resentment in others.

Collaborative: People who tend to use the collaborative style try to meet the needs of all involved. They tend to be highly assertive but cooperative.

Compromising: These individuals try to find a solution that will at least partially satisfy everyone. The compromiser expects everyone including himself to give up something.

Accommodating: This individual seeks to meet the needs of others at their own expense. They are not very assertive but are highly cooperative.

Avoiding: People using this style avoid the conflict altogether. While this can be useful at times, it is often a weak and ineffective approach.

Figure 12.1 combines the Balswick's styles of conflict management with the Kilman Conflict Resolution Grid. You can see from the grid, avoidance or withdrawal produces the least results in conflict management. The more we value the relationship over seeking our own interests, the more likely we are to try to resolve the conflict in a positive manner for all persons involved. The converse is also true: the less we value the relationship, the more likely we are to avoid resolution or the more likely we are to compete to win. Both of these can be extremely damaging to a relationship if used consistently.

The more we place value on mercy in a relationship, the greater the likelihood of working toward resolution of conflict. When justice and fairness are the goals, the couple is more likely to compete to achieve what each one considers fair in the relationship. In the New Testament, Jesus repeatedly calls Christians to be merciful. Mercy in a marriage prevents spouses from battling over what is "fair." Fair in a marriage is not always equitable or good for the marriage.

Ephesians, chapter 5, gives couples guidance regarding their relationship.

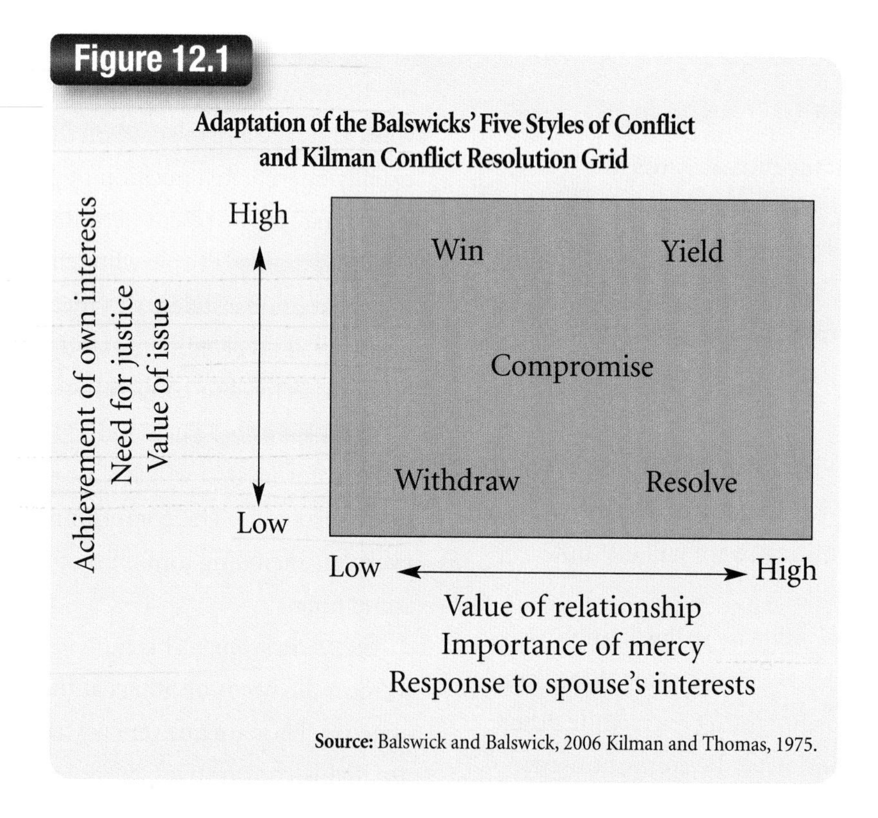

Source: Balswick and Balswick, 2006 Kilman and Thomas, 1975.

Ephesians 5:21 calls husbands and wives to "submit to one another out of reverence for Christ." When spouses respond to each other's needs and interests, they are more likely to resolve their conflicts. Couples who are more focused on their own self interests are more likely to compete against each other, with self interest at the forefront.

Constructive Conflict Management

American culture—including its movies, television shows, and popular songs—seems to assert that people who truly love each other will never quarrel. In reality, quite the opposite is true. Conflict in intimate relationships is inevitable. The more intensely couples love, the more intensely they will disagree. The key to marital fulfillment is not the avoidance of conflict, but the successful management of conflict. These are skills which take many years to develop.

Because children have underdeveloped conflict management skills, they frequently quarrel and fight with their siblings and friends. As people mature, they learn more constructive ways to resolve differences.

Twelve Rules for Fair Fighting

Conflict management skills are learned skills, not ingrained abilities. The success of families hinges on their ability to learn these important skills. The Balswicks (2006, p.124) suggest the following 12 rules for fair fighting:

1. One issue only. Identify the issue and don't veer from it.
2. Choose the time and place. Agree on a neutral place and time.
3. Be prepared. Know and abide by the rules. Bring a proper attitude.
4. The past is the past. Refuse to "bring up the past" in a current fight.
5. No surprise punches. Emotion-laden areas are off limits.
6. No hitting below the belt. Sensitive areas divert the issue.
7. Don't dismiss. Don't be flippant or make light of problems presented.
8. No "why"-questions allowed. Blame or accusation often lies behind "why" questions.
9. Dyad vs. triad. Keep it between the two of you—no third person allowed.
10. Don't ridicule. Ridiculing is rude. No put-downs or name-calling.
11. Veto power. Signal technical error when rules are broken.
12. Break at the end of each round. Short breaks ensure bodily rest.

Five Steps to Resolve Conflicts

Balswick and Balswick (1999) suggest five steps to resolve conflicts.

1. *Identify the Issue.* Most family conflicts involve more than one issue. Family members may disagree about which issue is the real one. The first task is to prioritize the issues. Come to an agreement about what issue to tackle first. Focus on that issue until it is resolved and then move on to the next.
2. *Choose the Right Time and Place.* Some conflicts can be constructively resolved immediately. If emotions are intense, however, it is better to allow a "cooling off" period. Choose a time when you can have privacy and all parties are not under undue stress. For example, it is not a good idea to hash out the family's future the night before a big project is due. It is not a good time to unload all your grievances at a formal dinner with friends and family present. Choose a time and place when you will have sufficient stress-free time and the necessary privacy to resolve the issue. See Sidebar 12.3 for an illustration of choosing the right time.
3. *Begin with a Positive Stroke.* Say something nice about one another before discussing what improvements are needed. This will soften the blow of criticism and enable everyone to listen and respond attentively.
4. *Express Anger Without Abusing One Another.* Anger is not wrong, but it must be controlled so it is not abusive. The Bible says, "Be angry but do not sin; do not let the sun go down on your anger" (Ephesians 4:26 NRSV). Use "I" statements ("I feel angry") rather than "you" statements ("You make me angry"). This makes you take ownership of your feelings instead of putting the blame on someone else. Anger which is verbally or physically abusive is sinful.
5. *Avoid Triangles.* Do not pull in someone else to side with you. Two against one is never fair. While children should be exposed to constructive conflict resolution by their parents, it is never appropriate to force them to take sides.

Choosing the right time and place can determine the likelihood of resolving a conflict.

When families stick to the rules of fair fighting, they will be able to resolve their conflicts constructively and in a manner which does not destroy the relationship. Instead, they will find that by working together to solve their problems, they have honored one another and strengthened their relationship.

Focus on the Positive

In their extensive research into marriage, the Gottman Institute (2004) found the first few minutes of an interaction can be crucial in setting the tone for its outcome. They recommend softening the impact of your words before unleashing critical statements in anger. According to them, it is *not* a good idea to say whatever you are thinking. Couples who begin to tolerate hurtful statements and bad behavior from one another begin to destroy their relationship. It is best to learn to interrupt long, heated discussions and focus on the positive, rather than the negative. See Sidebar 12.4 for some important tips on facilitating communication in a marriage.

Sidebar 12.3
Constructive Conflict Resolution: Waiting for the Right Time

Gary and I don't really fight. I mean, not the "knock-down-drag-out-dirty" kind of fights that you see on TV. Sure, we disagree—*a lot*. But we always try to find some middle ground. I remember a time when Gary wanted to buy a new car, and I thought we just shouldn't be spending money on things like that. One day, he dragged me along to look at cars. It was a Sunday afternoon, when the dealerships were closed, so we wouldn't be bothered by a salesperson. But I couldn't get interested in any of the cars. So, we decided to give it some time, since it was clear we weren't going to come to any agreement. I was too busy with some situations at work to even think about buying a new car at that time. I'm glad he didn't push it, because I didn't want to deal with it just then. Sometimes, the best resolution is to agree to disagree and give it some time.

A couple of weeks later, my car broke down while I was at lunch. It was only a dead battery, but it delayed me enough to make me late for a meeting. That was all I needed to convince me it was time for a new car! We were able to find a car that was reliable and economical (my requirements), while being sporty and fun to drive (his requirements). In this way, we resolved the conflict. So, we both benefited.

—Anonymous

Destructive Conflict

When families avoid conflict or do not follow guidelines for constructive resolution, conflict can erupt violently, resulting in relationship-destroying consequences.

Avoidance behaviors (withdrawing or the silent treatment) can seem to maintain peace, but without any constructive resolution, these kinds of behaviors can eat away at the relationship. Often conflict which is avoided erupts in an inappropriate emotional outburst, leaving all parties wondering, "What happened?" It is better to face the conflict and deal with it than to pretend it does not exist.

Sidebar 12.4
Marriage 101 Tips

Seek help early. The average couple waits 6 years before seeking help for marital problems (keep in mind, half of all marriages that end do so in the first 7 years). This means the average couple lives with unhappiness far too long.

Edit yourself. Couples who avoid saying every critical thought when discussing touchy topics are consistently the happiest.

Soften your "start up." Arguments first "start up" because a spouse sometimes escalates the conflict from the get-go by making a critical or contemptuous remark in a confrontational tone. Bring up problems gently and without a blaming tone.

Accept influence. A marriage succeeds to the extent that the husband can accept influence from his wife. For example, a woman says, "Do you have to work Thursday night? My mother is coming that weekend, and I need your help getting ready." The husband replies, "My plans are set, and I'm not changing them." This guy is in a shaky marriage. A husband's ability to be influenced by his wife (rather than vice-versa) is crucial. Research demonstrates that women are already well practiced at accepting influence from men, and a true partnership only occurs when a husband can do so as well.

Have high standards. Happy couples have high standards for each other. The most successful couples are those who, even as newlyweds, refused to accept hurtful behavior from one another. The lower the level of tolerance for bad behavior in the beginning of a relationship, the happier the couple is down the road.

Learn to repair and exit the argument. Successful couples know how to exit an argument. Happy couples know how to repair the situation before an argument gets completely out of control. Successful repair attempts include changing the topic to something completely unrelated; using humor; stroking your partner with a caring remark ("I understand that this is hard for you"); making it clear you're on common ground ("This is our problem"); backing down (in marriage, as in the martial art Aikido, you have to yield to win); and, in general, offering signs of appreciation for your partner and his or her feelings along the way ("I really appreciate and want to thank you for . . ."). If an argument gets too heated, take a 20 minute break and agree to approach the topic again when you are both calm.

Focus on the bright side. When discussing problems, happily married couples make at least 5 times as many positive statements to and about each other and their relationship as negative ones. For example, they might say, "We laugh a lot" instead of, "We never have any fun." A good marriage must have a rich climate of positivism. Make deposits to your emotional bank account.

Source: Gottman Institute, 2004.

The Myths of Family Violence

An extremely destructive form of conflict is the use of violence. Abuse is an extreme and violent adaptation to a need to control one's family. Our culture has many misconceptions regarding violence in families. The following myths are taken from the Domestic Violence Awareness Handbook (2008).

Myth 1: Family violence is rare. While statistics on family violence are not precise, millions of children, women, and even men are physically abused each year.

© iStockphoto.com / fredpal

Expressing anger is not wrong as long as it is controlled and not emotionally or verbally abusive.

Myth 2: Family violence is confined to the lower class. In fact, violence occurs in all social classes. Police records, victim services, and research have shown abuse exists equally in all socioeconomic groups, regardless of race and culture. While abusers come from all walks of life, some types of families are more prone to abuse than others. People in families who experience structural strain (e.g., intermarriage, many children, unemployment, social isolation, or special needs children) are more prone to violence.

Myth 3: Alcohol and drugs are the real cause of abuse in the home. While many abusers also use drugs and alcohol, these are two separate problems. Abusers, whether intoxicated or high, typically control their behavior until they are in private, where abuse can go undetected.

Myth 4: Battered spouses like being hit and/or are responsible for the violence; otherwise, they would leave. While people generally feel sorry for battered children because they are helpless to stop the violence, battered spouses are often blamed for their own situation. Many people do not understand why battered spouses may feel trapped in their marriages, seemingly powerless to support themselves away from their abusive spouses.

Myth 5: Children who are abused will grow up to be abusers. While people from violent homes are more likely to become violent themselves, the cycle is not automatic. It is possible to break the cycle of violence and form a family life remarkably different from the family of origin (Widom & Brzustowicz, 2006).

Myth 6: Domestic violence is a "loss of control." Violent behavior is a choice. Abusers use violence to control their victim. Domestic violence is about using control, not losing control (Domestic Violence Handbook, 2007).

© iStockphoto.com / juanmonino

An extremely destructive form of conflict is the use of violence.

Violence in Families

There are many different behaviors used by one person in a relationship to control the other. Many of these behaviors do not result in physical harm, yet they are abuse. The following are examples of abuse (Domestic Violence Handbook, 2007):

- name-calling and putdowns
- preventing a partner from contacting family and friends
- withholding money
- preventing a partner from getting or keeping a job
- actual or threatened physical harm
- sexual assault (even by one's spouse)
- stalking
- intimidation

Violence can be criminal: such as some type of physical assault, sexual abuse including any type of forced or unwanted sexual activity, and stalking. Emotional, psychological, and financial abuse are not criminal behaviors, but they are forms of abuse.

Why does conflict sometimes result in violence? In a culture which often does not encourage constructive conflict resolution, unresolved conflict can erupt into a dangerous situation. Two cultural factors seem to contribute to violence in families:

1. The cultural expectation that good families do not experience conflict;
2. A culture filled with violence.

A Culture of Violence. Our culture often encourages families to avoid conflict. As a result, family members are sometimes not encouraged to share their feelings. At the same time, the media often presents violence as an acceptable way to manage differences. On television shows and in movies, violence gets attention and gets results.

A victim will learn to do anything to avoid a violent confrontation. In this way, one person has successfully controlled another person. For example, violence becomes an effective way to control children—but it does not encourage them to make their own decisions and to recognize natural consequences for bad behavior. When parents discipline their children physically, they must take care not to allow their anger to be abusive. Society has a

Intimidation even without physical violence is still abuse.

About one forth of family violence is committed by women.

responsibility to protect children and intervene when the aberration of physical discipline—physical abuse—occurs.

Statistics. According to the U.S. Department of Justice (Longley, 2005), family violence accounted for 11% of all reported and unreported violence between 1998 and 2002. Of these offenses against family members, 49% were a crime against a spouse, 11% a parent attacking a child, and 41% an offense against another family member. Seventy-three percent of family violence victims were female and 76% of persons who committed family violence were male. Family violence is generally underreported because of the cultural belief that what happens within the family is private and out of fear of what might happen if it is reported.

Spouse Abuse

About 1 in 5 couples each year will experience at least one violent episode in their marriage (Rennison, 2003). Spouse abuse often starts in courtship and escalates in marriage. It may begin as a light slap during a frustrating argument. With each new conflict, the abuse may get worse. Victims of abuse often feel they deserve the abuse and have no alternative but to live in the abusive relationship. Warning signs of a possible abuser include extreme jealously, an attempt to control, and a tendency to blame others. Victims are often isolated from others, so they may feel they have nowhere else to go (American Psychiatric Association, 2005).

Male Dominance. Spousal abuse is more common in traditional marriages where the husband is dominant. By traditional, we are referring to a contemporary version of a nineteenth-century model of marriage in which the husband and wife share one identity—the identity of the husband. In chapter 6, we examined how today's traditional marriage differs from previous versions. However, certain elements remain, including a clear definition of roles. Husbands are the primary providers and make most of the decisions. Wives care for the children and the home, especially while the children are young.

In the case of spousal abuse, people who adhere to traditional gender roles may believe the husband *should* control the wife and children. In addition, if a man with traditional gender attitudes is denied access to power in the economic world (e.g., being unemployed or underemployed), he may compensate by trying to command more power in the home. This explains why spouse abuse is more common in marriages with traditional gender roles (Carter & McGoldrick, 2005; Esqueda & Harrison, 2005).

Marital Rape. Another disturbing phenomenon associated with spouse abuse is marital rape. This is a particularly vicious form of control because it violates the cultural norm that sexual intimacy is highly valued and privatized. In a culture which views sex as an act of love, rape becomes a particularly intrusive form of abuse. The Centers for Disease Control and Prevention (2006) reports a woman is more likely to be forced into a nonconsensual sexual act with her husband than with a stranger. Recent findings on the effects of pornography on the brain, and the resultant increase in aggression, helps explain why there is often a link between pornography and male sexual aggressiveness or abusiveness with their female partners (Seto, Alexandria, & Barbaree, 2001; Vega & Malamuth, 2003; Weaver, 2004).

Abusers are usually very remorseful and caring after an episode of abuse, sparking hope in the victim that it won't happen again.

Why Do They Stay? Why do spouses stay in an abusive relationship? Studies have shown over half of abused women return to their abusive relationships after discharge from a shelter (Mills, 2003). Mills goes on to suggest several reasons women stay in abusive and violent relationships. They stay because they have an intimate relationship or an emotional connection to their abuser, their children and the life they have built. Some stay for religious reasons, viewing divorce and remarriage as non-options. Some women see no other alternatives for providing financially and emotionally for themselves and their children. Still other women lack the self-esteem, possibly the result of many years of abuse, to make the decision to leave and act on it. Some women return because of ongoing threats of violence toward them or their children. When they return, they likely have less confidence and personal power, making them even more susceptible to abuse in the relationship.

Even women who successfully leave the abusive relationship are likely to return to the relationship many times before finally making the break (Mills, 2003). These women struggle with trying to decide what they should do. "They are deeply conflicted about how to address the abuse while trying to preserve what they value in their relationships" (Mills, 2003, p. 30). See Sidebar 12.5 for a battered woman's firsthand account.

The Cycle of Violence. Often the abused who choose to stay in such a broken relationship do not understand the powerful cycle of violence (see Figure 12.2). After the abused leaves, the abuser will notoriously seem very remorseful—full of apologies, offering gifts and promises it will never happen again. But once they reunite, the abuser is likely to return again to the same means of violence. This time it may be even more severe in a twisted view toward making sure the abused won't leave again. Thus, the cycle continues, each time more intense than before:

conflict violence apology reconciliation
conflict violence apology reconciliation
conflict violence apology reconciliation

The abuser actually thrives on this relationship. When not angry, he or she may be a very nice person—in public. But inside the privacy of the home, anger can erupt

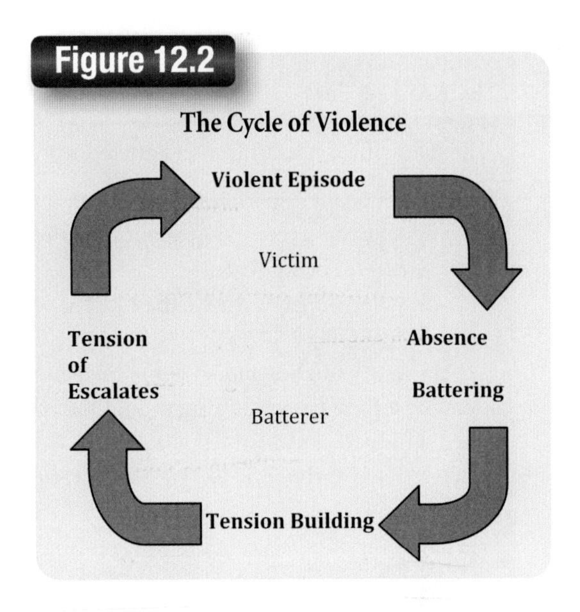

without warning and without the control so carefully cultivated in public. Fearful the spouse will leave, the abuser can seem to be quite remorseful. But this abusive behavior is a symptom of a deep personality problem which cannot be cured overnight. Even with professional help, abusive spouses have a difficult time changing.

Child Abuse

You will recall from chapter 7, the problem of child abuse is staggering. For instance, roughly 12 children in 1,000 are victims of abuse, usually at the hands of their parents. Girls are slightly more likely to be victims than boys. Young children, especially those under age 3, are more likely to experience abuse and neglect than older children. (Child Welfare Information Gateway, 2007).

SIDEBAR 12.5
There Are No Ears

(The following is a letter from a battered woman who attended a presentation on battering.)

You will never be able to realize how it felt to sit there looking like a well-dressed, middle-class woman, knowing that you were talking about me. It was the very first time I have ever heard anyone say I wasn't wrong for being beaten!

I will give you my own firsthand experiences and hope that it will be useful to you. I am presently married to the man who beats me, so I will have to remain unidentified.

I am in my thirties and so is my husband. I have a high school education and am presently attending a local college, trying to find the education I need to support myself. My husband is a college graduate and a professional in his field. We are both attractive people and, for the most part, respected and well-liked. We have three children and live in a middle-class home with all the comforts one would possibly want.

I have everything, except life without fear.

For most of my married life, I have been periodically beaten by my husband. What do I mean by "beaten"? I mean those times when parts of my body have been hit violently and repeatedly, causing painful bruises, swellings, bleeding wounds, unconsciousness, or any combination of those things.

I have had glasses thrown at me. I have been kicked in the abdomen when I was visibly pregnant. I have been kicked off the bed and hit while lying on the floor—while I was pregnant. I have been whipped, kicked, and thrown, picked up, and thrown down again. I have been punched and kicked in the head, chest, face, and abdomen on numerous occasions.

I have been slapped for saying something about politics, having a different view about religion, for swearing, for crying, for wanting to have intercourse. I have been threatened when I wouldn't do something I was told to do. I have been threatened when I have stated bitterly that I didn't like what he was doing with another woman. Each time my husband has left the house and remained gone for days.

Few people have ever seen my black-and-blue face or swollen lips, because I have always stayed indoors feeling ashamed. My husband on a few occasions did call a day or so later to provide me with an excuse that I could use for returning to work, the grocery store, the dentist appointment, and so on. I used the excuses—a car accident, oral surgery, things like that.

"Why didn't you seek help?" you might ask. I did. I went early in our marriage to a clergyman who, after a few visits, told me that my husband meant no real harm, that he was just confused and felt insecure. I was to be more tolerant and understanding. More important, I was to forgive him for the beatings, just as Christ had forgiven me from the cross. So, I did.

Things continued the same. I turned next time to a doctor. I was given little pills to relax me and told to take things a little easier. I was "just too nervous."

I turned to a friend, and when her husband found out, he accused me of either making things up or exaggerating the situation. She was told to stay away from me. (She didn't, but she could no longer help.)

I turned to a professional family guidance agency. There I was told that my husband needed help and I should find a way to control the incidents. But I couldn't control the beating—that was his decision.

I called the police one time. They not only didn't respond to the call, but they called several hours later to ask if things had "settled down." I could have been dead by then!

continued

Sidebar 12.5
There Are No Ears *continued*

I have nowhere to go if it happens again. No one wants a woman with three children. Even if someone is kind enough, they wouldn't want to become involved in what is commonly referred to as a "domestic situation." Everyone I have gone to for help has somehow wanted to blame me and to vindicate my husband.

No one has to "provoke" a wife beater. He'll hit when he's ready and for whatever reason he wishes. I know that I do not want to be hit. I know, too, that I will be beaten again, unless I can find a way out for myself and my children. I am terrified for them also. As a married woman I have no recourse but to remain in the situation, which is causing me to be painfully abused.

I have suffered physical and emotional battering and spiritual rape all because the social structure of my world says I cannot do anything about a man who wants to beat me. Society says that I must be committed to a man, without any opportunity for an education and earning capacity. It says that my children must be subjected to the emotional battering caused when they see their mother's beaten face or hear my screams in the middle of the night.

I would like to write more, but that would take a book—and there is no market because there are no ears.

Thank you,
Jane Doe

Child abuse can be caused by any combination of the following factors:

- situational factors—a stressful marriage, economic stress, a child with special needs
- psychological factors—especially of the abuser, such as poor control, certain personality traits
- social factors—violent role models and a culture which encourages aggressive behavior

When these factors combine with family conflict, the result too often is violence. Such abuse can start out rather benign but escalate into violence under the wrong circumstances. For example, a parent who spanks a child may become frustrated with the child's continued bad behavior and graduate to an electrical cord, causing welts and bruises. Such beatings often get even more severe as frustration grows over the inability to control the child's behavior. Inflicting physical trauma may stop the bad behavior for the moment; but then other bad behaviors will inevitably emerge, since the physical abuser has little interest in building character (in contrast to appropriate physical discipline). See chapter 7 for a more thorough discussion of child abuse.

Strategies for Victims of Domestic Violence

An important first step to solving the problems of family violence is to identify the victims and the abusers. Because the family so often is private, many of these victims suffer in silence, isolated from people who can help. They often hesitate to report family violence because the most common second step after identifying victims and abusers is to separate them. Victims are often very reluctant to separate themselves from their abusers, even when their well-being is endangered. The victims would rather live with the abuser than face an uncertain future away from the family. The cultural expectation in our society is children need a mother and father and should not be separated from them. Victims often underestimate the severity of their situation. Thus, a big part of convincing victims to leave is to provide them with a safe alternative situation.

Many agencies will help victims adjust to a new lifestyle. Survivors of abuse need people who believe in them and who will help them find the resources (education, housing, jobs) they require to survive on their own. They need to be loved and accepted for who they are apart from their marriage.

Victims of abuse often offer excuses, refusing to believe there is a problem. They often feel the abuse is their fault.

People who experience the death of a loved one go through stages in the grief process. The battered person also goes through stages before making the final decision to leave an abusive relationship. In explaining battered person syndrome, the Family Social Services Administration (2002) describes the four psychological stages the battered person experiences:

1. *Denial:* Victims will refuse to believe there is a problem and may offer excuses for the violence. They may call each incident an "accident" and believe it will not happen again.
2. *Guilt:* Victims acknowledge a problem, but feels it is their own fault. If they would only act a certain way, the violence would not happen. They believe they somehow "deserve" to be beaten.
3. *Enlightenment:* Victims recognize the abuse is wrong but stay committed to their relationships. They will remain in the abusive situation, hoping they can work things out.
4. *Responsibility:* Victims will make the decision to leave the relationship and take responsibility for their own lives. At this stage, it is important for the victims to have a support system which will empower them to take control of their lives.

A Christian Perspective

The Bible can teach us something about conflict. Beginning with Adam and Eve (Genesis 3), we see classic examples of marital conflict. Adam and Eve argued with one another about who was to blame for the first sin. Later, Sarah was upset that Abraham fathered a son by another woman, even though she engineered the situation (Genesis 16–22). Rebekah misled her husband so her second-born son would receive his father's inheritance (Genesis 27).

These marriages were blessed by God, but certainly contained much strife and conflict. Marital infidelity, deception, and conflict mark page after page of the Old and New Testaments. These examples point to our flawed, sinful natures. There is also much wisdom about marriage and family life in the Bible. For example, Proverbs is full of advice to parents. It is a tribute to marriage when Jesus Christ is referred to as a bridegroom (John 3:29) and the Church as His bride (Revelation 21:2; 22:17).

A Christian Response to Spousal Abuse

The ideal Christian marriage is a covenant, reflecting God's covenant love for us. Still, sometimes things go wrong and the marriage ends. In the next chapter, we will examine divorce and remarriage. In the case of marital abuse, some Christians believe it is sinful to break up a marriage for any reason. They believe the abused spouse must tolerate the abuse because it will identify her with Christ, the Suffering Servant.

Thankfully, these Christians are rare. Most religious leaders today agree God does not intend for anyone to be put in danger by remaining in an abusive situation. A good resource for church leaders seeking to advocate for a Christian approach to family violence is the Faith Trust Institute (www.faithtrustinstitute.org {accessed June 23, 2009}). Christians are called to respect the sanctity of human life, not to abuse anyone for any reason, nor even to stand by and tolerate such. God wants to deliver abusers from their sins of violence. Separating the abusers from their victims is an important first step. Often, the separation is a way to proactively identify the problem and cause the abuser to seek help. In some cases, the abuser may repent and through therapy be changed. It is possible the family can then be reunited.

A Christian Response to Family Violence

Family violence continues to be a problem for families who are ill-equipped to handle conflicts constructively. Christians can serve as role models for constructive conflict resolution. At the same time, Christians can help change a society which in many ways supports violence as a means to resolve conflicts.

The good news is efforts to educate and reduce violence in families appear to be having an impact. In 2005, the U.S. Justice Department announced the rate of family violence fell by more than one half between 1993 and 2002, from an estimated 5.4 victims to 2.1 victims per 1,000 U.S. residents 12 years old and older. Half of the victims were abused by their spouse, about 10% were children abused by a parent and about 40% involved abuse by another family member.

Christians need to lead the way to be Christ's hands and feet in extending mercy to victims and justice to abusers. They need to continue to spread Christ's message of peace and hope in a world full of violence. In their own families, Christians can be important role models of peace and compassion in dealing with family conflicts.

Summary

Conflict in family relationships is inevitable. The more people love each other, the more intensely they will disagree. If families do not utilize constructive conflict management skills, conflicts can tear a family apart.

Constructive conflict management includes looking at the disagreement from a different perspective. Instead of placing blame on a personality flaw, family members should seek to change the situation contributing to the conflict.

Rather than avoiding conflict in order to keep the peace, a family must utilize the rules of fair fighting to peacefully resolve conflicts. This includes finding the right time and place, sticking to the issue, active listening, and maintaining a good attitude.

Destructive conflict can result in violence. About 1 in 4 couples will have a violent episode at some point in their marriage. Many parents utilize some appropriate (even biblical) physical forms of discipline with their children; but for some families, this can escalate into physical abuse. Destructive conflict tends to run in a cycle of conflict, violence, apology, and reconciliation; each time the violence becoming more intense than before. The best solution for a violent family is to separate the abuser from the victims. Personality change for the abuser does not come easily. However, it is very difficult for victims to leave their abusers because they fear life outside the family. Victims need to be supported in establishing a life away from the abuser.

Christians can help reduce destructive conflict by promoting constructive conflict resolution. They can act as models of Christ's peace in a world filled with violent images.

Questions for Thought

1. In your experience, what most often leads to conflict in the family?

2. Offer both a constructive and a destructive resolution to each of these situations:
   a. A newly married couple must decide where to spend the holidays.
   b. A teenage son wants to drive the car to school.
   c. A dual-income couple must decide how to handle an unexpected pregnancy.
   d. A teenage daughter no longer wants to share her room with her younger sister.
   e. A wife gets a long-awaited job offer, but it means moving or commuting 100 miles.

3. This chapter has offered some general ways the Church can deal with conflict in families. Can you think of some specific ways your church could minister to families who are experiencing conflict?

Resources

Books:

A Child Called It by Dave Pelzer. A memoir of Pelzer's abusive childhood. (Orion, 2001)

The Wounded Heart: Hope for Adult Victims of Child Sexual Abuse by Dan Allender. Healing for victims of child abuse. (NavPress, 2008)

The Shack by William Young. The Shack wrestles with the timeless question, "Where is God in a world so filled with unspeakable pain? (Windblown Media, 2008)

Movies

The Burning Bed (NR). Depicts the moral ambiguities and painful questions of where justice lies in domestic violence

If Someone Had Known (NR). Story about a physically abusive husband that is killed in self defense

Video resource list on family violence:

http://www.mincava.umn.edu/documents/films/filmvid/filmvid.html (accessed June 23, 2009)

National Domestic Violence Hotline at 1-800-799-SAFE (7233) or TTY 1-800-787-3224.

Website:

http://www.helpguide.org/mental/domestic_violence_abuse_types_signs_causes_effects.htm (accessed June 23, 2009)

Safety planning:

1. http://www.abanet.org/tips/publicservice/DVENG.pdf (accessed June 23, 2009)
2. http://www.ncadv.org/protectyourself/MyPersonalSafetyPlan.php (accessed June 23, 2009)

Divorce and Remarriage

13

Jesus said, "Moses provided for divorce as a concession to your hardheartedness, but it is not part of God's original plan."

—Matthew 19:8 MSG

© Jupiter Images

Our contemporary culture tends to view almost everything, including relationships and marriage, as disposable. This hedonistic attitude of "me first" permeates our society and endangers many of our social and religious norms. Under the popular philosophical system of utilitarianism, the highest good appears to be what works for *me now*. Therefore, people fall in and out of "love," slipping in and out of relationships almost as often as they change clothing styles. Certainly, this is not what God intended when He ordained marriage. We must remember marriage was God's idea, not ours.

All divorce is hurtful, even the most civilized and "friendly" divorce. When a man and woman marry, they become one—a mystical blending of body with soul and spirit. By entering into the marriage covenant, two independent and separate persons together become a new person. Spiritually, divorce is a severance, a destruction of that new person.

God, in His infinite wisdom, knew the hurt and devastation divorce would cause and wanted to shield His children from the pain. Yet, even when God says no, His people often refuse to listen. In the shadow of Adam and Eve, who ate the forbidden fruit, bringing sin into the world, we continue to make the same mistakes and suffer similar consequences. The consequences of divorce are especially painful and long lasting.

Divorce: The Death of a Relationship

Marriage vows often contain this statement from Matthew 19:6b: "Therefore, what God has joined together, let man not separate." Older translations use the phrase "let not man put asunder" (KJV, RSV). Divorce tears a couple apart; it separates the two halves (puts asunder the oneness) of the marriage covenant. In essence, the relationship is put to death. As a metaphor, death is not too strong in describing divorce. People experience divorce as a kind of death. Grief—mourning the death of a relationship—characterizes the period leading up to and following a divorce.

The idea of divorce connotes that a marriage has taken place; however, it has become increasingly acceptable in society, though not in the church, for both men and women to have a series of monogamous partners throughout their lifetime which may or may not include marriage—serial monogamy. Breakups of these unmarried relationships can have consequences similar to divorce, especially for children.

In this chapter, we will examine the causes and consequences of divorce, as well as review the related issues of single parenting, remarriage, and stepfamilies.

Divorce Statistics

The divorce rate rose sharply in the 1970s and 1980s, but actually declined slightly in the 1990s and early 2000s. (see Figure 13.1 along with related Figures 3.1 and 3.2 in chapter 3) We have heard it said that half of all marriages will end in divorce. However, if present trends continue, about 4 in 10 marriages will end in divorce. Most of these people will remarry or re-partner to form stepfamilies.

While this sounds encouraging, it is important to remember the United States still has one of the highest divorce rates in the world (World Divorce Statistics, 1996–2005). Seven times more children are affected by divorce now than at the turn of the century (Fields, 2003). Children who commute between separated parents are now commonplace. One in two children will live in a single-parent family at some point in the child's life, and 1 in 3 children will be born to unmarried parents

Figure 13.1

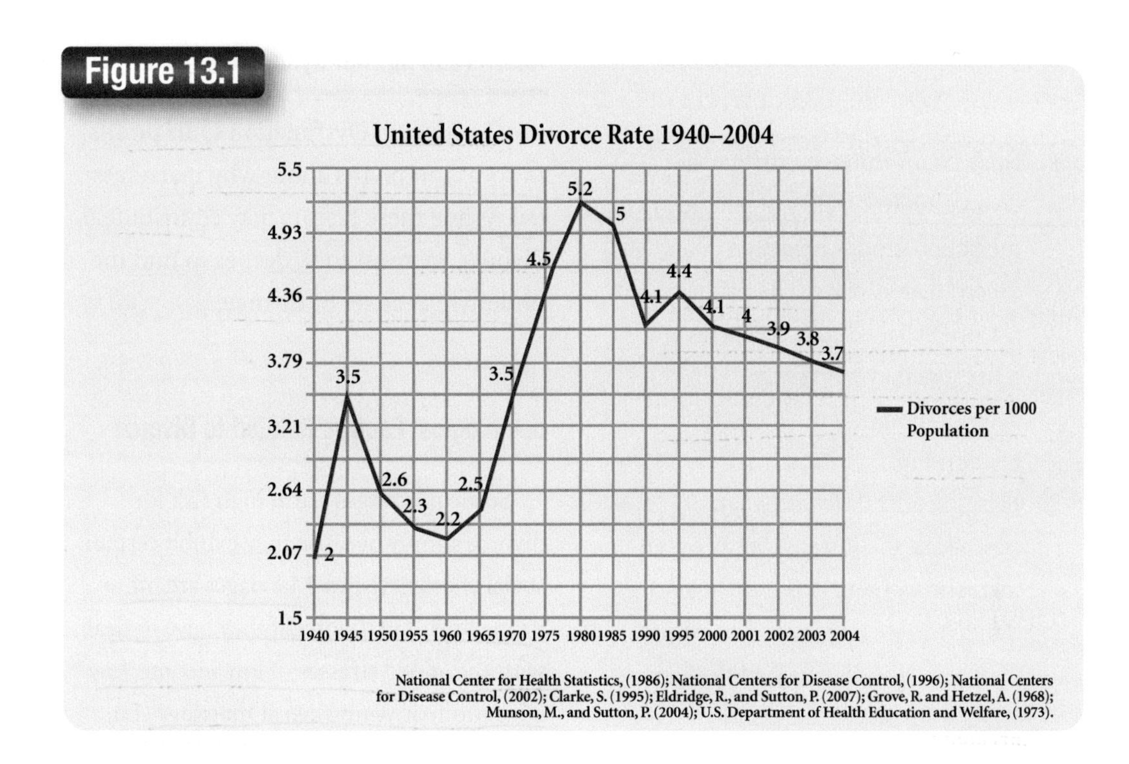

National Center for Health Statistics, (1986); National Centers for Disease Control, (1996); National Centers for Disease Control, (2002); Clarke, S. (1995); Eldridge, R., and Sutton, P. (2007); Grove, R. and Hetzel, A. (1968); Munson, M., and Sutton, P. (2004); U.S. Department of Health Education and Welfare, (1973).

(Children and Families in Crisis, 2004). Some critics claim this collapse of the traditional family is a greater cause of poverty than any shortcomings in the economic or the political system. Despite these statistics, 90% of all Americans marry and most people remarry after a divorce (Mintz, 2001).

The Causes of Divorce

Marital Dysfunction Quiz

Why do people divorce? Take the following quiz, based on Gottman's research (1995), to see if you can identify the primary reasons for divorce:

1. T or F Affairs are the primary cause of divorce.
2. T or F Gender differences cause divorce.
3. T or F Communication problems cause marital conflicts.
4. T or F Unsuccessful marriages have little or no *quid pro quo* (give something to get something).
5. T or F Marriages end because partners stop loving each other.

Answers to Marital Dysfunction Quiz

1. **False.** Many things contribute to divorce. Only 20–25% of people in mediation groups report an affair caused their divorce. The primary reason (80%) couples seek a divorce is because they perceive a deterioration of intimacy in their relationship.
2. **False.** Gender differences can complicate the interactions between men and women. However, if gender differences were the primary cause of divorce, the divorce rate would be 100% for heterosexuals, and homosexual relationships would thrive.
3. **False.** While failure to communicate is often problematic, distressed couples actually communicate quite clearly what they feel and mean—no holding back. Even clear communication can be harmful if it is hurtful or blaming in tone.
4. **False.** Research demonstrates a lack of quid pro quo is not the primary problem for ailing couples, but neither is it a problem for happy couples (Gottman, 1995).
5. **False.** Lastly, couples break up because their level of satisfaction with the relationship decreases, not because they stop loving each other (Sprecher, 1999).

The Marital Dysfunction Quiz points to common myths about why marriages fail. While these factors may contribute to divorce, we must look deeper to find the underlying causes of divorce.

Sociological Factors Related to Divorce

Some marriages are at high risk for divorce simply because they exhibit certain social characteristics. Marriages are more prone to end in divorce if they have to deal with the added stresses of low income, low education, or young age at marriage (Lu, 2006). Studies conclude that women who marry before the age of 18 have a 48% chance of separation or divorce within the first 10 years of marriage, while women who are at least 25 years of age or older when they marry have a 24% chance of separation or divorce (Bramlett & Mosher, 2002).

Factors related to a high risk of divorce include, low income, low education, young age at marriage and careers that require a lot of time away from home.

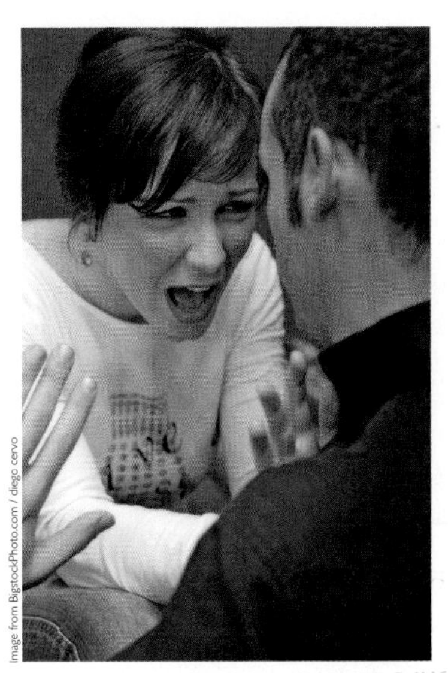

Image from BigstockPhoto.com / diego cervo

If left unchecked, criticism and defensiveness can lead to contempt.

Additional factors related to a young age of marriage are a lack of a college education and the addition of children before age 20. Some teenage couples marry because of a premarital pregnancy; statistics indicate a higher divorce rate among those with a premarital pregnancy (Lu, 2006).

In addition to age and education, statistics indicate people in certain careers are more prone to divorce. High divorce rates occur in couples who spend a considerable amount of time apart in job-related activities. Certain highly stressful occupations are also associated with a higher divorce rate: physicians, police officers, firefighters, or military personnel (Knox & Schacht, 1999).

Other high-risk factors include interracial marriage, unemployment, previous divorce, and a courtship of less than 6 months (Lu, 2006). It would appear two of the simplest ways to avoid divorce are to stay in college and avoid a premarital pregnancy.

Social-Psychological Factors Related to Divorce

Based on his groundbreaking work in behavioral observation methodologies, John Gottman has developed a method which predicts, with 94% accuracy, which newlywed couples will remain married and which will divorce 4 to 6 years later. He is also 81% accurate in predicting which marriages will survive after 7 to 9 years (Gottman, 2000). He has identified what he refers to as the four types of behavior which are particularly corrosive in a marriage:

1. *Criticism*: Most marital conflicts start with criticism. Wives are more prone to criticize than husbands. Criticism is presenting a problem as though the other person has a defective personality. Note that criticism is different from *complaining*, which reflects unhappiness without attributing it to the other person's personality. The book of Proverbs says, "Gentle words cause life and health, griping brings discouragement (15:4 TLB). Proverbs 17:9 (TLB) says, "Love forgets mistakes; nagging about them parts the best of friends."
2. *Defensiveness:* Both genders are equal-opportunity offenders of this predictor of divorce. Basically, defensiveness is just what it says it is.

continued

You defend. Instead of seeing what part of your partner's criticism might be true, you simply defend your point and desire to be right. Thus, a defensive partner denies responsibility for any part of a problem. Here is what Proverbs says: "The fool who provokes his family to anger and resentment will finally have nothing worthwhile left" (Proverbs 11:29 TLB). Therefore, criticism begets defensiveness; defensiveness begets more criticism, and defensiveness leaves little room to see your partner's perspective.

3. *Contempt:* According to Gottman, it takes 20 positive comments to make up for one "zinger." It is easy to see that couples in this criticism/defensiveness pattern are moving quickly downhill in terms of building a caring, warm relationship. Contempt is the suggestion you are *superior* in some way to the other person. This is often seen in a very specific facial expression—one side of the mouth is drawn further to the side, creating an "unhappy" dimple—and is often accompanied by a roll of the eyes.

   The result: couples become emotionally divorced. All the passion and energy which once filled the relationship have now turned into a seething ember of hostility in their souls. The writer of Proverbs says, "It is better to live in a corner of an attic than in a beautiful home with a cranky, quarrelsome woman" (25:24 TLB) and "A quarrelsome man starts fights as easily as a match sets fire to paper" (26:21 TLB).

4. *Stonewalling:* Stonewalling is defined as avoidance of the issue in any way possible—refusing to engage and provide feedback. It can be verbal, as in a comment, or nonverbal, as in walking away. Stonewalling prevents resolution of conflict, and as conflict grows, so does resentment. In contrast, Proverbs 25:12 (TLB) states, "It is a badge of honor to accept valid criticism."

While all of these behaviors appear in good marriages, the balance between positive and negative interactions is a critical factor in predicting marital success. In good marriages, according to Gottman, the ratio of positive to negative interactions is typically 5 to 1 (5 positive interactions for every 1 negative interaction), even during times of conflict. Therefore, couples are more prone to divorce when negative comments and behavior begin to outweigh positive ones (Gottman, 1995, 1999).

Many men meet criticism with stonewalling—refusing to engage or give feedback.

Figure 13.2 shows three models illustrating certain factors involved in divorce.

Causes of Divorce: Three Models.

- The enduring dynamics model suggests behavior patterns between spouses are established early in a marriage. These can fortify stability in the marriage or lead to instability and divorce (Huston, Niehaus, & Smith, 2001).
- The disillusionment model explains how marriage partners idealize one another early in their relationship. After a while, they begin to see each other differently or as they "really are," which can lead to disillusionment and divorce (Huston, Niehaus, & Smith, 2001).
- The emergent-distress model suggests early marital happiness can be destroyed by negative marital disagreements (Kurdeck, 2002).

Figure 13.2

Models Used to Explain Divorce

Model	Early Marriage	Difficulty	Result
Enduring Dynamics Model (Huston, Niehaus, & Smith, 2001)	Establish patterns of behavior that last throughout marriage	Stability or instability in the relationship is created by behavior patterns	Stability is the single factor that distinguishes who stays married and who divorces
Disillusionment Model (Huston, Niehaus, & Smith, 2001)	Romanticize and exaggerate partners good qualities	Begin to see real person which leads to disillusionment	Learn to love the real person or marriage may end
Emergent – Distress Model(Kurdeck, 2002)	Begin blissfully happy and affectionate	Disagreements create distress and negativity	Resolve differences or negativity can lead to divorce

Olson's Five Types of Marriage and Top Ten Dimensions.

David Olson and his colleagues have been studying marriage since the 1980s. They came up with five different types of marriages based on dimensions important for marital happiness (Olson & Fowers, 1993)

1. Devitalized
2. Conflicted
3. Traditional
4. Harmonious
5. Vitalized

They concluded the most common type of marriage was the devitalized marriage. In this marriage type, a couple expresses dissatisfaction in all dimensions and has usually considered divorce.

Couples in conflicted marriages were dissatisfied with marital communication, conflict resolution, their partner's personality, and their sex lives. They were satisfied with their children, their religious lives, and the use of leisure time. In other words, dissatisfaction stemmed from things within the relationship, and satisfaction stemmed from things outside the relationship.

Image from BigstockPhoto.com / marylooo

Conflicted couples find satisfaction from things outside the relationship such as children, religion, and leisure time, but are dissatisfied with things within the marriage.

Couples in what Olson and Fowers termed a traditional marriage were dissatisfied with communication, conflict resolution, and sex, but were satisfied with family and friends, religion, and leisure time. These traditional couples were one of the most satisfied of all types in how they handled their children and parenting duties. Like conflicted couples, traditional couples found satisfaction in things outside their marriage.

Couples in harmonious marriages reported relatively high relationship quality. Couples in vitalized marriages reported the highest levels of satisfaction across all nine dimensions (Olson & Fowers, 1993).

In a later study, Olson and Olson, using previous research, came up with 10 specific issues, or dimensions, important for happiness in married couples:

1. Personality issues
2. Communication
3. Conflict resolution
4. Couple flexibility
5. Financial management
6. Leisure activities
7. Sexual relationship
8. Children and parenting
9. Family and friends
10. Religious orientation

In this study, happily married couples had significantly higher levels of communication, flexibility, closeness, personality compatibility, and conflict resolution than unhappy couples (Olson & Olson, 2000).

Other Factors Related to Divorce

Certain premarital factors have been found to be key in determining which couples have a greater likelihood of marital distress. Two factors in particular, premarital interaction (such as emotional invalidation) and poor conflict resolution, play key roles in the development of marital distress. Lower premarital happiness plays a role in later marital distress, while higher religiousness on the wife's part is associated with marital happiness (Clements, Stanley, & Markman, 2004).

It is common to cite "lack of loving" as a cause of divorce. Susan Sprecher has concluded, if satisfaction and commitment increase over time, love also will improve. If levels of satisfaction decrease, the couple may stop loving as well. Her research suggests satisfaction and commitment are more important to couples than love, at least as these factors relate to a couple's staying together (1999).

From a different perspective, a group of attorneys reported these as the most common reasons their clients gave for seeking a divorce: poor communication, financial problems, a lack of commitment to the marriage, a dramatic change in priorities, and infidelity. Still common but less frequent, their clients reported these additional reasons for seeking a divorce: failed expectations or unmet needs; addictions and substance abuse; physical, sexual, or emotional abuse; and lack of conflict resolution skills (American Association of Matrimonial Lawyers, 2000).

Sidebar 13.1

"If we want less government, we must have stronger families, for government steps in by necessity when families have failed."

—*Jimmy Carter, 1976*

For therapists, some of the most difficult areas to treat are lack of loving, addictions of all kinds, and extramarital affairs, all of which create some of the greatest damage to a marriage. Some of the most common reasons given as causing a divorce are infidelity (the most common reason), followed by incompatibility, alcohol or drug use, and growing apart (Amato & Previti, 2003).

Types of Divorce

Once a couple makes the decision to divorce, it comes under the scrutiny of the court and the court's representatives. Thus, the family becomes a *public* family instead of a *private* family. (see Sidebar 13.1) Five different types of divorce exist, each with varying amounts of court intrusion. These are fault divorce, no-fault divorce, uncontested divorce, contested divorce, and simplified divorce.

Fault Divorce

Some states still allow fault divorces. In a fault divorce, one spouse must have done something wrong—the spouse must be "at fault" for the failure of the marriage. These wrongdoings, called "grounds for divorce," include adultery, physical or mental cruelty, desertion, confinement in prison, physical incapacity (for the purpose of sexual intercourse), and incurable insanity. If the defending spouse does not want the divorce, he or she has to deny the wrongdoing and defend that denial in court.

Image from BigstockPhoto.com / edisaacs

The decision to divorce brings a couple under the scrutiny of the court making them a public family instead of a private family.

No-Fault Divorce

Since 1970, an increasing number of states have enacted no-fault divorce laws, making it easier for a couple to get out of a marriage. A no-fault divorce means no one is at fault for the failure of the marriage. Misconduct does not matter in a no-fault divorce. The basis for dissolving the marriage may simply be "incompatibilities" or "irreconcilable differences." A no-fault divorce does not usually require any explanation or proof of a problem. In most states, it does not matter if the other spouse consents to the divorce or not.

Uncontested Divorce

An uncontested divorce can take one of two courses. Either one spouse does not respond to the other spouse's request for a divorce, or that spouse agrees to every detail of the decision, including division of marital property, debts, child support, alimony, and child-custody issues.

Contested Divorce

If an agreement cannot be reached on every issue, then the divorce is referred to as a contested divorce, and the couple has to take its issues before a judge. Contested divorces increase the costs involved and generally create more turmoil for the family.

Image from BigstockPhoto.com / cpephotoshop

In response to the rising divorce rate and the ease with which marriages are ended, a few states have added the option of covenant marriage which makes divorce more difficult.

Simplified Divorce

Available in some states, a simplified divorce speeds up the divorce process and usually keeps it out of the court. Simplified divorces are uncontested, no-fault divorces with no disagreements on the settlement. State laws differ on simplified divorce. Some states require the couple to fill out forms and have a judge approve the settlement agreement. In other states, couples can seek a simplified divorce if no financial debts and no dependent children (under the age of 18) are involved. Simplified divorces generally are granted very quickly and are usually less expensive and less stressful for the parties involved.

The Covenant Marriage Option

While no-fault divorce and simplified divorce have made the process of divorce easier, is easier always better?

Georgia State Representative Brian Joyce, while introducing a bill to end no-fault divorce, made this observation: "All around us, every day, we see the bitter fruit of the breakdown of the family . . . I believe the breakdown of the family is a direct result of our 'no-fault' laws . . . Why should a couple invest in a marriage when it can be dissolved for no reason at all?" (Joyce, 2001).

In response to the rising divorce rate and the ease with which marriages are ended, a few states have added covenant marriage as a response to no-fault divorce. In a covenant marriage, couples agree to counseling before marriage and to accept more limited grounds for divorce. These grounds typically are limited to abuse, a felony with jail time, or adultery. By making it more difficult to divorce, covenant marriage provides both spouses the security and motivation to work on their marriage, knowing the partners share an equal commitment to the covenant.

Three states have currently passed covenant marriage laws: Louisiana enacted it in 1997, Arizona in 1998, and Arkansas in 2001. Since 1997 about 20 states have either considered or are considering covenant marriage bills (Covenant Marriage, 2004). While it is really too early to determine if covenant marriages lower the divorce rate, there are some interesting differences between people who opt for a covenant marriage compared to standard marriage. People who choose covenant marriage are much less likely to have cohabited, tend to be more educated, hold more traditional beliefs, believe they have social responsibility to marry and have children, and to have attended premarital classes than those who choose a standard marriage. Covenant marriage partners differ from traditional marriage partners in communication practices, in that they are less likely to respond to conflict with sarcasm or hostility, possibly because of higher motivation to resolve conflict or the impact of premarital classes. Lastly, covenant marriage partners, not surprisingly, differ from standard married couples in religiosity. (Covenant Marriage, 2004; Sanchez, Nock, Wilson, & Wright, 2006). Because of the differences in these two groups of couples, it will be difficult to determine if marital stability is due to legal requirements or because of the couple differences. These differences in the two groups suggest covenant couples will have more stable marriage regardless of the terms of their legal unions.

The Consequences of Divorce

Is divorce really harmful? Researchers seem to respond on both sides of this question. As you will recall from chapter 3, divorce was relatively rare until the 1960s. The 1970s saw a doubling of the divorce rate, as baby boomers left their families in record numbers. For the next couple of decades, the prevailing view among analysts was that divorce was a brief crisis which would resolve itself. In this section, we will examine some of the current findings on the consequences of divorce.

Utterly Befuddled

In her book *The Case Against Divorce*, Dr. Diane Medved writes,

> I have to start with a confession: This isn't the book I set out to write . . . For example, I started this project believing that people who suffer over an extended period in unhappy marriages ought to get out . . . I thought that striking down taboos about divorce was another part of the ongoing enlightenment of the women's, civil-rights, and human potential movements of the last 25 years . . . To my utter befuddlement, the extensive

research I conducted for this book brought me to one inescapable and irrefutable conclusion: I had been wrong. Quite simply, I discovered in my research that the process and aftermath of divorce is so pervasively disastrous to body, mind and spirit that in an overwhelming number of cases, the "cure" that it brings is surely worse than the marriage's "disease." (1989, ch. 1).

Wallerstein and her colleagues (Wallerstein & Blakeslee, 2003; Wallerstein & Lewis, 2004), experienced something similar. Wallerstein and her colleagues began a study of 60 families with 131 children in the early 1970s. As she followed these families, she expected the children to feel a sense of relief at the marital separation in direct proportion to the amount of previous marital discord. This was not the case. After over a quarter of a century of following these families, she shocked the research community with her findings. Wallerstein and colleagues concluded that the emotional impact of divorce for children is cumulative, beginning with the parental separation and increasing over time and extending throughout adulthood. Adult children of divorce (adults whose parents divorced while they were young) essentially view life differently from their peers who have been raised in intact homes. Divorce affects the personalities of these adult children in their ability to trust, their expectations about relationships, and their ability to cope with change (Wallerstein & Blakelee, 2003; Wallerstein & Lewis, 2004). Wallerstein and her colleagues' research has been criticized because of its small, biased sample of only 60 families and no control group; it did, however, follow the same families over time.

© Jupiter Images

Some research findings indicate that the impact of divorce on children is cumulative and extends into adulthood.

Divorce: The Other Side of the Story

Not all researchers agree on the negative effects of divorce. Amato suggests that most children from divorced families do not experience the level of clinical problems Wallerstein found; however, he did find significantly lower measures of achievement, social adjustment, and well-being than adult children from intact families. He also noted gender differences in social adjustment, with boys showing a greater deficit in social adjustment than girls. Despite these problems, he suggests most children from divorced families grow up to be well-adjusted, successful people. The worst outcome for children, he says, is to remain in an intact family in which there is a chronic, high level of conflict. In this situation, children actually benefited from their parents' separation because it removed them from an adverse, unhappy environment (Amato, 2001).

Andrew Cherlin agrees the picture is not as grim as some researchers paint, although divorce still has negative effects. He suggests some of the problems attributed to divorce—such as school and behavior problems—were already present prior to the parents' separation. His work also implies most of the problems the children of divorced parents experience are due to long-standing psychological problems of the parents, poverty, racism, and the disabilities of the children (Cherlin, 1999; Cherlin, 2002; Cherlin & Furstenburg, 1991).

Hetherington and colleagues have been charting the psychological progress of children for over 25 years. They report less critically on the effects of divorce than some of their colleagues. However, they acknowledge certain very real increased difficulties. Twenty years after a divorce, they found, life improved for only about 20% of divorced adults, while 30% remained desperately unhappy (Hetherington & Kelly, 2002).

For children of divorce, Hetherington and colleagues found the first year to be the hardest for children, but the second year brought improvement. Boys typically rebelled against their mothers while girls tended to experience more stress and sometimes became sexually promiscuous. However, the majority of children of divorce were functioning within a normal range 20 years later, however, not without some lasting effects. Adult children of divorce have roughly double the divorce rate of those from stable families, due in part to less commitment to the permanence of marriage and fewer relationship skills. Children of divorce also were more likely to experience estrangement from their fathers. It seems very few fathers are able to maintain a vital relationship with their children; thus, two thirds of the boys and three quarters of the girls were found to have poor relationships with their fathers. Hetherington and colleagues admit many of the adult children she studied considered themselves permanently scarred by the experience of their parents' divorces (Hetherington & Kelly, 2002).

Ahrons (2004b) presents a very different view of the effects of divorce. She suggests "good divorces have been well-kept secrets because to acknowledge them in mainstream life threatens our nostalgic images of family" (p. 7). She insists divorce doesn't have to destroy children's lives or create a family breakdown if handled well. She interviewed 173 grown children whose divorcing parents she had interviewed 20 years prior. While she admits divorce is never easy for a family, her results show that children can and do adapt, and many actually thrive in the midst of family change. While she did find a full 20% of the adult children felt their parent's divorce had devastating effects on them and has left scars which would not heal, 80% feel their parent's decision to divorce was a good one, and they are better off or not affected by it (Ahrons, 2004b).

Regardless of which researcher comes closer to the truth, divorce affects people on many levels. It is fair to say the research as a whole suggests about 75-80% of children whose parents divorce will do fairly well. On the other hand, this means 20-25% will have more major difficulties. We will now examine the impact of divorce on society, educational achievement, family economy, personal well-being, family dynamics, and religious practice.

The Effects of Divorce on Society

Even when a divorce is amiable, it tears apart a family—the fundamental unit of American society. We should not be surprised that divorce profoundly affects our social fabric, particularly as it relates to the problems of crime, abuse, and addiction.

In a study of 171 cities with populations over 100,000, one study found the divorce rate predicted the robbery rate—the lower the rate of divorce, the lower the crime rate (Sampson, 1992). A different study found that children from divorced families were significantly more likely to become delinquent than children living with married parents (Demuth & Brown, 2004).

When parents divorce, most children suffer, at least initially. Not only do higher

Image from BigstockPhoto.com / alptraum

Children from divorced families are significantly more likely to become delinquent than children living in two-parent homes.

levels of crime accompany higher divorce rates, but also higher rates of child abuse. Child neglect is twice as high for separated and divorced parents than for intact families (Wallerstein & Blakeslee, 2003; Egami, 1996). Children of separated and divorced parents are 20% more likely to be abused, based on 10 years of research in Family Court (Brown & Alexander, 2007). Adolescent children whose parents divorce have been found to abuse drugs and alcohol more often than children whose parents are still married (Barrett & Turner, 2006).

The Effects of Divorce on Educational Achievement

Regardless of the child's age, divorce has a negative impact on the child's learning and achievement. Young children whose parents divorce are often afraid that both parents will abandon them. This leads to an inability to concentrate, particularly on schoolwork. Children frequently have difficulty sleeping. They fear falling asleep because the remaining parent might abandon them—after all, in a child's mind, if one parent can leave, why can't both? The resultant fatigue from sleeplessness then leads to even more difficulty concentrating.

Children of divorced families generally demonstrate lower preschool readiness; achieve lower educational performance at the elementary, secondary, and college levels; and exhibit a higher dropout rate in high school than their counterparts from intact families (Schneider, Atteberry, & Owens, 2005). Children from intact families maintained grade point averages 11% higher than their peers from divorced families. High school seniors from divorced households missed almost 60% more class periods than did those from intact families. These results are most pronounced for females, indicating females are more negatively impacted by divorce than are males (Ham, 2003). Those who graduate from high school are 16% less likely to attend college than students from intact households (Painter & Levine, 2000). Of those who started college, 57% completed a bachelor's degree compared to 90% in the comparison group (Wallerstein & Lewis, 2004).

The Effects of Divorce on Family Economy

Almost immediately after a couple separates, the family financial situation declines. Initially, the same income supports two households, as well as pays for legal fees, relocation costs, and other expenses related to family dissolution. Divorce results in a more significant decline in income for women than men. Wallerstein finds family income after a divorce drops more than 20%, resulting in a substantial number of women (with

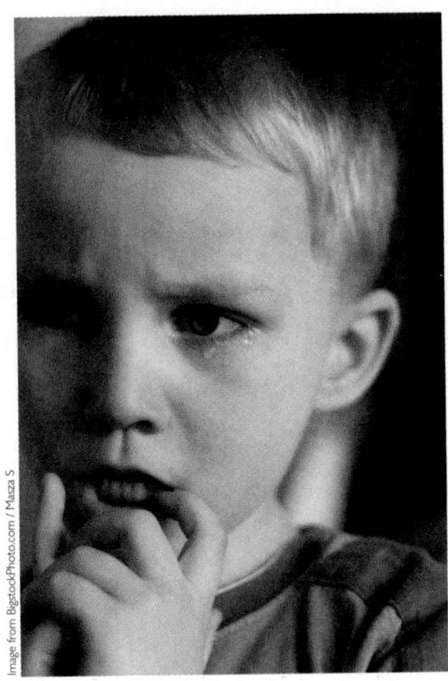

Children often find the pain and grieving following the separation of their parents overwhelming.

custody of children) who are living in poverty (Wallerstein, Lewis, & Blakeslee, 2000). This trend is far more severe for women and children, since most children of divorce reside with their mothers. Another study documents women experience a 30% drop in income level, as compared to a 10–15% increase for divorced men (Stafford, Eccles, & Schoeni, 2003).

The Effects of Divorce on Personal Well-Being

Immediate Effects on Children. In the immediate aftermath of divorce, children suffer from loneliness, fear, worry, sadness, anger, guilt, and feelings of rejection. Children of divorce are more likely to experience depression, withdrawal, and aggressive or impulsive behavior than children from intact families (Popenoe, 1995; Amato, 2001). Their routines are disrupted and their household is in disarray, frequently for years. They often face relocation to a new neighborhood, new school, and new friends, as well as the loss of old friends. Just when they need their parents the most to help them make sense of what is happening, they experience preoccupied parents who are also trying to cope with the stresses surrounding divorce (Hetherington & Kelly, 2002). Children often find the pain and grieving following the separation of their parents overwhelming.

Wallerstein found two thirds of the children she followed longed for their absent parent, and over one half experienced feelings of rejection from one or both parents. Less than 10% of the children experienced relief at the divorce (Wallerstein, Lewis, & Blakeslee, 2000). Children couldn't understand why one of their parents was gone and, subsequently, often felt their parent had abandoned them. If the father was the one who left, young boys often mistook their mother's criticism of their father as criticism of themselves. Both boys and girls frequently felt they were to blame for their parents' divorces (Wallerstein & Blakeslee, 2003).

Long-Term Effects on Children. Five years after a divorce, according to

Wallerstein's study, one third of the children were doing well and demonstrated high self-esteem. By and large, these were the children who had maintained loving relationships with both parents, including regular and frequent visitation with both parents. These children were also likely to have had a wide network of support in their extended families, schools, churches, and communities.

Slightly less than one third of the children were doing reasonably well, but continued to display anger, emotional neediness, general unhappiness, and only moderately good self-esteem.

Children in the last group, a little over one third of the children, were intensely unhappy and moderately to severely depressed. What surprised researchers the most was the unhappiness of these children was actually greater at 5 years (and later at 10 years) than it was one and a half years after the divorce (Wallerstein, Lewis, & Blakeslee, 2000).

Almost half of the children in Wallerstein's study entered adulthood as worried, underachieving, self-deprecating, and sometimes angry young men and women. Over the years, the boys in this study tended to achieve at lower levels in school, had poorer peer relationships, and demonstrated more problems handling aggression. However, their overall adjustment improved with time.

Adolescent girls from divorced families are more likely to engage in early sexual activity and to struggle with anxiety and guilt in their intimate relationships. This leads young women to engage in multiple relationships and impulsive marriages, often ending in divorce (Maher, 2003). Teen girls from divorced families are twice as likely to become pregnant than teens from intact families (Crowder & Teachman, 2004). Both young men and young women tend to lack an inner sense of how healthy marriages work, which causes anxiety in their adult relationships. Even those who go on to marry happily continue to have fears their marriages could dissolve at the first sign of conflict (Wallerstein, Lewis, & Blakeslee, 2000).

Impact on Children's Health. Divorce negatively impacts children's health. Children from divorced families have a greater risk of injury, asthma, headaches, and speech defects than children from intact families. They also are more likely to require professional help for emotional or behavioral problems than children living with both biological parents (Strohschein, 2005; Wade & Pevalin, 2004). In addition to health-related effects, divorce also influences suicide rates. Of all the factors contributing to teen suicide, divorce is the only factor consistently associated with both suicide and homicide rates in teens (Messner, Bjarnason, Raffalovich, & Robinson, 2006; Szumilas & Kutcher, 2008).

Impact on Well-Being of Adults. Just as children experience turmoil during a divorce, so do adults. Many adults report divorce is the most intense emotional period they have ever experienced. Following the separation, anger, rage, hurt, betrayal, and extreme loneliness persist for many months, lessening only with time. Many authors cite the pain and anger parents experience during and after a divorce as one of the major reasons children experience rejection—parents are in so much pain and anxiety, they just can't focus on their children's pain (Cherlin, 1999, 2002; Hetherington & Kelly, 2002; Wallerstein & Blakeslee, 2003). Adults often are tempted to jump quickly into another relationship to ease their pain. While this decision may help temporarily, the results are most often disastrous, because rarely do these relationships last.

The Effects of Divorce on Family Dynamics

Not only do parents divorce each other, but they also, in some respects, divorce their children. One of the primary effects of divorce on children is the deterioration of the relationship between the child and at least one of the parents, and sometimes both. In part, this is due to the self-absorption parents experience during the divorce process. Divorced mothers, despite their best intentions, are less able than their married counterparts to attend to the emotional needs of their children. Mothers are often so overwhelmed emotionally their childrearing practices suffer. They vacillate between harsh and permissive parenting styles. Mothers also can become emotionally dependent on their children, placing their children at a disadvantage.

Noncustodial divorced parents are less likely to have close relationships with their children than parents in intact families. This is especially true for noncustodial parents of younger children, who are more likely to drift away from regular contact with these young children. While more fathers are gaining custody of their children today, custodial fathers still represent only a small percentage of single parents—16.9% compared to 83.1% of custodial mothers (Grall, 2006). While noncustodial mother stereotypes exist—think of what goes though your mind when you think about a noncustodial mother—there are by far more stereotypes surrounding noncustodial fathers simply because there are so many more of them.

Divorced Dad Stereotypes. Ahrons (2004, p 96-117) offers some interesting ideas regarding divorced fathers. She categorizes them into three stereotypes (caution: remember stereotypes are generalizations and do not hold true for all or even most):

- *Disneyland dads* are fathers who use recreation to engage children, in place of providing real parenting. Ahrons points out the logistical difficulty of fathers who live a distance from the child and who do not have access to the child's belongings and toys. This limits fathers (or noncustodial mothers) in what they can do with their children. The noncustodial parent, usually the father, seeks out fun and exciting activities to do with the child; hence, the term "Disneyland dad."
- *Deadbeat dads* are fathers who do not pay child support. Ahrons suggests unemployment or financial difficulties related to maintaining a separate household, as well as meeting child support, are major challenges for these fathers.
- *Disappearing dads* are fathers who disappear by moving away, remarrying, cohabiting, or focusing all their attention on a new home, new family, or new relationship. This often occurs because of continuing conflict and litigation between the couple. The disappearing dad can also experience chronic feelings of guilt and loss because of the limited time he can spend with his child. It is sometimes easier to avoid contact with the children than to deal with the feelings of guilt and loss they have while with their children.

Mothers are often accused of restricting the visitation of fathers, which may be a way mothers, consciously or subconsciously, contribute to these stereotypes. For example, a mother might restrict visitation as punishment for lack of child support or for revenge. Unfortunately, little or no contact with the noncustodial parent increases the damaging effects of divorce on children. Research confirms children do best when they have continued contact with both parents, as long as there isn't high conflict between the ex-spouses (Bauserman, 2002).

Mothers can also be deadbeats. In fact, the percentage of mothers who do not pay child support is actually slightly higher than the percentage of men. According to the U.S. Census, in 2005, 43.1% of mothers who are ordered to pay child support pay some or all they owe, while 47.3% of fathers pay some or all of what they owe (Grall, 2007).

Adolescent and Grown Children. The ability to get along with peers is a social skill necessary for a happy family life, social life, and workplace life. Parental conflict accompanying divorce can jeopardize a young adult's sense of competence, leaving the young adult to feel emotionally immature (VanderValk, de Goede, Spruijt, & Meeus, 2007). In adolescence, all young people struggle with feelings of inadequacy, but this intensifies when parents divorce. Children of divorce view marriage differently than the children of intact families. Children of divorce tend to have more positive attitudes toward divorce, less favorable attitudes toward marriage, and are less likely to pursue marriage as a lifelong commitment (Kapinus, 2004; Wallerstein, Lewis, & Blakeslee, 2000).

The way grown children view their parents' divorces differs substantially from the way their parents view divorce. Wallerstein and colleagues found that 15 years after the divorce, 80% of mothers and 50% of fathers felt the divorce was good for them, while only 10% of the children felt positive about the divorce (Wallerstein, Lewis, & Blakeslee, 2000). This is in contrast to Ahrons' (2004b) findings that 80% of adult children of divorce felt their parents' decision to divorce was good and they have either benefited or not been affected by it.

The Effects of Divorce on Religious Practice

When families break apart, the foundation of their life together is shaken, even shattered. Divorce often disrupts the family's religious practice, which can have negative consequences. It is fairly common to see a drop-off in church attendance following a divorce. Children are more likely to stop practicing their faith after a divorce. In fact, adult children of divorce are between 2 and 3 times more likely to abandon religious practice than adults from intact families (Steakley, 2003). In a study of 1,500 people, half from divorced families and half from intact families, Marquardt (2005) found less than half from divorced families were members of a church compared to 63% from intact families. This creates potentially serious consequences, not only for the family, but for society as well. Religious involvement tends to improve people's physical and emotional health, and marital stability. It lessens adolescent sexual activity, crime, and the use of alcohol and drugs. A long-term decrease in religious worship after a divorce results in weakened families and weakened individuals.

The Church's Response to Divorce

By offering grace and forgiveness, churches can be supportive to divorced or divorcing families, which aids in the healing process. However, the church can also be instrumental in causing shame and guilt in individuals who divorce. Some conservative churches require divorced ministers to leave their positions. They may ask a divorced church member to leave a leadership position and permanently prohibit divorced individuals from certain church positions.

More than any other social organization, the church continues to perpetrate the stigma attached to divorce. While the church teaches grace and forgiveness of sin, many divorced individuals are made to feel divorce is the unpardonable sin. No wonder church attendance for divorced families often decreases or stops altogether.

Working Through Marital Difficulties

Divorce has consequences. While researchers may disagree on the severity of the consequences, they agree divorce wreaks havoc on adults and children. The good news is marriages can be saved. We routinely see marriages turn around. Even couples on the way to divorce can revitalize their relationships into healthy, satisfying marriages. Marriage counseling can be an effective tool to help couples work through their marital difficulties.

Unfortunately, most couples don't seek out a therapist until the marriage is nearly ruined. Not all counselors or psychologists have the training and experience to work through the complicated issues couples bring into therapy. It is important to find a therapist trained in couple and family therapy. Therapists who are clinical members of the American Association for Marriage and Family Therapy (AAMFT) have this kind of specialized knowledge and training to help couples restore the love and tenderness they long for in their marriages. A person of faith should seek a therapist who is sensitive to faith issues. A therapist with this kind of training can be found at www.therapistlocator.net (accessed June 23, 2009), a service of the American Association for Marriage and Family Therapy.

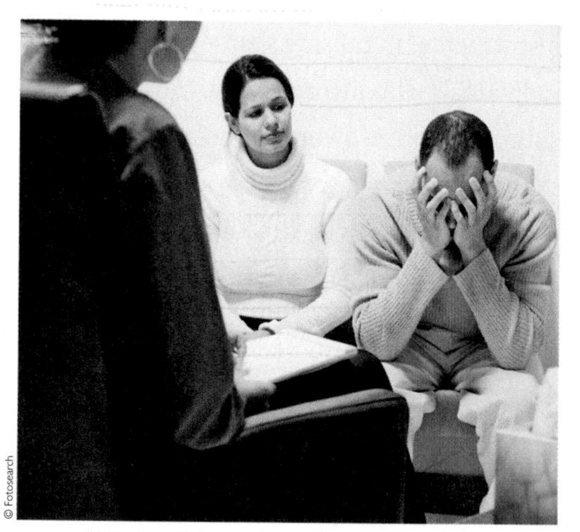

© Fotosearch

Unfortunately, most couples don't seek out a therapist until the marriage is nearly ruined.

Covenant Marriage Revisited

The biblical concept of "until death do us part" can be seen in a covenant marriage. In chapter 6, we equated a biblical model of marriage with covenant marriage. In our context here, we are referring to a modern concept of marriage which stems from a Christian, cultural, and political response to no-fault divorce. We looked at this earlier in the section on types of divorce.

In a covenant marriage, couples agree to attend premarital counseling. They also accept much more limited grounds for divorce. This serves to provide both spouses with the security and motivation to work hard to make a good marriage, knowing the other is committed to the same purpose.

This mutual commitment is promoted as the long-term foundation for marriage and family life, with benefits both for spouses and children. Sidebar 13.2 offers ideas for what couples can do before marriage to improve their relationship and to prevent

Sidebar 13.2
Preventing Divorce

- Commit to the marriage. Decide in advance that divorce is not a choice. This forces the couple to work out any difficulties in a different way.
- Make sure your expectations are appropriate. People often go into a marriage thinking they can change the other person. In truth, the only one we can change is ourselves. If you can't accept the way your spouse-to-be is today, don't get married.
- When problems seem overwhelming, get outside help. All marriages can benefit from counseling. Difficult marriages can be saved. Many churches offer marriage counseling or references to good counselors. Divorce is more expensive than counseling.
- Consider the cost of divorce. Divorce is financially draining. Think about all the costs involved, such as attorney fees, two homes instead of one, child support, and spousal maintenance. Financial costs are not the only consideration. Another cost of divorce is the heartache on everyone involved—especially the children.
- God tells us He hates divorce (Malachi 2:16). God's ideal and desire is one man and one woman "until death do us part." Remember that marriage is a vow, and not honoring that vow disappoints your family and friends, as well as God (Numbers 30:2).
- God's goal for each of us is to mature and become more like Him (Ephesians 4:13). God put your spouse into your life, so it is important to be accepting of his or her flaws.
- Honor and respect your spouse above yourself. Work on meeting your spouse's needs even when you don't feel like it or he or she does not deserve it. Making the first move toward an unloving spouse can be hard, but your spouse will usually reciprocate. Remember that feelings follow actions, so acting loving will bring about loving feelings.
- Preventing divorce is best done before marriage. Premarital counseling can help you prevent marrying too quickly, not knowing the other person well enough, or not being ready for the commitment of marriage. Make sure you can say that divorce is not an option and mean it—that you are willing to do whatever it takes to work out your differences.
- Before considering divorce, consider all the consequences to yourself, your spouse, and your children. Don't make hasty decisions based on emotions. Seek out help from family or friends. Remember, counseling from someone trained in marriage and family therapy can help.
- Marriage involves a great deal of work, patience, and commitment. Marriages that are on track can also be the source of incredible joy and satisfaction. If you are struggling in your marriage, don't give up. Continue to ask God to give you the strength, wisdom, and encouragement you need.

Source: Houdman, Matthews-Rose, Niles, eds. 2002–2006. Used by permission.

divorce. Note that while a covenant marriage serves a protective function for a marriage, is not an attempt to keep spouses or children in abusive relationships or in relationships with infidelity.

Single-Parent Families

Research clearly shows that children develop best when they live with two, happily married adults (Amato, 2003). Unfortunately, this is not always possible. One of the consequences of divorce is the single-parent family. Divorce is not the only way to create a single-parent family. An increasing number of women are choosing to raise a child conceived out of wedlock. In addition, a smaller percentage of children are raised by one parent following the death of the other parent. Single-parent families created by divorce are susceptible to all of the consequences of divorce: reduced income, emotional and behavioral symptoms in children, plus difficulties specific to single-parent families. As the divorce rate has increased and the stigma of having a child out of wedlock has decreased, the number of children living with only one parent has increased. Nearly 28% of all children under the age of 21 are living in single-parent households. The number of single mothers increased from 3 million to 10 million between 1970 and 2000 (Fields & Casper, 2001). In 2004, 70% of all children were living with both parents, 23.2% were living in mother-headed homes, and 3.2% in father-headed homes (Kreider, 2008). One in three children is born to unmarried parents, and 1 in 2 children will live in a single-parent family at some point in childhood (Children and Families in Crisis, 2004).

Image from BigstockPhoto.com / Creatista

One in three children is born to unmarried parents, and 1 in 2 children will live in a single-parent family at some point in childhood.

Financial Difficulties

Single-parent families created by the death of a spouse typically are financially better off than single-parent families created by divorce. After a divorce, single mothers often find it difficult to provide an acceptable standard of living for their families. Many rely on welfare for at least a period of time. Lack of child support exacerbates the financial difficulties, especially since less than 45% of mothers received the full amount of child support from the fathers of their children in 2003. The picture is only slightly better for fathers—46% of custodial fathers received the full amount of child support due them in 2003 (Grall, 2006).

Role and Task Overload

Another difficulty facing single parents is role and task overload. A single parent can find it overwhelming to take on the role of both mother and father. This is intensified by the likelihood of financial problems, forcing many single parents to work two jobs. Single parents who are trying to provide for their children often go without sleep and leisure time to meet the needs of their children. They experience social isolation, loneliness, and embarrassment in a society revolving around couples. Because many single parents shoulder the entire responsibility for the financial needs of their children, money becomes an important and pervasive concern for single parents (Anderson, 2003).

Unexpected Benefits of Single Parenting

Little has been written about the positive side of single-parent families. Parental and child health outcomes often are related to communication and social support. Single-parent families with larger networks of social support were found to have better physical and mental health. Good communication within the single-parent family was also related to positive mental and physical health outcomes (McCubbin, 2007).

While children are vulnerable to all the disadvantages of single-parent families, they also can benefit from this situation. Because children in single-parent families often have increased levels of responsibility, they frequently exhibit higher levels of autonomy than adolescents in other family types (Amato, 2001). Independence is a highly valued personal trait in our culture, and the increased independence of single-parent family members may be an important survival skill in our rapidly changing world.

Remarriage: A Blending of Two Households?

What is in a name? When it comes to stepfamilies, it can be a lot. The Vishers, well known for their research on stepfamilies, object to the term stepfamily because it suggests the new family will swiftly and easily blend together and it assumes a homogenous unit without a previous history or background (1992, 1996, 1997, 1998), On the other hand, the term stepfamily, which is the most popular term used in professional literature, is not without stereotypes, which often bring to mind images of fairy tales with "wicked stepmothers" (Claxton–Oldfield, 2000).

On the surface, remarriage sounds like the solution to the problems single-parent families face. Remarriage does provide some solutions, but it also creates new challenges:

> A stepfamily is assaulted on all sides by difficult and often divisive questions. How much control should a stepparent have over a stepchild? How much authority should a nonresidential parent exert over a child? How should a difficult former spouse be handled? How does an "ours" baby change the emotional dynamic in a stepfamily? Why is there a lack of "honeymoon effect" during the first years of stepfamily life? (Bray & Kelly, 1999)

In the next section, we will examine some of the complexities, challenges, and rewards of life in a stepfamily. The following statistics from the Census Bureau help to illustrate the complexity of North American families.

The Statistics of Remarriage

Estimating the number of stepfamilies in the United States is a complex task for several reasons. One, the definitions researchers use to define stepfamilies vary. The "official" estimates have been pieced together from the U.S. Census, the National Center for Health Statistics (NCHS) and various national surveys of American families. Due to budget limitations, the U.S. Census and the NCHS are no longer producing detailed reports of the trends in marriage, divorce and remarriage. Therefore, stepfamily estimates currently use data from the 1990s, making estimates outdated and underestimated (Stewart, 2007). According to 2001 data, 15% of all children under the age of 18 are living in stepfamilies, and 1 in 10 households containing children are stepfamilies (Kreider & Fields, 2005). In 2004, about 6.4 million children, just under one tenth of the nation's children were living with one stepparent and one biological parent (Kreider, 2008).

Stepfamilies are formed in several ways. We most commonly think of a stepfamily as one formed when a parent remarries after a divorce. One or both parents may bring a child or children from a previous marriage into the new relationship. Stepfamilies are also formed when a widow or widower with children marries after the death of their spouse. However, a growing number of parents bring a child from a previous, never-married relationship into the new marriage. Many cohabiting couples, who go on to marry, have a child or children from previous relationships. In 2001, 25% of children lived in single-parent families; 15% lived in stepfamilies; 3% lived with two cohabiting parents; and nearly 2% lived with at least one adoptive parent. Figure 13.3 graphically illustrates these percentages (Kreider and Fields, 2005).

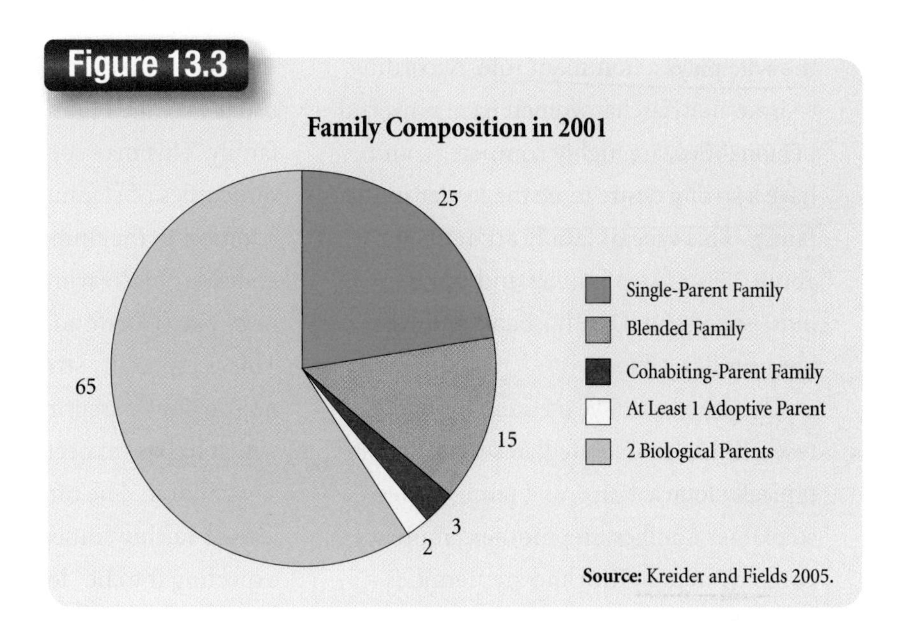

Source: Kreider and Fields 2005.

Types of Stepfamilies

Bray (1999) categorizes stepfamilies according to their adaptive styles for parenting, managing change, separating the first from the second marriage, and nonresidential parent(s). He identifies the first type of family as the neotraditional stepfamily. This family type ends up looking much like a nuclear family and has the best success for surviving the trials and disappointments of stepfamily life. Neotraditional families are close, loving families with compatible values. They score high on marital satisfaction and conflict resolution. Children in this type of family have a lower incidence of behavioral problems.

The second stepfamily type Bray describes is the romantic stepfamily. The romantic stepfamily strives for the same goals as neotraditional families—except they want to achieve everything *immediately*. They expect love, harmony, and closeness to happen almost instantaneously after the stepfamily is formed. In the critical first 2 years, romantic stepfamilies exhibit the highest degree of conflict and result in the highest failure rate. These families tend to either dissolve or develop into another type of family.

Bray's third stepfamily type is the matriarchal stepfamily. In this family form, the wife plays a dominant role. According to Bray, matriarchal women have powerful personalities, are highly competent, and have a strong desire to be the leader in the family. This type of family accounts for about 25% of stepfamilies and can be quite successful if the husband and wife have similar values.

Over the last 20 years, stepfamily research has proliferated. Research has typically focused on 1 of 4 family types: stepfather families, stepmother families, complex stepfamilies and stepfamilies with a mutual child. Of the roughly 10% of children living in a stepfamily, more than 8% reside with their biological mother and a stepfather (Kreider, 2008). These stepfather families are formed when a woman with children marries a man without children. It is often thought these families have the least difficulties of all stepfamilies. While some researchers have suggested this is because stepfathers take a noninvolvement role (White & Gilbreath, 2001), researchers find that many stepfathers develop satisfying relationships with their stepchildren. This is especially true when the stepfather takes a secondary parent role as warm and supportive, avoiding a direct disciplinarian role (Bray & Kelly, 2002; Hetherington & Kelly 2002; Sweeney, 2007).

Stepmother family types in which the woman with no children marries a man who has children can be more stressful than stepfather families, because mothers usually set the emotional tone for the family. This may contribute to the difficulties of stepmother families, in addition to the findings fathers tend to abdicate childrearing activities to their new wife (Norwood & Wingender, 1999). This is especially stressful for a wife with no previous parenting experience from which to base expectations of the new stepchildren. She often has a romanticized idea of raising someone else's children, expecting it to be "love at first sight."

Complex stepfamilies are families in which both spouses have biological children and are therefore also stepparents. These families are the most likely to re-divorce (Coleman, Ganong, & Fine, 2000). In addition to working out stepfamily difficulties, these families have the added burden of working out stepsibling relationships and disrupted birth order, where, for example, a youngest child may become a middle child in the new stepfamily (Ganong & Coleman, 2004).

The last type of stepfamily, the stepfamily with a mutual child, has not received much attention in the way of research. There has long been the sense, especially in popular literature, this child will bind or cement the family together; however, this has not been demonstrated in the research. Some of the few studies which have been done suggest that, especially if the child is born before successful stepfamily integration, the birth will complicate this integration (Bernstein, 1989). Parent-child interactional changes have been noted by investigators who have found disruption in both the stepmother–stepchild relationship and the stepfather–stepchild relationship (Ambert, 1986; Hobart, 1991). Other studies seem to contradict the previous studies and demonstrate benefits such as greater stepparent-stepchild involvement, closeness, warmth and overall integration with the addition of a shared child (Ambert, 1986; Hofferth & Anderson, 2003).

Stepfamilies created by divorce and remarriage are, by their very nature, created out of loss.

How Stepfamilies Meet Challenges

In 1978, Andrew Cherlin suggested that stepfamilies are incomplete institutions because our language, laws and customs do not accommodate them. While other researchers argue against this definition, institutional support for stepfamilies is skeletal. Stepparents often face non-inclusion by school systems, social organizations (such as youth groups and religious groups), and medical institutions (in which stepparents often have non-family status) (Ganong & Coleman, 2004; Stewart, 2007).

Stepfamily Timeline. All stepfamilies have ups and downs. The first 2 years tend to be the most difficult as family members struggle to sort out new relationships, come to terms with the ghosts of the first relationship, establish new roles, develop new rules, and work out conflict resolution. Hetherington and Kelly (2002) refer to this time period as a time of disorganization and turbulence. Stepfamilies are at their most vulnerable during this time. The next 1 to 3 years are a period of stabilization, which is often fairly tranquil, as the compromises made in the first 2 years continue to guide the family. Conflicts often arise again as children near adolescence. This can present a time of crisis for a stepfamily, just as it does in an intact family (Bray & Kelly, 1999; Hetherington & Kelly, 2002). Clinicians suggest that a strong couple relationship is the key to a strong stepfamily (Visher, Visher, & Pasley, 2003), and most research has found a positive correlation between the quality of the marital relationship and the quality of the stepparent-stepchild relationship (Stewart, 2007). In addition, when the couple is proactive in the family formation process and there is widespread acceptance of the new partner and marriage, it helps in the blending process and contributes to the success of the stepfamily (Michaels, 2006).

A Sense of Loss. Stepfamilies created by divorce and remarriage are, by their very nature, created out of loss. Adults suffer the loss of a relationship with a former husband or wife, even when they agreed the divorce was necessary. The loss includes the dreams and expectations of what the first marriage could have been. Parents experience the loss of a daily parent-child relationship. Most adults also experience changes in support from family and friends, a loss of a familiar community, school, or job, and loss of a familiar role in the family (Ganong & Coleman, 2004; Hetherington & Kelly, 2002).

Children experience many of the same losses as adults, plus the loss of both parents being present on a daily basis. Children also experience the loss of friends and family members, as well as their position in the family when step- and half-siblings are added to the family (Ganong & Coleman, 2004).

Conflict. New relationships are challenging for stepfamilies. The stepparent-stepchild relationship is critical for harmony in the new family. Love and concern do not develop quickly between stepparents and stepchildren, unlike the seemingly instant love parents experience for a new baby. Conflict and mistrust are created when stepparents try to rush the relationship (Carter & McGoldrick, 2005; Ganong & Coleman, 2004; Hetherington & Kelly, 2002). Support from the biological parent is essential for developing respect and trust of the stepparent. Conflict between the stepparent and the stepchild can become severe enough, especially with adolescents, to cause the breakup of the marriage. A strong, supportive couple relationship is an important mediating factor in this conflict (Visher, Visher, & Pasley, 2003).

A stepfamily can give children a broader definition of family, greater adaptability and coping, and a sense of belonging.

Stepsibling relationships can be difficult and create conflict. Often children reside in one household and visit another. This has been referred to as a "revolving-door family." The difficulty for children is they are always on the move—they lose a sense of permanence in any one place. In addition, when nonresidential stepsiblings come to visit, chores change, routines change, rules sometimes change, and an expectation of sharing can be uncomfortable for children.

Loyalties take on a unique place in stepfamilies. Children often are unconsciously resistant to their stepparent's attempts at a relationship, fearing this would demonstrate disloyalty to their other biological parent. This is difficult for stepparents to understand when they are trying so hard to develop a relationship. Children often fiercely defend an absent or intermittently absent parent, while becoming angry with their custodial parent and stepparent. It is as if they feel they can be angry at the parents they live with because they are secure with them, but fear getting angry at an absent parent for fear that parent might go away for good (Carter & McGoldrick, 2005; Ganong & Coleman, 2004).

Boundaries. Establishing clear boundaries is essential in stepfamilies. Because children belong to two different families, the boundaries around the stepfamily can become fuzzy, which can lead to anxiety and confusion. A stepfamily needs to experience its own separateness before it can experience a comfortable relationship between parents and stepparents in the children's two households (Carter & McGoldrick, 2005; Visher & Visher, 1988). Boundaries are a way of communicating the "rules of the house" and indicating who is included in the family. For example, boundaries communicate how the new family will handle dealing with ex-spouses, *his* children, *her* children, *our* children, grandparents, school conferences, and holidays, to name a few (Stewart, 2007; Visher, Visher, & Pasley, 2003). Once boundaries are established, spouses and children alike feel more comfortable in otherwise uncomfortable situations (Ganong & Coleman, 2004).

Finances. Finances are a struggle for most newly married individuals. Stepfamilies are no exception and actually can find finances to be more challenging. The financial picture for most stepfamilies is brighter than for either family before the marriage because of the combined income. However, some challenges do exist. The financial arrangements made at the time of divorce may seem unfair and unreasonable to either spouse in the new marriage, creating anger and a fertile battleground. Spousal maintenance and child support may result in a lower standard of living than would otherwise be possible. A husband may be hesitant to share financial matters with his new wife, especially if he feels his previous wife took advantage of him. Women who have gained competence and financial independence during their single-parent period may fear financial dependency. Inheritance issues become an issue, not only for the new couple, but also for the ex-spouses and grandparents (Carter & McGoldrick, 2005; Stewart, 2007).

The Rewards of Remarriage

You may remember the old TV series *The Brady Bunch*. A man with three sons marries a woman with three daughters. Their life together is full of fun, mischief, and goodwill. Any misunderstandings are minor and are quickly resolved. Each episode seems to end in "happily-ever-after" fashion. In real life, "happy-ever-afters" are rare. Though most American stepfamilies don't resemble the *Brady Bunch* fantasy, stepfamilies can be strong, satisfying families. Research has only recently moved from a deficits perspective to look at what makes a stepfamily successful (Visher, Visher, & Pasley, 2003). Despite the research evidence supporting the problems encountered in stepfamilies, there are many strong, successful stepfamilies. This strengths-based research can provide goals to help guide families in positive directions. The following are possible areas of strength which may be valuable to stepfamilies.

A Broader Definition of Family

Stepfamilies can give children a broader definition of family, a larger network for support, and a place to work out socialization. Stepparents, step-grandparents, and stepsiblings all can provide a wider family base from which children can learn and grow. This includes providing the child with a greater number of positive role models—people who care about the child and who can provide friendship and support. The increased number of people in the child's life provides an extra built-in support system, making more adults available for advice and encouragement. As a result, children can learn valuable social skills they might not have learned elsewhere as they interact with this wider circle of people (Olson & DeFrain, 2006).

Adaptability

Children who grow up in a stepfamily often reach adulthood with a greater capacity to adapt. They have learned through the experience of growing up how to cope with change, from experiencing a variety of family forms—family after death of a parent, family after divorce, single-parent family, cohabiting parents. They are exposed to a greater number of intimate adults (parents, stepparents, step-grandparents) than children in nuclear families. As a result, they may learn to be more tolerant of people. Stepchildren can learn firsthand about different lifestyles. They can also learn important interpersonal skills from this experience. Many stepchildren may become especially sensitive to other's emotional states because they have been intimately aware of their parents' feelings during the difficulties of divorce.

A Sense of Belonging

Stepfamilies can bring a source of comfort and belonging to children. After going through the difficulties involved in divorce, children often experience loneliness. Following an initial adjustment period to a new stepfamily, the addition of people in the child's life can decrease this loneliness. The child has more to do and more people to do things with (Olson & DeFrain, 2006). Children from stepfamilies tend to be more autonomous and independent than children in intact families. Following a divorce, they may have been expected to do things which were not required of them prior to the marital breakup. Children often take great pride in this achievement of independence. Long before their peers from intact families are able, children in stepfamilies can contribute tangibly to the well-being of their families.

Seeing the Family as a Reinvestment

Stepfamilies often represent a reinvestment. Adults have the opportunity to learn and grow from past mistakes, and all family members can benefit from lessons learned. Following a divorce, people are usually keenly aware of the fact they must work at relationships to achieve success. If they carry this sense into a second marriage, they will commit to working at building a family in which everyone can flourish. They will push themselves to communicate better, be more open to emotional risks, and be more willing to enter unknown territory in order to create a nurturing environment for their children, stepchildren, and new spouse.

Stepfamily members often have a greater sense of valuing those around them. This is useful in navigating the complex waters of life. Developmentally, children do not learn to value those around them until their late teens or early adulthood years. Children who experience divorce and remarriage, however, can learn early how to value those around them. This is an important relationship tool which will carry over to their young adult and adult relationships.

Building Trust

Trust is essential in working out the challenges the new stepfamily will face. It takes time and effort to overcome the ghosts seeming to haunt the new family.

To work through conflicts, families must employ clear communication, patience, and love (Visher, Visher, & Pasley, 2003). All families experience stressful times. It is important not to blame every problem or stressful situation on the stepfamily situation itself. Husbands and wives fight, children misbehave, adolescents rebel and eventually leave home. Jealousy, rejection, guilt, and anger, while more intense in stepfamilies, exist in all families. Understanding the negatives, as well as the positives of life in a stepfamily can decrease the disappointment and increase the enjoyment of this complicated family form (Visher, Visher, & Pasley, 2003).

The Church's Response to Remarriage

The church can be of assistance to stepfamilies. First, the church staff and congregation must display a nonjudgmental attitude—stepfamilies have enough guilt to deal with. The church can provide stepfamilies a loving, supportive place to grow. Classes on building strong stepfamilies can help normalize some of the transitions which occur in these families. Parenting support groups are helpful for all parents and can include some of the parenting variations stepparents encounter. The number of stepfamilies is increasing. By embracing, mentoring, and loving these families, the church can minister to those who most need Christ's love.

A Christian Perspective

It is clear that God hates divorce. He is a covenant-making, covenant-keeping God. It is also true God made allowances for divorce. When questioned by the religious leaders of His day, Jesus explained God allowed divorce because of the "hardness" of men's hearts (Mark 10:5). While divorce is a product of sin, and it has lasting consequences, it is *not* unpardonable. Jesus Himself allowed for circumstances in which divorce, though the exception, was an allowable choice (Matthew 19:8); and so divorce Jesus would allow cannot be sin.

But even when divorce is sinfully practiced, Romans 3:23 gives us good news, "all have sinned and fall short of the glory of God." This means everybody. Romans 5:12 further explains, "Therefore, just as sin entered the world through one man, and death through sin, and in this way death came to all men, because all sinned." This is a reference to the lasting consequences of sin—since the origin of humankind. Our hope comes from Romans 5:8: "But God demonstrates his own love for us in this: While we were still sinners, Christ died for us." We can also find hope in Romans

6:23: "For the wages of sin is death, but the gift of God is eternal life in Christ Jesus our Lord."

What an amazing Father we have. He warns us against taking a harmful path; yet, when we stubbornly go in that direction, He still welcomes us back when we confess our sin. Even more amazing, God promises His children they need not remain in sin, but may have their hearts changed (Ezekiel 11:19; 2 Corinthians 5:17).

Yes, God hates divorce, and in particular the circumstances of violence and unfaithfulness which are at its root (Malachi 2:16); but He loves us and wants us to love Him. He even wants to change our hearts, so that divorce is not the first avenue choosen when confronting difficulties in marriage. Instead, He asks us to follow a biblical-covenant marriage model, one reflecting His covenant love for us.

Summary

Our culture embraces a "me now" attitude, which has led to the deterioration of many of our cultural and social norms, including the permanence of marriage. This chapter has examined the increase in the divorce rate since the 1950s and the impact of divorce on poverty. Among the causes of divorce are these: young age at marriage, lack of college education, low income, and premarital pregnancy. These factors all lead to a greater risk of divorce. Other factors include the ways spouses interact with one another, disillusionment, negativity, dissatisfaction with the relationship, and lack of commitment.

Researchers debate the consequences of divorce. On the negative side, many researchers have found the effects for children to be cumulative, even lasting a lifetime. The higher the divorce rate in a community, the higher the crime rate will be. Children from divorced families are more likely to be involved in alcohol and drugs, to have lower educational achievement, to have more health problems, and to have a higher suicide rate than children from intact families. Parent-child relationships are compromised following a divorce. Children's social confidence and social skills are jeopardized, which later can make successful marriage difficult for the adult children of divorce.

On a more positive side, some researchers suggest most children of divorce don't display the level of clinical problems suggested by the first group of researchers. They point to the children's resilience, increased independence, and increased responsibility as advantageous for their growth. While divorce admittedly has negative effects on children, these researchers suggest some of the problems children experience may have existed before the divorce.

Single-parent families are formed when parents divorce, cohabiting couples separate, or—in increasing numbers—women raise children out of wedlock. The number of single parents has increased dramatically: 1 in 3 children is born to unmarried parents, and 1 in 2 children will spend some time in a single-parent family. Single mothers have a lower standard of living than their married counterparts and often rely on welfare for a period of time. Half of all single mothers do not receive regular child support, which exacerbates their financial problems. In addition to financial difficulties, single parents also face role and task overload which can be overwhelming.

A growing number of people bring a child into a new marriage. While stepfamilies experience the same difficulties all couples experience, they also have more complex challenges. Some of these challenges include loyalties to absent parents, boundary fuzziness with children belonging to two different families, and financial struggles related to child support and spousal maintenance. Despite the challenges stepfamilies experience, they also reap rewards. Stepfamilies provide children with a broader definition of family, a larger network for support and socialization, decreased loneliness, and greater independence and autonomy.

Questions for Thought

1. As it relates to marriage and family, how does our culture reflect a "disposable" society?
2. What are the most serious effects of divorce on families? On children? What consequences would you add that we have not mentioned in this chapter?
3. In your experience, which of these groups is better prepared to help families who have experienced divorce/remarriage: social agencies or the church? Explain your answer.
4. How can the church better minister to stepfamilies and divorced individuals?

Resources

Books:

Hope for the Separated: Wounded Marriages Can Be Healed by Gary Chapman. (Moody Publishers, 2005)

Saving Your Second Marriage Before it Starts by Les and Leslie Parrot. (Zondervan, 2001)

Two Homes by Claire Masural (author) and Kady Macdonald Denton (illustrator). (Candlewick, 2003)

Divorce and Remarriage in the Church by David Instone-Brewer. (IVP Books, 2006)

Movies:

Stepmom, (PG 13). DVD . A sad, yet heartwarming story of a divorced family and the challenges they face

Mrs. Doubtfire, (PG 13). Comedy about the lengths a dad will go to maintain contact with his children

Website:

American Association of Marriage and Family Therapists: http://www.therapistlocator.net (accessed June 23, 2009). Look for a marriage and family therapist near you to help with marriage counseling, processing your divorce, or pre-marital/blended family work.

14 Building Strong Families

Though one may be overpowered, two can defend themselves.
A cord of three strands is not quickly broken.

—Ecclesiastes 4:12

Image from BigstockPhoto.com / andres

Our discussion thus far should lead you to the conclusion marriages and families are complex, multidimensional entities. Because of the nature of marriage and family, we have most often targeted the many challenges couples and families face. If marriages and families were problem-free, we would not need to write this book. Threaded throughout our analysis you have found a Christian perspective. We have intentionally included this to highlight positive ways to approach difficulties, as well as to counter any negative conclusions you might draw. Christians are not "better" than anyone else. They do not have all the answers and they certainly make many mistakes. Paul the Apostle said, "I can do everything through Him who gives me strength" (Philippians 4:13). The Christian perspective holds out that promise: What we *cannot* do in our own strength, God *can* do in His strength through us. This chapter will first explore what characteristics are common in strong families, then compare similarities between family strengths and family resiliency. The final portion of this chapter includes suggestions for healthy family functioning.

What Determines a Strong Family?

Is there such thing as a strong family? If so, just what would a strong family look like? Is there such thing as a normal family? You may be asking yourself these questions: Do I come from a strong family? How can I make my family a stronger family?

Strong Family Quiz

Before we look at family strength, take the quiz in Figure 14.1:

Figure 14.1

Strong Family Quiz

	1 Never	2 Seldom	3 Usually	4 Always
1. When trouble hits my family, we pull together as one unit.				
2. The members of my family are committed to our family.				
3. My family members talk behind each other's backs.				
4. My family has a faith that is valued and shared by all members.				
5. My family enjoys being together.				
6. My family has trouble sharing emotions.				
7. My family argues a lot when we are together.				
8. In my family, we speak directly about things that bother us.				
9. In my family, each member feels valued and appreciated.				
10. Family members are able to openly express affection for each other.				
11. My family has trouble solving problems when they arise.				
12. In my family, members feel close to one another.				
13. I often feel misunderstood by my family.				
14. I am proud of my family.				
15. I feel comfortable sharing my feelings with my family.				

Now, reverse scores for statements 3, 6, 7, 11, and 13 (1 becomes 4, 4 becomes 1, 3 becomes 2, and so forth)

SCORE = 55

Strong Family Quiz Results

While this quiz has no scientific value, it will give you some indication of how you think your family "rates" on the strong family scale.

- 60: This is the maximum score, indicating you feel you have an extremely strong family.
- 45–59: From your perspective, your family falls in the "fairly normal" range, where most families are.
- Less than 45: You perceive a need for improvement in the area of your family's strengths.

What Experts Say About Family Strengths

What makes a family strong? What strengths constitute a strong family? These are questions researchers have asked for many years. The word strength in this context means a powerful attribute or an inherent asset a family possesses. Herbert Otto (1962) was one of the first to look at intact families in terms of their strengths. He suggested family strengths are interrelated and, taken together, they yielded what he called "family strength." Over the last 30 years, researchers have continued to refine Otto's thinking, suggesting families which exhibit these various family strengths are "strong families." Sidebar 14.1 presents 13 propositions about strong families.

John Stinnett and Nick DeFrain are two of the leading researchers, who have built on Otto's work since the 1970s. They have been writing about family strengths for the past 25 years and have authored dozens of books and many more articles.

Stinnett, DeFrain and their colleagues have conducted the most extensive studies of family strengths. In the last 30 years of study, these researchers have collected family-strengths data on more than 10,000 families from more than 20 countries around the world, including the United States (DeFrain, 1999; DeFrain & Stinnett, 2002). While researchers differ in their definition of "strength," they have come to surprisingly similar conclusions about specific family strengths.

In all of the data collected regarding strong families, six major qualities or themes appear consistently. These qualities or themes are common in the lives of strong families across the United States and in countries around the globe (Stinnett & Walters, 1971; Stinnett & Sauer, 1977; Stinnett, Chesser, & DeFrain, 1981; Stinnett, 1983; Stinnett & DeFrain, 1985; DeFrain, Fricke, & Elmen, 1987; DeFrain, DeFrain, & Lepard, 1994;

SIDEBAR 14.1
Propositions from a Strength Perspective

- All families possess strengths. Families encounter different struggles and have different ways of dealing with their struggles. Their strengths help them to adapt.
- If all you look for are problems in a family, then that is what you will find. Look for strengths and you will find them.
- Our weaknesses do not help us solve problems; our strengths do. An essential function of a family is to solve its own problems. It is important to maximize family strengths rather than focus on shortcomings.
- Family structure is not as important as family function. There are many diverse family types, each of which can be a strong family. Looking at the family structure tells little about the family's potential for growth.
- A strong marriage is essential to a strong family. The couple's relationship is the foundation upon which the family is built.
- Strong families usually produce strong kids, who then create their own strong families.
- Strengths develop over time. They are tested and grow through family transitions and challenges.
- Periods of crisis can tear families apart or be the catalyst for growth. Strong families work together to overcome their problems.
- Most families across the globe have considerable strengths.
- Every family is a culture unto itself. No two families are alike.
- Families from different cultures are more alike than different.
- Strong families are not perfect. All families, even the strongest families, have trouble getting along.
- Families have strong emotional connections. Family members have a sense of "belongingness" to one another. This allows families to pull together to withstand adversity.

Source: Adapted from DeFrain, J. 1999; DeFrain, DeFrain, and Lepard 1994; Xie, DeFrain, Meredith, and Combs 1996.

DeFrain, 1999; Stinnett, Stinnett, DeFrain, & DeFrain, 1999; DeFrain & Stinnett, 2002; DeFrain, Cook, & Gonzalez-Kruger, 2004; Olson & DeFrain, 2006).

The Family Strengths Framework. These six qualities form the basis for the "family strengths framework" developed by DeFrain and Stinnett (2002). This model includes the following strengths:

- Commitment
- Appreciation and affection
- Positive communication
- Enjoyable time together
- Spiritual well-being
- Ability to cope with stress and crisis

Figure 14.2

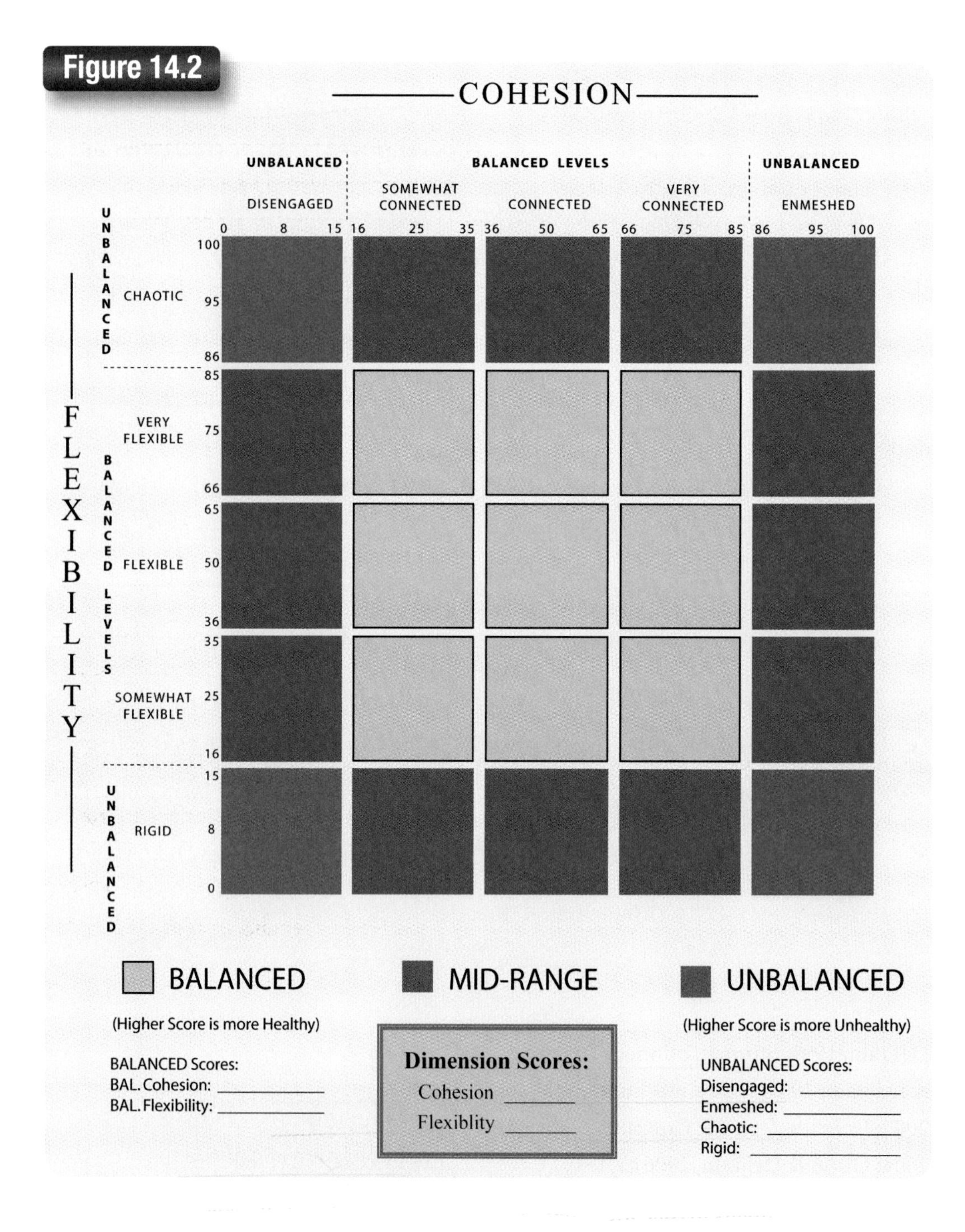

COHESION
UNBALANCED
BALANCED LEVELS
UNBALANCED
DISENGAGED
SOMEWHAT CONNECTED
CONNECTED
VERY CONNECTED
ENMESHED
0 8 15 16 25 35 36 50 65 66 75 85 86 95 100
FLEXIBILITY
UNBALANCED
CHAOTIC
100 95 86
85 75 66
VERY FLEXIBLE
BALANCED LEVELS
FLEXIBLE
65 50 36
SOMEWHAT FLEXIBLE
35 25 16
UNBALANCED
RIGID
15 8 0
BALANCED
MID-RANGE
UNBALANCED
(Higher Score is more Healthy)
BALANCED Scores:
BAL. Cohesion: ___________
BAL. Flexibility: ___________
Dimension Scores:
Cohesion _______
Flexiblity _______
(Higher Score is more Unhealthy)
UNBALANCED Scores:
Disengaged: ___________
Enmeshed: ___________
Chaotic: ___________
Rigid: ___________

The Circumplex Model of Family Systems. Another measure of family strength is the "circumplex model of family systems" (Olson, Russell, & Sprenkle, 1989). This model is conceptually consistent with the family strengths model and has been used as the basis for over 700 studies, assessment, and treatment of families (see Figure 14.2) (Kouneski, 2001).

The circumplex model looks at three dimensions:

1. *Family cohesion or closeness*—the emotional bonding between family members or the sense of togetherness versus separateness
2. *Family flexibility*—the family's ability to change its leadership, roles, and rules when necessary
3. *Communication*—the family members' honesty, clarity of speaking, and listening

A Comparison of Models. If we were to place these two models side by side, we would see the following similarities, as illustrated in Figure 14.3.

In the circumplex model, *cohesion* is most like *commitment* and *time together* in the family strengths model. *Flexibility* (circumplex model) is most like the *ability to cope with stress* and *spiritual well-being* (family strengths model). *Communication* (circumplex model) is most like *positive communication* and *expression of appreciation and affection* (family strengths model).

In defining a strong family, we would conclude a strong family exhibits these six major qualities or themes: commitment, appreciation and affection, positive communication, time together, spiritual well-being, and the ability to cope with stress and crisis. These strengths are interrelated and do not operate independently of each other. Each of these family strengths will be the focus of the remainder of this chapter.

Figure 14.3

Family Strengths Model	Circumplex Model
Commitment	Cohesion
Time together	Cohesion
Ability to cope with stress	Family flexibility
Spiritual well-being	Family flexibility
Positive communication	Communication
Expression of appreciation and affection	Communication

Commitment

Strong families typically are very committed to each other. They value the things which make their family special. They invest time in one another, share in family activities, and promote one another's happiness (DeFrain & Stinnett, 2002; Olson & DeFrain, 2006). Foundational to family commitment is the pledge the husband and wife make to each other: "For this reason a man will leave his father and mother and be united to his wife . . . So they are no longer two, but one. Therefore what God has joined together, let man not separate" (Matthew 19:5–6). Therefore, commitment involves fidelity. How can you build family commitment?

Image from BigstockPhoto.com / slocummedia

Traditions such as birthday celebrations bind a family together and give them a common history.

Set Family Goals

To foster family commitment, set family goals. This allows all members of the family an opportunity to share what is important to them. This kind of involvement also brings about a commitment to see that the goals are met.

Practice Family Traditions

Traditions bind a family together and give them a common history. They make a family feel special and create warmth and closeness. Traditions can be as simple as stories at bedtime, prayers before going to sleep, or pancakes on Saturday morning. They can be more elaborate—such as an annual trip to a favorite destination. If you have a storyteller in your family, encourage that person to carry on the tradition of passing down favorite family stories. Not only are these stories entertaining, but they can instill a sense of building a legacy. Encouraging family members to pass stories on to subsequent generations also will foster generativity (concern for establishing and guiding the next generation).

Develop a Family History

In a related vein, involve family members in developing and deepening a family history. An excellent way to do this is to encourage family members to talk to older relatives about their lives (where they lived, what their family upbringing was like, what kind of lifestyles they lived, what they did for a living). In the process, the family will learn more about its ancestry and cultural heritage. Use a tape recorder to capture these stories and save them for the future. This can be a fun activity for every family member, including young children.

Sacrifice for Unity

In times of trouble, strong families remain loyal to each other and work on their problems together. They see themselves as a team, with a family identity and a sense of unity. When outside pressures such as work threaten to upset family priorities, strong families will make the necessary sacrifices to safeguard family well-being.

Interestingly, sacrifice in strong families also includes altruism—selfless concern for the welfare of others. The highest family values include human virtues—compassion, concern, and altruism. These virtues build strong kids, strong families, and strong communities.

> For God so loved the world that he gave his one and only Son, that whoever believes in him shall not perish but have eternal life.
>
> —John 3:16

> And I am convinced that nothing can ever separate us from God's love. Neither death nor life, neither angels nor demons, neither our fears for today nor our worries about tomorrow—not even the powers of hell can separate us from God's love. No power in the sky above or in the earth below—indeed, nothing in all creation will ever be able to separate us from the love of God that is revealed in Christ Jesus our Lord.
>
> —Romans 8:38–39 NLT

Appreciation and Affection

Just as God loves each of us, the members of strong families love one another. They appreciate the unique contributions of each family member. In what ways do families express appreciation and affection?

Communicate in Word and Action

Strong family members express their appreciation for one another in words and actions. They verbally communicate how special each member is—not just because of *what* each person *does*, but because of *who* each person *is*. In the hustle and bustle of daily life, it is easy to fall into the habit of taking each other for granted, forgetting the importance of letting family members know how much they are appreciated.

- "That was a mighty good dinner, Mom."
- "Thanks, Dad, for putting gas in my car."
- "Hey, Emily, you did a great job of coloring that picture!"

Strong families communicate positively with one another. They pay attention when someone says or does something deserving of a compliment. Instead of becoming jealous because of a family member's achievement, they join with that family member in celebrating the achievement. They recognize special talents, gifts, skills, and achievements, and bring them to the attention of others—both inside and outside the family (DeFrain & Stinnett, 2002; Olson & DeFrain, 2006).

Deal with Conflict Constructively

Every family member will make mistakes, but strong families find ways to encourage, love, and support each other in spite of mistakes. They freely give love and respect, not as a way to "buy" love, but as a way to express true affection.

Conflict occurs in every family, even strong families. Family members get mad, criticize, and correct each other. Strong families are able to deal with conflict in such a way that it does not destroy a family member or harm the family's well-being. Strong families employ constructive conflict resolution methods to build up family relationships rather than tear them apart.

Remember the Little Things

It is not necessary to throw a party or post a compliment on a billboard to express appreciation. Family members can do this in simple, ordinary ways. For example, you can write a note and put it in a family member's backpack, purse, or briefcase. Notes can become family keepsakes, treasures to be read over and over, each time giving the reader a new sense of how he or she is appreciated. Planning a special date with a son, daughter, or spouse also communicates you care and want to spend time with this family member.

All families have conflict but strong families are able to deal with conflict in a way that does not harm family members of their well-being.

Gifts especially tailored for a person are an excellent way to show appreciation. It does not have to be a big thing. Give your daughter a charm for her charm bracelet. Put batteries in your dad's flashlight. Slip some new crayons in your kid sister's backpack. Make a gift certificate for your wife: "This certificate entitles the bearer to one back rub upon request." These are personal, uncomplicated ways to demonstrate affection and appreciation.

Treat Family Like Company

Home is often thought of as the place to flop down and chill out. Family members have the "privilege" of seeing each other without makeup or combed hair. However, good manners and common courtesy can demonstrate that someone matters to you—even if it is "just" family.

An old song says "You Always Hurt the One You Love" (Roberts & Fisher, 1944). Does this have to be true? Instead of taking our family for granted, what if we treated them like "company?" Imagine how appreciated family members would feel. What if we *asked* a family member to do something, instead of *demanding*? What if we *thanked* a family member who passed the butter, instead of just grunting? What if we asked for a family member's opinion and then actually listened to the answer? What if we avoid that all-too-familiar sarcastic edge to our comments?

Positive Communication

It seems natural to say communication is a key to strengthening families—or any relationship, for that matter. How to make communication positive is the challenge. Strong families communicate in positive ways, expressing their thoughts and feelings authentically, and listening attentively to the thoughts and feelings of others. Strong families communicate intimately—they share their fears, their hopes and dreams, their joys and sorrows, their experiences, their needs, and their growth. Not only do they *talk* about these things, but they take time to *listen* and *respond* to each other (DeFrain & Stinnett, 2002; Olson & DeFrain, 2006). Virginia Satir expresses the keys to good communication: "The greatest gift I can receive from anyone is to be seen by them, to be heard by them, to be understood by them, and to be touched by them" (1976, 1).

When someone takes another's side and really understands the person, something

> So also, the tongue is a small thing, but what enormous damage it can do. A great forest can be set on fire by one tiny spark.
>
> —James 3:5 TLB

> A word aptly spoken is like apples of gold in settings of silver.
>
> —Proverbs 25:11

Strong families communicate in positive ways, expressing their thoughts and feelings and listening to the thoughts and feelings of others.

special happens. Unfortunately, family members often become involved in their own busy schedules, allowing the pressures of the moment to block true understanding.

"Tommy hit me in school, Daddy," the little girl says softly.

"Uh-huh, that's nice," a very preoccupied dad replies, scrambling to get to work on time.

Model God's Understanding

God models the kind of understanding which hears and responds. When Christian songwriter Dottie Rambo ministered to her unsaved, dying brother, he remarked that the Lord surely would not want a person like him after the wicked life he had lived. She helped him to realize God did indeed want a person just like him, after which she wrote the song titled: "He Looked Beyond My Fault and Saw My Need" (Rambo, 2003). This is the kind of understanding we need to give every member of our family.

Make Time to Talk

Busy lifestyles often get in the way of taking time to talk. Talking about feelings cannot be rushed; it takes time. Turn off the TV to avoid distractions. You cannot have meaningful dialogue "during commercials," because your mind is focused on what will follow the commercial. However, take advantage of whatever time is available to you. You can give your undivided attention, even in short periods of time: chauffeuring a child to an after-school activity, washing dishes, or getting ready for bed.

Family games can encourage talking. Create a personal family game by writing down questions like these: "If you could be anyone you wanted to be, who would you want to be and why?" "What animal would you like to be?" "Is it ever OK to tell a lie?" Make sure the questions are appropriate for all family members. Put the questions in a box and draw them out, one family member at a time. Encourage one another to answer the questions as honestly as possible.

Speak Clearly

While it is important to be honest in what you say, you do not want to be rude. Be sure to exhibit tact and concern for everyone's feelings.

Use "I" messages when sharing your thoughts and feelings. "I" messages will help you take responsibility for your thoughts and feelings, without criticizing or making incorrect assumptions. This allows the other person to listen without getting defensive.

Here's an example of how to use an "I" message with clear communication:

> "I feel [insert feeling] when you [comment on what the other person is doing which makes you feel this way] because [suggest a reason why you might feel this way, such as, 'My mother used to call me lazy when I did not get things done']. I need [tell the other person what you need from him or her right now]."

Be specific. No one is a mind reader. When things are left for interpretation, they are often perceived incorrectly. Avoid using words such as *never* and *always*—they are rarely correct and put the other person on the defensive. Try focusing on a specific issue, rather than on the other person. For instance, "You are always late" becomes "I am upset you were late getting home, which made me late for my meeting."

Listening is a gift we give to those we care about.

When the family has a problem, make kind and helpful suggestions. Avoid criticizing another's actions without providing an alternative action. This prevents the person from feeling frustrated and helpless.

Learn to Listen

Listening is one of the most powerful ways to express love to another person. The goal of good listening is to hear, understand, and accept the other person's feelings and views. It is important to note that acceptance doesn't mean you necessarily agree with the other person, only that you have listened closely enough to understand what the other person is trying to say. Understanding another's point of view means you avoid lectures. Lectures cause people to tune out the speaker or become defensive.

Listening involves more than just hearing words. It also involves watching the other person's body language. Pay close attention to their eyes and upper lip. These can provide clues about how someone is feeling. Are the eyes clear or red, dry, or watery, wide open or partially closed? A quivering upper lip usually indicates the person is upset, while a straight or slightly tight lip generally indicates stress.

Employ active listening skills. This involves clarifying what you are hearing another person say. It means listening closely to the words and observing the body language, rather than developing your own response while the person is still talking.

What to Avoid

Avoid saying, "I understand." This trivializes the other person's problem and actually suggests an unwillingness to understand. No two people have had the exact same experience, so saying you understand isn't necessarily true.

Avoid giving advice unless the other person asks for it—or you are talking about your own experience and feel qualified to draw a conclusion from it. When you give unwanted advice, you minimize the other person's problem and communicate an unwillingness to listen more deeply.

Avoid statements such as this: "Everyone feels that way once in a while." This minimizes a person's pain. Understand that a person's pain is unique to each person. Do not assume to know how someone feels.

Avoid telling another person he or she doesn't feel a certain way. Remember, everyone is unique, and our feelings are unique to our situations. Even when the situation seems identical, what you feel may not be the same as what someone else feels.

Acknowledge or Identify the Other Person's Feelings

To show you are listening, acknowledge the other person's feelings by rephrasing what the person has said, or respond by interpreting what you think the other person is feeling. Be careful not to minimize or invalidate those feelings. Instead, use statements such as these: "You look really sad"; "That must be really difficult for you to deal with."

Ask the other person to share more. By expressing your desire to understand this person's point of view, you help in overcoming a sense of vulnerability. Sharing intimately—especially about complex topics—can be difficult. By showing you are interested and you care, you make it easier for them to open up.

Time Together

Strong families spend time together because they enjoy one another. Spending time together is one way to show love and caring. We saw in earlier chapters family time often suffers as the result of over-full work and school schedules. In too many families, family time is little more than an assortment of household duties, after-school activities, and errands. Quality family time is time spent together as a family to build and share positive experiences. Families can accomplish this by scheduling one night a week for the family only. Activities can include eating meals together, doing projects together, watching a movie together, or playing games (DeFrain & Stinnett, 2002; Olson & DeFrain, 2006). These kinds of family rituals have been associated with greater marital satisfaction, family satisfaction, and greater well-being of children (Leon & Jacobvitz, 2003).

> These commandments that I give you today are to be upon your hearts. Impress them on your children. Talk about them when you sit at home and when you walk along the road, when you lie down and when you get up.
>
> —Deuteronomy 6:6–7

> May your fountain be blessed, and may you rejoice in the wife of your youth.
>
> —Proverbs 5:18

Many parents feel their children really do not want to spend time with them. According to Stinnett and DeFrain (1985), when 1,500 school-age children were asked what they thought made a happy family, the most frequent answer was "doing things together." Not money, cars, big houses, or televisions, but time spent together.

The ideal amount of family togetherness depends on the age and structure of the family. Families with young children naturally spend more time together because young children require more care. Families with adolescents usually spend less time together because adolescents spend more time with their friends as they make the transition to young adulthood. Single parents may spend more time with their children if there are no other adults in the household. They may spend less time with their children if they are working multiple jobs to make ends meet. Either way, single parents need to make time for adult interaction, even if this means arranging for childcare.

Image from BigstockPhoto.com / Kzenon

Strong families spend time together because they enjoy one another.

Strong families know how to balance togetherness and separateness (Olson & DeFrain, 1999; Olson & DeFrain, 2006). Family time should be satisfying for all family members. Children will be more amenable to family time if they see their parents giving up activities to spend time with them. It is important to have one-on-one time with every child. This can be difficult for families to accomplish, especially with several children in the family. Because this is a way to help children feel valued and loved, parents should strive for one-on-one time with children. One recommendation is a "date night" with each child once a month.

Parents need alone time to nurture their relationship.

As important as it is for parents to arrange for one-on-one time with their children, it is equally important for parents to foster regular alone time for themselves. By nurturing their own relationship, they strengthen the marriage. Since children learn from their parents how marriages work, this also is a good way to model positive marital relationships for them. The stronger the marriage, the better the modeling children receive about marriage and family life. In our busy world, parents often neglect their own relationship. As their children grow older, parents may discover their neglected relationship is deteriorating. Courtship (remember that term from chapter 5?) should continue through all the years of a marriage.

Spiritual Well-Being

According to research, strong families share a high degree of religious orientation. (Krysan, Moore, & Zill, 1990; Larson & Olson, 2004; Olson & DeFrain, 2006; Stinnett & DeFrain, 1985). In addition to attending church together, they often pray together and read the Bible and other inspirational materials together. They share the ups and downs of their faith with one another. Because they have a common belief in something greater than themselves, they share common values and beliefs, giving them a sense of unity and purpose. Their spirituality provides guidelines by which the family lives. Spirituality also may reinforce family traditions and family history (Olson & DeFrain, 1999; Olson & DeFrain, 2006).

It is important to distinguish between spiritual and religious in regard to well-being. Religious refers to more public and external systems linked to denominations, while spiritual focuses on private, more universal beliefs (Erisman, 2004). Families define spirituality in different ways. However, common themes include unity, development of virtue, integrity, and kindness. Agreement on spiritual beliefs is strongly linked to more successful marriages (Larson & Olson, 2004). To promote spirituality, families may observe a devotional or prayer time every day. They may seek out inspirational settings (camping in a forest, a vacation to the mountains) to demonstrate God's wonders and their place as stewards of God's earth. Marriage and family therapists often encourage Christian couples to spend time each day in couple devotions. This frequently provides the motivation for parents to also have devotions with their children.

Spiritual well-being acts as a nerve center within each human being which promotes sharing love and compassion for others. When spiritual ethics are observed in the family setting, love, care, benevolence, and compassion result. Therefore, expression of family spiritual well-being can often be observed in service to others outside the family.

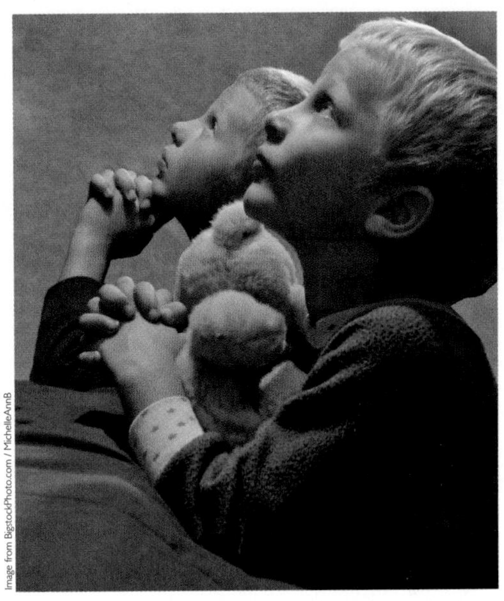

Strong families have a common belief in something greater than themselves, they share common values and beliefs, giving them a sense of unity and purpose.

Whatever is true, whatever is noble, whatever is right, whatever is pure, whatever is lovely, whatever is admirable—if anything is excellent or praiseworthy—think about such things.

—Philippians 4:8

Train a child in the way he should go, and when he is old he will not turn from it.

—Proverbs 22:6

Faith is an important component of spiritual well-being. Faith fosters gratitude and hope, allowing a family to recognize even the little things in life as special events. Faith provides a way to put successes and failures into perspective. It also reinforces families during stress and crisis.

The Ability to Cope with Stress and Crisis

Strong families have the ability to adapt to changing circumstances. Certain roles and rules govern who does what in the family, how to manage situations, and how to express emotions within the family. While these roles and rules establish continuity and stability for the family, they require flexibility when a crisis occurs. To cope with change, strong families can adapt their family patterns, establishing new patterns for family tasks, division of labor, habits, rules, and roles. Flexibility is also required when families enter transition periods, such as marriage, birth, adolescence, departure and reentry of grown children, remarriage, stepsiblings, aging, and death (Olson & DeFrain, 1998; DeFrain & Stinnett, 2002).

Image from BigstockPhoto.com / andres

Humor is an excellent coping tool for families experiencing stress and crisis.

> Do not be anxious about anything, but in everything, by prayer and petition, with thanksgiving, present your requests to God.
>
> —Philippians 4:6

Foster Resiliency

The ability to adapt to life's varying circumstances is a measure of resiliency. Family resiliency and family strengths are strongly linked. Families who *believe* in their ability to overcome difficulties most often do. Strong families foster resiliency when they teach problem-solving skills, provide non-critical support, and facilitate a sense of togetherness. When family members learn these skills, they receive the tools necessary to shape their lives positively and to overcome the difficulties they will face in life. The difference between a family which falls apart in a crisis and a family which pulls together most often is resiliency. Walsh (1998, 2003) identifies family resilience as a flexible construct encompassing different family strengths, in different contexts, at different points in the family life cycle. In other words, she suggests resilient families do not display all the characteristics of family strengths, at all times, in all situations. Walsh organized the key components of family resilience into three areas.

Belief system

- The capacity to make meaning out of adversity
- A positive outlook including hope, optimism, and confidence
- Transcendence and spirituality which provides meaning in people's lives

Organizational patterns

- Flexibility with openness to change but stable with authoritative leadership
- Connectedness which is supportive, respectful, and seeks reconnection
- Social and economic resources with adequate social support and financial means

Communication and problem solving

- Clarity which includes clear, consistent messages
- Open emotional expression including shared feelings and empathy
- Collaborative problem solving, including shared decision making and focus on goals

Teach Problem-Solving Skills

One way to improve a family's ability to manage stress or a crisis is to improve family problem-solving skills. Discuss a problem with the whole family and ask for suggestions on how to solve the problem. Help each family member think he or she is a part of the solution. When a crisis occurs, the family will be ready to draw on solutions it already has discussed.

For example, a family should work out an escape plan in the event of a fire. Once a month, the family should review the plan to see if anything has changed since the last meeting. Repetition cements principles into memory.

Laugh a Little

Never forget the power of humor during difficult situations. Humor is an excellent coping tool for families experiencing stress and crisis. It can strengthen the family and give a sense of perspective and power in a difficult situation.

Humor changes brain chemistry. It causes a release of endorphins, increasing our sense of well-being, improving our reasoning powers, and making us less sensitive to pain. Laughter also reduces stress. Humor has also been shown to have positive benefits on physical health (Boyle & Joss-Reid, 2004). Families who have joy in their lives are more likely to feel good about themselves. It seems fairly obvious having a sense of humor helps families cope with life's stresses and crises. Humor can ultimately be used as a coping tool for families.

A Christian Perspective

Families who are characterized by these six character strengths: commitment, appreciation and affection, positive communication, time together, spiritual well-being, and the ability to cope with stress and crisis, are better able to meet the challenges of raising a family in today's complex world. Their united strengths enable them to draw upon one another's resources. They become a source of strength to one another and an example to other families. We need to keep in mind that both individually and collectively as families, the source of our strength is in Christ. As we looked at in the beginning of this chapter, what we *cannot* do in our own strength, God *can* do in His strength through us.

Successful families celebrate their sense of family and its strength. They look for positive ways to develop new family strengths. Most of all, strong families give credit to God for carrying them through life's many complexities. Strong families realize Jesus Christ became a human being by being born into a family. They understand the Father and the Son enjoy a relationship which is a family relationship. And strong families accept that they, as God's image-bearers, are called to honor family in all its stages, assuring that family remains the foundational building block of contemporary society.

Summary

Research has identified six major qualities or themes common to strong families across the globe. These qualities are commitment, appreciation and affection, positive communication, time together, spiritual well-being, and the ability to cope with stress and crisis.

The family who models *commitment* sets family goals, practices family traditions, develops family history, and is willing to sacrifice for family unity.

The family who models *appreciation and affection* communicates in word and action, deals constructively with conflict, remembers the "little things," and treats family like "company." These families appreciate the unique contributions of each family member. Family members express love and respect freely, not as a way to buy love, but as a way to express sincere affection.

The family who models *positive communication* makes time to talk, speaks clearly, learns to listen actively, acknowledges and identifies the other person's feelings, and avoids statements which will invalidate what another is feeling.

The family who models *time together* focuses on making family time quality time. They work and play together and enjoy one another's company. They have learned how to balance togetherness and separateness. Couples make it a priority to find time together for themselves apart from children.

The family who models *spiritual well-being* shares a high degree of spirituality, including common values and morals. They spend regular devotional time together and find ways to acknowledge God in the ordinary and special events of their family life.

The family who models *the ability to cope with stress and crisis* has learned the meaning of "resiliency." They adapt readily to changing circumstances, teach their children problem-solving skills, provide non-critical support, and foster togetherness.

Questions for Thought

1. If you and your family were to form family goals, what do you think they would be? What goals would you include?

2. Do you think it's realistic to treat family like "company"? Why or why not?

3. What other qualities do you think characterize a strong family?

Resources

Books:

The Five Love Languages by Gary Chapman. (Northfield Publishing, 1995)

The Seven Principles for Making Marriage Work by John M. Gottman and Nan Silver. (Orion, 2004)

A Parent's Guide to Building Resilience in Children and Teens: Giving Your Child Roots and Wings by Kenneth R. Ginsburg. (American Academy Of Pediatrics, 2006)

Movies:

A Family Thing, (PG). Two half brothers find one another and an unlikely family they never knew.

Second Hand Lions, (PG). Two unlikely bachelors find the meaning of family with their nephew.

Websites:

1. *Marriage enrichment*—Weekend to remember conference website: http://www.family life.com/site/c.dnJHKLNnFoG/b.3204559/k.F5BB/Attend_a_conference.htm (accessed June 23, 2009)
2. *Focus on the Family* website with information on couples, families, and parenting: http://www.focusonthefamily.com (accessed June 23, 2009)
3. *Free online personality typing test* (like MBTI): http://www.humanmetrics.com/cgi-win/JTypes2.asp (accessed June 23, 2009)

Epilogue

The Future of the Family

You are the salt of the earth . . . You are the light of the world.

—Matthew 5:13–1

© iStockphoto.com / nataq

What's Ahead for the Family?

Authorities on the family would have us believe that we're seeing "the decline of the American family." However, statistics don't seem to support that affirmation. For example, the divorce rate reached a peak in the early 1980s and has leveled off since that time (see chapter 12). Though many are getting divorced today, Americans as a whole have not given up on marriage and family. We continue to marry, although at a later age (see chapter 3 and 5). Even those who have experienced a divorce are likely to try marriage again, indicating they still believe in marriage (see chapter 12). Although abortion remains high in America (see chapter 4), we continue to have children.

Many reasons contribute to the declining or stabilizing divorce rate. For the most part, Americans marry at an older age. Many young people finish college first and establish their careers before getting married. Many delay childbearing until they are financially stable. These factors mean they will be less likely to divorce (see chapter 12). People have become more receptive to marriage therapy as a way to strengthen our marriages.

One of the strongest pieces of evidence behind America's continuing support of marriage and family is the high enrollment of students in college-level marriage and family classes. These students recognize that family issues are challenging. Still, they are hopeful about the future of their own families. Students in these classes also are likely to experience lower divorce rates.

Twenty-first-century American families look different from those in previous generations. There is a larger percentage of multiracial and multiethnic families today than ever before (see chapter 11). Many are blended families or stepfamilies. Today's American families are more likely to be headed by a single parent than before. Most often, both parents have careers, so children are entrusted to multiple caretakers. Men are more active in family life today than in previous generations. It is not unusual for a man to be home with his children while his wife works outside the home (see chapter 9).

The fact that American families "look different" from earlier historical versions is not so much the issue as how families will continue to deal with future challenges.

Modern Families Face Challenges

Chapter 14 demonstrated that a strong family is a resilient family, a family with an ability to adapt to change. Change is the hallmark of American society. Among the many changes the American family has faced in the last century, we would identify these three as having the most dramatic impact on the American family:

1. *Cultural diversity:* Our society has become more culturally diverse. Families are more multiethnic and multiracial. A changing cultural climate also means that family composition is different. We cannot assume that all families share the same patterns of behavior (see chapter 11).
2. *Working mothers:* More mothers have moved into the workforce. This has changed family dynamics. Women have more input in decision-making, and other family members share household duties (see chapters 6 and 7). Family size has decreased. Couples delay childbearing and so have fewer children. Women are choosing to pursue career interests before they have children and also after their children are raised (see chapters 3, 5 and 7).

3. *Premarital sex:* With the advent of reliable birth control, sexual behavior has become increasingly separated from married life. Of course, extramarital sex has always plagued humanity since the Fall, but today couples are more likely than ever to be sexually active before marriage and to live together before marriage (see chapter 4).

What the Experts Say about Family Challenges

Balswick and Balswick (1999) summarize some of the challenges families face as they adapt to contemporary social changes. You may find some dilemmas embedded in their discussion.

Loss of Moral Authority

Political and social diversity means less agreement about family values. This loss of moral authority may result in privatization of the family. What this means, ironically, is that in a country of diverse cultures, one family may not have much in common with another family. Devoid of a community that promotes a singular conception of the family, married couples are left to struggle privately to apply their faith to the competing interests of home and career.

Some Christian family experts have advocated a return to *traditional family values*. It is not easy to identify what is meant by "traditional." Is it the eighteenth- and nineteenth-century model, the pre-World War II model, or the 1950s model? Thus, returning to traditional family values is not likely to provide much guidance in a society that is dramatically more complex than the "good old days." It may be that old patterns of family life are not practical in modern society. Clearly one needs to look more closely at the biblical model of marriage (see chapter 6) as a viable and time-tested way to deal with changing cultural climates.

Mixed Messages

The increasing complexity of communication forms in contemporary society has contributed to the speed of communication and variety in communication ability. For example, a cell phone now can take pictures and send them via e-mail; that same cell phone can download music, allow you to view a football game or connect to the Internet. However, not everyone is at the same level technologically. Often, changes occur so rapidly that the cell phone purchased last month is already obsolete. Technology itself may present obstacles to communication if some people are not able to "keep up with the Joneses." More important, messages often are contradictory. This has produced a "generation gap" in which younger family members often receive messages in music and videos that contradict the messages they receive at home. The language of communication may mystify adults who cannot understand the slang their children use to communicate.

Isolation of the Nuclear Family

Related to loss of moral authority, people often find that increased mobility means less community structure for raising a family. One of the most significant changes for the modern family is the increasing isolation of the nuclear family. Previous generations relied on extended family members, not only for financial support and childrearing assistance, but also to help provide a sense of community. Today's communities are increasingly fractured, the result of people coming and going. This can lead to diminished parental authority and the development of a separate youth culture that challenges parental values. As families sometimes grow suspicious and fearful of the larger society, nuclear families sometime become even more privatized, and isolated, limiting children's interaction with diverse culture and ideas.

The "Commodified" Family

To become "commodified" means to allow things to become more important than relationships. This was ushered in with the Industrial Age. With the disintegration of family farms and small family businesses, families gradually became units of consumption instead of production. Work was separated from family life, as husbands and wives left their homes for substantial periods of time. They did this to bring in money to meet the family's demands for more and more things (see chapter 3).

Modern Families Can Have Hope

Modern American families are unique adaptations of a society which is increasingly diverse, mobile, and materialistic. Some of these adaptations are extremely stressful on marriage and family relationships.

"You are the salt of the earth; but if the salt has become tasteless, how can it be made salty again? . . . You are the light of the world. A city set on a hill cannot be hidden; nor does anyone light a lamp and put it under a basket, but on the lampstand, and it gives light to all who are in the house. Let your light shine before men in such a way that they may see your good works, and glorify your Father who is in heaven" (Matthew 5:13–16 NASB).

In the verses above, Jesus referred to salt and light as metaphors. In His time, salt was used not only as seasoning, as it is today, but also as a preservative. In biblical times, people did not have refrigerators. So, when they pulled fish from the lake, they salted it to keep it from spoiling. Jesus means for His people to salt the earth—to bring flavor and preservation. In the context of marriage and family, we see this as meaning that Christians should enhance the world by their presence. No one is drawn to a joyless, sour, podium-thumping Christian. We are drawn to people who are energetic and positive in their approach to life, who enrich the world by being in it, and who seek to preserve the values that keep the world sane.

Jesus uses light to illustrate that Christians are meant to be the light of the world. They cannot just hold on to the light themselves, keeping it hidden under a basket. Light means nothing if it doesn't spill out into the dark. Light exposes things that often take place only in the dark. Light illuminates, clarifies, and levels the playing field.

We can act as "salt and light" in the world, transforming our culture so that it comes to appreciate the significance of family. Here are some examples of what Christians can do:

Defuse Commodification

We can strive to defuse the commodification of American life (Balswick & Balswick, 1999). By living more simply and refusing to accumulate excess goods, individual families can avoid the trap of being a slave to working outside the home. Parents who spend less time on the job can spend more time with their families.

Encourage Family-Friendly Policies

We can encourage employers to consider more family-friendly policies, such as flexible schedules, more family leave, and work-at-home options. Write your senators and representatives about this, suggesting tax breaks or other benefits to companies who offer family-friendly policies. These kinds of policies enable parents to give their families the attention they deserve.

Model a Covenant Marriage

Rather than seeing marriage as a legal *contract,* couples can rediscover the idea of *covenant.* In a covenant, the spouses view marriage as mutual submission to God and to one another.

Be a Beacon

Matthew 5:14 asks us to see ourselves as "the light of the world." Rather than isolating and insulating ourselves from the world, Christian families need to reach out to others in the community. We need to see ourselves as beacons in a troubled world. If we are pessimistic, we will feel overwhelmed by the negative forces operating in the world today. If we are optimistic, we will work with the church to offer constructive ways to thwart cultural deterioration. In that way, we will bring hope to the hopeless.

Stay Healthy as a Family

Work to ensure the health of your family. This may involve family therapy to deal with issues from the past and to help you gain strategies to deal with the future. Sometimes this means accepting things that cannot be changed in order to move forward into the future.

Conclusion

This book marks the end of a journey and what we hope will be the beginning of another. We have balanced our scientific study of marriage and family with a consideration of what it means to be a covenant family—a family that honors God's call to make a difference in the world. Now it is time for students to apply these principles to real-world families.

Each of us is born to a family, our family of origin. We have seen that families can and do look "different" from one another. Families vary in composition, change over time, and differ according to culture. We also have seen that God's design for marriage and family is able to override these variations. Certain "non-negotiables" will ensure the stability of the family for centuries to come.

Christian families can be salt and light. Keep your humor, keep an optimistic outlook, and, above all, keep your faith. Christians know that ultimately God is in control. God created us in His image. He put us into families because He knows we thrive on close, personal relationships. This God—who cares enough to provide us with families for our own joy and comfort—will certainly make sure that family as a social institution survives, no matter what obstacles the future may bring. Our job is to work with God to make it happen.

Resources

Books:

American Families and the Future: Analyses of Possible Destinies by Roma S. Hanks, Barbara H. Settles, and Marvin B. Sussman. (Routledge, 1993)

The Marriage Mentor Manual by Dr.'s Les and Leslie Parrott. (Zondervan, 1995)

Website:

Time Magazine article from 1970 on future of the family—very interesting: http://www.time.com/time/magazine/article/0,9171,944265,00.html (accessed June 23, 2009)

Glossary

abortion: A medical procedure used to end a pregnancy.

abuse: An extreme and violent adaptation to a need to control one's family.

active listening: A communication technique in which each participant in a discussion repeats what the other said before responding.

affect: The outward expression of emotion.

agape: A Greek word, describing unconditional love, as in commitment.

altruism: Unselfishly giving time, energy, and money to others without expectation of return.

assimilation: A process by which an immigrant fully integrates themselves into the community.

assisted reproductive technology (ART): Different medical interventions used to assist an infertile couple in becoming pregnant.

assortative partnering: Choosing a partner based on physical characteristics.

attachment: The physical and psychological connection of an infant to its primary attachment figure (parent or primary caregiver).

authentic sexuality: Balswick and Balswick's concept that one must balance the natural sex drive with sociocultural family teaching about sex and God's plan for sex.

authoritarian parenting style: Demanding and directive, but not responsive to the child.

authoritative parenting style: Demanding, but in a loving, supportive way.

baby boomer: In a general sense, everyone born between 1946 and 1964.

battered person syndrome: The stages through which a battered person eventually develops the motivation to leave: denial, guilt, enlightenment, and responsibility.

beat culture: A group of writers, artists, musicians, and other cultural icons who helped to shape an aesthetic of societal change following World War II.

biblical model of marriage: A marriage model that stresses covenant, grace, empowerment, and intimacy.

bicultural: Adoption of language and norms of two cultures.

caring: One of the Nichols' life-cycle core tasks, it involves the level of affection and concern that exists between the spouses.

case history: A way of scientifically gathering data by an in-depth look at one or more marriages or families.

celebrity stage of parenting: Begins before the baby is born with changes in extended family status and a sense of being special but at the same time feeling ambivalent.

child abuse: Any form of treatment which could potentially harm a child.

cognitive restructuring: The strategy of juggling home, work, and family by concentrating on the things which really matter and ignoring the rest.

cohabiting couples: Two people living together in a marriage-like arrangement without the benefit of marriage.

cohabitation: Refers to an unmarried couple living together.

cohesive/individuated marriage: These couples combine gender equality with intimacy which allows for personal freedom. These couples value renewal, affection, support and companionship. They have a low rate of divorce.

commitment: One of the Nichols' life-cycle core tasks, it involves the level of devotion and dedication to the marriage and to a spouse; the decision to further a loving relationship.

commodified family: As families increased consumption of goods, the family itself became a commodity to help make the money necessary to make purchases.

common-law marriage: A mutual agreement made by a cohabiting couple to present themselves as a married couple. A few states legally recognize these as marriages after the couple cohabits for a certain number of years.

communication: One of the Nichols' life-cycle core tasks, it involves how couples develop patterns of communication at each stage of the marriage.

companionate love: High in intimacy and commitment, but low in passion.

companionate notion of marriage: A family ideal which differed from the patriarchal form, focusing on the emotional bond between two people and reflecting affection and equality between husbands and wives.

compassionate family: A family ideal in which husbands and wives are both friends and lovers, and parents are their children's "pals."

compatibility: The capacity to live in harmony with someone whom we enjoy being with, who will listen and support us, and share many things in common with.

complementary style of conflict: The couple acts in opposite ways.

Comstock Act: Restricted distribution of contraceptive information and devices, as well as pornographic literature.

conflict and compromise: One of the Nichols' life-cycle core tasks, it relates to how couples learn to compromise and resolve conflicts.

conflicted marriage: Dissatisfaction stems from internal marriage concerns; satisfaction stems from external concerns.

conjugal family: Husband, wife and children

conservation of energy theory: Suggests we seek to acquire and maintain resources.

constructive conflict: Managing disagreements with the rules of fair fighting. This results in a resolution strengthening the relationship.

consummate love: Passion, commitment, and intimacy are all in equal proportions.

contested divorce: The spouses cannot reach an agreement, so take their issues before a judge.

contract: One of the Nichols' life-cycle core tasks, it involves how a couple clarifies its expectations of one another.

cooperative family economy: All family members are expected to contribute to the family economy.

core tasks: In the Nichols' marital life cycle, these are the changes that must take place in each stage. They are grouped in five areas: commitment, caring, communication, conflict/compromise, and contract.

covenant marriage: Couples agree to counseling before marriage and accept more limited grounds for divorce.

covenant: A reciprocal relationship between two people and God in which both parties swear to be faithful.

cult of true womanhood: A 19th century idea that supported four basic attributes of female character: piety, purity, submissiveness, and domesticity.

cultural assimilation: "To make similar"; to blend into a larger culture and lose the unique norms and values which distinguish a minority culture from a dominant culture.

cultural pluralism: Different ethnic groups coexist in the same society, with each group celebrating its unique cultural norms while adhering to the laws of the larger society.

culture: The values, beliefs, and norms characterizing a group in a particular place and time.

cycle of violence: Conflict, violence, apology, and reconciliation. With each repetition, the violence can escalate.

demandingness: Baumrind's term for parental control, based on how parents work to integrate a child into the family whole.

democratic family: More gender-balanced family of the mid- to late 1800s which had two functions: emotional and civil. It was to meet the emotional needs of family members and to teach good citizenship skills.

dependent variable: Part of a hypothesis which specifies an *effect.*

destructive conflict: Disagreements which are not constructively resolved, resulting in avoidance, coercion, or violence. These kinds of conflict often destroy the relationship.

devitalized marriage: Dissatisfaction in all nine dimensions of marriage.

differentiation: The process through which a married person separates from the family of origin and establishes a new family.

disengaged marriage: These couples have the second highest rate of divorce. There is little emphasis on intimacy and a great deal of emphasis on independence so couples drift along until they drift apart.

disillusionment model: Couple's idealized view of one another deteriorates and can lead to divorce.

domesticity: A view that a woman's role was to devote herself to her husband, domestic duties, and childcare.

dyadic formation theory of mate selection: Suggests relationships begin with attraction and proceed through six stages.

embryo adoption: Implantation of a frozen embryo from another couple into the uterus.

emergent-distress model: Negativity corrodes happiness of early marriage.

endogamy: Choosing a mate within one's status group.

enduring dynamics model: Behavior patterns established early will lead to stability or instability.

equity theory of mate selection: Similar to exchange theory, it requires equity and fairness in what people give and receive in the relationship.

equity: Justice and fairness in relationships.

Erickson's eight stages: The eight stages of Erik Erickson's development theory of the human life cycle, from infancy to death.

eros: A Greek word describing romantic physical desire, as in passion.

ethnic group: A group of people who share a common cultural heritage.

ethnocentrism: The belief one culture is superior to others.

evolutionary theory of mate selection: Characteristics we find attractive in a mate have to do with survival of the species—the potential for childbearing and child rearing.

exchange theory of mate selection: Based on the exchange of social and material resources; it suggests that we select a mate who is more or less our equal.

existing data: A way of scientifically testing a hypothesis by using public records.

experiment: A scientific way of gathering data by using a control group and an experimental group in a highly controlled environment.

expressive role: In a marriage context, tending to the emotional needs of the family; typically, the wife's role.

extended family: This includes a nuclear family, and all aunts, uncles, cousins, and grandparents.

facts: Objective and verifiable observations.

familism: The strong feelings of loyalty, reciprocity and solidarity found in Hispanic families

family cohesion: The emotional bonding between family members or the sense of togetherness versus separateness.

family flexibility: The family's ability to change it's leadership, roles, and rules when necessary.

family form: Describes the type and sometimes the composition of a family.

family life cycle: A series of emotional and intellectual stages through which families pass from childhood through retirement.

family manager stage of parenting: From age 2 to 4 in which the parent determine the meaning of "good enough parent".

family of origin: The family into which one is born and raised.

family of procreation: The family created when a couple marries and has children.

family of production: A family which is responsible for producing and providing for its own needs.

family remodeler stage of parenting: The departure stage in which parents must adjust to the child leaving home.

family strength: Herbert Otto's term for intact families who exhibit interrelated strengths.

family-wage economy: A family type in which the father is the breadwinner and the mother and children are not expected to help augment the family income.

fatuous love: High in passion and commitment, but low in intimacy.

fault divorce: One spouse must be at fault for the marriage's failure. These faults are called "grounds" for divorce.

fertility window: The 100-120 hours per month in which a female can conceive.

fictive kin: Intentional family-like relationship between friends; non-blood relatives served as family for the children of slaves separated from their parents.

gamete intrafallopian transfer (GIFT): A medical procedure that involves transferring both eggs and sperm into the fallopian tube so fertilization takes place in the woman's body.

generation gap: Marked philosophical and cultural differences between societal generations. This term came into use in the 1960s, as the youth culture developed its own styles of dress, slang expressions, and music preferences.

generativity: Concern for establishing and guiding the next generation; The ability to contribute to future generations, ensuring the continuation of society.

glass ceiling: Organizational, attitudinal, and societal barriers keeping women from advancing up the career ladder.

harmonious marriage: High relationship quality in marriage.

hedonism: The belief pleasure and happiness are the primary goals of life.

hedonistic: Believing sex is just for pleasure and recreation.

Homestead Act: Provided land for people willing to move to the Midwest and Plains states, allowing them to become landowners.

homogamy: Choosing a mate who is similar to oneself.

hooking up: Getting together for casual sexual interaction with no expectation of relationship.

hypotheses: Assumptions that scientists test and from which they draw conclusions. Scientists formulate predictions about the relationship between two or more variables in a hypothesis.

ideal mate theory of mate selection: Suggests people form a fantasy image of their ideal mate and then search for someone who comes close to filling the image.

immediate gratification: Satisfying an impulse to attain something now, whether it is financially feasible or not.

in vitro fertilization: A medical procedure in which a woman's egg is removed, fertilized by sperm (from her husband or a donor), and then implanted in her (or a surrogate's) uterus.

independent variable: Part of a hypothesis which specifies the *cause.*

indulgent parenting style: More responsive and less demanding of certain behaviors.

Industrial Revolution: (1750–1830) A time of rapid advancement in every area—philosophical, religious, political, scientific, and economic.

instrumental role: In a marriage context, providing the primary financial support for the family; traditionally, the husband's role.

intermediate value stage of SVR theory: Evaluating another's values, such as attitudes toward religion, sex, career, and family.

intimacy: The feeling of closeness between two people.

intracytoplasmic sperm injection (ICSI): A medical procedure in which a single sperm is injected into a mature egg then the embryo is transferred to the uterus or fallopian tube.

Levinger's relationship stage theory of mate selection: Suggests relationships go through a series of stages as couples mature.

Levinson's eras: A developmental theory focusing on four stages or eras: childhood and adolescence, early adulthood, middle adulthood, and late adulthood.

looking-glass self: Charles Cooley's concept that through our interactions with other people—same sex and the opposite sex—we get feedback about ourselves.

male menopause: Psychological and hormonal changes which occur in men between the ages of 40 and 55.

marriage: A social, economic, and legal covenant between a man and a woman.

matriarchal stepfamily: Wife plays the dominant role in the stepfamily. Can be quite successful if husband and wife have similar values.

matrilineal family: Ancestry is traced through the mother's bloodline, common in early Native-American families.

melting pot: A metaphor used to describe a nation in which various cultures blend together into a unified society.

menopause: A period of hormonal change beginning with a woman's last menstrual cycle and marking the end of a woman's reproductive years.

midlife crisis: Period of introspection and reevaluation of life occurring in people between their late thirties and early fifties.

midlife: Also known as the middle years or middle age, this period occurs approximately from 40 to 65 years of age.

monochronic: Time is linear and sequential, moving forward in segments, so most often, only one thing can be done at a time.

monogamy: A form of marriage in which a person has one spouse at a time. This is the law in all 50 states of the United States.

morning-after pill: Controversial form of birth control used as emergency contraception after unprotected intercourse.

mutual submission: A relationship which is characterized by mutual giving and receiving.

nativism: An ideology or policy of favoring the interests of native inhabitants over those of immigrants.

natural family planning: A method of birth control in which a woman determines her 'fertility window' and avoids sexual intimacy during that time to avoid pregnancy.

neotraditional stepfamily: Stepfamily is close and loving, having values similar to a nuclear family. This is the most successful stepfamily type.

New Deal: Instituted by the government between 1933 and 1945, this series of relief programs was intended to stimulate economic recovery and bolster the male breadwinner role.

nice-girl dilemma: Occurs when a religious woman cannot accept her own sexual drives and will deny that she is in a sexual relationship, even to the point of refusing to plan to prevent pregnancy.

no-fault divorce: No explanation or proof of a problem is necessary for a divorce to be granted.

nuclear family: This includes parents and children living together in one household.

nurturing/nurturance: Parental responsibility to foster a child's development, giving the child a loving, caring environment in which the child can grow to full potential.

operatic marriage: These couples have the third highest divorce rate. Their volatile relationships are marked by heated arguing following by passionate lovemaking. These couples are more prone to emotional and physical abuse contributing to their high divorce rate.

pantraditionalism: An interest in returning to one's roots or "old ways." For example, pantraditional Native-Americans who had been assimilated are seeking to re-embrace their previously lost native culture, values, and practices.

parallel style of conflict: The couple retreats or avoids one another.

parent image theory of mate selection: Suggests we marry someone most like our opposite-sex parent.

passion: The drive which produces romance.

paternal determinism: The belief that if you parent your children properly, they will turn out well.

patriarchal authority: Belief men have authority over women and children and are responsible for their behavior.

patrilineal family: Ancestry is traced through the father's bloodline.

perimenopause: Signaling the approach of menopause, these hormonal changes can occur in women as early as their mid-thirties.

personality-based conflict: Blames a conflict on a personality flaw. The assumption is if that person will change, the conflict will disappear.

philia: A Greek word describing friendship love, as in intimacy.

polychronic: Time is nonlinear, circular, or cyclical. It is looser in structure; many things can be done at once.

polygamy: Marriage in which there are multiple spouses. There are two types:

polyandry: One woman married to more than one husband.

polygyny: One man married to more than one wife.

prejudice: discrimination carried out by individuals.

Progressive Reform Movement: In the early 1900s, this movement inspired laws to restore the embattled family. Examples included compulsory school attendance, child labor restrictions, and the Pure Milk Act.

propinquity: Physical proximity.

psychodynamic theory of mate selection: Suggests we search for those who most closely fit what we experienced in our early childhood. This is an attempt to get what we feel we needed or missed as we were growing up.

psychosocial crisis: In Erickson's developmental theory, this is a challenge which must be overcome before a person can move from one stage to the next.

Puritans: Settled in New England and were the strictest of the religious groups in the New World.

pursuer–distancer marriage: The most common type of marriage that has the highest divorce rate. One partner seeks more intimacy and the other partner becomes more aloof.

Quakers: Established colonies in Pennsylvania, Delaware, and New Jersey, the least patriarchal and most liberal of the Colonies.

racial group: A group of people who share a common biological heritage which results in distinctive physical attributes.

racism: Discrimination carried out by institutions (courts, schools, businesses, etc) that reflect the dominant culture.

redemptioner: A person who agreed to a period of servitude in return for passage to the New World; a redemptioner might also serve on behalf of a child.

relativism: The belief that ethical truths depend on—are relative to—those who hold them. Thus, premarital sex is seen to be acceptable under the "right" conditions.

role stage of SVR theory: Share activities to build relationship.

role strain: A clear idea of one's role but neither the time nor the energy to fulfill it to ones expectation.

role theory: Suggests experiencing ambiguity and/or conflict within a role has undesirable effects on an individual.

romantic stepfamily: Strives for the same goals as neotraditional families—except they want to achieve everything *immediately*. This stepfamily type has the highest degree of conflict and highest failure rate.

salad bowl: A metaphor used to describe a nation in which the various cultures retain their identities as they mix with one another to form a larger society.

sandwich generation: A period of time when adults become responsible for the well-being of their aging parents at the same time they are still raising their own children.

scale: Used to measure the strength of responses, often using a numerical value of 1 to 5.

second shift: Arlie Hochschild's term for the work women do at home when they return home from their jobs.

self-centered love: Fromm's idea of love, which is conditional on obedience.

selfless love: Fromm's idea of unconditional love.

serial marriage: A series of multiple marriages which take place after the death of a spouse or divorce.

serial monogamy: A series of sometimes long-term monogamous relationships which may or may not include marriage,

sexual double standard: Premarital sex is OK for men but not for women.

simplified divorce: Uncontested, no-fault divorce; no disagreements on the settlement.

single-parent family: A family consisting of one parent and children formed after divorce, death of a spouse, breakup of cohabiting couple, or single person with a child.

situational conflict: Stems from circumstances other than personality flaws, although certain situations may exacerbate a personality flaw.

sponge stage of parenting: From birth to age 2 in which the new parent attaches to the child and identifies as a parent.

stage 1: In the Nichols' marital life cycle, this stage involves separating from parents and establishing an identity as a couple.

stage 2: In the Nichols' marital life cycle, this stage involves early marriage and the early addition of children.

stage 3: In the Nichols' marital life cycle, this stage involves the middle years of marriage, during which couples examine the integrity of their relationship.

stage 4: In the Nichols' marital life cycle, this final stage of marriage involves reviewing the successes of a couple's married life, anticipating the losses to come, and seeking fulfillment in their remaining time together.

stage theories of mate selection: Describe how we move through distinct stages as we develop.

stepfamily: A family formed when two people marry and bring a child from a previous marriage or relationship into the present marriage.

Sternberg's triangular theory of love: Characterized by intimacy, passion, and commitment.

stimulus stage of SVR theory: Evaluating people based on physical appearance.

Stimulus-Value-Role (SVR) theory of mate selection: Suggests people select friends and partners through a three-stage model, filtering out people in each stage.

storge: A Greek word describing our natural affection for things and people.

strength: A powerful attribute or inherent asset a family possesses.

strong family: A family who exhibits six major qualities or themes: commitment, appreciation and affection, positive communication, time together, spiritual well-being, and the ability to cope with stress and crisis.

superwoman syndrome: The strategy of juggling home, work, and family by trying to "do it all."

survey: A questionnaire or interview used to collect data systematically.

symmetrical style of conflict: Both parties react to each other in similar ways.

systematic observation: A scientific way of gathering data by carefully observing some behavior.

time: A social construct meaning different things in different cultures.

tithe: To give a portion of your income to God.

traditional family: A nostalgic image of families which include a husband, wife and their biological and adopted children.

traditional marriage: A stable marriage in which partners have defined traditional roles. As long as both spouses agree on the roles and one partner doesn't decide to change them, they have a low rate of divorce; (Olson-Fowers definition) Dissatisfaction in areas of communication, but satisfaction with external marriage factors.

travel agent stage of parenting: Elementary through middle school years in which parents must adjust to the child's autonomy.

uncontested divorce: Either one partner fails to respond to requests for a divorce, or there is total agreement on the settlement.

uninvolved parenting style: Few demands and unresponsive to the child.

value stage of SVR theory: Evaluating a person based on similar values.

Victorian family: Ideology of the 1800s which viewed men as the breadwinner and women too pure and innocent to work.

vitalized marriage: Highest levels of satisfaction in all nine dimensions of marriage.

volcano dweller stage of parenting: Adolescent years in which parents must support their teen(s) while maintaining their own authority and responsibility for their teenager.

zygote intrafallopian transfer (ZIFT) or Tubal Embryo Transfer: A medical procedure similar to IVF but the young embryo is transferred to the fallopian tube instead of the uterus.

References

Acemoglu, D., Autor, D., & Lyle, D. (2002). Women, war and wages: The effect of female labor supply on the wage structure at mid-century, (NBER working papers 9013). *National Bureau of Economic Research.* Retrieved August 18, 2008, from http://ideas.repec.org/p/nbr/nberwo/9013.html

Adler, R., Rosenfeld, L., Proctor II, R., & Proctor, R. (2004). *Interplay: The Process of Interpersonal Communication.* New York: Oxford University Press.

Ahrons, C. (2004). *We're still family: What grown children have to say about their parents' divorce.* New York: HarperCollins.

Alan Guttmacher Institute. (2001, July). Teenagers' sexual and reproductive health. *Facts In Brief.* Retrieved August 31, 2009, from http://www.guttmacher.org/pubs/fb_teens.html

Alan Guttmacher Institute. (2006, September). Facts on American Teens' Sexual and Reproductive Health. *In Brief.* Retrieved August 31, 2009, from http://www.guttmacher.org/pubs/fb_ATSRH.html

Alfano, S. (2005). Kids of same-sex parents do fine. *CBSNews.com.* Retrieved October 18, 2009, from http://www.cbsnews.com/stories/2005/10/12/health/webmd/main938234.shtml

Allegretto, S. (2005). Basic family budgets: Working families' incomes often fail to meet living expenses around the U.S. (Briefing Paper #165). *The Economic Policy Institute.* Retrieved November 29, 2008, from http://www.epi.org/content.cfm/bp165

Amato, P. (2001). Children of divorce in the 1990's: An update of the Amato and Keith (1991) meta-analysis. *Journal of Family Psychology, 15*(2), 355–370.

Amato, P. (2003). For the sake of the children. *Council on Contemporary Families.* Retrieved July 10, 2008, from http://www.contemporaryfamilies.org/subtemplate.php?t=factSheets&ext=fact4

Amato, P. (2005). The impact of family formation change on the cognitive, social, and emotional well-being of the next generation. *The Future of Children, 15*(2), 75-86. Retrieved October 18, 2009, from http://futureofchildren.org/futureofchildren/publications/journals/article/index.xml?journalid=37&articleid=107§ionid=694

Amato, P., & Booth, A. (1997). *A generation at risk: Growing up in an era of family upheaval.* Cambridge, MA: Harvard University Press.

Amato, P., & Priviti, D. (2003). People's reasons for divorcing: Gender, social class, the life course and adjustment. *Journal of Family Issues, 25*(5), 602-626.

Amato, P., Booth, A., Johnson, D., & Rogers, S. (2007). *Alone together: How marriage in America is changing.* Cambridge, MA: Harvard University Press.

Ambert, A. (1986). Being a stepparent: Live-in and visiting stepchildren. *Journal of Marriage and Family, 48*(4), 795-804.

Ambert, A. (2001). *Families in the new millennium.* Boston: Allyn and Bacon.

American Association of Matrimonial Lawyers. (2000). *Making marriage last: A guide to preventing divorce.* Retrieved November 29, 2008, from http://www.collaborativedivorcebc.org/articles/marriage.html

American Psychiatric Association. (2005). *Let's talk facts about domestic violence.* Retrieved August 31, 2009, from http://www.healthyminds.org/Document-Library/Brochure-Library/Domestic-Violence.aspx

Anderson, C. (2003). The diversity, strengths and challenges of single-parent households. In F. Walsh (Ed.), *Normal Family Processes (*3rd ed., pp. 121-152). New York: Guilford Press.

Anderson, N., & Anderson, P. (2003). *Emotional longevity.* New York: Penguin Putnam, Inc.

Anderson, V. (1992). *New England's generation: The great migration and the formation of society and culture in the seventeenth century.* New York: Cambridge University Press.

Andersson, G., Noack, T., Seierstad, A., & Weedon-Fekjaer, H. (2004). The demographics of same-sex "marriage" in Norway and Sweden, Rostock, Germany. *Max-Planek Institute for Demographic Research.* Retrieved August 2, 2008, from http://www.demogr.mpg.de/papers/working/wp-2004-018.pdf

Ang, R., & Goh, D. (2006). Authoritarian parenting style in Asian societies: a cluster- analytic investigation. *Contemporary Family Therapy, 28*(1), 131-151.

Antonucci, T., & Schulz, R. (2003). Families, social support, and caregiving. In W. R. Hazzard, J. P. Blass, J. B. Halter, J. G. Ouslander, & M. E. Tinetti (Eds), *Principles of geriatric medicine and gerontology*, (5th ed., pp. 255-263). New York: McGraw-Hill.

Aquilino, W., & Supple, A. (2001). Long-term effects of parenting practices during adolescence on well-being outcomes in young adulthood. *Journal of Family Issues, 22*(3), 289-308.

Are Mormons still involved in polygamy? (2001). *Analysis of an LDS Press Release on Polygamy.* Retrieved August 4. 2008, from http://www.absalom.com/mormon/apostasy/polygamy.html

Aronwald, R. (2005). Work/family researchers seek to disarm nostalgia trap. *Parent Map.* Retrieved July 24, 2005, from parentmap.com/index.php?option=com_content&task=view&id=288&Itemid= 206

Aughinbaugh, A., & Gittleman, M. (2003, February). Maternal employment and adolescent risky behavior. *Bureau of Labor Statistics,* (working paper 366). Washington, DC: U. S. Department of Labor. Retrieved July 4, 2008, from http://econwpa.wustl.edu/eps/lab/papers/0302/0302002.pdf

Austin, S., Jun, H., Jackson, B., Spiegelman, D., Rich-Edwards, J., Corliss, H., & Wright, R. (2008). Disparities in child abuse victimization in lesbian, bisexual, and heterosexual women in the Nurses' Health Study II. *Journal of Women's Health, 17*(4), 597-606.

Axinn, W., & Thornton, A. (2000). The transformation in the meaning of marriage. In L. J. Waite and A. de Gruyter (Eds.), *The ties that bind: Perspectives on marriage and cohabitation* (pp. 127–165). New York: Aldine de Gruyter.

Bailey, B. (2004). From front porch to back seat: A history of the date. *OAH Magazine of History, 18*(4), 23-26.

Balsam, K., Beauchaine, T., Mickey, R., & Rothblum, E. (2005, August). Mental health of lesbian, gay, bisexual, and heterosexual siblings: effects of gender, sexual orientation, and family. *Journal of Abnormal Psychology, 114*(3), 471-476.

Balsam, K., Rothblum, E., & Beauchaine, T. (2005). Victimization over the life span: a comparison of lesbian, gay, bisexual, and heterosexual siblings. *Journal of Consulting and Clinical Psychology, 73*(3), 477-487.

Balswick, J. O., & Balswick, J. K. (1999). *The family: A Christian perspective on the contemporary home.* Grand Rapids, MI: Baker.

Balswick, J., & Balswick, J. (2006). *A Model for Marriage*. Downers Grove, IL: Intervarsity Press.

Balswick, J., & Balswick, J. (2008). *Authentic human sexuality*. Downers Grove, IL: Intervarsity Press.

Balswick, J., & Peck, C. (1971). The inexpressive male: A tragedy of American society. *The Family Coordinator, 20*(4), 363-368.

Bankruptcy filings drop 61% in March 2007 12-month period. (2007, June 27). *U.S. Courts*. Retrieved November 29, 2008, from http://www.uscourts.gov/Press_Releases/bankruptcyfilings062707.html

Bankruptcy filings rose in March 2006 12-month period quarterly filings lowest since mid-80s. (2006, May 26). *U.S. Courts*. Retrieved November 29, 2008, from http://www.uscourts.gov/Press_Releases/bankruptcyfilings052606.html

Barbarin, O. (1993). Coping and resilience: Exploring the inner lives of African-American children. *Journal of Black Psychology, 19*(4), 478–492.

Barber, N. (2000). *Why parents matter.* Westport, CT: Bergin and Garvey.

Barna Group Ltd. (2005) Annual Barna Group survey describes changes in America's religious beliefs and practices. Retrieved October 10, 2009, from http://www.barna.org/barna-update/article/5-barna-update/181-annual-barna-group-survey-describes-changes-in-americas-religious-beliefs-and-practices

Barna Group, Ltd. (2006, November 3). *Morality continues to decay.* Retrieved November 28, 2008, http://www.barna.org/barna-update/article/5-barna-update/129-morality-continues-to-decay

Barrett, A., & Turner, R. (2006). Family structure and substance use problems in adolescence and early adulthood: Examining explanations for the relationship. *Addiction, 101*(1), 109–120.

Basic family budget calculator. (2005). *Economic Policy Institute*. Retrieved November 29, 2008 from http://www.epi.org/content/budget_calculator

Bateson, G. (1979). *Mind and nature: A necessary unity.* New York: Dutton.

Baumrind, D. (1966). Effects of authoritative parental control on child behavior. *Child Development, 37*(4), 887–907.

Baumrind, D. (1967). Childcare practices anteceding three patterns of preschool behavior. *Genetic Psychology Monograph, 75*, 43–88.

Baumrind, D. (1971). Current patterns of parental authority. *Developmental Psychology Monographs, 4*, 1–102.

Baumrind, D. (1991). The influence of parenting style on adolescent competence and substance use. *Journal of Early Adolescence, 11*(1), 56–95.

Baumrind, D. (1996). The discipline controversy revisited. *Family Relations, 45*(4), 405–414.

Baumrind, D. (2001, August 21). *Does causally relevant research support a blanket injunction against disciplinary spanking by parents*? Symposium conducted at the annual meeting of American Psychological Association.

Bauserman, R. (2002). Child adjustment in joint-custody versus sole-custody arrangements: A meta-analytic review. *Journal of Family Psychology, 16*(1), 91–102.

Baylies, P. (2004, February 20). Exclusive at-home dad survey results. *At Home Dad Newsletter.* Retrieved August 24, 2008 from http://www.angelfire.com/zine2/athomedad/index.blog?topic_id=17189

Bays, D. (2005). The foreign missionary movement in the 19th and early 20th centuries. *National Humanities Center*. Retrieved November 28, 2008, from http://nationalhumanitiescenter.org/tserve/nineteen/nkeyinfo/fmmovementd.htm

Bean, F., & Stevens, G. (2003). *America's newcomers and the dynamics of diversity*. New York: Sage.

Bearman, P., & Brückner, H. (2001). Promising the future: Virginity pledges and first intercourse. *The American Journal of Sociology, 106*(4), 859-912.

Beedon, L., Southworth, L., & Gist, J. (2006). The state of 50+ America, 2006 research report. *American Association of Retired Persons,* Washington, DC. Retrieved July 7, 2008, from http://assets.aarp.org/rgcenter/econ/fifty_plus_2006.pdf

Bengtson, V. (2001). Beyond the nuclear family: The increasing importance of multigenerational bonds. *Journal of Marriage and Family, 63*(1), 1-16.

Bergman, M. (2007, March 27). Single-parent households showed little variation since 1994. *Newsroom* (CB07-46). Washington, DC: U.S. Census Bureau. Retrieved November 28, 2008, from http://www.census.gov/Press-Release/www/releases/archives/families_households/009842.html

Berkin, C. (2005). *Revolutionary mothers: Women in the struggle for America's independence.* New York: Alfred A. Knopf.

Berstein, A. (1989). *Yours, mine and ours.* New York: Scribner's.

Bianchi, S., Milkie, M., Sayer, L., & Robinson, J. (2000). Is anyone doing housework? Trends in the gender division of household labor. *Social Forces, 79*(1), 191-228.

Bianchi, S., Robinson, J., & Milkie, M. (2006). *Changing rhythms of American family life.* New York: Sage Foundation.

Biography for Celeste Holm. (n.d.). Retrieved October 3, 2008, from http://www.imdb.com/name/nm0002141/bio

Bogle, K. (2007, August). Hooking up and the sexual double standard among college students. *Paper presented at the annual meeting of the American Sociological Association, New York City.* Retrieved August 11, 2008, from http://www.allacademic.com/meta/p184479_index.html

Bookwala, J. (2005). The role of marital quality in physical health during the mature years. *Journal of Aging and Health, 17,* 85-104.

Bornstein, M. (1998). *Refocusing on parenting.* Paper presented at Parenthood in America Conference. Retrieved November 28, 2008, from http://parenthood.library.wisc.edu/Bornstein/Bornstein.html

Bos, H., & van Balen, F. (2008). Children in planned lesbian families: stigmatization, psychological adjustment and protective factors. *Culture, Health and Sexuality, 10*(3), 221-36.

Bos, H., van Balen, F., & van Den Boom, D. C. (2004). Experience of parenthood, couple relationship, social support, and child-rearing goals in planned lesbian mother families. *Journal of Psychology and Psychiatry, 45*(4), 755-64.

Bos, H., van Balen, F., & van Den Boom, D. C. (2007). Child adjustment and parenting in planned lesbian-parent families. *American Journal of Orthopsychiatry, 77*(1), 38-48.

Bowlby, J. (1969). *Attachment* (1st ed.). New York: Basic Books.

Boyce, T. & Hart, B. (1966). The Monkees [Recorded by The Monkees]. On *The Monkees: Greatest hits* [CD]. Rhino Records (October 24, 1995).

Boyd-Franklin, N. (2003). *Black families in therapy: Understanding the African-American experience.* New York: Guilford.

Boyle, G., & Joss-Reid, J. (2004). Relationship of humor to health: A psychometric investigation. *British Journal of Health and Psychology, 9*(1), 51-66.

Boyse, K. (2008). *Television.* Retrieved November 28, 2008, from http://www.med.umich.edu/1libr/yourchild/tv.htm

Bradford, W. (1850). History of Plymouth plantation. *Modern history sourcebook.* Retrieved November 28, 2008, from http://www.fordham.edu/halsall/mod/1650bradford.html

Bramlett, M., & Blumberg, S. (2007). Family structure and children's physical and mental health. *Health Affairs, 26*(2), 549-558. Retrieved July 5, 2008, from http://content.healthaffairs.org/cgi/content/abstract/26/2/549?ck=nck

Bramlett, M., & Mosher, W. (2002). Cohabitation, marriage, divorce, and remarriage in the United States. *Vital and Health Statistics, 23*(22). Hyattsville, MD: National Center for Health Statistics. Retrieved July 10, 2008, from http://www.cdc.gov/nchs/data/series/sr_23/sr23_022.pdf

Bray, J., & Kelly, J. (1999). *Stepfamilies: Love, marriage and parenting in the first decade.* New York: Broadway.

Brinkley, D. (2003). *New York public library American history desk reference, The.* New York: Hyperion.

Brizendine, L. (2008). One reason women don't make it to the C-suite. *Harvard Business Review, 86*(6), 36.

Brown, C. (2002). *Rosie's mom: Forgotten women workers of the first World War.* Boston: Northeastern University Press.

Brown, G. (2003). Child's play. In C. Levander & C. Singley (Eds.), *The American child: A cultural studies reader.* New Brunswick, NJ: Rutgers University Press.

Brown, K. (1996). *Good wives, nasty wenches, and anxious patriots.* Chapel Hill, NC: University of North Carolina.

Brown, T., & Alexander, R. (2007). *Child abuse and family law.* Sydney, Australia: Allen & Unwin.

Brunner, E. (1997). Socioeconomic determinants of health—stress and the biology of inequality. *BMJ 314*(7092), 1472–1476.

Bucks, B., Kennickell, A., & Moore, K. (2006). Recent changes in U.S. family finances: Evidence from the 2001 and 2004 survey of consumer finances. *Federal Reserve Bulletin, 2006.* Retrieved August 24, 2008, from http://www.federalreserve.gov/pubs/bulletin/2006/financesurvey.pdf

Bulcroft, R., Bulcroft, K., Bradley, K., & Simpson, C. (2000). The management and production of risk in romantic relationships: A postmodern paradox. *Journal of Family History, 25*, 63-92.

Burgard, S., Brand, J., & House, J. (2007). Toward a better estimation of the effect of job loss on health. *Journal of Health and Social Behavior, 48*(4), 369-384.

Burke, P. (2008). *Disability and impairment: Working with children and families.* Philadelphia, PA: Jessica Kingsley Publisher.

Burns, E. (2001). Aging and the immune system. *HealthLink, Medical College of Wisconsin.* Retrieved July 8, 2008, from http://healthlink.mcw.edu/article/999210348.html

Buss, D. (2006). Conflict in Married Couples: Personality Predictors of Anger and Upset. *Journal of Personality, 59*(4), 663-688.

Buss, D., Shackelford, T., Kirkpatrick, L., & Larsen, R. (2001). A half century of American mate preferences: The cultural evolution of values. *Journal of Marriage and the Family, 63*(2), 491-503.

Calvert, K. (1992). *Children in the house: The material culture of early childhood, 1600–1900.* Boston: Northeastern University Press.

Cameron, P. (2006). Children of homosexuals and transsexuals more apt to be homosexual. *Journal of Biosocial Science, 38*(3), 413-418.

Cameron, P., & Cameron, K. (2002). Children of homosexual parents report childhood difficulties. *Psychological Reports, 90*(1), 71-82.

Caplow, T., Hicks, B., & Wattenberg, B. (2000). *Religion. The first measured century.* Washington, DC: American Enterprise Institute Press.

Carson, D., Dail, P., Greeley, S., & Kenote, T. (1990). Stresses and strengths of Native-American reservation families in poverty. *Family Perspective, 24*, 383–400.

Carter, B., & McGoldrick, M. (Eds.). (1989). *The changing family life cycle: A framework for family therapy* (3rd ed.). New York: Gardner Press.

Carter, B., & McGoldrick, M. (Eds.). (1999). *The expanded family life cycle.* Boston: Allyn and Bacon.

Carter, B., & McGoldrick, M. (Eds.). (2005). *The expanded family life cycle: Individual, family, and social perspective* (3rd ed.). Boston, MA: Allyn and Bacon.

Carter, J. (1976). Statement in New Hampshire, Aug.3, 1976 during the Presidential Campaign, Cited in S. Brotherson & J. Teichert, Value of the law in shaping social perspectives on marriage. *Journal of Law and Family Studies, 3*(1), 23-56.

Cashell, B. (2007, March 20). Who are the middle class? *CRS Report for Congress.* Retrieved July 30, 2008, from http://assets.opencrs.com/rpts/RS22627_20070320.pdf

Casper, L., & Bianchi, S. (2002). *Continuity and change in the American family* (p. 3). Thousand Oaks, CA: Sage.

Casper, L., & Bryson, K. (1998, March). Co-resident grandparents and their grandchildren: Grandparent-maintained families. *Population Division Working Paper (26),* Washington, DC: U.S. Census Bureau. Retrieved November 28, 2008, from http://www.census.gov/population/www/documentation/twps0026/twps0026.html

Cayton, M., Gorn, E., & Williams, P. (1993). Family structures. *Encyclopedia of American social history.* New York: Scribner.

Centers for Disease Control and Prevention. (2006). Understanding intimate partner violence. *Fact sheet.* Retrieved August 26, 2008, from http://www.cdc.gov/ncipc/dvp/ipv_factsheet.pdf

Chao, R. (1995, August). Beyond authoritarianism: A cultural perspective on Asian-American parenting practices. *Paper presented at American Psychological Association, New York.* Retrieved November 28, 2008, from http://www.eric.ed.gov/ERICDocs/data/ericdocs2sql/content_storage_01/0000019b/80/14/55/f1.pdf

Chapman, A. (2007). In search of love and commitment. In H. P. McAdoo (Ed.), *Black families* (4th ed., pp. 285–296). Thousand Oaks, CA: Sage.

Cherkas, L., Aviv, A., Valdes, A., Hunkin, J., Gardner, J., Surdulescu, G., Kimura, M., & Spector, T. (2006). The effects of social status on biological aging as measured by white cell telomere length. *Aging Cell, 5*(5), 361–365.

Cherlin, A. (1978). Remarriage as an incomplete institution. *American Journal of Sociology, 84*, 634–650.

Cherlin, A. (1999). Going to extremes: Family structure, Children's wellbeing and social science. *Demography, 36*(4), 421-428.

Cherlin, A. (2002). *Public and Private Families.* New York: McGraw-Hill.

Cherlin, A. (2004). The deinstitutionalization of marriage. *Journal of Marriage and Family, 66*(4), 848-861.

Cherlin, A., & Furstenburg, F. (1991). Longitudinal studies of effects of divorce on children in Great Britain and the United States. *Science, 252*(5011), 1386–1389.

Cherlin, A., & Furstenburg, F. (1997). The future of grandparenthood. In M. Hutter, Ed. *The family experience.* Boston: Allyn & Bacon.

Child Welfare Information Gateway. (2004). *How many children were adopted in 2000 and 2001?* Washington, DC: U.S. Department of Health and Human Services. Retrieved November 28, 2008, from http://www.childwelfare.gov/pubs/s_adopted/s_adopted.pdf

Child Welfare Information Gateway. (2007). *Child maltreatment 2007: Summary of key findings.* Washington, DC: U.S. Department of Health and Human Services, Administration on Children, Youth and Families. Retrieved July 5, 2008, from http://www.childwelfare.gov/pubs/factsheets/canstats.cfm

Children's Defense Fund. (2004). Children and families in crisis. *The State of America's Children: 2004*. Washington, DC: Children's Defense Fund.

Children's Defense Fund (2005). *State of America's children: 2005*. Washington, DC: Children's Defense Fund.

Children's Defense Fund. (2007). Defining poverty and why it matters for children. Washington, DC: Children's Defense Fund.

Childs, E. (2005, August 14). The "Problem of the children:" White and black families' opposition to becoming multiracial. *Paper presented at the meeting of the American Sociological Association, San Francisco, CA*. Retrieved July 30, 2008, from http://www.allacademic.com//meta/p_mla_apa_research_citation/0/2/4/9/2/pages24920/p24920-1.php

Christakis, N. (2006, May 18). Mortality after the Hospitalization of a Spouse. *New England Journal of Medicine, 354*, 2190-2191.

Cicirelli, V. (2003). Influence of mothers' and daughters' paternalism beliefs on caregiving decision making. *Research on Aging, 25*, 3-21.

Clark, S. (1995, March 22). Advance report of final divorce statistics, 1989 and 1990. *Monthly Vital Statistics Report, 43*(9) supplement. Hyattsville, MD: National Center for Health Statistics. Retrieved November 28, 2008, from http://www.cdc.gov/nchs/data/mvsr/supp/mv43_09s.pdf

Claxton-Oldfield, S. (2000). Deconstructing the myth of the wicked stepparent. *Marriage and Family Review, 30*(1-2), 51-58.

Clayton, O., Mincy, R., & Blankenhorn, D. (Eds.). (2003). *Black fathers in contemporary American society: Strengths, weaknesses and strategies for change*. New York: Russell Sage Foundation.

Clements, M., Stanley, S., & Markman, H. (2004). Before they said "I do": Discriminating among marital outcomes over 13 years. *Journal of Marriage and Family, 66*(3), 613-626.

Cochran, S., Mays, V., & Sullivan, J. (2003). Prevalence of mental disorders, psychological distress, and mental health services use among lesbian, gay, and bisexual adults in the United States. *Journal of Consulting and Clinical Psychology, 71*(1), 53-61.

Cochran, S., Mays, V., Alegria, M., Ortega, A., & Tekeuchi, D. (2007). Mental health and substance use disorders among Latino- and Asian-American lesbian, gay, and bisexual adults. *Journal of Consulting and Clinical Psychology, 75*(5), 785-794.

Cohan, C., & Kleinbaum, S. (2002). Toward a greater understanding of the cohabitation effect. *Journal of Marriage and Family, 64*, 180–192.

Cohany, S., & Sok, E. (2007, February). Trends in labor force participation of married mothers of infants. *Monthly Labor Review Online, 130*(2). Retrieved August 18, 2008, from http://www.bls.gov/opub/mlr/2007/02/art2abs.htm

Cohen, J., & Agiesta, J. (2008, June 22). 3 in 10 Americans admit to race bias. *Washington Post*.

Coleman, M., Ganong, L., & Fine, M. (2000). Reinvestigating marriage: Another decade of progress. *Journal of Marriage and Family, 62*, 1288-1307.

Coles, R. (2006). *Race and family: A structural approach*. Thousand Oaks, CA: Sage

Collins, P. (2000). *Black feminist thought: Knowledge, consciousness and the politics of empowerment* (2nd ed.). New York: Routledge.

Conway, J., & Conway, S. (2001). *Traits of a lasting marriage*. Wheaton, IL: Tyndale House.

Cooley, C. (1922). *Human nature and the social order*. New York: Charles Scribner's Sons.

Cooney, R. (2005). *Taking a new look—The enduring significance of the American woman suffrage movement*. Santa Cruz, CA: American Graphic Press. Retrieved November 28, 2008, from http://www.americangraphicpress.com/articles/index.html

Coontz, S. (1992). *The way we never were: American families and the nostalgia trap.* New York: Basic Books.

Coontz, S. (1999, November). The American family. *Life Magazine,* 79, 90, 92, 94. Retrieved October 19, 2009, from http://academic.evergreen.edu/c/coontzs/a10.html

Cotter, D., England, P., & Hermsen, J. (2007). Moms and jobs: Trends in mothers' employment and which mothers stay home. *Council on Contemporary Families.* Retrieved June 28, 2008, from http://www.contemporaryfamilies.org/subtemplate.php?t=factSheets&ext=momsandjobs

Courtney, C. (2004). Dateless in Christianville. *Today's Christian Woman, 26*(4), 42.

Covenant marriage. (2004). *Marriage Issues.* Washington, DC: National Conference of State Legislatures. Retrieved July 11, 2008, from http://www.ncsl.org/Default.aspx?TabID=123&tabs=858,55,56#858

Covey, S. (1995). *First things first.* New York: Fireside.

Cowan, C., Cowan, P., Heming, G., Garrett, E., Coysh, W., Curtis-Boyles, H., & Boyles, A. (1985). Transition to parenthood: His, hers, and theirs. *Journal of Family Issues, 6*(4), 451–481.

Cox, M., & Gunn, J. (1999). Studying conflict and cohesion in families: An overview. In M. Gunn (Ed.), *Conflict and cohesion in families: Causes and consequences* (pp. 1-11). Hillsdale, NJ: Erlbaum.

Cozzens, L. (1998). *The civil rights movement 1955–1965: Introduction.* Retrieved November 28, 2008, from http://www.watson.org/~lisa/blackhistory/civilrights-55-65/index.html

Crittenden, A. (2001). *The price of motherhood: Why the most important job in the world is still the least valued.* New York: Metropolitan Books.

Crohn, J. (1998). Intercultural couples. In M. McGoldrick (Ed.), *Re-visioning family therapy: Race, culture, and gender in clinical practice* (pp. 295–308). New York: Guilford Press.

Crowder, K., & Teachman, J. (2004). Do residential conditions explain the relationship between living arrangements and adolescent behavior? *Journal of Marriage and Family, 66,* 721–738.

Crowder, K., & Tolnay, S. (2000). A new marriage squeeze for black women: The role of racial intermarriage by black men. *Journal of Marriage and Family, 62*(3), 792-807.

Crutcher, R. (2006). Spiraling through the glass ceiling: Seven critical lessons for negotiating leadership positions in higher education. *Business Network.* Retrieved May 20, 2008, from http://findarticles.com/p/articles/mi_m0NKR/is_3_92/ai_n16714102?tag=artBody;col1

D'Augelli, A., Grossman, A., Salter, N., Vasey, J., Starks, M., & Sinclair, K. (2005). Predicting the suicide attempts of lesbian, gay, and bisexual youth. *Suicide and Life-Threatening Behavior, 35*(6), 646-660.

Daniels, R. (2002). *Coming to America: A history of immigration and ethnicity in American life.* New York: HarperCollins.

Daly, K. (2001). Deconstructing family time: From ideology to lived experience. *Journal of Marriage and Family, 63*(5), 283–294.

Daly, K. (2004). The changing culture of parenting. *The Vanier Institute of the Family.* Retrieved May 29, 2008, from http://www.vifamily.ca/library/cft/parenting.html

Daly, K., & Hawkins, L. (2005, July/August). Fathers and the work-family politics. *Ivey Business Journal, 69*(6).

Daniel, C., & Fogarty, K. (2007). "Hooking up" and hanging out: Casual sexual behavior among adolescents and young adults today, (document no. FCS2279). *Department of Family, Youth and Community Sciences, University of Florida.* Retrieved August 11, 2008, from http://edis.ifas.ufl.edu/pdffiles/FY/FY100200.pdf

Darroch, J., Landry, D., & Oslak, S. (1999). Age differences between sexual partners in the United States. *Family Planning Perspectives, 31,* 160–167.

DeFrain, J. (1999, Winter). Strong families around the world. *Journal of the Australian Institute of Family Studies, 53*, 6–13.

DeFrain, J., & Stinnett, N. (2002). Family strengths. In J. J. Ponzetti et al (Eds.), *International encyclopedia of marriage and family.* New York: Macmillan Reference Group.

DeFrain, J., Cook, G., & Gonzalez-Kruger, G. (2004). Family health and dysfunction. In R. J. Coombs (Ed.), *Family therapy review.* Mahwah, NJ: Lawrence Erlbaum.

DeFrain, J., DeFrain, N., & Lepard, N. (1994). Family strengths and challenges in the South Pacific: An exploratory study. *International Journal of Sociology of the Family, 24*(2), 25–47.

DeFrain, J., Fricke, J., & Elmen, J. (1987). *On our own: A single parent's survival guide.* Lexington, MA: Lexington Books/Health.

Del Castillo, R. (2007). La Familia. In S. Ferguson (Ed.), *Shifting the center* (pp. 99-114). New York: McGraw-Hill.

Demuth, S., & Brown, S. (2004). Family structure, family processes, and adolescent delinquency: The significance of parental absence versus parental gender. *Journal of Research in Crime and Delinquency, 41*(1), 58–81.

DeNavas-Walt, C., Proctor, B., & Smith, J. (2007, August). Income, poverty, and health insurance coverage in the United States: 2006. *Current Population Reports, Consumer Income* (P60-233). Washington, DC: U.S. Census Bureau. Retrieved July 31, 2008, from http://www.census.gov/prod/2007pubs/p60-233.pdf

Denisiuk, J. (2004, November). Evolutionary versus social structural explanation for sex differences in mate preferences, jealousy, and aggression. *Great Ideas in Personality.* Retrieved May 28, 2008, from http://www.personalityresearch.org/papers/denisiuk.html

Department of Health and Human Services. (2005, February 18). Annual update of the HHS poverty guidelines. *Federal Register, 70*(33), 8373–8375.

Deutch, F., Kokot, A., & Binder, K. (2007). College women's plans for different types of egalitarian marriages. *Journal of Marriage and Family, 69*(4), 916-929.

Diagnosing Birth Defects. (2005). *The American College of Obstetricians and Gynecologists.* Retrieved June 23, 2009, from http://www.acog.org/publications/patient_education/bp164.cfm

Diller, J. (2004). *Cultural diversity: A primer for the human services* (2nd ed.). Belmont, CA: Brooks/Cole.

Dobson, J. (1996). *Dare to discipline.* Wheaton, IL: Tyndale House

Doherty, W. (2001). *Take back your marriage.* New York: Guilford Press.

Domestic Violence Awareness Handbook. (2008). *U.S. Department of Agriculture, Safety, Health and Employee Welfare Division.* Retrieved August 26, 2008, from http://www.usda.gov/da/shmd/aware.htm

Domestic Violence Handbook. (2007). Retrieved August 30, 2008, from http://www.domesticviolence.org/

Donnally, M. (1986). The American Victorian woman: The myth and the reality. New York: Greenwood Press.

Downs, B. (2003, October). Fertility of American women, June 2002. *Current Population Reports* (P20-548). Washington, DC: U.S. Census Bureau. Retrieved November 29, 2008, from http://www.census.gov/prod/2003pubs/p20-548.pdf

Downs, T., & Downs, J. (2003). *Fight fair!* Chicago: Moody Press.

Dunifon, R., & Kowaleski-Jones, L. (2002). Who's in the house? Race differences in cohabitation, single parenthood and child development. *Child Development, 73*(4), 1249-1264.

Durr, M., & Hill, S. (2006). *Race, work and family in the lives of African-Americans.* New York: Rowman and Littlefield.

Dush, C., Taylor, M., & Kroegar, R. (2008). Marital happiness and psychological well-being across the life course. *Family Relation,* 57(2), 211-226.

Dye, J. (2005, December). Fertility of women: June 2004. *Current Population Reports* (P20-555). Washington, DC: U.S. Census Bureau. Retrieved May 27, 2008, from http://www.census.gov/prod/2005pubs/p20-555.pdf

Eagle, B., Miles, E., & Icenogle, M. (1997). Inter-role conflicts and the permeability of work and family domains: Are there gender differences? *Journal of Vocational Behavior, 50*(2), 168–184.

Eagly, A., & Wood, W., (1999). The origins of sex differences in human behavior: Evolved dispositions versus social roles. *American Psychologist, 54*, 408–423.

Eaton, D., Kann, L., Kinchen, S., Shanklin, S., Ross, J., Hawkins, J., Harris, W., Lowry, R., McManus, T., Chyen, D., Lim, C., Brener, N., & Wechsler, H. (2008, June 6). Youth Risk Behavior Surveillance-United States, 2007. *Surveillance Summaries,* 57(SS04), 1-131. Washington, DC: Department of Health and Human Services. Retrieved October 3, 2008, from http://www.cdc.gov/mmwr/preview/mmwrhtml/ss5704a1.htm

Edin, K., & Kefalas, M. (2005). *Promises I can keep: Why poor women put motherhood ahead of marriage.* Berkley, CA: University of California Press.

Edin, K., & Reed, J. (2005). Why don't they just get married: Barriers to marriage among the disadvantaged. *The Future of Children, 15*(2), 117-137.

Egami, Y. (1996). Psychiatric profile and sociodemographic characteristics of adults who report abusing or neglecting children. *American Journal of Psychiatry, 153*, 921–928.

Egle, U., Hardt, J., Nickel, R., Kappis, B., & Hoffmann, S. (2001). *Early stress and its long-term effects on health-State of the art and implications for future research.* Retrieved May 28, 2008, from http://www.v-r.de/data/materialien/zfpm-0204/egle.pdf

Elder, G. (1999). *Children of the Great Depression: Social change in life experience.* Boulder, CO: Westview Press.

Eldridge, R., & Sutton, P. (2007, July) Births, marriages, divorces, and deaths: Provisional data for November 2006. *National Vital Statistics Report, 55*(18). Hyattsville, MD: National Center for Health Statistics. Retrieved August 20, 2009, from http://www.cdc.gov/nchs/data/nvsr/nvsr55/nvsr55_18.pdf

Elgar, K., & Chester, A. (2007). The mental health implications of maternal employment: Working versus at-home mothering identities. *Australian e-Journal for the Advancement of Mental Health (AeJAMH), 6*(1). Retrieved July 4, 2008, from http://74.6.239.67/search/cache?ei=UTF-8&p=maternal+employment+role+strain&fr=yfp-t-305&u=www.auseinet.com/journal/vol6iss1/elgar.pdf&w=maternal+employment+employer+role+strain&d=bRn5Cy72RAeu&icp=1&.intl=us%20

Emerson, M., Yancey, G., & Chai, K. (2001). Does race matter in residential segregation? Exploring the preferences of white Americans. *American Sociological Review*, 66, 922-935.

Employee burnout: America's newest epidemic. (1991). *Stress...at Work* (NIOSH pub no. 99–101). Cincinnati, OH: National Institute of Occupational Safety, 1999. Retrieved August 25, 2008, from http://www.cdc.gov/niosh/docs/99-101/default.html

Engermann, K., & Owyang, M. (2006, April 1). Social changes lead married women into labor force. *The Regional Economist.* Retrieved August 18, 2008, from http://www.allbusiness.com/public-administration/administration-economic-programs/4071376-1.html

Epstein, B. (2002). Feminist consciousness after the women's movement. *Monthly Review*, 31-37.

Erickson, E. (1950). *Childhood and society.* New York: Norton.

Erickson, E. (1963). *Childhood and society.* New York: Norton.

Erickson, E. (1968). *Identity: Youth and crisis.* New York: Norton.

Erisman, M. (2004). Spiritual and moral identity formation within the family. *The Family Psychologist, 20*(2), 9-12.

Esqueda, C., & Harrison, L. (2005). The influence of gender role stereotypes, the woman's race, and level of provocation and resistance for domestic violence culpability attributions. *Sex Roles, 53*(11-12), 821-834. doi 10.1007/11199s-005-8295-1

Ethics of reproductive technology debated, the. (2008). *The American College of Obstetricians and Gynecologists.* Retrieved August 16, 2008, from http://www.acog.org/from_home/publications/press_releases/nr05-05-08-2.cfm

Etzioni, A. (1977). The family: Is it obsolete? *Journal of Current Social Issues, 14*(4).

Evans, S. (1989). *Born for liberty: A history of women in America.* New York: The Free Press.

Everything you need to know about online dating: 10 singles offer their been-there-done-that advice. (2005, March 9). *Christianity Today.* Retrieved August 11, 2008, from http://www.christianitytoday.com/singles/newsletter/mind50309.html.

Facts at a Glance 2007. (2007). *Child Trends*, (Pub. No. 2007-12). Retrieved May 28, 2008, from http://www.childtrends.org/_docdisp_page.cfm?LID=D6F165A5-00B3-4D76-ABACFD97F248817C

Fairtlough, A. (2008, April 21). Growing up with a lesbian or gay parent: Young people's perspectives. *Health and Social Care*, 1365-2524.

Faludi, S. (1991). *Backlash: The undeclared war against American women.* New York: Doubleday.

Family Social Services Administration. (2002). *Hands of hope: Domestic violence prevention and awareness handbook.* Marion, IN: Family Service Society.

Feagin, J., Early, K., & McKinney, K. (2001). The many costs of discrimination: The case of middle-class African-Americans. *Indiana Law Review, 34*, 1313–1360.

Federal Interagency Forum on Aging-Related Statistics. (2004, November). Nursing home utilization. *Older Americans 2004: Key indicators of well-being.* Federal Interagency Forum on Aging-Related Statistics. Washington, DC: U.S. Government Printing Office. Retrieved November 28, 2008, from http://www.agingstats.gov/agingstatsdotnet/Main_Site/Data/Data_2008.aspx

Federal Interagency Forum on Child and Family Statistics. (2008). *America's children in brief: Key indicators of well-being, 2008.* Federal Interagency Forum on Child and Family Statistics, Washington, DC: U.S. Government Printing Office. Retrieved July 31, 2008, from http://www.childstats.gov/pdf/ac2008/ac_08.pdf

Fertility Awareness Methods. (2008). *FPWA Sexual Health Services.* Retrieved May 28, 2008, from http://www.fpwa.org.au/healthinformation/informationsheets/fertilityawareness/

Fields, J. (2004). America's families and living arrangements: 2003. *Current Population Reports* (P20-553). Washington, DC: U.S. Census Bureau. Retrieved June 1, 2009, from http://www.census.gov/prod/2004pubs/p20-553.pdf

Fields, J., & Casper, L. (2001). America's families and living arrangements: March 2000. *Current Population Reports* (P20–537). Washington, DC: U.S. Census Bureau. Retrieved May 28, 2008, from http://www.census.gov/prod/2001pubs/p20-537.pdf

Fischer, D. (1989). *Albion's seed: Four British folkways in America.* New York: Oxford University Press.

Fisher, H. (2004). *Why we love: The nature and chemistry of romantic love.* New York: Henry Holt and Company.

Fleeson, W. (2004). The quality of American life at the end of the century. In O. Brim, C. Ryff, & R. Kessler (Eds.), *How healthy are we?* Chicago: University of Chicago Press.

Flexner, E., & Fitzpatrick, E. (1996). *Century of struggle: The woman's rights movement in the United States* (3rd ed.). Cambridge, MA: Belknap Press.

Fraley, R. (2004). *A brief overview of adult attachment theory and research.* Retrieved May 28, 2008, from http://www.psych.uiuc.edu/~rcfraley/attachment.htm

Francis, R. (2006). Frequently asked questions about the ERA. *National Council of Women's Organizations.* Retrieved May 28, 2008, from http://www.equalrightsamendment.org/faq.htm

Friedan, B. (1963). *The feminine mystique.* New York: W.W. Norton.

Friedman, S., & Greenhaus, J. (2000). *Work and family—Allies or enemies?: What happens when business professionals confront life.* New York: Oxford University Press.

Fromm, E. (1956). *The art of loving.* New York: Harper and Row.

Galinsky, E. (1999). *Ask the children: What America's children really think about working parents.* New York: William Morrow.

Galinsky, E., Bond, J., & Hill, E. (2002). *Why workplace flexibility. When work works: A status report on workplace flexibility.* New York: Alfred P. Sloan Foundation.

Gallo, L., Troxel, W., Kuller, L., Sutton-Tyrrell, K., Edmundowicz, D., & Matthews, K. (2003). Marital status, marital quality, and atherosclerotic burden in postmenopausal women. *Psychosomatic Medicine, 65*(6), 952–962.

Ganong, L., & Coleman, M. (2004). *Stepfamily relationships: Development, dynamics, and interventions.* New York: Kluwer Academics/Plenum Publishers.

Gardyn, R. (2002, July 1). The mating game. *American Demographics.* Retrieved July 4, 2008, from http://findarticles.com/p/articles/mi_m4021/is_2002_July_1/ai_89374138?tag=content;col1

Garrett, E. (1990). *At home: The American family, 1750–1870.* New York: Harry N. Abrams, Inc.

Garrett, M., & Pichette, E. (2000). Red as an apple: Native-American acculturation and counseling with or without reservation. *Journal of Counseling and Development, 78*, 3–13.

Gaventa, B. (2008). Spiritual and religious supports: What difference do they make? *EP Magazine, 38*, 66–68.

Gemery, H. (1980). Emigration from the British Isles to the New World: Inferences from Colonial populations. In P. Uselding (Ed.), *Research in economic history* (pp. 179-231). Greenwich, CT: Jai Press.

Gerasimos, S. (1991). *Plato Freud: Two theories of love.* New York: Wiley-Blackwell.

Gerson, K. (2007). What do women and men want? *The American Prospect, 18*(3), a8-a11. Retrieved October 17, 2009, from http://www.prospect.org/galleries/current_issues/v1/TAP_ISSUE_2007_03.pdf

Gerstel, N., & Sarkisian, N. (2006). Marriage: The good, the bad, and the greedy. *Contexts, 5*(4), 16-21.

Gilligan, C. (1982). *In a different voice: Psychological theory and women's development.* Cambridge, MA: Harvard University Press.

Gilligan, C. (1991). Women's psychological development: Implications for psychocounseling. In C. Gilligan, A. G. Rogers, and D. L. Tolman (Eds.), *Women, girls and psychocounseling: Refraining resistance* (pp. 5–32). New York: Haworth Press.

Gilligan, C. (2008). Exit-voice dilemmas in adolescent development. In D. Browning (Ed.), *Adolescent identities: A collection of readings* (pp. 141-156). New York: The Analytic Press/Taylor & Francis Group.

Ginsberg, A. (1996). *Beat culture and the new America: 1950–1965*. New York: Whitney Museum of American Art.

Glenn, E. (2007). Split-household, small producer, and dual wage earner: An analysis of Chinese American family strategies. In S. Ferguson (Ed.), *Shifting the center* (pp. 114-131). New York: McGraw-Hill.

Glenn, N., & Marquardt, E. (2001). *Hooking up, hanging out, and hoping for Mr. Right: College women on dating and mating today*. New York: Institute for American Values.

Goldberg, A. (2007). (How) does it make a difference? Perspectives of adults with lesbian, gay, and bisexual parents. *American Journal of Orthopsychiatry*, *77*(4), 550-562.

Golden, C., & Katz, L. (2002). The power of the pill: Oral contraceptives and women's career and marriage decisions. *Journal of Political Economy*, *110*(4), 730-770.

Goldman, H., Rye, P., & Sirovatka, P. (Eds.). (1999). Older adults and mental health. *Mental Health: A Report of the Surgeon General* (pp. 336–381). Rockville, MD: Department of Health and Human Services.

Golombok, S., Perry, B., Burston, A., Murray, C., Mooney-Somers, J., Stevens, M., & Golding, J. (2003). Children with lesbian parents: a community study. *Developmental Psychology*, *39*(1), 20-33.

Goodman, C. (1999). Reciprocity of social support in long-term marriage. *Journal of Mental Health & Aging*, *5*(4), 341-357.

Goodman, C., & Silverstein, M. (2006). Grandmothers raising grandchildren: Ethnic and racial differences in well-being among custodial and coparenting families. *Journal of Family Issues*, *27*(11), 1605-1626.

Goodman, J., Schlossberg. N., & Anderson, M. (2006). *Counseling adults in transition: Linking practice with theory*. New York: Springer.

Gottman Institute. (2004). *Marriage Tips 101*. Retrieved August 26, 2008, from http://www.gottman.com/marriage/self_help/.

Gottman, J. (1995). *Why marriages succeed or fail: And how you can make yours last*. New York: Simon & Schuster.

Gottman, J. (1999). *The marriage clinic: A scientifically based marital therapy*. New York: Norton.

Gottman, J. (2000). *The seven principles for making marriage work*. New York: Three Rivers Press.

Gottman, J., & DeClaire, J. (2001). *The relationship cure: A 5 step guide to strengthening your marriage, family, and friendships*. New York: Three Rivers Press.

Gottman, J., Levenson, R., Swanson, C., Swanson, K., Tyson, R., & Yoshimoto, D. (2003). Observing gay, lesbian, and homosexual couples' relationships: Mathematical modeling of conflict interaction. *Journal of Homosexuality*, *45*, 65-91.

Gould, R. (1993). Transformational tasks in Adulthood. In G. H. Pollock and S. I. Greenspan (Eds.), *The course of life, vol. VI: Late adulthood*. Madison, CT: International Universities Press.

Grall, T. (2006, July). Custodial mothers and fathers and their child support: 2003. *Current Population Reports* (P60–230). Washington, DC: U.S. Census Bureau. Retrieved from http://www.census.gov/prod/2006pubs/p60-230.pdf

Grall, T. (2007, August). Custodial mothers and fathers and their child support: 2005. *Current Population Reports* (P60-234). Washington, DC: U.S. Census Bureau. Retrieved July 12, 2008, from http://www.census.gov/prod/2007pubs/p60-234.pdf

GrandFacts (2007, October). *A State fact sheet for grandparents and other relatives raising children*. Washington, DC: American Association for Retired Persons. Retrieved July 6, 2008, from http://www.grandfactsheets.org/doc/National%202007%20New%20Template.pdf

Green, J., & Winters, M. (2002, November). Public school graduation rates in the United States. *Civic Report, 31*. New York: Manhattan Institute for Policy Research. Retrieved May 28, 2008, from http://www.manhattaninstitute.org/html/cr_31.htm

Greenwood, J., Seshadri, A., & Yorukoglu, M. (2005). Engines of liberation. *Review of Economic Studies, 72*, 109-133.

Grove, R., & Hetzel, A. (1968). *Vital statistics rates in the United States 1940–1960*. Hyattsville, MD: National Center for Health Statistics. Retrieved May 28, 2008, from http://www.cdc.gov/nchs/data/vsus/vsrates1940_60.pdf

Gurian, M. (2002). *The Soul of the child: Nurturing the divine identity of our children*. New York: Atria Books.

Guttmacher Institute. (2006, September). Facts on American teens' sexual and reproductive health. *In Brief*. Retrieved May 28, 2008, from http://www.guttmacher.org/pubs/fb_ATSRH.html.

Guttmacher Institute. (2008). State policies on later-term abortions. *State Policies in Brief*. Retrieved May 28, 2008, from http://www.guttmacher.org/statecenter/spibs/spib_PLTA.pdf

Guttmacher Institute. (2008, July). Facts on induced abortion in the United States. *In Brief*. Retrieved May 28, 2008, from www.guttmacher.org/pubs/fb_induced_abortion.html

Haddock, S., & Rattenborg, K. (2003). Benefits and challenges of dual-earning: Perspectives of successful couples. *The American Journal of Family Therapy, 31*(5), 325–345.

Haddock, S., Zimba, S., Zimmerman, T., & Current, L. (2001). Ten adaptive strategies for family and work balance: Advice from successful families. *Journal of Marriage and Family, 27*(4), 445-458.

Hahn, S. (2004). *Swear to God: The promise and power of sacraments*. New York: Doubleday.

Hall, L. (2000). *The Cleavers don't live here anymore*. Cincinnati, OH: Servant Publications.

Ham, B. (2003). The effects of divorce on the academic achievement of high school seniors. *Journal of Divorce and Remarriage, 38*(3/4), 167–185.

Hamilton, B., Martin, J., & Sutton, P. (2004, November 23). Births: Preliminary data for 2003. *National Vital Statistics Reports, 53*(9). Hyattsville, MD: National Center for Health Statistics. Retrieved May 28, 2008, from http://www.cdc.gov/nchs/data/nvsr/nvsr53/nvsr53_09.pdf

Hamilton, B., Martin, J., & Ventura, S. (2006, November 21). Births: Preliminary data for 2005. *Health E-Stats*. Retrieved May 28, 2008, from http://www.cdc.gov/nchs/products/pubs/pubd/hestats/prelimbirths05/prelimbirths05.htm

Hamilton, R. (1958, October). Song for a fifth child. *A Gift of Poetry*. Retrieved May 28, 2008, from http://www.agiftofpoetry.com/Mother_To/mother_birth_song_for_fifth.htm

Hamilton, T. (2003). Abortion, theologically understood (2001). In S. Hauerwas, *The Hauerwas reader* (pp. 601-622). Durham, NC: Duke University Press.

Hanson, S. (1985). Healthy single-parent families. *Family Relation, 35*, 125–132.

Hartup, W., & Laurson, B. (2000). Conflict and context in peer relations. In C. Hart (Ed.), *Children on playgrounds: Research and perspectives and applications*. Albany, NY: SUNY Press.

Hashaw, T. (2007). *The birth of black America: the first African-Americans and the pursuit of freedom at Jamestown*. New York: Carroll & Graf Publishers.

He, W., Sengupta, M., Velkoff, VA. & DeBarros, KA. (2005). 65+ in the United States: 2005. *Current Population Reports*, (P23-209). Washington, DC: U.S. Census Bureau. Retrieved November 29, 2008, from http://www.census.gov/prod/2006pubs/p23-209.pdf

Henry, N., Berg, C., Smith, T., & Florsheim, P. (2007). Positive and negative characteristics of marital interaction and their association with marital satisfaction in middle-aged and older couples. *American Psychological Association, 22*(3), 428–441.

Herzog, E., Gara, M., & Rosenberg, S. (2006). The abused child as parent: Perception of self and other. *Infant Mental Health Journal, 13*(1), 83-98.

Hetherington, E., & Kelly, J. (2002). *For better or worse: Divorce reconsidered.* New York: Norton.

Hetzel, L., & Smith, A. (2001). The 65 years and over population: 2000. *Census 2000 Brief Series* (C2KBR/01-10). Washington, DC: U.S. Census Bureau. Retrieved May 28, 2008, from http://www.census.gov/prod/2001pubs/c2kbr01-10.pdf

Hewlett, S., Luce, C., & Servon, L. (2008). Stopping the exodus of women in science. *Harvard Business Review, 86*(6), 22-24.

Hirsch, J. (2003). *A courtship after marriage: Sexuality and love in Mexican transitional families.* Los Angeles, CA: University of California Press.

Hobart, C. (1991). Conflict in remarriages. *Journal of Divorce and Remarriage, 15*, 69-86.

Hobfoll, S. (1989). Conservation of resources: A new attempt at conceptualizing stress. *American Psychologist, 44*, 513–524.

Hochschild, A. (1989). *The second shift.* New York: Viking Press.

Hochschild, A. (2007). The emotional geography of work and family life. In S. Ferguson, *Shifting the center* (3rd ed., pp. 683-697). New York: McGraw-Hill.

Hofferth, S., & Anderson, K. (2003). Are all dads equal? Biology versus marriage as a basis for parental investment. *Journal of Marriage and Family, 65*, 213-232.

Hofferth, S., & Sandberg, J. (2001). How American children spend their time. *Journal of Marriage and Family, 63*(2), 295–309.

Homelessness in the United States and the human right to housing. (2004). *The National Law Center on Homelessness and Poverty.* Retrieved August 1, 2008, from http://www.nlchp.org/content/pubs/HomelessnessintheUSandRightstoHousing.pdf

Houdman, M., Matthews-Rose, P., & Niles, R. (Eds.). Preventing divorce—What are the ways. *All About Life Challenges.* Retrieved July 13, 2008, from http://www.allaboutlifechallenges.org/preventing-divorce-faq.htm

How many people experience homelessness? (2009). *National Coalition for the Homeless.* Washington, DC. Retrieved August 1, 2008, from http://www.nationalhomeless.org/factsheets/How_Many.html

How much debt can we afford? (2005, December 5). *Des Moines Business Record Online.* Retrieved November 29, 2008, from goliath.ecnext.com/coms2/gi_0199-5067624/How-Much-Debt-Can-We.html

How welfare begat daycare (2001). *The Howard Center for family, religion and society, 15*(01). Retrieved November 29, 2008, from http://www.profam.org/pub/nr/nr_1501.htm

Hugo, V. (2004). *The quotations page* (quotation no. 31616). Retrieved November 28, 2008, from http://www.quotationspage.com/quote/31616.html

Hungerford, T., Rassette, M., Iams, H., & Koenig, M. (2002, Fall). Trends in the economic status of the elderly, 1976–2000. *Social Security Bulletin, 64*(3), 12-21. Retrieved May 28, 2008, from http://www.ssa.gov/policy/docs/ssb/v64n3/v64n3p12.pdf

Huston, T. (2003). The success of a marriage. *Psychology Today.* Retrieved May 28, 2008, from http://www.psychologytoday.com/articles/pto-20030703-000001.html

Huston, T., Niehaus, S., & Smith, S. (2001). The early marital roots of conjugal distress and divorce. *Current Directions in Psychological Science, 10*(4), 116–119.

Hutcheon, P. (1995). Evolutionary theory in Freud, Piaget and Skinner. *World Futures, 44*, 203-11.

Hyde, J. (1991). *Half the human experience: The psychology of women.* Lexington, MA: Heath.

Ingersoll-Dayton, B., & Krause, N. (2005). Self-forgiveness: A component of mental health in later life. *Research on Aging, 27*, 267–289.

Joe, J. (2001). Out of harmony: Health problems and young Native-American men. *Journal of American College Health, 49*, 237–242.

Johnson, B., & Johnson, J. (2004). *Global issues and change*. Marion, IN: Triangle Publishing.

Jones, D. (2008, January 2). Female CEOs make more gains in 2007. *USA Today*. Retrieved November 28, 2008, from http://www.usatoday.com/money/companies/management/2008-01-02-women-ceos_N.htm

Jordan, J., Kaplan, A., Miller, J., Stiver, P., & Surrey. J. (Eds.). (1991). *Women's growth in connection; Writings from the Stone Center*. New York: Guilford Press.

Joyce, B. (2001). Favorite quotes on divorce reform. In J. Crouch (Ed.), *Americans for divorce reform*. Retrieved May 29, 2008, from http://patriot.net/~crouch/quotes.html

Judice Powell, C. (2005). *Interracial marriage: Black women and white men*. PhD. dissertation, Northwestern University, United States—Illinois. Retrieved October 18, 2009, from Dissertations & Theses: Full Text.(Publication No. AAT 3200957).

Kahn, R., Wolfe, D., Quinn, R., Snoek, J., & Rosenthal, R. (1964). *Organizational stress: Studies in role conflict and ambiguity*. New York: Wiley.

Kaiser Family Foundation. (2005). *U.S. teen sexual activity*. Washington, DC: The Henry J. Kaiser Family Foundation. Retrieved May 28, 2008, from http://www.kff.org/youthhivstds/upload/U-S-Teen-Sexual-Activity-Fact-Sheet.pdf

Kalil, A. & DeLeire, T. (2002). Parental job loss and early adolescent adjustment in black and white families. *JCPR Working Paper*. Chicago, IL: McCormick Tribune Foundation. Retrieved October 17, 2009, from http://www.eric.ed.gov/ERICDocs/data/ericdocs2sql/contentstorage01/0000019b/80/29/ce/a8.pdf

Kamp Dush, C., Cohan, C., & Amato, P. (2003). The relationship between cohabitation and marital quality and stability: Change across cohorts? *Journal of Marriage and Family, 65*(3), 539-549.

Kapinus, C. (2004). The effect of parents' attitudes toward divorce on offspring's attitudes: Gender and parental divorce as mediating factors. *Journal of Family Issue, 25*(1), 112-135.

Karis, T. (2003). How race matters and does not matter for white women in relationships with black men. *Journal of Couple & Relationship Therapy*, 2(2/3), 23-40.

Kastner, L. (2004, October 21). In B. Meltz, '*FWB' trend distorts the lessons of sex and love*. The Boston Globe. Retrieved August 10, 2008, from http://www.boston.com/yourlife/family/articles/2004/10/21/fwb_trend_distorts_the_lessons_of_sex_and_love/

Kelch, O. (2008). African-American grandparent caregivers: Stresses and implications for counselors. *The Family Journal, 16*(1), 43-50.

Kessler, R., Mickelson, K., Walters, E., Zhao, S., & Hamilton, L. (2004). Age and depression in the MIDUS survey. In O. Gilbert, C. Ryff, and R. Kessler (Eds.), *How healthy are we?* Chicago: University of Chicago.

Kiecolt-Glaser, J., Glaser, R., Cacioppo, J., & Malarkey, W. (1998). Marital stress: Immunologic, neuroendocrine, and autonomic correlates. *Annals of the New York Academy of Sciences, 840*, 656-663.

Kiecolt-Glaser, R., Glaser, R., Cacioppo, J., MacCallum, R., Snydersmith, M., Kim, C., & Malarkey, W. (1997). Marital conflict in older adults: endocrinological and immunological correlates. *Psychosomatic Medicine, 59*(4), 339-349.

Kilman, R., & Thomas, K. (1975). Interpersonal conflict-handling behaviors as reflections of Jungian personality dimensions. *Psychological Reports, 37*, 971-980.

Kimmell, T. (2009, September 25). Sex with no strings attached; the new "relationship." *dailywildcat.com*. Tucson, AZ: The University of Arizona. Retrieved October 28, 2009, from http://wildcat.arizona.edu/opinions/sex-with-no-strings-attached-the-new-relationship-1.529499

Kirby, J. B., & Kaneda, T. (2002). Health insurance and family structure: The case of adolescents in skipped-generation families. *Medical Care Research and Review, 59*(2), 146-165.

Kliman, J., & Madsen, W. (2005). Social class and the family life cycle. In B. Carter, & M. McGoldrick, *The expanded family life cycle,* New York: Allyn and Bacon.

Knox, D., & Schacht, C. (1999). *Marriage and family: A brief introduction.* Belmont, CA: Wadsworth.

Knox, D., & Schacht, C. (2004). *Choices in relationships: An introduction to marriage and the family* (8th ed.). Belmont, CA: Thompson Wadsworth.

Koczyriski, S. (2004). Conflicts in Marriage. *Pedagogy Studies, 75*, 44-49.

Koenig, H., George, L., & Peterson, B. (1998). Religiosity and remission of depression in medically ill older patients. *American Journal of Psychiatry, 155*(4), 536-542.

Kounseki, E. (2001). *The family circumplex model, faces II, and faces III, overview of research and applications.* St. Paul, MN: Department of Family Social Science. Retrieved October 19, 2009, from http://www.facesiv.com/pdf/faces_and_circumplex.pdf

Kreider, R. (2007). Living arrangements of children: 2004. *Current Population Reports* (P70-114). Washington, DC: U.S. Census Bureau. Retrieved July 13, 2008, from http://www.census.gov/prod/2008pubs/p70-114.pdf

Kreider, R., & Fields, J. (2005). Living arrangements of children: 2001. *Current Population Reports,* (P70-104). Washington, DC: U.S. Census Bureau. Retrieved July 14, 2008, from http://www.census.gov/prod/2005pubs/p70-104.pdf

Kreis, S. (2002). The triumph of science and the heavenly city of the eighteenth century philosophy. *The History Guide.* Retrieved May 28, 2008, from http://www.historyguide.org/intellect/lecture9a.html

Kroger, J. (2004). *Identity in adolescence: The balance between self and other.* New York: Routledge.

Krysan, M., Moore, K., & Zill, N. (1990). *Identifying successful families: An overview of constructs and selected measures.* Washington, DC: Child Trends, Inc.

Kulikoff, A. (1986). *Tobacco and slaves: The development of southern cultures in the Chesapeake, 1680–1800.* Chapel Hill, NC: University of North Carolina.

Kurdeck, L. (2002). Predicting the timing of separation and marital satisfaction: An eight-year prospective longitudinal study. *Journal of Marriage and Family, 64*(1), 163–179.

Kurdek, L. (2004a). Gay men and lesbians: The family content. In M. Coleman & L. Ganong (Eds.), *Handbook of contemporary families: Considering the past, contemplating the future* (pp. 96-115). Thousand Oaks, CA: Sage.

Kurdek, L. (2004b). Are gay and lesbian cohabitating couples really different from heterosexual married couples? *Journal of Marriage and Family*, *66*(4), 880-900.

Kurdek, L. (2005). What do we know about gay and lesbian couples? *Current Directions in Psychological Science*, *14*(5), 251-254.

Lachman, M. (2004). Development in midlife. *Annual Review of Psychology, 55*, 305–331.

Lachman, M., & Firth, K. (2004). The adaptive value of feeling in control during midlife. In O. Gilbert, C. Ryff, and R. Kessler (Eds.), *How healthy are we?* Chicago: University of Chicago.

Laird, J. (2005). Lesbian and gay families. In F. Walsh (Ed.), *Normal Family Processes* (3rd ed.). New York: Guilford Press.

Lamborn, S., Mounts, N., Steinberg, L., & Dornbusch, S. (1991). Patterns of competence and adjustment among adolescents from authoritative, authoritarian, indulgent, and neglectful families. *Child Development,* 62, 1049–1065.

Landry, B. (2000). *Black working wives: Pioneers of the American family revolution.* Los Angeles, CA: University of California Press.

Larson, A., & Olson, D. (2004). Spiritual beliefs and marriage, A national survey based on ENRICH. *The Family Psychologist, 20*(2), 4-8.

Larzelere, R. (1998, April). Combining love and limits in authoritative parenting: A conditional sequence model of disciplinary responses. *Paper presented at Parenthood in America Conference, Madison, WI.* Abstract. Retrieved May 28, 2008, from http://parenthood.library.wisc.edu/Larzelere/Larzelere.html

Larzelere, R., & Kuhn, B. (2000). Child outcomes of nonabusive and customary physical punishment by parents: An updated literature review. *Clinical Child and Family Review, 3*(4), 199–221.

LaSala, M. (2002). Walls and bridges: How coupled gay men and lesbians manage their intergenerational relationships. *Journal of Marital and Family Therapy, 28*(3), 327-339.

Lee, S., & Edmonston, B. (2005). New marriages, new families: U.S. racial and Hispanic intermarriage. *Population Bulletin, 60*(2). Washington, DC: Population Reference Bureau. Retrieved May 28, 2008, from http://www.prb.org/pdf05/60.2NewMarriages.pdf

Lee, S., Daniels, M., & Kissinger, D. (2006). Parental influences on adolescent adjustment: Parenting styles versus parenting practices. *The Family Journal, 14*(3), 253-259.

Lee, Y. (2005). Measuring the gender gap in household labor: Accurately estimating wives' and husbands' contributions. In B. Schneider and L. Waite (Eds.), *Being together, working apart* (pp. 229–247). Cambridge, UK: Cambridge University Press.

Leisure time on an average day. (2007). *Bureau of Labor Statistics.* Washington, DC: United States Department of Labor. Retrieved October 20, 2009, from http://www.bls.gov/tus/charts/chart9.pdf

Leon, K., & Jacobvitz, D. (2003). Relationship between adult attachment representations and family ritual quality: A perspective longitudinal study. *Family Process, 42*(3), 419-432.

Levinger, G. (1976). A social psychological perspective on marital dissolution. *Journal of Social Issues, 32*(1), 21–47.

Levinger, G. (1999). Duty toward whom? Reconsidering attractions and barriers as determinants of commitment to a relationship. In J. M Adams & W. H. Jones (Eds.), *Handbook of interpersonal commitment and relationship stability* (pp. 37-52). New York: Kluwer/Plenum.

Levinson, D. (1997). *The seasons of a woman's life.* New York: Knopf.

Levinson, D., Darrow, C., Klein, E., Levinson, M., & Braxton, M. (1978). *The seasons of a man's life.* New York: Knopf.

Lewin, A. (2005). The effect of economic stability on family stability among welfare recipients. *Evaluation Review, 29*(3), 223-240.

Lewis, C. S. (1960). *The four loves.* New York: Harcourt, Brace.

Lichter, D., Qian, Z., & Mellott, L. (2006). Marriage or dissolution? Union transitions among poor cohabiting women. *Demography, 4,* 223-240.

Lindau, S., Schumm, P., Laumann, E., Levinson, W., O'Muircheartaigh, C., & Waite, L. (2007). A study of sexuality and health among older adults in the U.S. *New England Journal of Medicine, 357*(8), 762-774.

Lino, M. (2005). *Expenditures on children by families, 2004,* Miscellaneous publication no.1529–2004. Washington, DC: U.S. Department of Agriculture, Center for Nutrition Policy and Promotion. Retrieved August 22, 2008, from http://www.cnpp.usda.gov/Publications/CRC/crc2004.pdf

Little, L. (2005). *Children of same-sex parents do as well as other children.* Concurrent Seminar F340, Presented October 10, 2005 at the American Academy of Pediatrics 2005 National Conference and Exhibition. Retrieved October 17, 2009, from http://www.medscape.com/viewarticle/514477

Llagas, C. (2003). *Status and trends in the education of Hispanics*, (NCES 2003–008). U.S. Department of Education, National Center for Education Statistics. Washington, DC: U.S. Department of Education. Retrieved August 25, 2008, from http://nces.ed.gov/pubs2003/2003008.pdf

Longley, R. (2005). Rate of family violence dropped by more than one-half from 1993 to 2002. *About.com*. Retrieved August 26, 2009, from http://usgovinfo.about.com/od/defenseandsecurity/a/famviolence.htm

Longmore, M., Manning, W., Giordano, P., & Rudolph, J. (2004). Self-esteem, depressive symptoms, and adolescents' sexual onset. *Social Psychological Quarterly, 67*(3), 279-295.

Lowry, R. (2001, May 28). Nasty, brutish, and short: Children in daycare and the mothers who put them there. *National Review*. Retrieved August 24, 2008, from http://findarticles.com/p/articles/mi_m1282/is_10_53/ai_74362320?tag=artBody;col1

Lu, C. (2006, August 10). *Risk factors for marital distress and divorce among stable, happy married couples*. Paper presented at the annual meeting of the American Sociological Association, Montreal Convention Center, Montreal, Quebec, Canada. Retrieved July 10, 2008, from http://www.allacademic.com/meta/p104997_index.html

Lubin, A. (n.d.). What's love got to do with it? The politics of race and marriage in the California Supreme Court's 1948 Perez and Sharp Decision. *OAH Magazine of History, 18*(4), 31-34.

Lundberg, U. (2005). Stress hormones in health and illness: The roles of work and gender. *Psychoneuroendocrinology, 30*(10), 1017–1021.

MacCallum, F., & Golombok, S. (2004). Children raised in fatherless families from infancy: A follow-up of children of lesbian and single heterosexual mothers at early adolescence. *Journal of Child Psychology and Psychiatry, 45*(8), 1407-1419.

Maccoby, E., & Martin, J. (1983). Socialization in the context of the family: Parent-child interaction. In E. Hetherington (Vol. Ed.) and P. Mussen (Ed.), *Handbook of child psychology: Volume 4. Socialization, personality, and social development* (pp. 1–101). New York: Wiley.

Madathil, J., & Benshoff, J. (2008). Comparison of importance of marital characteristics and marital satisfaction for Asian Indians in arranged marriages and Americans in marriages of choice. *The Family Journal, 16*, 222-230

Madden, J. (Director). (2001). *Captain Corelli's mandolin* [Motion picture]. Los Angeles, CA: Universal Studios.

Madden, M., & Lenhart, A. (2006, March 5). Online dating. *Pew Internet and American Life Project*. Retrieved May 28, 2008, from http://www.pewinternet.org/PPF/r/177/report_display.asp

Maher, B. (2003). Patching up the American family: Friends of the family. *WorldandI.com, 18*(1), 56.

Makinwa-Adebusoye, P. (2001, June 18). *Sociocultural factors affecting fertility in sub-Saharan Africa* (UN/POP/PFD/2001/2). Department of Economic and Social Affairs, Population Division. Retrieved August 4, 2008, from http://www.un.org/esa/population/publications/prospectsdecline/makinwa.pdf

Manning, W., Giordano, P., & Longmore, M. (2006). Hooking up: The relationship contexts of "non-relationship" sex. *Journal of Adolescent Research, 21*(5), 459-483.

Marcia, J. (1966, May). Development and validation of ego identity status. *Journal of Personality and Social Psychology, 3*(5), 551–558.

Marks, D., Nesteruk, O., Swanson, M., Garrison, M., & Davis, T. (2005). Religion and health among African-Americans: A qualitative examination. *Research on Aging, 27*(4), 447–474.

Marks, L. (2005). How does religion influence marriage?: Christian, Jewish, Mormon, and Muslim perspectives. *Marriage and Family Review, 38*(1), 85–111.

Marks, L., Hopkins, K., Chaney, C., Monroe, P., Nesteruk, O., and Sasser, D. (2008). Together, we are strong: A qualitative study of happy, enduring African-American marriages. *Family Relations, 57*(2), 113–266.

Marks, L., Nesteruk, O., Swanson, M., Hopkins-Williams, K., & Davis, T. (2006). Stressors in African-American marriages and families: A qualitative study. *Stress, Trauma, and Crisis: An International Journal, 9*(3-4), 203–225.

Markus, H., Ryff, C., Curhan, K., & Palmersheim, K. (2004). In their own words: Well-being at middle life among high-school-educated and college-educated adults. In O. Brim, C. Ryff, & R. Kessler (Eds.), *How healthy are we?* Chicago: University of Chicago.

Marquardt, E. (2005). *Between two worlds: The inner lives of children of divorce*. Bethel, CT: Crown.

Martin, H. (1973). [Cartoon]. *The New Yorker, 48*(51).

Martin, P., Specter, G., Martin, M., & Martin, D. (2003), Expressed attitudes of adolescents toward marriage and family life. *Adolescence, 38*(150), 359-367.

Martin, S. (2000). Diverging fertility of U.S. women who defer childbearing past age 30. *Demography, 37*(4), 523-533.

Marus, R. (2005, May 17). Federal judge strikes down Nebraska amendment banning gay marriage. *Associated Baptist Press*. Retrieved May 28, 2008, from http://www.abpnews.com/index.php?option=com_content&task=view&id=444&Itemid=118

Massey, D. (1993). *American apartheid: Segregation and the making of the underclass*. Cambridge, MA: Harvard University Press.

Matthews, T. (1995). *The religion of the slaves*. Retrieved May 28, 2008, from http://www.wfu.edu/~matthetl/perspectives/twelve.html

Mattingly, M., & Bianchi, S. (2003). Gender differences in the quantity and quality of free time: The U.S. experience. *Social Forces, 81*(3), 999-1030.

Mayo Clinic Staff. (2007). Male menopause: Myth or reality? *MayoClinic.com* (No. MC00058). Retrieved July 6, 2008, from http://www.mayoclinic.com/health/male-menopause/MC00058

Mayo Clinic Staff. (2008). Morning-after pill: Emergency birth control. *MayoClinic.com* (No. AN00592). Retrieved May 28, 2008, from http://www.mayoclinic.com/health/morning-after-pill/AN00592

McAdoo, H. (Ed.). (2007). *Black families*. Thousand Oaks, CA: Sage Publications.

McCord, H. (2007). Family: Where "God Is with Us". *Catechist, 41*(3), 8.

McCreary, L., & Dancy, B. (2004). Dimensions of family functioning: Perspectives of low-income African-American single parents. *Journal of Marriage and Family, 66*(3), 690-701.

McCubbin, M. (2007). Family stress and family strengths: A comparison of single- and two-parent families with handicapped children. *Research in Nursing and Health, 12*(2), 101-110.

McCullough, M., Hoyt, W., Larson, D., Koenig, H., & Thoresen, C. (2000). Religious involvement and mortality: A meta-analytic review. *Health Psychology, 19*(3), 211-222.

McDonald, J. (2007). What are the major sources of income for Americans age 65 and over? *Fast Facts from EBRI*, (FFE #69). Washington, DC: Employee Benefit Research Institute. Retrieved July 10, 2008, from http://www.ebri.org/pdf/publications/facts/fastfacts/fastfact121207.pdf

McElroy, W. (2001, May). The free soil movement, part 1. *Freedom Daily*. Retrieved May 28, 2008, from http://www.fff.org/freedom/0501e.asp

McGinnis, S. (2003). Cohabitating, dating, and perceived costs of marriage: A model of marriage entry. *Journal of Marriage and Family, 65*(1), 105–116.

McGoldrick, M. (2003). Culture: A challenge to concept of normality. In F. Walsh (Ed.), *Normal family processes: Growing diversity and complexity* (3rd ed.). New York: Guilford.

McGoldrick, M., & Carter, B. (2003). The family life cycle. In F. Walsh (Ed.), *Normal family processes: Growing diversity and complexity* (3rd ed.). New York: Guilford Press.

McMinn, L. (2004). *Sexuality and holy longing: Embracing intimacy in a broken world.* San Francisco: Jossey-Bass.

McNall, S. (1983). *Plains families: Exploring sociology through social history.* New York: St. Martin's Press.

Medora, N. (2005). International families in cross-cultural perspective: A family strengths perspective. *Marriage and Family Review, 38*(3), 47–64.

Medved, D. (1989). *The case against divorce* (ch. 1). New York: Ballantine.

Meezan, W., & Rauch, J. (2005). Gay marriage, same-sex parenting, and America's children. *Future Child, 15*(2), *97-115.*

Melmed, M. (2008, January 23). Hearing on investing in early education: Paths to improving children's success. *Paper submitted to the Committee on Education and Labor, U.S. House of Representatives.* Retrieved July 4, 2008, from http://www.zerotothree.org/site/DocServer/1-2308_Investing_in_Early_Education_Testimony.pdf?docID=4841

Messner, S., Bjarnason, T., Raffalovich, L., & Robinson, B. (2006). Nonmarital fertility and the effects of divorce rates on youth suicide rates. *Journal of Marriage and Family, 68*(4), 1105-1111.

Michaels, M. (2006). Factors that contribute to stepfamily success: A qualitative analysis. *Journal of Divorce and Remarriage, 44*(3-4), 53-66.

Miller, J. (1986). *Toward a new psychology of women.* London: Penguin Books.

Miller, P. (1989). *Theories of developmental psychology* (2nd ed.). New York: Freeman.

Miller, P. (2001). *Theories of developmental psychology* (4th ed.). London: Worth Publishers.

Miller, R. (2001, April). Do children make a marriage unhappy? *Marriage and Families, 5*, 13-18. Retrieved May 28, 2008, from http://contentdm.lib.byu.edu/cdm4/document.php?CISOROOT=/MarriageandFamily&CISOPTR=116&REC=6&CISOSHOW=8

Mills, L. (2003). *Insult to injury: Rethinking our responses to intimate abuse.* Princeton, NJ: Princeton University Press.

Milton, J. (2001). *Complete poems of John Milton, The Harvard classics, vol. IV*, 1909–14. New York: P.F. Collier & Son. Retrieved September 8, 2008, from www.bartleby.com/4/

Minino, A., Heron, M., Murphy, S., & Kochanek, K. (2007). Deaths: Final data for 2004. *National Vital Statistics Reports, 55*(19). Hyattsville, MD: National Center for Health Statistics. Retrieved August 24, 2007, from http://www.cdc.gov/nchs/data/nvsr/nvsr55/nvsr55_19.pdf

Mintz, S. (2001, Summer). Does the American family have a history? Family images and realities. *OAH Magazine of History,* 4–10.

Mintz, S. (2004). *Huck's raft: A history of American childhood.* Cambridge, MA: Belknap Press of Harvard University Press.

Mintz, S. (2007a). The Puritan mind. *Digital History.* Retrieved May 28, 2008, from http://www.digitalhistory.uh.edu/historyonline/us4.cfm

Mintz, S. (2007b). The roots of American economic growth: The laboring poor. *Digital History.* Retrieved May 28, 2008, from http://www.digitalhistory.uh.edu/database/article_display.cfm?HHID=612

Mintz, S., & Kellogg, S. (1988). *Domestic revolutions: A social history of American family life.* New York: The Free Press.

Moen, P., & Roehling, P. (2004). *The career mystique: Cracks in the American dream.* Lanham, MD: Rowman and Littlefield.

Moitozo, S. (2005). *Tiny book of homeschooling.* Lewiston, ME: North Atlantic Regional High School.

Molina, E. (2000). Informal non-kin networks among homeless Latino- and African-American men. *American Behavioral Scientist, 43*(4), 663-685.

Morton, L. (2004). Upper or elite class. *Public Relations Quarterly, 49*(4), 30-32.

Mosher, W., Chandra, A., & Jones, J. (2005). Sexual behavior and selected health measures: Men and women 15-44 years of age, United States, 2002. *Advance Data from Vital and Health Statistics* (No. 362). Hyattsville, MD: National Center for Health Statistics. Retrieved August 2, 2008, from http://www.cdc.gov/nchs/data/ad/ad362.pdf

Mroczek, D. (2004). Positive and negative affect at middle age. In O. Gilbert, C. Ryff, and R. Kessler (Eds.), *How healthy are we?* Chicago: University of Chicago.

Multifetal Pregnancy Reduction. (2007). *The American College of Obstetricians and Gynecologists, ACOG Committee Opinion No. 369.* Retrieved May 28, 2008, from http://www.acog.org/from_home/publications/ethics/co369.pdf

Munson, M., & Sutton, P. (2004). Births, marriages, divorces, and deaths: Provisional data for 2003. *National Vital Statistics Reports, 52*(22). Hyattsville, MD: National Center for Health Statistics. Retrieved July 28, 2008, from http://www.cdc.gov/nchs/data/nvsr/nvsr52/nvsr52_22.pdf

Muraco, M. (2006). Intentional families: Fictive kin ties between cross-gender, different sexual orientation friends. *Journal of Marriage and Family, 68*(5), 1313–1325.

Murstein, B. (1987, November). A clarification and extension of the SVR theory of dyadic pairing. *Journal of Marriage and Family, 49*(4), 929-933.

Musick, M., Wilson, J., & Bynum, W. (2000). Race and formal volunteering: The differential effects of class and religion. *Social Forces, 78*(4), 1539-1570.

Mutchler, J., Baker, L., & Lee-Seung, A. (2007). Grandparents responsible for grandchildren in Native-American families. *Social-Science Quarterly, 88*(4), 990-1009.

Nakajima, H. (1994). Stress and health. *World Health, 47*(2), 3.

Nash, G. (2006). *The unknown American revolution: The unruly birth of democracy and the struggle to create America*. New York: Penguin.

National Center for Disease Control. (1996). Marriage and divorce. *Vital Statistics of the United States, 1988, vol 111*. Hyattsville, MD: National Center for Health Statistics. Retrieved November 28, 2008, from http://www.cdc.gov/nchs/data/series/sr_23/sr23_022.pdf

National Center for Disease Control. (2002). Cohabitation, marriage, divorce, and remarriage in the United States. *Vital Statistics of the United States, 2002, 23(22)*. Hyattsville, MD: National Center for Health Statistics. Retrieved November 28, 2008, from http://www.cdc.gov/nchs/data/vsus/mort88_2b.pdf

National Center for Health Statistics. (1973). 100 years of marriage and divorce statistics United States, 1867–1967. *Vital and Health Statistics, 21*(24), (DHEW publication no. (HRA) 74-1902). Rockville, MD: National Center for Health Statistics. Retrieved November 28, 2008, from http://www.cdc.gov/nchs/data/series/sr_21/sr21_024.pdf

National Center for Health Statistics. (1986). Marriage and divorce. *Vital Statistics of the United States, 1982, vol. 111,* DHHS pub no. (PHS) 86-1103. Hyattsville, MD: National Center for Health Statistics. Retrieved November 28, 2008, from http://www.cdc.gov/nchs/data/vsus/mgdv82_3.pdf

National Center for Health Statistics. (1989). Compilations of data on natality, mortality, marriage, divorce, and induced terminations of pregnancy. *Vital and Health Statistics, 24*(1), DHHS Publication No. (PHS) 89-1951. Hyattsville, MD: National Center for Health Statistics. Retrieved November 28, 2008, from http://www.cdc.gov/nchs/data/series/sr_24/sr24_001.pdf

National Center for Health Statistics. (1996). Provisional vital statistics for August 1995. *Monthly Vital Statistics Reports, 44*(8). Hyattsville, MD: National Center for Health Statistics. Retrieved November 28, 2008, from http://www.cdc.gov/nchs/data/mvsr/mv44_08.pdf

National Center for Health Statistics. (2002). Births, marriages, divorces, and deaths: provisional data for 2001. *National Vital Statistics Reports, 50*(14). Hyattsville, MD: National Center for Health Statistics. Retrieved November 28, 2008, from http://www.cdc.gov/nchs/data/nvsr/nvsr50/nvsr50_14.pdf

National Council on Aging. (2002). *American perceptions of aging in the 21st century,* Item No. RES6 Research Publications. Washington, DC: National Council on Aging. Retrieved July 7, 2008, from https://www.ncoa.org/Downloads/Chartbook.pdf.pdf

Neuharth, D. (1989). *If you had controlling parents: How to make peace with your past and take your place in the world.* New York: HarperCollins.

Newman, D., & Grauerholz, L. (2002). *Sociology of families.* Thousand Oaks, CA: Sage.

Newman, K. (1999). *No shame in my game: The working poor in the inner city.* New York: Knopf.

Nichols, W., & Pace-Nichols, M. (1993). Developmental perspectives and family therapy: The marital life cycle. *Contemporary Family Therapy, 15*(4), 299–315.

Nightlight Christian Adoptions. (2008). *What is embryo donation and adoption?* Retrieved November 28, 2008, from http://www.nightlight.org/Snowflakesfacts.pdf

Norwood, P., & Wingender, T. (1999). *The enlightened stepmother: Revolutionizing the role.* New York: Avon.

Nouriani, M. (2006). Infertility. *Frequently Asked Questions.* Washington, DC: U.S. Department of Health and Human Services, Office on Women's Health. Retrieved May 28, 2008, from http://www.womenshealth.gov/faq/infertility.pdf

Ogunwole, S. (2006). We the people: American Indians and Natives in the United States. *Census 2000 Special Report* (CENSR-28). Washington, DC: U.S. Census Bureau. Retrieved August 2, 2008, from http://www.census.gov/prod/2006pubs/censr-28.pdf

Olson, D., & DeFrain, J. (1999). *Marriage and the family: Diversity and strengths* (3rd ed.). New York: McGraw-Hill

Olson, D., & DeFrain, J. (2006). *Marriages and families: Intimacy, diversity and strengths* (5th ed.). New York: McGraw-Hill.

Olson, D., & Fowers, B. (1993, July). Five types of marriage: An empirical typology based on ENRICH. *Family Journal, 1*(3), 196–207.

Olson, D., & Olson, A. (2000). *Empowering couples: Building on your strengths.* Minneapolis, MN: Life Innovations.

Olson, D., McCubbin, H., Barnes, H., Larsen, A., Muxen, M., & Wilson, M. (1983). *Families: What makes them work.* Beverly Hills, CA: Sage.

Olson, D., Russell, C., & Sprenkle, D. (1989). *Circumplex model: systematic assessment and treatment of families.* New York: Hayworth.

Online dating magazine media center: Abbreviated online dating facts and stats. (2007). *Online Dating Magazine.* Retrieved June 23, 2009, from http://www.onlinedatingmagazine.com/mediacenter/onlinedatingfacts.html

Ory, M., Hoffman, M., Hawkins, M., Sanner, B., & Mockenhaupt, R. (2003). Challenging aging stereotypes: Strategies for creating a more active society *American Journal of Preventive Medicine, 25*(3), *164-171.*

Otto, H. (1962, February). What is a strong family? *Marriage and Family Living, 24*(1), 77–81.

Page, L. (1999). *Stress and energy: Reduce your stress and boost your energy.* Del Rey Oaks, CA: Healthy Healing Publications.

Paige, R. (2005). Sexual orientation, parents and children. *Proceedings of the American Psychological Association, Incorporated, for the legislative year 2004. Minutes of the meeting of the Council of Representatives, July 28 & 30, 2004, Honolulu, HI.* Retrieved July 5, 2008, from http://www.apa.org/pi/lgbc/policy/parents.html

Painter, G., & Levine, D. (2000). Family structure and youths outcomes: Which correlations are causal? *Journal of Human Resources, 35*(3), 524-549.

Parke, M. (2003). Are married parents really better for children? What research says about the effects of family structure on child well-being. Washington, DC: Center for Law and Social Policy. Retrieved November 29, 2008, from http://www.eric.ed.gov/ERICDocs/data/ericdocs2sql/content_storage_01/0000019b/80/1b/05/49.pdf

Parkin, S. (2000). Nearly half of older Americans say "These are best years of my life," National survey shows. *Myths and Realities of Aging Project.* Washington, DC: National Council on Aging. Retrieved November 28, 2008, from http://www.ncoa.org/content.cfm?sectionID=105&detail=43

Parkman, A. (2004). Bargaining over housework: The frustrating situation of secondary wage earners. *The American Journal of Economics and Sociology, 63*(4), 765–795.

Parsons, T. (1997) *Sources and stages of mate selection, relationship development, and marriage.* Ph.D. dissertation, The Fielding Institute, United States-California. Retrieved October 19, 2008, from Dissertations & Theses: Full Text database. (Publication No. AAT 9809580).

Patterson, C. (2000). Family relationships of lesbians and gay men. *Journal of Marriage and Family, 62*(4), 1052-1069.

Pattillo-McCoy, M. (1999). *Black picket fences: Privilege and peril among the black middle-class.* Chicago: University of Chicago Press.

Paul, E., McManus, B., & Hayes, A. (2000). "Hookups": Characteristics and correlates of college students' spontaneous and anonymous sexual experiences. *The Journal of Sex Research, 37*(1), 76-88.

Pellis, S., & Pellis, V. (2007). Rough-and-tumble play and the development of the social brain. *Current Directions in Psychological Science, 16*(2), 95-98.

Perrin, C. (2002). Technical report: Coparent and second-parent adoption by same-sex parents. *Pediatrics, 109*(2), 341-344.

Pietromonaco, P., & Barrett, L. (2000). The internal working models concept: What do we really know about the self in relation to others? *Review of General Psychology, 4*(2), 155-175.

Pinderhughes, E., Bates, J., Dodge, K., Pettit, G., & Zelli, A. (2000). Discipline responses: Influences of parents' socioeconomic status, ethnicity, beliefs about parenting, stress, and cognitive-emotional processes. *Journal of Family Psychology, 14*(3), 380–400.

Pippert, T. (2003, August 16). Applying family theories to fictive kin: Postmodernism meets exchange theory. *Paper presented at the annual meeting of the American Sociological Association, Atlanta Hilton Hotel, Atlanta, GA.* Retrieved August 5, 2008, from http://www.allacademic.com/meta/p106311_index.html

Phillips, J. & Sweeney, M. (2005). Premarital cohabitation and marital disruption among white, Black and Mexican-American women. *Journal of Marriage and Family, 66,* 296-314.

Place, M., Hulsmeier, J., Brownrigg, A., & Soulsby, A. (2005). The family adaptability and cohesion evaluation scale (FACES): An instrument worthy of rehabilitation? *Psychiatric Bulletin, 20*(29), 215-218.

Pleck, J. (1999). Balancing work and family. *Scientific American, 10*(2), 38–43.

Polakow, V. (2007). *Who cares for our children? The child care crisis in the other America.* New York: Teachers College Press.

Popenoe, D. (1995). *Life without father.* New York: Martin Kessler Books.

Popenoe, D. (2002, March). The top ten myths of marriage. *The National Marriage Project, Information Brief.* Retrieved November 28, 2008, from http://marriage.rutgers.edu/Publications/MythsMarriage.pdf

Post, S. (Ed.). (2007). *Altruism and health: Perspectives from empirical research.* New York: Oxford University Press, USA.

Post, S., Neimark, J., & Moss, O. (2007). *Why good things happen to good people: The exciting new research that proves the link between doing good and living a longer, healthier, happier life.* New York: Broadway.

Pruthi, S. (2007). Abortion: Does it affect subsequent pregnancies? *MayoClinic.com* (No. AN00633). Retrieved November 28, 2008, from http://www.mayoclinic.com/health/abortion/AN00633

Qian, Z., & Lichter, D. (2007). Social Boundaries and marital assimilation: Interpreting trends in racial and ethnic intermarriage. *American Sociological Review, 72*(1), 68-94.

Rambo, D., [Artist]. (2003). *He Looked Beyond My Fault and Saw My Need.* Nashville: Benson.

Ramirez, J., Crano, W., Quist, R., Burgoon, M., Alvaro, E., & Grandpre, J. (2004). Acculturation, familism, parental monitoring, and knowledge as predictors of marijuana and inhalant use in adolescents. *Psychology of Addictive Behavior, 18*(1), 3-11.

Ramsey, D. (2007). The truth about credit card debt. Retrieved July 29, 2008, from http://www.daveramsey.com/etc/cms/index.cfm?intContentID=3478

Redefining family. (2005). *The Colonial Williamsburg Foundation.* Retrieved June 28, 2008, from http://www.history.org/Almanack/life/family/famhdr2.cfm

Reeves, T., & Bennett, C. (2004). We the people: Asians in the United States. *Census 2000 Special Report* (CENSR17). Washington, DC: U.S. Census Bureau. Retrieved May 28, 2008, from http://www.census.gov/prod/2004pubs/censr-17.pdf

Religion in Eighteenth-Century America. (2006). Library of Congress, Religion and the founding of the American republic. Retrieved May 28, 2008, from http://www.loc.gov/exhibits/religion/rel02.html

Rennison, C. (2003). Intimate partner violence, 1993-2001. *Bureau of Justice Statistics: Crime Data Brief* (NCJ 197838). Washington, DC: U.S. Department of Justice. Retrieved October 12, 2009, from http://www.ojp.usdoj.gov/bjs/pub/pdf/ipv01.pdf

Ritter, E. (2005). Parenting styles: Their impact on the development of adolescent resiliency. *Dissertation Abstracts International, 66*(1-B), 621. (UMI No. AAI3161747).

Roberts, A., & Fisher, D. (1944). "You always hurt the one you love" [Recorded by the Mills Brothers]. On *You always hurt the one you love* [record]. Decca Records.

Roberts, S. (2007, January 16). 51% of women are now living without a spouse. *New York Times.* Retrieved June 28, 2008, from http://www.nytimes.com/2007/01/16/us/16census.html

Robinson, J., & Godbey, C. (2005). Time in our hands. *The Futurist, 39*(5), 18-23.

Rodriguez, N., Consuelo, B., Paez, N., & Myers, H. (2007). Exploring the complexities of familism and acculturation: Central constructs for Mexican origin. *American Journal of Community Psychology, 39*(1-2), 61-77.

Roessler, R., Chung, W., & Rubin, S. (2006). Family-centered rehabilitation case management. In R. Roessler & S. E. Rubin, (Eds.). *Case management and rehabilitation counseling* (4th ed.). Austin, TX: PRO-ED.

Rogers, S., & May, D. (2003). Spillover between marital quality and job satisfaction: Long-term patterns and gender differences. *Journal of Marriage and Family, 65*(2), 352–369.

Rollins, B., & Feldman, H. (1970). Marital satisfaction over the family life cycle. *Journal of Marriage and Family, 32*(1), 20–28.

Romich, J. (2007). Sharing the work: Mother-child relationships and household management. *Journal of Early Adolescence, 27*, 192-222.

Ronnau, J., & Shannon, P. (n.d.). A strengths approach to helping Native-American families. *Indian Child Welfare Manual*. Olympia, WA: Department of Social and Health Services. Retrieved August 15, 2008, from http://www1.dshs.wa.gov/CA/pubs/mnl_icw/appendixA_2.asp

Rotondo, D., Carlson, D., & Kincaid, J. (2003). Coping with multiple dimensions of work-family conflict. *Personnel Review, 32*(3), 275-296.

Rouse, L. (2002). *Marital and sexual lifestyles in the United States*. Birmingham, NY: Hayworth Press.

Ryff, C., Magee, W., Kling, K., & Wing, E. (1999). Forging macro-micro linkages in the study of psychological well-being. In C. Ryff and V. Marshall (Eds.), *The self and society in aging processes*. New York: Springer.

Saad, L. (2008, May 19). Cultural tolerance for divorce grows to 70%. *Gallup.com*. Retrieved August 10, 2008, from http://www.gallup.com/poll/107380/Cultural-Tolerance-Divorce-Grows-70.aspx

Sabatelli, R., & Bartle-Haring, S. (2003). Family-of-origin experiences and adjustment in married couples. *Journal of Marriage and Family, 65*(1), 159-169.

Sage, G. (2001). Worldview: Identity and prevention in American Indian communities. In J. Trimble & F. Beauvais (Eds.), *Health promotion and substance abuse prevention among American Indian and Alaska Native communities: Issues in cultural competence*. Washington, DC: Department of Education. (ERIC Document Reproduction Service No. ED 452 006) Retrieved July 30, 2008, http://www.eric.ed.gov/ERICDocs/data/ericdocs2sql/content_storage_01/0000019b/80/16/f5/dd.pdf

Sahardi, J. (2005, April 19). Lucrative degrees for college grads. *CNNMoney.com*. Retrieved May 29, 2008, from http://money.cnn.com/2005/04/15/pf/college/starting_salaries/

Sample, I. (2006, July 20). Low position on social status ladder linked to faster aging. *guardian.co.uk*. Retrieved May 28, 2008, from www.guardian.co.uk/science/2006/jul/20/lifeandhealth.medicineandhealth

Sampson, R. (1992). Crime in cities: The effects of formal and informal social control. In M. Tonry and N. Morris (Eds.), *Crime and justice* (pp. 271–301). Chicago: University of Chicago Press.

Sanchez, L., Nock, S., Wilson, J., & Wright, J. (2006). Is covenant marriage a policy that preaches to the choir? A comparison of covenant and standard newlywed couples in Louisiana. *Center for Family Demographic Research*. Bowling Green, OH: Bowling Green State University. Retrieved July 11, 2008, from http://www.bgsu.edu/downloads/cas/file35343.pdf

Santore, D. (2008, December). Romantic relationships, individualism and the possibility of togetherness: Seeing Durkheim in theories of contemporary intimacy. *Sociology, 42*(6), 1200-1217.

Sapolsky, R. (2004). Social status and health in humans and other animals. *Annual Reviews of Anthropology, 33*, 393–418.

Sarkisian, N., & Gerstel, N. (2004). Kin support among Blacks and Whites: Race and family organization. *American Sociological Review, 69*(6), 812-837.

Sassler, S. (2004). The process of entering into cohabitating unions. *Journal of Marriage and Family, 66*(2), 491-505.

Satir, V. (1976). *Making contact*. Mellbrae, CA: Celestial Arts.

Saunders, P. (2002, December). The direct and indirect effects of unemployment on poverty and inequality. *Social Policy Research Center,* (Discussion Paper No. 118). Retrieved August 24, 2008, from http://www.sprc.unsw.edu.au/dp/DP118.pdf

Savage, J. (2007). *Teenage: The creation of youth 1875-1945*. New York: Viking

Scanzoni, L., & Scanzoni, J. (1981). *Men, women, and change: A sociology of marriage and family* (2nd ed.). New York: McGraw-Hill.

Scharff, D., & Scharff, J. (2005). The Primmer of Object Relations (2nd Ed.). Lanham, MD: Jason Aronson Inc.

Schlessinger, L. (2000). *Parenthood by proxy: Don't have them if you won't raise them.* New York: Cliff Street Books.

Schmitt, M., Kliegel, M., & Shapiro, A. (2007). Marital interaction in middle and old age: A predictor of marital satisfaction? *International Journal of Aging and Human Development, 65*(4), 283-300.

Schneider, B., Atteberry, A., & Owens, A. (2005). *Family matters: Family structure and child outcomes.* Alfred P. Sloan Center on Parents, Children and Work. Chicago, IL: The University of Chicago

Schoenborn, C. (2004). Marital status and health: United States, 1999–2002. *Advance Data from Vital and Health Statistics,* (No. 351). Hyattsville, MD: National Center for Health Statistics. Retrieved August 5, 2008, from http://www.cdc.gov/nchs/data/ad/ad351.pdf

Schore, A. (1997). Early organization of the nonlinear right brain and development of a predisposition to psychiatric disorders. *Development and Psychopathology, 9*(4), 595–631.

Schore, A. (2000). Attachment and the regulation of the right brain. *Psychology Press, part of the Taylor Francis Group, 2*(1), 23–47.

Seaman, P., Turner, K., Hill, M., Stafford, A., & Walker, M. (2006). Parenting and children's resilience in disadvantaged communities. *Joseph Rountree Foundation.* Retrieved August 1, 2008, from http://www.jrf.org.uk/knowledge/findings/socialpolicy/0096.asp

Segerstrom, S., & Miller, G. (2004). Psychological stress and the human immune system: A meta-analytic study of 30 years of inquiry. *Psychological Bulletin, 130*(4), 601-630.

Selected caregiver statistics. (2001). *Family Caregiver Alliance,* (No. FS-SCS200506). San Francisco, CA: California Department of Mental Health. Retrieved November 28, 2008, from http://www.caregiver.org/caregiver/jsp/content_node.jsp?nodeid=439

Seltzer, J. (2000). Families formed outside marriage. *Journal of Marriage and the Family, 62,* 1247-1268.

Seto, M., Alexandria, M., & Barbaree, H. (2001). The role of pornography in the etiology of sexual aggression. *Aggression & Violent Behavior, 6*(1), 35-53.

Sharlin, S., Kaslow, F., & Hammerschmidt, H. (2000). *Together through thick and thin: A multinational picture of long-term marriages.* Binghamton, NY: Haworth Press.

Sheehan, G., & Noller, P. (2002). Adolescent's perceptions of differential parenting: Links with attachment style and adolescent adjustment. *Personal Relationships, 9*(2), 173-190.

Sheehy, G. (1995). *New Passages: Mapping your life across time.* New York: Random House.

Sheehy, G. (2006). *Passages: Predictable crises of adult life.* New York: Ballantine.

Silenzio, V., Pena J., Duberstein, P., Cerel, J., & Knox, K. (2007). Sexual orientation and risk factors for suicidal ideation and suicide attempts among adolescents and young adults. *American Journal of Public Health, 97*(11), 2017-2019.

Simmons, T., & Dye, J. L. (2003, October). Grandparents living with grandchildren: 2000. *Census 2000 Brief,* (No. C2KBR-31). Retrieved July 6, 2008, from http://www.census.gov/prod/2003pubs/c2kbr-31.pdf

Simmons, T., & O'Neil, G. (2001, September). Households and families: 2000. *Census 2000 Brief,* (No. C2KBR/01-8) Retrieved November 28, 2008, from http://www.census.gov/prod/2001pubs/c2kbr01-8.pdf

Slater, S., & Mencher, J. (1991). The lesbian family life cycle: A conceptual approach. *American Journal of Orthopsychiatry, 61*(3), 372-382.

Smalley, G., & Trent, J. (2004). *The blessing* (Rev. ed.). Nashville: Nelson.

Smedes, L. (1976). *Sex for Christians*. Grand Rapids, MI: Erdmans Publishing.

Smith, C. (2005). *Soul searching: The religious and spiritual lives of American teenagers*. New York: Oxford University Press.

Smith, K. (2002). Who's minding the kids? Childcare arrangements: Spring 1997. *Current Population Reports, (*P70-86). Washington, DC: U.S. Census Bureau. Retrieved May 16, 2008, from http://www.census.gov/prod/2002pubs/p70-86.pdf

Smith, S. (1991). Sociodemographic differentials in mate selection processes. *Journal of Marriage and Family, 53*, 928–940.

Sneed, J., Johnson, J., Cohen, P., Gilligan, C., Chen, H., Crawford, T., & Kasen, S. (2006). Gender differences in the age-changing relationship between instrumentality and family contact in emerging adulthood. *Developmental Psychology, 42*(5), 787-797.

Sprecher, S. (1999). I love you more today than yesterday: Romantic partners' perceptions of changes in love and related effect over time. *Journal of Personality and Social Psychology, 76*(1), 46–53.

Stacey, J. (1996). *In the name of the family: Rethinking family values in the postmodern age*. Boston: Beacon Press.

Stacey, J., & Biblarz, T. (2001). Does the sexual orientation of parents matter? *American Sociological Review*, *66*(1), 159-183.

Stack, S., & Wasserman, I. (2007). Economic strain and suicide risk: A qualitative analysis. *Suicide & Life-Threatening Behavior*, *37*(1), 103-12.

Stafford, F., Eccles, J., & Schoeni, R. (2003). *Panel study of income dynamics*. Institute for Social Research, University of Michigan. Retrieved May 29, 2008, from http://psidonline.isr.umich.edu/Guide/Overview.html

Stanley, S., Rhoades, G. & Markman, H. (2006). Sliding vs. deciding: Inertia and the premarital cohabitation effect. *Family Relations,* 55, 499-509.

Stanley, S., Whitton, S., & Markman, H. (2004). Maybe I do: Interpersonal commitment and premarital or nonmarital cohabitation. *Journal of Family Issues*, *25*(4), 496-519.

Statham, J. (2007) The effect of family poverty on children. *Community Care*, 1701 (29 Nov): 24-5.

Statistics. (2008). A publication of Christian Oriented Education, Inc. In *Financial Freedom*. Retrieved November 29, 2008, from http://www.coeinc.org/AllPages/9Sections/Sidebar/financialstatistics.htm

Steakley, K. (2006, April 10). Fumbling childhood: The bad results of a good divorce. *BreakPoint*. Retrieved November 29, 2008, from http://www.breakpoint.org/features-columns/articles/1762-fumbling-childhood

Stein, R. (2007, July 13). Plan B use surges, and so does controversy. *WashingtonPost.com*. Retrieved August 15, 2008, from *http://www.washingtonpost.com/wp-dyn/content/article/2007/07/12/AR2007071202146.html*

Stein, R. (2007, July 22). Teen sex rates stop falling, data show. *WashingtonPost.com*. Retrieved June 23, 2009, from www.washingtonpost.com http://www.washingtonpost.com/wp-dyn/content/article/2007/07/21/AR2007072101275.html

Steinberg, L., Darling, N., & Fletcher, A. (1995). Authoritative parenting and adolescent adjustment: An ecological perspective. In P. Moen, G. Elder, & K. Luscher (Eds.), *Examining lives in context: Perspectives on the ecology of human development*, (pp. 423–466). Washington, DC: American Psychological Association.

Sternberg, R. (1986). A triangular theory of love. *Psychological Review, 93*(2), 119–135.

Sternberg, R. (1987). Liking versus loving: A comparative evaluation of theories. *Psychological Bulletin, 102*(3), 331–345.

Sternberg, R. (1998). *Love as a story*. New York: Oxford.

Sternberg, R. (2000). *Cupid's arrow: The course of love through time*. Cambridge, UK: Cambridge University Press.

Sternberg, R., Hojjat, M., & Barnes, M. (2001). Empirical test of aspect of a theory of love as a story. *European Journal of Personality, 15*, 199-218.

Stewart, S. (2007). *Brave new stepfamilies*. Thousand Oaks, CA: Sage.

Stewart-Brown, S. (1998). Emotional wellbeing and its relation to health. *British Medical Journal, 317*, 1608–1609.

Stinnett, N. (1983). Strong families. In D. Mace, *Prevention in family services: Approaches to family wellness*, (pp. 175–189). Beverly Hills, CA: Sage Publications.

Stinnett, N., & DeFrain, J. D. (1985). *Secrets of strong families*. Boston: Little, Brown.

Stinnett, N., & Sauer, K. (1977). Relationship characteristics of strong families. *Family Perspectives*, (Fall), 3–11.

Stinnett, N., Stinnett, N., DeFrain, J. & DeFrain, N. (1999). *Creating a strong family*. West Monroe, LA: Howard Publishing.

Stinnett, N., & Walters, J. (1971). Parent-child relationships: A decade of research. *Journal of Marriage and Family, 32*(4), 70–111.

Stinnett, N., Chesser, B., & DeFrain, J. (Eds.). (1981). *In search of strong families*. Lincoln, NE: University of Nebraska.

Strauss, M. (2001). *Beating the devil out of them: Corporal punishment in American children* (2nd ed.). Somerset, NJ: Transaction Publishers.

Strauss, M., & Stewart, J. (1999). Corporal punishment by American parents: National data on prevalence, chronicity, severity, and duration in relation to child family characteristics. *Clinical Child and Family Review, 2*(2), 55–70.

Strohschein, L. (2005). Parental divorce and child mental health trajectories. *Journal of Marriage and Family, 67*(5), 1286-1300.

Suleiman, L. (2003). Beyond cultural competence: Language access and Latin civil rights. *Child Welfare Journal, Mar/Apr*, 185-200.

Sweeney, M. (2007). Stepfather Families and the Emotional Well-Being of Adolescents. *Journal of Health and Social Behavior, 48*(1), 33-49.

Swindoll, C. (2006). *Marriage: From surviving to thriving*. Nashville, TN: Thomas Nelson.

Szumilas, M., & Kutcher, S. (2008). Youth and suicide. *Canadian Medical Association Journal, 178*(3), 286.

Tarman, A. (2003). International adoption rate in U.S. doubled in the 1990s. (excerpt from, What drives U.S. Population Growth {PDF:559KB}) Washington, DC: Population Reference Bureau. Retrieved November 28, 2008, from http://www.prb.org/Articles/2003/InternationalAdoptionRateinUSDoubledinthe1990s.aspx

Tasker, F. (2005). Lesbian mothers, gay fathers, and their children: A review. *Journal of Developmental and Behavioral Pediatrics, 26*(3), 224-240.

Taylor, H., & Naison, M. (2000). Epilogue: African-Americans and the dawning of the postindustrial era. In H. Taylor & W. Hill, *Historical roots of the urban crisis: African-Americans in the industrial city, 1900-1950*. (pp.275- 286). New York: Taylor Francis.

Teachman, J. (2003). Premarital sex, premarital cohabitation, and the risk of subsequent marital dissolution among women. *Journal of Marriage and Family, 65*(2), 444–455.

The Futurist. (2005, September/October). Stay-at home dads: At-home dads can benefit children and mothers. *The Futurist, 39*(5), 12-13.

The history of Chinese immigration. (2000, Spring). *The Brown Quarterly*, 3(4). Retrieved May 8, 2008, from http://brownvboard.org/brwnqurt/03-4/03-4c.htm

The real issue of poverty. (2005). *Community Care, 1587*, 5. Retrieved August 1, 2008, from ProQuest database, http://proquest.umi.com/pqdweb?did=899723441&sid=1&Fmt=3&clientId=48621&RQT=309&VName=PQD

Thomas, K., & Kilmann, R. (1974). *Thomas-Kilmann conflict mode instrument.* Palo Alto, CA: Consulting Psychologists Press, Inc.

Thompson, W., & Hickey, J. (2005). *Society in Focus.* Boston, MA: Pearson.

Toliver, S. (1998). *Black families in corporate America.* Thousand Oaks, CA: Sage Publications.

Troxel, W., Matthews, K., Gallo, L., & Kuller, L. (2005). Marital quality and occurrence of the metabolic syndrome in women. *Archives of Internal Medicine, 165*(9), 1022-1027.

Trussell J., & Kowal, D. (2004). The essentials of contraception: Efficacy, safety and personal consideration. In R. A. Hatcher et al., *Contraception Technology* (18th ed.) (pp. 221-252). New York: Ardent Media.

Tucker, M. (2000). Marital values and expectations in context: Results from a 21-city survey. In L. Waite (Ed.), *The ties that bind: Perspectives on marriage and cohabitation.* New York: Aldine de Gruyter.

Tweedell, C. (2002). *Sociology: A Christian approach for changing the world.* Marion, IN: Triangle Publishing.

U.S. Bureau of Labor Statistics. (2009). *Economy at a glance.* Washington, DC: U.S. Department of Labor. Retrieved July 30, 2009, from http://www.bls.gov/eag/eag.us.htm

U.S. Census Bureau. (1949). *Historical statistics of the United States, 1789–1945.* Washington, DC: U.S. Department of Commerce. Retrieved July 30, 2008, from http://www.questia.com/library/book/historical-statistics-of-the-united-states-1789-1945-by-united-states-bureau-of-the-census.jsp

U.S. Census Bureau. (1994). *Race of wife by race of husband.* Washington, DC: U.S. Census Bureau. Retrieved July 29, 2008, from http://www.census.gov/population/socdemo/race/interractab1.txt

U.S. Census Bureau. (2003). Households by type and size: 1900 to 2002. *Statistical Abstract of the United States* (No. HS-12). Hyattsville, MD: National Center for Health Statistics. Retrieved May 28, 2008, from http://www.census.gov/statab/hist/HS-12.pdf

U.S. Census Bureau. (2004). Special Edition, National Adoption Month (November). *Facts for Features* (CB04-FFSE.12). Washington, DC: U.S. Census Bureau. Retrieved May 28, 2008, from http://www.census.gov/Press-Release/www/2004/cb04ffse-12.pdf

U.S. Census Bureau. (2005a). Back to School. *Facts for Features* (CB04-FF.12). Washington, DC: US Census Bureau. Retrieved July 10, 2008, from http://www.census.gov/Press-Release/www/2004/cb04-ff12.pdf

U.S. Census Bureau. (2005b). *Marital history for people 15 years old and over by age, sex, race and ethnicity: 2001.* Washington, DC: U.S. Census Bureau. Retrieved August 10, 2008, from http://www.census.gov/population/www/socdemo/marr-div/p70-97-tab01.html

U.S. Census Bureau. (2005c). Mothers Day: May 8, 2005. *Facts For Features* (CB05-FF.05-2). Washington, DC: U.S. Census Bureau. Retrieved August 24, 2008, from http://www.census.gov/Press-Release/www/releases/archives/facts_for_features_special_editions/004109.html

U.S. Census Bureau. (2006a). American community survey: children's characteristics. *American Fact Finder* (S0901). Washington, DC: U.S. Census Bureau. Retrieved November 29, 2008, from http://factfinder.census.gov/servlet/STTable?_bm=y&-qr_name=ACS_2006_EST_G00_S0901&-geo_id=01000US&-ds_name=ACS_2006_EST_G00_&-_lang=en&-format=&-CONTEXT=st.

U.S. Census Bureau. (2006b). American community survey: households and families. *American Fact Finder* (S1101). Washington, DC: U.S. Census Bureau. Retrieved June 29, 2008, from http://factfinder.census.gov/servlet/STTable?_bm=y&-geo_id=01000US&qr_name=ACS_2006_EST_G00_S1101&-ds_name=ACS_2006_EST_G00_&-redoLog=false

U.S. Census Bureau. (2006c). Births, deaths and health. *USA Statistics in Brief-Vital Statistics and Health*. Hyattsville, MD: National Center for Health Statistics. Retrieved June 16, 2008, from http://www.census.gov/compendia/statab/files/vital.html

U.S. Census Bureau. (2006d). *Estimated median age at first marriage, by sex: 1890 to the present, (table MS-2)*. Washington, DC: U.S. Census Bureau. Retrieved November 28, 2008, from http://www.census.gov/population/socdemo/ms-la/tabms-2.txt

U.S. Census Bureau. (2006e). Nation's population one-third minority. *Newsroom* (CB06-72). Washington, DC: U.S. Census Bureau. Retrieved June 28, 2008, from http://www.census.gov/Press-Release/www/releases/archives/population/006808.html

U.S. Census Bureau. (2007a). Household income rises, poverty rate declines, number of uninsured up. *Newsroom* (CB07-120). Washington, DC: U.S. Census Bureau. Retrieved July 9, 2008, from http://www.census.gov/Press-Release/www/releases/archives/income_wealth/010583.html

U.S. Census Bureau. (2007b). *Married couples by race and Hispanic origin of spouses: 1970 to 2006* (Table 59). Washington, DC: U.S. Census Bureau. Retrieved July 3, 2008, from http://www.census.gov/compendia/statab/tables/09s0059.xls

U.S. Census Bureau. (2007c). Poverty: 2006 highlights. *Current population survey, 2007 annual social and economic supplement*. Washington, DC: U.S. Census Bureau. Retrieved May 29, 2008, from http://www.census.gov/hhes/www/poverty/poverty06/pov06hi.html

U.S. Census Bureau. (2007d). The American community-blacks: 2004. *American Community Survey Reports* (ACS-04). Washington, DC: U.S. Census Bureau. Retrieved July 29, 2008, from http://www.census.gov/prod/2007pubs/acs-04.pdf

U.S. Census Bureau. (2007e). The American community-hispanics: 2004. *American Community Survey Reports* (ACS-03). Washington, DC: U.S. Census Bureau. Retrieved July 29, 2008, from www.census.gov/prod/2007pubs/acs-03.pdf

U.S. Census Bureau. (2008a). Nearly half of preschoolers receive child care from relatives. *Newsroom* (CB08-31). Washington, DC: U.S. Census Bureau. Retrieved February 28, 2008, from http://www.census.gov/Press-Release/www/releases/archives/children/011574.html

U.S. Census Bureau. (2008b). Teenagers-Live births, birth rates, and fertility rates by Hispanic origin status: 1990 to 2005. *Statistical abstracts of the United States, 2008*. Washington, DC: U.S. Census Bureau. Retrieved August 10, 2008, from http://www.census.gov/prod/2007pubs/08abstract/vitstat.pdf

U.S. Department of Agriculture. (2009). Food distribution programs, history and background, Section 1. *Food and Nutrition Service*. Retrieved July 31, 2009, from http://www.fns.usda.gov/fdd/aboutfd/History/history1-ccc1933.htm#top

U.S. Department of Health and Human Services, Administration on Aging. (2004). *A profile of older Americans: 2004*. Retrieved August 25, 2008, from http://www.aoa.gov/AoAroot/Aging_Statistics/Profile/2004/Index.aspx

U.S. Department of Health and Human Services, Administration on Aging. (2007). *A profile of older Americans*. Retrieved July 9, 2008, from http://www.aoa.gov/AoAroot/Aging_Statistics/Profile/2007/index.aspx

U.S. Department of Health and Human Services, Health Resources and Services Administration. (2007). *Women's Health USA*. Rockville, MD: U.S. Department of Health and Human Services. Retrieved August 1, 2008, from http://mchb.hrsa.gov/whusa_07/popchar/0204wp.htm

U.S. Department of Health and Human Services. (2006). Infertility. *Frequently Asked Questions*. Retrieved May 28, 2008, from http://www.womenshealth.gov/faq/infertility.htm#a

U.S. Department of Health and Human Services. (n.d.). Scope of stress in the American workplace. *Stress at Work* (NIOSH Publication No. 99–101). Cincinnati, OH: National Institute for Occupational Safety and Health.

U.S. Department of Health Education and Welfare. (1973). 100 years of marriage and divorce statistics: 1867-1967. *National Vital Statistics System, 21*(24). Rockville, MD: National Center for Health Statistics. Retrieved July 1, 2010, from http://www.cdc.gov/nchs/data/series/sr_21/sr21_024.pdf

U.S. Department of Labor. (2008a). Employment characteristics of families. *News* (USDL 09-0568). Washington, DC: U.S. Department of Labor, Bureau of Labor Statistics. Retrieved August 18, 2008, from http://www.bls.gov/news.release/pdf/famee.pdf

U.S. Department of Labor. (2008b). Married parents use of time, 2003-06. *News* (USDL 08-0619). Washington, DC: U.S. Department of Labor, Bureau of Labor Statistics. Retrieved August 20, 2008, from http://www.bls.gov/news.release/pdf/atus2.pdf

Unell, B., & Wyckoff, J. (2000). *The 8 seasons of parenthood: How the stages of parenting constantly reshape our adult identities*. New York: Times Books.

University of Alberta (2006, February 9). Long-term poverty affects mental health of children. *Science Daily*. Retrieved September 22, 2009, from http://www.sciencedaily.com /releases/2006/02/060206171449.htm

Unknown. *God as parent*. Retrieved November 28, 2008, from http://soli.inav.net/~catalyst/ inspire/children.htm

Urban Institute, The. (2000). *A new look at homelessness in America*. Retrieved August 1, 2008, from http://www.urban.org/url.cfm?ID=900302

Urdang, L. (Ed.). (2001). *The timetables of American history (millennium edition)*. New York: Touchstone.

Using Preimplantation Embryos for Research. (2006). *ACOG, Committee Opinion,* (No. 347). Washington, DC: American College of Obstetricians and Gynecologists. Retrieved August 16, 2008, from http://www.acog.org/from_home/publications/ethics/co347.pdf

Vaillant, G.E., & Mukamal, K. (2001). Successful aging. *American Journal of Psychiatry, 158*(6), 839-847.

VanderValk, I., de Goede, M., Spruijt, E., & Meeus, W. (2007). A longitudinal study on transactional relations between parental marital distress and adolescent emotional adjustment. *Adolescence, 42*(165), 115-36.

Vega, V., & Malamuth, N. (2003, May). "A mediational-hierarchical model of sexual aggression" *Paper presented at the annual meeting of the International Communication Association, Marriott Hotel, San Diego, CA*. Retrieved August 23, 2008, from http://www.allacademic.com/ meta/p112131_index.html

Ventura, S. & Bachrach, C. (2000). Nonmarital childbearing in the United States, 1940–1999. *National Vital Statistics Reports, 48*(16). Hyattsville, MD: National Center for Health Statistics. Retrieved August 28, 2008, from http://www.cdc.gov/nchs/data/nvsr/nvsr48/nvs48_16.pdf

Visher, E., & Visher, J. (1988). *Old loyalties, new ties: Therapeutic strategies with stepfamilies*. New York: Brunner/Mazel.

Visher, E., & Visher, J. (1992). *How to win as a stepfamily* (2nd ed.). New York: Brunner/Mazel.

Visher, E., & Visher, J. (1996). *Therapy with stepfamilies*. New York: Brunner/Mazel.

Visher, E., & Visher, J. (1998). Stepparents: The forgotten family members. *Family and Conciliation Courts Review, 37*(4), 444-451.

Visher, E., Visher, J., & Pasley, K. (1997). Stepfamily therapy from the client's perspective. *Marriage and Family Review, 27*(1-2), 191-213.

Visher, E., Visher, J., & Pasley, K. (2003). Remarriage families and stepparenting. In F. Walsh (Ed.) *Normal family processes* (3rd ed.), (pp. 153-175). New York: Guilford Press.

Votruba-Drzal, E. (2006). Economic disparities in middle childhood development: Does income matter? *Developmental Psychology,* 42, 1154–1167.

Voydanoff, P. (2002). Linkages between the work-family interface and work, family, and individual outcomes: An integrative model. *Journal of Family Issues, 23*(1), 138–164.

Wade, T., & Pevalin, D. (2004). Marital transitions and mental health. *Journal of Health and Social Behavior, 45*(2), 155-70.

Waite, L. (2001). 5 marriage myths, 6 marriage benefits. *Marriage and Families, 5*, 19-25.

Waite, L., & Gallagher, M. (2001). *The case for marriage.* New York: Random House.

Waller, M., & McLanahan, S. (2005). "His" and "her" marriage expectations: Determinants and consequences. *Journal of Marriage and Family, 67*(1), 53-67.

Wallerstein, J., & Blakeslee, S. (2003). *What about the kids? Raising your children before, during and after divorce.* New York: Hyperion.

Wallerstein, J., & Lewis, J. (2004). The unexpected legacy of divorce: Report of a 25-year study. *Psychoanalytic Psychology, 21*, 353-370.

Wallerstein, J., Lewis, J., & Blakeslee, S. (2000). *The unexpected legacy of divorce: A 25-year landmark study.* New York: Hyperion.

Walsh, F. (1998). *Strengthening family resilience.* New York: The Guilford Press.

Walsh, F. (2003). Family resilience. In F. Walsh, *Normal family processes*, (pp. 399-423). New York: Guilford.

Warne, T., & McAndrew, S. (2008). Painting the landscape of emotionality: Colouring in the emotional gaps between the theory and practice of mental health nursing. *International Journal of Mental Health Nursing, 17*(2), 108-115.

Warren, N. C. (1998). *Finding the love of your life: Ten principles for choosing the right marriage partner.* Colorado Springs: Focus on the Family.

Watson, J. (1928). *Psychological care of infant and child.* New York: W. W. Norton and Co.

Weaver, J. (2004, November 18). Effects of pornography addiction on families and communities. *Presented before the Senate Committee on Commerce, Science and Transportation, Washington, DC.* Retrieved August 30, 2008, from http://www.obscenitycrimes.org/Senate-Reisman-Layden-Etc.pdf

Weber, S. (2008). Parenting, family life, and well-being among sexual minorities: Nursing policy and practice implications. *Issues in Mental Health Nursing, 29*(6), 601-618.

Webster, B., & Bishaw, A. (2007). Income, earnings and poverty data from the 2006 American community survey. *American Community Survey Reports,* (ACS-08). Washington, DC: U.S. Census Bureau. Retrieved August 1, 2008, from http://www.census.gov/prod/2007pubs/acs-08.pdf

Wedekind, C., & Furi, S. (1987, October). Body odor preferences in men and women: Do they aim for specific MHC combinations or simply heterozygosity? Proceedings of The Royal Society B. *Biological Sciences, 264*(1387), 1471–1479.

Wei, W. (1995). *The Asian-American movement.* Philadelphia: Temple University.

Weitoft, G., Hjern, A., Haglund, B., & Rosén, M. (2003). Mortality, severe morbidity, and injury in children living with single parents in Sweden: a population-based study. *The Lancet, 361*(9354), 289-295.

Welter, B. (1976). *Dimity convictions: The American woman in the nineteenth century.* Athens, OH: Ohio University Press.

West, E. (1994). Families in the west. *OAH Magazine of History,* (Fall, 1994). Retrieved May 28, 2008, from http://www.oah.org/pubs/magazine/west/west.html

What grown-ups understand about child development: A national benchmark survey. (2002). Danbury, CT: DYG, Inc. Retrieved June 28, 2008, from http://www.buildinitiative.org/files/grown-ups.pdf

White, J., & Niell, J. (2002). *The same-sex controversy.* Minneapolis, MN: Bethany House.

White, L., & Gilbreath, J. (2001). When children have two fathers: Effects of relationships with stepfathers and noncustodial fathers on adolescent outcomes. *Journal of Marriage and Family, 63*(1), 155-167.

Widom, C., & Brzustowicz, L. (2006). MAOA and the "cycle of violence:" Childhood abuse and neglect, MAOA genotype, and risk for violent and antisocial behavior. *Biological Psychiatry, 60*(7), 684-689.

Williams, B., Sawyer, S., & Wahlstrom, C. (2005). *Marriages, families and intimate relationships.* Boston MA: Pearson.

Wilson, M., Kohn, L., & Lee, T. (2000). Cultural relativistic approach toward ethnic minorities in family therapy. In J. F. Aponte and J. Wohl (Eds.), *Psychological intervention and cultural diversity* (2nd ed.), (pp. 92–109). Boston: Allyn and Bacon.

Wilson, R., Mendes de Leon, C., Barnes, L., Schneider, J., Bienias, J., Evans, D., Evans, D., & Bennett, D. (2002). Participation in cognitively stimulating activities and risk of incident Alzheimer disease. *Journal of American Medical Association, 28*(6), 742-748.

Winn, P. (2006). Another victory for marriage. *CitizenLink.com, Focus on Family Action.* Retrieved June 27, 2008, from http://www.citizenlink.org/CLtopstories/A000000629.cfm

Winnicott, D. (1989). *The family and individual development* (reprint edition). London and New York: Routledge.

Women in the labor force: A databook. (2007). *U.S. Department of Labor Statistics, (report 1002). Washington, DC: U.S. Department of Labor.* Retrieved August 18, 2008, from http://www.bls.gov/cps/wlf-databook-2007.pdf

Women's history in America presented by Women's International Center. (n.d.). Abstract. Retrieved June 28, 2008, from http://www.wic.org/misc/history.htm

Woodson, C. (1921). *The history of the Negro church.* Washington, DC: The Associated Publishers. Retrieved June 28, 2008, from http://docsouth.unc.edu/church/woodson/woodson.html

World divorce statistics 1996–2005. (2005). *Divorce Magazine.com.* Retrieved July 26, 2008, from http://www.divorcemag.com/statistics/statsWorld.shtml

Wuthnow, R. (2007). *After the baby boomers.* Princeton, NJ: Princeton University Press.

Xie, X., DeFrain, J., Meredith, W., & Combs, R. (1996). Family strengths in the People's Republic of China. *International Journal of Sociology of the Family, 26*(2), 17–27.

Yancey. G. (2002). Who interracially dates: An examination of the characteristics of those who have interracially dated. *Journal of Comparative Family Studies, 33*(2), 177-190.

Yellin, E. (2004). *Our mother's war: American women at home and at the front during World War* II. New York: Simon and Schuster.

Yeung, W., Linver, M., & Brooks-Gunn, J. (2002). How money matters for young children's development: Parental investment and family processes. *Child Development, 73*(6), 1861–1879.

Yllo, K. (2007). Gender, Diversity and Violence. In S. Ferguson (Ed.), *Shifting the center* (3rd ed.). New York: McGraw-Hill.

Youth Happiness Study. (2007). MTV and the Associated Press. Retrieved June 13, 2008, from http://www.mtv.com/thinkmtv/about/pdfs/APMTV_happinesspoll.pdf

Zanden, J. (1977). *Social psychology*, (pp. 112–113). New York: Random House.

Zeiss, A., & Kasl-Godley, J. (2001). Sexuality in older adults. *Generations, 25*(2), 18–25.

Zemon-Gass, G., & Nichols, W. (2007). "Take me along"- A marital syndrome. *Journal of Marriage and Family Therapy, 1*(3), 209-217.

Zhang, D., & Rusch, F. (2005). The role of spirituality in living with disabilities. *Journal of Religion, Disability and Health, 9*(1), 83-98.

Zhou, M., & Gatewood, J. (2000). *Contemporary Asian-American: A multidisciplinary reader.* New York: New York University Press.

Zweig, M. (2004). *What's class got to do with it? American society in the twenty-first century.* New York: Cornell University Press.

Zylan, Y. (2000). Maternalism redefined: Gender, the State and the politics of daycare, 1945-1962. *Gender and Society, 14*(5), 608-629.

Index

A

AAMFT 124, 360
Abortion 79, 95, 97, 148-152
Acquired immunodeficiency syndrome (AIDS) 93
Active listening 336
Adams, John 37
Adaptability 370
Adolescence 179, 180, 199, 208, 211
Adoption 153, 154
Affect 216, 219
Affection 381, 383-385
African-Americans 33, 34, 36, 46, 47, 56, 66, 69, 286-289
Agape 108-110
Age at first marriage 63, 72
Aging 197, 198, 208-210, 212, 215, 216, 219-223, 226, 227
Altruism 265-383
Amendment 47, 57, 78
American Revolution 36
American woman Suffrage Association (AWSA) 44, 57
Appreciation 217, 381, 383-385
Arranged marriage 54, 85, 86, 109
Asian-Americans 85-87, 287, 291
Assimilation 34
Assisted reproductive technology (ART) 151
  Embryo adoption 153
  Gamete intrafallopian transfer (GIFT) 153
  In vitro fertilization (ART) 153
  Intracytoplasmic sperm injection (ICSI) 153
  Zygote intrafallopian transfer (ZIFT) 153
Attachment 161, 163, 181
Attributes of God 187, 188, 191-193
Authentic sexuality 92, 93, 128
Authoritarian parenting 172
Authoritative parenting171, 174, 177, 178

B

Baby 148-151, 163, 166-168, 175-177, 194
Baby boomer 207, 218, 233
Balance 2, 68, 92, 116, 124, 129, 134, 140, 169, 192, 194, 205, 212, 232, 247, 250, 252-254, 263, 264, 270, 278, 279, 289, 307, 344, 390, 395
Battered person syndrome 334
Beat Culture 66, 67
Biblical model of marriage 141, 142, 156, 360, 399
Biblical revelation 12
Bicultural 286
Biological 9, 11, 135, 143, 175, 181, 284
Birth control 144-147
Birth rate 10, 31, 38, 44, 68, 72-74, 78, 80
Boundary 165, 166, 168, 183, 194, 204
Bowlby, John 161, 181
Bradford, William 26
Budget 122, 268, 269, 271-275, 277, 281

C

Case history 14
Child abuse 182, 195, 212, 246, 331, 333
Child characteristics 176
Child depravity 31, 32
Child Rights 160
Childless couples 11, 60
Chinese-American 48, 71
Christian marriage 18, 20, 38, 113, 142, 155, 225, 254, 335
Christian parenting 187, 188, 193, 225
Circumplex Model 381
  Family cohesion 290, 293, 381
  Family flexibility 381
Civil Rights Act 64, 66
Civil Rights Movement 47, 66
Civil War 36, 39, 44-46, 57, 64
Cohabitation; Cohabiting 6, 7, 9, 11-13, 68, 75, 128, 129, 132, 135, 137, 365
Cohesion 70, 169, 381
Colonial America 27, 39
Colonies 26, 28-34, 36, 51
Commerce 37, 42
Commitment task 217
Commodified family 37, 42
Common-law marriage 5-7
Communication 129, 134, 136-138, 156, 228, 253, 346-348, 350, 363, 381, 385, 393, 399
Communication task 202, 203, 205, 217
Companionate love 120
Companionate notion of marriage 38-40
Compassionate childrearing 38, 40
Compassionate family 58
Compatibility 110
Comstock Act44
Conflict management styles 319
  Accommodating 321
  Avoiding 322
  Collaborative 321
  Competitive 321
  Compromise 321
  Resolve 320
  Win 320
  Withdrawal 320
  Yield 320
Conflict styles 317
  Complementary style of conflict 317
  Symmetrical style of conflict 317
  Parallel style of conflict 317
Conflict types 317-319
  Personality-based conflict 317, 318
  Situational conflict 318, 319
Conjugal family 299
Conservation of energy theory 264
Constructive conflict 315, 323-325, 335, 336, 384
Consummate love 120, 121
Contempt 344
Contested divorce 349
Contract task 206, 218
Control 170, 173, 194, 195,215, 327, 335
Coontz, Stephanie 55, 77
Cooperative economy 39
Cooperative family economy 58
Cortisol 182
Cost of raising children 270
Covenant xii, xiii, 4, 17-19, 141, 156, 192, 335
Covenant marriage 349, 350, 360, 401
Credit cards 268, 273, 274
Criticism200, 343, 344
Cult of true womanhood 39
Cultural assimilation 34, 285, 290
Cultural diversity 285, 311, 398
Cultural interconnection 35
Cultural pluralism 286, 311
Custody 5, 29, 65, 241, 244, 305, 348, 355, 357
Cycle of violence 331

D

Dating 83-91, 93, 98, 100-105
Daycare 245
Deadbeat dads 358
Death 223, 227, 340, 360
Defense of Marriage Act (DOMA) 7
Defensiveness 343, 344
Deism 33
Delayed childbearing 143
Demandingness 170, 171
Democratic family 41, 51
Dependent variable 14
Destructive conflict 315, 325, 336
Devitalized marriage 346
Differentiation 134
Dimensions of Love 108, 109
Disability 303, 309
Disappearing dads 358
Disillusionment model 345
Disneyland dads 358
Diversity 23
Divorce 61, 62, 74, 75
  Adolescents 356

Adults 340, 351, 352
Children 340, 355, 356, 357
Church response 359
Consequences 350
Education 354
Family dynamics 357
Finances 354, 362
Health 356
Preventing divorce 360, 361
Religious worship 359
Society 353
Well-being 355, 357
Divorce rate 61, 62, 74, 341
Divorce statistics 340
Divorce, types of 348
Contested divorce 349
Fault divorce 348
No-fault divorce 348
Simplified divorce 349
Uncontested divorce 348
Divorced dad stereotypes 357
Domestic duties 30, 39, 45, 236, 242, 253
Domestic violence 303, 316, 326, 327, 334
Domesticity39, 233, 234
Dual-income 231, 232, 238, 244, 246, 247, 251, 252, 255
Dual-career families 244, 248

E

Early-middle-years family 210, 211
Economy 76
Education 40, 113, 271
Egalitarian 234, 238, 241, 248, 254, 291, 299
Elderly 75, 218, 220-224, 228, 229
Emancipation Proclamation 36, 46
Emergent-distress model 345
Emotional well-being 219, 228
Employees 250, 260, 266, 267
Empty-nest 201, 210
Endogamy 112, 113
Enduring dynamics model 345
Energy 263-265, 267, 278
Enlightenment 37, 38, 51, 334, 350
Equal Rights Amendment (ERA) 236
Equity 254
Equity theory of mate selection 117
Eras 199, 200, 228
Erickson, Eric 162, 179, 180, 198-200, 202, 228
Eros 108, 109, 124
Estrogen 115
Ethnic group 284, 285
Ethnicity 284, 285, 306
Ethnocentrism 285, 308, 311
European settlers/immigrants 24, 25-27, 33
Evolutionary theory of mate selection 114, 115
Exchange theory of mate selection 116
Existing data 14
Experiment 15
Expressive role 140
Extended family 10, 21, 134, 168

F

Facts 15, 21
Faithfulness 18, 189, 192, 291
Family
Breakdown 353
Democratic family 41, 51
Form 38, 41, 51
History 382, 394
Institution 402
Nuclear 9, 10, 16, 21, 78, 80, 400
Single-parent 11, 178, 249, 362-364, 370, 374
Traditional 24, 61, 80, 81, 140-142, 399
Family composition 365, 398
Family dynamics 205, 210, 211
Family flexibility 381
Family form 38, 41, 51
Family life cycle 2, 118, 119, 206
Family of origin 10, 11
Family of procreation 11
Family of production 29
Family strength strong family 377, 378, 379, 381, 383, 398
Family strengths framework 379
Ability to cope with stress and crisis 392, 393
Appreciation and affection 383-385
Commitment 382
Positive communication 385-388
Spiritual well-being 390, 391
Time together 389, 390
Family strengths model 381
Family time 166, 252, 260-263, 280, 390, 395
Family-wage economy 58
Fatuous love 120
Federal Marriage Protection Amendment (FMA) 7
Female-headed family 303, 311
Feminist 68, 236
Fertility window 148

Fictive kin 11, 35
Finances 270, 271, 276, 369
Freedom 20
Friendship Love 109

G

Gay/lesbian parents 178
Gender 177
Gender roles 28, 39, 67, 88, 105, 142, 237, 241, 329, 330
Generation gap 65, 66
Generativity 198, 216, 382
German immigrants 50
Glass ceiling 234
Goals 279, 382
Gottman, John 138, 139, 307, 317, 341, 343, 344
Government 347
Grandparent 212-214, 222, 223
Great Awakening 33, 51
Great Depression 58, 76, 80
Grief 223, 224, 340

H

Harmonious marriage 346
Hedonism 225
Hispanic-Americans 70, 178, 289
Holiday 35, 286
Homestead Act 45, 51
Homogamy 112, 113
Hooking up 89, 90, 105
Human papilloma virus (HPV) 93
Humor 114, 187, 252, 326, 393, 402
Hypothesis 13-15

I

Ideal mate theory of mate selection 116
Identity 180, 211, 248, 259, 295, 329, 383
Independent variable 14
Individuation 130
Indulgent parenting 170, 171, 180, 181, 194
Industrial Revolution 10, 37, 42, 51, 179
Infatuation Love 109
Infertility 151, 153
Instant gratification 272
Institution of family 24, 51, 80
Instrumental role 140
Internet dating 90
Interracial marriage 86, 87, 343
Intimacy 4, 18, 92, 98, 103-105, 109, 119-121, 123, 124, 130, 131, 138-142, 156, 177, 198, 199, 205, 330
Irish-Americans 50

J

Japanese-Americans 49, 71, 258
Job satisfaction 247, 248, 264

K

Keeping company 84
Ku Klux Klan 69

L

Langham Act 245
Later years 202, 216-220, 222, 223, 226, 228
Later-middle-years family 210, 211
Latino 289
Levinson, Daniel 199, 200, 228
Levinson's eras 199
Living expenses 135, 268 269
Looking-glass self 88
Loss 202, 217, 220, 223, 227, 327, 368, 399
Love xii, 16-20, 107-111, 119, 120, 121-124, 136, 137, 188, 191-193
Lower class 297, 301, 327
Lower-middle-class 300
Loyalties 369, 374

M

Male menopause 209
Marital core tasks 202
  Caring 204
  Commitment 204
  Communication 205

Conflict/compromise 205
Contract 206
Marital dysfunction quiz 341, 342
Marital life cycle 202
Affirmation and preparation 203
Consolidation and celebration 217
Expanding the base 203
Mating and marriage 202, 203
Marital rape 330
Marital satisfaction 206, 207, 220, 221
Marriage counseling 360
Marriage patterns 138-140
Cohesive-individuated 140
Disengaged 139
Operatic 139, 140
Pursuer-distancer 138, 139
Marriage rate 60
Marriage types 346
Conflicted 346
Devitalized 346
Harmonious 346
Traditional 346
Vitalized 346
Mate Selection 88, 112
Matrilineal 25
Melting pot 285, 286
Menopause 209, 210, 228
Mexican-Americans 49, 214, 289
Middle age 197, 207, 219
Midlife crisis 208, 225, 228
Midlife transition 208
Money 267, 268, 270-273, 276, 277, 280, 281, 317, 328
Monochronic 258, 280
Monogamy 5, 6
Moralistic Therapeutic Deism 79
Morality of caution 99
Morality of concern 99
Morality of law 99
Morality of personal relationships 99
Morning-after pill 145, 148
Myths 13, 65, 100, 135, 155, 216, 326

N

National Woman Suffrage Association (NAWSA) 44
Native-Americans 24-26, 292, 293
Nativism 50
Natural family planning 144
Neglect 182
New Deal 59
New World 26-29, 31, 33, 51
Newlywed 343
Nice-girl dilemma 101
Nichols, William 130, 202, 203, 205, 217, 228
No-fault divorce 348
Nuclear Family 9, 10, 16, 21, 78, 80, 400
Nursing homes 212, 222
Nurturance 161, 194
Nurture 44, 170, 175, 177, 192, 194, 195, 304

O

Obedience 159, 162, 172, 193, 194, 300
Olson, David 346

P

Pantraditionalism 292
Parent image theory of mate selection 116
Parental demandingness 170
Parenting 2, 40, 159, 161-165, 174-180, 183, 187, 188, 192-195
Parenting goals 159
Parenting stages 162
Celebrity 163, 194
Sponge 163, 194
Family manager 163, 194
Travel agent 164, 194
Volcano dweller 164, 194
Family remodeler 164, 194
Plateau parent 165, 194
Rebounder 165, 194
Parenting style 174
Authoritarian parenting 172
Authoritarian-directive 172
Non-authoritarian-directive 173
Authoritative parenting 171, 174, 177, 178
Indulgent parenting 171
Uninvolved parenting style 174
Parenting style 174-177
Paternal determinism 225
Patriarchal authority 29, 30
Patrilineal 25
Patriot 36
Perimenopause 209
Personality 175, 317

Philia 108, 109
Physical Appearance 114, 116, 117, 176
Pioneer 45, 51
Polyandry 6
Polychronic 258, 259, 277
Polygamy 6, 21
Polygyny 6, 21
Pornography 316, 330
Positive communication 379, 385, 394
Poverty 50, 70, 74, 167, 182, 212-214, 219, 224, 250, 269, 270, 290, 293, 296, 301-303, 341, 355
Pregnancy 41, 60, 90, 93, 95-97, 99, 143, 148, 149, 178, 182, 212, 286, 302, 343
Prejudice 56, 86, 287, 293
Premarital counseling 122, 123, 125, 360, 361
Premarital sex 92-98, 104, 128, 399
Preventing divorce 361
Priorities 253, 277-281
Problem-solving 136, 392, 393, 395
Progressive Reform Movement 56
Propinquity 112
Protection 159, 160
Psychodynamic theory of mate selection 115
Psychosocial crisis 198
Psychosocial development 198, 199
Pure Milk Act 56
Puritan 29-32

Q

Quaker 32, 47

R

Race 284, 285
Racial group 284, 285
Racism 56, 287, 293
Redemptioner 28
Relationship stage theory of mate selection 118
Relativism 93, 105
Religion 28-30, 33, 34, 39, 47, 57, 79, 113
Remarriage 363, 364, 368, 370, 372
Resiliency 392, 395
Resources 264, 265, 276-281
Responsiveness 161, 166, 170, 174-176
Risk factors 307, 343
Role 167
Role strain 167, 264
Role theory 264, 280

S

Salad bowl 286
Same-sex families 304, 306
Same-sex unions 7, 21, 67, 310
Sandwich generation 77, 212
Savings 266, 274, 275, 281
Scale 14
Second shift 235
Self-in-relation theory 199
Self-centered Love 108
Self-giving Love 109
Selfless Love 108, 109
Seniors 3
Serial marriage 27
Serial monogamy 6
Sexual double standard 96
Sexuality 90, 92, 104, 105, 128, 221
Simplified divorce 349
Single parent 11, 178, 249, 362-364, 370, 374
Singleness 102-104
Slavery 32-36, 46, 47
Social Class 113, 215, 295, 309
Socioeconomic 175, 176, 195
Spouse abuse 329, 330
Stage theories of mate selection 117
Stay-at-home mothers/fathers 242, 262
Stepfamily 11, 363-372
Stepfamily types 365
  Matriarchal stepfamily 365
  Neotraditional stepfamily 365
  Romantic stepfamily 365
Sternberg's triangular theory of love 119
  Commitment 119, 120
  Intimacy 119, 120
  Passion 119, 120
Stewardship 276, 277, 278
Stimulus-Value-Role (SVR) theory of mate selection 117
  Role stage 117
  Stimulus state 117
  Value stage 117
Stonewalling 344
Storge 108, 109, 124
Stress 181, 182, 265-267, 276, 277, 316, 379, 392-395
Strong family 377, 378, 379, 381, 383, 398
Submission xiii, 19-21, 30
Suffrage 43, 44, 56, 57
Superwoman syndrome 236
Survey 14
Systematic observation 15, 21

T

Task overload 363, 374
Teen sex 94-97
Teenager 94-97, 164
Television 12, 54, 62, 67, 69, 92, 104, 263, 328
Testosterone 115
Theories of Mate Selection 112, 117, 119
Therapy 124, 204, 335, 360, 402
Time 258-263
Tithe 277, 281
Tolerance 32, 33
Traditional family 24, 61, 80, 81, 140-142, 399
Traditional marriage 3, 4, 6
Transition to parenthood 165, 167-169, 194
Trust 160-162, 189, 194, 199, 371
Types of marriage 5, 346

U

Uncontested divorce 348
Unemployment 58, 70, 76, 182, 250, 251, 327, 358
Uninvolved parenting 174
Upper-class 296, 298
Upper-middle-class 298, 299

V

Victimization 182, 183
Victorian family 39
Victorian Ideal 38
Violence 326-331, 333-336
Vitalized marriage 346

W

Wallerstein, Judith 351, 352, 354-357, 359
Warren, Neil Clark 122, 123
Watson, John 24, 55
Wedding 4, 5, 38, 104, 129
Well-being 214-216, 218, 219, 355, 357, 390, 391, 395
Widows 56, 209, 227
Womanhood 39
Women who work outside the home
  First generation - revolution 234-236, 242, 243, 255
  Second generation - counter revolution 236, 237, 242, 255
  Third generation – renegotiation 237, 238, 242, 255
Women's revolution 234-236, 255
Work stress 266, 267
Working class 297-300, 311
World War I 58, 59
World War II 59, 60, 232, 255

Y

Youth culture 65, 66, 80, 400

About the Authors

Dr. Cynthia Tweedell, Ph.D.

Dr. Tweedell has taught Sociology and Marriage and Family classes for over 25 years. She and her husband have been married over 30 years and they have two children. She has an M.A. in Sociology from University of North Carolina-Greensboro; an M.A. in Education from University of Chicago; and a Ph.D. in Human Services from Walden University. She is currently Executive Director of the Council for Christian Colleges & Universities (CCCU) Center for Research in Adult Learning.

Cynthia Tweedell with husband, Bill, and children, Matthew and Rebecca

Barbara A. Riggs, RN, Ph.D., LMFT

Dr. Riggs is an associate professor at Indiana Wesleyan University where she teaches primarily Marriage and Family Therapy (MFT) courses. She is the MFT Program Director for Indiana Wesleyan University and also serves as the Indianapolis Site Director for the Indiana Wesleyan Counseling Program. She continues to have a small private practice at Eagle Creek Counseling Services, which she founded in 1992 and managed for 12 years before selling the business.

Barbara Riggs with her husband Randy, and daughters Jennifer, Melissa and Mandi and their grandson Collin.

Dr. Riggs is the President-elect for Indiana Association for Marriage and Family Therapy, as well as chairing the Training and Education Committee for IAMFT. She has been an American Association for Marriage and Family Therapy (AAMFT) Approved Supervisor for 10 years and teaches the Approved Supervisor Refresher Course for Indiana. She has been a clinical member of AAMFT since 1985.

She graduated from Purdue University (Purdue) in 1988 with a Ph.D. She has a M.S. in Nursing from Indiana University and worked as a nurse practitioner and taught nursing for several years before attending Purdue. As a registered nurse, she continues to utilize her medical knowledge as she works with clients.

She actively serves on several boards as a board member and on various committees. She does frequent mission work in the Philippines where she recently wrote the curriculum for a Certificate in Counseling that would equip Filipino Pastors and Teachers to better serve the Filipino people.

Dr Riggs has a deep faith in God and is excited to see what God has next in store. This text is only one example of how God opens doors and allows us to use our gifts and talents.